D1766158

SIBELIUS

A COMPOSER'S
LIFE AND
THE AWAKENING
OF FINLAND

GLENDA DAWN GOSS

THE UNIVERSITY OF CHICAGO PRESS

Chicago and London

The University of Chicago Press, Chicago 60637
The University of Chicago Press, Ltd., London
© 2009 by The University of Chicago
All rights reserved. Published 2009.
Paperback edition 2012
Printed in the United States of America

21 20 19 18 17 16 15 14 13 12   2 3 4 5 6

ISBN-13: 978-0-226-00547-8 (paper)
ISBN-10: 0-226-00547-X (paper)

This book has been supported by grants from the Finlandia Foundation National, Pasadena, California;
the Lloyd Hibberd Publication Endowment of the American Musicological Society;
and Svenska kulturfonden (the Swedish Cultural Foundation in Finland).

Library of Congress Cataloging-in-Publication Data

Goss, Glenda Dawn.
Sibelius: a composer's life and the awakening of Finland / Glenda Dawn Goss.
p. cm.
Includes bibliographical references and index.
ISBN-13: 978-0-226-30477-9 (cloth : alk. paper)
ISBN-10: 0-226-30477-9 (cloth : alk. paper) 1. Sibelius, Jean, 1865–1957—Appreciation—Finland.
2. Nationalism—Finland—20th century. I. Title.
ML410.S54G68 2009
780.92—dc22
[B]
2009013833

♾ This paper meets the requirements of ANSI/NISO Z39.48-1992 (Permanence of Paper).

SIBELIUS

TABLE OF CONTENTS

PART III

TAIDE KUULUU KAIKILLE—ART BELONGS TO ALL

321

ILLUSTRATIONS

PREFACE
Methods and Miracles, Debts and Confessions

Awakenings happen in myriad forms and in every place. This volume represents a series of personal revelations in connection with Finland, a land that could hardly be further away in every sense from coastal Georgia, where I first came to know the music of Jean Sibelius. (That his music took hold in that sandy soil provides more than adequate testimony to its tenacious power.) Through a series of circumstances that now seem preordained—including the preservation of the composer's letters in the Olin Downes collection at the University of Georgia, where for many years I was a professor of musicology—this biography advanced step by jerky step to completion. Its pages were begun in the early 1990s (the purpose behind *Jean Sibelius: A Guide to Research*). Yet it was only in 1998, when I was asked to join the Sibelius critical edition and produce an authoritative score of the seminal *Kullervo* choral symphony, that I stepped through the looking-glass and entered the altered reality essential for bringing this book to fruition.

Part of that reality was being immersed for nearly a decade in Sibelius's manuscripts, a particularly satisfying aspect of working with the critical edition, which I was privileged to lead as editor-in-chief during a crucial four years.[1] Above all, the thousands of pages connected with *Kullervo*—an autograph manuscript of 456 leaves, a full set of parts from the first performances in 1892, and the composer's sketches and rehearsal scores, their fragile leaves still smelling faintly of cigars and even now glowing with the distinctive colors and decorative curlicues of a golden age—drew me deeper and deeper into Finland's turn-of-the-century world and forced a confrontation with the powerful forces that prompted a young Finn to create a work filled to the brim with some of the most compelling ideas of the day.

Another part of that reality was even more, well, real. In connection with the work of the critical edition, I brazenly asked a scholar whom I knew only by reputation, Rainer Knapas, to lead me through readings of Finland's literature. To my everlasting wonder and benefit, he magnanimously agreed. In a moment of stunned comprehension at the point when our sessions began spinning off into matters social and political, artistic and architectural, historical and historiographical, I realized that Rainer Knapas was a miraculous embodiment of cultural and historical knowledge. He is, in fact, one of the leading figures in the so-called Helsinki tradition of historiography, and it was he who pointed me down many of the avenues for traveling into the new world of understanding explored here. A number of his important studies in the history of ideas appear in the notes and the bibliography; his gently made but incisive comments vastly improved the text, yet it is impossible to credit all the insights and assistance he so freely shared. My debt to Rainer Knapas remains insurmountable.

The extraordinary Erik Werner Tawaststjerna (1916–1993) was another of those "real" figures. I was fortunate enough to meet him as well, albeit only briefly, and to be encouraged by him (there *is* a larger point here, not just a bald-faced attempt to upgrade myself by an academic equivalent of Beethoven's kiss on the forehead of the young Liszt). In his *Jean Sibelius*, published in five Finnish volumes, five Swedish volumes, three English volumes, and a single Russian one, and also in his many supplementary articles, radio broadcasts, and newspaper columns, Tawaststjerna made the most thoroughgoing investigation of the composer's life that has ever been undertaken. He brought to light letters, diary entries, and manuscript annotations at a time when few were known. Although today several collections of Sibelius letters have been published, an annotated edition of his diary has appeared, and vast quantities of new research are available, from detailed analyses of most of the major compositions to documentary material reproduced on the World Wide Web, virtually all of this work was spurred by Tawaststjerna's lifetime of pioneering endeavor. It was he who placed the study of Jean Sibelius on a solid foundation. Like all Sibelius scholars, I have benefited immeasurably from his work and from the labor of his translator, Robert Layton, who generously and repeatedly placed his exceptional skills in the vastly underappreciated art of translation in the service of all who love learning about music (and who wrote a fine Sibelius biography of his own).

The generational difference between these two mentors is significant. Tawaststjerna began his Sibelius work during the cold war, a time when the notion of a self-determining Finnish people struggling against impossible odds—the forces of nature, the conquering Swedes, the oppressive Russians—and heroically overcoming them all was deeply embedded in attitudes and historical writings of every kind. When a younger generation of Finnish historians led by such scholars as Matti Klinge and Tuomo Polvinen began to question the received version of the country's history, a debate ensued that is still going on today. At issue have been such questions as whether the period of Russian rule was truly an offensive parenthesis on the way to realizing a preexisting Finnish "nation"— the notion itself a kind of Finno-Ugric manifest destiny; whether the Finnish-speaking peasants were indeed self-determining actors scripting a play about their own destiny; and whether the widely used term *oppression* even correctly described the entire period of autonomy under the Russian emperors. These were the attitudes advanced by the leading historian of Tawaststjerna's generation, Eino Jutikkala (1907–2006), whose selective choice of facts avoided casting any favorable light whatsoever upon the Russian period. Negative opinions of Russia were widespread, a result of the horrors Finns suffered at Soviet hands during World War II and its aftermath, when they were forced to cede their beloved Karelian territory (whose significance is dealt with in chapter 8) to the Soviet Union.

Answering these important questions has helped to bring about an appreciation of the benefits to Finland of being part of the Russian Empire, benefits that were nowhere more splendidly manifest than in the arts, whose spectacular bloom created a Finnish golden age. The younger generations have also begun to raise other questions—about the construction of heroes as part of the national awakening, an activity that elevated a few stars—such as Jean Sibelius—to near-cult status; about the Finnish civil war in 1918 (a full half century elapsed before reconciliation between the two halves of the Finnish population was undertaken); and about how Finland's landscapes and history had been transformed into *lieux de mémoire* by Finnish-minded leaders in the nineteenth century before the majority of Finns even knew they had a *mémoire*. The altered reality created by these shifting perspectives has shaped the present account, which diverges fundamentally from Tawaststjerna's orientation while shamelessly benefiting from his magnificent accomplishment. I believe, from all I have learned of Erik Tawaststjerna, that this big-hearted, self-correcting scholar would have led the way in these and other new interpretations were he still working today.

Along with Tawaststjerna's volumes, there have, of course, been other Sibelius biographies, a number of which have been of value to the present study, and they will be noted in due course.[2] Here mention must be made of only one, Harold E. Johnson's (1915–1985). To Finns it might seem heresy to mention Johnson's name on the same page as that of Erik Tawaststjerna, for the American's assessment of Sibelius, in a biography just prior to Tawaststjerna's, caused an uproar in Finland. Yet it was Johnson's *Jean Sibelius*, published in 1959, that prompted the Sibelius family to request Erik Tawaststjerna to write a more balanced approach to their famous relative. And in turning to Johnson's pages today, I find much that is valuable, that rings true, and that offers edifying asides important for readers who are not Finns. As an outsider, Johnson had an eye for what those unfamiliar with Finnish history and culture needed to know to understand Sibelius. If he refused to treat the composer with the exaggerated deference that his iconic image had come to demand in Finland, it was ultimately to the benefit of Sibelius's wider reputation. And it was Johnson who led the way in consulting the primary music sources and correspondence and endeavored to locate and preserve these materials for scholarly use.

This brings us to what I call "the Route 66 syndrome," the idea that only an insider (that is, native-born) can write about a topic. I ruefully confess to having noticed with dismay some of its symptoms in myself. They turned up when the Finnish scholar Markku Henriksson mentioned that he was writing a book about Route 66, based on seminars he had given at the University of Helsinki. My reaction was visceral: how on earth could any foreigner *possibly* understand the symbolism of a highway, a television show, a concept that my generation of Americans had grown up with? How could he have the *feeling*, the experience? The very impertinence.

Well. Markku Henriksson has written a perceptive study of Route 66.[3] He also (unwittingly, since I have not shared with him the news of my affliction) taught me a valuable lesson. Sometimes it helps to be an outsider to appreciate the unique qualities of a culture, to ask the "obvious" questions, to articulate truths that go unremarked within a society where "everybody knows." The function of the outsider is particularly important in Finnish society, which represents what Edward T. Hall called a "high-context culture"[4]—a close-knit population in which few rules are stated and missing information is filled in with shared assumptions or even well-tuned imagination. The situation works well for Finns, but it is dangerous for the rest of us, especially those from "low-context" societies (including most North Americans, many Anglo-Europeans, and Germans), with our dramatically different cultural backgrounds, vastly different assumptions about the world, and precious little inside knowledge about Finland and how it really works.

Those of us who are outsiders thus have a special role to play in representing one culture to another, although we have an obligation to play it well. In my case, I almost missed Finland, because as a young professor, my loves were Renaissance music and culture. Belgium, a former seat of the Habsburg rulers, was the European milieu in which I lived and studied. But trying to convey the far-off world of the Renaissance to American university students in the late twentieth century was always a difficult proposition. In the search for new ideas and fresh perspectives, I turned to the rich collection of Olin Downes papers in the Hargrett Rare Book and Manuscript Library in Athens, Georgia. Olin Downes's enthusiasms, which positively radiate from the pages of his writings, led me to Sibelius and to the decision to write a book on the relationship between a *New York Times* critic and a composer from Finland. The view from only one side of the Atlantic Ocean, however, is undeniably a limited one. In a benighted moment of crusading zeal for finding the "real" Sibelius for that book, I mortgaged the house (the University of Georgia having no such thing as sabbaticals) and, with my two young teens in tow, sailed across that ocean on a rusty Italian freighter to a country with which we had

had no previous contact and where we knew absolutely no one. We stayed for a year. Since that audacious (some called it foolhardy) introduction to Finland in 1989–90, I returned to live, work, and teach in the country for more than a decade, studying and using its languages and learning its mores through unforgettable and sometimes unbelievable events.

I relate this background at the behest of my publisher in order to shed light on how this volume evolved and to demonstrate the personal engagement with Finns, their culture, and their living history that I have been so fortunate to have. These experiences also explain the tone of my writing. I found that to relate the extraordinary and stirring dimensions of Sibelius's story in "neutral" academic prose not only drained the life from a great human drama, but also went against its grain, congealing in humdrum, artificial language a false "Sibelian" image of the kind all too often purveyed. His story—and Finland's—requires a human voice, a voice that does not spare hard truths, yet manages to find the humanity and levity in life's vicissitudes whenever possible—as Finns do themselves and, contrary to his image, as Sibelius did too.

Over the decades of puzzling out this story, my debts to the living as well as to the past have accumulated—and not just within the narrowly defined realm of musicology. It is always a great pleasure to acknowledge these dues, because each represents a human connection in the all-too-solitary business of scholarly research and writing. Providentially, two such connections in the form of exceptionally fine dissertations appeared as the present volume was being completed: Janne Gallen-Kallela-Sirén's "Axel Gallén and the Constructed Nation: Art and Nationalism in Young Finland, 1880–1900," and Derek Fewster's *Visions of Past Glory: Nationalism and the Construction of Early Finnish History*. In the freshness of their examinations of the Finnish context in which Sibelius lived and composed and in pointing the way to essential Finnish sources, both writers have contributed to a more balanced view of Finland's golden age and thereby informed my own thinking. Specific matters will be acknowledged in their proper places, but I would like to draw attention here to the overall importance of their work. Furthermore, I had the incomparable additional benefit of Derek Fewster's generous comments on a late stage of my manuscript.

Another vital human connection has been George C. Schoolfield, who possesses a surpassing knowledge and understanding of Finland, its literature, and its culture. His outstanding scholarship, a portion of which appears in the bibliography, his invaluable outsider's perspective, and, not least, his unfailing humor have been guiding lights. Lest one think humor an odd and even frivolous thing to mention in the context of a serious study, I have to make another true confession: its lack in the source materials presented one of my greatest challenges. (By contrast, working with the Olin Downes collection was pure pleasure for the tongue-in-cheekiness, reverberant Victorian prose, and out-right hilarity exercised by letter and newspaper writers.) Humor provides a crucial means of getting at hard, serious truths (Charlie Chaplin's film *The Great Dictator* comes to mind). As it turns out, the humor issue belongs to the larger story, one of the dark lega-cies of Finland's awakening (it is discussed in chapter 5). Still, those engaged in ferreting out that story must have some relief from its almighty gravity; Professor Schoolfield's deft and often witty touch has been absolutely indispensable for the vivacious way he enlightens his readers on the most momentous of matters. That enlightenment happily extended even to the present text, which Professor Schoolfield read closely and com-mented on with unsurpassed expertise.

Thankfully, one source of humor is Sibelius himself, particularly as a correspondent. And I have Gitta Henning to thank for initiating me, with good humor of her own and unfailing goodwill, into the delicate art of tuning in to the composer's ironic prose and Swedish-speaking Finn's wit. Gitta Henning, who for more than a quarter of a century assisted Erik Tawaststjerna in his biographical research and without whom those vol-umes would not have been completed,[5] appears to have performed the astounding feat of having read, multiple times, every one of the thousands of Sibelius letters preserved in the National Archives. Not only did she help with the tedious processes of proofreading and making the index, she also heroically agreed to assist in the translations, in the course of which she exhibited a superb ability to achieve the perfect nuance from whichever of the several languages we were dealing with. Her linguistic skills and our discussions of these texts revealed more of the man than mountains of dry facts and sterile analyses have ever done. The translations have been enormously improved by her generous assis-tance, while any errors there remain embarrassingly my own.

Where the Swedish language is concerned, it was Margareta Örtenblad Thompson, formerly at the University of Georgia, who started me on its study, a path along which Carmen von Boehm Tawaststjerna also steered my steps, and I learned enormously from both of them. After translating *The Hämeenlinna Letters*, Margareta Örtenblad Thomp-son agreed to join in translating the composer's diary into English. Although we never finished that overambitious project, what I learned from her in the process was priceless, and a number of the diary translations used here reflect her perceptive input. A further Swedish connection has been the professor and leading James Joyce scholar Hans Wal-ter Gabler of the University of Munich, who spent a portion of his childhood in Sweden and came to know the Adolf Paul family well. Our stimulating discussions and his assis-tance with materials connected to both Paul and Joyce have contributed new insights to this project.

Over the years I have had the privilege of being able to pursue Sibelius research in a number of great institutions, and the generosity and helpfulness of people in each not only improved the outcome, but also immensely increased its pleasures. In retrospect, it seems inconceivable that my Sibelius work should have begun in Georgia—but so it did, at the beautiful Hargrett Library. The personnel there still stand out for their kindness, competence, and keen interest in the work and readiness to assist in every way. Numerous forays were also made into the Library of Congress, especially the Performing Arts Library, where Kevin Lavine has been an unfailing source of detailed information, ready assistance, and enthusiasm about matters Finnish.

In Finland, the institutions I have come to know well include the National Library, the National Archives, and the Sibelius Academy Library in Helsinki, and the Sibelius Museum in Turku. To name all who assisted me would require listing just about everyone on their respective staffs. Here I am forced to be somewhat more selective, yet to all those who have repeatedly come to my assistance, I express my great gratitude.

The National Library, where the great majority of Sibelius's music manuscripts and many letters are deposited, necessarily served as the principal locus of my research. Mention must be made of Petri Tuovinen's tireless and cheerful delivery to the reading room of manuscripts by the pound and, together with Ilona Fors, readiness to answer countless questions; of Liisa Koski's repeated interlibrary loans on my behalf; of Matti Munnukka's generous help with the university map collections; and of Kari Timonen's skilled photographing of manuscripts, maps, and other documents.

In Finland's National Archives, Marja Pohjola and the many staff members showed the same professionalism and kindness as have the numerous librarians at the Sibelius Academy, where Mikko Ikkala expertly digitalized the illustrations from the academy's collections. Without the marvelously reliable Inger Jakobsson-Wärn and Sanna Linjama at the Sibelius Museum in Turku I would have been at a loss time and again. At the Department of Prints and Photographs in the National Museum, Sirkku Dölle, Seija Martin, and Hannu Häkkinen spent days helping to find just the illustrations I sought; at the Central Art Archives, Heleena Hätönen, Johanna Helin, and Susanna Sääskilahti located artists' correspondence and artworks; at the University Archives, Susanna Pennanen hauled out masses of fading documents at my request; at Finland's National Broadcasting Company, Pekka Gronow and Martti Haapakoski responded unfailingly to endless appeals for information; and at the Finnish Music Information Center, Risto Korhonen readily answered all queries. The historian Tuomo Olkkonen generously shared materials from his personal library and discussed historical events with me in detail, while Seija Lappalainen has been an unfailing resource of essential information on matters from Martin Wegelius to Russian connections to Finland. Anneli Asplund of SKS readily assisted my search for the folk-song sources of various Sibelius works. The art historian Leena Lindqvist, whose

Järnefelt studies have been invaluable, has been vital in supporting other aspects of the project.

Although in a sense this volume has been underway for nearly twenty years, the end stages were decisively facilitated by two research awards. The first came from the Paul Sacher Institute in Basel, Switzerland, in 2005. A four-month immersion in Stravinsky music manuscripts, correspondence, and other materials for a music-editing study opened new sources and wider perspectives that turned out to be invaluable for this project, especially in connection with Finns and their Saint Petersburg links, although the Finland-Russian cultural connections still await full investigation. The other was an award from the National Endowment for the Humanities. To both institutions I express my deep gratitude.

Nor would it have been possible to produce such a study without the many permissions so graciously given: first and foremost, by the Sibelius heirs, for use of musical examples and other documentary and iconographic materials; secondly, by Sibelius's various publishers (Breitkopf & Härtel and Robert Lienau in Germany; Wilhelm Hansen in Copenhagen; and Fennica Gehrman Oy in Helsinki, where Ari Nieminen gave ready assistance), as well as by G. Henle Verlag, where Dr. Wolf-Dieter Seiffert cordially and promptly gave permission for use of the Haydn example; and thirdly, by the various institutions and private owners of the many artworks who willingly acquiesced to their use.

As the book began to go into production, other people and agencies stepped forward with much-needed support: Kathleen Kuzmick Hansell, music editor at the University of Chicago Press, who, with enthusiasm and personal knowledge of the Nordic world, helped to steer the volume through the byways of publishing with a professionalism, expertise, and goodwill that are unmatched in my experience; James Hepokoski, brilliant analyst of Sibelius's and others' music, who carefully read the whole manuscript and, in his magnificent and inspiring way, made important and meticulous comments; and Hedvig Rask of Svenska litteratursällskapet i Finland, who lent her superb proofreading and indexing skills. In addition, various foundations generously awarded grants to help with illustrations, music examples, production, and other costs: the Finlandia Foundation National, Pasadena, California; the Lloyd Hibberd Publication Endowment Fund of the American Musicological Society; and Svenska kulturfonden (the Swedish Cultural Foundation in Finland). To each I express my deep appreciation.

As every scholar knows, it is friends and family who nourish the heart and provide sanity's touchstone. In my case, these included Elisabeth Airas, who helped deconstruct Finland's golden ages to the accompaniment of Crimean tomatoes from her garden and homemade pasta from her kitchen; Alexandra Andersson, who also verified my German translations and discussed the whole enterprise with infinite patience and real (or really well-feigned) interest; Henrik Ekberg, on whose deeply appreciated historical research and splendid editorship of *Uppslagsverket Finland* I relied again and again, while the historical tours on which he guided me through some of Finland's most meaningful spaces made the past come alive; Patricia Dunlap Hämäläinen, whose wonderful paintings nourished my thinking as much as did our discussions of art, life, and philosophy; Carl Henning, whose enthusiastic perspective on Finnish history sharpened my own insights and who, with Gitta Henning, showed the ultimate in true friendship—"kitchen-testing" the manuscript; Kristiina Hildén, who provided unforgettable tours of Sibelius's summer town of Lovisa; Vivienne Sinclair and Leo Vuosalo, who, along with lively discussions and infinite support, assigned me the pleasurable task of editing and annotating the journalist Paul Sjöblom's writings about Finland; Anu Virkkunen and Henry Fullenwider, with whom there were frequent insightful discussions of language and cross-cultural living; and Laura Youens and Richard Wexler, whose immersion in Renaissance musicology kept me in touch with my first musical passions.

It was my children who braved the ocean crossing that first time and who added their talents to my efforts—Beth in making the photograph for the book jacket and James in perceptively discussing issues of language and style. They have been my life's linchpins, along with my parents and my sister, Angela Carin, who provided refuge from the endless Finnish winters and kept me grounded (the rolled eyes, the cleared throat) when my constant talk about Sibelius and Finland went on and on and—as she gently reminds me—*on*.

Glenda Dawn Goss
HELSINKI, FINLAND/SAINT SIMONS ISLAND, GEORGIA
SUMMER 2007

PRACTICAL QUESTIONS
Names and References

However much one longs to avoid anachronisms, the challenge in writing about Finland presents near-insurmountable difficulties. Names that Sibelius knew in Swedish (Tavastehus, Helsingfors, Åbo) are widely known today, especially by visitors to Finland, only by their Finnish designations (Hämeenlinna, Helsinki, Turku), even though the Swedish names are still fully in use. For the sake of clarity Finnish names have reluctantly been decided upon, with the exceptions of Åland, Lovisa, Mariehamn, and Vasa; however, the chart on p. xxv gives the dual names of places mentioned in this volume.

A further complicating factor is that name changes continue apace in present-day Finland. Together with the already confusing linguistic picture (thanks to which every official institution has names in both languages of the land), the unwary can easily be led astray. An example is the university library. It was once part of the institution known as the Imperial Alexander University. After Finland's independence, the institution began to be called the University of Helsinki, and the library's name changed accordingly. Then, in the summer of 2006, the library's name metamorphosed again: it became the National Library of Finland. Yet the siglum HUL (for Helsinki University Library) was deeply and inextricably entrenched in the Sibelius literature, not least in such important reference sources as Kari Kilpeläinen's *Jean Sibelius Musical Manuscripts at Helsinki University Library*, as well as in hundreds of books and articles. Hence, HUL is used here for primary sources housed in what is now styled the National Library of Finland.

There have been the inevitable no-win choices with transliterations. In Finland some spellings of Russian names, such as Sinebrychoff (the founder of a brewery whose products are still marketed under that name), are firmly entrenched in Finnish culture. Others, such as Bobrikov (who was always troublesome), appeared even in his own time in multiple forms, including Bobrikov, Bobrikow, and Bobrikoff (Sibelius once referred to him as "Bobba"). Because the spelling Bobrikov is widely used today, including in many studies in English, some of which are also cited in the text, it seemed the better part of valor to use it. In books as in life, there are no perfect—or perfectly consistent—solutions.

A further problem has concerned what to call works of art. Unlike musical compositions, which even in manuscript form often have a title, artworks may not have a fixed designation. Around the turn of the century, Finnish artists often unveiled their creations for the first time at the Paris salons, where the works were given French titles. Back in Finland, these artworks acquired Finnish and Swedish names. Because today the Finnish-language titles are the most likely to be encountered in reference books and Internet searches, I have generally used a Finnish designation together with an English translation, although there are some exceptions.

Unless otherwise indicated, names and dates of Sibelius's compositions, their first performances, and their source locations are based on the composer's thematic catalog, *Sibelius-Werkverzeichnis*, designated SWV, compiled by Fabian Dahlström. Quotations from Sibelius's diary are taken from Professor Dahlström's annotated edition of that document, *Dagbok, 1909–1944*, and cited simply as *Dagbok* with the date of the entry, page numbers being given only when the composer left the exact day unspecified. With diary texts and other documents readily available in published form (such as the composer's letters to Uncle Pehr, transcribed and translated in the *Hämeenlinna Letters*), the original Swedish texts have not been included.

In the endnotes, sources are cited only by the author's last name and a short title. Full publication information will be found in the bibliography. Articles in symposia, conference proceedings, and newspapers are not enumerated separately there, but the endnotes supply bibliographical particulars whenever such articles are cited. The bibliography also omits recordings and editions other than the Sibelius critical edition, but the endnotes provide full details.

In a few cases, conventions have been devised to distinguish among several books by the same author all having the title *Jean Sibelius*. Erik Tawaststjerna's many volumes are given sigla plus a volume number (see the Abbreviations section below). Karl Ekman Jr.'s biography *Jean Sibelius*, first published in 1935, is always followed by a year in order to designate whether the English translation by Edward Birse is meant (1936) or the revised and enlarged volume (1956), considered Sibelius's "authorized" biography but never translated from Swedish into English.

Because there are so many citations from Sibelius's correspondence with Axel Carpelan, Aino Järnefelt, Adolf Paul, Christian "Kitti" Sibelius, and Martin Wegelius, only the correspondents and dates are given for these letters. Their file locations are listed in the bibliography;[6] file locations of other letters are given with their citations.

A word about spellings: changes in Swedish and Finnish over the last 150 years mean that consistency is an unattainable goal. The general policy is that in quotations from correspondence and other primary documents, original spellings have been preserved. In titles of Sibelius's compositions, spellings conform to those in his thematic catalog (SWV). Sibelius's original title (whether Swedish, Finnish, or German) is given first, followed by an official English translation, generally also the one used in SWV. As for *runo* (pl. *runot*), meaning "poem," the Finnish term has been retained to avoid the misleading connotations of the often-used English translation "rune."

Dates are not always given at the first mention of a figure, but rather at the place it seemed most natural so as not to interrupt the flow of the narrative. Dates for all individuals, where they are known, will be found in the index.

ABBREVIATIONS

Dagbok	Jean Sibelius, *Dagbok, 1909–1944*
ETF	Erik Tawaststjerna, *Jean Sibelius* [Finnish volumes]
ETL	Erik Tawaststjerna, *Jean Sibelius* [Robert Layton's English translation]
ETS	Erik Tawaststjerna, *Jean Sibelius* [Swedish volumes]
FMQ	*Finnish Music Quarterly*
HUL	Helsinki University Library (National Library of Finland)
JSW	*Jean Sibelius Works*
KVS	Kansanvalistusseura (Society for the Enlightenment of the People)
NA	Kansallisarkisto (National Archives of Finland)
SFA	Sibelius-perheen Arkisto (Sibelius Family Archive), NA
SHS	Suomen Historiallinen Seura (Finnish Historical Society)
SibMus	Sibelius Museum, Turku, Finland
SKB	*Suomen kansallisbiografia* (The National Biography of Finland)
SKS	Suomalaisen Kirjallisuuden Seura (Finnish Literature Society)
SLS	Svenska litteratursällskapet i Finland (Society of Swedish Literature in Finland)
SWV	*Sibelius Werkverzeichnis*
WSOY	Werner Söderström Osakeyhtiö
YL	Ylioppilaskunnan Laulajat (Helsinki University Male Voice Choir)
YLE	Suomen Yleisradio (Finnish Broadcasting Company)

TOWNS AND PLACE-NAMES

Finnish Name	Swedish Name
Ahvenanmaa	Åland
Espoo	Esbo
Hämeenlinna	Tavastehus
Hamina	Fredrikshamn
Helsinki	Helsingfors
Järvenpää	Träskända
Käkisalmi	Kexholm
Katajanokka (an area of Helsinki)	Skatudden
Kauniainen	Grankulla
Lapinjärvi	Lappträsk
Loviisa	Lovisa
Maarianhamina	Mariehamn
Mikkeli	Sankt Michel
Mustasaari	Korsholm
Naantali	Nådendal
Oulu	Uleåborg
Pori	Björneborg
Porvoo	Borgå
Rauma	Raumo
Tampere	Tammerfors
Turku	Åbo
Vaasa	Vasa
Viapori (later Suomenlinna)	Sveaborg
Viipuri	Viborg

SIBELIUS

Introduction

AN UNSOLVED MYSTERY

For those who appreciate elegantly solved mysteries, the strange case of composer Jean Sibelius and his lapse into silence has never been satisfactorily explained. The outline of his story goes something like this:

In a remote corner of a faraway land, a strangely gifted youth imagined music of such beauty and power that within his lifetime those imaginings became staple works of orchestras the world over. His sparkling violin concerto was well on its way to setting a record as the one most often recorded during the entire twentieth century. His symphonies and symphonic poems resonated in concert halls throughout the Nordic lands, across Europe, around England, and even in distant North America. Chamber works, solo songs, choral music, dramatic numbers, piano pieces all flowed from his pen.

Then the music stopped.

His supporters (for this is a man with decided proponents and opponents) say that the composer's self-criticism grew to such proportions that it shut down his creative faculties completely (the self-criticism being somehow construed as bespeaking the great man's modesty). His detractors point to the composer's all-too-comfortable state pension and eventual prosperity or sagely nod their heads and murmur sanctimoniously about intemperance and the ill effects of unbridled consumption of alcohol.

Yet all these explanations leave a bad taste behind. On the one hand, the self-criticism argument forces one to ask how and why Sibelius differed from other creative artists who, throughout history, have exercised self-criticism of their own. On the other hand, the derogatory judgments fail to stand up to close scrutiny: Sibelius began receiving state support before a single one of his seven numbered symphonies was composed and without it might well have frittered all his time away in "sandwich pieces" to feed his growing brood of daughters. And can alcohol really be the explanation? After all, the composer lived well into his ninety-second year, to all appearances in good spirits (the psychological kind) and robust health.

Whatever the solution to this enigma, it is potentially of real importance, and not just to mystery lovers. It matters to all who are dismayed by the awful specter that human creativity is something that can be irretrievably lost.

THE SCENE OF THE CRIME

Like any good detectives, then, we must visit the scene of the crime—in this case, Finland—and unearth buried clues; ask hard questions of those now silent witnesses such as newspapers, diaries, memoirs, and music manuscripts; and, not least, establish a sense of what has been called the geography of biography. Indeed, Finland's geographical and botanical features—the woodlands and waterways, the flora and fauna that make up its natural world—have long dominated the image propagated of Sibelius and his music. "Apprenticeship of a Nature Lover" reads the opening chapter of a mid-twentieth-century Sibelius life story. From the words of his first biographer, Erik Furuhjelm, in 1915—"Sympathy for nature appears to be the primary, the Ur-characteristic of Sibelius"[1]—to the Web pages of Finland's Ministry for Foreign Affairs, where as recently as January 2006 Sibelius appeared (along with the Finnish architect Alvar Aalto) under the heading "National Identity in the Forests,"[2] Sibelius has been represented as "firmly rooted in the forests," his identity securely tied to the Finnish nation through its trees, flowers, birds, and lakeshores. Why, the very titles of his music *prove* the contention: from early settings of Finnish nature poems (Runeberg's *När sig våren åter föder* [*When Spring Once More Comes to Life*]) to the last orchestral tone poem, *Tapiola*, which evokes the dwelling place of the forest god, a handful of undeniably great works along with a slew of little ones bear the names of Finnish trees, Finnish flowers, Finnish nature myths, and Finnish landscapes.

Yet the romanticized nature image conceals and distorts. In particular, it misrepresents geopolitical realities, since an essential part of that image is the notion of "little Finland," a small nation in relation to the great powers of the world, albeit one that encompasses natural beauty, abundant natural resources, and a determined and heroic people. The same artificial and anachronistic notion continues in the refrain endlessly repeated in the country today, "Suomi on pieni maa" (Finland is just a small country).

The facts give a rather different picture. Territorially, present-day Finland is larger than the United Kingdom.[3] Historically, Finland and its people were part of the kingdom of Sweden for six centuries (ca. 1155–1808/9), then belonged to Imperial Russia for more than one hundred years (1808/9–1917). Finland and its inhabitants have been formed as much by their symbiotic political relationships as by their natural environment. Being part of first one, then another enormous power relentlessly sculpted, altered, and shaped the country's history, languages, and literature. Simultaneously, those same forces formed the unspoken attitudes, deepest assumptions, and creative manifestations of its people.

The scene of the crime thus reveals anything but a simple solution to the mystery. Instead, it forces us to consider an array of complicating factors, not least the roles of the powerful realms of Sweden and Russia, which throughout Sibelius's lifetime and for centuries before that had molded his country. Sibelius spoke the language of the first realm, while living, until the age of fifty-two, as a citizen of the second. And he was born into these unusual surroundings at an exceedingly propitious time: music and the arts *mattered*. They were part of what Finns needed to formulate, demonstrate, and celebrate their golden ages of the past and create self-definition in the present vis-à-vis the great powers between which they were compressed.

Incited by the push-pull of the giants on either side of Finland, Sibelius and a handful of his predecessors and contemporaries set out to compose, conduct, draw, paint, poetize, sculpt, and versify what it meant to be Finnish, to inculcate a sense of pride in being Finnish, and through these activities to awaken their fellow Finns to their uniqueness, their separateness, and ultimately the possibilities of nationhood. They succeeded spectacularly, creating a world that so impressed its lustrous accomplishments upon those who encountered it that the epithet "golden age" was bestowed on their era and its artistic expressions. It was fitting that such a gilded epoch should have been born in regal surroundings—Imperial Russia, a realm of nearly unimaginable wealth and splendor. Of its surface glitter, Sibelius was supremely aware. He recognized it—and adored it. As he once wrote, "It's the surface sparkle people fall for. But I love this sparkle, because when you march over worries and so on with a tiara on the back of your head, then life becomes so dramatic. Not this drab gray."[4]

To the extent that this golden age existed, a narrowly Finnish outlook was, paradoxically, not part of its character. Rather, during this time what was Finnish and what was more broadly European were inextricably mixed. It was also during this time that forces unforeseen by the creators of Finland's golden age were awakened: a desire for equal rights, for better working conditions, for improvement in the daily lives of ordinary working people. It is said that children eat their fathers, and Finland's revolutionary awakening was no different. In its train those who crafted its precepts and envisioned its artistic shapes either went into exile, were smothered into silence, or were turned into empty icons, all their creative juices sucked dry.

The hard truth about the Sibelius mystery, and one of the reasons for the difficulties in getting to the heart of it, is that this mystery compels us to confront things we would rather avoid for the sake of social or political correctness, such as class. The language of class difference permeates the correspondence of Sibelius and his contemporaries, colors their perceptions, and shapes their art. Such language raises hackles among many in "democratic" America, but without it we can have no meaningful discussion of Finland, its history, or its creative artists. We have to get over any squeamishness that might arise from speaking about nationalism, social class, linguistic prejudice, elitism (as in the arts), and, not least, the price of regime change, even when or especially when that change is to a democratic system, because all of these uncomfortable truths belong to the gritty reality of Sibelius and Finland's story, a story that has acquired unusual currency in our time. Its significance goes beyond human curiosity about how other people lead their lives and how they solve the central problems of existence. In an era when regime change is promoted for the common good, it is important to understand all of its costs.

The difficulties are undeniable. Who would want to argue that in weighing the benefits of living in a militant democracy against those of living under increasingly autocratic emperors, the gain in human welfare of the one might come at the cost of the creative force engendered by the other? Yet the fact is that, with the series of events that culminated in the Bolshevik Revolution, Finland's secession from Russia, and its launch into independence, Jean Sibelius's creativity—like that of so many of his generational compatriots—came to an end. To be sure, the end came gradually. But come it did—within a mere ten years of the country's declaration of nationhood.

However "self-critical" Sibelius may have been, to ignore the impact of the cultural and political climate on his and other creative minds is to leave out the most startling and important part of their story. As Sibelius once observed about himself, "I'm not suited for 'writing' music. All [music] has to be *experienced*."[5] Composers, writers, and artists inevitably reflect experiences on their home turf and its tensions in relation to the outer world to which they also belong, and where they travel. To understand Sibelius, to try and fathom the mystery of his lost creativity, mortifyingly played out on an international stage, requires understanding more fully the world from which he came. It is to that end that this book is written.

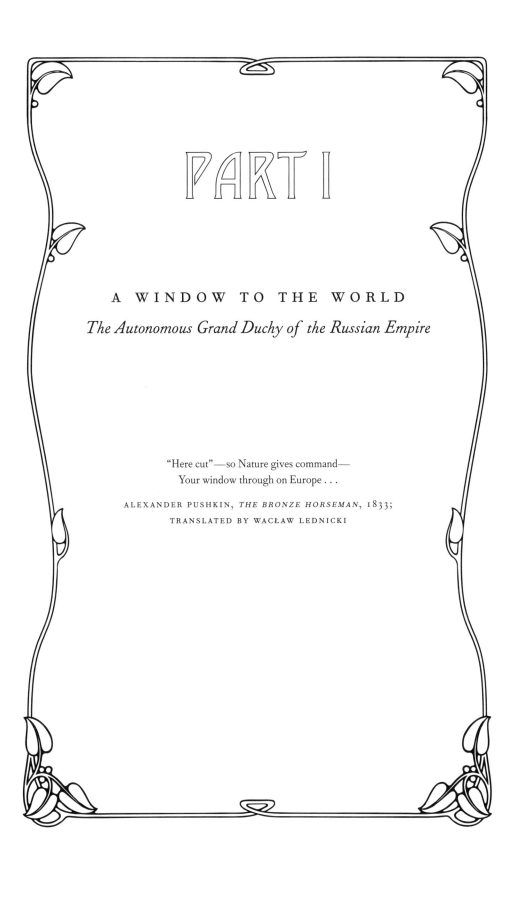

PART I

A WINDOW TO THE WORLD

The Autonomous Grand Duchy of the Russian Empire

"Here cut"—so Nature gives command—
Your window through on Europe . . .

ALEXANDER PUSHKIN, *THE BRONZE HORSEMAN*, 1833;
TRANSLATED BY WACŁAW LEDNICKI

❦ 1 ❦

Finland's Nature
Vårt Land—Our Land

Gray mists churned and eddied around the prow of the ship. Occasionally, the
vapours parted, affording a glimpse of rocky outcropping or stony island looming
terrifyingly close. Still the ferry kept to port, the pilot skillfully maneuvering past first
one, then another tall ship gliding by, their triple masts cloaked in the haze. Slowly,
out of the wet, hovering clouds a shoreline, a harbor, then a town emerged from the
fog. Finland, like Brigadoon, rose magically from the sea.

"A TRAVELLER'S NOTEBOOK," 1989

To approach Finland from the sea is to come upon a mysterious and alien land that
appears to rise miraculously out of rocks, mists, and marine depths. The metaphor of emergence is apt: geologists say the land is indeed rising, the consequence
of its release from ice sheets that formed during the last ice age. Finland has been rising
figuratively as well: in the early twenty-first century the country is enjoying a booming
economic and artistic golden age. Finland is held aloft as a model for its humane social
programs, educational achievements, technological excellence, and artistic attainments.
With the global success of Finnish products ranging from Nokia telephones and utilitar-
ian modern art forms to an astounding crop of world-class conductors, singers, composers, and even prizewinning rock groups, Finland stands at the forefront of technology
and education, and of medical, social, and musical accomplishment. Yet a long and terrible history involving countless personal sacrifices underlies the success of the Finns and
their mysterious, waterladen country.

To outsiders, Finland's exotic qualities begin with its faraway location, a good fourteen days' journey from North America by sea—in favorable weather. Although Finland
has been a part of the European Union (and its constituent European Community) since
1995, the country's isolation from central Europe, many of whose citizens consider Finland the end of the world, is such that its southernmost city and capital, Helsinki, rarely
shows up on central European television weather maps, although Stockholm and Moscow

9

are regularly identified. Situated on the northern periphery of Europe, the land stretches from the Arctic Circle (within which approximately one-third of Finland lies) to the Baltic Sea. The Gulf of Bothnia forms its western border; the Gulf of Finland its southernmost limit. Thousands of miles of shoreline, lakefront, and coastal marsh meander across its face and around its borders, which taper off into strikingly beautiful archipelagos. Yet if the inland and outbound waters of the west and south give Finnish nature much of its special character, the eastern boundary imparts distinctive qualities of another kind. For some eight hundred miles—a border longer than that of any other western country—Finland's frontier adjoins Russian territory.

Some say geography is destiny, and there is no better example than Finland and its environmental place next to the global giant that so profoundly shaped twentieth-century history. In Finland, East and West converge as nowhere else on earth. And from that convergence this story flows.

THE NATURAL LANDSCAPE

The geographical position, of course, explains the characteristics of the land. Even though the last ice age was about ten thousand years ago, its effects are starkly visible still today: gravelly ridges called *eskers* and smooth, oval hills, or *drumlins*, thought to be the work of glaciers. The glaciers also left shallow depressions that filled with water, creating the "Land of a Thousand Lakes" immortalized by the national poet Johan Ludvig Runeberg (1804–1877) in the first canto of his *Fänrik Ståls sägner* (*Tales of Ensign Stål*). Had Runeberg been more scientific and less poetic, he would have had to describe his country as having around 190,000 lakes that provide a system of interconnecting waterways. The interlaced channels link Finland's interior and the sea as neatly as any network of modern highways. Even the Baltic Sea has the characteristics of a large lake: it has no tides, and it is relatively static and shallow. And only in recent years, geologically speaking, did it open out to the Atlantic Ocean.

From ancient times water provided the most natural and affordable means of transport. Nearly five thousand miles of inland waterways wander through the Finnish countryside, with another five thousand miles in coastal fairways.[1] These water routes were the reason that, when railroads began transforming central Europe in the 1830s and 1840s, most Finns deemed such technology extravagant and unnecessary. When finally Finland's first railroad was built, it was to connect two ports: Helsinki and a little town nestled alongside Lake Vanajavesi called Hämeenlinna. And when the railroad tracks turned east toward Saint Petersburg—their ultimate destination—their route was again geographically determined: they ran along the ridge named Salpausselkä, a rim left where the glacier had stopped, which facilitated construction in a way that going directly east from Helsinki could not.

Despite Runeberg's poetic eloquence, not everyone has found beauty in the land, especially because the country's wetlands give rise to rich bogs, called *suo* in Finnish (at one time thought to be the root source of the country's Finnish name, Suomi, although that theory is generally discredited today). The artist Albert Edelfelt (1854–1905), whose limpid canvases turned Finland's most luminous face to the world, was known to comment on the "unutterable monotony" of the Finnish landscape; Axel Gallén (1865–1931), later known as Akseli Gallen-Kallela, who loved Finland fiercely, lamented the country's flatness.[2] When the celebrated violinist Leopold Auer (1845–1930) travelled through Finland on his way to Stockholm, he left with a dismal impression:

> Both in Finland and this part of Sweden nature wears a sad and monotonous aspect; there are forests of wretched little firs and pines, broken by clearings showing small hollows filled with muddy water, gray and leafless brush, and an occasional small lake, or some great rocks dating from the volcanic epoch. Remnants of unmelted, grimy snow bordered the ditches on either side of the railroad tracks . . . the general effect was depressing.[3]

Yet however aesthetically it is defined, the idea of the land, "*our* land," a word which in both Finnish (*maa*) and Swedish (*land*) means "country" as well as "land," has a central place in the national psyche and its beliefs, thanks not least to the emotional power of Finnish poetry and song. One need look no further than the erstwhile national anthem, a combination of Runeberg's verses and Fredrik Pacius's music, whose title is *Vårt land* (*Our Land / Country*; see fig. 1.1).

Finland's geographical position, between 60° and 70° north, also determines the climate. And that climate is dominated by winter. "Winter is the only real season of the year," wrote Toivo Pekkanen in his novel *Nuorin veli* (*The Youngest Brother*); "winter is indeed of our essence: snow, ice and cold are a part of our nature. Winter never betrays us. Its arrival is a certainty."[4] Finnish winter means "vehement darkness" (Olaus Magnus's all-too-apt description) and, until very recent times, a band of sea ice that girdled the country. A fragment of one of Runeberg's poems preserves a Finn's proud if laconic perspective on Finnish winters:

Vi [är] Europas förpost mot naturen,	We are Europe's outpost against Nature
Mellan isar är vår lager skuren	Our fame has been cut out of ice
Och vårt bröd vi ryckt ur is och snö.[5]	And our bread we hacked out of ice and snow.

Figure 1.1. J. L. Runeberg, *Fänrik Ståls sägner* (*Tales of Ensign Stål*), opening canto, from the
edition illustrated by Albert Edelfelt (Porvoo, 1900). India ink and gouache.
The National Library of Finland. Photo: Kari Timonen.

To outsiders, the shivery horrors of winter have long fed delicious tales of tongues
and lips excruciatingly frozen against drinking cups, of forts defended with water poured
upon the walls, of "stockades [converted] into unassailable barriers of ice, that shone like
'looking-glasses'. . . [;] of rivers turned to marble; of reindeer sleighs drawn at the speed
of a bird's flight; . . . of people so mutilated by cold that they were deficient of arms and

legs; of the northern lights and of the low altitude of the sun which cast a man's shadow ten times as long as himself upon the flat white snow."[6]

Those who struggle and overcome such conditions must be heroic indeed. And in truth, even though the effects of sea and air mean that Finnish winters are often warmer than at similar latitudes elsewhere, real dangers exist: the first Finn who managed to compose a symphony, Axel Gabriel Ingelius (1822–1868), was sadly not the first Finn to freeze to death. And the latitude produces inevitable and profound psychological effects: the rhythm of daylight and darkness that brings the spectacular white nights of summer also delivers the long, smothering night that reigns from November to February, abetting drinking, depression, and suicide. For Finns, hell is not a place of eternal fire and melting heat. It is cold so bitter that even teeth and toenails freeze.

Both the long, slow geologic processes and the climate are part of Sibelius's story. For they have left their marks not just on the terrain, but also on the people and their politics. Throughout recorded history the country's inhabitants have seemed strange to outsiders. From Tacitus (ca. 55–120), who described the Finnish Lapps as living in barbarism and misery, to Herman Melville (1819–1891), who wrote in *Omoo: A Narrative of Adventures in the South Seas* (1847) that seamen believed Finns to be possessed of the gift of second sight and the power to wreak supernatural vengeance, Finnish people have appeared to be a race apart. Indeed, to one another they appeared unusually homogeneous, as Zachris Topelius observed in his *Boken om vårt land* (*Book of Our Country*).

People who live in a geographical region so emphatically removed from the mainstream unavoidably experience its psychological and practical effects. Over the centuries Finns have cultivated great self-reliance, strong family ties, fierce pride in their land and its dark moods, and their famous *sisu*, a quality perhaps best rendered in English as "true grit." Their capacity for drink is legendary, their taciturnity a subject of humor, even among themselves. The Italian pianist and composer Ferruccio Busoni (1866–1924) encountered the notorious reticence exactly one hour after his first endeavor to begin a conversation with a Finnish colleague: "every attempt," he grumbled, ". . . rebounded as if against a stone."[7] The granite of the archipelago was not the only rocky part of life in Finland.

THE LANDSCAPE OF POLITICS

As surely as it shaped its people, Finland's geography has shaped the country's political and economic history. Lying between Sweden and Russia, Finland has belonged to both, and both have left impressions on the culture as indelible as the glaciers left upon the land. Finland presents a unique point of contact between west and east. From the west came the Swedes, with their Christianity, vibrant trade, and social progress. The Finns' long history as part of Sweden reaches back to the 1200s, when much of Finland was under Swedish jurisdiction.[8] With the Peace of Nöteborg (Pähkinälinna) in 1323, the first of several borders distinguishing Finland from Russia was established. During the following centuries Sweden's political, administrative, and ecclesiastical power structures enveloped the Finns. Finland was to become still more like Sweden with the accession to the throne in 1523 of Gustav Vasa, the king who centralized administrative power in Stockholm and broke the hold of the Catholic church. The Reformation he brought to his kingdom, which included Finland, had consequences reaching down to the present.

Early in the nineteenth century, other political forces altered the balance of power in the Nordic region and with it, Finland's history. Alexander I, Emperor and Supreme Ruler of All Russia, and Napoleon I, meeting at Tilsit in 1807, agreed to join their formidable might in a bid to conquer the world and divide it between them.[9] For Alexander, the proximity of his capital, Saint Petersburg, made Finland strategically important as a buffer zone against outside aggression. In 1808 he ordered his troops across the Finnish border. Although the Finnish soldiers were entirely loyal to Sweden and the fighting was brutal, the Swedes were defeated. In the aftermath of that war, the area of Finland was annexed to Russia as an autonomous grand duchy and, for the first time in history, defined with exact borders in the Treaty of Hamina in 1809.

There can be no doubt that the status of grand duchy had definite advantages. Whereas previously the Finns had merely been one of many parts of the great Swedish kingdom, now Finland was both geopolitically defined and autonomous. The new ruler even assured the Finns "membership in the family of nations"—*placée désormais au rang des nations*. The geopolitical definition and the status of autonomy were key factors enabling a Finnish national culture to evolve.[10] Indeed, fostering such a culture appears to have been one of the Russian emperors' goals. As conceived in imperial terms, the policy of autonomy was based on the belief that political loyalty to the new rulers and distance from the old ones could be ensured by continuing the established institutional structures. The same policy was followed in other countries annexed by Russia (such as Poland and the Baltic provinces).

Finland's local, central administration thus continued as before, managed by local elites on the same Gregorian calendar as before, only under the watchful eye of an imperially appointed governor-general. The emperors even allowed Finland a special juridical position with its own constitution and its own Diet of Four Estates (not convened, however, until 1863), and they encouraged the development of the Finnish language. In a word, the conditions for developing a strong national profile and the impetus for a national "awakening" flourished under the Russian emperors in ways that almost certainly would not have happened had Finland remained simply a remote region of the Swedish realm. Rather than "self-determining agents," the Finns were part of a grand imperial plan, and their change of status, from Swedish province to grand duchy, was far more than an administrative shift. Finland was now joined to a huge realm, one fast approaching one-sixth of the world's territory and rapidly expanding

> from Perm to Tauris,
> From the cold rocks of Finland to the flaming Colchis,
> From the stunned Kremlin
> To the walls of stagnant China,
> Flashing its steel bristles,
> Will not the Russian land rise?[11]

In 1830, when Adrien Brué, the geographer to the French king, mapped the world, he showed the Russian Empire stretching from Finland's western coast (the area called Ostrobothnia) to Alaska ("Amérique russe," which Russia sold to the United States only in 1867) (see fig. 1.2).

Despite the uncertainties of its future, Finland belonged to a domain of incalculable resources, abundant wealth, possibilities not previously imagined. New ways of thinking, no less than the altered political status, would affect everyone in the land.

THE NATURE OF FAMILY

> In the cold my song was resting,
> Long remained in darkness hidden.
> I must draw the songs from Coldness,
> From the Frost must I withdraw them.

KALEVALA, RUNO I, LINES 79–82, TRANSLATED BY W. F. KIRBY

It was the Russian Empire that determined where Jean Sibelius was born. Hämeenlinna had long been a garrison town and a service and training center for Russian troops.[12] It was the place where, on December 15, 1854, Emperor Nicholas I had established a sixth Sharpshooter Battalion, part of the increased defense prompted by the misbegotten Crimean War. By 1859 the sharpshooter unit had been converted to a training battalion. And when in that year a doctor was needed, the position was filled by a deeply loyal Finnish physician named Christian Gustaf Sibelius (1821–1868). A mature thirty-eight-year-old from Lovisa who had studied at the Imperial Alexander University in Helsinki (the institution formerly located in Turku), Christian Sibelius had served his emperor on the ship *Finland*, part of the imperial fleet guarding the Finnish coast.[13] By the time he

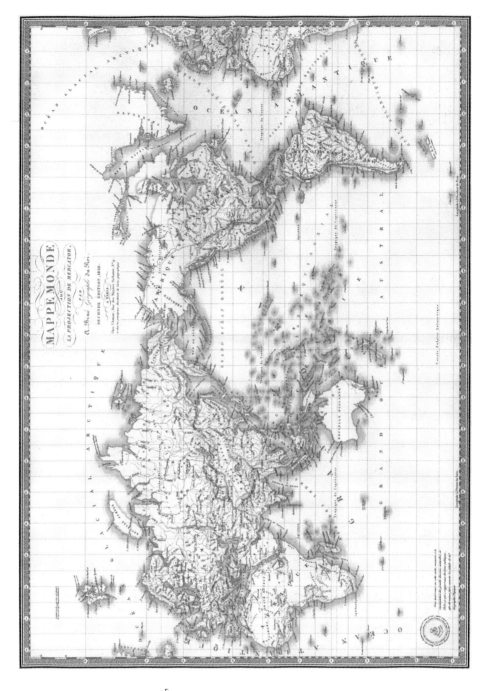

Figure 1.2. The Russian Empire's reach, from its western border Finland to "Russian America" (Alaska) in the east. Adrien Brué, *Atlas classique de Géographie physique, politique, ancienne & moderne*, 2nd ed. (Paris: Chez l'Auteur, 1830). Plate 10: Mappe monde. The National Library of Finland. Photo: Kari Timonen.

settled down in Hämeenlinna, the training center had been dismantled, so Christian Sibelius became the chief physician for the Sixth Hämeenlinna Battalion. The only other physician in the town, Otto Blåfield, perhaps seeing his chance, moved away, leaving his colleague to care for all of Hämeenlinna's citizens. Evidently this turn of events presented no special problem. Christian Sibelius had worked elsewhere as town doctor and in that very year completed a dissertation in gynecology.

The best-known picture of Christian Sibelius to survive shows a somewhat self-satisfied Finnish burgher dressed in starched collar and waistcoat adorned with a watch chain. A physique more pudgy than robust betrays a love of fine wines and good foods. His curly hair recedes, and he looks off to the side through wire-rimmed glasses, right eyebrow slightly lifted. The downward curve of his mouth conveys a moue of distaste, probably at having to sit for a photographer. All indications are that his first son's fun-loving nature came through the father's genes. So did other traits. Christian Sibelius adored cigars, whose rich, distinctive aroma permeated the very fabric of his life: his waistcoats and trousers, his books and medical records were redolent of their fragrance. As a young man, the doctor also loved singing and poetry. Known for his guitar playing, his singing (during his university studies he had joined Finland's oldest men's choir, Akademiska Sångföreningen), his hunting, and his generosity, Christian Sibelius spent lavishly, regardless of whether the money he dispensed was his.

The Hämeenlinna assignment, together with other events of the 1860s, shaped the lives of all the Sibelius family. It was there that the doctor's bachelor habits came to an abrupt end. The received tale is that his peers decided on Maria Charlotta Borg (1841–1897), daughter of a Lutheran minister, and set about arranging an introduction, after which a passionate courtship ensued.[14] The real story appears to have been rather less romantic. Sibelius was told that an inebriated Christian had come into the Borg home one evening after carousing with his Hämeenlinna companions and woozily picked out one of the young ladies.[15] That the engagement was one of convenience there is little doubt. The couple who married on March 7, 1862, were not even buried together.

But in the early 1860s that sad end was still in the future. Three children were born in due course: the first, Linda Maria, on November 27, 1863; the last, Christian, on March 28, 1869. It was the middle child, Johan Christian Julius, who arrived on a Friday in the darkest month of the year: December 8, 1865. That day the lead article in the local weekly, *Hämäläinen*, was devoted to the bitter weather: minus 17 degrees Celsius (1 degree Fahrenheit), so frigid that the lakes had frozen solid. The ice meant that it was possible to cross safely, even with a carriage, but the huge amounts of snow were causing difficulty in the countryside. The weather was an early harbinger of a catastrophe that would soon engulf all of Finland as well as other parts of Russia. The unseasonably early, bitter, and long-lasting cold led to massive crop failures, desperate hunger, and record numbers of deaths. In December 1865, however, there was rejoicing in the Sibelius household. Christian announced the new arrival to his brother Pehr: "He will be christened Johan Christian Julius and we will call him Janne, in memory of our departed brother"—Captain Johan "Janne" Sibelius.[16]

Janne Sibelius was enormously blessed to have arrived at this moment in the history of his land. The roll call of infants born in the 1860s reads like a panoply of Finland's finest: Juhani Aho; Axel Gallén; Arvid, Armas, and Eero Järnefelt; Pekka Halonen; Carl Gustaf Mannerheim; Oskar Merikanto; Venny Soldan-Brofelt; Helene Schjerfbeck; and Ellen Thesleff. Parents of Finnish children born in the 1860s had reason to expect a stable and even prosperous future for their offspring. In contrast to the period under Emperor Nicholas I, when a person "could not move, one could not even dream; it was dangerous to give any sign of thought—of the fact that you were not afraid,"[17] the grand duchy was thriving under Alexander II, who had assumed the throne in 1855, bringing peace and prosperity.

Whereas Nicholas I had censored, fined, and stifled the life out of his subjects, closing Russia's iron door and launching into the ill-fated Crimean War, his son had other ideas. In 1856 Alexander II ended the war that Nicholas had begun. By the 1860s the country had embarked upon a time of reform and rejuvenation, including the abolition, in 1861, of serfdom in Russia. Even though the Finns had no serfs, Alexander's actions signaled a spirit of individual liberation that pervaded the land and benefited Finns in matters from education to banking. Finland's beloved children's author, Zachris Topelius the Younger, heralded this moment in a patriotic poem, *Islossningen i Uleå älv* (*The Ice Breaking on the Oulu River*). The pride of being part of such a liberal-minded empire shone through: "O let me be worthy of my country/by sunlight and by night"; its opening stanza proclaimed, "Free I was born, and free I want to die." No more fitting words could have greeted the birth of Finland's sons and daughters of the 1860s.

ʊʊʊʊ

Despite the rosy prospects, the 1860s held tragedy for many, and the Sibelius family was not immune. By 1868 crop failures had led to a desperate state of affairs. The Finns were starving. With undernourishment exacerbated by plague, people began dying in record numbers: 14,500 in March 1868; 20,600 in April; 25,200 in May.[18] Conditions threatened to overwhelm the medical community, which was engulfed in caring for victims of typhus and other epidemics. A full one-tenth of the country's doctors perished. Christian Sibelius was among them. On July 7, 1868, at the age of just forty-seven, he breathed his last, stricken by typhus, his first son not yet three, his second son not yet born.

The plague that ravaged the population revealed a shadow side of the tranquil image promoted of Finland: neither the emperor nor his liberalizing advances could fend off the scourge. Nor did the tragedy evoke compassion from society's upper echelons, which exhibited regrettable hypocrisy and callous indifference toward the poor, who were the hardest hit.

Christian's death dealt the family a heavy blow. Although a new generation of Sibeliuses had emerged during the 1860s with the three births in Hämeenlinna, eerily, the lives of three brothers were exacted from the older Sibelius generation during the same decade: Carl Edvard, a surveyor, who died in 1863; Johan Matias Fredrik, the sea captain, who died in 1864; and Christian in 1868. Of the once large clan, there were now only the men's mother, Catharina Fredrika (1792–1879); one surviving brother, Pehr (1819–1890); and a sister, Evelina (1832–1893).

Among the family members, the plague's cruelest effects were felt by Christian's young wife, Maria Charlotta. She had been left destitute; despite his prominent position in Hämeenlinna, Christian Sibelius had managed money poorly, and his death cast the family into bankruptcy.[19] Maria Sibelius, young, pregnant, and evidently stunned by the tragic turn her life had taken, was now dependent on a small widow's pension. Sorrow and humiliation perhaps help to account for the increasing intensity of her introspection and religious obsessions. After all the household items had been auctioned against the debts, she took the one recourse open to her: she moved with her children into the Hämeenlinna home of her mother, the formidable Katarina Juliana Haartman Borg (1812–1892). Within months her third child was born, named Christian after the abruptly departed father; the family called him Kitti. Sibelius, too, christened Johan Christian Julius, bore his father's name, and the seeds of his later ambivalence in how he signed himself— alternately pushing "Christian" to third place in the name order, then pulling it back— were evidently sown in that crucial figure's unexpected and unwonted extinction.

LUTHERAN FOREBEARS

The Sibelius household now changed dramatically. Instead of a vigorous and life-loving set of parents, suddenly the family circle was predominantly female and cloyingly religious. Maria's father, Gabriel Borg, had been a Lutheran pastor and a school headmaster. He died in 1855, and his morose-looking widow settled in Hämeenlinna, the region from whence she had come. Mrs. Borg—Katarina Juliana—was born a Haartman, a clan marked by "a sense of the realities unencumbered by imagination or grace," as Sibelius once dryly put it.[20] Signs of imagination or fantasy in her grandchildren were considered fibbing and merited severe scolding. The household included "Mormor's" three grown daughters, the other five children having died or moved away: Julia (1850–1909, twin to Otto, a math teacher), who taught piano and had nervous troubles; Thekla (1839–1912), plagued with hypochondria; and Maria, who sank ever deeper into religious fervor. Maria's letters to her children overflow with religious concerns—worries about their psalmbooks, details of church sermons, and such expressions as "God, our God, help! And lead us! to do right in all things and give us health and strength to work."[21]

All the adult members of the household voiced similar sentiments. Expressions of God-fearing belonged to the society and to the times. When Maria's cousin Fredrik Borg (1847–1907) wrote to his relative, he was wont to begin his letters with such apostrophes as "Our Lord Jesus Christ, peace be to you all! Grace, Mercy and the peace of God our Father and of Jesus Christ our Lord! Amen."[22] No "Dear Marias" here, but sermonizing epistles of the most intense and unctuous kind. His letter of October 1879 characteristically overflows with biblical quotations—from Daniel, chapters 6 and 9; with lectures on King David (with a citation of Psalm 32:5—"I acknowledged my sin unto thee, and mine iniquity have I not hid: I said, I will confess my transgressions unto the Lord; and thou forgavest the iniquity of my sin"); and with citations from 1 Timothy 1:5—"When I call to remembrance the unfeigned faith that is in thee, which dwelt first in thy grandmother Lois, and thy mother Eunice; and I am persuaded that in thee also." Fredrik signed the letter "Din kusin och trosbroder Fredrik" (Your cousin and brother in faith, Fredrik), then continued the biblical deluge on the letter's verso with 1 John 4:9, 1 John 3:1, Philippians 4:5, 2 Corinthians 12:9, and more.

After a visit from the "cousin and brother in faith," Maria's brother Otto declared: "As far as his religiosity is concerned, it's one thing I will always appreciate about him."[23] Sibelius, who became extremely skilled at ambiguous and ironic meanings, evidently learned a thing or two from Uncle Otto.

~2~

Pillars of Finnish Identity

Whoever desires to describe the evolution of the mind must also consider its religious side, for it is one of the most important and influential phases of the history of the mind of man in the Nordic countries.

MINNA CANTH TO PASTOR ELIS BERGROTH, SEPTEMBER 27, 1886; TRANSLATED BY PAUL SJÖBLOM

LUTHERANISM AND THE FINNS

The copious moralizing expressions that permeate the Sibelius-Borg family correspondence hold the keys to understanding not only Sibelius, but also the Finns. As the writer and activist Minna Canth (1844–1897) insisted, "In the representation of no other nation is the religious side of the psyche so important as in that of ours."[1] For most Finns, that "religious side" was Lutheran. Lutheranism had dominated the religious life of Finland and Sweden ever since Gustav Vasa introduced the Reformation into his kingdom in the sixteenth century. Since that time, the Lutheran church has been the state church, and so it remained even through the years of Finland's autonomy, although the Orthodox faith, operating under the Holy Synod in Saint Petersburg, made its appearance in the grand duchy and, controversially, was the faith of the Karelians.[2]

The cornerstone of the Finns' religious side was the Bible, the implacable basis for the stern instruction of children and the unyielding source for the chastisement of adults. The Good Book read by the Sibelius family had been translated into the language spoken in their home, Swedish, by disciples of Martin Luther himself, Olaus Petri (1493–1552) and his brother Laurentius (1499–1573). The Petri version of the Bible was used in Finland right up until 1907, when the Gustaf V translation appeared. The sheer weight of the Petris' tome imparted an uncompromising and fearsome message—*anything* could be suppressed with it.

Lutheranism's severe and unyielding teachings have left their imprint even on modern Finns. Self-discipline and hard work are some of its lessons. So is obedience to authority, which helps to account for the unheard-of levels of popularity enjoyed by Finland's presidents: in 2003, for instance, President Tarja Halonen experienced a jaw-dropping 94 percent approval rating.[3] Lutheranism also explains the high literacy rate (the Lutheran church having implemented reading and writing requirements as a precondition for marriage as early as the eighteenth century), the uniform church tax, and a law—a *law*—against blasphemy. It has contributed to the deep conservatism in Finnish society and the regimented way in which matters are often carried out (evident in such ordinary things as notebook paper—lined not only horizontally, but also vertically, a printed and none-too-subtle injunction to "stay within the lines!" determined by some unseen authority.)

In Finland, there is no separation of church and state. Previously, there was no separation of church and school either. School days began with a prayer and the singing of a psalm. Pupils lined up by class, psalmbooks in hand, to attend the morning ceremony. For pupils in elementary school, the day also ended with prayer. Musical impressions were more likely to be excruciating than inspiring: schoolteachers usually accompanied the pupils on a harmonium or a small pump organ. Few teachers could have been called musicians; it was rather a matter of educators being required to master twenty or thirty psalms on the keyboard as part of their training. The result was often a dreadful hunt-and-peck musical experience in a lethally slow tempo, with the "organist" pumping madly while searching wildly for the next note.

The school curriculum required courses in religion and church history, which included readings from Luther's sermons and David's psalms. As is still the custom, most Finnish children attended confirmation school, where they received special religious instruction in the texts and doctrines of Lutheranism. Its culmination was a public profession of faith in a ceremony before the assembled congregation during which the initiates recited biblical passages from memory, declaimed church doctrine, and sang hymns. Although the particulars are no longer known, there can be no doubt that the Sibelius siblings, the grandchildren of a Lutheran minister, went through this coming-of-age ceremony.

Lutheranism's musical aspects—its chorales and hymns—were also regular features of services in which the Sibelius children participated. One of Janne's early letters to Uncle Pehr mentioned that Kitti was singing in Abbé Georg Joseph Vogler's *Hosianna* during an Advent service, still part of the Christmas ritual in Finland.[4] To be Finnish meant to be inculcated with the sounds of Lutheranism. It is no coincidence that Alexander Glazunov (1865–1936), exactly Sibelius's age and a frequent visitor to Finland, designed his C major *Fantaisie finnoise* to culminate on a stern and mighty blast of *Ein' feste Burg* or that the same hymn returns in the Russian composer's *Finnish Sketches*.[5]

Little attention has been paid to the Bach chorales, Lutheran hymns, and organ preludes that Sibelius heard as a child, but his compositions—with their hymnlike textures, their sometimes cloying harmonies, even their titles (such as *Religioso*, op. 78, no. 3, its manuscript dedicated "to my beloved brother Christian" in 1919)—give irrefutable testimony to this upbringing. Such features surface not just in the early works, but also show up among the very last pieces Sibelius composed: the hymnic compositions for the Masons; the organ works *Präludium*, *Postludium*, and *Intrada*; and the *Three Introductory Antiphons* and *God's Blessing* (*Herran siunaus*), written for the standardized edition of liturgical melodies in Finland. The deep impressions of the early Lutheran experiences endured in other ways, as will be seen.

For all its benefits, Lutheranism has its shadow side. The joyless version often practiced in the Nordic countries has supplied plenty of grist for literary mills, from August Strindberg's *The Red Room* to Isak Dinesen's *Babette's Feast*. Lutheranism engendered guilt and bred emotional distance, even among family members. It forced upon the Finns, people of passionate inclination, an uncompromising insistence on rules and punishment. Although some found outlets in creative expression, for many the psychological and emotional consequences of the Lutheran straitjacket in combination with the endless winter darkness were depression, alcoholism, domestic violence, or suicide. Of all the Sibelius siblings, the most terrible price would be paid by Sibelius's sister, Linda Maria, perhaps because, unlike her brothers, she had fewer opportunities to escape the oppressive home atmosphere. Already as a young person she was described as "religious."[6] The memento of hers preserved today in the Sibelius birthplace in Hämeenlinna is a prayer book. As an adult, Linda spent far too much of her sad life in mental institutions. The youngest sibling, Christian, the peacemaker and family caretaker, became a psychiatrist.

More usefully, religion provided something to rebel against. Already as a child, Sibelius exhibited a sense, if not of rebellion, then at least of being apart from this austere and inflexible atmosphere. At the age of ten he drew a picture of himself in a hot-air balloon soaring freely over the correct, constrained world of prim parasols and stiff top hats below (see fig. 2.1). His "acting out" in later years, from alcoholic binges to abandoning his wife to creditors for days at a time, may have owed as much to rebellion against the grim straits and rigid thinking of his upbringing as to his middle position in the sibling order and the business-as-usual behavior of men of his time.

Yet the Lutheran stamp was upon his brow. It was not just that he often pondered

Figure 2.1. The Sibelius family, with Uncle Pehr peering through his telescope at Janne in a
balloon. Childhood drawing by Sibelius, 1875.
Hämeenlinna City Archives.

on religion (in letters to his fiancée he confided that everyone in his family was *very* religious except himself),[7] or that he imbued a number of his works with spiritual content. To others around him, from friends to biographers, he made such comments as "How a man can get along without religion I can't understand."[8] Biblical images flicker through the pages of the diary he began keeping more or less regularly in 1909: here is doubting

Thomas; there is the uncompromising, grave, and somber God of his youth. But it is the words of Martin Luther that run through its pages like a sacred leitmotif: *Hier stehe ich, ich kann nicht anders.*

FINNS' LITERARY HERITAGE

While the Lutheran Bible inculcated in children of Sibelius's generation the moral values and ethical ideals of good Finns, three additional books supplied the other cornerstones for constructing a Finnish identity: Johan Ludvig Runeberg's *Fänrik Ståls sägner* (*The Tales of Ensign Stål*, 1848, 1860); Zachris Topelius's fabulously successful school classic, *Boken om vårt land* (first published in 1875); and Elias Lönnrot's academic compilation of oral poetry, the *Kalevala* (1835, revised and expanded in 1849).[9] Of these texts, only the *Kalevala* was originally written in Finnish. And, like the Bible, it was available in Swedish translation. Thus, by the time Sibelius was ten years old, the four great pillars of his country's literature and the base on which a solid Finnish identity was being molded were firmly and securely in place.

No other Nordic country has this kind of literary foundation. And it is no coincidence that, with the exception of the Bible, these literary Goliaths were created in the nineteenth century. They were the Finns' self-conscious endeavors to describe how they saw themselves and what they desired to be at a time when the leaders of this small group of people were preoccupied with establishing a distinct profile, formulating a national history, and constructing an image of what being Finnish meant vis-à-vis the world. As key factors in shaping Finnish self-image, these literary mainstays and, equally crucial, the opposition to them generated a creative tension that infused Finland's art, literature, music, theater, and later its films, through the nineteenth and much of the twentieth centuries. This dynamic tension is part of what makes Finland's story, and Sibelius's, unique. Jean Sibelius and his contemporaries did not come out of a cultural wilderness: the ground had been thoroughly and splendidly prepared. And it was largely prepared in Swedish.

RUNEBERG AND THE *TALES OF ENSIGN STÅL*

Johan Ludvig Runeberg, the poet laureate of Finland, the man who endeared himself to his countrymen with his deeply patriotic *Tales of Ensign Stål*, who crafted poems, short stories, and literary criticism, who inspired others to verbal and even musical expression, wrote very little about himself.[10] The main outlines of this doughty icon's life are well known: how the great fire in Turku that destroyed the university there destroyed his hopes for a career; how in Helsinki he was unable to obtain a position at the Imperial Alexander University; how he spent most of his adult life as a *gymnasium* (high school) teacher in the town of Porvoo in eastern Finland. Personal, human details—his tyranny over generations of aspiring youths; his passionate love affairs that sorely tried his plain but gifted wife, Fredrika; and his conflicted attitudes toward nature, love of which did not prevent him from laying strychnine-laced bait for some of its creatures—were hardly the stuff of national legends.

And a legend his manly ego aspired to be, a goal in which to all appearances he succeeded. In Finland the people paid him their respects—with statues, a museum, a day, even a pastry in his honor. All the way from Hämeenlinna, Janne Sibelius, only six or seven years old, accompanied his mother on a pilgrimage to visit Runeberg in person (Christian Gustaf had once studied with the great man). A handful of years later, Sibelius, now eleven, journeyed again to Porvoo—to lay flowers at the poet's newly dug grave.

The Finns were not alone in paying homage to this poet. Accolades came from abroad as well, for Runeberg's Swedish-language verses had achieved renown in Sweden. He had made the themes of his poetry—the nature, the religion, the patriotism that so intimately shaped the lives and attitudes of the Finns—universal. With classic, cool distance, Runeberg fashioned the immortal from the familiar:

Barn av våren	Child of the spring,
Rov för höstens vind,	Prey of autumn's wind,
Blomma, säg vi dröjer tåren	Flower, why does a tear
På din späda kind?	Tarry on your delicate cheek?[11]

Pressing romanticism's familiar images—flowers, seasons, swans—into simple forms, his verses sounded fresh and new, especially by comparison with earlier Swedish-language poetry, whose verbose, gothic images had bombastically glorified a Scandinavian past. And the simplicity of his language, ennobling drifting leaves, soaring swans, and freezing lakes in short lines, simple words, and easy forms made his poems exceptionally singable.

In Runeberg's vision, the beauty of Finland's natural landscapes was in harmony with the nature of the people who inhabited it—the moderate, stable, contented Finns. That view of ordinary people in an Arcadian idyll dominated his epic *Elgskyttarne* (*The Elk Hunters*), written, not coincidentally, in hexameter in imitation of the ancient Greeks. For this poet's classic vision was more in keeping with the aesthetics emanating from Saint Petersburg, where the Age of Enlightenment ideals held sway in courtly and aristocratic circles, than with the German-Swedish romanticism churning in the west and south.[12]

If love of Finnish nature was "in the poet's blood," so was religion, which Runeberg taught, along with Greek and Latin, at the *gymnasium* and to which in a sense he was married: Fredrika Tengström Runeberg (1807–1879) was the daughter of a Lutheran archbishop.[13] In the 1850s Runeberg even penned hymn texts for the Evangelical Lutheran Church. A number are still in use, but some were considered too artistic for the simple tastes of the Finnish people and were reworked, albeit over the poet's objections. Runeberg offered an alternative to the harsh Lutheran dogma. In *Kyrkan* (*The Church*), a poor man who is repeatedly thwarted in his attempt to attend church finally decides to worship on a small island in a mist-covered lake. In Finland's evocative nature, the poet seemed to say, lies the real church.[14] In the poem's final stanza, the morning sun rises over the lake. That image would acquire powerful currency.

Of all Runeberg's poetry, it was the patriotic *Tales of Ensign Stål* that supplied Finns with the central images and strongest vision of who they aspired or saw themselves to be. When part 1 was released at Christmastime in 1848, half the print run of two thousand was sold within a few days.[15] The release of part 2 in 1860, also at Christmas, likewise met with success (the role of market forces might well be credited for at least some of that success). Both parts awakened powerful emotions: as one of Finland's leading newspapermen, August Schauman, recalled on hearing the poems read aloud (a frequent mode of presentation in nineteenth-century Finland), "Our hearts pounded, tears flooded our eyes, our souls were uplifted."

Part 1 dwelled on idealized images of the land and its people; part 2 was devoted to history, heroism, and the courage and patriotism shown in the war of 1808–9. Every Finn knows the *Tales'* very first canto, "Vårt land, vårt land, vårt fosterland" (Our land, our land, our fatherland), the source of the phrase "land of a thousand lakes" and, since 1848, sung as the country's national anthem: "O Land, du tusen sjöars land, / der sång och trohet byggt" (O Land, thou land of a thousand lakes, / Where song and honor dwell). As recently as one hundred years ago, literate Finns could recite much more—even all—of the *Ensign Stål* cantos from memory.

Throughout Sibelius's creative life, the images of the character and soul of the people propounded in the *Tales* resonated—literally—in the air. As Zachris Topelius observed, never had a work of poetry been greeted with such admiration or inspired such devotion in Finland: "Few countries and few eras," said he, "can boast of such lofty tales, so proud, so warm, such masterful descriptions of events and persons."[16] In the strength and scope of their lines—tales of military heroes in epic trochaic tetrameter entwined with expressions of simple love of the land and its bounty—unfolds the same rich background against which Sibelius's life and music played out: "pure" country life versus the decadent seductions of the city; pious obedience versus fierce independence; patriotism, rebellion, and, overall, deep humanity.

Fifty years after part 1 appeared, Jean Sibelius was inspired to set one of *The Tales of Ensign Stål* to music, composing a stirring men's chorus with orchestra. *Sandels* is a story woven around a Swedish general who dallies over his morning meal while enemy Russians threaten the Finnish troops. Suddenly, the general reveals that he is afflicted with neither cowardice nor indifference: he leaps to his feet and courageously leads his men to victory. By 1898, when Sibelius composed *Sandels*, circumstances in Finland had fanned patriotic passion to new heights. Even though from the moment of their publication the *Tales* had been sought after by the educated classes, in the 1890s they were being re-released in massive numbers to the population, and the Finnish artist Albert Edelfelt was making bold, deeply patriotic, and anti-Russian illustrations to accompany a new edition published in 1900 (shown in fig. 1.1). Like so much else in the visions of the founding fathers, the currency of Runeberg's images of the Finns became self-fulfilling prophecy.

For Sibelius, who set more poems of Runeberg to music than those of any other bard, the poet of Porvoo proves an invaluable guide to a man finding his way, both as a composer and as a Finn, through the complicated, interwoven paths of national sentiment and modernist creative thought. With the exception of the *Sandels* episode, Sibelius selected Runeberg's lyrical works for musical setting, conspicuously choosing those with the most modern, even potentially Symbolist, content.[17] The earliest date from 1888— two choral settings from Runeberg's *Third Book* of poems (1843), both composed for mixed choir. One begins *Hur blekt är allt* (*How Pale Is All*), a strophic setting of three verses the poet had called *Höstkvällen* (*Autumn Evening*). The other is *Tanke, se, hur fågeln svingar* (*Imagine, See How the Bird Swoops*), with its telltale lines "Även du har dina vingar / Och din rymd att flyga i" (You too have your wings / And your mighty space in which to fly).[18] The conventional romantic musical language of both settings gives no indication that their composer would ever do anything more than stay boringly earthbound. Only the texts hint at his dreams and ambitions:

Klaga ej att du vid gruset	Lament not that to the heavy earth
Som en fånge binds ännu;	You are still bound like a prisoner;
Lätt som fågeln, snabb som ljuset,	Light as a bird, quick as the light,
Mer än båda fri är du.	You are freer than either.

In the course of the 1890s, Sibelius mined Runeberg's poetry for many more texts. The six songs assembled as op. 13 included the psychologically rich verses of *Under strandens granar* (*Beneath the Fir Trees*), *Drömmen* (*The Dream*), and *Till Frigga* (*To Frigga*). Across a thirty-year span and well into the second decade of the twentieth century, Sibelius set to music many more Runeberg poems, all adroitly and meaningfully chosen, from the seldom-heard duet *Tanken* (*The Thought*) to the exquisite solo *Norden* (*The North*) and the cycle of six Runeberg songs written toward the end of World War I. Runeberg's shade hovers over even such instrumental works as *The Village Church* and *The Bard*. Sibelius absorbed the poet's classical vision of balance and moderation, his minimalist compression, and his pantheistic beliefs until they were part of the composer's own identity.

ZACHRIS TOPELIUS, *THE BOOK OF OUR LAND*, AND *SCÈNES HISTORIQUES*

If Runeberg's image has shape-shifted into that of an egocentric and distant genius, Zachris Topelius (1818–1898), the other dominant literary figure in nineteenth-century Finland, is remembered as a gentle and benevolent, if anti-intellectual, character, a writer of children's stories who was ultimately killed by the kindness of his effusive admirers: he expired during the lavish festivities in celebration of his eightieth birthday, in the year Sibelius composed Runeberg's *Sandels*.[19] Known to be quite narrow-minded about trends of the 1880s, Topelius became synonymous with the naively idealistic, sidelined as sentimental and saccharine, the nodding, grandfatherly bard embodied in the statue that stands today in a Helsinki park, a venerable storyteller enfolding solemnly listening children.

The younger Topelius was feistier and juicier. He too has been honored in a sculpture. This one stands on Helsinki's Esplanade: *Saga och sanning—Saga and Truth*—is its name. Two young lasses—nude—face in opposite directions, the flame of truth in the hand of one, the bluebird of happiness in the hand of the other. The symbols point to the Topelius who was a newspaper editor, history professor, and eventually rector of the Imperial Alexander University, a man who pursued a number of passionate love affairs whose progeny was a clutch of erotic poetry (it remained in manuscript). Some of his patriotic verses rang with sentiments so astonishingly anti-Russian that they failed to pass the censors. Meanwhile, his ideas about the education of girls shocked the locals. Topelius, remaining true to his Christian ideology, upheld the belief that all things made by God had rights, even women. As university rector, he fought for women's entitlement to advanced study. These radical ideas, apparent by the 1860s, contributed to the adoption of equal suffrage in Finland in 1906, and Zachris Topelius was one of the first to take up such questions. He also awakened Finnish society to other issues needing reform, from nature preservation to animal rights.

Topelius played a more direct part in Finland's musical life than did Runeberg. He too wrote hymn texts that can still be found in Finnish psalmbooks. He wrote the libretto—in Swedish—for the first opera to be composed in Finland: *Kung Karls jakt*

(*The Hunt of King Charles*); Christian Gustaf Sibelius had sung in its chorus when the work was premiered in 1852.[20] Occasionally Topelius even set some of his own poems to music, but it was mainly other composers, from Karl Collan to Fredrik Pacius, who mined the bard's verses for song texts.

Jean Sibelius did too. Sibelius almost certainly first encountered Topelius's works through the children's stories, for the tales of this Hans Christian Andersen of Finland formed part of every Finnish child's life. Among the most adored was a cycle of historical novellas, *Fältskärns berättelser* (*The Tales of a Field Surgeon*, 1853–67), together with *Läsning för barn* (*Readings for Children*, begun the year of Sibelius's birth and eventually running to eight volumes, 1865–96). In his twenties, the fledgling composer played one of his works for Topelius; although shamefully convinced he had not made a good impression, Sibelius fervently declared, even many years later, that he was "the most devoted admirer [Topelius] could have wished for."[21]

It seems fitting that, just as Topelius's books and stories were among the most widely read in Finland, Sibelius's settings of this poet's words are among the best-known of his country's songs, even more than a century after their creation. *Julvisa* (*Jouluvirsi* [*Christmas Song*]) is performed every yuletide by choirs and congregations all over the land; Finns know it by heart, although today most of them sing it in Finnish rather than in the poet's original Swedish:

Giv mig ej glans, ej guld,	Give me no splendor, no gold,
ej prakt	no pomp
i signad juletid;	at blessed Christmastide;
giv mig Guds ära, änglavakt	give me God's glory and angel hosts
och över jorden frid!	and peace o'er earth so wide!

The hymn's huge popularity shows up in the nearly three pages of editions and arrangements listed in the Sibelius works catalog; as late as 1954 the composer himself was arranging the hymn for boys' choir and organ.[22]

Topelius's poetic message resonated with Lutheran teachings, and Sibelius's setting recalls countless hymns he had known from childhood: a syllabically set text; standard, four-measure phrases underpinned by long pedal points; pious, diminished-seventh chords sugaring the non-too-adventurous harmony—music as sweetly sentimental as the poetry, a hymnic embodiment of the writer the Finns called "the fairy tale uncle" (see ex. 2.1).

It is hardly surprising to find that the hymn belongs to the composer's op. 1—hardly surprising, that is, until the date of composition is mentioned: 1909, the same time the radical Fourth Symphony was begun. Nor were the simple hymns of op. 1 the only time

EXAMPLE 2.1. SIBELIUS, *JULVISA*, OP. 1, NO. 4, MM. 1–12.

BY PERMISSION OF FENNICA GEHRMAN OY, HELSINKI.

the mature Sibelius turned to Topelius (or manipulated his opus numbers): he created a recitation with strings out of Topelius's version of Anna Maria Lenngren's *Countess's Portrait*, a gentle spoof on familiar figures in eighteenth-century Swedish life.[23] In 1914 he made a setting of Topelius's poem *Orion's Belt* (op. 72), although the music has been lost. Such a jolting disconnect indicates something of the depth and resonance of childhood experiences within a composer confronted by radical changes in a tumultuous world.

Topelius also produced some of the key texts of Finnish nationalism and self-definition. In his poetry, love of the country's natural landscapes combined with keen beliefs about its history. The result was often so strong a sense of historical scenes that whole poems could be called *scènes historiques*. In other works Topelius enshrined Finland's landscapes in forms so graphic that he gave sanctity to what, in the eyes of many, had previously represented harsh conditions and cruel fate. One such work was an annotated collection of lithographs: *Finland framstäldt i teckningar* (*Finland Presented in Pictures*), initially published in installments. There, Topelius lovingly intermingled his deep attachment to nature and an aesthetic appreciation of the land and its history with patriotism.[24]

Never before had Finland's nature received such treatment, and the pages of these handsome illustrations together with their historical and geographical texts fostered pride in the fatherland, nurtured a national consciousness, and promoted a collective sense of sacred mission. Together with its successor, *En resa i Finland* (*A Trip through Finland*), which Topelius never quite finished, *Finland framstäldt i teckningar* established the canonic images of Finland's natural scenery, invested devotion and significance in the terrain, and elevated Finland's landscapes through one man's personal vision to "sites of memory" to which Finns added ever more layers of meaning.

What underpinned these and other writings was Topelius's belief that history was equated with time, and geography, with space. And what united these seemingly inseparable concepts were the Finnish *folk*, a people indivisible, under God, divinely chosen. These ideas took their most influential form in still another Topelian volume. Its cumbersome title needed an editor's hand—*Läsebok för de lägsta lärowerken i Finland: Boken om vårt land*—but the work known widely as *The Book of Our Land* powerfully shaped the Finns' self-image for decades. In this volume, first published in 1875, Topelius assembled a variety of proverbs, riddles, and lyrical songs; he hailed and explained Finland's literature, especially the *Kalevala*; and not least, he expressed admiration for its ruling emperors. His focus, however, was on Finland's people—in his vision, God-fearing, obedient, perseverant, industrious, tough, freedom loving—and on the people's history and geography. Notably, the book was one of the first volumes to emphasize geography as an independent science.

The Book of Our Land provided the Finns with one of their central texts. Quickly adopted as a fundamental primary-school reader, the volume reached thousands of Finnish pupils and was used for generations. Although written in Swedish, it was immediately translated into Finnish and over time revised by its author, and later by others; there have been no fewer than twenty subsequent editions in Swedish and fifty-three in Finnish.[25] Well into the twentieth century, the volume, especially under its Finnish title, *Maamme kirja*, was still serving its national purpose. The writer Väinö Linna (1920–1992), who penned a canonic volume of his own, *The Unknown Soldier*, identified *The Book of Our Land* as one of his earliest literary influences; Topelius's tome even provided the point of departure for Linna's celebrated trilogy *Under the Northern Star*, whose unforgettable first words are "In the beginning was the swamp, the hoe—and Jussi."[26]

Linna's actual words were "Alussa olivat suo, kuokka—ja Jussi," because Linna wrote his novels in Finnish. Topelius had shown remarkable foresight when he wrote in the early editions of *Boken om vårt land*, "Swedish literature in Finland will slowly fall into silence."[27] It was a prediction that would chillingly apply to Jean Sibelius.

A QUESTION OF LANGUAGE

Surely, eyebrows are being raised and throats cleared. Foundations of *Finnish* identity in the *Swedish* language? A Finnish national poet, Finnish national texts, Finland's national composer, all writing in Swedish and speaking Swedish as a mother tongue? The circumstances of two strong and radically different languages in Finland—one an Indo-European tongue closely related to German and the other an exotic and extremely challenging Finno-Ugric language whose closest relatives today are Karelian and Estonian—indeed call for explanation. Although modern Finland is one of the few nations in the world where more than 90 percent of the population speak the same language, bilingualism nevertheless represents one of the most important, yet least understood, aspects of its history.[28] It was a crucial component of Finnish society that was quite strong up until World War II and endures to this day, in matters from the mundane to the professional. The complications are considerable, and they must be kept in mind when approaching almost any Finnish topic.

To begin with, until the end of the nineteenth century the concepts of a "mother tongue" and of labeling themselves by linguistic group were foreign to most Finns, although there were "Finnish-minded" Finns—*Fennomaani*—from at least the 1860s. Runeberg's example, however, can stand for many: he wrote his works in Swedish and identified himself as a Finn. Within the two-language framework it was perfectly possible to change position in any one of a variety of ways: you could be born into one language, then wholeheartedly adopt the other; you could adapt to the other language as needed; you could change one or more of your names to the other language; you could use a pen name in one tongue and your given name in the other. When in the 1890s statistics began to be taken to sort out where the linguistic divides might be, people were forced to identify with one group or the other, and the answer was generally given according to the language of the *gymnasium* a person had attended. Yet even the most stubborn and radical advocates of the Finnish language were fluent in Swedish. Those in academic life had to be, because in many cases Finnish words did not yet exist for certain scholarly concepts.

It was not until the 1910s that the phrase "Finland-Swede" was invented to designate the antagonistic position between Finland's Swedish speakers and the extreme Fennomans. The epithet fueled a fundamental misconception: that Finland-Swedes are of Swedish origin. But in fact among Finns of both language groups there are those with Swedish ancestors and those with wholly Finnish (or Russian or Baltic) ancestors.[29] The mix prevents any reductive simplification.

There are also other language groups in Finland—the three languages found among the Sámi of Lapland, for example, and the languages of the Roma and the Russians. Today the Sámi and Roma languages are protected under the constitution, but they constitute only a tiny minority (around 1 percent) of an already small population. In Sibelius's time the upper classes often spoke German, especially in the area around Viipuri in southeastern Finland; in 1813 the language of instruction in all twenty schools in Viipuri province was German, and one of their teachers, *Oberlehrer* L. Purgold, confidently predicted that German would become the language of all Finland.[30]

The Viipuri situation highlights what was largely accurate about bilingualism in Finland, namely, that it was (and is) found mostly among minorities. In nineteenth-century Finland, that meant the upper class. The habit is abundantly evident in Sibelius's letters to Aino in the period after their marriage, where he flows from one language into the other and back again at will. Like Sibelius, most of the leaders of the national movement came from Swedish-speaking homes. It was they who adopted the majority tongue in the service of the greater goal of securing their country's future.

The Roots and Consequences of Bilingualism

The roots of this linguistic history reach deep into the past, a consequence of Finland's long centuries as part of Sweden.[31] As far back as the Middle Ages, many of the people known as Finns spoke a common, non-Indo-European tongue, albeit in various dialects, and many state and judicial affairs in Finland were conducted orally in Finnish. But when the power-lusting, long-reigning Gustav Vasa came to the Swedish throne in 1523 (which he ruled until 1560), he changed the lives of Finns irrevocably. Managing his realm like a ruthless tycoon, this suspicious-minded dictator consolidated every possible power into his royal hands. His relentless grasp extended to the Roman Catholic church, whose influence he shrewdly usurped and replaced with the Reformation, having identified its interests as utterly his own. The consequences were immediate—and for the Finns profound.

Luther, of course, had opened the way for vernacular languages to replace Latin in the church. In predominantly Finnish-speaking regions of the land, Finnish could be heard in church services, a practice aided considerably after the Finn Mikael Agricola (1510–1557), who had studied with Luther and Melanchthon in Wittenberg, translated the New Testament and other Lutheran texts into Finnish. Completed in 1543, Agricola's New Testament translation was published five years later, establishing a firm basis for the linguistic development of Finnish and demonstrating that a widely spreading bilingualism was already in place.

Nevertheless, the use of Swedish as the administrative language of the kingdom of which Finns were a part, as well as the language of culture and education, contributed to a devastating split in Finnish society. It was bad enough that the language of commerce, civil, and administrative affairs was Swedish, which put anyone without Swedish skills—meaning the vast majority of Finnish peasants—at a supreme disadvantage. What was worse was that the linguistic difference also divided the Finns by culture, by class, by wealth, and by position. At its most extreme, two separate nations have lived—and do live still—in Finland.

With the annexation of Finland to Russia as an autonomous unit in 1808–9, the linguistic picture suddenly changed. Finnish was no longer the minority language vis-à-vis Swedish.[32] Moreover, the Russian emperors encouraged the use of Finnish, the weapon of choice in their determination to eradicate the Swedish past, its culture, and its loyalties from the minds of their new subjects. In 1828 the emperor established a lectorate in Finnish at the Imperial Alexander University in Helsinki. In 1831 he sanctioned the founding of the Suomalaisen Kirjallisuuden Seura (Finnish Literature Society), and a few years later he looked favorably upon its project to publish the Finnish-language epic, the *Kalevala*. In 1850 his imperial hand created a university professorship in the Finnish language. Not only was this professorial chair one of the very first such positions, but furthermore, the Finnish and Russian chairs remained the only ones in modern languages for more than two decades at Finland's university. Meanwhile, research on Finno-Ugric philology was instigated at the prestigious Academy of Sciences in Saint Petersburg.

For their part, Finnish leaders, all of whom spoke Swedish, had not been slack about advancing the Finnish language. In 1880 Finns who spoke Swedish as the language of the home (a group to which the Sibelius family belonged) constituted just 14.3 percent of the population.[33] Nevertheless, their education and fluency in the idiom and mores of the dominant culture put them in the upper class culturally and in positions of leadership administratively. Even though the numbers of Swedish speakers were small, their influence was great.

J. V. SNELLMAN AND THE NATIONAL MOVEMENT

The most forward-thinking Swedish speakers advocated adopting Finnish as the national language. In their view, linguistic unity was a sure means of rallying the Finnish-speaking majority to the national cause and thereby maintaining the country's treasured autonomy. A key figure in this movement was Johan Vilhelm Snellman (1806–1881). Born in Stockholm of a Finnish father and raised in Sweden until the age of twelve, Snellman became one of the central figures advancing the idea of a Finnish nation as a political entity.[34] Snellman's practical and patriarchal philosophy (equality for women was a foreign concept to this forefather) was a mix of Hegelian, Lutheran, and Herderian elements and included the belief that individuals had moral obligations to their nation (a conviction he put into practice in his own life). He maintained that society should be a civic, not a bureaucratic order, and that the national spirit, not religion, should be its guiding principle.

In furtherance of these beliefs, Snellman supported educating the masses, on the one hand, and "nationalizing" the educated, on the other, meaning, in effect, rallying the elite minority to change their language from Swedish to Finnish (although Snellman himself never acquired much more than a rudimentary command of Finnish). Along with achieving such pragmatic benefits for his countrymen as Finnish currency (the *markka*) in 1860, Snellman won a major linguistic advance when the emperor signed the Language Edict in 1863, giving Finnish equal status to Swedish in matters involving the Finnish-speaking population and paving the way for full language equality.

It was thus for the sake of the national cause that many Swedish-speaking Finns changed their language—and even their names—from Swedish to Finnish. Some adopted pen names: Aleksis Kivi, for instance, who remained Alexis Stenvall but used a Finnish name in his literary endeavors. Others changed their names legally. The Forsman family presents one of the most disconcerting cases in point: the archnationalist born with the Swedish name Georg Zacharias Forsman adopted the lip-curling Finnish pen name Yrjö-Koskinen. Assuming a name of "the people" in no way deterred him from accepting ennoblement—as Yrjö Sakari Yrjö-Koskinen; the paterfamilias's son was bewilderingly called Yrjö Koskinen Yrjö-Koskinen.[35] Such formulations, reformulations, and mutations daze even the most diehard devotees of Finnish history.

However convoluted, this background explains the seemingly paradoxical circumstance that the majority of those passionately working for a distinctively Finnish identity were Swedish speakers: Snellman, Topelius, the Cygnaeuses, Carl Gustaf Mannerheim, Martin Wegelius, Robert Kajanus, Albert Edelfelt, and Axel Gallén, to name but a few. Today, when flattened academic summaries have sapped the life from the suasions and sermons of the converted, it is easy to miss the irony, but on the original pages of pamphlets, newspaper articles, and personal letters, the great creators of and apologists for Finnish-language literature and Finnish arts, even bilingual Lönnrot and the literary giant Aleksis Kivi, often made their cases for the Finnish national cause in Swedish. Although some, such as Topelius, envisioned a bilingual Finland with "one nation, two languages," others, such as Snellman, who knew nary a word of Finnish beyond an exchange of pleasantries, fanatically insisted on "one nation, one language," eradicating their own language in the process.

By the latter part of the nineteenth century, many families were beginning to put their young children into the new Finnish-language schools, a choice seen as assuring their future. Hämeenlinna, a regional administrative center for southern Finland and strategic military headquarters, had one of the newest such institutions, Hämeenlinnan normaalilyseo (the Hämeenlinna Normal School), founded in 1873 as part of a highly significant initiative: "enlightenment" through public education in the Finnish language. For the Sibelius children, the location of the school in their hometown was fortunate indeed, a consequence of the internal Russian-Swedish-Finnish tensions: intended for Helsinki, the lyceum was shifted to small-town Hämeenlinna thanks to Casimir von Kothen (1807–1880), a pro-Russian, pro-Swedish-language Finn who, as vice chancellor of the university and later director of Finland's school board, saw little need for a school with Finnish-language teaching in the capital.[36] The Sibelius family enrolled the two boys, who, in studying Finnish, learning Finnish folksongs, and reading the *Kalevala*, acquired the veneer of another culture. For Sibelius, the Finnish-language education did not replace his Swedish-language inheritance, but instead fruitfully enriched and opened his outlook.

THE *KALEVALA*

The fourth rock on which the Finns built the temple of their national identity was the *Kalevala*, the collection of folk poetry collected, assembled, and edited by Elias Lönnrot (1802–1884). The *Kalevala* was the only one of the Finns' four literary pillars originally written in Finnish. Its importance is as difficult to define as it is to overstate. Its value had relatively little to do with the work's intrinsic literary worth and everything to do with what it was believed to prove. After all, few clamored to read and reread its pages; the first edition's limited run of 500 copies took more than a decade to sell.[37] But with the *Kalevala*'s first appearance, in 1835, the publisher (the respected Finnish Literature Society) proclaimed the volume to be Finland's "national epic." So, uncontested, it has remained. Thus, from a publisher's advocacy promulgated on the wave of a swelling national consciousness, the *Kalevala* began to acquire a central role in shaping the national identity.

The *Kalevala*'s very existence belonged to the larger picture of Finland's national awakening, and the background to its creation belongs here.

Defining a National Agenda

The swell of national consciousness generated intellectual thought waves as early as the eighteenth century, but as with so many other issues, the annexation of Finland to Russia caused it to billow into a full-blown surge. In 1809, when Emperor Alexander I met with his new subjects in Porvoo for the first time and acknowledged newly defined Finland's special rights, the concept of "Finnishness" hardly existed. But the emperor's actions strengthened the waves already being made, most effectively by scholars in Turku, the seaport in southwestern Finland.[38] An intellectual meeting ground for currents coming from Sweden and further afield, the Turku university, founded in 1640 and called the Royal Academy, was counted as one of the Swedish universities.[39] It provided the locus of a flourishing Finnish patriotism arising from a thirst for knowledge, a love of the land, and ideas about improving the people's well-being as a means of ensuring prosperity for all.

The professor of rhetoric at the Royal Academy, Henrik Gabriel Porthan (1739–1804), had decisively advanced the study of Finnish poetry and history with his five-volume *De poësi Fennica* (published between 1766 and 1778). Yet it was Porthan's students, the so-called Turku Romantics, who realized the potential of his and his compatriots' ideas by turning to their history, retrieving—or sometimes inventing—it, undertaking the collection of folk poetry and folk ways, and promoting the Finnish language. As one of them, Carl Axel Gottlund (1796–1875), put it, "Just as an independent nation cannot exist without a fatherland, no fatherland can exist without poetry. For what is poetry except the crystal in which nationality mirrors itself, the spring from which the nation's original feeling arises to the surface."[40] To these radical students has been attributed the rallying cry of obscure origin but later fame, "Swedes we are no longer, Russians we cannot be, therefore, let us be Finns."[41]

The lofty national purposes to which the Turku Romantics aspired came to be associated with students (all of whom were men) and with stirring, youthful ideals: unite the people with a common tongue, awaken national pride by exalting Finland's heroic past, and develop artistic traditions from an authentic Finnish foundation. Music was to have an essential place among those traditions, and in a way that glorified the cult of masculinity. Across Europe, men's choirs were being used to express political and especially patriotic opinion, and now student songs began to sound from the streets and parlors of Turku.[42] One of the most outspoken of the Turku Romantics was Adolf Ivar Arwidsson (1791–1858), a man connected to central figures in Sweden's romantic movement and founder of a newspaper, *Åbo Morgonblad*, that championed the national movement. Arwidsson made significant contributions to the musical life of his land, partly through his promotion of national men's choirs, partly by producing a three-volume national folk-song anthology, *Svenska fornsånger* (published in Stockholm in 1834, 1837, and 1842), to which he devoted almost a decade and a half. With the Turku Romantics, art and politics joined common cause.

The ideals of these early patriots, far from being inherently Finnish, came from Europe, and their philosophical precepts were German. Johann Gottfried von Herder (1744–1803) had promoted the belief that a people's language usage, literature, and history must be built on cultural roots; where lost, those roots could be reclaimed through the poetry, songs, and other traditions of ordinary folk.[43] It was symptomatic of the time that national thought was sparked by and inextricably mixed with international ideas, and the results were on full display in the ideals of the Turku Romantics: they embraced notions formulated and articulated abroad, yet their Fennocentric goals prompted their countrymen to begin using the zealous term "Fennomania," a name that gradually came to refer to language politics and the Finnish national movement.[44]

The Turku Romantics' most ambitious goals were linguistic. Even though they were Swedish-speaking, they aspired to forsake their home language, "convert" to using Finnish, and persuade their Swedish-speaking countrymen to do the same. Plenty of people thought their ideas preposterous. "Geese all speak the same tongue, it is true," sniped one, "but they do not form a nation."[45] It was the start of a long conflict over linguistic usage and superiority that would be waged throughout Jean Sibelius's creative life.

As for those lofty and patriotic goals for the arts, well, who could possibly dream that a country like Finland—"too cold, too poor, and, let us say without timidity, too uncivilized for the magnificent and colorful flowers, those southern sun maidens, of pictorial art to gain an enduring footing in its snow-covered granite soil"[46]—could produce anything of artistic value? Finland did not have any art museums. It had no sustainable orchestra, no regular opera, no ballet company. In theater, not only did the language question make for an uncertain literary and dramatic future, but worse, many were convinced that the language of the majority—Finnish—would be unable to "spawn anything but ABC books."[47] Finnish was an idiom for geese, not poetry. The notion of developing Finnish artistic traditions looked as laughable and out of reach as linguistic conversion.

Despite the naysayers, a handful of idealists, fired by the exhilarating possibilities, set out to study folk poetry and folk music as a patriotic duty. They initiated a long and fruitful activity that eventually generated the largest folk archive of its kind in the world.[48] Their endeavors led to a series of accomplishments so brilliant, so dazzling that the Finns could claim not one, but several golden ages. The Turku Romantics may not themselves have fulfilled their principal goals. But they articulated a national agenda— "let us be Finns"—and encouraged the national movement, which they aided and abetted with copious research into the folkloric heritage of "true Finnishness," generating a momentum that enabled others to carry out their goals in ways beyond their own wildest imaginings.

The "Founding Fathers"

Three young men who arrived in Turku in 1822 to study at the university would profoundly change the social, civic, and linguistic landscape: Johan Ludvig Runeberg,
Johan Vilhelm Snellman, and Elias Lönnrot. The contributions of the first two to the
national movement have already been explored. It was the third figure, a medical doctor
with a passion for collecting folk tales, who created the *Kalevala* from a collection of
oral folk poems gathered during his numerous trips throughout the area known as Karelia. Lönnrot titled his anthology *Kalewala: taikka: Wanhoja Karjalan runoja Suomen
kansan muinoisista ajoista* (*Kalevala: or, Old Karelian Poetry from the Antiquity of the
Finnish People*).[49] Rooted, as Lönnrot and his contemporaries believed, in the Finnish
people's history, the *Kalevala* embodied the linguistic, historical, and cultural ideals
of the Turku Romantics. Topelius, whose father, Zacharias Topelius the elder, had
also collected folk poems and had published the multivolume *Suomen Kansan Wanhoja
Runoja* (*Old Poems of the Finnish People*), devoted an entire chapter in his *Book of Our
Land* to the *Kalevala*, which he presented in a condensed version for impressionable
young Finns:

> Everywhere it has been thought that the *Kalevala* is one of the most remarkable
> folklore products [that has] ever appeared, and the Finnish nation has been con-
> sidered fortunate to possess such a work. For no folklore collection in the world
> is like the *Kalevala*. It reflects the character of the Finnish people, and although
> much in it appears pagan and strange to our age, there is in it a profound wis-
> dom, a simple beauty, and a moving love of the fatherland.[50]

With its tales of heroes tongue-twistingly called Väinämöinen, Lemminkäinen, Ilmarinen,
and Kullervo, the *Kalevala* gave Finns a literary monument that won praise from foreigners, the Finnish litmus test of worth—people like the Brothers Grimm in Germany and
Henry Wadsworth Longfellow (1807–1882) in America. Longfellow modeled his *Song
of Hiawatha*—"By the shores of Gitchee Gumee / By the shining Big-Sea-Water . . ."—
directly on the *Kalevala*'s trochaic tetrameter—"I will sing the people's legends, / And
the ballads of the nation." Here was a classic worthy of Homer, an epic capable of holding its own with other landmarks of world literature. Even better in the view of many,
the *Kalevala* not only gave Finns a great literature, it also gave them a history, or at least
the means for constructing one. Even though the poems had been edited and fashioned
into a unity according to a plan of Lönnrot's creation, they were widely believed to show
that Finland had a splendid, heroic past both ancient and independent. They proved that

a sovereign Finnish nation had been blessed with its own gods, traditions, cultural values, and ways of life; here was a cultural continuity that validated the Finns as a separate entity.[51]

With the appearance of the *Kalevala*, the fourth foundation stone of Finnish identity was rolled ringingly into place.

～3～

Nineteenth-Century Finland
Scènes historiques

SCENES FROM CHILDHOOD: LIFE IN A FINNISH GARRISON TOWN

While young Sibelius's inner world was molded by stories, poems, and Bible verses in Swedish, growing up in a garrison town of the Russian Empire impressed formative experiences of another kind upon his small person. The setting was both picturesque and historical. Tavastehus, as Sibelius knew it—Hämeenlinna in Finnish—the oldest inland town in Finland, lies beside the waters of Lake Vanajavesi.[1] *Linna* means castle, and a castle fortress, parts of which date from the mid-thirteenth century, forms the town's most distinctive landmark. International trade had long preceded the castle's construction. Already in the early medieval period the Ox Road (Härkätie) led westward, connecting Hämeenlinna via Turku to Scandinavia. Remnants of commerce as ancient as 1,000 years old still survive in the region in the form of silver jewelry hoards and caches of western and oriental coins.

Over its long past Hämeenlinna has had many faces, but when fire raged through its streets in 1831, the stage was set for it to acquire the look the Sibelius family was to know. The design, originally ordered by the Swedish king, Gustav III, was replanned by none other than Carl Ludvig Engel (1778–1840), the German architect of Helsinki's imperial style. Drawn on a grid pattern, a new Hämeenlinna rose from the ashes, its pretty, single-storied Empire-style buildings spaced well apart, its tree-lined lanes and areas designated for parks and deciduous trees safeguarding against future fiery destruction.

The Russian emperors required more ominous places of residence: barracks. These too were given names, *Linnan kasarmi* (the barracks for the Russian military) and *Suomen kasarmi* (the barracks for the Finnish troops). By the time Sibelius was ten years old, Hämeenlinna's population of 3,672 citizens had been augmented by some 1,256 Russian

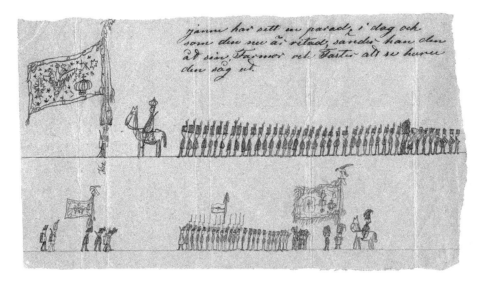

Figure 3.1. The emperor's military might on parade in Hämeenlinna. The text reads: "Janne saw a parade today and now that it's drawn, he sends it to his grandmother and aunt for them to see what it looked like." Childhood drawing by Sibelius, 1875. The National Archives of Finland.

infantrymen, artillery troops, and Cossacks. The townspeople were sometimes called upon to provide for the military men. In the summer of 1875 it was decreed that 198 kitchens and 158 horse stalls should be handed over for military use; the citizens feared these demands would be their ruin.[2]

Still, that same military on parade could shake a person to the core. When the troops marched to the blare of the military band, brass and woodwinds blasting, the great crashing drums reverberating from every side, the buildings of Hämeenlinna's central square threw back the mighty sounds in thunderous echoes in a thrilling display. Battalion bands normally consisted of eight wind players and eight drummers, a makeup reflecting the general European situation in the latter part of the eighteenth century.[3] For the Russian emperors the bands played a vital role: their awesome sounds conveyed the power of the empire itself.

A scene from the year 1875 featuring such a parade greatly displeased the Russian general who was reviewing the troops. Those echoes! Those delays! Lagging beats! Inaccurate timing! In defiance of all the laws of physics, the general angrily reprimanded the bandmaster—in public—for those out-of-sync reverberations. Ten-year-old Janne Sibelius captured this historical *tableau* in an astonishingly detailed drawing (see fig. 3.1). Over seventy men march across the page, standing at attention in two long rows, their hat plumes meticulously penciled, their bayonet-embellished rifles precisely aligned. At the head of the parade sits the general astride a giant horse, an enormous, onion-shaped hat dwarfing his smallish head. The Russian double eagle looms from a splendid banner, flanked by the imperial crown and the Orthodox cross, while a tiny figure standing at attention beneath the banner and holding a rifle is identified in small handwriting as "Kitti." Bringing up the rear, behind a priest bearing a sacred icon, is the band, its players trumpeting their spine-tingling sounds on two horns, two bassoons, two clarinets, and four flutes. A second row of soldiers, fierce weapons at the ready, marches across the lower part of the page, where more imperial banners wave.

For an impressionable, sensitive-eared boy it was the beginning of a love affair with musical sound, the very essence of the music of the spheres. The first musical experience to leave visible traces, possibly the very first to find its way into small Janne Sibelius's heart, the military parade reverberated for decades from other pages written in his hand, its sounds and images sculpting powerful symphonic shapes in which sound and space merged, and symphonic aftershocks echoed through his orchestras (see ex. 3.1). It reverberated in his head still when, in the ninth decade of his life, he recounted this episode to Otto Andersson.[4]

EXAMPLE 3.1. SIBELIUS, *SKOGSRÅET*, MM. 238–42.
© BREITKOPF & HÄRTEL, WIESBADEN.

The Military Influence

The military shaped the life of the town. It attracted Russian merchants: nurserymen, such as Wasili Kuriatkin, from whom young Sibelius bought seedlings and whose imposing gravestone in the local cemetery eclipses many another in size and embellishment; and families such as the Novoschiloffs and Bogdanoffs, whose children were the Sibeliuses' playmates.[5] It brought Russian delicacies: blinis and caviar, which Janne discovered at the home of his friend Kostya, the son of a Russian colonel. And it brought the railroad.

In 1862 the first railroad tracks, built to the broad Russian gauge of 1.524 meters or five feet, reached Hämeenlinna from Helsinki. Their destination reflected the need to move troops as well as to connect the country's lake district with the import-export harbor of Helsinki. This first stage in the building of Finland's railroads was followed by the laying of tracks to Saint Petersburg. By 1870 the trip between the capital cities was only a matter of hours.

Some, who held with the waterways that had served the Finns so well for centuries, saw in the railway an emperor's folly. But another scene from Hämeenlinna life—the arrival of the first "fire horse" (*tulihevonen*)—erupted in great celebration.[6] On January 31, 1862, the fine-looking engine christened *Lemminkäinen* puffed into Hämeenlinna station pulling a passenger car and several freight cars. The station was crammed with well-wishers young and old, bearded and hatted, besotted and tipsy. People greeted each other joyfully, shook hands, blew kisses, and drank toasts to the railroad boss, to the railroad engineers, to *Lemminkäinen*, and to Finland.

The composer Frans Hoyer did more than drink a toast. He commemorated the event in music: the *Helsingfors–Tawastehus Jernban Galopp* (*Helsinki–Hämeenlinna Railway Galop*), written for piano. Steaming across its cover is a gravure of the *Lemminkäinen*; below appears a dedication to the wife of Platon Ivanovich Rokassovsky, Finland's well-liked governor-general (1861–66) who braved the *Lemminkäinen* and traveled to Hämeenlinna in person to thank the good townspeople personally for welcoming the ruler's largesse (they had, of course, little choice). The *Galop* went through at least three editions, the third printed by December 1865 (see figs. 3.2a and b). With its opening tremolo, its blue notes, its authentic whistle, and its programmatic annotations— "Signal for Departure," "The Passengers Climb on Board," "The Train Goes over a Bridge," "Arrival in Hämeenlinna"—the *Galop* gaily recalled the delicious excitement of that momentous historical scene.

The railroads moved more than goods and troops: they also transported musicians. Thanks to the railroad, Hämeenlinna was one of the few towns outside Helsinki where traveling artists were sure to appear. Within a decade the Finnish singers Emmy and

Figure 3.2a–b. Frans Hoyer, *Helsingfors–Tawastehus Jernban-Galopp* (*Helsingfors–Hämeenlinna Railway Galop*), ca. 1862. The Sibelius Museum.

JERNBAN-GALOPP.

Lorenz Nikolai Achté were visiting Hämeenlinna. So were other talented national singers: Johannes Hahl and Filip Forstén, the latter accompanied by his cousin, the pianist
Ina Forstén.[7] Gradually international stars began to arrive: the pianists Carl Pfeiffer and
Sophie Menter, a pupil of Liszt; the violinists Anton Sitt and Gerhard Brassin; and even
the "Violin King" himself, August Wilhelmj.

Some of the military men also contributed their share of music. The bandmaster of
the Onegan regiment was Gustaf Levander (1824–1895), at least until he resigned in the
wake of his public censure, for it was Levander who had been disciplined that day when
little Janne made his parade drawing. Thereafter Levander gave music lessons to the
town's children. Another music-loving figure at the Hämeenlinna garrison, a Lieutenant
Jaroschevsky, led in founding the town's concert association. And every townsperson was
familiar with the military band. For Janne Sibelius, the most powerful musical effects of
his impressionable childhood were bound up with the high, the mighty, and the imperial.

A Parallel Universe

Long after Sibelius had been turned into a national icon, many of his contemporaries
were pressed into recording their impressions of the boy who became their national composer. The value of such recollections is uncertain, for, intentionally or not, most people
gild their memories with an emotional patina shaded by time and wishful thinking. Especially where national celebrities are concerned, the veneer of imagination and veneration
frequently conceals more than it conserves. Only in the consistencies among accounts
may something approaching truth be illuminated.

One of those consistencies touches on the parallel universe Sibelius seemed to
inhabit. It appears to have been his world since childhood. It was noticed by his family
and observed by his teachers, one of whom, Eva Savonius (who founded the Swedish-
language girls' school in Hämeenlinna), recorded another scene from childhood:[8]

One cold winter day Janne went missing. He was only six. When eventually he
turned up, he told his frantic mother that he had been watching a large house on fire. He
had joined the brigade, he said, carrying buckets of water to put out the flames until he
was miserably wet and cold. In spite of all efforts, the house burned to the ground. But
when pressed to tell where the fire was, he could not say. Then his mother realized that
his clothes were perfectly dry. Had he actually carried water, they asked? Well, no, he
said. Could he recall anything at all about where the fire took place? Finally, he admitted,
there was no fire. But he had *imagined* a house burning down as he stood by the waters
of Lake Vanajavesi, how it would look, and how he would rush in heroically and douse
the flames.

Miraculously, that vivid imagination survived the repeated onslaughts of the well-meaning. His Aunt Julia, for example. One of the town's piano teachers, Julia was naturally pressed into service to instruct her niece and nephews. Her dismal lack of success may be gauged by the fact that only Linda took to the instrument. To be fair, perhaps her instruction of the young Janne yielded depressing results because of his ears. The earliest photographs show a solemn boy already sprouting enormous "catchers of sound," as Karl Flodin later called them. Those ears gave the impression that, like the furry antennae of the Finnish hare, they were never still, but quivered constantly in response to the slightest echo, unaccustomed vibration, dissonant clang, falling snow, creak of boots, the raucous hullabaloo of birds, the hiss of spitting fire, the ticking of clocks, the echoing emptiness. The sensitivity of these ears was, if not legendary, certainly annoying. Another of Aunt Julia's students, Alma Pomoell, found, to her chagrin, a small voice accompanying her lessons. The voice came from beneath the piano. It repeated over and over again, "You played the wrong note, do you hear? You played it wrong"; then, "You are hitting the wrong note again, why do you play it wrong?" and finally, "Why in heaven's name do you play so horribly?!"[9]

In that tale emerges another consistency, one that is borne out by his music, namely, a feeling for beauty, for the "rightness" of sounds, which, it seems, belonged to Sibelius's very being from an early age. And "wrong" sounds usually came from pianos.

Later Finnish nationalists who were in the business of promoting Sibelius as a young genius claimed that already at the age of ten, the prodigious youngster was showing his future path in a composition for strings, *Vattendroppar* (*Water Droplets*), a little piece for violin and violoncello, but involving no piano. This claim combined several elements in the national movement—the belief in a young Finnish Orpheus, an exaggerated reverence for Finnish nature, and one of those running-water metaphors whose currents eventually coalesced into a surge of righteous resistance to Russian imperialism.

The truth was more prosaic. At the age of ten, Janne was making childish, if detailed, drawings, though he did manifestly dislike the piano. It seems unlikely that *Vattendroppar* comes from so early a time. Yet whatever its date, the symbolic meaning of those twenty-four measures cannot be gainsaid: they reveal indisputably that Sibelius thought compositionally in terms of vibrating strings. Not for this composer "orchestrating" a piano draft: the thrum and twang of strings, the reedy honking of woodwinds, the resonant flaring of brass—in the very physicality of sound lay the essence of music.

However reluctant a piano student he later was ("the piano cannot *sing*," he once protested in frustration), Sibelius eventually acquired some ability on the thing. It was on the advice of a man in the family, his Uncle Pehr, that he finally returned to the instrument as a means of improving his music-reading skills.[10] In many other ways it was thanks to Uncle Pehr that Sibelius's life in music began. Significantly, Pehr Sibelius was not a professional musician; he was among the many businessmen who were building the solid foundation on which Finland's economy was thriving. And Janne Sibelius would be just one of the many beneficiaries.

NEW VISTAS: OUR LAND, OUR INDUSTRIALIZED LAND

In the year of Sibelius's birth, a Finnish engineer by the name of Fredrik Idestam (1838–1916) established a small pulpwood plant no more than fifty miles from Hämeenlinna on the lower falls called Tammerkoski. Three years later, in 1868, Idestam built a second plant some nine miles further west, naming his venture for the river beside which the plant stood: Nokia. Thus was born the business that evolved into one of the most spectacularly successful of modern Finland. Nokia's world-class enterprise grew out of imperial Finland's nurturing forests, a manifestation of the same phenomenon as the composer Jean Sibelius, namely, the shared project of building a Finnish national identity.

Acknowledging the development of Finland's economy through industry and technology is not just a nod to comprehensiveness in weaving Sibelius's story. The musical phenomenon of Sibelius would hardly have been possible without his country's industrial success and economic stability. The economic base provided the foundation that enabled the creation of art museums, symphony orchestras, opera companies, and theater troupes. It made possible the pursuit of the education that enabled people to appreciate art, music, and theater. It meant funds to travel abroad for study.

At the very time the Sibelius children were being raised on the idyllic, agrarian vision of Finland, the image poetized, pictured, and promoted by Runeberg and Topelius, industrialization was spreading across the country. And just as it had changed central Europe, the Industrial Revolution was profoundly changing Finland's natural and economic landscapes.[11] The country's abundant resources of wood and water represented possibilities for previously unimagined wealth. The development of Finland's forest industry had begun in the seventeenth century with tar, vast amounts of which were needed by the sailing fleets of the Netherlands and Great Britain.[12] Some two hundred years later the development of steam-driven mills transformed that industry in startling ways. Operating around the clock, the steam mills replaced the water-driven wheels, which were capable only of limited daily production, and marvelous possibilities ensued. While England and the Netherlands remained important markets for wood, the large, newspaper-thirsty populace of Russia guzzled Finnish pulp and paper. Finland's open trade borders with Russia (meaning that customs were not levied on goods, and exports were accomplished with ease) encouraged the growing industry.

With its plentiful forests, proud sailing traditions, navigable waterways, and powerful rapids, Finland was splendidly positioned to enter the world economy. Further enhancing its position were trends far beyond its borders: in 1860, London's slashing of timber duties; in 1861, from Saint Petersburg, imperial endorsement of a proposal to abolish political restrictions on the sawmill industry; in 1879, the emperor's decision to abolish workers' guilds, which boosted both innovation and profitability. In the homeland the nationalist ideology, promoted by university-educated Fennomans who were vigorously advocating the virtues of Finnish ingenuity and self-sufficiency, was driving the momentum forward. The effect on the economy was wondrous. Logs were floated downriver to be loaded on ships leaving for Europe. Sailing vessels and soon steamships, from towns such as Lovisa, Helsinki, and Turku, plied the waters of the Baltic Sea, laden with Finnish products for markets in England, Spain, and even distant South America. A whole infrastructure arose to support this activity: sawmills, pulp mills, shipbuilders, ship suppliers, cloth factories, banks, dry goods, sugar mills.

The men of the Sibelius family were up to their sizable ears in this commerce. And their activities were based in one of Finland's eastern port towns, Lovisa, named for Sweden's Queen Luise Ulrike, sister of Frederick the Great. Despite its pretty name, a delicious air of mystery and danger lurked around the town. The sea fortress Svartholm, at the mouth of Lovisa Bay, formed part of a chain of defense reaching from Lovisa to Hanko. The town itself, tucked into the ragged edge of Finland's eastern coast, provided a well-known haven for smugglers, pirates, and sea captains. The coastal location and proximity to the Russian border had given the town strategic value in the days when Finland was part of the Swedish Empire. In the nineteenth century, Lovisa's importance had shifted to trade, seafaring, and pleasure, this last thanks to its renowned spa. And it was trade that attracted the very first Sibelius there.

In the early nineteenth century, a country boy called Johan Mattsson (1785–1844) made his way from his home village of Lapinjärvi to Lovisa, some sixteen miles away. He found a position with Pehr Mårten Unonius, a merchant from a family of Swedish sea captains and ship owners.[13] Within ten years Mattsson, who had become Pehr Unonius's bookkeeper, was positioned to buy the business, a prospering retail trade in grain and grocery items, in partnership with Henrik Lindroth.[14] Business urbanized Mattsson. He decided to take a Latin surname, such as his employer had had, and settled on Sibelius, after the landholding where he was born, Sibbe. He too became a respected local figure: he was elected a city elder and named an honorary alderman.

The position with Unonius proved to have many benefits. One was the merchant's attractive niece, Catharina Fredrika Åkerberg (1792–1879), whom the man now called Johan Sibelius married. There were also the opportunities afforded the couple's four sons, three of whom followed the business direction of their father and entered Lovisa's closely interlinked world of commerce.

The first son, Johan Matias Fredrik Sibelius (1818–1864), the one called Janne, went to sea. Pursuing a familiar career path for ambitious Lovisa business-oriented men, he became the first captain and part owner (with the Unoniuses and Anders Sundman) of a barque called the *Ukko*. The *Ukko* was launched in the autumn of 1856 at the Siksala shipyard, a 237-last ship that could accommodate a crew of seventeen. Like other vessels belonging to the Lovisa merchants, the *Ukko* regularly made the long journey to and from Cádiz, exchanging Finland's forest gold for salt and returning with other exotica tucked into its hold—Spanish oranges, Havana cigars, lace mantillas, and, of course, contraband. The *Ukko*'s globe-trotting captain went by the name "Jean Sibelius" in urbane company. A formal photograph showed him stuffed uncomfortably into suit, bow tie, and topcoat, bandy legs askew, fists self-consciously clenched. In real life this Jean Sibelius cut a dashing figure—a man gloriously alive in a white summer suit commandingly astride the afterdeck of his ship, waving his white straw hat in farewell on his way to ports as far-flung as Saint Petersburg, Cornwall, and Havana.[15]

The second son, Pehr Ferdinand (1819–1890), bore the name of his father's mentor. He too went into business, initially working for his father. But like his older brother, Pehr sailed away from the perhaps too-sheltering embrace of the parental home. He went out not upon the wide sea, but to the port town on the other side of Finland, Turku, where his grandfather Mathias Åkerberg had once lived. The youngest boy, Carl Edvard (1823–1863), was the shortest lived, though he also profited from the land: he became a surveyor. Only the fourth brother, Christian Gustaf, deviated from the family business tradition: he became a physician and amateur musician, in the mode of his Åkerberg grandfather.

Although Lovisa's commercial scenes thus revolved around import and export, its domestic scenes were gently weighted with tradition—and music. In the Sibelius household, the grandmother, the well-born, well-starched Catharina Åkerberg, displayed the good manners, correct deportment, and aristocratic bearing of her Swedish ancestors. She brought to life Runeberg's *Tales of Ensign Stål*, relating to her grandchildren real-life episodes of the fierce war that had changed all of Finland. And unlike the practical Borg grandmother, who disdained music making as a frivolity, Catharina Åkerberg had a special enthusiasm for music: her father had played violin, her mother's family had owned a clavier at a time when few did, and a forebear, Jakob Dannenberg, who hailed from Brandenburg and had served in the Viipuri cavalry, had reputedly been a trumpeter.

Catharina Åkerberg Sibelius died in 1879, but in the family's red clapboard house under the Siberian pea trees she left her grandchildren a musical legacy: her daughter, with the musical name of Christina Vilhelmina Evelina (1832–1893). By the time the Sibelius children began regular summer visits to Lovisa, Aunt Evelina had taken on a musical role in their lives. She played piano, hammering out four-hand versions of Beethoven symphonies with friends such as Elise Stenbäck. Short and plump, she adored her niece and nephews, she adored music (about which she once said, "For music's sake I wish I could live my life once again, for with an instrument and despite all my ignorance, I have known a life without words"), and she adored being part of their joyful lives. Aunt Evelina nurtured their musical passions in a way that made up for the ninny-isms of Aunt Julia. The piece grandly titled *Aunt Evelina's Life in Music*, which Sibelius allegedly improvised at a young age, may be more hagiography than fact, but his aunt's devotion to music was real.

UNCLE PEHR

Of all the relatives, it was Johan and Catharina Sibelius's longest-lived son, Pehr, who played the most vital role in the children's lives. As the sole surviving man on the Sibelius side, Uncle Pehr served as a surrogate father to Maria's children. And it was characteristic that his practical and generous contributions to their upbringing involved both music and commerce.

Like his father, Uncle Pehr took a position as a bookkeeper with a leading merchant in a port town. In his case, the merchant was Abraham Kingelin (1788–1849) and the town, Turku, the proud and thriving little metropolis on Finland's western side, enlivened by intellectual, political, and cultural activity, thanks especially to its university and its patriots, the Turku Romantics. From the thirteenth century until 1812, Turku had been the capital of Finland. But with the country's annexation to Russia, the emperors wanted to move the seats of administration and learning further away from the potentially corrupting Swedes, and Turku lost both its administrative significance and its university to Helsinki. The town suffered further losses when, during the night of September 4–5, 1827, it was ravaged by a devastating fire. Thereafter, the growing success of the forest industry and useful trade connections with Russia brought about a happy reconstruction of the town as a flourishing port. One of its architects was Abraham Kingelin.[16]

Kingelin had regular and close contacts with merchants abroad, and the ships he and his various partners operated sailed from Turku to Saint Petersburg, Stockholm, and South America, bearing products from such Finnish enterprises as the Billnäs iron works and various sawmills and returning with Russian and other products, salt, and coffee.

Good relations with Russia held the key to prosperity, as Kingelin well knew, and he assiduously cultivated his steamship line to Saint Petersburg. He also supplied sails for the vessels and sold saws and the products of the saws. In addition, he envisioned a sugar factory that would produce two million pounds of sugar a year, enough to supply more than half of Finland's needs.

Kingelin's success as entrepreneur and agent was part of what was fueling Finland's economic awakening. It was as much a part of the national movement as Sibelius and his artistic contemporaries. And many of these leading industrialists, merchants, and businessmen interested themselves in Finland's arts. Some of them were amateur practitioners; others supported the arts with their patronage. However much he later resented their philistinisms, Sibelius received regular financial support from Finland's business community. And in his early years that support came from Uncle Pehr.[17]

Pehr Sibelius eventually left Kingelin's employ to establish a seed store, which he managed, after a fashion, from 1859 almost until his death. After a fashion because, even though Maria Sibelius looked to him for financial and other advice, Uncle Pehr's management followed the dictates of its quiet-spoken owner's heart rather than the balance sheet. Seeds that germinated before sale were promptly discarded, and profit margins fell accordingly. Evidently, the store succeeded in spite of its owner, because the uncle always seemed able to give financial assistance to his ever-needy nephew. Uncle Pehr was, after all, a bit of a soft touch—as young Sibelius discovered at an early age. Someone once convinced his uncle that, unless sufficient warnings could be gathered, a fire so great would be ignited in Siberia that the glow would be seen from Mars. In support of this doomsayer, Uncle Pehr generously loaned the fellow money: predictably, both man and money vanished.

Uncle Pehr too had the Sibelius ears, the most outsized of them all, their hugeness on full display astride his broad forehead with its thinning hair. His quiet speech, gentle mien, and formal attire (he was regularly depicted with a silk top hat on his head or in his hand) belied the unconventional character beneath the starched shirt and severely knotted cravat. He joined the volunteer fire brigade in 1846, a sure means of showing commitment to his adopted town, where the memories of that catastrophic fire live still. The volunteer fire brigades were also an indication of the Finns' passion for organized activity; by the 1860s the brigades espoused semi-military ideals and were considered training grounds for self-government.[18] Pehr Sibelius's views about these matters have not been systematically explored, but his volunteerism speaks forcefully for his awareness of the national movement. So too, as will be seen, does his correspondence.

Uncle Pehr's most exotic, some said eccentric, activity was stargazing. Passionate about astronomy, he owned a telescope (depicted by his nephew in the hot-air-balloon drawing). The enchantment with the stars took some dramatic turns. Uncle Pehr rented a site where he was sure falling meteors could be observed, and there he watched patiently, night after night. During one Christmas holiday Janne Sibelius went along. More than half a century later, the aging composer claimed to remember still "how *beastly* cold" he had been.[19] Most everyone agreed that Pehr Sibelius was an original character, good-hearted and helpful. And his peculiar passions were not without fruitful musical issue. When his nephew composed an early violin sonata, he explained to his uncle that its third movement ("fresh and spirited as well as romantic") depicted a meteor falling down into the midst of a group celebrating Midsummer Eve (see ex. 3.2).[20]

EXAMPLE 3.2. SIBELIUS, VIOLIN SONATA IN F MAJOR, THIRD MOVEMENT, MM. 31–35. BY PERMISSION OF FENNICA GEHRMAN OY, HELSINKI.

Among the uncle's most charming features was his humor. For despite the Lutheran straitjacket, the men of the Sibelius family were not lacking in wit. Into a homemade booklet given the title "Pehrs Wis-Bok" ("Pehr's Little Book of Wisdom"), Uncle Pehr copied word games, poems—mostly doggerel written by his brothers and friends—drinking songs, stories, and aphorisms. A group of riddles in the same booklet has the heading "The Merry Nutcracker or a Selected Collection of 101 Entertaining Riddles for Pastime in Leisure Hours copied out by Pehr Ferdinand Sibelius."[21] It was compiled in Lovisa in February and March of 1835. Penmanship was another of Pehr Sibelius's many skills. In his elegant hand he wrote out poems, song verses, proverbs, music. Among his most intriguing handwritten scores, mostly of songs and choral works, appears Carl Maria von Weber's *Freischütz*, arranged for string quartet. The arrangement is Joseph Küffner's, but the parts are in Pehr Sibelius's hand.

It was the interest in music—the passion they shared—that seems to have drawn young Sibelius most strongly to his uncle. In Turku, Pehr took lessons in music theory with the German-born Conrad Greve (1820–1851), *Kapellmeister* of the Grenadiers' Battalion and founder of Turku's Musical Society (to which his grandfather Mathias Åkerberg had also belonged). Uncle Pehr was deeply involved with the town's choral and orchestral ensembles. And he loved the violin. He regaled his nephews with tales of the great virtuosi, such as Wilhelm Ernst (1814–1865), whom he heard in Stockholm and Saint Petersburg. He even played the violin himself, after a fashion, and was notorious for practicing far into the night, playing the same concerto over and over until the neighbors verged on hysteria. As his nephews and niece grew older, he joined them in playing chamber music. Best of all, Uncle Pehr owned a fine and intriguing pair of violins.

PEHR'S VIOLINS

In the late seventeenth century a violin bearing the name Stainer and the date 1695 was built somewhere in central Europe. Its name referred to the renowned violinmaker Jacob Stainer. Stainer had gone to his own maker long before, having died in 1683, but his instruments were in such demand that forgeries by distinguished craftsmen—such as Giovanni Battista Gabrielli, William Forster, and the brothers Lorenzo and Tomaso Carcassi—circulated as "Stainers." Until the end of the eighteenth century the Stainers were prized for their silvery tone—the celebrated *voce argentina*—and valued even above the Cremona violins.

    Almost two centuries passed. Then one day the path of the forged fiddle led to Saint Petersburg. The reasons for the violin's travel to Russia and why it was cast aside for sale remain unknown, although they may have been related to the changing styles and growing preference for the stronger timbre of Cremonas. What is known is that the Stainer intersected with the Sibelius family in Russia's capital. In the early 1860s the sea captain Jean Sibelius, who regularly brought treasures of all kinds from his wide-ranging voyages, purchased two violins from a Saint Petersburg market. One was the Stainer. Captain Johan gave the instruments to his brother Pehr.[22] There, lovingly played and cared for, they awaited the next chapter in their fate. It would open in 1881.

    The year was a momentous one. Terrorism roiled the Russian capital. The previous year, on February 17, revolutionary nihilists set off a bomb in the Winter Palace in their campaign to rid the country of Alexander II. A benevolent father in the eyes of the Finns, Alexander II presented a serious obstacle to the full regeneration of Russian society in the view of the revolutionaries. The object of their hatred had been entertaining the prince of Bulgaria when a quantity of dynamite meant to blow his imperial person to smithereens succeeded instead in killing ten of the Finnish Guards on duty and grievously wounding thirty-six.[23] Helsinki newspapers solemnly reported that the whole of Saint

Petersburg was decked out to celebrate the sparing of the emperor's life. Other assassination attempts also proved futile—until the inauspicious day of March 13, 1881. As Alexander was returning to the Winter Palace from a military parade, a bomb hidden beneath his armored sledge exploded. The emperor leaped from the vehicle, only to be struck by a second explosive. It blew off his legs.

The ghastly news shocked the Finns as much as the Russians. Helsinki's Swedish-language daily, *Hufvudstadsbladet*, published a special issue on March 14 about the dreadful deed. On March 15 the same paper devoted its entire front page to the assassination. Services were held in Helsinki in both languages of the land. And there were rituals not only in the capital's Orthodox Cathedral, but also in the Lutheran Nicholas Church. Mourners thronged to the ceremony. In Hämeenlinna, too, the weekly paper, *Hämeen Sanomat*, devoted its front page to the murder. In this town, whose citizens lived closely and sometimes grudgingly with Russian soldiers, the lead article began conspicuously with the words: "The land of the Finns has met with unspeakable sorrow. Alexander II, our noble, beloved ruler, is dead."[24] The emperor whose very name the Finns believed to be synonymous with liberal values, benevolent actions, and enlightened rule had been ominously silenced.

To the Russian throne now ascended Alexander III (1845–1894). A Goliath of a man who had commanded Russian regiments during the Russo-Turkish War (1877–78), Alexander could strike a blow with the mere force of his steely gaze. He was known to straighten horseshoes with his bare hands.[25] And he now directed all of his enormous strength to unbending what he saw as the misguided reforms begun by his father. Francophile where his father had been Germanophile, reactionary where his father had been liberal, Alexander governed from three principles—orthodoxy, autocracy, and *narodnost*, or belief in the Russian people.[26] He stiffened censorship and overturned reforms. Matters from law to education were thrown into turmoil, human rights among them: because women had been among the terrorists, women were forbidden to attend the university.[27] And Alexander curbed the rights of many minorities, especially Jews. Pogroms "cleansed" the country; between April 1881 and June 1882, a million Jews fled. Poles, Lithuanians, Afghans, Turkestanians, Georgians, Ukrainians—one and all were harassed. The Baltic provinces were threatened with increased Russification measures. Ministers with even the remotest interest in constitutional rights were dismissed. Meanwhile, the revolutionaries went underground or abroad, there to foment further unrest.

Yet simultaneously with these repressive and reactionary measures, this most xenophobic of emperors began promoting large-scale industrial development in a bid to attain for his empire its rightful place among civilized nations. Iron, coal, and steel industries, the drilling of Caucasian oil fields, electrical and chemical plants, textile production, railways—these and more burgeoned and boomed. And although the initiative came from the Russian state, the financing and management came, often as not, from Europeans and Americans. Along with investments, factories, and powerful new banks, foreigners began arriving in Saint Petersburg. Nevsky Prospekt sprouted a bewildering crop of advertisements for companies such as International Harvester and Singer, the sewing-machine manufacturer. The Swedish family Nobel became the largest foreign investors in the Baku oil fields, followed later by the Shibayevs and Rothschilds.

The economic boom promoted by this Alexander proved to be the most advanced Russia had ever experienced. It invigorated all the empire, not least Saint Petersburg and the nearby grand duchy of Finland. The inhabitants saw themselves as part of a much more open world, into which they traveled and from which ideas and, not least, investments came. As one of them described that time:

> People who lived there [in Saint Petersburg] were essentially newcomers, and so always ready to try something new. It was the capital of Russia, after all, so it naturally drew to itself people who were willing to experiment and who lived in hopes of being recognised as people who had something special to contribute. People automatically thought in revolutionary terms rather than in terms of rebellion. We're going to change something, they said, therefore, let's change it entirely. And this was, certainly at the end of the 19th century, what was so very special about Saint Petersburg. And this applied not just to the political scene, but it applied also to literature, the theatre, to the ballet, and to music.[28]

Ironically, diehard and despotic though he was, Alexander III, in pursuit of the magnificence he deemed appropriate for signifying the grandeur of his realm, supported art as an essential component of his nationalistic program. He became a leading patron of the Russian school of realist artists known as *peredvizhniki*. His personal collection of paintings formed the basis of a museum housed in the Mikhailovsky Palace that opened to the public in 1898.

Music and theater acquired special opulence. The monopoly on the ballet had ended with the death of Alexander II, making possible for the first time private entrepreneurship in concert and theater performance and signaling a new era in Russian ballet, out of which came the Tchaikovsky ballets. Among composers, Alexander III favored Tchaikovsky and, oddly, despite his belief in *narodnost*, disliked the works of the Mighty Five (the name used for the Russian nationalist composers Mily Balakirev, Alexander Borodin, César Cui, Modest Musorgsky, and Nikolai Rimsky-Korsakov). It helped that the emperor loved music, or at least, military music. He himself played the baritone horn; while still czarevich, he had organized a small military band.

Finland's music had a special place in this Alexander's steely heart: Adolf Leander (1833–1899), "the father of Finnish brass music," was rumored to be his preferred band-master, and the Finnish Guards Band (Suomen kaartin soittokunta), among his favorites. Within a year of being crowned emperor, Alexander had a court orchestra, the Court Musicians' Corps. Founded in Saint Petersburg in 1882, the corps was supported by the Imperial Chancel, headed by Alexander Taneyev, a pupil of Rimsky-Korsakov. Its pur-pose was to entertain the ruler and the imperial entourage on Sundays and holidays. In the very same year a Philharmonic Society Orchestra was miraculously founded in Alex-ander's westernmost capital, Helsinki; so was a musical conservatory. The prospects for imperial musical culture looked promising indeed.

It was Alexander Benois (1870–1960), the Russian stage designer, director, and art historian, who insisted to the end of his days that the reign of Alexander III had been "in general, extremely significant and beneficial" for the arts and prepared the way for the cultural flowering in the early twentieth century, Russia's so-called Silver Age.[29] Whether or not that assessment is true, what is undeniable is that for Janne Sibelius, during Alex-ander's reign the music began.

THE MUSIC BEGINS

"I want so much to learn to play the violin . . . I would also like to learn to play
the violoncello!"

SIBELIUS, LETTER TO HIS UNCLE PEHR SIBELIUS, JUNE 19, 1881

The impact of the new emperor on a young boy in Hämeenlinna would be profound, though not, of course, immediately apparent. Instead, 1881 marked a special turning point for other reasons: Janne Sibelius turned sixteen. No longer did Linda, the big sister, need to watch over her younger brothers like a second mother (she was always calling for them like they were a couple of small dogs: "Kitti! Janne! Where are you? Jannnée! Kittiiiii!").[30] Instead, the activities of the extended family revolved around music.

Although as a teenager Sibelius may not yet have been aware of what has been described as "the unceasing tug-of-war between a critically disposed society (obshchestvo) and the oppressive regime,"[31] he was beginning to speak with a new voice. It sounds out in correspondence with Uncle Pehr, to whom he had written since childhood. Earlier his epistles had related interests familiar to boys everywhere—stamp collecting, ice skating, sledding, duck hunting. Now the pages of his letters expressed other concerns—musical ones. Sibelius wanted to study violin and violoncello both. Having neither, he asked his uncle for the loan of one of those instruments from the Saint Petersburg market. For a family whose financial means were as limited as the Sibeliuses', the violin was probably the instrument easiest to obtain.[32] And thanks to Uncle Johan, two violins belonged to the family. In due course one of the violins arrived in Hämeenlinna. It was not the Stainer, but the lesser of the two bought by Uncle Johan. Still, Sibelius could begin lessons, which he undertook with the former leader of Hämeenlinna's military band, Gustaf Levander.

The meaning and importance of that violin cannot be underestimated. Oh, it was not a fine violin. But the sounds from its resonant body and glimmering strings filled young Sibelius with a joy and sensation of beauty such as he found virtually nowhere else. It shows through all his compositions: the exquisitely drawn-out cantabiles, which he tried to make even the clunky piano emulate—the directive is liberally sprinkled throughout the piano works. There are the infinitely vibrating tremolandi (see ex. 3.3) and the

EXAMPLE 3.3. SIBELIUS, *CASSAZIONE*, MM. 1–6. BY PERMISSION OF FENNICA GEHRMAN OY, HELSINKI.

lifelong efforts to produce a "sound screen," whether with string timbre or by means of other instruments (see ex. 3.4).

Music now began to fill the pages of his correspondence—indeed, his whole life. Sibelius could no more hold back its floods than he could alter the shape of Lake Vanajavesi. He performed at the Hämeenlinna lyceum, where his friend August Ferdinand Ringvall (1865–1941), educated at Tsarskoje Selo, had started a small orchestra. They performed marches and dances, staged dramatic works, played through *Norma*, and presented an *Ave Maria* (Schubert's? Gounod's?) at a school convocation. Sibelius had arranged the parts, using a pair of singers, a piano, a harmonium, four violins, and a violoncello.[33] Outside school he played duets with Anna Tigerstedt (1860–1946), the daughter of the town's doctor, Theodor Tigerstedt. Those two made up half a string quartet, the other half being completed by their teacher Levander on viola and the local pharmacist, Hugo Wilhelm Elfsberg, on violoncello.[34] Sometimes Elfsberg's wife joined them on

EXAMPLE 3.4. SIBELIUS, *KAIUTAR*, OP. 74, NO. 4, MM. 1–9. © BREITKOPF & HÄRTEL, WIESBADEN.

piano. They played Schubert, Beethoven, and Haydn. Is it any wonder that in those circumstances Haydn's illustrious "Russian Quartets," dedicated (ca. 1781) to the Russian grand duke who became Emperor Paul I in 1797, made a powerful impression? A quarter of a century later, Sibelius was still capitalizing on their lessons. The earlier composer's timeless examples on the power of silence to speak (see ex. 3.5) were redefined for a Finnish milieu (see ex. 3.6).

Sibelius expressed his love for Haydn's music in a letter of gratitude to Uncle Pehr for repairing the violin, which had cracked:

> I could never have imagined that my violin could ever achieve such a sound in its timbre, such an artistic quality that I have never before heard in a violin. When I play on it, I am filled with a strange feeling; it is as though the insides of the music opened up to me, and Haydn's sonatas with their deep, serious sounds almost make it holy.[35]

At the end of 1884 Elfsberg sold his pharmacy and moved to Helsinki. The dissolution of the town quartet left Sibelius little choice but to compose for ensembles that he and his siblings could manage, nameless duos for piano and violin, and trios, such as the

EXAMPLE 3.5. JOSEF HAYDN, STRING QUARTET IN E-FLAT, "OP. 33, NO. 2," FOURTH MOVEMENT, MM. 148–72; ED. GEORG FEDER AND SONJA GERLACH (MUNICH: G. HENLE VERLAG, 1974). BY PERMISSION OF THE PUBLISHER.

EXAMPLE 3.6. SIBELIUS, *TAPIOLA*, MM. 26–32.
© BREITKOPF & HÄRTEL, WIESBADEN.

one in A Minor for Violin, Cello, and Piano. Sibelius was possessed of a sociable nature, and from the outset he made music with others. Solo practice was necessary, but he still craved company. Was it then that he found his much-vaunted inspiration in nature? The reality was something other than the romanticized image promoted later. As he explained to Uncle Pehr:

> The day before yesterday I played outside on the slope on the large rock that you saw, and imagined that the entire slope was an orchestra. The crows were the oboes, the magpies the bassoons, the sea gulls the clarinets, the thrushes the violas, the chiffchaffs the violins, the pigeons the violoncellos, the pine thrushes the flutes, the cock on the farm the concertmaster, and the pig the percussionist. You can just imagine that I was in a dangerous position and had to make a speedy retreat because the violas started dirtying me; I moved to another place a little lower down, but it was even worse. They tried very hard to drown me out, but they were beaten by your
>
>   Janne[36]

"A Celebrated Violinist at Any Price"

As Sibelius's school days came to an end, his family's prime concern revolved around how their eldest son, who inhabited a world utterly alien to the rest of them, would earn a living. His only goal was "to be a celebrated violinist at any price."[37] The Borgs, who relegated musicians to the same category as wandering organ grinders, illiterate entertainers, and dancing bears, were horrified. They spewed forth stern advice and pressured their hapless relative to consider something practical—law, civil service, pharmacy (although Maria knew her Janne: "Mamma says that I am too impractical to be a pharmacist. She may be right; I just don't know," he wrote disingenuously to Uncle Pehr).[38] Still wide eyed, he also wrote that he needed money; asked his uncle's advice on taking out an insurance policy; and wanted counsel on what profession to pursue. It was Pehr Sibelius who followed the early loan of the violin with financial loans, enabling his nephew to have the musical education he so clearly craved.

In the summer of 1885 Janne Sibelius, his mother, his sister Linda, and Aunt Evelina all moved to Finland's capital, Helsinki. The family legacy proved difficult to breach outright. Just as his father had done, the son enrolled in the Imperial Alexander University, and, again like his father, he registered in the physical-mathematical faculty, evidently with the harebrained idea of studying medicine. Then he changed his mind and matriculated in the faculty of law. Meanwhile, he registered as an "irregular student" at the newly founded Music Institute. The trait of indecision that was to become a way of life had showed up early. It almost always masked underlying and powerful desires connected to his art.

Fortunately for Sibelius, those desires seemed to be blessed with a lucky star; less lyrically, it could be said that those blessings were often a consequence of imperial beneficence. For now, in Mother Russia's westernmost outpost, the empire was about to bestow a second gift on a musical son. The first had been his violin. The second was a violin teacher: Mitrofan Timofeyevich Wasiljeff.

4

Imperial Helsinki

"HELSINKI OF THE CZARS"

Helsinki of the Czars: so the capital of Finland has aptly been called.[1] There the benevolence of the Russian emperors, which gave both economic benefit and visual shape to Finland, is perhaps at its most conspicuous, for Emperor Alexander I built Helsinki as a showcase. Whereas Sweden's capital, Stockholm, is constructed like a bulwark, concealed along the coastline and filled with tiny medieval alleyways, Helsinki thrusts boldly out into the sea (see fig. 4.1). Its majestic and spacious plan announces pure imperial Saint Petersburg: Union Street sweeps grandly down from a rise to the north (today commanded by the granite shaft of the Kallio Church) and back up again, to the high hilltop on which the Imperial Observatory stands. Overflowing at the avenue's approximate center, magnificent Senate Square opens up and out to the sky, a Finnish complement to a similar plaza in Saint Petersburg. The monumental, classically designed Nicholas Church, crowned with cupolas reminiscent of Saint Isaac's, breathtakingly dominates the square.[2] The Nicholas Church is Lutheran; in the near distance soar the onion-shaped domes of the Orthodox cathedral called the Uspensky.

All these features, the most Petersburgian of them the work of German architect Carl Engel, are still stupendously on display in modern Helsinki. But other aspects of the town Sibelius knew are not. Street names, for instance. Some honored imperial family members: Konstantin, Sofia, Vladimir, Mikael, Elisabeth. Union Street (Unioninkatu), whose name remains, commemorated the unification of Finland and Russia. At the foot of the Esplanade, which runs through the city from east to west, the Russian double eagle sat atop a stone monument to the Empress Alexandra, marking the spot where her highness's royal extremity first graced Finnish soil, in 1833 (the monument stands there still).[3] A bust of Alexander I by Russian sculptor Ivan Martos (1754–1835; his tribute to Minin and Pozharsky adorns Moscow's Red Square) stood in the university's Festival Hall. Such

Figure 4.1. Helsinki viewed from the south harbor, 1893. Photograph by Daniel Nyblin. The
National Museum of Finland, Department of Prints and Photographs, Helsinki.

lofty and regal surroundings could not help but impart something of their spirit to the
city's inhabitants.

Part of that loftiness came from the university, which the Russian emperors had
moved from Turku to Helsinki in 1828.[4] It was to honor the university's imperial bene-
factor, Alexander I, that Alexander's successor and brother, Nicholas I, named the newly
erected institution Kejserliga Alexanders Universitetet i Finland—the Imperial Alexander University in Finland. The emperors enlarged and modernized the university and in
so doing positioned it to become central to the country's life. Not only did the institution
have a monopoly on education for professions from agriculture and forestry to the ministry and medicine, but also it became the focal point around which Finland's intellectual
life revolved: politics, economics, and journalism no less than literature, art, and music.

Along with its Russian names and imperial architecture, the town showed the Russian influence in still other ways. As in Petersburg, droshkies clopped through the cob-
bled streets. (For Helsinki residents, "a closed droshky [was] like something out of Won-
derland; a land whose realization is to be found in the words 'St. Petersburg.'")[5] Along
with Orthodox churches, there were Russian schools and eventually a Russian theater

named after Alexander II. On the city center's easternmost peninsula, called Kataja-nokka, military barracks went up as early as 1820. And then there was the island fortress in Helsinki's harbor: Sveaborg, or, in Finnish, Viapori. A part of the archipelago so close to Helsinki that you can swim to the island, Viapori formed a strategic part of the empire's outer defensive line. This military base was governed directly from Saint Petersburg right up until the end of 1917 (after which it would quickly and grandly be rechristened Suomenlinna—"Finland's Castle"—in late May 1918 as part of the nationalizing of public spaces). During the Crimean War, Sveaborg's ramparts were bombarded by Anglo-French fleets. Today the island is a UNESCO heritage site.

One of Finland's most prominent artists, Albert Edelfelt, called attention to some of the more elusive qualities that made nineteenth-century Helsinki very nearly unique: "The aspect of the town [was] gay and clean," he observed in his article "Sketches in Finland," published, of all places, in *Harper's New Monthly Magazine*; though "to be just, we must confess that these fine white houses do not constitute the whole town; the moment you leave the principal streets you find the usual wooden houses characteristic of Sweden and of the little Russian towns—low houses composed of a single story, and generally painted yellow."[6] Still, the artist's keen eye did not fail to miss the clean air: "The total absence of coal smoke in this country, where only wood is burnt, makes our towns clean, and explains that limpid and transparent sky which seems to spread out its blue expanse immediately behind the houses." Helsinki probably had the least homogeneous population of any city in Finland:

> Swedish fishermen with their sailor look, Finns in short cloaks, Russian soldiers [some ten thousand] wearing long gray overcoats and with their heads wrapped up in the "bashlik," Russian vegetable sellers in the traditional costume of the mujiks, Israelites in long caftans; and all this crowd of people, smoking all the while like chimneys, dance and stamp on the frozen ground to keep their feet from freezing entirely.

For a boy from the small garrison town of Hämeenlinna, Helsinki opened up a whole new world. As Sibelius wrote to Uncle Pehr shortly after arriving in 1885, "I am completely delighted with Helsingfors; once one gets a taste for it, Tavastehus is no longer good enough."[7] Earlier that same year another outsider, one far better traveled, recorded his impressions of the town: Hans von Bülow (1830–1894), who had been conducting the Russian Musical Society concerts in Saint Petersburg, arrived in Helsinki on a frigid January day: "I have taken great inner strength into the Russian New Year," he wrote home to Germany, "but am I still in Russia?"

Here [in Helsinki] time is reckoned according to European time; also there is so much German, Finnish, and Swedish spoken here, and prices are no longer reckoned in rubles, but in marks and pennies, but which have only the value of French francs and centimes—even the stamps are different, as you see. *Enfin*, the town is wonderfully original—my [hotel] windows look out over the marketplace and the colorful milling crowd—in the background numerous ships are frozen fast. Hotel the height of elegance, luxurious, but not expensive—the food to die for. But there is an enormous lack of time. The people follow me with respect, worship. A deputation of white cravats from the Orchestra, the Music School, and so on. Hospitality to excess. And at the concerts devoted listening and then furious applause.[8]

In those years Helsinki's harbor routinely froze with the onset of cold weather, and the winter months meant long periods of isolation and darkness. Then the city echoed with gay laughter and flirtatious banter, waltzes and polkas, wind bands and violin serenades, all pouring forth from glittering salons, *gemütlich* drawing rooms, concert *salles*, and dance halls. In the city of "white cravats," Sibelius gravitated to its musical glitter.

"FIRE AND LIFE": MITROFAN WASILJEFF

At the time Janne Sibelius was debating whether to pursue law, pharmacy, or music, composer and critic Martin Wegelius (1846–1906) was building up the new music school he had helped to establish, Helsingfors Musikinstitut (the Helsinki Music Institute). In the spring of 1885 the institute's principal violin teacher, the Czech Anton Sitt (1847–1929), had been enticed to the position of concertmaster in the equally new Helsinki Philharmonic Society Orchestra. And so Wegelius recruited Mitrofan Timofeyevich Wasiljeff to fill Sitt's position. The new man probably came from Saint Petersburg, because he had played in the imperial court quartet, but more precise details are lacking.[9] He came highly recommended by one of the Rubinsteins (whether Anton or Nikolai is not clear) and commanded one of the institute's highest salaries.

Wasiljeff was of another ilk entirely from the kindly Levander, Sibelius's music teacher in Hämeenlinna. Mysterious even now, when most of his life remains shrouded in uncertainty, the dark-eyed, black-haired Wasiljeff radiated glamour. To the inexperienced Janne Sibelius, the pale, slender Russian seemed *very* talented: "[He] plays with fire and life, and possesses a colossal technique. He is delicate in appearance, rather tall, thin, with black hair, a mustache and whiskers and two black eyes in his head" (see fig. 4.2).[10]

The one picture known of Wasiljeff proves the young student's eyes to have been as

Figure 4.2. Mitrofan Wasiljeff and his pupils, ca. 1886; Sibelius is in the top row, left.
The Sibelius Museum.

keen as his ears.[11] The teacher poses with his pupils: the Hämeenlinna contingent, Janne Sibelius and Anna Tigerstedt, stand tall in the background; four others gather to the teacher's left and right. Unlike the rest, Janne gazes off in his own direction. But it is the romantically handsome Wasiljeff, with his tantalizing mustache, those dusky eyes capable of smoldering, who draws the attention. His delicate hands, in such contrast to his dark, curling locks, lie nervously in his lap. One slim foot points forward. Even in the photograph those eyes on which Sibelius commented stand out. In largely blue-eyed Finland, where dark eyes spawn wariness and distrust, those orbs were sure to invite suspicion and break hearts.

Wasiljeff had several languages at his command: Russian, German, French, and even a little Swedish, according to Sibelius. Although French had cachet as the cosmopolitan language of sophisticated tastes, Sibelius spoke it little (although he had studied some French at the Hämeenlinna Normal School). So Wasiljeff conducted the lessons in German—on a Stradivarius.

For decades Wasiljeff's role in educating Janne Sibelius was edited out of biographical accounts of the composer. The idea of a *Russian's* helping to shape the national icon was more than most Finns could stand in the aftermath of the horrible events of the first half of the twentieth century. Yet Sibelius's letters from the 1880s show that the impact of this slim and handsome Slav was profound. There was the "glitter" of his magnificent instrument. His bow alone had cost the unheard-of sum of 100 rubles back in 1817, a detail Sibelius reported to Uncle Pehr at least twice. Then there was the violin itself: it dated from 1610 or 1710 or 1723, Sibelius could never quite remember the year, but it was *old*, it was authentic, and it had come through a Polish baron. At last, Janne Sibelius was touching musical royalty.

Then there was Wasiljeff's "colossal technique." And the teacher set about imparting some of it, beginning with improving Sibelius's tone. Scales, arpeggios, bow exercises—the pupil worked through them diligently, trying to develop his cantilena.[12] His efforts required practical adjustments. Only a few weeks into the lessons Sibelius was writing to Uncle Pehr that Wasiljeff found his bow far too heavy; so the teacher ordered a new one, "directly from a factory so it will be almost fifty percent cheaper that way."[13] Wasiljeff directed his charge to improve his sound further with a higher bridge for Uncle Pehr's violin, which the nephew had again borrowed for his studies. Step by step, Wasiljeff emphasized a lighter approach to playing than Sibelius had previously learned. As the young man reported to his uncle on studying Charles-Auguste de Bériot's Seventh Concerto: "I had practiced a lot for it, because it has to be played in an entirely different manner than I have played before. You see, I played it too much in the classical way, *heavily* and correctly. Instead, it should sound brilliant and free, almost like an improvisation. The tempi vary quite a lot."[14] The effect on Janne Sibelius's own tentative efforts at composing could hardly have been more dramatic. What better description than sounding "brilliant and free, almost like an improvisation" could there be of the so-called *Korpo* Trio (the Trio in D Major) for violin, violoncello, and piano, written the second summer after Sibelius began studying with Wasiljeff? It overflows with numerous, whimsical changes of tempo and abundant leggiero markings, and not just for the violin (see fig. 4.3). And how better to explain the effervescence that enters Sibelius's music in other works of 1885–87, such as the E minor violin piece, with its bouncing, nimble writing for the bow?[15]

Little by little, the pupil was turned in a more Gallic direction. Rodolphe Kreutzer and Jacques-Féréol Mazas, Jacques-Pierre Rode and that great Italian inspiration to the French, Giovanni Battista Viotti, as well as the Belgians Henri Vieuxtemps, Bériot, and Alexandre-Joseph Artôt—young Sibelius worked through their etudes and exercises, practiced their concertos, and dreamily fiddled through their fantasias.[16] Some of these violinists had played personal roles in the musical life of the Russian Empire and enjoyed imperial favor. Rode, for instance, was enormously popular in Saint Petersburg, especially between 1803 and 1808, when he was solo violinist to Emperor Alexander I.

Figure 4.3. Sibelius, *Korpo* Trio, second movement, opening bars. HUL 0533. © Breitkopf & Härtel, Wiesbaden. The National Library of Finland. Photo: Kari Timonen.

Likewise, Vieuxtemps had been an influential part of the city's cultural scene (from 1846 to 1851) as violin professor at the Saint Petersburg music conservatory. Artôt (1815–1845), whose mezzo-soprano niece, Marguerite-Joséphine Désirée Artôt, was briefly engaged to Tchaikovsky, was a great favorite of the imperial family; Artôt dedicated his dazzling *Souvenirs de Bellini* to a Russian grand duchess.[17]

These practitioners produced a flood of variations, with titles such as *Airs variés* and *Fantasia*. Above all, they fostered an art that emphasized technical facility, elegance of playing, imagination, and the "bouncing bow"—a fitting musical counterpart to Saint Petersburg's salon culture, with its light, witty conversation, captured by Pushkin in *Eugene Onegin*:

> The conversation sparkled bright;
> The hostess kept the banter light
> And quite devoid of affectations;
> Good reasoned talk was also heard,
> But not a trite or vulgar word,
> No lasting truths or dissertations—
> And no one's ears were shocked a bit
> By all the flow of lively wit.[18]

Is it any wonder that Janne Sibelius, fired with virtuoso ambitions and nurtured on the Franco-Belgian repertoire by a representative of the imperial culture that favored and rewarded such music, decided after only seven months of study with Wasiljeff to adopt the French form of his name? "Jean," he wrote to Uncle Pehr, "is my music name."[19]

"DA-DA-DA DOO": HERMANN CSILLAG

In 1887 life at the Music Institute changed. The fiery Wasiljeff vanished. He was last heard on the evening of May 21, 1887, in a Music Institute concert, playing a trio by Carl Goldmark. The following autumn his place was taken by Hermann Csillag (1852–d. after June 1922), "(pronounced Tschillag) . . . a first-rate violinist and excellent teacher," Janne, now Jean, Sibelius told Uncle Pehr.[20] But more experienced musicians, among them the incomparable Ferruccio Busoni, who arrived at the institute that same year, regarded the new man with skepticism. Csillag had a talent for being offensive, observed Busoni. Csillag claimed to have studied at the Hochschule in Berlin, had taught violin in Rotterdam, and thereafter traded on his early successes, hauling out old concert programs and reviews as proof.[21] Busoni was not impressed. Furthermore, Csillag's mode of teaching boded ill for any serious violin student: "He subscribes to an outmoded, mannered (Viennese) school. He scoops all the time and is unable to play so much as a third without slithering through it in microtones. He also plays in such a way that, when a triplet crops up, he has to drag it out really slowly."

"Da-da-da-doo—that's how it sounds," said Busoni.[22]

For his part, Sibelius mentioned only the violinist's broad tone, assured technique, crystal-clear playing. And true to form, he was seduced by the surface sparkle; this time it was Csillag's opinion of the value of Uncle Pehr's violin, the Stainer, which Sibelius had on loan: "Csillag praised your violin, but said that it's too bad its tone is so weak; otherwise it would be worth thousands. It is hard to say if it is entirely authentic, but at least the top is authentic. It has the same timbre as Professor Laub's instrument, the most expensive violin in the world (120,000 francs)."[23]

With Csillag (who at thirty-five was already considered old by his pupils), Sibelius performed in the institute's string quartet, just as he had done earlier with Wasiljeff. (Busoni found the custom of pupils playing with their instructors in the conservatory's ensembles altogether unsettling.) But around this time Sibelius's performance dreams began to spiral downward. He had been plagued by dreadful bouts of stage fright from his very first appearances in public. The attacks did not diminish with time. And now an increasing number of physical complaints began to well up. Boils interfered with his practice, an old shoulder injury acted up, and the institute's director, Martin Wegelius, finally sent him off for physical therapy at the clinic of the anatomy professor, Georg August Asp.

At this remove, it is difficult to know just how serious these complaints really were or to judge the nature of Sibelius's illnesses, some of considerable length. What does emerge from the correspondence with Uncle Pehr is his nephew's dissatisfaction with his progress on the violin and his gradual realization that he lacked the virtuosity required of a star performer. All Csillag's encouragement and high marks—in categories from diligence to progress and ability—made little difference in the face of the pupil's technical limitations. Right then Jean Sibelius's career might have foundered—and with it the central role of music in the Finnish national movement—but for two crucial individuals: Martin Wegelius and Ferruccio Busoni. The one involved him directly in the national agenda; the other showed him the international stage on which it should be played out.

A NATIONAL AGENDA FOR MUSIC:
MARTIN WEGELIUS

For anyone at all familiar with Finnish music history, the name Wegelius summons up the image of a dry, lackluster pedagogue, to be dutifully acknowledged for his pioneering role in the dreary field of music education before quickly turning one's attention elsewhere. In real life Wegelius was a complicated and versatile man, that rare figure who combined the gifts of vision, leadership, and organization with a love of music and literature.[24] In these gifts, and in the parallels and differences of his life vis-à-vis Sibelius's, lies Wegelius's importance, not just for the younger composer's personal development, but also for Finland's musical awakening.

Like most of Finland's leading figures in this era, Wegelius came from a family of Swedish-speaking Finns, and, like many, he too was stamped from birth by his family's deep religiosity. Born on Luther's name day, November 10, Martin bore the great reformer's name. The Wegelius home religion, however, was severe: the family were Pietists, Lutherans who consider all pleasures sinful and desire for any kind of decoration, even window curtains, vainglorious display. Nevertheless, the family tolerated Martin's musical interests and supported his literary pursuits, both of which he cultivated with more or less equal enthusiasm. This upbringing explains much about his later reactions to some of Sibelius's music.

Wegelius eventually decided to combine his loves of music and literature by composing vocal music, both choral and solo works. Although he began his studies with the German musician Richard Faltin (1835–1918), who held the position of music instructor at the Imperial Alexander University, the lack of professional music schools in Finland meant that Wegelius had to seek instruction abroad. It was symptomatic of prevailing attitudes that, despite the musical life and education flourishing in nearby Saint Petersburg, Finland's musicians headed for Germany. Little irony was seen in the fact that the emperor's largesse enabled Finns to cultivate a German musical education, because Germany and Austria were the clearly acknowledged homes of superior musical accomplishment. Thus, with an "Alexander stipend" in hand (awarded by the Imperial Alexander University), Wegelius headed first to Vienna, where he immersed himself in music theory, composition, and piano with the organist Rudolph Bibl in 1870–71, and then to Leipzig for a further two years of study.

The enthusiasm for Germany's musical tradition that shaped Wegelius's outlook and teachings made its impact on an entire generation of Finns, thanks in no small part to Wegelius's most important activities in his homeland. For even though he was a pianist, composer, critic, and conductor, even for a time of the Finnish Opera, Wegelius found his greatest satisfaction in the practice and fundamentals of education. He established a number of organizations, yet his central, most splendid gift to the musical life of his land was the Helsinki Music Institute (today the Sibelius Academy), of which he was one of the principal founders. When the Norwegian composer Edvard Grieg (1843–1907) declined the invitation to be its first director, Wegelius assumed those responsibilities. From the time of the conservatory's opening in 1882 until his death twenty-four years later, Wegelius served as its director. He also wrote many of its textbooks, both in music theory (some of which are still in use, albeit in revised form) and in music history (a three-volume general history of music, which has as its unfortunate guiding principle Joseph Arthur Comte de Gobineau's racial superiority of Aryans).[25]

On many fronts, then, Wegelius was passionately involved in the collective national project of enlightening the people of his land through education and cultivating their potential, in this case through music, an arena in which Finns would prove to be spectacularly successful. Wegelius was supremely conscious of his role. His seemingly airy dismissal of Sibelius and of Finland's music history ("in Finland the history of music must first be *made* before it can be written")[26] has been regarded as shortsighted, but it has too often been quoted out of context. Wegelius was emphasizing the work and continuity of the national movement, through Pacius in the case of music, in which he and many others were deeply involved and which provided the essential foundation on which Jean Sibelius and others of his generation would build: "And probably the generation growing up now shall in this respect both experience and be able to create far more significant things than we have."[27]

Wegelius thus forcefully acknowledged the national project that was the shared goal of leading nineteenth-century Finns. His words also reflect a closely related concern—Finland's history. If that history could not be discovered, then it would have to be invented. As early as 1843 Topelius had published a provocative essay, "Äger finska folket en historie" ("Do the Finnish People Have a History?"). More than half a century later the question was being taken up by Arvid Järnefelt (in his article "Onko Suomella historiaa" ["Does Finland Have a History"], published in *Nuori Suomi*, 1900).

Martin Wegelius's role in creating that history was paramount.

Composition Lessons

In the spring of 1887 Sibelius began composition lessons with Wegelius. Up to now composing had largely been a way for the young man to assuage his hunger for making music on the violin. In Hämeenlinna, it had been the surest means of obtaining music to suit the resources at hand. A slew of untitled works for violin and piano, violin and cello, or violin alone written during Sibelius's student years in Helsinki testify to the same need.

Before Wegelius, Sibelius had been self-taught in composition. In 1884 he acquired a copy of Johann Christian Lobe's *Lehrbuch der musikalischen Composition* (whose fifth edition was revised by the eminent Hermann Kretzschmar, 1848–1924) and made his way through its pages, which inspired him to compose a piano trio and a piano quartet.[28] His absorption of Lobe's emphasis on periodic structure showed up even decades later (see fig. 4.4).

Now Sibelius submitted to the same formal training that would be given to other aspiring young Finns, from Armas Järnefelt and Ilmari Krohn to Erkki Melartin, Selim Palmgren, and Toivo Kuula. Wegelius began to reign in Sibelius's wild flights of fancy with methodical, even pedantic instruction—exercises in counterpoint, fugues, systematic practice of every kind. Though orderly teaching may have been exactly what was needed, the young violinist's compositional efforts seemed temporarily to lose their luster. Wegelius's own compositions were solid, if unremarkable works (a list may be found in Karl Flodin's Wegelius biography). The tense, cramped handwriting in the manuscript of his *Oceanidernas sång* (*Song of the Oceanides*, 1868; see plate 1), its text taken from the last scene of Topelius's *Prinsessan af Cypern* (*The Princess of Cyprus*), personifies his sternness, uprightness, and control. Yet its mythical topic and title had possibilities that would not be lost on the coming generation of musical nationalists.

Not least, under Wegelius's guiding hand, Sibelius began to develop a consciousness of what it meant to be a *Finnish* composer. On May 31, 1888, an ensemble led by Csillag and comprised of the Sibelius brothers and Anna Tigerstedt premiered Janne Sibelius's Theme and Variations in C-sharp Minor. The young composer wrote ecstatically to Uncle Pehr that he "was applauded and called back almost countless times. It was so unexpected for the large audience to hear a string quartet by a Finn, because no Finn has ever composed anything in this genre."[29] To go where no Finn had gone before, to show what Finns could do—already the aspirations and the vocabulary of the national movement were coloring his perceptions, shaping his outlook, and spurring him to action.

THE MAN FROM TRIESTE: FERRUCCIO BUSONI

For Janne Sibelius the move from small Hämeenlinna to the capital of his country had been a giant step into the wide world. But for Ferruccio Busoni, born in Empoli, raised in Trieste, and schooled in Germany where he then taught, Helsinki was a petty small town and artistic backwater. Although he praised the city's cleanliness and described its coast as among the most beautiful he had ever seen, he also drew a not altogether flattering

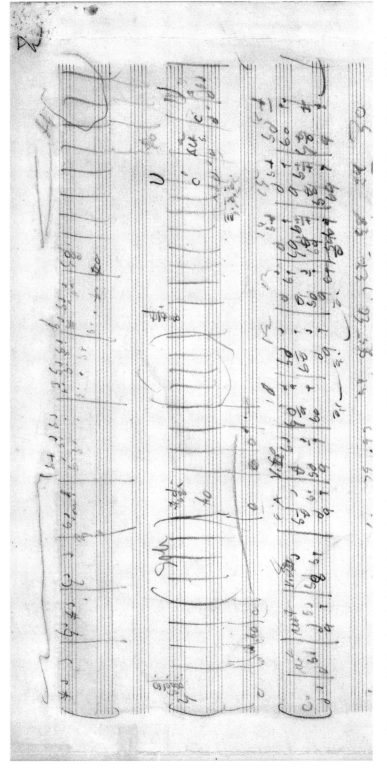

Figure 4.4. Sibelius, draft for the Fourth Symphony's second movement. HUL 312, p. [2]. © Breitkopf & Härtel, Wiesbaden. The National Library of Finland. Photo: Kari Timonen.

picture of the town.[30] He despaired of the living conditions—the foul water, the stink-
ing, ever-present dogs, the difficulty of making himself understood—and the discourag-
ingly low musical standards—no regular opera company, only a miserable theater where
works such as *La traviata* were sung in Swedish; the absence of any planned teaching curriculum at the conservatory; and the necessity of having to be content with "reproducing or imitating *a fragment* of that which has been achieved elsewhere."[31] He expressed
dismay at the loose attitude toward women, which resembled Gomorrah, he said. He
especially deplored what he saw as the wretched, backward outlook toward Jews, who
were restricted by law to a small, fixed population, required to live in their own quarter,
and subject to being transported across the border if, through childbirth, their numbers
exceeded the permitted limit.

Busoni saw immediately the dangers faced by an impressionable young man in the
Finnish capital, conditions that bedeviled Sibelius and many others. One of the first
things to be apparent was the quantity of drinking: "In this country one drinks very
heavily. Schnapps is called for all day, before and after lunch, for breakfast and to fill in
any idle moments."[32] Conditions at the institute also took him aback. When asked about
the educational program, Wegelius calmly replied that there was no specific program,
method, or materials envisioned or selected for teaching the students; "one could perhaps
take the Inventions of Bach as a starting point." It may have been for this reason that after
he left Helsinki, Busoni helpfully dedicated the development sections of his *Invenzioni a
due voce* and the *Invenzioni a tre voci* of Bach (1892) to the Helsinki Music Institute.

Busoni also complained that the "Music Institute" (the very name caused him to
shudder) could hardly even boast a string quartet: students (Sibelius being one) played
the inner parts, the insufferable Csillag scraped away on first violin, and the violoncel-
list, Wilhelm Renck, the cello "professor," was, to put it charitably, still at the beginning
of his career, having until recently been a traveling salesman. And everywhere, as in all
small towns, Busoni observed, rivalry and petty envy reigned.

But the worst hazard of all was the constant exposure to low standards. Everything
was praised; everything was "good," everyone "talented." Would his own abilities fall as
a result?

What the Finns saw in Busoni was happily recorded by one of his students, the
Swede Adolf Paul (1863–1943). Busoni was small and slender (see fig. 4.5),

> with full brown beard, gray eyes, young and gay, with a long gray overcoat with
> long tails, a small round cap perched proudly on his thick artist's curls, and an
> enormous Saint Bernard [in fact, a Newfoundland hound], which lay down and
> looked so sternly at the pupils during lessons that it wasn't worth playing wrong

notes. His master laughed so hard when he saw our finger exercises that he had to hold his sides.[33]

The main thing in playing piano, Busoni lightheartedly told his pupils when he saw them struggling with elaborate finger motions, was not how the fingers went up but how they came down.

For Sibelius, Busoni was something of a revelation. There was the quick wit. He could be sardonic, his criticisms devastating—"trained geese," he was heard to call his

Figure 4.5. Ferruccio Busoni. Photograph of a portrait by Emil Fuchs
(London, 1897) printed in *Ateneum*, November 15, 1898.
The National Museum of Finland, Department of Prints and Photographs, Helsinki.

students. "One knows what one means, doesn't one?" he commented to a pianist who had just played a composition of his own; "illness is a sign of lack of talent" was his acerbic riposte when another missed a lesson, allegedly due to sickness.[34] His repartee was legendary. Encountering Wegelius one day as the director was leaving his counterpoint class, Wegelius greeted the pianist, "Sie sind ja ein Meister der Pünktlichkeit, Busoni!" to which Busoni promptly rejoined, "Und Sie ein Meister der Kontrapünktlichkeit."[35]

A student later in Busoni's thrall, the Milwaukee-born composer and pioneer of electronic music Otto Luening (1900–1996), recalled an evening with Busoni, Richard Strauss, and friends at the Tonhalle in Zurich. Strauss held forth, proclaiming how opera had moved as far as it possibly could in the direction of gargantuan Wagnerian proportions, how it had come to the point that now composers needed to reduce the means, restore the Mozartean orchestra, bring back the numbers—those arias and recitatives! those duets! the ensembles!—and achieve clarity, *clarity* in both music and drama. Yes, yes, back to Mozart, Strauss had tendentiously concluded. This speech was met with thundering silence.

Then Busoni spoke. "It took you a long time to discover this, Dr. Strauss." The two of them, said Luening, were not on speaking terms for five years.[36]

Then there was Busoni's music. Even though in later years Sibelius scrawled into his diary the rhetorical "Why must this great pianist compose?",[37] the lucid, transparent qualities of Busoni's works, their melodious sounds and rhythmic clarity, their dramatic effectiveness, and their profound but not ponderous brevity reinforced the aesthetic precepts Sibelius had learned from Wasiljeff and pointed up the contrast to the heavy Germanic style in which he had been instructed as a youth. Nor was Sibelius's experience unique. After having heard laborious German music for almost five years, Otto Luening had also reluctantly fallen under Busoni's spell. On hearing the Italian conduct his *Arlecchino* and *Turandot* at the Zurich Opera, a deeply surprised Luening came away enchanted.[38]

Perhaps most seriously of all, this European, younger than Sibelius (by a few months), was already an accomplished professional. Busoni set a standard Sibelius had not previously encountered and brought the crosswinds of the wider musical world into Finland. Busoni was, after all, the most extensive personal contact Sibelius had ever had with anyone outside the Russian Empire. For the first time, the Hämeenlinna boy was exposed to the standards and requirements that would be expected of a world-class virtuoso. And the realization changed his life's direction profoundly. Busoni became quite central to Sibelius's life. Around the Italian there now gathered a coterie of lively comrades: Janne Sibelius; a couple of brothers by the name of Järnefelt, Armas and Eero; and Adolf Paul. These young upstarts were destined to play important roles in the rest of each other's lives.

～5～
Crosswinds

No other western country has quite the same crosswinds as Finland. Most often they blow from the southwest, though sometimes they gust from the northeast. To underestimate these currents can spell disaster for travelers, whether on land or sea. No less forceful have been the metaphorical crosswinds, which, owing to the country's geographical position between east and west, have decisively affected virtually every aspect of Finnish life. In the nineteenth century, economic and administrative gusts affecting Finland blew in not only from Russia, but also from England, whose powerful financial centers helped to shape the Finnish economy. Meanwhile, the fresh air of new intellectual ideas wafted in from both directions, and especially from Scandinavia.

SCANDINAVIAN CURRENTS

Finns did not (and do not now) consider themselves Scandinavian, any more than they considered themselves Russian. Not only does their history diverge sharply from Scandinavia's, but also their linguistic circumstances are unique. One of their languages, Finnish, is a world apart from most modern tongues except Estonian, so far in fact that only the most obstinate foreigners ever learn it. Fortunately, Finland's other language, Swedish, allows its practitioners entrée into the wider Nordic community. The ease with which speakers of Swedish, Danish, and Norwegian understand each other's written speech facilitated a network of newspapers, literary journals, and personal contacts across the Nordic countries that nourished a strong intellectual community.

Sibelius's debt to the literature of Scandinavia runs deep. One need look no further than his song texts: the Swedes Viktor Rydberg and Ernst Josephson take second place only to the Swedish-speaking Finns J. L. Runeberg and K. A. Tavaststjerna. Other Swedes—Adolf Paul and August Strindberg—provided libretti for Sibelius's theater works, among which also appear translations into Swedish of Maurice Maeterlinck's *Pelléas et Mélisande* (by Bertel Gripenberg) and into Danish of Shakespeare's *The Tempest* (by Edvard Lembcke). For Danes also made their impact on the Finns. As a child, Janne Sibelius read the stories of Hans Christian Andersen. As a student in Helsinki, he composed a melodrama for narrator and string quartet to texts from *The Little Mermaid*.[1] And as an adult, he read the work of Georg Brandes (1842–1927), in whose Goethe biography he met "much of pure genius. But so much cynicism!"[2] The gestation of many of his greatest works, from *Kullervo* to the last symphonies, included the reading of great literature. As A. N. Wilson has observed of Tolstoy, it was as if "the absorption in a different mind engaged in an analogous creative process released something within him."[3]

As Sibelius was coming of age, the charismatic Brandes, dubbed the "Danish King of Literature" by Willy Burmester, was exerting enormous influence on the Nordic literary world.[4] Born into a Jewish family, Brandes had come under the spell of the French critics Hippolyte Taine and Ernest Renan as well as the Englishman John Stuart Mill, whom the Dane met in Paris and whose *Subjection of Women* he translated. With a reformer's zeal, Brandes set about his mission: liberating his countrymen from their cultural isolation and provincialism. In 1871 he began a series of lectures at the University of Copenhagen that had repercussions as far away as Finland and Saint Petersburg (the talks were eventually published in six volumes as *Main Currents in Nineteenth Century Literature*, 1872–90). A brilliant synthesizer of other men's ideas, Brandes introduced central Europe's most radical thinkers to his Nordic contemporaries, adding to Taine, Renan, and Mill the aesthetic theories of Arthur Schopenhauer, poetry of the romantic satanists, the novels of George Sand, and the scandalous viewpoints of Friedrich Nietzsche, whom he befriended and with whom he corresponded.

Even though he was evidently not much of an original thinker himself, Brandes had the enviable ability to articulate new ideas so forcefully that his attitudes and beliefs animated aesthetic talk in Nordic salons and restaurants from 1870 until the end of the century. Brandes exhorted his audiences to embrace progressive ideas, reform society, and break through into modernism. He widely promoted the breakthrough idea, both in speech and in writing (as in the essay "Det moderne gjennembruds maend" ["Men of the Modern Breakthrough," 1883]). With his swashbuckling style, flamboyant dress, and angry insistence—shouted in lofty tones—that mental salvation was impossible without a knowledge of "foreign devils," he gleefully offended conservatives (who branded him an "atheist Jew") and thrilled youthful firebrands to the core.

In the late 1880s, under the influence of Nietzsche, Brandes developed a philosophy of aristocratic radicalism. He expressed its tenets in his study *Aristokratisk radicalisme*

(*On Aristocratic Radicalism*, 1889) and revealed its precepts in his biographies of "great men"—Goethe, Michelangelo, Shakespeare, Julius Caesar, and Voltaire. As he grew older, Brandes lost none of his relish for defying convention and denouncing tyrannical thinking: his *Sagnet om Jesus* (*Jesus: A Myth*, 1925) made him, if possible, even more enemies.

A friend of such leading Scandinavian writers as Henrik Ibsen, August Strindberg, and Bjørnstjerne Bjørnson, Brandes also made connections in Finland, where he came to lecture. Some of his works were translated into Finnish by the leading realist and social crusader Minna Canth. For a time Brandes's scolding refrain exhorting all who would listen to address social ills, in combination with the cold drafts of evolutionary and positivist science blustering into Finland from England, turned literary and artistic concerns away from national folk topics and toward realism (a direction shown in Finnish-language literature by Aleksis Kivi). In 1880 Henrik Ibsen's realist drama *A Doll's House* was staged in Helsinki. The Finns had admired Ibsen for his nationalism, so a play harping on radical social issues was a fiasco with the public. Among Finnish intellectuals its scandalous lines fueled debates on morality, the position of women in society, and other social issues, loosening tongues and escalating emotions for decades.

By the time Sibelius moved to Helsinki in 1885, realism pervaded Finland's plays, novels, and artworks. That very year signaled a tipping point: Minna Canth's play *Työmiehen vaimo* (*The Workingman's Wife*) appeared. So did Juhani Aho's novel *Papin tytär* (*The Parson's Daughter*) and a startling canvas by Axel Gallén called *Akka ja kissa* (*Old Woman and a Cat*), whose central subject—a gnarled peasant woman observing a cat in a homely farmyard—highlighted "the people" in a way hardly seen before in Finnish art. Canth's writings challenged complacent, upper-class society by exposing the pitiless labor conditions of the working men and women in Finland, the inequality of Finnish women, and the overall poverty of the working classes. Aho likewise dealt with controversial issues, including the "woman question"—her education, her position in society—matters that greatly exercised Helsinki's educated citizens during the 1880s. A few years later K. A. Tavaststjerna (1860–1898) dramatized the stark class contrast in Finland in his novel *Hårda tider* (*Hard Times*, 1891), an account of the famine and typhus-infested years of the 1860s during which his mother had died of the same plague that took Jean Sibelius's father. With the help of Aho, Tavaststjerna adapted the novel for the stage in a Finnish version retitled *Uramon torppa* (*Uramo's Croft*).

As a music student in Helsinki, Sibelius's connection with literature, rather than being replaced by music, thrived along with it. In part, this was owing to the company he kept—Wegelius adored literature, Busoni had his own literary bent (he wrote the libretti for most of his operas), and Sibelius's closest companions, especially his fellow students Adolf Paul and the Järnefelt brothers, Armas and Eero, read widely. Paul eventually left music to become a writer.

Together, they sniggered over *The Red Room*, subtitled *Scenes of Artistic and Literary Life*, a parody of Stockholm society by August Strindberg (1849–1912). Much of its hilarious action takes place in Bohemian haunts where young men "who had found themselves in that peculiar state that begins when one leaves the parental roof and continues until one has one's own" congregated, there to drink themselves into oblivion while seeking their mission in life.[5] The parallels to the young Finns' own lives were deliciously close. The author lampooned those elements of society they were regretfully coming to know: newspaper editors, who should be a bit stupid, because stupidity was always accompanied by a conservative turn of mind; publishers, who enlighten the public with market propaganda; politicians, about whom the less said the better; proselytizers, who "had succeeded in making it fashionable to be sinful" and for whom the pursuit of grace was a sport; theater critics (the one in *The Red Room* turns out to be deaf); and artists themselves. This kind of satire was new in Swedish fiction, and it made Strindberg nationally famous.

Sibelius admitted to being obsessed with Strindberg. So were many others—the Norwegian author Knut Hamsun (1859–1952), for example, who would receive the Nobel Prize for literature in 1920. (Hamsun got to know Sibelius, even composing a poem "Sibelius" in which the Finn is called *en Fan i al Norden*—"a Devil in the North.") For Hamsun, Strindberg was "the most important author of his country, perhaps of our times. He is a supreme genius, a brain on horseback, charging his own way, leaving all others far behind."[6]

The literature of Scandinavia, whether fiction, poetry, or biography, helps to explain Sibelius and his contemporaries in ways that Finnish-language literature does not. Finland's Scandinavian and Russian neighbors have often wondered at Finnish plays, movies, and stories, whose characters seem so depressed, so introverted, so lacking in humor. Finnish artworks are somber as well. The men are perpetually grim visaged; only women smile, and then only tentatively. And yet anyone at all acquainted with Finns quickly experiences their wit, their wry jesting, and their infinitely creative comic side. That side was clearly in evidence among the Sibelius men and was passed on to Janne Sibelius, who made it one of his most endearing traits.

One explanation for the disconnect between illusion and reality is that the national mission—to create a Finnish identity politically, artistically, industrially, and musically—was a deeply serious affair, a question even of survival. In view of that mission, humor was suspect, a sign of light-mindedness, the trivializing of a momentous goal. Moreover, the very pillars of Finnish identity had inculcated the idea that the men of Finland, at least, were grave and stern.

Consider the *Kalevala*. As the epic was interpreted by the orchestrators of the national movement, the *Kalevala* forcefully proved that laughter did not belong to the character of Finnish men. Eliel Aspelin (1847–1917), who added Haapkylä to his Swedish name in 1906, and who was a passionate Fennoman, an aesthetician and literary historian, an activist in numerous cultural organizations, and a figure deeply involved in the Finnish movement, observed that not for nothing was Väinämöinen called *vaka vanha Väinämöinen*—serious old Väinämöinen. Or that Kullervo, breaking his knife on that stone cruelly baked into his loaf of bread, vowed revenge on "woman's jeering, housemaid's mocking" (*naisen naurun, piian pilkan*). Laughter, whether derisive and scornful or mindless and silly, was the province of women. Finnish men, claimed Aspelin, *never* laugh in the *Kalevala*. They were silent and serious. Aspelin even went so far as to publish an eighteen-page article titled "On Crying and Laughing in the *Kalevala*" to prove his point.[7]

In Sweden wit and satire flourished, especially in the eighteenth century during the reign of Gustav III. But this lightness did not reach Finnish-language writing, whose literature was based on the Bible, law, and authority. No humor there. And even though old Finnish folk-song texts can be funny (a heritage that Aleksis Kivi had tried to exploit), nineteenth-century Finnish leaders held the strong conviction that humor had no place in fulfilling the national hopes. There are clear indications that a stern nature was self-consciously adopted (made, not born) as a way of separating Finns from "merry Swedes" and promoting national definition.

The gloom inevitably reached into music.[8] Older Finnish folk songs have been handed down in major keys. But during the awakening, especially in the years of "oppression" at the end of the nineteenth century, composers were rewarded for writing in minor mode: such music succeeded in being praised, published, and performed. Ironically, those choices fostered a quality of "Russianness," for which the only acceptable term in Finland, of course, was not Russian, but "Slavic."

Whatever the combination of factors behind the long faces, Sibelius dutifully presented a dour image to the world, not only in stone-faced photographs but even sometimes in person: the British composer Arnold Bax (1883–1953) once remarked that Sibelius gave the impression of never having laughed in his life.[9] The reality was otherwise. Witty repartee, merrymaking, *le bon mot* belonged to Sibelius's private side, as his correspondence, his diaries, and long-forgotten (or conveniently laid aside) photographs prove. And his student years showed him, not inappropriately, at the height of indulging in comical and witty pleasures. For these pleasures, he needed friends, and the group around Busoni provided the most frequent excuses for indulging in companionable amusements.

WESTERN CURRENTS: ADOLF PAUL

Sibelius's connections to Scandinavian literary currents in his student years came not only through Wegelius, who read widely in Swedish literature, but also through fellow student Adolf Paul (see fig. 5.1). Paul's real name was Georg Wiedersheim-Paul, and he was a Swede, born in Skåne of a German father and a Swedish mother.[10] The boy's relationship to Finland began early: the family came to the country when their son was nine. A defiant spirit showed up early too: Paul rebelled against the name his parents had bestowed upon him and then defied their plans for him to study agriculture. Instead, Georg, now Adolf, enrolled at the Helsinki Music Institute with the idea of becoming a pianist.

Under Busoni's tutelage, Paul advanced enough to be able to play the piano part in Janne Sibelius's Quintet in G Minor in its first full performance on October 11, 1890, in Turku. A shared obsession with E. T. A. Hoffmann had brought composer and pianist together. Sibelius acknowledged their mutual literary passion in the way he usually dealt with strong feelings—in music. He dedicated to Paul a piano suite called *Florestan* (1889). Its title and textual annotations evoked Hoffmann's *Kreisleriana*, whose incarnation in Schumann's like-named work they had heard Busoni play in Helsinki the previous December.[11]

Paul's technical shortcomings and the lure of success in the world of letters dampened the blaze of his musical will. He found a new ambition—writing about "great men" he knew. Had his friends seen what was coming, they might have been warier. *En bok om en människa* (*A Book about a Human Being*), published in Stockholm in 1891 and dedicated to Sibelius, portrays an egocentric, irresponsible, childish Janne, thoughtless chaser of beautiful women, thinly disguised under the name Sillén. The similarity of the name to Sellén, one of the starving artists in August Strindberg's *The Red Room*—the "genius-child" whom his peers recognize as endlessly talented—was not lost on Sibelius or any of the others in the Helsinki pack who had guffawed over Strindberg's satire. Although a later Sibelius worshipper (Axel Carpelan) dismissed Paul's book as a "kitchen midden of semi-digested insights into the artist's work and frenetic life,"[12] with its debut the person of Jean Sibelius joined the Swedish-language literary streams. So did Busoni a few years later when Paul dedicated *A Book*'s sequel, *Med det falska och det ärliga ögat* (*With the Deceitful and the Honest Eye*, 1895), to Busoni, "my friend."

ADOLF PAUL.

Figure 5.1. Adolf Paul. Photograph from an unidentified newspaper, 1890s. The National Museum
of Finland, Department of Prints and Photographs, Helsinki.

Paul's idolization of Sibelius was a matter of self-interest: he was convinced that
he, Paul, would write the libretto to which his musical friend would compose a magnificent opera, thereby making both their fortunes. When Paul relocated to Berlin in 1889,
he turned to full-time writing and pandering to intellectuals, spending his days with the
bizarre Stanisław Przybyszewski, the smoldering Dagny Juel, the tormented Edvard
Munch, and the eccentric Strindberg. Although the first three unwittingly lent their idiosyncrasies to some of the characters in *With the Deceitful and the Honest Eye*, it was
Strindberg who starred in the sometimes acerbic volume *Min Strindbergsbok: Strind-
bergsminnen och brev* (1915; Stockholm: Norstedt, 1930).

Strindberg, never one to take offense lightly, avenged himself not once, but twice.
He turned Paul into a Finn (a true insult coming from a fellow Swede): Paul is "the unim-
portant, uncultured Ilmarinen" in *Fagervik och Skamsund* (*Fair Haven and Foul Strand*,
1902); later, Strindberg seats this comer among the dishonored guests at a dinner for
dunces in *Svarta fanor* (*Black Banners*, 1907). Paul's last volume, *Profiler: Minnen av stora
personligheter* (*Profiles: Memories of Great Personalities*, 1937), proved that the gravita-
tional pull of the powerful stayed with him to the last. He died in poverty, infatuated with
another "great man": Adolf Hitler.

EASTERN CURRENTS: THE JÄRNEFELTS

If Busoni and Paul brought the air of Scandinavia and central Europe into Finland, it was the Järnefelt brothers, Armas and Eero, who put Sibelius in contact with Saint Petersburg intellectual circles and with a personal, ethically grounded sense of national aspiration. The boys were two of a great brood, and all who lived into adulthood showed a prodigious array of talents. The patriarch, August Alexander Järnefelt (1833–1896), was born near Viipuri and spent his various careers in the service of the Russian emperors.[13] Although he came from a family of modest means, Alexander Järnefelt proudly traced his kinship lines to the Stuarts of England; it was even claimed that patrician blood of the Roman Claudius circulated in his stalwart veins.

Alexander Järnefelt became a Russian military topographer and served an apprenticeship with the celebrated astronomer Wilhelm Struve (1793–1864) in the Nicholas Observatory at Pulkova (near Saint Petersburg) in 1861. In 1870 Järnefelt was named head of the Finnish section of the Russian army's topography office in Helsinki. He then began cultivating a second, administrative career. He was appointed governor, first of the province of Mikkeli, then of Kuopio, and finally of Vasa. In 1894 he was promoted to the position equivalent to defense minister for Finland. An enormously well-educated man who spoke and published his scientific essays in Russian, General Lieutenant Järnefelt had been born into a Swedish-speaking home, learned Finnish as a child, and came to believe that Finnish should be the country's first official language as well as the language of the intelligentsia. He raised his many children to speak Finnish, meanwhile ensuring that they also learned Russian, Swedish, French, and German.

The life of this paterfamilias demonstrated for all to see that Finnish nationalism and imperial loyalties, far from being mutually exclusive, could go hand in hand. Alexander even married into Russian intelligentsia: his wife, Elisabeth Clodt von Jürgensburg (1839–1929), born in Saint Petersburg, came of a family deeply involved in the cultural life of the Russian capital. Sculptures by her uncle, Peter Carlovich Clodt (1805–1867), bedeck the city: his fearsome steeds even today guard the Anichkov Bridge, and his statue of Nicholas I looms over Saint Isaac's Square. Elisabeth's brother, Michael Clodt von Jürgensburg (1832–1902), an artist associated with the Russian school of *peredvizhniki*, taught painting at the Petersburg Academy.

Alexander brought Elisabeth to Finland after their marriage in 1858, and the couple settled in Kuopio. Elisabeth's stunned realization of the true meaning of life in a provincial Finnish town was later given literary expression by one of her sons in a lengthy novelistic work, *My Parents' Story*.[14] Elisabeth spurned Swedish, learned Finnish, and set about organizing a salon (whatever else?), to which her versatile and growing brood of children contributed: Kasper (1859–1941), who became a professional translator and literary critic; Arvid (1861–1932), a devotee of Tolstoy who eventually became one of Finland's leading authors; Eero (1863–1937), who studied art with his uncle in Saint Petersburg at the Academy of Arts from 1883 to 1885; Armas (1869–1958), musician, composer, and eventually conductor; and Aino (1871–1969), born into the first generation of Finns to bear a *Kalevala* name, highly intelligent and linguistically well schooled.[15]

Elisabeth Järnefelt's cultural background and her later Tolstoyan awakening left its indelible imprint upon her offspring.[16] The mother taught her children that art must be grounded in ethics. It should be for everyone, and it should be truthful. The artist must be true, above all, to himself, and the surest path to that truth was through familiar subjects—national subjects, for instance. But national did not mean provincial or isolated. Indeed, it was through the national that wider European ideals could be attained, the lofty ideal embodied in the Järnefelts' motto: *kansallisen kautta yleiseurooppalaiseen*—through the national to the all-European.

It was Armas Järnefelt (see fig. 5.2) who introduced his new friend, Janne Sibelius, to the family. In 1887 Armas had abandoned his law studies at the university and enrolled in the Helsinki Music Institute. He and Sibelius studied composition together with Wegelius; while Janne fiddled, Armas had piano instruction with Busoni. From 1890 to 1893, Järnefelt studied with the punctilious Albert Becker in Berlin, but it was Wagner who ignited his passions, and eventually he conducted Wagner's music dramas numerous times in Finland.

Armas Järnefelt cut a fine figure. With his unruly hair, twirling mustache, and aristocratic face, he had the look of an aesthete. He wore a pinkie ring on his right hand, and he tied his silk cravats in delicate swoops that drooped elegantly from his neck. Ambitious to compose, to conduct Wagner, to make a name for himself, Armas Järnefelt was perhaps too much of a musical rival to become Sibelius's close friend. Instead, it was his brother Eero, the artist, and their pretty sister, Aino, who became the most important to Janne Sibelius.

Christened Erik Nikolai (czarist names being widely popular in Finland), Eero (see fig. 5.3) was the Järnefelt brother closest in age to Sibelius. Like the rest of the family, he was thoroughly steeped in the goals of the national mission: building a Finnish-minded spirit and creating Finnish art. His paintings, both landscapes and realistic portraits, contributed steadily to the collective Finnish identity—splendid contemporary documents that show the artist's affinity with the prevailing currents of realism and with the family's belief that "Only the truth is constant."[17] As for Aino, more anon.

Figure 5.2. Armas Järnefelt with Max and Kax. Photograph by Daniel Nyblin. Armas Järnefelt Archive,
the National Archives of Finland.

The Järnefelts, with whom Sibelius was closely involved from the late 1880s and into
whose family he married in 1892, linked the composer to the national movement in a way
that was constant, personal, and vital. From this point forward, his life was so intricately
entwined with his country's national awakening that even had he so desired, no escape or
avoidance of its great mission was possible.

Figure 5.3. Gunnar Berndtson, *Eero Järnefelt*. Oil on canvas, early 1890s.
The National Archives of Finland. Photo: Erkki Vaalle.

"DEAR SIBELIUS, YOU HAVE FALLEN DOWN FROM THE MOON"

What his contemporaries saw in Janne Sibelius emerges from contemporary photographs, paintings, and memoirs. That he cut an imposing physical figure is beyond doubt. A high forehead, broad as Finland was wide, "rose like a Corinthian capital" from a starched collar and silk cravat,[18] its height magnified by the rising pompadour of an unruly head of hair. Photographs have darkened those locks, but the young Sibelius had light-colored hair. Above a magnificent Roman nose, sloping eyebrows imparted a hooded, sad look to his eyes, but those eyes could pierce with "a look all blue." All the features—forehead, saucer-shaped ears, broad nose—could have been hewn from Finnish granite, with the exception of the mouth, which betrayed an artist's sensitivity and nervous energy.

And the composer bristled with nervous energy. Conversation with him "darted about like a hare in the undergrowth," gasped one interviewer. As any listener to the early works knows, in these years Sibelius was far from calm. Again and again, his hands ran nervously and elaborately through his thick hair. And hair he had in abundance. A bushy, thick mane stood up in a crest or waved wildly, an aureole of power. Like Samson. Slim, intense, hirsute, and mighty, Sibelius was wired.

His contemporaries frequently described him in color: Juhani Aho said he looked "all gray." Aho may have been color-blind: almost everybody else said he looked all blue, even brilliantly blue (as Karl Flodin put it, "a look of blue brilliancy"). Men as well as women testified to the intensity of those glittering azure eyes. And his very words were vividly tinted in multitoned hues; he tossed around "colours and sounds as if they were bright glass balls, made colours resound and sounds glow, so that A major became blue and C major red, F major green and D major yellow."[19]

And his speech! Dazzling and deep, Sibelius's voice resonated with bass tones, as do the voices of most Finnish men. Even as an old man, the strength of that splendid voice carried power, presence, conviction.[20] His speech revealed a nature that was not uncomplicated. Busoni found him complex and difficult to make out; he sensed that Sibelius was never quite at ease in his company, taking on a childish, ingratiating manner that left the composer-pianist feeling awkward.[21] The same attitude showed in the nephew's dealings with his Uncle Pehr, naive and manipulative all at once. Karl Flodin described him in similarly quixotic terms:

> There was something peculiarly fascinating about his slender figure. It was as if his straightforward nature always wanted to meet one with open arms. But you were never sure whether there was not, after all, some mockery behind it. His speech overflowed with paradoxes and metaphors, without allowing you to realise what was serious and what only played on the surface like bubbles born of odd caprices in his quick brain.[22]

Yet when the childish shaded into childlike, Janne Sibelius could be mesmerizing. Alexander Järnefelt's eyes were said to light up when he was around, and Hanna Wegelius remarked, "It's strange, but Jean inspires only admiration in everyone, even though he makes no effort at it."[23]

During summers in Lovisa both Sibelius brothers enchanted their friends (the Sucksdorffs and the Stenbäcks) and acquaintances (a Mrs. Terechoff, wife of one of the town's leading Russian industrialists, and many of Lovisa's spa visitors). It was in Lovisa that

Alma Söderhjelm (1870–1949), later a history professor and writer but then a blossoming teenager, got such memorable impressions of the handsome Sibelius boys.[24] Meeting Christian was exactly the same, she said, as if someone suddenly opened a window to let in the fresh morning breeze. Happy and positive, manly and young was what he was. Even back then his voice conveyed his personal magnetism. One simply *had* to follow him, whether it was sailing along the coastline or whirling around the dance floor. Christian Sibelius was interested in science and debate and always had the right—and the last—word. He could suddenly say something that would make everything clear. A shining intellect, a character of gold, the family had no worries about Christian.

The other brother, Janne Sibelius, pale and handsome, slender and sensitive, seemed to live in a world of his own, even at the rather advanced age of twenty-four. One day, said Alma Söderhjelm, as his mother sat serving coffee and visiting with her friends in the drawing room, the door opened and in walked Janne. He seated himself at the piano and began to play, apparently without noticing anyone else in the room. Ladies loved this strange and attractive being. His delicate, sympathetic, attentive nature emanated something they adored. Alma said he stood above them, speaking so interestingly and knowing so much. He spoke about Macbeth and how he wanted to write a symphony on Macbeth's story. He read stories aloud, then played on the piano how the story should go. As for dancing, he did not dance himself because he was a "sick patient," so he played for others to waltz, only you couldn't really dance to his music. It started in good time, but soon began to go into roulades and runs. With one brother Alma Söderhjelm gained a new perspective on life. With the other for the first time she met—so she said—a genius.

In his last year of study at the Helsinki Music Institute, Sibelius attended a masked ball. He showed up disguised as a Finnish folk singer, chanting and thrumming out songs on the *kantele*, a kind of Finnish psaltery. Then he changed into a red domino (probably a loose cloak with a mask that hid the upper part of his face) and demonstrated a new feat: bouncing like a rubber ball. Partygoers shrieked with laughter. Meanwhile, a wondrous conglomeration of masked figures milled about the dance floor: an old, run-down piano teacher who strolled around with a butterfly; a prince accompanying a shop vendor; a hundred-year-old man on whom everyone took pity; a schoolmaster dressed like a donkey (the evening's real hit); a mewing cat, a neighing horse, a crowing rooster, and masses of fat men and ladies. Even one of Santa's elves was there. It was the elf who sharply eyed the red domino figure and announced, "Now dear Sibelius, you have fallen down from the moon."[25]

Otherworldly, outlandish, fantastical—Janne Sibelius appeared alien indeed to many Finns. His impulsive and capricious nature showed up in his conversations, his correspondence, even his musical notation. It is a feature that prevents uncomplicated assessment of the man and his music and is the quicksand in which many have foundered. It is all too easy to believe that Sibelius's letters, his diary ("Oh, You Glorious Ego!"), and his statements to interviewers (especially those asking such vacuous questions as "Who is your favorite composer?") mean precisely what they say. Beware the biographer who misses the mockery, who fails to hear the irony, who takes Sibelius's pronouncements at face value. Not for nothing did he and his cohorts compare themselves to Don Quixote.

THE DON QUIXOTES

It was the perceptive Busoni who captured in music the spirit of these funny, fledgling Finns. They seemed to gravitate naturally to the silvery-tongued Italian who could jest with them in Swedish and German, and who was so close to them in age, yet so cosmopolitan and artistically superior. Busoni's glamorous appeal was heightened by his lovable pet, the great Newfoundland hound he called Lesko, who faithfully (some thought ominously) attended the music lessons. Sibelius, Paul, and the Järnefelts formed a close circle around Busoni, who dubbed his coterie of Nordic friends "the Leskovites" and eventually paid it tribute in his Second Orchestral Suite, op. 34a. One longs to say he "immortalized" them, but because the work has been almost forgotten, both in concert halls and even by scholars, immortality hardly applies.

Yet neither as a musical composition and certainly not as a cultural document does the suite deserve its obscurity. Although in the year of its creation (1895) Busoni complained to his mother about the lack of interest in the piece ("it's too difficult to digest for stomachs used to sorbet, lemonade and sugared almonds," he observed sardonically), a hundred years later it was still not commercially recorded.[26] Even now, few Busoni scholars discuss it—and even fewer Sibelius scholars. Yet in its pages Busoni brought to life one of Finland's foremost artistic circles, placing Sibelius and his closest contemporaries in a context that captures *la verité* of their idea world—their comic sides, their personal qualities, their preoccupations—in a way few other documents have done.

Busoni dedicated his suite "To the Leskovites in Helsingfors (1889)" and named each of the four movements for one of the group: "Sibelius" (the first movement), "Adolf Paul" (the second), "Armas Järnefelt" (the third), and "Eero Järnefelt" (the fourth). The cuteness of the dedication, which exalts the dog above any of the other companions, lends the suite a frivolous air. Yet the work's real wit—and its deeper layers of meaning— become apparent through the titillating subtitle: *Geharnischte Suite*, or *The Armoured Suite*. Its imagery points in the direction of that madcap nobleman Don Quixote. The valiant Spanish knight lent his aristocratic courage to many young artistic types. Knut

Hamsun saw him in Strindberg, the "brain on horseback, charging his own way, leaving all others far behind." Richard Strauss concocted the Don's most famous musical adventures in his eponymous tone poem, dated 1897. Sibelius too invoked the Don's likeness. In January 1891, writing from Vienna, he attempted to lure his fellow Leskovite Paul to join him: "Come here in the spring. We'll go to the Prater and party and live it up. In a way we're both artistic Don Quixotes. It's good enough—then you at least plagiarize Cervantes."[27] The same metaphor recurs in other letters both then and later, and shows up in his diary, where, as late as June 5, 1912, he refers to Paul as his "comrade-in-arms."

Perhaps the Järnefelts, sons of a literature-loving Russian mother, had appropriated Don Quixote as the Leskovites' artistic ideal. The idea had been made current by the author and playwright Ivan Turgenev (1818–1883), whose essay "Hamlet and Don Quixote," written in the 1850s, became widely known after his celebrated lecture on the topic in 1860. Turgenev's scheme for classifying his contemporaries was widely discussed in intellectual circles: were you a Hamlet, a self-doubting skeptic, a ditherer, an incompetent dreamer? Or were you a Don Quixote, blazing with mad passion for your ideals? Were you led by your head or your heart? The answer was vital—and for Turgenev incontestable: "Only that man who is led by his heart finds the right way."[28]

For the exuberant Leskovites, the answer was also unequivocal: they were the radical new Don Quixotes burning with zeal for their ideals, however wacky and weird others might find them. Not for them discouragement or daunting setbacks. As comrades-in-arms, they would march forth to build a Finnish golden age carried through by indomitable will. For Finns fired with idealism and passion to stand up and fight for their heritage and prove the true nobility of their natures, the image fit superbly. Sibelius once compared his *Lemminkäinen* to a cocky, aristocratic count: "I would want more pride in us Finns. Not 'every helmet askew!' What do we have to be ashamed of? This idea runs through 'Lemminkäinen's Homeward Journey.' As a personage, Lemminkäinen is the like of any count. He is an aristocrat, absolutely an aristocrat!"[29]

The artists of Sibelius's generation held on to their admiration of Don Quixote's blind faith and fanatical adventures and to their feelings of oneness with the quirky knight for many years. More than two decades after the Leskovites had disbanded as a regular group and gone their various ways, Sibelius bought a horse and named it Rosinante.[30] In that same decade, the artist Axel Gallén was turning fifty, a milestone that caused him to reminisce on the national aims he had shared with his compatriots. In the spring of 1915, Gallén wrote to Sibelius, his "close comrade-in-arms," invoking the brave knight who followed his heart: "I was able to stand my ground against the storm of homage by thinking of Cervantes' splendid hero, who, too, was not scared . . . . Soon it will be your turn, and then: Evoe, Evoe! You will not need, however, to compare yourself to the Knight of La Mancha, for you have never had to defend yourself against windmills and hogs-heads."[31] In that, of course, Gallén was mistaken.

The Armoured Suite

Busoni armed the Leskovites every bit as fully as Don Quixote was equipped: in the suite's revised orchestration from 1903, the band sallies forth from an orchestra kitted out with a battery of trumpets, trombones, horns, tubas.[32] The comrades are accompanied by side drum and bass drum, triangle and glockenspiel, cymbals and timpani. Neither clashes nor conflict, dissent or confrontation intimidates these knights in armor. They have the passion of their beliefs, although there are the occasional distractions.

In the first movement, dedicated (naturally) to Sibelius, the confident martial theme skips to a second subject of ardent tenderness (marked espressivo dolcissimo), a musical wooing of a fictive Dulcinea who momentarily distracts the knight errant. It is the Sibelius music that, in Busoni's personification, is the most complex of that of all the four allies. Beginning allegro moderato e deciso, it opens with low woodwind growls, the sound Sibelius had by 1903 made unforgettable in the opening bars of *Finlandia*.

Busoni skillfully captured his friend's musical essence along with his human qualities: flurries of nervously mad action alternating with episodes of quiescent meditation in which the strings murmur a placid background to a vocally expressive English horn melody. Along with the frolicsome changes of mood and key, there are the kinds of dizzying harmonic juxtapositions that gave Sibelius's composition teachers heart palpitations. And best of all, the movement rises to an agitated section of great fury, with orbiting repetitions, the stylistic weapon with which Sibelius assaulted the bastions of sonata form, then closes with wisps of sensual delights flitting through the orchestra, whispering of lascivious distractions.

The second movement, "Kriegstanz—Danza guerresca," belongs to Adolf Paul. Its self-possessed allegro risoluto unfolds in less complex harmonic space—F major—and in classically phrased, platitudinous themes. The opening chords, loudly proclaimed on three trumpets, are to be played "möglichst kräftig und kurz, jedoch klangvoll wieder-zugeben." They announce a more transparent character, the one who constantly aspired to grand schemes, yet was everlastingly relegated to the periphery of greater men. It is into Paul's movement that Rosinante lumbers, announced by a clumsy dissonance at quasi presto agitato e deciso and followed by a flurry of motives and militaristic effects that conjure up images of the knight who battled an army of sheep.

With the third movement, dedicated to the Wagner fanatic Armas Järnefelt, the chivalrous hero turns Wagnerian. The title, "Grabdenkmal—Momento funèbre," together with the pace and key (an andante grave that begins in E minor but ends in A major), the throbbing timpani, the murky brass colors, and the long pedal points all convey adoration for the Demon of Bayreuth. The sorrowing Siegfried-like themes (the score's page 72) suggest that it is Wagner—Armas Järnefelt's idol and the giant all serious nineteenth-century musicians would eventually have to lay symbolically to rest—who is being carried to his grave.

Busoni launched the Leskovites' final assault, "Ansturm—Assalto," in the suite's longest movement, dedicated to Eero Järnefelt. The artist's delicate build and gentle pursuits seemed poles apart from the charging knight, but this Järnefelt's innate nature emerges in the tempo indication, allegro impetuoso, and the whimsical uses of 6/4 time. The full horn choir blares courageously hopeful, victorious triads, yet the zany string background, fluttering through broken chords, and the tipsy-sounding theme stumbling awkwardly downward can only give substantial hope to any enemy with ears to hear. Even the allegretto marziale, instead of sounding like a fierce and foreboding militaristic advance, lurches along out of sync. But as blind conviction will sometimes do, stubborn insistence on the truth as you passionately believe it to be wins the day—the reiterated octave/fifth and resolute chords claim victory, albeit not in any triumphal C major, but in the D minor gloaming of a Finnish winter.

~6~

From Russian Empire to Musical Empire

IMPERIAL PATRONAGE

By 1889 Janne Sibelius had in hand almost all of the ingredients essential to creativity: tools (education, a violin), economic support (thanks to Uncle Pehr), and like-minded spirits (above all, the Leskovites). Now, at the close of his Helsinki study years, the fourth essential ingredient was presented to him: the chance to travel abroad. On May 30, 1889, a small notice in *Nya Pressen* announced the most recent travel awards conferred by the grand duchy's senate: 3,000 marks each went to Axel Gallén and Emil Wikström; 2,000 marks apiece were awarded to "music students I. H. R. Krohn and J. C. J. Sibelius."

The tiny size of this six-line announcement belied its huge significance. Fostering Finnish arts and sciences was a key aspect of Finland's national awakening and at the same time the happy outcome. And it was not just allowed, it was encouraged—out of Russian self-interest, as a means of securing Finnish loyalties. In the country's early years as a grand duchy, the emperors had made funds available for scientific endeavors in the Finnish language. Gradually, support spread to other disciplines. In 1839 the Finnish Science Association received funding for ecclesiastic and educational purposes. In 1842 the aesthetician and historian Fredrik Cygnaeus (1807–1881) received the first of those "Alexander stipends"—awards granted through the Imperial Alexander University for study abroad. Cygnaeus had justified his application with the argument that "in central Europe [can be found] increased broad education in general, deeper knowledge of languages, lands, and people, increased experience and wider horizons for the head and for the heart."[1]

With the economic prosperity that began to blossom under Alexander II, the patronage broadened to Finland's arts.[2] In 1863 the senate granted the first travel stipends to artists. The following year, for the first time, funding was given to the Finnish Society of

Fine Arts—3,000 rubles to finance its activities. In 1870 the composer Martin Wegelius was among the recipients of the emperor's largesse. By 1888 singers and instrumentalists had begun receiving support. The groundswell rushed onward. Between 1891 and 1913 study grants were awarded to seventy artists, forty-three actors and actresses, and forty composers. Funding was given to writers, and then, by degrees, to organizations such as theaters and orchestras. Pensions comparable to salaries were bestowed. In proportion to the need and the available resources, support for the arts in Finland had never been as great as during what later was called the "first period of [Russian] oppression."[3]

Artistic Finns thus went off to live for a time in the great European cities, especially Paris (where Gallén and Wikström headed), Berlin, and Rome; in 1908 one Finnish traveler observed that "nowadays just about the whole of civilized Finland is abroad. All the artists—around 30—are in Paris, while writers and musicians are in Italy."[4]

Sibelius too would eventually head for Italy. But in 1889 no pupil of Martin Wegelius could seriously consider studying anywhere other than the German Empire. In Wegelius's eyes the Germanic race epitomized human accomplishment, and Germany's musical triumvirate—Bach, Beethoven, and Wagner—was very nearly sanctified. For other reasons as well, Berlin, the capital of the German Reich since 1871, attracted young Nordic students in large numbers. Although architecturally new, overblown, and downright ugly, linguistically Berlin offered an environment of relative ease for speakers of Swedish, Danish, or Norwegian. And Sibelius was not there to study architecture, but to hear and study music. For that, Berlin was widely recognized. It had distinguished educational institutions—the Hochschule für Musik, the Stern Conservatory, the Scharwenka Conservatory, the university; it had splendid orchestras, fine choral ensembles, outstanding opera houses, solo recital programs, and music festivals. Indeed, the critic Romain Rolland (1866–1944) was of the opinion that *there was too much music in Germany*" (the emphasis is his).[5] Yet those from the Russian Empire took a different view. The composer Arthur Lourié (1892–1966) described Berlin at the beginning of the twentieth century as the center, not just of European music, but of the world.[6] And in 1889 Berlin was surging toward that glittering global status. Despite its resistance to German hegemony, Imperial Russia had no objection to Germany as a *musical* destination, where even an "emperor" reigned—in the person of Richard Strauss.

The idea was for Sibelius to study with Albert Becker (1834–1899). The aspiring pupil had probably heard Becker's unremarkable music in Helsinki: the cantata *Die Wallfahrt nach Kevlaar*, a setting of a sentimental ballade by Heinrich Heine for soloists, chorus, and orchestra, performed on November 30, 1886; or *Frühlings Begräbnis*, played in February 1889. Solid, Germanic works they were, reverberant of "civilization." And so on a hopeful Saturday in September, Sibelius boarded one of the steamships that by now regularly plied the Baltic waters, the one that had been christened for the Russian emperor—*Storfursten* (*The Grand Duke*, his majesty's title in Finland). However elevated its namesake, the *Storfursten* was no luxury liner. Busoni, whose first journey to Finland had been aboard this steamship, had expected rather more from the vessel that sat so gracefully in the water. He found it small, cramped, and comfortless. Yet Sibelius seemed happy: his long-awaited wish "to get out" was coming true. Even so, the defenses of insecure youth had been raised. He wrote to Uncle Pehr: "There are three musicians on board, one poet, one painter, and an architect, so the arts are well represented on the *Storfursten*. There are also several merchants, including a traveling salesman in wine named Stahl, who said he knows you. In general one must distrust people in order not to be deceived."[7]

The *Storfursten* was carrying other young Finns to European centers—Ilmari Krohn to Leipzig, Eero Järnefelt and Juhani Aho to Paris. Also aboard was Werner Söderhjelm (1859–1931), a writer, philologist, and historian, one of the many siblings of Alma. Söderhjelm wrote to his mother from the ship about the congenial Aho and Järnefelt and "the musician Jean Sibelius," whom he described as "a very decent and talented boy, especially placed under our care."[8]

It is unfortunate that the Söderhjelms did not keep the talented boy more strictly under their care, for in this first year away from home, Sibelius's personal extravagances began to manifest themselves on a far broader scale than ever before. As with many young people on first leaving the parental environment, once in Berlin, Sibelius acted out recklessly. His inability to manage money and his utter lack of consideration for others created real hardships on his family, especially his loyal brother Christian, who was always counseling, soothing, assisting, and patching up. In *En bok om en människa*, Adolf Paul depicted the behavior of Sillén, the Sibelius stand-in, as thoroughly immature:

> His many whims were the most childish imaginable and, far from being brilliant, belonged more to a spoiled brat than to a full-grown man. . . . He was a polished egotist. If he craved anything—a cigar costing two crowns, for example— he suffered unspeakably and was the most miserable man in the world until he had the desired object in his hand. Then he would become quite indifferent and throw away his expensive cigar without thinking about it. He derived his pleasure not from the ownership of something but from the longing for it. And his naïveté![9]

A photograph of the naive one taken in Berlin by Albert Grunder and inscribed to Uncle Pehr shows a rather uncertain-looking young man with mustache and lower-lip hair, an insecure youth trying to give the impression of a man of the world. Attired in wide cravat, waistcoat, and high collar, with a full head of hair atop a wide forehead and the prominent ears clearly visible, Sibelius gazes out from under sloping eyebrows. But he looks slightly to one side, not proudly and directly into the camera. His lack of confidence and feelings of inferiority would be among the challenges the year would force him to confront.

Artists coming to Europe's great capitals from the Russian Empire often experienced feelings of insecurity.[10] The insecurities were exacerbated by German chauvinism, which has to be experienced to be believed. Though greatly admired by the Finns for their civilized and highly accomplished society, much-vaunted Germany made a different impression on a daily basis. Sibelius complained to Uncle Pehr, "Certainly here in Germany they know how to put you down. The only thing for it is to put them down in return. . . . You can be sure that it takes a lot where such an unknown country as Finland is concerned."[11] Aino Järnefelt's word was "plebs." When a decade later she visited the city as Sibelius's wife, she was aghast at the bad taste and mocked the language ("Ach!! wie wunderschön!! dassss ist hübsch, wirklich schööön!"), "but organization! Quite exemplary."[12]

But affronts and slurs by the Germans would not be the worst of the year's occurrences. That unhappy honor was reserved for his illness.

PLAYING WITH FIRE

Sibelius had not been in Berlin a week before he was admitted to a hospital. Just which institution he entered is not known. The time and circumstances would point to Charité, the largest and likeliest hospital to have taken in foreign patients in the nineteenth century. Surviving records leave the question open, perhaps owing to the nature of his illness. As he explained to Adolf Paul from his sickbed, "I have, as you probably know, syph[ilis]."[13]

For young men of every generation, reaching maturity involves sowing wild oats. Sibelius's high life had begun in Helsinki. Even though he lived with his mother, Aunt Evelina, and Linda, activities of his "pack life" with Busoni and company were a frequent topic of letters, conversations, and bemused observations by others. And perhaps the most lethal of those activities was prostitution.

The "golden era" of Helsinki's prostitution culture flourished from the 1860s to the 1880s.[14] It thrived in bordellos with such outlandish, non-Nordic names as Eldorado, Alhambra, Mesopotamia, Philadelphia, and the particularly fearsome-sounding Green Hell. Despite its deeply Lutheran foundations, nineteenth-century Helsinki was no differ-

ent from other growing cities in its ready availability of prostitutes, nearly all of whom
were infected with venereal disease. In an effort to curb syphilis and gonorrhea, regular
checkups were begun for women prostitutes, and in 1847 the first venereal disease inspection office was opened in Helsinki. But the diseases still spread, owing to the ineffective-
ness of available condoms and to carelessness.

The carelessness was compounded by alcohol. The old saw of "wine, women, and
song" was never crooned louder than in Helsinki. It was often hard to tell whether the
wine or the women came first. Even as late as the 1950s there might be little difference
between a waitress and a prostitute in Finland. If a woman's job was to serve drinks, then
her morals were under suspicion. Likewise, women who went to restaurants without male
company were regarded with a jaundiced eye. (The later, oft-told story of Aino Sibelius
sending Kajanus into the restaurant König to fetch her husband reflected the social mores:
no self-respecting lady would have entered such an establishment alone.)

Among the students, the habit was to attend the theater, followed by an evening in
Helsinki's restaurants and trips to the bordellos. Although members from all groups of
society availed themselves of the bordellos' services, students appear to have been among
the most frequent patrons, especially of the "high-class" Swedish-speaking prostitutes
who were brought to Helsinki from Stockholm. Statistics tell the tale: to cite just one example, in the period from February 1905 to October 1907 the number of venereal diseases by social group in Helsinki included 495 cases among the students of the Imperial
Alexander University and the Polytechnic institute. Since the number of university students in 1906 was only 1,281, and a mere 377 were enrolled in the Polytechnic, those 495
cases represent a very high percentage indeed.[15]

Neither class nor background mattered; sons of Finland's leading families patronized the bordellos. Police records from the 1870s disclose an altercation in a brothel with
two sons of none other than the great Snellman. Among the artistic types with whom
Sibelius kept company, the use of prostitutes was well-known. Juhani Aho wrote about it
in his novel *Yksin*; the artist Hugo Simberg died in 1917 of syphilis.

Prostitution was not a criminal offense until 1889, although sexual intercourse before
marriage was against the law. Students' encounters with prostitutes were more or less
a one-time thing, a "man's experience," initiated by more worldly companions. Yet it
was an experience that could exact a terrible price. While the custom was heartbreaking
for women, the effect on men could also be devastating. Syphilis—devious, incurable,
deadly—was the great danger. A person could believe himself cured and recovered,
only to be plagued after a decade or more with new symptoms. If untreated, such symptoms included behaviors similar to what is known as Alzheimer's today; among infected
mothers-to-be, infant mortality was as much as 90 percent. Less dramatically, even with

treatment, the illness could leave a person with a shaking hand, subject to depression and decreased creative powers.

Before the introduction of penicillin, the treatment of choice involved heavy-metal therapy, either by injection or with ointments. If an upper-class youth suspected that he was infected, he would most likely be treated by a private physician. Yet because venereal diseases were such a stigma, these records were almost always destroyed. In the absence of medical records or DNA evidence, it is not possible at the remove of more than a century to arrive at a diagnosis of Sibelius's maladies. Nor should it be of any interest whatsoever except for one thing: the possibility of its devastating long-term effects on Sibelius's creativity and thus the solution to the conundrum about a man whose abandonment of composition has mystified for so long.

What evidence remains consists of unscientific comments in letters, reports of illnesses that plagued Sibelius from the 1880s (some of which were almost certainly due to his king-sized hypochondria), and such documented evidence as changes in handwriting, onset of tremors, and loss of creative power. From the list of "ten clues to secret syphilis" presented by Deborah Hayden in her recent study of the disease and artistic genius,[16] a number coincide with what is known of Sibelius's life: letters revealing the infection to close friends and family; sudden change from good health to chronic, relapsing illness; a fear of infecting others; visits to many doctors and practitioners; reports of deafness; swings from euphoria to depression; fear of death; changes in handwriting; and tremors. As the street doggerel had it,

> There was a young man from Back Bay
> Who thought syphilis just went away
> He believed that a chancre
> Was only a canker
> That healed in a week and a day.
> But now he has "acne vulgaris"—
> (Or whatever they call it in Paris);
> On his skin it has spread
> From his feet to his head,
> And his friends want to know where his hair is.[17]

Even before leaving Helsinki, Sibelius was not well. "Because of his long illness," his spring term report read, "Herr Sibelius cannot receive any certification in violin playing."[18] His letter written onboard the *Storfursten* assured Uncle Pehr, "if only my health holds up, I shall certainly work."[19] The correspondence from Berlin goes further. Sibelius revealed his infection both to Adolf Paul and also to Christian: "Dear Brother, don't go the way I have gone; don't play with fire. This is my ruin, as it has been the ruin of so many others."[20] The problems—and his descriptions of them—continued the following year, when he reported such bizarre symptoms as *Eierstocks Entzündung* (an infection in the ovaries) and a tumor in the stomach. One letter even made direct reference to that fatally seductive combination of sex and alcohol: writing with surprising frankness to Wegelius, Sibelius disclosed that in his new *Scène de ballet*, there was "something of 'intoxication' and 'thigh.'"[21]

Sibelius's closest companions knew his habits all too well. Busoni captured their essence in *The Armoured Suite*. Adolf Paul, another carousing partner, was particularly eager to record his friend's promiscuity in *A Book about a Human Being*. He portrayed the Sillén/Sibelius character as a "the slickest skirt-chaser of us all," with the skirt-chaser offhandedly insisting, "He who wants, takes."[22] The image of the beguiling ladies' man persisted. In 1919 Paul was writing to Sibelius: "People don't have to know everything. If they did, that Leporello index of yours would constitute not one forbidden book, but a whole library."[23] This character is not Sibelius the national hero, but the Sibelius depicted by Eero Järnefelt in the early 1890s, chin thrust belligerently forward, eyebrows disdainfully arched, eyes cast sullenly downward (see fig. 6.1).

Syphilis has changed the course of history and caused endless suffering of innocents (the actions of Ivan the Terrible, Henry VIII, and possibly Adolf Hitler can be attributed to the insanity caused by syphilis).[24] Sibelius suffered for his sins—not only in physical symptoms, but also emotionally: on a rainy, sleet-slick Christmas Eve in Berlin he wrote a letter to his mother in which recognition of his own shortcomings and yearnings for Finland were poignantly entertwined: Kitti and Linda were the good and competent siblings, he wrote sadly, but he, the "poor wild bird," was turning out well at last, he assured her.[25] He implored his mother, surely the best mother who could be found, not to forget him—a plea he earnestly repeated.

Although in December 1889 Sibelius was being prematurely optimistic, he did "turn out well at last"—not only professionally, but also physically. His long, remarkably healthy life (hypochondria aside), the even longer life and good health of his wife, Aino, and the general good condition of five of their six children (only one of whom did not survive childhood) all indicate that if Sibelius did contract syphilis, he was probably self-cured—a healing that takes place in the majority of cases.[26] It is also possible that Sibelius was inoculated for syphilis; he reassured Aino that he had been vaccinated for her sake.[27] In the days before penicillin, one remedy was inoculation with malaria, a therapy for which Julius Wagner von Jauregg received the Nobel Prize in 1927.[28]

Thus, although his Lutheran-induced shame may have haunted him deeply, the reasons for the great tragedy of Sibelius's creative life must ultimately be sought elsewhere.

Figure 6.1. Eero Järnefelt, *Sibelius*, early 1890s. Oil on canvas. Private collection.
Photo: Matti Ruotsalainen.

MUSICAL LIFE IN BERLIN

In view of his illness, it is ironic that the first opera Sibelius heard in Berlin was *Don Giovanni*. Opera, seriously lacking in Helsinki, thrilled, surprised, and disappointed him. Along with Mozart's music, he heard operas of Verdi (*Otello*), Amilcare Ponchielli (*La Gioconda*), and Wagner (*Tannhäuser, Lohengrin, Der fliegende Holländer, Die Meistersinger von Nürnberg*). He listened to Strauss conduct *Don Juan*, von Bülow direct the Philharmonic Orchestra, and possibly Carl Goldmark premiere his *Ouverture zum Gefesselten Prometheus*.[29] There were concerts of Bach, Beethoven, Berlioz, Brahms, Liszt, Meyerbeer, and Moszkowski performed by legendary violinists, pianists, harpists, and singers. Charles Gregorovich played Damrosch's Violin Concerto no. 2 (a work still in manuscript) and Moszkowski's Violin Concerto op. 30. Von Bülow played Beethoven's Piano Concerto no. 5.

Sibelius's letters, vividly fabulizing this great musical world, were copied out, circulated, and eagerly devoured by his family. Similarly piquant details went to Wegelius. The magical reactions on hearing the third movement of Beethoven's Razumovsky Quartet, op. 59, no. 1, gave irrefutable proof that the lively imagination of the six-year-old who had conjured up a life-threatening fire crackling on the shore of Lake Vanajavesi had lost none of its startling synesthetic power to see, smell, and feel through music:

> When the Adagio was played, I imagined being in a colonnaded walk. There was moonlight. On the left side was a solid wall; on the other side, a wonderful garden with birds of paradise, seashells, palm trees, and other things. All was dead and still, the shadows were long and sharp, and it smelled like it does in an old library. Nothing was heard except sighs. It was Beethoven who sighed. When the theme in F minor returned for the second time, he sighed really deeply.— After a while everything was transformed into big lakes where the water was red and above them, God was playing the violin. Gradually, I noticed that it was [Joseph] Joachim who was drawing his bow, [Heinrich] de Ahna and the other players joined in, and last of all, there was I myself, J. Sibelius.[30]

Sibelius's state grant was for violin study, for which he was obliged to find a teacher. Yet he did not seek out Joseph Joachim, the most celebrated teacher in all Berlin, at that time director of the Königliche Hochschule für Musik. Instead there were lessons with Fritz Struss (1847–d. after 1912), a Joachim disciple.[31] In the 1929 edition of Hugo Riemann's famous *Musik-Lexikon* Struss is praised as a "distinguished violinist," and the pages of such publications as the *Allgemeine Musik-Zeitung* are filled with announcements of his performances, often in conjunction with celebrated artists. Struss was affiliated with the Scharwenka Conservatory, among other Berlin institutions.[32] But Sibelius did not formally enter the conservatory. Nor did he enroll at the prestigious Hochschule für Musik (even though he lived just opposite it),[33] despite some urgings from Wegelius via Christian (in a letter of November 11, 1889). Whether it was a question of money or confidence is not clear, but it was a pattern that would be repeated the following year in Vienna.

Struss turned out to be less than genial and was replaced by a shadowy figure named "Sachse."[34] Yet it was Struss's colleague at the conservatory who loomed largest in Sibelius's Berlin experience: a teacher named Albert Becker.

THE LUTHERAN HERITAGE REVISITED:
ALBERT BECKER

Albert Ernst Anton Becker, born in Quedlinburg, some 125 miles southwest of Berlin, was a thoroughly earnest German *Kleinmeister* with a weighty academic reputation.[35] Born into a family of devout Lutherans, the young Becker had resisted his family's attempts to coerce him into the ministry and studied music instead. There he was blessed with success. By the 1850s he had composed two symphonies, one of which, the Symphony in G minor, was premiered at Potsdam in 1859 and received a second prize from Vienna's prestigious Gesellschaft der Musikfreunde.

But it was not with his symphonies that Becker made his mark or for which Sibelius went to him for instruction. Psalms, motets, *geistliche Lieder*, sacred cantatas, and religious oratorios dominated his works list. It was the example of the great Johann Sebastian Bach that had turned Becker to sacred music and shown the way in which devout Lutheranism could be manifest in music.[36] Becker's Mass in B-flat Minor, composed in 1878, had its first performance in a place of great significance to Lutherans and Bach lovers: Leipzig's Thomaskirche. And Becker had paid solemn homage to the four hundredth anniversary of Martin Luther's birth (November 10, 1483) with a *Reformation Cantata*, op. 28, in 1883.

Becker settled in Berlin, composing and teaching, and over time became a decorated and elevated member of Berlin music circles. His insecurities smothered beneath the folds of his elaborate robes, his watery eyes a bit vacant (or self-absorbed—it was difficult to tell which behind the thick glasses), Becker ensconced himself in the secure confines of his pedantic world, encouraged by the empty titles lavished upon him. In 1881, when he married Magdalena Ratke, daughter of the sculptor Eduard Ratke,[37] those titles began to accrue. In that year he was appointed teacher of composition at the newly founded Scharwenka Conservatory, although he continued to give private lessons. The next year he joyfully accepted the lofty honorific of Königlicher Professor. In 1883 he became an associate of the Royal Academy of Arts.

In 1889 Becker was appointed to the prestigious directorship of Berlin's Königlicher Domchor (a position once held by none other than Felix Mendelssohn). In that capacity he served until his death, even though he was offered the post of Thomaskantor in Leipzig. The kaiser himself intervened to persuade Becker to remain in Berlin. Eventually Becker was awarded an order of the Fatherland, the Rother Adler-Orden, fourth class, no doubt aided by his musical conservatism and the favor he curried with the political establishment with such items as a festival cantata composed for the kaiser's ninetieth birthday and the oratorio *Selig aus Gnade*, which was premiered on March 7, 1890, in memory of Kaiser Wilhelm I.[38]

Not everyone was impressed. Although Hermann Kretzschmar (1848–1924), one of the founders of the Bach-Gesellschaft and part of the Berlin musical establishment, acclaimed the Mass in B-flat Minor and praised the secular cantata *Die Wallfahrt nach Kevlaar*, Heinrich Dorn (1804–1892) found little to admire in Becker's music. A composer and teacher as well as music critic, Dorn pronounced Becker to have "too much intellect and too little imagination; too much art and too little 'nature.'"[39] Such was to be Sibelius's experience. "I am in the midst of studying fugues" was his dismal complaint to Uncle Pehr; the most positive thing he could find to say had to do with the glitter: Becker's income—100 rubles a day!—enabled him to live like an old-fashioned composer.[40] His first meeting with the venerable personage left him in less than awe. As he famously reported to Martin Wegelius, "Becker is a fuddy-duddy from head to toe" (Sibelius's exact term, *peruk*, referred to the Swedish word *perukstock*, meaning a wigblock, an oft-used metaphor for a stiff pedant); "when he saw my quartet he nearly had a heart attack (in particular he could hardly get over the fact that I had used the minor and major form of the same triad in immediate alternation)."[41]

Wegelius was indignant. On October 4, he wrote back, firmly admonishing Sibelius, in a letter beginning "Mon cher Jean!," to calm down. The man who composed the B-flat Minor Mass and *Die Wallfahrt nach Kevlaar* is *no* "fuddy-duddy from head to toe"— "that you can put out of your mind." Wegelius knew his former pupil and his Achilles' heel: the inability to distinguish gold from glitter. Both, he reproved sternly, sparkle in the sun.[42]

But Wegelius was not named "Martin" for nothing. He revered the Lutheranism of his colleague. Moreover, he too had set Heine's *Wallfahrt nach Kevlaar* text, a sentimental tearjerker that relates the tale of a mother who travels with her deathly ill son to Kevlaar to ask the intervention and healing of the Virgin, only to arrive too late to save the boy. Becker's setting alternates between a cappella, four-voice chorale writing, recitativelike dialogue between mother (alto) and son (a baritone), and stirring orchestral passages, and Wegelius was himself stirred.

Sibelius had little choice but to put his head down and trudge through fugues and counterpoint, analyses and hymnals. Still, he was discouraged. On the reverse side of a receipt from Becker, dated October 14, 1889, he sternly admonished himself to be a man! Develop harmoniously! Work intelligently! "*Si male nunc et olim sic erit*," he finished his note to himself. "You are the child of so many prayers and intercessions that it is impossible God will leave you."[43]

Just why Martin Wegelius should have urged Sibelius, who was particularly interested in orchestration, to study with this didactic exponent of German choral music is not entirely clear. The most likely explanation seems to be that Wegelius believed his former pupil needed strict discipline. As he explained in his somewhat sarcastic "Mon cher Jean" letter, "the reason that he disciplines you in this strict style is indeed to give you the power to be *free*."[44] Wegelius was also well aware that Becker's star as a composer had been on the rise. The Mass in B-flat Minor had come to the attention of Franz Liszt, on whose recommendation it had been premiered at Leipzig's Thomaskirche in May of 1879.[45] Wegelius, no less than his former pupil, had a yen for what glittered in the eyes of the establishment—and for what would best serve to produce a Finnish composer to advance the national cause at home and abroad.

Neither Becker nor Berlin prompted Sibelius to compose any great works. The pupil was as yet too inexperienced and too immature, the realities faced in the Berlin year too bitter, and Becker's instruction—"Lieber langweilig, aber im Stil" (Better boring but in strict style)[46]—too pedantic to prod a puerile composer into writing awe-inspiring music. Still, the year was far from fallow. Despite the all-too-evident alternation between revelry and illness,[47] there is irrefutable proof of hard work. Somewhat surprisingly, Sibelius preserved the evidence: contrapuntal settings of the Mass Ordinary, where settings of the Kyrie, Gloria, Credo, and Agnus Dei perform dutiful imitations of ploddingly crafted leading motives; a cappella choral works (*Hallelujah, Hallelujah*), most of them based on Lutheran chorales; settings for chorus and full—*full*—orchestra of *Herr, Du bist ein Fels* and *Herr erzeige uns deine Gnade und hilf uns*.[48] Merely writing down the drafts and fair copies of these settings was the labor of hours, though surely not of love. By November Sibelius was muttering that he knew the German psalmbook back to front. *Herr Gott, mein Heiland, ich schreie Tag und Nacht vor Dir* (*O Lord, My Salvation, I Cry Out to Thee Day and Night*) and *Sei mir gnädig* (*Be Thou Merciful unto Me*) had begun to acquire desperate, ironic meaning. He found himself caught up in an environment as conservative and Lutheran in its way as the one he had left back home.

However bizarre it seems to come upon a collection of sacred Sibeliana, these choral and orchestral settings were serving as unwitting dress rehearsals for a certain choral symphony that Sibelius would begin the next year. A violin concerto written years afterward would include a lavish "Bachian" cadenza in its first movement. The resonance of those chorale studies would echo down the decades, in *Musique religieuse* (op. 113), for instance, into which, Beckerlike, Sibelius incorporated Philip Nicolai's chorale *Wachet auf, ruft uns die Stimme*.[49] The Lutheran heritage long continued to leave its mark.

Other works from the months in Berlin had personal associations of other kinds; the Quintet in G Minor was one. The straitlaced Wegelius grimly objected not only to its poor piano writing (what was such a pathetic pianist as Janne doing writing a piano quintet in the first place!), but especially to the parts his wife Hanna thought were a little bit autobiographical—*à la bonheur*, as he put it. Wegelius huffed and puffed about a com-

EXAMPLE 6.1. SIBELIUS, ADAGIO IN D MINOR, MM. 1–16.
BY PERMISSION OF FENNICA GEHRMAN OY, HELSINKI.

poser keeping his gropings to himself.[50] The first movement's seductive chromatic theme and its capricious tempos—now racing dazzlingly forward, now distractedly lingering over a surprising modulation to a C major chord (is it allegro or grave?! demanded Wegelius, a man who liked to have things *clear* and who believed in staying within the bounds of convention)—came all too close to incarnating the creator himself.

And then there was that mournful D Minor Adagio. A theme and variations written for string quartet, it begins with a sixteen-measure lament (see ex. 6.1). The peculiar chromatic twists and odd little rhythms sound like the idiosyncrasies that might be heard in, well, in family ensembles, for instance. In the year of the Adagio's composition, the Sibelius family ensemble lost a member: Uncle Pehr. The last words of this uncle as he lay dying in Turku had voiced the cultural hopes of the Turku Romantics: "Janne shall be something great for his fatherland!"[51]

It has been thought that Sibelius left no expression of sorrow whatsoever for this uncle, who died on January 4, 1890—a rather startling omission on the death of a man Sibelius viewed as occupying his father's place "here on the earth."[52] But no such fault should be placed at the nephew's door: the peculiar nature of his Adagio's theme, its instrumentation for the ensemble in which he and his uncle had played together, and its character of faithfulness and constancy—expressed in nine full variations—not to mention the quirky whimsy of some of those variations leave little doubt that the Adagio was a memorial for Pehr Sibelius.

Uncle Pehr's steadfast presence had been a constant theme throughout all of Janne Sibelius's life, and the nephew's musical homage shows insight and genuine sorrow. When, at the close, the hymnlike theme is restated for the last time, now an octave higher than at the beginning, the completion of its final cadence is interrupted: a poignant, full measure of silence ensues before the music comes to a close on a dark and sorrowing D minor chord.

PART II

HERÄÄ SUOMI! —AWAKE, FINLAND!

POLITICAL MANEUVERING, 1889–90

The very year Sibelius went abroad for the first time marked a pivotal phase in the wider course of events. For while Finnish nationalism had been rising, so had nationalism in Russia, with inescapable consequences for the Finns. In the autumn of 1889 Alexander III approved plans to consolidate Finland's postal, customs, and financial institutions with the empire's. When the "postal question" was signed into a manifesto, on June 12, 1890, Finns employed by the postal service found themselves under the authority of the Russian interior ministry, forced to circulate Russian stamps, and expected to exhibit competency in the Russian language.

The pendulum had reversed its inevitable swing. After years of largely peaceful existence under the emperors, the Finland Sibelius had known for his entire lifetime was changing. As the politician and leading Fennoman Agathon Meurman (1826–1909) observed in his tract *Finland förr och nu* (*Finland Before and Now*, 1890), "The existence of this little people, happy within itself, beside the Russian one, wounds Russian national sensibilities."[1]

Russian nationalists had long viewed Finland and its special status with suspicion, irritation, and even hostility. Now, after the diverting attentions of the Russo-Turkish War of 1877–78, they fixed the grand duchy in their cross-hairs.[2] During the 1880s a series of legal questions had begun to drive a wedge between the empire and its grand duchy, and all too soon the effects were felt. One of those questions had to do with Finnish criminal law, which Alexander's advisors wanted to consolidate with the empire's. More chilling was the attempt to call into question the very constitutional basis on which Finns believed their autonomy rested. In 1886 the Finnish senator Leo Mechelin had brought out his *Précis du droit public du grand-duché de Finland*, claiming in effect that Finland was "a constitutional monarchy, a state in a real union with Russia."[3]

In 1889 Kesar Filippovich Ordin, a Russian nationalist and historian serving as the imperial court's *gofmejster* (*Hofmeister*), published a response to Mechelin's *Précis* entitled *Pokorenie Finlyandii* (*The Conquest of Finland*). The battle over "the Finnish question" was joined. In this 950-page opus in two parts supplemented with more than 310 pages of appendices, Ordin challenged Finland's position as an autonomous unit within the empire, insisting that the grand duchy had only "local autonomy." The Russian press launched a veritable campaign against Finnish autonomy, with hundreds of its articles showing up in translation in Finland's newspapers. Over the next two decades the Finns responded in literary kind, publishing demeaning parodies of Ordin and of hostile Russian newspapers threatening the innocent "Maid of Finland," who made her debut at this moment as the personification of Finland (see fig. II.1). The question was taken up across Europe as well. The whole debate was symptomatic of attitudes that were to shape Finnish historiography well into the twentieth century: the Finns' devout belief that a conquering emperor's solemn promise amounted to a legal treaty guaranteeing Finland's existence as a constitutional state.

The reigning emperor, Alexander III, and his empress, Dagmar of Denmark, actually viewed Finland with considerable favor. Nevertheless, Alexander yielded to the nationalists on certain issues, which, though largely token, had implications that provoked anxiety among those who paid attention to such things. The postal manifesto had been one such issue, a roar evidently intended to intimidate the subjects of the Russian Bear. The manifesto's defective implementation showed up in the Finnish stamps that continued to circulate on which growled the Finnish Lion. In the snarling standoff, plans were broached to consolidate Finland's customs and financial institutions with those of the empire, but they really amounted to very little in the early part of the decade.

Figure II.1. K. F. Ordin (the barking dog) and three Russian newspapers threaten the "Maid of Finland" in her press debut as a symbol for the nation in the satirical journal *Matti Meikäläinen*, 1890. The title of the journal is a name that is the Finnish equivalent of John Doe. Photo Kari Timonen.

Still, the very attempts at redefining and restricting Finns' prized autonomy, coming after years of peaceful and largely stable life as part of the Russian Empire, rekindled a latent patriotism and stoked the fires of a simmering national pride—and it wrought wondrous effects on the cultural lives of the Finns.

THE NATIONAL MOVEMENT

In a study of the social preconditions for national awakenings, Miroslav Hroch has identified the basic stages in the development of small European nations.[4] The first involved an isolated group, usually intellectuals, who were passionate about the language, culture, and history of the nationality to be "awakened." This group lacked formal organization, their interest being motivated by a thirst for knowledge, yet theirs was a necessary phase in raising a national consciousness. Where the raised consciousness ultimately led, in Hroch's view, was to national awareness on the part of the masses, thanks to the rise of a broad national movement with a solid organizational structure. Between these phases, the one characterized by scholarly interests, the other being mass diffusion of patriotism, lay a decisive epoch of patriotic agitation, what Hroch called "the fermentation process of national consciousness," a phase driven by a group of patriots who believed that their mission in life was to spread national consciousness among the people.

In Finland those three stages had been precipitated by the country's annexation to Russia. The first stage was manifested above all among the Turku Romantics, who had raised their scholarly voices in support of establishing a national identity for the Finns.[5] The consciousness of nationalism they had raised fermented in the endeavors of the next generation, among whom were the "founding fathers," Runeberg, Lönnrot, and Snellman. Although the patriotic poetry of Runeberg and the *Kalevala* of Lönnrot established the basis for what was considered Finnish, the writings of Snellman, including two seminal articles in 1844 (in his publication *Saima*), more broadly introduced the idea of a national consciousness and fueled the national movement. As Snellman put it:

> How can there be a national literature without a clear-cut national spirit; and where does the consciousness for this come from, if it is not to be found in the nation? Turn whichever way you wish. There is no national literature without a conscious national spirit, for the former is nothing more than the expression of the latter, and that in its turn only exists as the antithesis of other nationalities, principally of that which threatens its existence.[6]

The work of building that consciousness remained for some decades the province of the academic and cultural elite, the intelligentsia, also characteristic of the awakening of small nations.[7] The elite in Finland were Swedish-speaking, and many had connections to the Imperial Alexander University, where student activists banded together in student "nations" (*osakunta* in Finnish, a concept dating from the Middle Ages).

The university-and-student orientation was prominently on display at mid-century when, stimulated by the first publication of the *Kalevala*, boosted by Runeberg's sympathetic poetic images of Finns, and fortified above all by a vast quantity of alcohol, the spring jubilee called Flora Day was staged, on May 13, 1848. Celebrating the season when the long night of winter finally gives way to an intense and gorgeous springlike summer is a very old tradition in the Nordic countries. That particular May, while students in Paris, Vienna, Dresden, and elsewhere were manning the barricades and one Richard Wagner was arguing so passionately for democratic reform of the German national theater that he was forced to flee his country, students in Finland gathered to sing choruses and acclaim the emperor.[8] In 1848 the Finnish national spirit still accommodated imperial reality and imperial benefits, and even demonstrated imperial loyalty (as Snellman insisted that it should).

But a shift was occurring—and it was evident in music. Flora Day was the first time on record that Finland's knolls, forests, and watery shores echoed with the happy combination of Runeberg's poem *Vårt land* (idealizing Finnish landscapes, exhorting high moral values, and reflecting resignation to fate's vicissitudes) and Fredrik Pacius's music, allegedly tossed off in mere days' time with liberal debts to a German drinking song, *Papst und Sultan*. Runeberg's lines, the first verses of his *Tales of Ensign Stål*, had been intentionally written as a national song, an anthem for students to express their love of the fatherland; for it was from the young, the founding fathers believed, that the nation should come forth.[9]

As the 1840s waned, the largely peaceable example of Flora Day gave way to an acrimonious linguistic struggle drawn out over some two decades, sapping energies and rousing tempers. These years were marked by Snellman's fanatical pursuits to promote the Finnish language, the rise of a zealous Finnish-spirited contingent, and the emergence of various national associations and interest groups, some of which eventually began to coalesce into political parties. And among the most influential were the Fennomans, led by men who fit Hroch's description of patriots who "saw their mission as the spreading of national consciousness among the people."[10]

The Fennomans' outspoken leader was Yrjö-Koskinen—the very Yrjö-Koskinen who had changed his name from its Swedish form, Georg Forsman, to that daunting Finnish substitute. By the 1860s Yrjö-Koskinen was claiming that the ideology of the Fennomans represented "the sacred will of the people" (*kansan pyhä tahto*), proof of which were associations and public meetings where "the people" expressed their desires, which the intelligentsia would carry out.[11] Yrjö-Koskinen also championed the consistent use of Finnish as the language of the country and believed "education and enlightenment in the national spirit" to be the most effective ways of preventing the horrid weeds of socialism from taking root.

Yrjö-Koskinen was not alone; other leaders, such as Agathon Meurman and J. J. F. Perander, played important roles in the Fennoman Party. So did the work of a certain Lieutenant-General Alexander Järnefelt. And by the 1870s the collective efforts of the upper classes and the clergy to foster a national consciousness had coalesced into a national movement, clearly evident in the different kinds of associations that had rapidly begun to emerge—with tremendous consequences. There were youth clubs, workers' associations, educational societies, choirs and bands, theater groups, book and literary societies, voluntary fire brigades, women's groups, and not least, temperance unions, these last destined to become the largest mass organization in Finland.[12] Largely secular, often reform minded, mainly patriotic, and passionate, all would contribute in one way or another to the breaking down of the old privileged social order. But the organization that had a central role in promoting the national awakening was founded by Yrjö-Koskinen. It was called Kansanvalistusseura.

KANSANVALISTUSSEURA—LIGHT TO THE PEOPLE

Kansanvalistusseura was originally a bilingual association whose Swedish name—Folkupplysningssällskapet—is unfortunately no less difficult for foreigners to pronounce. The unwieldy appellation—which translates as Society for the Enlightenment of the People—enshrined the organization's lofty ideals.[13] (In the 1990s the official English translation was the "Society for Culture and Education"; today the organization goes by the even more neutral moniker "KVS Foundation," which, for ease of reference, will largely be used here.) Yrjö-Koskinen, together with K. A. Castrén and Jaakko Päivärinta, founded the KVS in 1874, and it quickly became a hub of national ideology. Its aims were embedded in its name: *kansanvalistus* means "enlightenment of the people," which was to be achieved through "public education." The entire vocabulary referred to the enterprise of promoting a national consciousness.

Finnish leaders took educational aims very seriously. Snellman was a case in point. Although skeptical of the society, Snellman had nevertheless been promoting the ideas it took up: "education of the nation and nationalization of the educated" was his theme.[14] As another leading figure maintained, "What greater, more sacred responsibility is there than to serve the [Finnish] people, improve their position, [and] disseminate enlighten-ment [*valistusta*] and education [*sivistystä*] to its great masses."[15]

Members of the KVS wholeheartedly embraced the goal of promoting public enlightenment. And their motto—"Light to the People"—indicated how the concept of public enlightenment had become synonymous with national awakening—*kansallinen herääminen*.[16] Images of dazzling light and metaphors of arising and awakening filled their orations, delivered in rhetoric as impassioned as the Turku Romantics'. The phrase *Herää Suomi!*—Awake, Finland!—began to echo through association halls, public meet-ings, and articles in the press.

To deliver the light that would awaken that consciousness, the society engaged in strategically gauged activities. In its first years, publishing was its most important func-tion. It published educational materials; lists of recommended books; and an illustrated yearly calendar with patriotic poetry, stories, and current events meant to inform the public, of which annual print runs ran into the thousands. Gradually, its activities spread to promoting a public library system, a key concern of the light bringers, who under-stood the importance not only of reading but of what was being read.[17] Municipal librar-ies, considered as important as if not more vital than elementary education, grew by leaps and bounds—from a mere 19 in 1849 to nearly 1,500 in 1900—thanks to the efforts of Finnish-minded nationalists. Nevertheless, like much else in closely regulated Finland, there were rules: reading was supervised, and stacks were closed (no browsing!). The people's literary choices were guided by unseen hands.

Another key activity promoted by the KVS was song festivals. Collective singing provided a sure means of cultivating allegiance to a group. Singing together height-ened the sense of shared pride, engendered feelings of nationalism, and encouraged group identity. The music festivals inaugurated by the KVS in 1884 grew into enormous patriotic events that would reach deep into Sibelius's life. And the first time was in that pivotal year of 1889, when, in connection with the upcoming KVS song festival, Chris-tian Sibelius directed a letter to his brother in Berlin.[18] The KVS was holding a competi-tion for new compositions to be written either for four-voice chorus (men's, women's, or mixed voices) or for brass septet (for which reason the jury was to include Adolf Leander, Finland's esteemed "father of brass music"). In true Herderian fashion, each composition was to be based on a Finnish folk song or a Finnish national dance, and choral works would need to have Finnish-language texts. Christian promised to send his brother some Finnish lyric poetry, and his words show once again how keenly aware of the national movement were the members of the Sibelius family: "It's a shame you have so little time; otherwise, you could, for example, compose a choral cycle to some episode of the Kalevala or such. I'll also try to get some Finnish folk songs and dances for you."[19]

Sibelius evidently considered submitting a choral work as his contest entry. Wegelius was certainly pushing him in this direction ("Why haven't you written any choral music?" he demanded in a letter dated May 6, 1890). Wegelius's expectations, together with the choral writing the young composer was being forced to produce for Becker, make it seem a bit odd that Sibelius submitted a piece not for chorus, but rather for brass septet and triangle, an imminently forgettable Allegro that was indeed forgotten for almost a century. Perhaps he did not want to reveal his uncertainty in setting the language of the national movement to music (a problem he was still worrying about the following year).

Sibelius dutifully included two folk songs in his Allegro, both taken over wholesale from a relatively new anthology called *Folk Songs of Mäntyharju* collected in eastern Finland and recently published by Eemil Sivori (1864–1929), a nationalist active in the Finnish musical world around Viipuri.[20] Almost certainly it was Christian Sibelius who had sent Sivori's anthology to his brother.

It seems unlikely that Becker ever saw the Allegro. It won no prize and was neglected for over a century. Its significance only recently became clear: from the folk tunes Sibelius borrowed to meet the contest requirements emerged the main theme of *Kullervo*, begun in 1891. At a time when Becker was reining in his pupil to write strict fugues, contrapuntal exercises, and chorale settings, a brass septet composed for the purpose of awakening a national consciousness offered fertile ground for ideas to germinate. And perhaps it was because of this uninspired, folkish Allegro that on February 11, 1890, when the Finnish conductor Robert Kajanus (1856–1933) arrived in Berlin to conduct his *Aino*, the folk-song qualities and Finnish texts of this nationalist symphonic poem, which Sibelius now heard for the first time, made such a deep impression.

～ 7 ～

Finland from Afar

A CENTRAL EUROPEAN MILIEU

Until Jean Sibelius went to Vienna, he was just one of a number of promising Finns in whom the country's cultural hopes were vested. In Helsinki the dashing conductor-composer Robert Kajanus held the Finnish public in thrall. In the visual arts Albert Edelfelt, Eero Järnefelt, Axel Gallén, Emil Wikström, and others were making names for themselves, not only at home, but also in Paris. On the stage Ida Aalberg (1858–1915) was winning plaudits far beyond Finland's borders. Jean Sibelius, whose ambition equaled theirs but who was the despair of his most devoted teacher (Wegelius) and a man for whom friends "foresaw a meteoric rise and sudden extinction,"[1] was known only for a few successful chamber works, a brass piece, and a string of small things for piano, violin, and voice. He had been unable to complete his violin studies at home. After his year in Berlin, Becker found him "interesting" and "decidedly gifted," but only "*when* he has matured as the result of further studies" would [his talent] excite high expectations.[2] As yet Sibelius had little to offer.

The Vienna year changed all that. It was a common experience. Most of the young Finns who went abroad discovered that the gold at home glittered more brilliantly from afar. Juhani Aho, living in Paris, found to his delight that in the minds of the French, "we [Finns] have gold in our midst."[3] Aho's experience was repeated countless times among the artists and composers who traveled abroad. During Sibelius's study on the European continent, his personal ambition and latent talents were catalyzed by the broad literary and intellectual currents to create pure Finnish gold. And that gold was dazzlingly displayed in *Kullervo*.

Kullervo represented an astounding technical as well as creative breakthrough. The first musical venture into *Kalevala* territory and the first symphony, this most grandiose work ever composed by its creator burst forth after a strict diet of contrapuntal exercises, chamber works, and Lutheran discipline force-fed by Martin Wegelius and Albert Becker. Although their fundamentalist regimen probably served to hone an unruly youth's technical skills, political, intellectual, and emotional currents fanned the creative fires in a young composer whom companions regularly described as impassioned, volcanic, fiery. No portly, hairless establishment icon this, but a fiercely electric, magnificently maned Don Quixote who stirred hearts as well as ears and left both atingle.

What were the magical ingredients that transformed budding talent into pure gold? Love—of woman, of fatherland, of life, not always distinguishable. No small dose of determination. And sufficient distance from home to allow the true meaning of the national heritage to come clearly into focus.

"THIS OUR LOVE IS IN FACT OUR LIFE"

They met when she was just turning sixteen. She was the highly cultivated, well-educated daughter of a Finnish military officer, high in the emperor's service, and a Russian aristocrat. Sibelius later said it was love at first sight: "I already loved you then."[4]

But Sibelius seems to have fallen in love again and again, with one beauty after another. Betsy Lerche, for example, for whom he composed a little waltz, *A Betsy Lerche* (1889). Its flirtatious instructions, in French—"Avec élégance," "Douce," "Avec force," "À la Betzy," "Avec passion"—preserve a memoir of their attraction. It also showed Sibelius's cosmopolitan orientation, both Gallic and Petersburgian (French was Russia's courtly language and the language of Betsy's mother, the daughter of a diplomat in Saint Petersburg). Then there were those *souvenirs* for other young sweethearts—*Valse fantastique*, *Lulu valse*, *En visa* (*A Song*, "a keepsake from J. S.")—many inspired by summer's white nights in Lovisa, where blooming lasses like Alma Söderhjelm lost their hearts to Janne Sibelius.

Gradually, though, the field had narrowed to "the prettiest girl in all Finland"— Aino Järnefelt, whose charms radiate even in black and white from the photograph taken in 1890 by Daniel Nyblin (himself a key figure in the national movement) (see fig. 7.1).[5] Aino's brothers were Sibelius's "comrades-in-arms." Aino herself was "practical and can cook, etc. etc. Healthy too, and delightful in every way"; so said her beloved.[6] Not least, Aino's family, at once imperialist and Finnish minded, were deeply involved in the national movement to promote the identity and the uniqueness of the Finns. They also set great store by Russian intellectual life and the artists, writers, musicians, and composers who gilded life in Mother Russia with exquisite beauty.

The impact of this family on Sibelius's life was profound. Two of its members, Armas and Eero, already belonged to his circle of friends. In marrying into the clan, he

Figure 7.1. Aino Järnefelt, 1890. Photograph by Daniel Nyblin. The National Museum of Finland, Department of Prints and Photographs, Helsinki.

formally entered into the milieu enamored of Saint Petersburg intelligentsia. Simultaneously, he allied himself securely with his country's highest aspirations and most important enterprise.

Janne and Aino became secretly engaged during the summer of 1890. Not until November did Sibelius make his family aware of this turn of events. Their reaction was clearly not what he had hoped for. "You must not think that this engagement is like the previous ones," he wrote, strenuously pressing his point.[7] In early December he was complaining to his "dear girls, Maria and Evelina," that he was really annoyed that they *still* had not congratulated him on his engagement. "Linda, Uncle Otto, [Aunt] Hilma and others have written and congratulated me while from you, my nearest and dearest, not one word. Don't think it is some kind of prank; it is certainly quite serious."[8] He signed off with "Write now to your own lonesome Janne" and then added a peevish postscript: "Surely it is a little curious that you of all people would forget me so." He repeatedly assured them that this time was serious, that Aino was a dear girl, that they could rest easy now that he was engaged. A further plea brought up another aunt: "I believe [Julie] too will think I have good taste."[9]

Yet they had heard it all before. In the family's silence echoes a weariness and skepticism of the antics and irresponsible behaviors of their precocious but exasperating boy. And well they knew their Janne, whose ways hardly changed in Vienna, despite an outpouring of love in his letters to Aino. By spring he was writing to Wegelius about his anxieties over "bad pollutions" from his none-too-abstemious living, a desire to be "clean" for Aino, and his fear of impotence.[10] By the time he returned to Helsinki the story was going around that Janne Sibelius had utterly forgotten his engagement to Aino Järnefelt. Two weeks went by without the bridegroom's troubling to seek out his alleged fiancée. When in some desperation—or annoyance—Aino sought him out, he was quite embarrassed and stuttered, "Ah jassoo!"[11] She should have been warned.

The lovely Aino, whose devotion to Sibelius would be sorely tried over the sixty-five years of their marriage, has remained in the background of Sibelius's life. The role was how she seems to have wanted to play it. She suffered her mother's mood swings, at times appearing deeply depressed, bearing slights in resentful silence, or slipping away to her parental home when life with the composer became too difficult. Fabian Dahlström's publication of Sibelius's diary has deconstructed the myth of the long-suffering icon and shown the more human, if less lovable, side of Aino in the relationship. Yet her smile was pure sunshine, and her faith in the destiny of her beloved a lifeline that could pull a drowning man to the shore of sanity. No Haydnesque mate here, rolling her hair in the creator's manuscripts. Aino knew, with that deep soul knowing, that Jean Sibelius would fulfill Uncle Pehr's prediction—he would be something great for the fatherland. It was she who encouraged him to compose symphonies, she who managed the home so that he could create, she who pulled them back again and again from the brink of economic disaster with her gardening, her faithful copying of his scores, her home schooling of the children, and her unshakable convictions, however far to the right they sometimes veered.

There is no doubt that Aino kept him involved with the ongoing national movement. From the start, her Finnish-mindedness nurtured his commitment to the larger cause and kept Sibelius abreast of its developments at home while he was abroad. Her passions, her gift for languages, and her delight in great literature (an enthusiasm she and Janne shared) inspired him to improve his Finnish-language abilities and to turn serious attention to the *Kalevala*. Sibelius, well skilled from a young age in putting into his letters what people wanted to hear, may have been more interested in impressing his fiancée and her family of influential Fennomans and literary cognoscenti than in speaking his heart when he wrote earnestly: "I'm reading the Kalevala diligently and already understand Finnish much better. . . . In my opinion the Kalevala is completely modern. I think it is nothing but music, theme with variations. The actions always subordinate to moods: gods [are] men, Väinämöinen [is] a musician, and so on."[12] Yet it is undeniable that his enthusiasm for composing a work on the *Kalevala*, already suggested a year earlier by his brother, now acquired unstoppable momentum, powered by the combination of love for Aino and his swelling national fervor and energized by events in the homeland.

Significantly, Aino's enormous influence is nowhere more exuberantly evident than in *Kullervo*, that strange tale of a weirdly flawed Karelian hero turned into a European-style symphony. When Aino and Janne fell in love, a Finnish symphony was an oxymoron. With one long-forgotten exception, a symphony by the unfortunate Axel Gabriel Ingelius written in 1847, no Finn had ever composed a symphony.[13] Finnish symphonic poems there were as well as aspirations to compose operas. But a symphony, that highest and mightiest Germanic musical genre of them all, had remained beyond the ken of Finns. Now, in 1891, Sibelius arrived in Vienna fired with zeal to compose a symphony. "I've begun to think about a new symphony"; "I now have in mind a symphony"; "I'm now working on a new symphony"; "I'm hoping much of my symphony"; "I'm continuing to get clarity in my symphony":[14] these were the refrains that sounded from his Vienna letters. The resulting choral symphony, *Kullervo*, which wedded Finland's *Kalevala* myths, Finnish-language poetry, and the country's growing and symbol-laden men's choir tradition to symphonic movements in such traditional designs as a sonata form (movement 1), a variation-filled lullaby (movement 2), and a march (movement 4) resulted as much from his Don Quixote–like zeal to break a lance for his beloved and secure a musical victory for Finns as from the inspiration of the great symphonists he heard in Vienna, especially Beethoven and Bruckner.

And a gallant knight's worshipful adoration of his Dulcinea pulses throughout the *Kullervo* score and its source materials. She appears in direct tributes: "As recently as today," Sibelius wrote to Aino, "when I sat at the piano and composed [*Kullervo*], I thought that when you, Angel, are here with me, you sit beside me or in my arms and help me with kisses."[15] Aino's name appears in profusion throughout the sketches. And there is that single, highly meaningful change that Sibelius made in *Kullervo*'s text, replacing "money" (*raha*) with "desire" (*halu*) to account for Kullervo's success in seducing the lovely maiden (his unrecognized sister, whom he meets by chance). The composer's gloss on that change—a wordless duet murmured between two amorous and throaty oboes, which merge in lovingly entwined counterpoint before soaring into the ether in unison (mm. 262–74)—invests "desire" with hidden layers of whispered meanings. A magical word—and a secret word, because there seems little doubt that *halu* lay among the mysterious "seven words" that Janne and Aino devised to express their amorous feelings.[16]

Sibelius's love for Aino sparked other powerful emotions that year. Jealousy, for one. Sibelius had a rival for Aino's hand: Juhani Aho (1861–1921). An enthusiastic participant in the Järnefelts' Kuopio salon, Aho had fallen in love with Aino's mother, Elisabeth, older by twenty-three years. When the obvious futility of that relationship finally dawned on him, he turned his attentions upon Aino. In the novella *Yksin* (*Alone*), Aho's main female character, "Anna," is a stand-in for Aino. Romantic yet realistic, *Yksin* titillated its readers with some of the most vivid eroticism ever to surface in Finnish literature. Aho certainly knew whereof he wrote: his capacity for the priapically unconventional was plain for all to see, not least in his later menage à trois with his wife, the artist Venny Soldan, and her sister, which produced offspring with both.

Literature, which ever exerted a powerful force on Sibelius, set off extreme reactions now. He first read *Yksin* during Christmas 1890; by February he had read it ten times.[17] He was disturbed to the point of considering challenging Aho to a duel. Maybe Pushkin's unhappy fate deterred him (he sent Aino a copy of *Eugene Onegin* in April 1891). To her he also admitted his jealousy: "You'll probably think I'm a fool, a Don Quixote."[18] He excused his decision to abstain from shooting Aho on the basis, of all things, of advancing national aims (if ever there was proof of the power of the people!). "If he were a prosperous businessman with a fatty heart, I would laugh at him, but Finland needs people such as he and so there you are."[19]

"ALL OF VIENNA IS RINGING WITH WALTZES AND LAUGHTER"

Most of all, Vienna defined what Finns and Finland were—and what they were not—in ways that could only happen in a foreign atmosphere.[20] "This air is making me crazy," Sibelius wrote to Wegelius; "my head is full of waltzes, and they all remind me of Schubert's."[21] Sibelius came up with a waltz of his own, the *Scène de ballet* for orchestra. A work bearing all the marks of Vienna, its opening theme recalls the beginning of Mozart's *Jupiter* Symphony (albeit in F-sharp minor). Its 473 measures contain a quixotic mix that grotesquely reinterprets the idea of a waltz, one that "cocked a snook at the public," as the first listeners observed. The *Scène* fit Alma Söderhjelm's description of her friend

Janne's waltzes: they started normally enough, but soon began to swoop and whoosh and zoom off exuberantly.

Along with the swoops, Sibelius riddled long passages with hemiolas and melancholia. He also, bizarrely for him, threw in some castanets: a splash of realism from *Carmen*? He had heard the Austrian soprano Pauline Lucca (1841–1908) sing the sensuous gypsy at a private soirée and "was absolutely mad about her," or so he told Wegelius.[22] Were those castanets a manifestation of the *espagnolisme* seducing many Finns? Albert Edelfelt, for instance, who was a fan of Pablo de Saraste, came to know the Spaniard personally and traveled to the Alhambra seeking inspiration. Whatever the story behind the *Scène*, its manic composer declared, "I have never cried so much as when I composed it," perhaps an unconscious echo of Runeberg, who, in the course of his passionate extramarital affairs, had also written to a friend that he had "wept many a pillow wet."[23]

If he wept copiously while composing the *Scène*, Sibelius, who was clearly bedazzled by the demimonde on offer in Vienna and whose own highs and lows were swinging in manic curves, found that the lows bruised his ego, but left no permanent damage. Although Berlin had been Sibelius's first encounter with the arrogance of the Germanic mind and the implacable conviction of its musical superiority, its patronizing condescension toward outsiders, and its stereotyping of Nordic men as barbarians, it was not the last. When his new teacher, Carl Goldmark (1830–1915), flatly criticized his themes as "contrived,"[24] Sibelius bridled. A disastrous violin audition he played in early January 1891 for Jakob Moritz Grün (1837–1916), the crusty concertmaster of the Vienna Philharmonic Orchestra, greatly sobered him and reawakened an "old antipathy" for everything German.[25] The way a person deals with such episodes shows his mettle, and "the doctor's boy from Finland" (as he told Aino) showed that his was made of steel.

Yet hand in hand with the tears went laughter in this eternally superficial metropolis. "I happened to join a whole group of merry musicians and painters with their models," he wrote to his mother after being at the opera; "one of them had a big wine bottle and it went all around. I am half dead with laughter."[26] He found the high life and the aristocratic few quite to his taste. Writing to Aino about having spent an evening in the company of the alluring Lucca, he self-importantly reported that he "was presented to a lot of people all belonging to the aristocracy here."[27] He expounded on that sentiment the next month, writing, "There exists an aristocracy throughout the world, and by that I don't mean those with titles, but those who feel deeply and have views that others cannot understand. This is the aristocracy I love."[28] He had found his niche, but it was going to cause problems.

Along with all the superficialities Sibelius cultivated in order to be an *homme du monde* in that capital—silk top hats, crisply pressed white linen shirts, the best opera seats, fine dining, expensive cigars—he absorbed the city's music. The stunning impact of Beethoven's Ninth Symphony and Bruckner's Third, as played in that cradle of the symphonic art, shows up in his correspondence and, more profoundly, in his music manuscripts. Guided by his erstwhile teachers, Goldmark and Robert ("Serenade") Fuchs (1847–1927), Sibelius was steered toward the classics—Haydn, Mozart, and Beethoven—whose magnificent achievements were on splendid display. But forbidden fruit ever tempts the young. Warned away from Berlioz and Wagner, Sibelius was conspicuously on hand for the latter's *Tristan and Isolde*. He joined the Wagner Society. And he witnessed *Siegfried*.

Siegfried—a Nordic hero, the progeny of brother-sister love, of incestuous behavior utterly scandalous to conventional morality. What more seductive milieu than Vienna in which to experience that powerful opera so fully in tune with the zeitgeist? For Vienna was home not only to dazzling opera and leading symphonists, but also, by this time, Sigmund Freud (1856–1939).[29] Although no direct connection between Freud and Sibelius has been found, around Freud crystallized many issues swirling through discussions of nineteenth-century intellectuals: from the psychological importance of mythic archetypes to the increasingly heightened awareness of human psychological and sexual depths, from moralistic social movements promoting birth control, reining in prostitution, and fighting venereal disease to innovative studies of the human psyche, sexual symbolism in folklore, and genetic psychology.

The effect of these widely discussed ideas on Sibelius and his *Kullervo* was profound. In an important sense the chief product of Sibelius's Vienna year—the *Kullervo* symphony, with its portrayal of a mythic archetype from the *Kalevala* and a hero caught up in such universal issues as murder, incest, and suicide—spectacularly realized that Järnefelt vision: through the national to the all-European.

TITANIC SYMPHONY: KULLERVO

The year 1892 exploded, quite literally, across the Nordic countries. Unrest in the Russian Empire, exacerbated by terrible famine, led to a year of bombings. Arvid Järnefelt published his word portrait of Tolstoy.[30] And Jean Sibelius unleashed a work of gigantic fury on the Helsinki public. Suddenly, the purveyor of pleasant chamber pieces and reluctant composer of chorales had metamorphosed into a symphonist of grandiose proportions. The size, the audacity, the brazenness of *Kullervo* can easily be overlooked by those living in an era of gigantism and oversaturation on everything from MTV to pornography. But in 1892 Helsinki the work had the effect of a volcanic eruption.

Even before this, Sibelius had gleefully commented about his far tamer Overture in

E Major and *Scène de ballet* that both were so far from "the public and Auntie tastes that I rejoice."[31] In five movements scratched furiously across hundreds of pages, *Kullervo* required not only the full complement of orchestral instruments, but also a choir of vigorous men's voices to sing Finnish texts taken straight from the *Kalevala*, a baritone to execute the title role, and a mezzo-soprano to sing the part of the sister. And if these dimensions were not enough to jolt a town that had never before heard a Finnish choral symphony—indeed, only once, long years before, had they heard a Finnish symphony at all—the appearance of the Kullervo story in music was a spectacular coup. Kullervo is the most tragic—and the most flawed—of the *Kalevala* heroes. Endowed from youth with Herculean power, he is sold into slavery after his family is apparently slain by murderous relatives. Yet in the way of fairy tale and myth, the family members have after all survived, a circumstance that leads to the young man's unwitting seduction of his sister. Kullervo rides off to wage war and avenge the violence against his clan with still more violence, but returns to the site of the incest to take his own life.

Just one year before the symphony's unveiling, paintings of Kullervo submitted for a *Kalevala* illustration contest had provoked Helsinki's intellectual community, and sensibilities were still raw.[32] Among the contest's five participants—Axel Gallén, Gallén's teacher Sigfrid August Keinänen (1841–1914), Johan Kortman (1858–1923), Louis Sparre (1863–1964 [*sic*]), and Eero Järnefelt—two had submitted no fewer than six paintings each with episodes from Kullervo's story. Sparre's were potentially the most shocking: his watercolor *Kullervo ja hänen sisarensa reessä* (*Kullervo and His Sister in the Sledge*) broke a virtual taboo in its depiction of the "hero" in the act of seduction. But as a foreigner—a Swede—Count Sparre was not taken as seriously as his peers (even though he was the brother-in-law of Carl Gustaf Mannerheim, who was to become a famous national hero.) Still, Sparre belonged to Sibelius's circle of friends.

Even more intimately connected to the composer was Eero Järnefelt, his future brother-in-law, who had painted the triptych *Kullervon urotöitä lapsena* (*Kullervo's Heroic Deeds as a Child*). Neither the triptych nor Järnefelt's three other paintings, *Untamon joukon ja kylän hävitystä* (*The Destruction of Untamo's Clan and Village*, sometimes called *Kullervon kosto* [*Kullervo's Revenge*]), *Kullervon lähtö kotoaan* (*Kullervo's Departure from Home*), and *Kullervon kuolema* (*Kullervo's Death*), earned any prize in the competition (Gallén had won the contest with a painting called *Sammon taonta* [*The Forging of the Sampo*]). Even worse for Järnefelt, Thiodolf Rein (1838–1919), a philosopher and the university rector, had launched a scathing attack on the artist, using his review as a vehicle to rail against realism (so prominently on display among the entries) for portraying the sacred *Kalevala*. Rein charged that Järnefelt had left Kullervo, the hero who had honorably fallen on his sword, lying "with *his face turned away*, his bleeding back reminiscent of a carcass on an operating table."[33] (Vivid words those—and some of the strongest descriptions left of Järnefelt's canvases. All have disappeared, presumably destroyed in the wake of Rein's censure.)

The *Kalevala* illustration contest signified a pivotal moment in the artistic life of the homeland. Not only did it show that the subject of Kullervo was in the air—and in a bold and audacious way—but this moment also served as the point of departure for a series of *Kalevala* works on a monumental scale by Axel Gallén.[34] Arguably, the most spectacular would be *Kullervon sotaanlähtö* (*Kullervo Departs for War*) (see plate 2).

A Symphony Rooted in Song

Sibelius's decision at just this moment to compose a monumental work himself—a symphony—on the *Kalevala*, and specifically on the Kullervo episodes, dramatically revealed the close connections among art, artists, and political issues. Moreover, the specifics of his ambitious goal—to unite the Finns' living musical and poetic traditions with the preeminent structure of Germanic musical accomplishment—showed just how keenly aware of the national project and its aims he was.

Later, when the political and aesthetic climate had changed, Sibelius emphatically denied ever having used the obvious—folk song—to achieve that goal.[35] Yet folk song permeates *Kullervo*. During the work's composition Sibelius journeyed east to hear the famed traditional folk singer Larin Paraske; he came away with inspiration for *Kullervo*'s second movement. More startling is that while composing his symphony, Sibelius had in hand not just one, but at least two folk-song collections. One was Eemil Sivori's; his *Folk Songs of Mäntyharju* furnished Sibelius with melodies not only for that brass Allegro, but also for *Kullervo*, whose motto theme follows the outlines of Sivori's "Tuomen juurella" ("Underneath the Birdcherry Tree"). It was the other collection, however, that was the problem, perhaps one reason the whole enterprise was later denied: it was Russian. The exact source Sibelius used has yet to be determined: whether it was one of the editions of Nikolai Lvov and Ivan Prach's celebrated anthology, a resource mined by Tchaikovsky, Rachmaninoff, Rossini, Beethoven (for the Razumovsky Quartets), and many others, or Rimsky-Korsakov's *100 Russian Folk Songs*, which incorporated a substantial portion of the Lvov-Prach repertoire, is unclear.[36] What is clear is that Sibelius, like so many before and after him, found in Russian folk song a rich resource for compelling themes: the jaunty tune in *Kullervo*'s fourth movement (mm. 142–47), for one, which is reminiscent of the later *Danse russe* in *Petrushka* for the simple reason that Igor Stravinsky used the same source;[37] the throbbing, endlessly repeating theme in the third movement, for another, which Sibelius skillfully placed in the service of seduction (Leoš Janáček would find a more sinister use for it when he later composed his "Russian" opera *From the House of the Dead*).[38]

In 1892 national songs were on the national agenda, and mining Lvov-Prach or Rimsky-Korsakov seemed natural: Finland was, after all, part of the Russian Empire, whose culture was deeply admired (it seems highly probable, in fact, that the Russian songs came to Sibelius through the Järnefelts, many of whose Russian-produced musical editions are still in Ainola's cupboards). Moreover, many of the "folk" melodies in these collections circulated in Karelia, where the *Kalevala* itself had originated (to these two concepts, the "folk" and Karelia, we will return later). Upper-class and artistic Russians regularly visited Finnish Karelia, where some, including Rimsky-Korsakov and Ilya Repin, had homes.[39] Sibelius, who was just then finding his way in composing orchestral music, even incorporated a Rimsky-like tribute in *Kullervo*, whose first movement shifts into a section (at rehearsal letter S) evocative of *Shéhérazade*. It was only in retrospect, when *Kullervo* was identified as marking the birth of Finnish music in a fiercely independent Finland and Sibelius was being promoted as "so original" and "purely Finnish," that the stigma of anything borrowed or remotely Russian became insupportable.

Of the borrowed tunes identified thus far in *Kullervo*, none was quoted exactly, yet their shapes and spirit gave the music its authenticity. As *Päivälehti*'s critic Oskar Merikanto wrote breathlessly, "we recognize [the melodies] as our own, even though we had never heard them before."[40] Yet in truth those melodies had been heard—in lands that Finns and Russians shared. Even while Merikanto was struggling to identify what was the quintessentially Finnish "ours" in Sibelius's new music, he unwittingly fingered a deep truth about artistic Finns in the 1890s: they drew things in rather than keeping them out. That wide-open embrace was an essential part of their creative lives.

ഇരുരുഇരു

In its titanic musical incarnation, *Kullervo* was elevated to monumental proportions. Here titanism reached its zenith: hundreds of pages of sketches and scores; five huge movements (Sibelius had envisioned even more); the maximum number of instruments possible in the Helsinki orchestra, including a tubist and extra trumpeters. Three oboes and three clarinets stretched the resources even further; and a raucous men's choir numbering as many as the orchestral players generated splendid martial effects, thanks to their unison part-writing. Just to get so many orchestral and vocal parts readied for the premiere—thousands of pages—required no fewer than eight copyists, who received the pages of score only days before the scheduled performance.[41] Their frantic haste shows in the parts, where the inevitable copying errors, hurried misinterpretations, and overlooked measures caused havoc in rehearsal and, inevitably, in the performance.

When Sibelius nervously stepped onto the podium to conduct, the public was primed. Merikanto had been whetting the public's appetite for a "huge native composition." The novelty of the event and the electrifying conducting of the tall, slim young composer, his hair a plush, unruly crest, his altogether gray-blue color belying the volcano beneath, fueled public enthusiasm. Merikanto's rapturous and grandiose plaudits— "He caresses our ears with Finnish tones. . . . We look at one another and whisper 'magnificent!'"—have reverberated through the literature on Sibelius, as have the words from the *Kalevala*, imprinted on the blue-and-white ribbon adorning the giant laurel wreath that Robert Kajanus handed to the composer: "That way now will run the future, / On the new course, cleared and ready."[42] *Kullervo* was primitive, it was raw, it was flawed— and it was utterly spellbinding. For the first time, the national movement had produced a musical achievement worthy of its high ideals.

Young Finland and the Carelian Call to Arms

FINNISH VOLCANOES

Kullervo made Sibelius the man of the hour. In the wake of this triumph, Jean was able to marry his Aino. They set out for a honeymoon in Karelia, their trip financed by a grant from the Imperial Alexander University in support of Sibelius collecting folk songs for the national movement. (This was the occasion when he hauled a piano through the wilderness; Sibelius's ideas about rural living were rather rarified.)

In the 1890s Karelia, *Kalevala*, and *kansalainen* (meaning a Finnish citizen) issues were in the ascendancy in a powerful way. Asked to compose a work for the tenth jubilee of the university men's choir, Ylioppilaskunnan Laulajat (YL), Sibelius stunned the musical community with *Venematka* (*The Boat Journey*). Everybody expected one of the usual saccharine serenades. Instead, to the opening lines of the *Kalevala*'s fortieth *runo*, which tell how Väinämöinen set off with Ilmarinen and Lemminkäinen to steal the Sampo (a magical object that would bring good fortune to its owner), Sibelius created a staccato, syllabic, declamatory men's-choir version of a runic song, its upper parts in the *runo* singers' signature rhythm, its basses supplying vocal drones (see ex. 8.1).

Venematka also had the effect of a bomb, Sibelius recalled gleefully.[1] This and other remarks of the 1890s, together with remarkably consistent descriptions by his contemporaries, reveal a composer who in this decade was an angry young man, a figure of titanic energy. Axel Törnudd, who had described *Kullervo*'s premiere as being "like a volcanic eruption," observed that in those days "the Goddess of fury was . . . Sibelius's genius, titanism his ideal"; the gifted I. K. Inha described the composer's movements even at home as being "like a volcano."[2]

Eero Järnefelt made one of his finest interpretations of Sibelius at just this time. It shows a handsome and smartly dressed yet vulnerable young adult, still unsure of his

EXAMPLE 8.1. SIBELIUS, *VENEMATKA*, MM. 1–4.

© BREITKOPF & HÄRTEL, WIESBADEN.

place in the world. The long, delicate hands, the huge ears (those "catchers of sound"), the proud coiffure—all are on full display. Yet it is the piercing eyes that haunt the mind. They draw the viewer in and even now, after the lapse of decades, convey the burning intensity of a soul's inner passion (see plate 3).[3]

Angry young men come of age in every time and place, but at the end of the nineteenth century the stance was honed into a fine art.[4] It was a time when Sibelius's brother-in-law Arvid Järnefelt and compatriot Juhani Aho were flabbergasting Finland's good Lutherans with their blasphemous novels. The artists Axel Gallén and Magnus Enckell were scandalizing the gentry with their paintings of fresh corpses and naked youths. Even after the turn of the century, the unveiling of Ville Vallgren's fountain on Helsinki's central market square in 1908, its centerpiece the luscious Havis Amanda unencumbered by clothing and surrounded by phallus-shaped sea lions, caused an uproar. As George Antheil, America's angry young man and "bad boy of music," would learn in Berlin and Paris, riotous audiences and public notoriety did so boost a reputation.

The public to which Sibelius's youthful titanism was displayed was being increasingly democratized and educated. And the tensions and interactions between it and its composers, writers, and artists shaped the artistic results. Early in 1893 the radical social worker and temperance leader Alli Trygg prevailed on Sibelius to write a national working-class hymn. He complied with *Työkansan marssi* (*The Workers' March*). Beginning "Workers, we rise!," its text (by J. H. Erkko) extolled the Christian values and happiness found in hard work. *Työkansan marssi*, for mixed choir, was published in a people's journal, *Viipurin Työväenyhdistys* (*Viipuri Workers' Association*), in 1896. It would not be the only time Sibelius collaborated with the citizens of Viipuri. Nor would it be the only time he participated in spreading music to an increasingly mass market. Taking up life again in the homeland, Sibelius plunged fully into the work of the national movement.

NUORI SUOMI—YOUNG FINLAND

Finnish leaders believed that from the young, the nation would come forth. And come forth it did in Nuori Suomi (Young Finland). The importance of Young Finland, which began taking shape in the 1880s, is best viewed against the background of internal power struggles going on among those involved in "awakening" the nation. The fault lines had broken open in 1877–78 during sessions of the Finnish diet, exposing a rift in the differently aligned four estates. Through the breach stepped the zealous and divisive factions identified as the Fennomans and the Svecomans, the latter also derisively called "Vikings." On the Fennoman side were the peasantry and clergy, united in their conservative, agrarian values. The clergy, traditionally Fennoman, were conspicuously pro-Russian as well; they tried to advance the upward mobility of their class through education—in the Finnish language—and through socially progressive and cultural programs.

Increasingly opposed to their ideas were the nobility and the bourgeoisie, who espoused liberal, pro-industrial, pro-Western ideals. Though loyal to the emperors, these two estates were determined to keep the social privileges they had acquired under the prevailing legal system, which was based on Swedish law. Increasingly Svecoman in orientation, these estates valued the Swedish language, which after all bore the legal traditions of Finland. Swedish resonated with their culture. Was it not the language of the founders of Finnish patriotism, Snellman, Runeberg, and Topelius?

Not surprisingly, Russia viewed such attitudes as nationalistic and chauvinistic. Yet the infernal squabbling among the factions, their splits and reconfigurations, served the Russians well, since it diverted the Finns from consolidating their energies into a uniform national effort. Albert Edelfelt, writing to a friend in January 1885, saw the situation clearly: "Our political conflicts—only race and language feuds—are unbearable. The Russians humiliate us as much as they can, and the more we fight with each other, the happier they are."[5]

As if the divisions between the Fennomans and Svecomans were not bad enough, differences within the Fennoman ranks began to sharpen as their status and influence improved.[6] With the dawn of the 1890s the ideological split became palpable, with differences of orientation and beliefs separating Old Finns (Vanhasuomalaiset) from Young

Finns, represented by Young Finland, Nuori Suomi.[7] The activist playwright Minna
Canth commented on the shifting scene in a letter to the theater director Kaarlo Bergbom
in September of 1892: warning that there was no greater obstacle to creating a Finnish
culture than Helsinki's old Fennomans, Canth claimed, "The concepts 'fennomania' and
'svecomania' no longer exist for me. They belong to the past. Now times are different";
echoing the cry of the Turku Romantics, she continued, "No power can any longer make
us Swedes, but we must take care we don't become Russians."[8]

The differences between the new factions (which continue to be reflected in the ideology of political parties in Finland today) arose out of the old Fennoman endorsement
of "altar and throne." Fennomans pledged allegiance to Finland's Lutheran church and
gave their loyalty to the emperor. Young Finns were anticlerical, socially progressive,
artistically avant-garde, Western oriented. They embraced rather than rejected Scandinavian culture, Brandesian ideals, and intellectual freedom. Initially, they also took a liberal
view of the language issue. And like the young everywhere, they relished the challenge
of conquering new domains.

Young Finland had its roots in the student circles of the Imperial Alexander University, among which there were many different allegiances and inner factions. Significantly,
the group also had roots outside politicized Helsinki, namely, in the Järnefelt circle in
Kuopio, in which Minna Canth had participated and where Elisabeth Järnefelt had been
a central, mentoring spirit. The circle's foremost members—the Järnefelts' most radical son, Arvid, and the writer Juhani Aho—wanted to "humanize Fennomania." Indeed,
the Järnefelt group's high-minded motto, "through the national to the all European"
(*kansallisen kautta yleiseurooppalaiseen*), unofficially served the Young Finns as well, for
the group was unreservedly oriented toward international thinking. As one of their key
members, Eino Leino, explained, they desired "cleaner air, a younger, more European
view of life, religious liberal-mindedness and tolerance, [and] power to the people in
national and social affairs."[9] Their ideals echoed those of other "young" circles around
Europe, such as Junges Deutschland, Jung-Wien, and Det unga Sverige.

It was symptomatic that Young Finland's official motto, proclaimed in a manifesto
published in their cultural periodical, also called *Nuori Suomi*, came directly from the
rhetoric of the national movement: "Valoa kansallemme!" (Light to Our People!).[10]
Their philosophical precepts likewise echoed the national rhetoric. Those precepts were
set forth in *Nuori Suomi*'s inaugural issue, Christmas 1891, by its editor and leading figure,
Eero Erkko (1860–1927). The Young Finns wanted public education and art—Finnish
art—for all. They advocated freedom of personal and ideological life. They pledged
to promote Finnish language and literature, which they would show to be capable of
expressing the highest and most abstract of ideals. With that agenda, Young Finland took

the lead in promoting art and politics, using their publications—their periodical and their newly founded daily newspaper, *Päivälehti*—to reach a wide public.

Nowhere is the central role of the arts in Finland's national awakening clearer than among the Young Finns. As the sculptor Emil Wikström (1864–1942) wrote idealistically to one of their central spirits, Axel Gallén, "What matters most is to live or die for art, for Finnish art! Let us grasp each other's hand and work together with our combined strength for its exaltation."[11] Although politically driven and given vigorous life by increasingly oppressive Russian policies, Young Finland fomented not riotous protests, but cultural and artistic demonstrations. As Gallen-Kallela-Sirén has observed, its members carried out their activities in that ill-defined realm between state and society; although they were serving a political function, by operating under the guise of culture they could avoid institutional restraints.[12] Suitably, the Young Finns' periodical *Nuori Suomi* was devoted to contemporary art, literature, and even music, singling out what was new and vital in Finnish cultural achievements. *Nuori Suomi* was welcomed by cognoscenti around the country and quickly became a cultural force to be reckoned with.

The Young Finns' cultural-political program was equally clear in *Päivälehti*, founded in 1889 and the chief instrument of their agenda.[13] Its editor, Eero Erkko, had been an active member of the Järnefelts' Kuopio salon. He and the other key figures—Aho, Gallén, the Järnefelts, Kasimir Leino, and Louis Sparre—put literary and artistic interests prominently on display. Such central issues to the Young Finns had largely been secondary to the Old Finns, whose newspaper *Uusi Suometar* (which no longer exists) gave short shrift to the arts.

By virtue of his age, interests, and established Järnefelt friendships, Jean Sibelius was inevitably drawn to Young Finland. The inaugural issue of *Nuori Suomi* proudly presented a facsimile of his *Perpetuum mobile*. Yet well before this, probably in 1889, Sibelius was photographed in the company of Young Finns at a time when plans for introducing *Päivälehti* were being finalized.[14] That was the summer when many of the group were showing their national activism by participating in a lottery.

LOTTERIES AND THE NATIONAL AGENDA

Lotteries have a long history in nation building. A means of raising funds for anything from fighting insurgencies to promoting public health, education, and welfare, lotteries have sometimes been compulsory, other times entirely voluntary. That master of seduction Casanova claimed to have invented the lottery; at the very least he managed to persuade Louis XV to establish the Loterie Royale. In truth, lotteries, sweepstakes, and games of chance go back to antiquity.

The idea of national lotteries surfaced in nineteenth-century Finland in connection with the national movement. It was broached by none other than Zachris Topelius. In an article entitled "Light to Our People" (in *Morgonbladet*, a Swedish-language Fenno-man newspaper) on April 14, 1875, Topelius proposed organizing public meetings with lotteries as a means of supporting the newly established KVS, the Kansanvalistusseura.[15] A great debate arose in the Finnish press, with Fennomans largely supportive while their outraged critics brayed over meetings open to "everybody" and the effect on public morals of "promoting gambling." In the end, market forces and mounting Fennomania won out, and lotteries caught on in an extravagant way.

Far more was involved in the lotteries than simply buying a ticket of chance. The faintly distasteful act of giving money to gamble for prizes was masked by the elaborate spectacle of the lottery soirée, which proved to be an ideal device for raising money in support of national causes and, at the same time, promoting social cohesion and Finnish identity in a guise that the imperial censors would approve. The beneficiary was usually announced as some worthy "educational" cause—a school, a library, an orchestra. The festivities surrounding the lottery drawings—the soirées—were turned into national celebrations. These entertainments—for entertainments they were, with music, drama, dancing, drinking, and eating mingled with the fund-raising—combined a rich brew of lusty student songs and militaristic marches with lavish *tableaux vivants* in which key events from Finland's myths, landscapes, and history were colorfully dramatized and accompanied by specially composed music.[16]

The soirées were planned by leading figures in the national movement who in turn drafted Finnish historians, writers, architects, university professors, students, artists, musicians, museum curators—in a word, a huge swath of educated society. Members of national theater groups organized and directed the *tableaux*. Archaeologists reconstructed national costumes and located authentic props. National artists designed, painted, and decorated sets and programs and sometimes even provided some of the prizes. Choruses, orchestras, and other musicians were brought in to sing, play dance music, and perform new works, which the country's composers were prevailed upon to compose. Even the prizes—from bona fide Finnish tools to framed pictures of domestic writers to new Finnish artworks—resonated with national meaning. The very spectacle was enough to take one's breath away. And when, at the end of the evening, the audience rose, as they almost always did, to sing *Vårt land*, national passions were stirred to thrilling heights.

Finns were by no means unique in these kinds of nationalist endeavors. The parallels with France, with which the Finns had strong ties through the artistic community, are instructive.[17] There, three major innovations had begun to unfold in the late 1860s: primary education (the secular equivalent of the church), imbued with national ideals;

public ceremonies, from Bastille Day to world expositions; and public monuments. The Finnish equivalents ranged from exact to similar: primary education imbued with national ideals; public ceremonies in the form of lottery soirées, art exhibitions, and music festivals; and public monuments, in monumental artworks (Gallén's *Kalevala* paintings and Sibelius's *Kullervo* symphony, for examples) and in the construction of public memorials (which took place on an even grander scale after the Civil War of 1918).

Although the Russian emperors and their censors gave consent to these activities, by tightening their controls at the beginning of the 1890s the emperors also unwittingly gunned the Finnish national movement into high gear. Had anyone been watching they would have observed that, during the 1890s, lotteries to raise funds for national enlightenment and education had begun to gather force in Finland.

THE FORMULA: THE SAVO-KARELIAN LOTTERY OF 1891

In the autumn of 1890 the Savo-Karelian student nation began bandying about the notion of staging a lottery. The elaborateness of their plans and their implementation on two March evenings in 1891 showed just how lavish, how artistic, and how historical these festivities could be. With them Sibelius's music would soon have very much to do.

Under the guise of raising money for public libraries, the Savo-Karelian gala followed a formula that proved both successful and capable of endless variation.[18] Held in Society House (Societetshuset or, in Finnish, Seurahuone), the elegant building facing the harbor in Helsinki's center, the two evenings (March 12 and 13, 1891) featured a prologue written by Kaarle Krohn, two *tableaux vivants* arranged by Axel Gallén, and special music composed by Robert Kajanus and Ilmari Krohn. Kajanus conducted the men of his orchestra as well as the university men's choir, YL. With its historical elements mixed with entertainment, the program resembled previous festivals "for the fatherland" and, as reported by "Tuomas" in *Päivälehti* (March 14, 1891), brought out representatives from both language groups.

The program unfolded as follows:

1. *March of the Thirty Years' War*
2. Prologue, written by Kaarle Krohn, presented by Ida Aalberg-Kivekäs
3. *Aino* Symphony by Robert Kajanus
4. *Tableau* of a wedding in Pohjola from the *Kalevala* by Axel Gallén, with incidental music composed by Ilmari Krohn
5. Songs for mixed choir:

    a. *Kansanlaulu* [*Folk Song*], arranged by Ilmari Krohn

    b. *Rauhan maa* [*Land of Peace*], Emil Genetz

    c. *Kansanlaulu* [*Folk Song*] for chorus and tenor solo, arranged by Richard Faltin

    d. *Vårsång* [*Spring Song*], Fredrik Pacius[19]

Half-hour intermission

6. "University Inauguration Ceremony in Turku 1640"—cortege and *tableau*, arranged by Axel Gallén, orchestral music by Robert Kajanus

7. Student songs appropriate to the evening (Ylioppilaskunnan Laulajat)

    1) a. *Savolaisen laulu* [*Song of the Man from Savo*], Karl Collan

       b. *Kaipaus* [*Longing*], Fredrik Pacius

       c. *Studentsång* [*Student Song*], Filip von Schantz

    2) a. *Hymn till Finland* [*Hymn to Finland*], Fredrik Pacius

       b. *Sotamarssi* [*War March*], Robert Kajanus

An evening that officially began and ended with military marches was bound to be rousing. Indeed, it might well be wondered why such a program would have been permitted in a land where the emperor's censors smothered every spark of separatist sentiment with their leaden pens, suppressing everything from newspapers to musical events. The reigning emperor, however, was Alexander III, that enthusiast of military music, especially brass music. And there was more to it. Developing the Finnish language and a national, Finnish (as opposed to Swedish) culture served the imperial purpose, which was to distance the Finns psychologically as far as possible from Sweden and, ultimately, enable the Russian language, Russian culture, and Russian loyalties to flourish among the Finns. As Governor-General Count Fyodor L. Heiden (1821–1900) put the situation to the emperor:

> The more successfully Finland's national culture and language are developed and the greater the degree to which these displace the Swedish language and Swedish influences, the more rapidly will the Russian language strengthen in the land, because Russian is culturally on a higher level than Finnish, nor will there be resistance if [Russian] is spread only to the educated classes and not made the language of administration, a position that, of course, belongs to the Finnish [language].[20]

Had the Russians fully realized the Savo-Karelian evening's underlying resonances, they might have viewed the thing differently. The country's finest representatives in the arts and the academy were on display—such as the Krohns, sons of the nationalist author and folklorist Julius Krohn (1835–1888). Both boys were following in the footsteps of their scholarly father: Kaarle (1863–1933) was becoming an internationally recognized authority on folklore, and Ilmari (1867–1960), a composer, critic, and folklorist, had already begun collecting what would amount to thousands of folk songs, some of which were heard during the evening. Of the other composers on the program, Pacius (1809–1891), Genetz (1852–1930), Faltin (1835–1918), and, above all, Kajanus represented the cream of the country's current crop.[21] Ida Aalberg, the first great star of the Finnish national theater and married to one of the most fanatical of the Young Finns, Lauri Kivekäs, had already made her international breakthrough.[22] Axel Gallén was emerging at the forefront of Finland's most nationally minded artists.

Then there were the program's shrewdly selected ingredients. The full title of the opening number, as everyone there knew, was *Finska rytteriets Marsch i trettioåriga kriget* (*The March of the Finnish Cavalry in the Thirty Years' War*), a marching song to a patriotic text by Topelius. Its verses related a theme dear to the hearts of Finnish men: the brave and legendary Finnish cavalrymen fighting religious oppression alongside the Swedish King Gustav II Adolf (1594–1632). Just whose setting of this traditional march was played is not clear from the program; perhaps it was Martin Wegelius's invigorating arrangement, whose unison vocal line (see ex. 8.2) delivers the poet's words with crystal clarity:

> The snowy north is our Fatherland,
> There our hearths throw sparks on its stormy strands.
> Holding the sword, our arms hardened like steel.
> Our hearts glowed with faith and honor.

Topelius had also written the words to von Schantz's *Student Song*, which begins "We are a Free People." Karl Collan's *Song of the Man from Savo* was also a march, to words of A. Oksanen (pseudonym for the university's rector, August Ahlqvist [1826–1889]). Together with Kajanus's *War March* and Pacius's *Hymn to Finland*, a more militant or nationalist program would have been difficult to put together.

Then there were Gallén's sensational *tableaux*. The first portrayed a wedding scene from the *Kalevala*, accompanied by Ilmari Krohn's music. Weddings were a favorite choice for national dramatizations everywhere (Smetana's *Bartered Bride* being a famous case in point): they afforded a chance to show off bright ethnic costumes in a ritual that pointedly emphasized the regeneration and continuity of a people.[23] The second *tableau*, the inaugural cortege and ceremonies at the Royal Academy of Turku, had an equally ideological subtext. The reason, of course, was the academy's association with the Turku Romantics and their highly influential successors, Lönnrot, Runeberg, and Snellman, all

EXAMPLE 8.2. MARTIN WEGELIUS, *FINSKA RYTTERIETS MARSCH I TRETTIOÅRIGA KRIGET*
(*THE MARCH OF THE FINNISH CAVALRY IN THE THIRTY YEARS' WAR*), MM. 1–8.

of whom had been university students in Turku. When the actor-protagonists trooped across the stage to reenact the cortege and the choir and orchestra dramatically struck up Pacius's hymn *Vårt land*, the audience, awash with patriotic spirits as well as the liquid kind, rose from every nook and corner of the hall to join in. As "Tuomas" observed, "No longer were we just watching an expertly organized *tableau*; we were living and experiencing the events ourselves."[24]

There were other choral numbers on the program, and multiple meanings could be read into them all. Of the pieces for mixed choir, Genetz's unctuous, hymnlike *Land of Peace*, fast becoming a staple of Finnish choral literature, projected a wish on everyone's minds. Hymns, easy to sing, were the musical incarnations of the Finns' Lutheran heritage. They harked back to Swedish and Western historical roots, as opposed to Orthodox Russian ones. The evening peaked with choruses for men. Choirs of stirring, youthful men's voices not only had unmistakable vigor, they also tapped into historical roots and celebrated both the cult of masculinity and the collective sense of "we Finns." They too were connected with the Royal Academy and the Turku Romantics, whose advocacy of men's choirs had been on their agenda for the nation.

On this patriotic evening, men's choruses were out in force. They even showed up in the misnamed *Aino* "symphony," Robert Kajanus's symphonic poem. With its title taken from the *Kalevala*, the work concludes with a robust male chorus, the men singing in mighty unison to Finnish-language texts. There were numerous other hearty songs, from Collan's *Savolaisen laulu* to Kajanus's belligerent *Sotamarssi*, for men's choir and orchestra composed to A. Oksanen's text, beginning:

Syttynyt on sota julma,	Cruel war has broken out,
Vihan liekki leimuaa;	The flame of hatred rages;
Punainen on Pohjan kulma,	Red is the North's corner,
Verta, tulta ennustaa[25]	It augurs blood and fire

—words offering delicious opportunities for reading contemporary issues into the soirée's events.

Not least of the evening's features was a lack of "separate but equal" division into Finnish and Swedish elements. Indeed, the evening stood out for its integration of the language groups. Antagonists will often unite in the face of a common enemy, and the bully in Saint Petersburg powerfully motivated the Finns to bond as one people.

Sibelius was in Vienna when the Savo-Karelian lottery took place. Yet its shrewdly crafted features stamped Finnish lotteries so indelibly that it would have been impossible to argue with so successful a formula for merging art and politics. Sibelius was soon to exploit their blueprint with stunning results. Returning from Vienna to take up life in Helsinki, Jean Sibelius was not stepping onto an empty stage.

THE PEOPLE'S CONCERTS

Sibelius has usually been depicted as hurtling first to national, then to international fame, as though on a trajectory as direct as that of a fired missile. *Kullervo* may have made his name a household word, but it was a word uttered mainly by educated, Finnish-minded Helsinki citizens. Ángel Ganivet, the Spanish diplomat who loved Finland and wrote about it during his service there in 1896 and 1897, did not mention this household word.[26] Sibelius's life after *Kullervo* was very like the musical scene in Helsinki, criss-crossed with various kinds of events, many if not most connected to the wider sociopolitical context. Then as now Helsinki resounded with musical happenings, and Sibelius's works could be heard at many of them. The parallel concert series familiar today to audiences of the Helsinki Philharmonic Orchestra have their roots in the ensemble's beginnings, when the conductor Robert Kajanus resourcefully planned both serious and popular concerts. Important, usually large works such as *Kullervo* belonged to the serious series and took place in the

solemn Festival Hall of the Imperial Alexander University. So-called popular concerts and
people's concerts (*folk konserter*) belonged at the very center of society life, presented in
the hall of the Volunteer Fire Brigade (Palokunnantalo) or in Society House.

Society House, another of Carl Engel's neoclassical buildings bordering Senate
Square, faces southward onto Helsinki's Market Square; since its completion in 1833, it
has undergone various renovations and today serves as City Hall.[27] But in the nineteenth
century its dining areas, gambling rooms, restaurants, main hall, and twenty-seven hotel
rooms, long the city's finest, echoed with the most glittering balls, operas, concerts, and
banquets in all of Finland. Its restaurants boasted French and Russian dishes *à la Berlin*.
The main hall, which at one time accommodated some 1,600 guests, still retains many of
its nineteenth-century features: parquet floors, dazzling chandeliers, soaring plinths, and
decorated ceilings. There Finland's first opera, Pacius's *Hunt of King Charles*, received
its premiere. The public sat around small tables, not stiffly ordered side by side.

By throwing in his lot with Kajanus and the orchestra in "people's concerts" and lottery soirées, Sibelius aligned himself professionally with the national movement. Both
types of events, with their consistent programming of compositions by Finns—Collan, Genetz, Armas Järnefelt, Kajanus, Krohn, Sibelius, Wegelius—promoted a sense of
national awareness among those present.[28] And a repertory of "light classics" bore out
one of the Young Finns' central aims: to make art available to all. "Sillén/Sibelius" had
claimed to have the same goals:

> It is only a sign of poverty to talk about "art for art's sake." All have a right to
> it—the shabby fellow as well as the over-refined, well-educated *salon* type. . . .
> To cast light on the great, the commonly human, that unites these two extremes
> is art's greatest task. That is why it is an unnatural crime to produce well-made,
> and well-dressed art works that can be understood only by a privileged few.[29]

High-minded talk for a man who insisted on starched linens, silk top hats, and the finest
leather shoes. Janne Sibelius may have had the illusion that he was composing for all—
"the shabby fellow as well as the over-refined, well-educated *salon* type"—but Helsinki's
concert venues were filled primarily with society's privileged upper classes—educated,
stylishly dressed Swedish-speakers boasting an overlay of painfully learned Finnish.

As the leading composer among the Young Finns, Sibelius was in demand to provide music for the lottery soirées. They offered opportunities that Sibelius not only took
advantage of, but positively thrived on. And so did the public. From the first time Sibelius
participated in a lottery soirée and produced the *Karelia* music to the lottery for the Press
Days, for which he composed *Scènes historiques I* and *Finlandia*, the pageantry and patriotism of national lottery soirées repeatedly fed his musical creativity. *Skogsrået, Maid in*

the Tower, *Islossningen i Uleå älv*, the intermezzi *Pan och Echo* and *Cortège, Musik zu einer Szene, Grevinnans konterfej*—all saw the light of day thanks to lottery commissions. Even *Song of the Athenians* had its day as a *tableau vivant* in a lottery soirée, within just months of being composed. His connection with the national agenda could not have been clearer.

Eastern Finns gave Sibelius his first opportunity to dip into the soirée baths. This time it was not the Savo-Karelians, but the Viipuri students who were organizing a lottery, to be held in the autumn of 1893. Although the smallest of the university's "nations," numbering only some eighty members, the Viipuri students hailed from the largest, most beautiful, most symbolic town in all Karelia. Since medieval times, Viipuri had been one of Finland's important cities, exceeded in ecclesiastical significance only by Turku. Multicultural and multilingual, cherished for its superb architecture, Viipuri flourished as a trading port for Novgorod and eventually became part of the Hanseatic League. In 1710 the city was conquered by Peter the Great, for whom it served as a key portal on the Russian Empire's western frontier.[30] Only when Russia annexed the rest of Finland in 1808–9 was "Old Finland" (the province of Viipuri) again joined to "New Finland."

Despite their rich heritage, the students of the Viipuri fraternity had failed to impress their contemporaries with the zeal of their national enthusiasm. In October 1892 an article in the *Viipurin Sanomat* complained that the Viipuri students showed the least interest of all the student nations in patriotic matters.[31] Stung into action, the group pushed forward with its budding plans for an event that would lavishly display Viipuri's ancient history, its landscapes, and its cultural heritage as the pearl of Karelia.

KARELIANISM

Karjala—Karelia or Carelia: for Finns, the very name evokes purity, strong emotions, and a welter of associations. Karelia includes territory on the present-day Karelian isthmus as well as the area known as Ingria, located along the southern shore of the Gulf of Finland and the banks of the Neva River.[32] For centuries Karelian borders have been contested and fought over, their gentle, fertile lands turned into battlefields of greedy conflict between the competing interests of Russian emperors and Swedish kings (see fig. 8.1).

Finns had a crucial stake in this border region. Certain areas, including those around Sortavala, Käkisalmi, and especially Viipuri, had long been home to people calling themselves Finns. And in the region's northeastern territories—including remote areas of "Finnish and Russian Karelia"—Lönnrot had collected the epic *runot* of the *Kalevala* and the lyric poems of the *Kanteletar*. Irrevocably bound up with these sacred texts, Karelia represented the very cradle of Finnish civilization, a *lieu de mémoire* whose landscapes and poetry had preserved unspoiled the true soul of the Finns, a place where the echo of

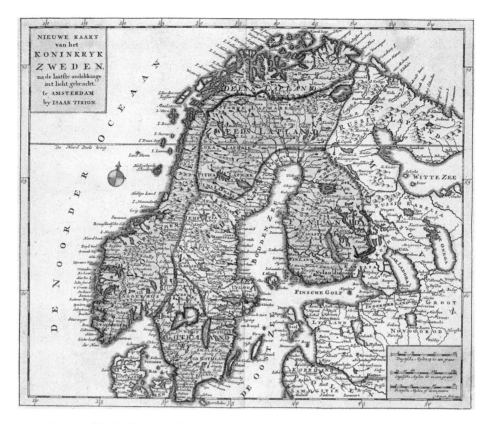

Figure 8.1. Karelia, Finnish and Russian. Copper engraving of Isaak Tirion, "New Map of the
Kingdom of Sweden" (Amsterdam, ca. 1744), after an original by J. Keijser, 1734.
The National Library of Finland. Photo: Kari Timonen.

the ancestors reverberated. Karelia also served another, equally important, purpose: by
imagining Karelia as a primitive, exotic space on their periphery, Finns could see themselves as advanced and modern.[33] Russian Karelians, meanwhile, viewed themselves as
Russian, and foreign visitors (including the Finns), as Swedes.

During the nineteenth century folklorists, ethnographers, and song collectors made
their way to the region to connect with its ancient landscapes and with what they believed
to be their authentic spiritual heritage. But it was the rising nationalist aims of Young
Finland that ignited what came to be called Karelianism.

Though as yet it had no name, the passion for Karelia blazed into public awareness
on October 1, 1890, from the pages of *Päivälehti*:

> What great success awaits those works of art originating from the land where
> the Kalevala was sung and where the folk have managed to preserve that true

Karelian "character" that elsewhere has been lost or sullied; we would, perhaps, better understand the nuances of the old poetry once the keen eye of the artist has revealed to us the place where the rune singers lived and from where they undoubtedly derived their greatest inspiration! In this respect folk art has already been of great help to our imagination, but implements, clothes and decorations are dead things and have little effect. What we need is skin and bones, light and shadow, we long to see the moods of nature and living people. In a word: we wish to feel the artistic side of Karelia.[34]

From today's perspective it is astonishing to realize that although Finns had literary accomplishments aplenty by 1890, including a revised and expanded *Kalevala* and the works of Aleksis Kivi and Minna Canth, in art and music they were much poorer. Juhani Aho, probably the author of the *Päivälehti* summons, put it succinctly: our art, he wrote, "does not have a past: our artists themselves act as the founders of our arts, which have no national pedigree."[35] Proving his point were the circumstances surrounding a contest to illustrate the *Kalevala* in the 1880s: the cry had gone up that national artists could not be found.

Now, in a bid to originate that art and spurred by the Russian emperor's threats against Finns' long-cherished rights, attention returned to that precious resource, the *Kalevala*, and to the realm whence it had come. Folklorists, photographers, poets, historians, ethnologists, writers, linguists, composers, and heaven knows who else began streaming into Karelia. As Eero Järnefelt described that heady time:

> We young artists rushed like explorers . . . to seek subject matter for our paintings from our own people and landscapes: and like youth always, we believed we had found the Finnish nation and its landscapes, the Kalevala and Kanteletar completely anew. They were for us like an untouched wilderness mysteriously lighted.[36]

Writers poetized Karelia, Arvi Jännes's verses *Karjala* (1889) being among the best-known late nineteenth-century examples. Composers celebrated it, turning Jännes's *Karjala* into choral jubilation. The composer-conductor Kajanus, one of the first to create musical works with Kalevalan titles, even met Lönnrot himself, an encounter that went down in fabled romance:

> The old man took out his kantele and showed me how he had written down the folk tunes he had collected. Because he did not know how to write music, he had invented his own numerical system. . . . For a long time I dreamed of the unattainable—that I would inherit Lönnrot's old kantele.[37]

Tellingly, the term "Karelianism" was coined only in retrospect, during the 1930s, by Yrjö Hirn (1870–1952), a literary historian and aesthetician, in a self-conscious for-mulation to describe the national activity.[38] It was in Hirn's company that Jean Sibelius had joined the rush to Karelia. The year was 1891, and Sibelius was in the throes of com-posing his *Kullervo* when, with Hirn, he travelled to Porvoo in eastern Finland to hear the astonishing Larin Paraske (ca. 1834–1904), the tiny Ingrian singer who had come to Finland "from Russian Karelia." Though unable to read or write, Paraske held in her memory untold thousands of Kalevalan verses. Her phenomenal memory of those lines and her hair-raising delivery of them (her screeching and sobbing made the hair of even the experienced Lönnrot stand on end) were legendary in her own time.[39] Sibelius, who like his contemporaries was evidently seeking national insights to put into practical use, made copious notes. What he came away with, no one knows for sure. Yet immediately after hearing Paraske's performance, Sibelius "found" the theme for his *Kullervo* lullaby. It goes in a folklike alla recitativo style, with drones in perfect fourths supporting a regu-larly phrased melody (see ex. 8.3). The lullaby had even started life in the so-called *Kale-vala* meter—five beats to a bar.[40]

The experience of Larin Paraske (about whom Sibelius rather pompously claimed to Aino, "We got to be such good friends, you know") and his honeymoon in Karelia, dur-

EXAMPLE 8.3. SIBELIUS, *KULLERVO*, SECOND MOVEMENT, MM. 1–4.
© BREITKOPF & HÄRTEL, WIESBADEN.

ing which he collected various folk songs, meant that when the chance came to compose the music for the Pro Carelia lottery, Sibelius had already had direct personal contact with these hallowed spaces and their artistic expressions.

THE PRO CARELIA LOTTERY

All these circumstances lay just below the surface of the Viipuri fraternity's commission, a play on burgeoning national enthusiasms. As the students were well aware, their province, Karelia, was one of the few without its own *kansanopisto* or "people's college," an institution for adult education and public enlightenment. To remedy this failing, their lottery would raise funds to establish such a school, and the means would be the formula made so successful by the Savo-Karelians—a soirée designed around patriotic *tableaux vivants*. The Viipuri event, however, would depict landmarks in Karelia's history. Their evening would display handicrafts made by Karelians. Their show would exhibit genuinely Finnish furniture and Finnish costumes. And they would feature prominent Karelian Finns.

The lottery prizes, of course, would be crucial. A volunteer army of over 200 ladies was drafted to help (their only apparent reward being their names announced in the newspapers). Participants could win anything from hardware (scissors, pliers, and other tools) to textiles, crafts, coffee sets, carpets, suites of furniture, and even original paintings by artists of the caliber of Albert Edelfelt and Väinö Blomstedt. Nearly nine hundred people would walk away with a prize of one sort or another. Meanwhile, ingenious ways had to be found to compensate the performers. Although Sibelius would be paid for his commission (as would Ernst Röllig, for copying out the parts),[41] the orchestra members received in payment 115 steins of beer. Students would be used to populate the *tableaux vivants* and sing the choruses, led by the university men's choir YL performing student songs and patriotic choruses—Kajanus's *Sotamarssi* and Emil Genetz's *Karjala*.

Such were the preparations that now began to unfold.[42] Karelian elements were out in force, beginning with the figure in charge: the Viipuri-born architect Johan Jakob ("Jac") Ahrenberg (1847–1914), a Swedish-speaking Finn, a scholar of Karelian history, and a writer who had even attracted attention abroad. There was the respected Gabriel Lagus (1837–1896). A poet and former rector of the Viipuri Gymnasium, Lagus was engaged at that very moment in writing Viipuri's history. Prevailed upon to produce a text for the occasion (J. H. Erkko having refused), Lagus complied—in Swedish. His eulogy, "Den 13 November 1893," extolled the birds and people, the light and the waterfalls of Karelia.[43] Linguistic diversity was part of Viipuri's proud cosmopolitan history; on the city's streets Finnish, Swedish, German, and Russian were all heard. For the Pro Carelia evening, along with the speeches and poetry in Finnish and Swedish, there were plans for a scene in French, although it had to be abandoned when the French-speaking actor fell ill.

The centerpiece was to be the *tableaux vivants*. Although each *tableau* evoked some aspect of Karelia, the unifying theme was that proudest of Karelian sites, Viipuri Castle. Unlike central Europe, where abundant cathedrals and castles testify to the antiquity and perpetuity of the nations, Finland has precious few such structures. Viipuri Castle, founded in 1293, was one of the few tangible proofs of Finland's ancient glory and of its Christian—and non-Orthodox—values, and the Pro Carelia lottery was celebrating the six hundredth anniversary of that glory. Almost every scene featured the castle, driving home the idea that here was a solid Finnish venue of history, ceremony, and cultural expression.

The *tableaux* were directed by Kaarlo Bergbom (1843–1906), cofounder (with his sister Emilie) of the Finnish National Theater. The *tableaux* were to be accompanied by newly composed music. Kajanus was induced to provide his orchestra, while Jean Sibelius was commissioned to write the musical numbers. There would, of course, be costumes—and not just imaginative stage designs. Ahrenberg had enlisted Theodor Schvindt (1851–1917), an archaeologist who had been excavating medieval burial grounds in Karelia, as his assistant. Schvindt's just-completed dissertation included illustrations of ancient Karelian outfits reconstructed from his research on the Iron Age.[44] His recreated historical attire went on public display for the first time in the Pro Carelia lottery soirée.

To design the stage sets, Ahrenberg recruited Axel Gallén and, toward the end, Gallén's friend Emil Wikström and the young Eliel Saarinen (1873–1950), then just twenty years old. Some of the sets seem to have been recycled from the Savo-Karelian lottery two years before. However, this time there was a handsome eighteen-page program booklet produced by the Finnish Literature Society, its covers made of elegant transparent parchment. Viipuri's red insignia with the historic date of 1293 decorated the front cover. Together with the liberal use of crowns in the illustrations, these emblems imparted a distinct aura of antiquity and royalty. Within the delicately sewn bindings, the first page opened to a vignette of Viipuri Castle, a rising sun in the background (see fig. 8.2). The booklet's pages, framed with intricate *Jugendstil* borders, bore verses from the "historic" *Kalevala*, printed in both Finnish and Swedish; authentic excerpts appropriate to each *tableau* taken from ancient chronicles; official letters, including a handsome facsimile of the oldest document in Finland's archives, the king of Sweden's guarantee of protection for the women of Karelia, dated 1316; and the historic speech made by Emperor Alexander I in December 1811 proclaiming the reunification of "Old Finland" with the rest of the grand duchy. The whole enterprise was steeped in history and attempts to demonstrate the ancient and the royal lineage of the Finns, all brought to life in vivid *tableaux*.

Figure 8.2. Pro Carelia lottery program, November 13, 1893; opening page showing Axel
Gallén's vignette of Viipuri Castle and verses from the *Kalevala*, *runo* 25.
The National Library of Finland. Photo: Kari Timonen.

The Pro Carelia Tableaux

TABLEAU I: 1293; A KARELIAN HOME, A MESSAGE OF WAR

The first scene opened in a *savupirtti* or smoke cottage, a space revered by Finns even
today for its connections to past generations. The time was the year of Viipuri Castle's
founding, a distant age when Finland had belonged to neither Sweden nor Russia. The
program texts were pointedly drawn from both the *Kalevala* and the *Kanteletar*, the
proofs that the Finns had enjoyed a high culture *before* being invaded by the neighbors.

Two singers, wearing Schvindt's reconstructed "Aino" dresses, serenely exchanged
a *runo* dialogue, chanting Lemminkäinen's words from the passage in the *Kalevala* that

precedes the hero's death. Here, however, Lemminkäinen invokes the god Ukko to lead him to his quarry: "Oi Ukko ylijumala, / tahi taatto taivahinen" (O thou Ukko, God of gods, / Thou, the father of the heavens!; *Kalevala*, *runo* 14, lines 13–14).The idyll suddenly breaks off: a youth, bow in hand, interrupts the placid singers; music of combat rings from the horns.

TABLEAU II: 1293; TORKEL KNUTSSON FOUNDING VIIPURI CASTLE

An excerpt from Olaus Petri's *Svenska krönika* on the founding of the castle along with a facsimile of King Birger Magnusson's letter of protection for the women of Karelia made up the program texts.[45] The *tableau* depicted Torkel Knutsson, the Swedish warlord whose coat of arms included the image of a lion (the talisman adopted by the Finns) and who led the Swedes against the Republic of Novgorod (the subtext: "fearsome Russia"). In the *tableau* Torkel Knutsson conquered Karelia and established the Castle at Viipuri.[46] Peasants heaved forth the castle's cornerstone, the Bishop of Västerås blessed it with a golden cross, monks prayed, and choirboys swung censers.

The Catholic elements carried potent messages: they reminded the audience that Knutsson's battle was not just about possession of the land, but also involved religion: the Catholic church versus the Orthodox.

TABLEAU III: 1333; LITHUANIAN DUKE NARIMONT RAISING TAXES FROM THE KARELIANS FOR MARTENS AND HAWKS

In a winter landscape the handsomely dressed Duke Narimont, surrounded by his soldiers, sat upon his horse.[47] The program excerpt, from Mathias Akiander's *Russian Annales*, related how Narimont, son of the Lithuanian Grand Duke Gedeminas and baptized with the name Gleb, had been given the lands of Ladoga, Orechow, Käkisalmi, Karelia, and half of Koporje. That an entire *tableau* would be devoted to this shadowy duke calls for some explanation. Narimont (ca. 1292–1348) was the first ruler of "Russian Karelia" to be identified.[48] Not only was he a royal, he also embodied ideals central to the nationalists, both territorial (his realm had included lands inhabited by Finns) and ideological (he waged warfare against "foreign oppressors"). Narimont also represented Finland's relationship to a great kingdom, Lithuania. No less important were his descendants: the Renaissance princess Katarina Jagellonica (about whom more will be heard) and Mikhail Mikhailovich Golitsyn (1675–1730), a Russian commander during the Great Northern War, who worked to limit czarist power and became known as "the Finns' god." Either to accompany or to follow the duke's scene, Sibelius created the rollicking orchestral music later arranged as *Intermezzo*, as effective a piece of theatrical galloping as has ever been composed and absolutely crucial to the *tableau*'s success, since the duke was sitting—and upon a *wooden* steed. The Finns might have liked comparing themselves to the ancient Greeks, but the wooden horse seems to have been the lottery equivalent of Macbeth's curse: it caused no end of broken ankles and other mishaps.

TABLEAU IV: 1446; KARL KNUTSSON IN VIIPURI CASTLE

Karl Knutsson Bonde was king of Sweden on several occasions and deposed nearly as many. He made Viipuri Castle a place of high culture and refined taste, as related in the excerpt from the *Karlskrönika* printed in the program. Also printed were the verses to the troubadour's song, *Dansen i Rosenlund*, performed for the king (by a Finnish baritone, a Mr. Kruskopf). All the music for this *tableau*, with its orchestrated ballade, remains intact in Sibelius's manuscript.

TABLEAU V: 1580; PONTUS DE LA GARDIE CONQUERING AND BURNING KÄKISALMI

The French-born commander Pontus de la Gardie (ca. 1520–1585), in a notable about-face after being captured by the Swedes, led a war against Russia. Pontus appeared at the city gates and proceeded to conquer and burn. A long field account of the deeds by de la Gardie himself was reproduced in the program. The audience was treated to the dreadful spectacle of Viipuri Castle in flames; evidently it was at this moment that the newfangled electric lights—four arc lamps—were put to good use in one of the evening's high points. To follow this scene (according to the orchestral parts), Sibelius composed the *March to an Old Motive* (the later Alla marcia of the *Karelia* Suite). From this point on, most of the original music manuscript pages have been thoroughly mutilated.

TABLEAU VI: 1710; THE SIEGE OF VIIPURI

Viipuri Castle, besieged by Peter the Great and his eighteen thousand troops, now fell to the enemy. The program text related that according to legend, as the emperor approached Håkon's Gate, he was met by a deputation, and a Miss Havemans handed him the key to the city.

TABLEAUX VII–VIII: 1811; THE PROVINCE OF VIIPURI REUNITED WITH THE REST OF FINLAND

This dramatic and musically illustrated history lesson was crowned with the joining of Old Finland to the rest of the country, certified by Emperor Alexander I himself, whose unification testament appeared in the program. The program did not distinguish the dividing lines between the last two *tableaux*, but Sibelius's later arrangement of material for the seventh scene, *Sjunde satsen ur Carelia*, provides a guideline. When the curtains rose for the last time, the white-clad "maid of Finland" (portrayed by one Selma Tavaststjerna) stood bearing a shield adorned with the Finnish lion, appropriated from the martyr Torkel Knutsson. Her right arm was draped protectively around a young Karelian woman; to her left posed a man from Häme (the architect Yrjö Sadenius).[49] Although at this place the manuscript has been destroyed, contemporary accounts make clear the concluding musical event: *Vårt land*, sung by the assembled choirs and enthusiastic public.

The Tableau *Music*

On that evening of November 13, 1893, attention to historical detail and ethnographic accuracy was everywhere on display. In that context Sibelius's *tableau* music has a significance not apparent from abbreviated concert renditions of the *Karelia Suite*. For the composer too had put into operation his Karelian findings, and they sounded off right from the first *tableau*.[50]

After the obligatory overture, which introduced themes to be taken up later, the orchestra ceded the leading role to the two *runo* singers. Their melody was every bit as authentic as their costumes: Sibelius had transcribed it the previous summer directly from the lips of the Karelian singer Pedri Shemeikka (1825–1915).[51] Few in Society House's stylish audience knew its origin, but no one missed the significance of the performers: there on stage, exchanging *runo* dialogues with Selma Tavaststjerna, was Larin Paraske herself. When the music of combat and the news that the Swedes had invaded brought the tranquil beginning to a halt, the implications were not lost on the audience: the scene immediately had to be repeated, not once but several times.

Sibelius availed himself of other authentic resources. During *tableau* IV, with the now fully constructed and Christianized castle transformed into a place of culture, he portrayed at least three "events" in the music. A minuet opened the scene, suggesting (however anachronistically) the aristocratic and "beautiful taste" (as the program pointed out) of the castle's inhabitants. Then a broadly spaced, octave-reinforced theme swelled forth, invoking the grandeur of the Karelian landscape. The scene ended with the troubadour performing *Dansen i Rosenlund*. The words of this ballad had been published by none other than Adolf Ivar Arwidsson, one of the Turku Romantics, who was identified in the program. Arwidsson had spent more than a decade and a half compiling a national folk-song anthology, the three-volume *Svenska fornsånger* (Stockholm, 1834–42). The source thus had great national resonance, and it had been put into Sibelius's hands by the enterprising Yrjö Hirn. Arwidsson's collection consisted mostly of texts, and although he included some tunes, none corresponds to the troubadour's song, which has long been believed to be original with the composer. Yet Sibelius may have drawn on an authentic source for this music too: the opening four measures recall the opening of *Kopparslagare visan* (*The Coppersmith's Chantey*), the folk song to which he had improvised variations at the piano just five years earlier.[52]

There were almost certainly other direct musical borrowings, a modus operandi that differed noticeably from that of *Kullervo*, where Sibelius had used folk songs chiefly as points of inspirational departure. Now, in the context of an evening when ethnographic precision was paramount, "authentic" musical sources were called for. Although not all the sources have been identified, Sibelius himself called attention to one of them: "Marsch nach einem alten Motiv" in the intermezzo between *tableaux* V and VI (the later Alla marcia). Someone, perhaps the composer, later erased the penciled words "Marsch nach einem alten Motiv," and the "old motive" is still being sought. Its designation in German suggests that its origins may lie among the many Germanic works that so profoundly shaped art music in Finland before the advent of the golden-age composers.

What is striking about this mixture of authentic borrowings is the variety of cultural models Sibelius used and what he viewed as his national roots. During the Viipuri lottery evening, he and his contemporaries put on display Finland's multiple traditions, both linguistic and cultural, and in the broadest possible historical context. In his *Karelia* music, Sibelius intermingled high-status international ingredients with Finland's "national" elements, just as he had done in *Kullervo*. In *tableau* I, he accompanied the *runo* singers not with the national instrument, the *kantele*, but with the orchestra, whose drone bass and pizzicato violins emulated the *kantele*'s sounds. In *tableau* II, he portrayed the laying of the castle's cornerstone first in the time-honored technique of sacred music—points of imitation—and then with a broad and spacious choralelike theme worthy of Smetana. In *tableau* III and with the appearance of the Lithuanian Duke Narimont, Sibelius conveyed a sense of the breadth of the Karelian realm and its wide-open spaces with bucolic horns and echo effects (a favorite device of Grieg), with muted trumpets faintly re-sounding the horns' opening gambit. He resorted to the fugal process again in *tableau* VI with the siege of Viipuri, when Peter the Great overwhelmed the castle, and for the grand finale Sibelius had arranged Pacius's *Vårt land*. And it was the Pacius hymn that drove the audience to ecstasy. As the composer told his brother later, the music was hardly heard for all the shouting and clapping.[53]

Today the music known as the *Karelia* Suite, arranged from the Pro Carelia *tableaux*, belongs to the popular repertoire classified as "easy" listening. Its often static and undemanding tonal language and the pictorial qualities evoked in its titles allow a kind of desiccated enjoyment of music from a distant corner of the earth. It seems to have been Kajanus, with his unfailing instinct for what worked with the Helsinki public, who guided

the choice of movements for the suite, with their unprovocative titles—Intermezzo, Ballade, and Alla marcia.[54]

But the *Karelia* music in its original setting was something else. Steeped in Finnish history, ethnicity, and landscape, the music as much as the events it portrayed placed
Finland's national aspirations within a conspicuously international context. The *tableaux*
and their music unfolded in surroundings connecting a broad swath of historical events
and countries from Sweden through Finland and into Russia and Lithuania and across
a time span of six centuries. It was a setting that brought Swedish speakers and Finnish
speakers together to honor one of Finland's most multicultural cities, and in a multi-
artistic way. Sibelius's musical conception of his national history was as wide-ranging as
Viipuri's own; it combined Bachlike chorales, Russian-Karelian *runo* song, Swedish folk
ballads, Lutheran hymns, Germanic fugues, and Grieglike techniques in a grand mix. If
this was the vision of a land and its future, then plurality was its watchword.

∾9∾

Science, Art, and Symbolism

TECHNOLOGY AND THE FINNS

When Sibelius moved from Lovisa back to Finland's capital in the winter of 1892, he joined a thriving small metropolis enjoying the benefits wrought by science, technology, and economic prosperity.[1] The city glowed with electric lamps. The air was filled with the ringing of telephones and the whistling of engines. The familiar droskies still rumbled through the streets, but less gratingly, thanks to the recently introduced rubber on their wheels. Although Finns had been slow to adopt gas lighting,[2] where telephones and electricity were concerned, they were quick off the mark. In 1877 Finns had adopted telephones, a mere two years after their invention by Alexander Graham Bell. In 1880 electricity lit up the popular park called Kaivopuisto.

The increased availability of venture capital aided this progress. In 1881 the emperor had agreed to grant loans in order to establish local telephone lines. A few years later, his imperial hand approved a similar undertaking for setting up long-distance lines. By the time the indefatigable British traveler Mrs. Alec Tweedie visited Helsinki in 1896, she found telephones, telegraphs, and electric lighting commonplace. A telegraph network laced the whole country. Nearly four thousand telephone subscribers covered the city of Helsinki (the larger population of Saint Petersburg, by comparison, could boast only five thousand telephones even five years later). By 1916 the density of Finland's telephone networks exceeded the rest of Russia's.

Technology lessened Finland's remoteness. The start-up of the Finnish steamship company known as FÅA—Finska Ångfartygs Aktiebolaget—in 1883 revolutionized mobility. Not only were Stockholm and Travemünde within easier reach, but so were Lübeck, Stettin, Bremen, Rotterdam, Antwerp, and the British Isles. Postal connections improved. In 1890 the launch of the first icebreaker, *Murtaja* (*The Breaker*), signaled the end of Finland's isolation during the long winter months.

Restaurant life changed along with street and concert life. When Sibelius left the Helsinki Music Institute for Berlin in 1889, Stockmann's department store was already an established institution (it had been in business since the 1870s), as was Paulig's coffee firm, begun in 1876.[3] In 1887 the last columns, ornamental pilasters, and decorative patterns were being completed on the new Hotel Kämp, designed by the architect Carl Theodor Höijer (1843–1910). The Kämp was one of Höijer's most beautiful interiors. It also boasted a peculiar modern contraption: a hydraulically powered elevator.

Far from being oblivious to the changing world, artists and intellectuals responded powerfully to it. That premier symbol of technological progress, the railroad, showed up in stories, paintings, photographs, and even musical compositions. Streetlamps, electric lights, bicycles, bridges, industrial smoke, and steamships perked up posters, etchings, and photographs. The Industrial Revolution may have come later to Finland than elsewhere, but its effects were no less spectacular, and artists were neither the least of its beneficiaries nor the last to respond. At the age of twenty-two, Sibelius, alerted by Uncle Pehr to the novel idea of recording music, speculated on the possibilities to the point of being inspired to invent an experimental chord:

> Once the vibrations can be stored, then I think this force dominates everything else. Who knows what results one might obtain? A very musical age will then begin. (The practical use of music will then have been found.) If, for example, one imagines a city with several factories, the cotton factories could, for instance, have low C; the sawmills, the [minor] second, E–F; the iron factories, G–A-flat; and all the other factories, C–D-flat. Then the following chord would result:

> This chord is a sexdecim chord which is not found in any music other than my experimental music. This chord has a highly peculiar effect on people and animals. I think that the many seconds vibrating in the air cause electricity, and this in turn is transformed into animal magnetism in people and animals which again remolds the activities of the entire animal kingdom. After a century in the city I have described, natives and animals would be highly peculiar. The task of the composer would be to compose pieces in which the tonal vibrations would be raised to the highest number possible. A profitable time for music![4]

Art and technology already mingle in Sibelius's piano work *Florestan*, composed the next year (1889). In this programmatic suite, Florestan attempts to entice an enchanting wood nymph to his side. When she vanishes, he returns home, sad and dejected. Already in this early work, the composer had come up with that haunting sound immediately recognizable as "Sibelian" (see ex. 9.1). Technically, it consists of a II6—I6 progression

EXAMPLE 9.1. SIBELIUS, *FLORESTAN*, PART 4, MM. 249–54.
BY PERMISSION OF FENNICA GEHRMAN OY, HELSINKI.

over a tonic-dominant ostinato, but its effect packs all the power of a steam engine. Its mournful descent echoes the distant, lonely whistle of a passing locomotive. The peculiar and unexpected merging of alluring nymph and modern technology echoed both out of the past—a sensitive-eared boy's upbringing in a railroad town—and into the future.

Since the late nineteenth century, Finns have made a specialty of fusing art and technology. Perhaps their most spectacular concord in Sibelius's time merged in Eliel Saarinen's monumental Helsinki railway station, designed in 1904, a shrine to art, high culture, and Finnish technological expertise. Elsewhere in the Nordic countries, common ground between art and science was being sought in literature. In his novel *To Be or Not to Be* (1857), Hans Christian Andersen had observed, "I am convinced that in our time, under the whirring of the turning wheels of machinery, the roar of steam, and the whole tumult, a new hero of literature will step forward, and in the very spirit of science."[5]

That hero, at least in the brave man's own eyes, was none other than the loopy Swede August Strindberg. Known to denizens of Helsinki for his uproarious social satire *The Red Room* and such naturalist plays as *Miss Julie*, Strindberg had altogether unexpected scientific proclivities. His (second) wife Frida, greeted one day by evil-smelling fumes emanating from the bedroom, found the great author conducting experiments with sulfur. Strindberg solemnly assured her that he could make gold—more or less. He believed

Figure 9.1. Oulu Bridge, 1890. Photograph by I. K. Inha.
The Finnish Railway Museum, Hyvinkää, Finland.

"in a primary matter, out of which all the rest has developed by splitting, condensa-
tion, diluting, copulating, crossing, etc.," and the evidence was tenderly preserved in his
Green Bag, in whose "billowing swaths of lime lay Strindberg's new theory that plants
have nerves. There sat the evidence that an element can split. There Newton was refuted,
famous astronomers led on *ad absurdum*."[6]

Not all artists and writers were as taken with science as was Strindberg. Many felt
horribly alienated from high-tech machines and the Industrial Revolution and either
clung to familiar modes of creating art or sought inspiration in the realms of indefinable
mystery and enigmatic symbolism.[7] Two images, both from 1890, speak eloquently of
the clash of worlds. The first is the photographer I. K. Inha's picture of the bridge over
the Oulu River in northern Finland, a site invested with great national pride. The angular, elegant steel forms a symmetrical archway over cleanly functional railroad tracks,
from which ironclad railings separate it. In the right foreground another sign of the new
technology, a velocipede, leans against an old wooden fence. Human life, dwarfed by the
modernist surroundings, appears in four small figures on a footbridge that parallels the

Figure 9.2. "A-i-a" (Adelaïde Ehrnrooth), *Två Finskors Lustvandringar II: Resor i Orienten* (*Two Finnish Ladies' Walking Tours*, Vol. II: *Travels in the Orient*) (Helsingfors, 1890). Scan: Mikko Ikkala.

railroad tracks (see fig. 9.1). The same year in which Inha captured his functional vision, "A-i-a" (as Adelaïde Ehrnrooth signed her name; see fig. 9.2) brought out the second of her travel books, a guide to the alluring, extravagant world of the Orient. Among the exotic scenes featured on the richly tinted gold-and-red covers loomed an inscrutable sphinx.

SYMBOLIST RESPONSE

Technological advancement represented a two-edged sword, ominous and threatening even as it delivered its dubious benefits. When, in 1896–97, Axel Gallén painted a water-color of railroad tracks, he placed a woman's decapitated head lying grotesquely on the ties. The brave but alien new world that positivist science had wrought frighteningly eluded human control. Why, it imperiled humankind's very existence! Worse, it challenged the essence of what it meant to be human. It was bad enough that Copernicus had demonstrated to mankind that he and his planet were not, after all, at the center of the universe.[8] Now scientific advances began accelerating with such terrifying speed that one onslaught after another assailed the human ego.

In 1859, in his *On the Origin of Species by Means of Natural Selection*, Charles Darwin shared with his fellow man the disturbing insight that humankind was not a cosmic design in the eyes and image of God, but merely the result of natural selection. No sooner had Darwin upset the apple cart of Garden of Eden theology than the subterranean and seemingly unfathomable realm of the subconscious began attracting serious attention. Even before Freud broached his theories, folklorists, artists, social critics, and authors were plumbing the scope and depths of the psyche.

The arts offered salvation, a means of restoring mankind's lost cosmic, biological, and psychological superiority. Myths, for instance, placed humans at the heart of the cosmos. So did ancient beliefs and religion. By exploring the human capacity for abstract thought and awareness of death—the source of human biological preeminence—and by teasing out the most deeply buried secrets of the soul, mankind might again find the way to the heart of the self. These were the solutions proposed by Freud himself in 1917; they could be a prescription for what has come to be called Symbolism.

Of Symbolism, Constantin Stanislavsky (1863–1938) observed: "It is a hard nut to crack—the Symbol. It is successful when it has its source not in the mind, but in the inner soul."[9] As a source for historical inquiry, the soul makes a difficult subject. As for its signs—namely, symbols and ideas—there is a tendency to reduce them to neatly labeled entities, the better to examine them. Ideas, however, are fluid, not rigid formulations; they shape-shift and mutate, metamorphosing under the influence of events and places, with one aspect of the flow now highlighted, now another. Shifting, swinging between poles, coalescing, and transmuting were the very essence of Symbolism, a name applied to the broad currents dominating the end of the nineteenth century and meaning different things to different people. Nevertheless, from the time Jean Moréas's manifesto *Le symbolisme* was published in *Le Figaro* on September 18, 1886, until 1905, when the new avant-garde movements began to appear, the set of ideas covered by the Symbolist umbrella shaped and transformed life and thought all over the European continent, the Nordic countries, Russia, and even faraway North America. Book illustrations, typography, theater, photography, films, art, music, dance—nothing was immune to its effects.

Moréas had proclaimed that Symbolism was hostile to objective description, declamation, or didactic teaching; the goal of the Symbolists was "the Idea," whose exact meaning remained vague. The point was "to depict not the thing but the effect it produces," as one of its proponents proclaimed.[10] The power and effect of such thought lay in the antidote it offered to the sterility of positivism.

Although associated especially with literature, Symbolism had an unmistakably Wagnerian dimension. The notions of using the great myths and fusing all the arts belonged to Wagner's *Gesamtkunstwerk*. In a hopelessly alienating and pessimistic world, a world being dramatically fragmented and compartmentalized by technology—bicycles and automobiles, telegraphs and telephones, railroads and their tracks, tunnels, and scaffolds—Symbolism offered hope for regaining lost unity and restoring "the natural and ancient links that man, as a thinking being, had established with the world."[11]

From its early focal points, Brussels and Paris, Symbolist ideas dispersed far and wide, carried back to homelands all over Europe by the young and by the printed word. In the process the ideas transformed and were themselves transformed as they combined and recombined with local attitudes and native trends. The Symbolists' affection for legends, sagas, ancient history, and national epics flowed naturally into the tributaries of national goals. For Finns struggling to formulate a national profile without isolating themselves from the vitalizing stream of contemporary thought, Symbolism presented an exquisite solution: an international rationale for nationalistic thought.[12] Symbolism showed how their nationalism served a higher purpose.

SYMBOLISM IN FINLAND

International Symbolist ideas had a direct conduit into Finland through the many young Finnish artists and writers who traveled to France to study.[13] After a stint in Paris preparing a doctoral thesis on Prosper Mérimée, Kasimir Leino (1866–1919, né Kasimir Agathon Lönnbohm), older brother of the more famous Eino, returned to Finland, where his lecture "New Trends in French Literature," delivered on November 9, 1891, jumpstarted his countrymen's fascination with Symbolist ideas. How readily the new thinking was adapted to the particular circumstances of the Finns was demonstrated by another Finn in Paris: the novelist Juhani Aho, who made the marvelous discovery that everyone has two native countries—one's own and France. The land of the Gauls had inspired him to make those Symbolist allusions to a "Golden Age" in Finland.[14]

Along with Finnish writers visiting Paris, the number of Finnish artists trooping into the city was legion: Väinö Blomstedt, Albert Edelfelt, Axel Gallén, Eero Järnefelt, Venny Soldan-Brofeldt, Beda Stjernschantz, Ellen Thesleff, Ville Vallgren, Georg Wettenhovi-Aspa, Emil Wikström, and more. The atmosphere, so different from Finland's, left few unmoved. As Blomstedt observed on arriving in the French capital in the autumn of 1891: "There is something new in the air right now in Paris. The art of ancient Assyria and Egypt has been elevated to an ideal."[15]

The alluring elements of mysticism, exoticism, and antiquity and their value for the creative imagination sparked similar sentiments among other members of Finnish intellectual circles. In early 1894 Adolf Paul wrote, somewhat weirdly, to Axel Gallén:

> The sphinx, the mother of the children of our souls, comes flying for an instant like a strange bird in a wonderful, overdone display of colors—for a moment it sits at our table, ready to fly away again in the next instant. And half mockingly, it tells us the most splendid sagas; it explains the most bizarre mysteries, sets jestingly before us the most adventurous predictions; it is the hermaphroditic soul in the whole entertainment, a sense of intoxication only that comes and flies away—with alcohol.[16]

While it would be a mistake to reduce the 1890s to a "Symbolist period" in Sibelius's life or in the lives of his artistic contemporaries for that matter, there can be no doubt that its ideas animated his own. The main themes underlying his works of these years all have connections to the wider backdrop of Symbolist thought, whose impulses provide a means of understanding the odd, even bizarre, conglomeration of Wagnerian crisis, Karelian enthusiasms, mystic orientalisms, fascination with death, and nationalistic expressions along with erotic and even supremely self-interested musical manifestations of the 1890s. There was the attempt to write an opera, *The Building of the Boat*, imagined on pompously recycled Wagnerian precepts. There were songs of exotic longing—

> I wish I were in Indialand
> and India were itself
> with pearls for stones and rubies for sand
> and castles that at a wave of Akbar's hand
> are dreamed up by a sacred river

—Gustaf Fröding's *Jag ville, jag vore*, which Sibelius set as op. 38, no. 5. There were new works on *Kalevala* myths. Even such clearly nationalist music as the numbers for the *Karelia tableaux* had conspicuous Symbolist elements. On a sketch for *Karelia*'s overture, Sibelius's red pencil scrawl reads: "A soul seeking peace." Not just idle doodlings these, for the composer crossed out "peace" and substituted "happiness." The text goes on: "Seeks but does not find. He feels tormented. He surrenders and tries to kill happiness. Bacchanal." And then, "I go in search of solitude by the side of a distant forest lake. It is evening. A lonely waterfowl [a swan?] sings sorrowfully."[17]

Soulful swans, forest scenes, and bacchanals—all were to be played out in the context of a remarkable band that posterity has called the Symposium.

HYVÄ VELI—THE SYMPOSIUM BROTHERHOOD

The circle is a well-established means for cultivating friendships and exchanging ideas. It also has deep and primitive roots: a group of men in a state of excitement whose fiercest wish is to be more, as Elias Canetti observed.[18] The circle involves rituals of sharing food and drink. It promotes feelings of power. And it promises a kind of safety in numbers that the individual alone does not possess.

From his student days Sibelius sought out circles of like-minded fellows in whose company he seemed to flourish. The Helsinki Leskovites had formed his chief social group in the late 1880s; the Euterpists would provide solace in the early twentieth century; thereafter, so would the Freemasons. In the early 1890s the circle occupying center stage among the Young Finns was christened the Symposium. The security of this group, Sibelius claimed later, "gave much to me at a time when I would otherwise have been more or less alone. The chance to trade thoughts with kindred souls animated by the same spirit and the same goals exerted on me a stimulating influence of the highest degree, strengthened me in my intentions, and gave me confidence."[19]

As is the nature of such groups, the Symposium circle was a changing constellation, shifting first one way and then another, a man now dominant moving to the group's edge and then back again. Yet even though the group's nucleus, so important to Sibelius, had begun to dissolve by 1894–95, the questions debated in the Symposium gatherings belonged to the central aesthetic and political concerns of the Young Finns. Religion, womankind, heroism, psychology, mythology, beauty, the *Kalevala*, Wagner, *Gesamtkunstwerk*, sexuality, creativity, and more spun together in a nocturnal web of sweetly scented tobacco, tinkling glasses, and trilling piano music. Themes from these diverse spheres took material form in Sibelius's and Armas Järnefelt's music and Kajanus's concert programs; in artworks by Axel Gallén, Pekka Halonen, Eero Järnefelt, and Magnus Enckell; and in the writings of Juhani Aho, J. H. Erkko, Arvid Järnefelt, and Eino Leino. The congruency of topics to which the diverse members gave their attention provides its own authentication of the group's power.

The Symposium circle has been given somewhat short shrift in accounts of the creative cycle of Sibelius's life, and indeed, its halcyon days were relatively short: from around the time of *Kullervo*'s premiere, in April of 1892, to November 1894, when Emperor Alexander III died unexpectedly. Yet all the major works from the years 1892 to 1896 and some thereafter, not to mention various compositional plans, some of which materialized only years later, can be traced to its aesthetic and philosophical discussions and to its fascination with such Symbolist notions as the occult, religious ecstasy, mystical self-communion, and Egyptian sphinxes.

The men gathered (for seldom were there respectable women) in the informal and lively way Strindberg described in *The Red Room*.[20] The elegant and elite Hotel Kämp has gone down in legend as the symbol of these evenings. There the publisher Wentzel Hagelstam slipped in to whisper his farewells that April of 1903 when he fled Finland to avoid arrest by Nikolai Bobrikov's soldiers.[21] But Kämp was the most expensive possible choice, a place where clients were expected to dress in white tie and tails. Notably, in relating these evenings to Karl Ekman, Sibelius mentioned instead the rococo setting at Catani's on the North Esplanade (overseen by its genial Italian host Giovanni ["John"] Catani, who had built the structure in 1890, and where Eino Leino was a regular, arriving early for breakfast and the morning paper); König's, on Mikaelsgatan (where only men were permitted to dine); the rustic artist-academic club Pirtti; and private homes.

At various times participants included Finland's leading artists, profoundest thinkers, and most prominent Young Finns: the Erkko brothers, Eero and Juhana Heikki (J. H.); the Brofeldt brothers (later called Aho), Pekka and Juhani; the Järnefelt brothers, Armas, Arvid, and Eero; the Swedes Adolf Paul and Louis Sparre; the poet Eino Leino; the multi-talented pianist, organist, song writer, opera pioneer, and music critic Oskar Merikanto, whose songs—largely set to poems in Finnish—fused folklike features with bel canto melodies and surpassed Sibelius's in popularity. There were also distinguished visitors such as the violinist Willy Burmester and pianist and the Liszt pupil Alfred Reisenauer (1863–1907). Benedictine flowed, cigar smoke wafted, music vibrated. Sibelius was wont to seat himself at the piano and, without regard for the passing hours, improvise for the assembled company.[22]

The circle generated endless stories, one of which is eventually repeated in one or more of its hundreds of variations to every visitor to Finland interested in the arts: Kajanus (or Järnefelt or Gallén or Leino or one of the others) left his compatriots at the Kämp for Saint Petersburg or a concert or some other faraway destination; on returning the next day to the table where all his colleagues still sat, the traveler was asked, What took you so long in the men's room? Although the story, which unaccountably even shows up in respected history books,[23] is probably apocryphal, the spirit that gave rise to it was not. For long, forgetful periods, time was suspended, and what mattered was com-

Plate 1. Martin Wegelius, *Oceanidernas sång* (*Song of the Oceanides*), 1868, autograph manuscript. The Sibelius Academy Library, Helsinki. Scan: Mikko Ikkala.

Plate 2. Axel Gallén,
*Kullervon sotaanlähtö
(Kullervo Departs for
War)*, 1901. Tempera
on canvas. Fresco in
Ylioppilastalo (the
University Student
House), Helsinki.
Ateneum Art Museum/
Central Art Archives.
Photo: Jukka Romu.

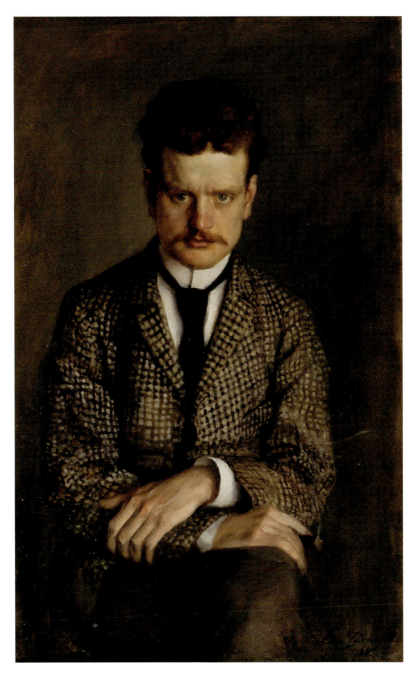

Plate 3. Eero Järnefelt, Sibelius in a checked jacket, 1892. Oil on canvas.
Private collection. Photo: Matias Uusikylä.

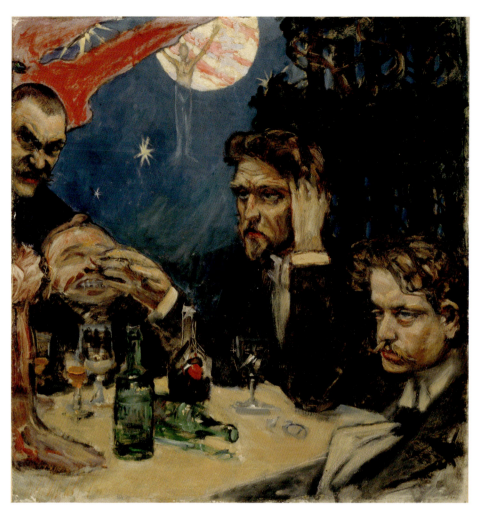

Plate 4. Axel Gallén, *Kajus-taflan* (*The Kajus Painting*), 1894. Oil on canvas. Gösta Serlachius Museum of Fine Arts, Mänttä, Finland/Central Art Archives. *Left to right*: Gallén, Oskar Merikanto, Robert Kajanus, Sibelius. Photo: Pirje Mykkänen.

panionship, serious discussion, and drinking. At the age of sixty, Sibelius was gravitating still to masculine gatherings (the Freemasons) and (alone) to the Kämp, about which he wrote into his diary, "The lemon table at the Kämp. The lemon, symbol of death—to the Chinese. However, Anna-Maria Lenngren sings, 'Buried with a lemon in the hand.' Such a blessing!"[24]

Sibelius's connections to certain members of the Symposium circle lasted a lifetime. With some of them, he undertook artistic ventures. He launched into an opera project with J. H. Erkko (who in 1895 had taken up the Kullervo story into a play of that title). He set Erkko's poems to music, as well as verses by Juhani Aho and Eino Leino. His relationship with the Järnefelt brothers was at once deeply personal and profoundly artistic. But the two members of the group who stood out in Finland's artistic life in general and in Sibelius's life in particular were Axel Gallén, the artist better known by his later name, Akseli Gallen-Kallela, whose ideas and works had conspicuous parallels to his own; and Robert Kajanus, founder of the Helsinki Orchestra. The glory days of the Symposium were the heyday of the Gallén-Kajanus-Sibelius triumvirate.

AXEL GALLÉN AND THE FINNISH RENAISSANCE

In 1885, at the time Sibelius enrolled at the Helsinki Music Institute, Axel Gallén had already been in Paris a year, studying art and "living in quite poor conditions," as the older artist Albert Edelfelt reported to his mother; "but little does it matter when one is nineteen and absolutely convinced one will become the leading painter in all the world."[25] The brazen young Gallén was even then building a reputation for cultivating revolutionary ideas and outrageous theories for art in Finland. Edelfelt continued, "He is living with a Norwegian, just as wild as he is. They're radicals, brave and bold." In 1889 Gallén returned to settle in Finland, at least for a time, and there to marry. He probably met Sibelius in the summer of 1889, when the composer spent at least some time in the company of the Järnefelt family in the countryside.[26]

The two men had much in common. Born in the same year into Swedish-speaking families, both were highly imaginative, ambitious, restless dreamers, determined to revolutionize their respective art worlds, and they had both been drawn into the nationalistic circle of Young Finns. They shared a fascination with the *Kalevala* and an enthusiasm for its homeland, Karelia. Both had spent their honeymoons in Karelian territory, and both had mined its treasures for their respective arts. Gallén, for his part, spoke persuasively and often about a "Finnish renaissance."

Yet despite the parallels, the two men were of vastly different fiber. Gallén, garrulous, full of life, charisma, and strong, freely expressed, opinions, filled up any space with the force of his personality. He was known to entertain his friends with mischievous imitations of the German Kaiser Wilhelm II and with his readiness for outlandish stunts. In Paris, the antics of Gallén and company (Eero Järnefelt, Emil Wikström, and the Norwegian Dörnberger) were familiar to the local police, for the visitors were wont to disturb the peace. It was the time of the Franco-Russian entente, and whenever the Nordic quartet was rounded up and commanded to identify themselves, the reply was always a cool "Alliance Franco-Russe!"[27]

A sly caricature the artist made of himself in 1890 shows a tall, slim man with an overlarge nose and a buzz haircut.[28] In point of fact, Gallén was handsome, handy, and virile. An avid sportsman and Finland's first alpine skier, he explored the Finnish wilderness on skis, a shotgun on his back. His sense of adventure earned him the title of the "artistic Stanley." Awesome stories spread about his feats. One tells of the time his canoe capsized in the middle of the sea; nothing fazed, he swam to shore and boarded a train for Malmi, only, in the nick of time, to realize that his train was on a collision course with an oncoming locomotive. "Quick as a dragonfly," the brave man launched himself through the window of the moving vehicle and landed—unscathed—on the nurturing Finnish earth.[29] True or false, the story is faithful to the character of the man, who was an early advocate of physical fitness and noticeably proud of his beautifully molded physique. On his fiftieth birthday, a Finnish sports magazine ran a feature article on Gallén in which his agility was likened to that of a panther.[30] Gallén—masculine, fit, dexterous—not only energized Finnish art; he embodied the very essence of what it meant to be Finnish.

By nature rebellious, larger than life, passionate, fanatical, and reckless, Gallén naturally gravitated to the Young Finns' radical circle. Their mouthpiece, *Päivälehti*, portrayed him in 1892 in unforgettable terms:

> Although he would be dressed in the latest Anglo-Parisian fashion—wide trousers, loose coat, elegant gloves, big floppy tie, a thick, silver-trimmed cane in his hand—or clad in high leather boots, sheepskin coat, fur-lined leather hat, wearing mittens, a gnarled stick in his hand, you know immediately from the gait, the height, the huge countenance visible from afar, and the snapping, twinkling eyes that it is Gallén coming.[31]

Gallén carried himself like a lord and had fantasies of nobility. His notebooks and correspondence preserve his dreams of being a knight-adventurer (of the Don Quixote type). He eventually built his own turreted castle, Tarvaspää, near Helsinki. His magnificent painting *Kullervo Departs for War* harks back to early Renaissance knighthood, an era that fascinated him: the fresco of this name in the Student House of the Imperial Alexander University bears a striking resemblance to the fresco by Simone Martini (ca. 1284–ca. 1344), *Guidoriccio da Fogliano*, that graces Siena's Palazzo Pubblica. The knight on horseback, his position, the direction of man and animal, the decorative appurtenances, even the startling blue of the background sky rendered Finnish what had once been medieval Italian seigneury.[32]

The light of self-assuredness shone brightly around Gallén. His superb rendering of contemporaries and bravura interpretations of the *Kalevala* gave Finland its face, created a uniquely Finnish art, and helped to create an identity for a nation just then in the process of becoming. His fantastical imagination and charisma attracted Sibelius, though he was too outsized, too competitive, too much Gallén to be an avid Sibelian supporter—he was, after all, the Axel around which the world should revolve. Instead, Gallén served a far more important role: he painted.

Those paintings glowed with sensual opulence and decadent content, bringing the men and ideas of the Symposium circle vividly to life. The brazen canvas that gave the group its name, *Symposion* (*The Symposium*), also called *Probleemi* (*The Problem*), and its companion, *Kajus-taflan* (*The Kajus Painting*), disgracefully showed Finland's finest in a state of either extreme inebriation or complete befuddlement (see plate 4). Wonderfully scandalous they were—as shocking as the *Kullervo* symphony. There sit Young Finns, the country's cultural present and future, sprawled with hooded eyes around tables strewn with wineglasses and liquor bottles, their revered heads wreathed in cigar smoke and unmistakably hallucinating bizarre, drug-induced fantasies. Weird sphinx-like wings undulate across the canvas of the *Symposium* and stretch sensuously along the wide gilded frame, vapors waft through the room, and a nude female ascends heavenward.

Improbably, Sibelius denied any need of Bacchus to fuel the Symposium discussions:

> Our seances were tremendously fruitful, any extravagance in the use of Bacchic favors not being at all necessary for deriving meaning and color. We let fantasy fly, thoughts play. The waves of discussion rose quite high. We talked about everything between heaven and earth, problems were flushed out and laid bare, but always in a spirit of optimism and liberation. We were going to make way for new ideas in every domain.[33]

High-minded language, that. (Of course, Kajanus wryly observed that Sibelius in his normal mood was like the rest of them when drunk.)[34] In any case, the mood of the Symposium evenings was created by the fortuitous mingling of Gallén's fantastic ideas ("It's a shame [he spends] more time philosophizing than on painting," Edelfelt had muttered), Kajanus's eloquent and often idealistic proclamations (Kajus being well-known for breast-beating pronouncements), and Sibelius's animated conversations, which veered from artful, ambiguous jesting to deepest seriousness.[35]

Yet there can be no mistake that theirs were philosophical discussions: Gallén's paintings gave proof of that too. As the artist's great-grandson has recently shown,[36] the precedent for two of the best-known works of this time, *The Kajus Painting* and *The Symposium*, was Peter Paul Rubens's *Four Philosophers with a Bust of Seneca* (1611–12), a precedent that makes an artist-as-philosopher interpretation inescapable: Gallén adopted the seating arrangement in Rubens's canvas, the depiction of friends as subject matter (although Rubens mixed the living and the dead), and even the inclusion and placement of the artist himself (Gallén leans out of the left corner, the very place Rubens appears in his *Four Philosophers*).

The fit among these three dominant artist-philosophers was not always an easy one. Gallén lorded over the less physically robust Sibelius. And as for Kajanus, he "dominated me completely," Sibelius grumbled about those years, although he—or rather, his compositions, as he realized—was a thorn in the flesh of those "rulers" (Kajanus and his sort).[37] The plaint was not just momentary self-pity; a long string of events bore out the friction in the none-too-perfect relationship. As early as the Vienna year Sibelius, in an irritatingly fawning letter to Kajanus, had pleaded: "Dear Brother, leave off all antipathy for me.—I am really your friend, so please be mine too!" Besides, he added in a postscript, "I won't live much longer, so you can risk it."[38] He could grovel when it was a question of getting a new work conducted. And for that, Kajanus was the man to know.

ROBERT KAJANUS: FINNISH NATIONALISM AND THE BIBLE

The later eclipse of Robert Kajanus's reputation by Sibelius's star has often obscured the firmament from the vantage point of the 1890s. Even Kajanus's own first biographer, Yrjö Suomalainen, who should have been his advocate, subscribed to the myth of great men harmoniously creating the nation:

> Robert Kajanus was completely convinced of Sibelius's greatness and for this reason he submitted to him, assuming the role of his faithful armor-bearer. Already at this time Kajanus had been faced with the task of considering the question: which is to be chosen, continuing his own composing or assuming the role of an apostle who spreads the new proclamation both in Finland and to the world? The decision which he reached was that his own composing could take second place, with interpreting Sibelius becoming his main purpose.[39]

Suomalainen added that on hearing a recent Sibelius composition at the Helsinki Music Institute, Kajanus grandly announced: "I was so charmed by what I heard then that I immediately decided: I shall not compose a note after this! But Wegelius broke my assertive promise: Don't be a fool! I left composing alone for ten or so years, but then I was unable to hold back any longer."[40]

Yet Suomalainen also quoted the modest man as saying, "Our influence on each other lasted until the Fifth Symphony. But after that [Sibelius] never asked me for advice in matters of orchestration" (evidently sending Sibelius into a fit of apoplexy).[41] And rather than stepping humbly aside when Sibelius was elected, fair and square, as the university's music director, Kajanus fought like a lion—and got himself instated instead. For the fact was, in the 1890s Robert Kajanus, conductor and founder of the Helsinki Philharmonic Orchestra, was the most powerful musical figure in Finland.

He came from the clan of Flodins (on his mother's side), of whom the best-known was the critic Karl. Proud, stern, and statuesque in appearance (some of his relatives attained prodigious heights), Kajanus cut a glamorous figure. When he stood before his three dozen or so men wielding his rapierlike baton of deadly ivory, he reigned omniscient. He was accustomed to being seen—and obeyed. His eyes pierced each player, his attention fastened on everything at once. At the end of each concert, Kajanus haughtily accepted the applause that was his due, an ancient victor receiving a salute. He ruled the world of orchestral music in Helsinki.[42] And nothing testified to that rule more dramatically than his "power show" in 1894 and 1895: *La damnation de Faust* by Hector Berlioz. In each of no fewer than eleven performances Kajanus conducted some 240 musicians, including harpists from Saint Petersburg and an operatic tenor from Mannheim, to bring off one of the most spectacular events in Finland's musical history.[43] His remarkable deeds extended to his private life: he was married no fewer than four times and along the way begot some eight children, three of whom became professional harpists.

Kajanus was furiously occupied with consolidating his musical command: recruiting and rehearsing musicians from other European centers; leading his orchestra in two regular concert series, popular and serious programs; cultivating links with other Nordic musical circles as well as with key imperial administrators; and establishing his own orchestra school (a rival of Wegelius's music institute), for which he hired Sibelius. No wonder Gallén made Kajanus the central figure in paintings that captured the mood, the aura, and the characters at the forefront of Helsinki's cultural and artistic life, the paintings whose finest representatives are *The Kajus Painting* and *The Symposium*. In neither work does Sibelius occupy the central position. It is Kajanus who sits at the head of the table—in Gallén's words, the master before the pupils.[44] Gallén, clearly among the worshipful, positioned Kajanus to occupy the light and draw the attention.

The others—Sibelius, Gallén, and Oskar Merikanto (whose head was famously modeled on a rutabaga)—are placed in positions secondary to the conductor. Especially striking is *The Kajus Painting*, in which Sibelius slouches with bleary and staring eyes while Kajanus dominates the table, contemplative and commanding. His place not only suggests his role as the circle's *symposiarchos*, it also befits the founder and conductor of an orchestra that for over a decade had succeeded where others had failed.

Although *The Kajus Painting* was once believed to have been a study for *The Symposium*, Janne Gallen-Kallela-Sirén has recently shown that the work is an independent composition begun in the autumn of 1893.[45] Gallen-Kallela-Sirén makes the case that *The Kajus Painting*, with its wondrous images in the sky, its darkened moon, its blood-red clouds, its bewitched young men, alludes not to the *Kalevala*, but to that other great pillar of Finnish identity, the Bible, and specifically, to a passage from Acts 2 (quoted here from the King James Version):

> 2:17: And it shall come to pass in the last days, saith God, I will pour out of my Spirit upon all flesh: and your sons and your daughters shall prophesy, and your young men shall see visions, and your old men shall dream dreams:
>
> 2:18: And on my servants and on my handmaidens I will pour out in those days of my Spirit; and they shall prophesy:
>
> 2:19: And I will shew wonders in heaven above, and signs in the earth beneath; blood, and fire, and vapour of smoke:
>
> 2:20: The sun shall be turned into darkness, and the moon into blood, before that great and notable day of the Lord come.

Executed at a time when Gallén was occupied with other biblical themes—*Ristiinnaulittu* (*The Crucified*), *Jeesus ja kiusaaja* (*Christ and the Tempter*), *Tuonelan joella* (*At the River of the Dead*), *Ad astra* (depicting the Resurrection)—and was expounding on biblical subjects in his correspondence, this painting and its visual symbols show powerful correspondences to the passage. In Gallen-Kallela-Sirén's stunning interpretation, Gallén's vision in *The Kajus Painting* unites the artistic avant-garde with biblical and nationalist themes.

Religion figured large among the Symposium discussion topics. How could it not among a group of rebellious young men brought up to be good Lutherans? As one of them, Juhani Aho, later had one of his characters remark in the novel *Kevät ja takatalvi* (*Spring and the Late Frosts*, 1906), biblical and *Kalevala* elements "must be amalgamated into one great Finnish culture, which one day will conquer even the world."[46] The leading Symposium members shared an interest in the Virgin Mary—Marjatta, as she is called in the *Kalevala* (improbably, Gallén even named his first-born child "Virgin

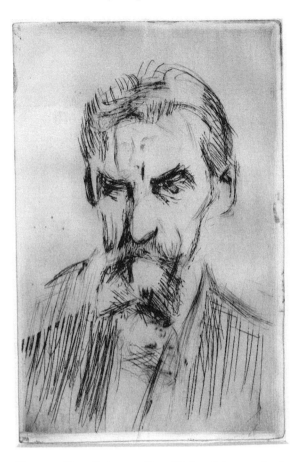

Figure 9.3. Hugo Simberg, etching of Robert Kajanus, undated.
The Sibelius Museum.

Mary"—Impi Marjatta). Between 1891 and 1895 Gallén was working on a triptych he eventually called *Marjatta* (*The Mary Myth*), its central panel showing Mary with the Christ child in her arms; on the right, Väinämöinen departs Finland in that famous boat, and on the left, to the strains of a Kullervo lookalike playing a birch-bark horn, a group of maidens cavorts while a brilliant red swan floats in the foreground. The jumble of pagan, Christian, and *Kalevala*-esque belonged to the nature of the group's ruminations and to their art. Gallén may have intended to join his *Lemminkäinen's Mother* canvas to his *Mary Myth* but changed his mind when he realized that it upset the balance between heathen and orthodox.[47]

These ideas did not pass Sibelius by. He too had great plans for a composition on the *Kalevala*'s Marjatta tale, although the idea did not begin to ripen until 1902, maturing in 1905, after which he abandoned the project.[48] Shades of death and resurrection also haunted its libretto, fashioned by Jalmari Finne (1874–1938): a son dies and is brought back to life by his loving mother with the intercession of nature in the form of an eagle descending on a sunbeam.

The Symposium triumvirate even shared quasi-religious experiences outside their highly charged evenings of swilling wine and spouting wisdom. Around the end of the century Kajanus and Sibelius attended the christening ceremony of Axel and Mary Gallén's children, Kirsti (born in 1896) and Jorma (born in 1898; little Impi Marjatta had died in 1895, barely four years old). In the woodland setting of Ruovesi, Sibelius improvised chorale variations at the piano, blissfully unmindful of the other chorale tune being sung by the bass-voice "choir," Kajanus and Mikko Slöör, Mary's brother. When the pastor tried to baptize Kirsti, she objected in no uncertain terms: "Go away! I've already washed!"[49]

Those who knew Kajanus knew that his religious connections ran deep. One of his brothers, Herman Kajanus (who was also an amateur composer), was a Lutheran minister who served the Saint Petersburg Finns at the Swedish Church of Saint Catherine.[50] But it was more than that. The very face of Robert Kajanus made people think of Jesus Christ. This was not just wishful Finnish thinking: observers in other Nordic lands noticed the resemblance.[51] Finnish artists turned Kajanus into a religious icon. Emil Wikström carved a massive reddish-gray granite head of the conductor that can only be described as Christlike (begun in 1906, it was not completed until 1914).

Not everyone, it must be admitted, approached the great man with reverence. The artist Hugo Simberg (1873–1917), one of Gallén's students, made a portrait of Kajanus in which the conductor jarringly resembles Rasputin (see fig. 9.3). Kajanus the Christ or Robert the Devil? Sibelius would have occasion to know them both.

ᔕ 10 ᔖ

Of Sagas and Springtime

THE SAGAS

It was just at this time, when Gallén, Kajanus, and Sibelius were bonding in long evenings of drink and philosophy, that Kajanus evidently pointed out the value of having something new for the Helsinki Orchestra's regular repertoire. The demanding, five-movement *Kullervo*, requiring chorus and soloists (and added rehearsal time) in addition to a large orchestra, was hardly suitable for frequent performances by the small Helsinki ensemble. Thus was *En saga* born—or perhaps reborn, because there is an unusual consistency in Sibelius's recollections that *En saga* started life as a chamber work. The grouping varies—from seven to eight to nine instruments, depending on the telling; the musical sources that would illuminate these stages seem not to have survived.[1] Yet evidently the germ of the work at least was already in existence.

Like the Kullervo myth, which spawned dramatic plays, poems, sculptures, paintings, frescoes, tone poems, and a symphony, ideas and enthusiasms about a saga figured among the shared interests of the Symposium group and gave rise to parallel literary, artistic, and musical manifestations. Right after its premiere on February 16, 1893, Gallén "interpreted" the work in a bizarre watercolor: a knobby apple tree sheltering a devilish-looking creature, with a glittering shower of snowflakes raining over scampering rats. The watercolor was eventually fitted into the left side of a triptych, with a portrait of Sibelius (from one of the Symposium paintings) on the right and a blank space below. There Sibelius was supposed to add something from *En saga*'s score: "les parfums, les couleurs et les sons se répondent."[2] Perhaps the Symbolist correspondences were just too far-fetched: for whatever reason, Sibelius never felt compelled to add any musical notation to the painting (see plate 5).

Sibelius revised *En saga* in 1902 and Kajanus conducted it in early November. Not long thereafter, Saint Petersburg–born Samuli Suomalainen (1850–1907), a newspaperman and member of the *Päivälehti* circle, published a literary interpretation of the piece. It appeared in his book of short stories and essays entitled *Andante, akkordeja iltahämyssä* (*Andante, Chords in Twilight* [Helsinki: Otava, 1903]), dedicated to Jean Sibelius. The several tales there with musical titles—"Impromptu," "Sydämeni laulu," and "Aleksis Kiven satu" ("Aleksis Kivi's Tale")—hint provocatively at Sibelian connections, given that Sibelius had written a set of six impromptus in 1893 and made a setting of Kivi's poem *Sydämeni laulu* (*Song of my Heart*) in 1898. Yet it was in "Aleksis Kivi's Tale" that there appeared to be more truth than fiction: a Sibelius-like young composer, "Johannes Seppälä," nicknamed "Janne," discusses revisions to a score called *En saga* with a conductor friend, "Robert Kajava." In the story, the tone poem is based on an episode from Kivi's famous novel *Seven Brothers*, depicting a hunt for a lynx. The creature tries to save itself by climbing a spruce tree but is shot. In fury, the tree shakes its branches, raining down sparkling snow upon the dying animal.[3]

The similarities between Gallén's and Suomalainen's renderings of *En saga* are so striking as to suggest that they were not merely coincidental.[4] Moreover, in the early 1890s Gallén was in the grip of a Kivi passion (an author to whom he had been introduced by none other than Eero Järnefelt, another Symposium participant).[5] In Gallén's usual voluble style he shared his latest enthusiasm with his companions, even translating passages of Kivi into Swedish for Adolf Paul. Thus, the connection between Sibelius's *En saga* and Kivi's lynx hunt may not be at all fanciful, at least in representing the idea world from which the various *En saga*s sprang.

It was an idea world resonant with national values. Already in *Finland framstäldt i teckningar*, Topelius had used that poetic word "saga" as a synonym for the "ancient history" of the Finns.[6] And that idea world was widely shared among members of the Symposium circle. When the handsome volume entitled *Finland i 19de seklet* (*Finland in the 19th Century*, edited by Leo Mechelin) was published in the year of *En saga*'s première, among its illustrations was a winter landscape by Eero Järnefelt: there a lynx crouches in the top of a tree, stalked by a hunter creeping over a snowbank (see fig. 10.1). The next year Adolf Paul penned a short story entitled "En saga ifrån ödemarken ("A Saga out of the Wilderness"), dedicated to Gallén (who designed the cover for a German edition), allegedly based on an episode Gallén had related involving a bear hunt (Paul was as convinced that he would do great things with Gallén as he was sure that he and Sibelius would be world-famous together).[7]

Gallén's writings at this time were filled with references to sagas. "In the world, in life, and in nature," he noted in a sketchbook in 1894, "there is nothing other than *beautiful sagas* and when the door is opened, step in and fill your soul to the full."[8] He and his student Hugo Simberg exchanged similar thoughts, and the latter's creation of a dreamlike painting entitled *Satu* (*Saga*), executed in 1895, signified a move away from naturalism and toward an art based on fantasy and feeling.[9]

VINTERLANDSKAP AF EERO JÄRNEFELT.

Figure 10.1. Eero Järnefelt, *Vinterlandskap* (*Winter Landscape*). Reproduced in *Finland i 19de seklet* (Helsingfors, 1893). The National Library of Finland.
Photo: Kari Timonen.

What is striking about these synchronicities is not only their simultaneity with the point in time when Sibelius's *En saga* was created, but also that the same idea world suggested itself even much later, to the ever-intuitive American critic Olin Downes (1886–1955); on hearing *En saga* in the 1930s, Downes rashly proclaimed, "When I hear this music I avow a carnal desire to discard the soft fat ways of life; to set out in oilskins, or something, for somewhere, to discover at least a desperate polar bear bent on conflict!"[10]

Oddly, in the 1890s Sibelius himself related his new work to the visual imagery not of any Finnish artists or Nordic tales, but to that of a Swiss painter, Arnold Böcklin (1827–1901), who was supplying the Symbolists with some of their most potent images. In a letter to Adolf Paul, dated December 10, 1892, Sibelius had announced: "I have a 'Saga' ready for orchestra. You ought to be attracted by it. It's delirious. I was thinking of Böcklin's pictures [when I composed it]. He does paint the air too bright, the swans too white, and the sea too blue and so on."[11] The wide appeal of Böcklin for enthusiasts of Symbolism appeared to rest on his being "one of the very few in whom the myth-building imagination of prehistoric peoples has arisen anew in our bustling, practical era: one of those who feel what the primitive German [*Urgermanen*] was feeling in the holy forests at twilight."[12] Although Böcklin's myth-building imagination may well have inspired Sibelius, one wonders if the mention of Böcklin was a Sibelian feint meant to divert attention from a too-obvious literary connection.

Yet whatever else can be said about it (and much has been), *En saga* is an extremely personal work. Sibelius eventually admitted that *En saga* had a subjective content (what composition does not?):

> Of all my works *En saga* is psychologically one of the deepest. I could almost even say that it contains my whole youth. It is an expression of a certain soul state. At the time I wrote *En saga*, I was experiencing very much that was distressing. In no other work have I revealed myself as in *En saga*. For this reason all interpretations are, of course, for me quite alien.[13]

Nearly half a century had passed between the time *En saga* was composed and this "explanation." Moreover, Sibelius, who was talking with Santeri Levas, probably related his recollection in Swedish. Levas published his conversations with the composer in Finnish, and his words are here rendered in English. Both the lapse of time and the language factors restrict our ability to understand fully what Sibelius was trying to convey, assuming that he himself knew what he had thought and felt decades earlier (a stretch in itself). The phrase "a certain soul state" has often been quoted, for it seems to sum up the essence of the work. Levas quotes Sibelius as having used the word *sieluntila*, literally, "soul situation."[14] Together with the next sentence—"I was experiencing very much that was distressing"—the conversation brings up the question of what on earth Sibelius could have meant. He had just married, to all appearances very happily, and neither his teaching nor his home life contained anything we know of that could be considered truly upsetting. Yet there *was* one thing distressing young, artistic, Symbolist-oriented Finns: that musical Goliath, Richard Wagner.

RICHARD WAGNER AND THE FINNS

Sibelius had seen his first Wagner operas in Berlin. After two evenings experiencing *Tannhäuser* and *Die Meistersinger*, he had written to Wegelius: "I've heard Meistersinger and Tannhäuser and am completely out of my mind. This music is just great. When we meet I'll tell you more about my impressions and what I felt. I had such a strange mixture of astonishment, disappointment, exaltation, and whatever."[15] It would have been difficult to find a more passionate Wagnerite in Finland than Martin Wegelius. Wegelius had attended the Bayreuth Festival's inaugural concerts in 1876 and reported on the events for the *Helsingfors Dagblad* (Finland's "first modern newspaper").[16] He had held lectures on the *Ring* cycle, with the pianist Karl Ekman Sr. performing the music examples. He wrote a biography of the master, though it remained unpublished. And he did what came to him so naturally—he organized. He founded a Finnish Wagner Society that lasted long enough for his *Näcken*, on which Sibelius collaborated, to be performed at one of its concerts.

Another leading Helsinki musician, the Danzig-born Richard Faltin, had also been along on that Bayreuth trip. Yet it was Robert Kajanus, Wegelius's archrival, who held the title of the first Finn to introduce Wagnerian musical style into his musical compositions. He did it with aplomb and Finnish mythology—and as early as 1881. His *Kullervon kuolema* (also called *Kullervon surumarssi* [*The Death of Kullervo* or *Kullervo's Funeral March*]) mingled unmistakably Wagnerian chromatic language with the folk song *Voi äiti parka ja raukka!* (*O Mother, So Pitiable and Poor!*). And his symphonic poem *Aino*, a Wagner-Liszt-*Kalevala* hybrid, allegedly opened Sibelius's eyes, or, more accurately, his ears, to similar possibilities.

Those born in Sibelius's generation also carried the torch for Wagner. It was well-known that Aino Järnefelt's brother Armas was as fanatical about Wagner as their sibling Arvid was about Tolstoy. After hearing Wagner in Berlin in 1890, Armas Järnefelt described his zealous reaction as ardently as any lover: "When Wagner came into my life, it came like a fever which caught a man in an overwhelming, uncritical ecstasy, and which cannot be compared to anything other than an ardent falling-in-love, which neither judges nor reconsiders, neither hears nor sees."[17] Needless to say, this Finn's works had a decidedly Wagnerian tone.

Wagnerian themes also wove through the Symposium discussions. And not just among the professional musicians. Gallén was wont to refer to his famous painting *Lemminkäi-nen's Mother* as his *Götterdämmerung*.[18] J. H. Erkko planned to collaborate with Sibelius on a Wagner-style opera, based on Nordic myth. Sibelius's love/hate reaction to Wagner thus did not take place in a vacuum. Its most acute and well-documented effects occurred in the years when the Symposium circle exerted its greatest influence—1892 to 1894.

It was only at the end of that time, in the summer of 1894, that Sibelius visited Bayreuth. If his letters can be believed, he immersed himself fully in the scores of the music dramas, including *Tannhäuser*, *Lohengrin*, and *Die Walküre*. Yet it was *Parsifal* that shook him. Before *Parsifal*, he had thought himself dried up (at the advanced age of twenty-nine). Now he realized the sap rose in him yet. His first words to Aino were: "Aino darling! I have just heard Parcival [*sic*]. *Nothing* in the world has ever made such an impression on me; it quite moves my innermost heartstrings. I had thought I was already a dead tree, but no, such is not the case."[19] The botanical metaphor was not original with Sibelius. It belonged to the Young Finns' vocabulary in the early 1890s, part of the ideology of awakening, growth, and rebirth. Eero Erkko had used a similar figure of speech in the very first issue of *Nuori Suomi* in 1891: "[The Young Finns party] has arisen just like a new branch from the side of an old pine tree."[20]

Parsifal, with its dimensions both religious and heroic, swan-rich and nationalistic, sent Sibelius into a tailspin of mingled ecstasy, self-doubt, and the snobbish criticism born of insecurity. Trotting between Munich and Bayreuth, he heard *Die Meistersinger*, the *Ring* operas (except *Das Rheingold*), *Tristan*, and another *Parsifal*. He had to reconsider his own opera, whose efforts now seemed feeble and inauthentic. At one moment he was finding "everything familiar and clear." At another he was finding fault with everything—music far too calculated, ideas that sounded "manufactured" (an ironic echo of Goldmark's criticism of Sibelius himself). And the contrived reverence! Droskies in which Wagner allegedly sat designated "historical"! The faithful worshipping at the shrine of the Master! The true believers acting as if they were receiving Holy Communion![21]

Yet Wagner's example had already challenged Sibelius earlier. Had he not created a kind of Finnish *Siegfried* in *Kullervo*, his operatic symphony featuring brother-sister incest? In 1893 the projected opera plan with J. H. Erkko could hardly have sounded more Wagnerian. Not only was it to have a libretto fashioned out of Nordic myth, but his ruminations about its very essence shamelessly regurgitated *Oper und Drama*:

> I must first explain in a few words what I have realized, after going through great sorrows, about music. I believe that music by itself, that is, absolute music, cannot satisfy us. It certainly arouses feelings and emotions, but something is

always left unsatisfied in our souls; we always ask "For what reason." Music is like the woman who can only become pregnant by a man. This man is Poësis. Tones attain their real power only when guided by poetic meaning. In other words, when text and tone unite.[22]

Now the time had come to perform the ritual that virtually every composer of Sibelius's generation would have to carry out: laying Wagner to rest.

Jean Sibelius was by no means alone in being thrown into a crisis ignited in the fiery furnace of Symbolist frenzy and Wagnerian angst. For many artists, the experience forced a complete renewal, a vast change in feeling and thinking; for some, it provoked a religious crisis, usually filled with mysticism and even tinged with theosophy or Catholicism.[23] In his case, Sibelius wrote of "great sorrows" and of "very much that was distressing" at this time (although with Sibelius, you could never be entirely sure—melodrama, irony, and nervous theatrics belonged to his very nature[24]).

Out of this disturbing welter came *En saga*. It bore all the hallmarks of its troubled birth.

TONE POEMS: A MUSICAL SOLUTION FOR A NATIONAL AGENDA

Part of Wagner's appeal to Finns in an era awash with nationalist aspirations and Symbolist impulses was his rejuvenating use of ancient myth. The crucial concept of ancient Finnishness ran through educated Finnish society during the 1890s, reflected in the importance given episodes from the *Kalevala* and Finland's early history as the appropriate sources for building a national art.[25] *En saga*'s title directly reflects that belief. No one could doubt that "a saga" alluded to something—a myth or a fairy tale, and surely a Nordic one—but exactly what? Did that enigmatic Swedish name bear some allusion to the Finnish *Kalevala*? The Grimm brothers? The Icelandic eddas? The very ambiguity belonged to Symbolism's veiled nature. More definite was Wagner's appeal for his spectacular use of the orchestra. And *En saga* delivers stunning orchestral passages—to the eye as well as to the ear. Those subdivided string arpeggios, for instance. Against the background of their sixteenth notes strides forth a manly theme in bassoons, cellos, and basses, its orchestration bearing striking similarities to the *Vorspiel* of *Parsifal* (see exx. 10.1 and 10.2). The correspondences resonate not only in the textures, but also in aspects of instrumentation—and in the sense of deep reverence in the face of the unknown.

Not least of Wagner's appeal was his overt nationalism. To devise a Finnish music drama would surely be among the highest and noblest of endeavors, the ultimate mani-

EXAMPLE IO.I. SIBELIUS, *EN SAGA*, MM. 34–41.
© BREITKOPF & HÄRTEL, WIESBADEN.

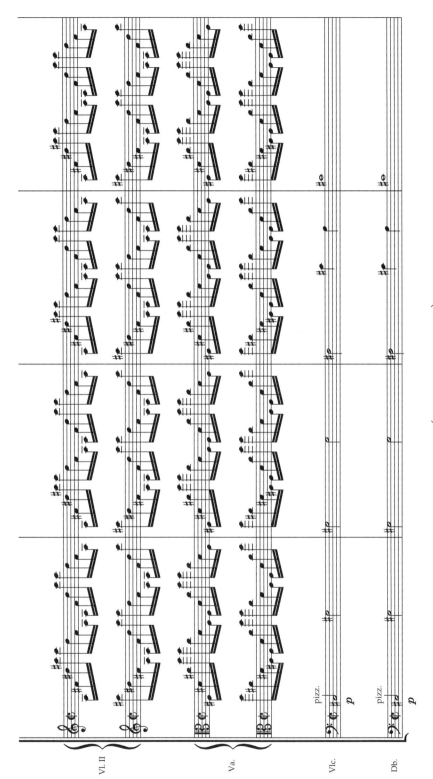

EXAMPLE 10.1. (CONTINUED ON NEXT PAGE)

EXAMPLE 10.1. (CONTINUED)

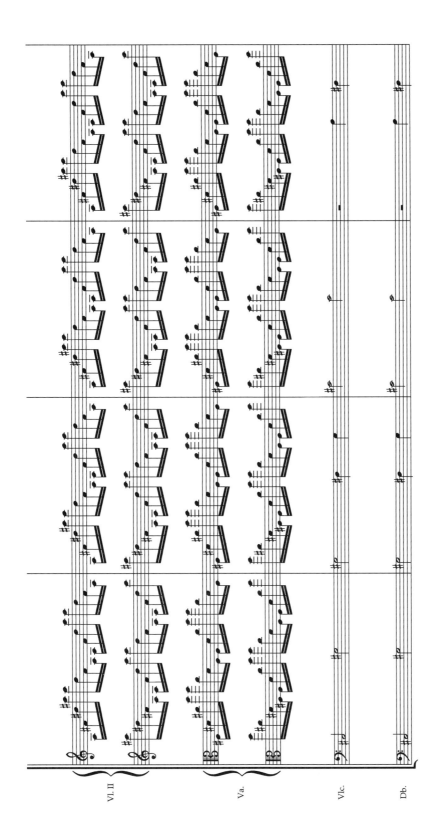

EXAMPLE 10.2. RICHARD WAGNER, *PARSIFAL*, VORSPIEL, MM. 6—11.

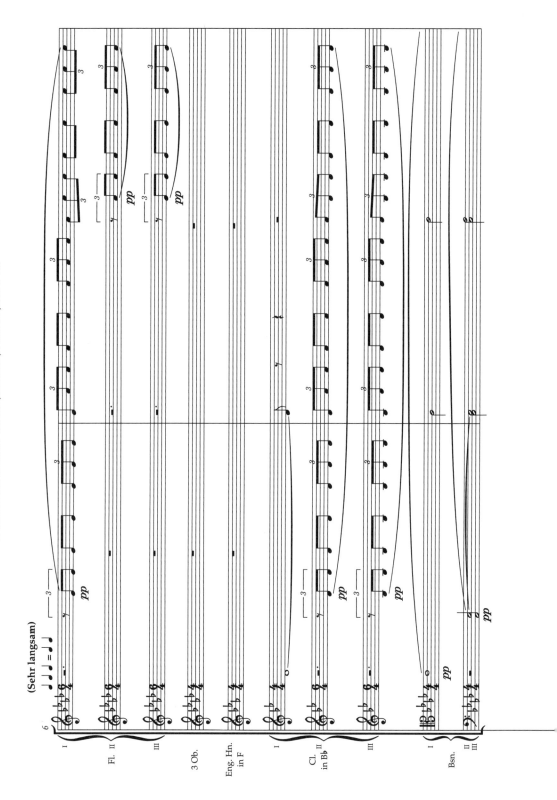

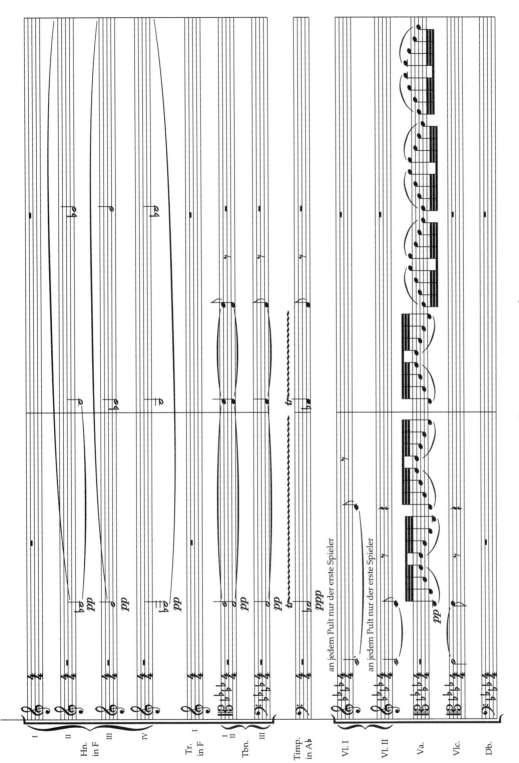

EXAMPLE 10.2. (CONTINUED ON NEXT PAGE)

EXAMPLE 10.2. (CONTINUED)

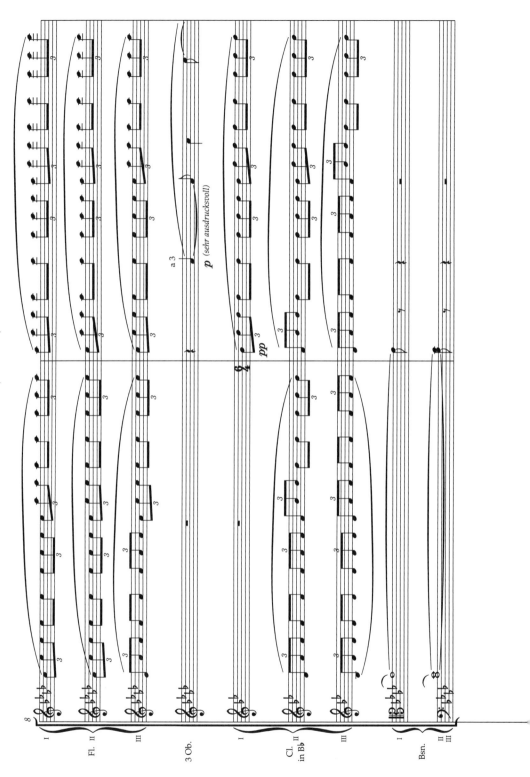

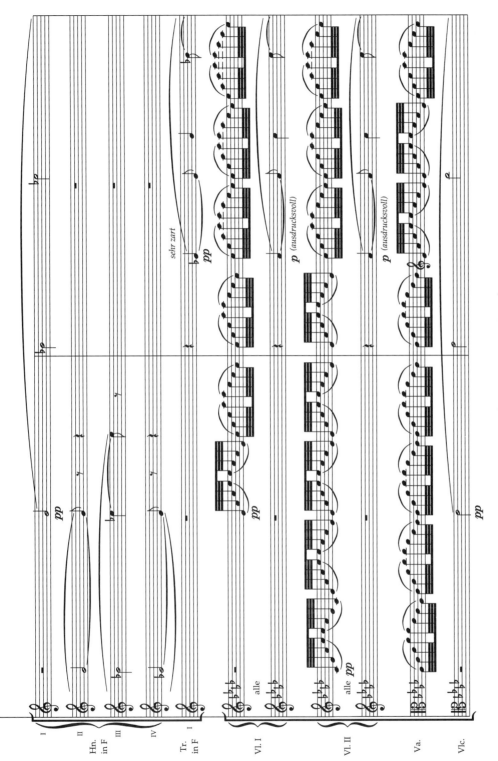

EXAMPLE 10.2. (CONTINUED ON NEXT PAGE)

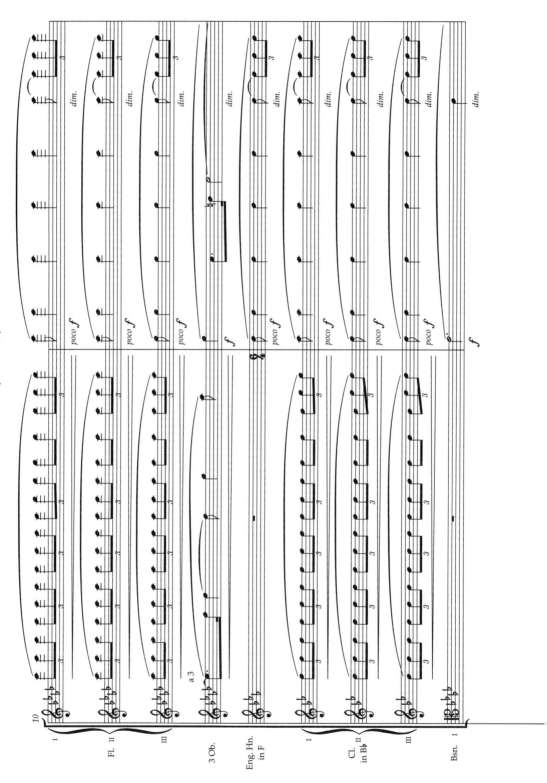

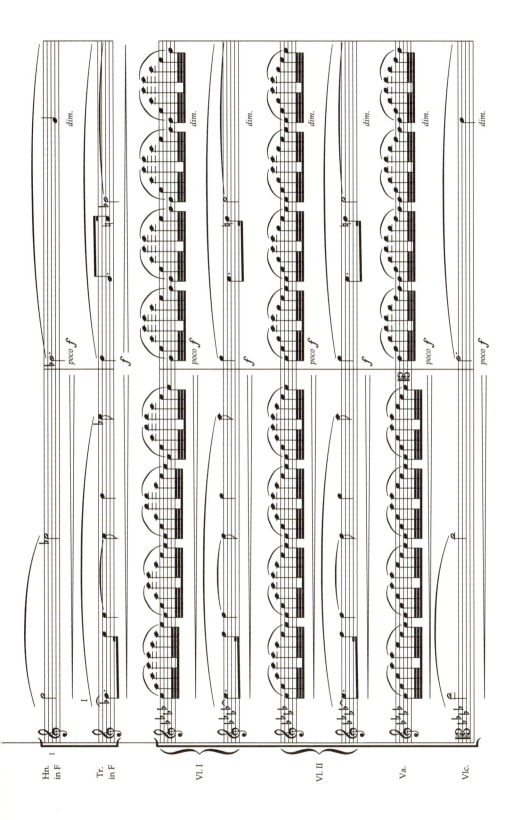

festation of that grand ideal "through the national to the all-European." And Sibelius, whose love of literature very nearly equaled his love of music, seemed the perfect composer to bring about a Finnish national music drama. Throughout much of his creative life, from the setting of that youthful libretto *Ljunga Wirginia*, written by his schoolmate Walter von Konow (1866–1943), to the abandoned plan for *The Building of the Boat* and the sadly unsuccessful *Maid in the Tower*, Sibelius entertained operatic dreams. But for a Finn, there were decided obstacles—and the central one was language.

In what tongue would a composer raised on Swedish-language poets and Lutheran Bible verses, whose solo songs are musical jewels refracting the beauties of Swedish-language poetry, compose his operas? The Young Finns, to which group Sibelius belonged by enthusiasm and marriage, resolutely promoted the Finnish language. But where, in late nineteenth-century Europe, was the market for opera in Finnish? Finland itself did not even have a regular opera company. Worse, for a composer with his eye on the world stage, it hardly seemed likely that Finnish-language operas would succeed as exports to Germany, the land of musical milk and honey, or to England, however sympathetic its audiences later proved to his symphonies. Singers would quail before the language, choruses cringe, audiences flee. Swedish, with its intimidating *å*'s, *ä*'s, and *ö*'s, was hardly any better. German, which Sibelius spoke and wrote, though not without error, might have been an option, but what German literature would have appealed to him? In composing well over a hundred solo songs in the course of a lifetime, he turned to German poems only nine times.

And so Sibelius turned away from opera. Instead, for the first time, he composed a symphonic poem, a "poetic solution" for instrumental music and a genre associated with advancing nationalism, albeit of the Austro-German sort.[26] Deeply rooted in literature and legend, those prescriptions for retrieving a national art, the symphonic poem was the ideal vehicle for conveying wordless nationalist aspirations and also for combining them with the Symbolist cult of the self. Sibelius claimed, "I have, I think, found myself again, musically speaking. I've discovered so many facts. I think that I'm really a music painter and poet. What I mean is that Liszt's view of music is closest to me. That symphonic poem (I meant 'poet' in that sense)."[27] The mention of Liszt may have been another feint—it was Richard Strauss, as Sibelius well knew, who was the kaiser of the *Tondichtung*. But the idea of being a "music painter and poet" stayed with him: two and half decades later Sibelius was describing himself as "poeta laureatus (♩)," the quarter note clarifying exactly what he was a poet of.[28]

There were, of course, those who disparaged the symphonic poem and "Liszt's view of music," men like the Russian critic German Avgustovich Larosh (1854–1904). Larosh mockingly called the newfangled genre a combination of "long sequences in unknown tonalities, fermatas, instrumental recitatives, colossal rumbling over a diminished-seventh chord, incomplete phrases transposed from one tone to another, and the obligatory tam-tam."[29] Others recognized the potential of the tone poem for conveying the experience of innermost being. Richard Pohl (1826–1896), critic and champion of music of the future, had credited Franz Liszt with developing "symphonic lyricism" and creating a genre that strives "through the medium of music toward the goal to which lyric poetry aspires, that of self-expression, the evoking of a human consciousness and its experiences."[30] In no other type of music do music and poetry come as close to Symbolist ideals as in tone poems, which evoke correspondences only hinted at, achieve "fluidity," and mingle the separate experiences of the senses in "perceptible surfaces created to represent their eso-teric affinities with the primordial Ideals" (to borrow the words of the Symbolist Mani-festo's author Moréas). The stream of consciousness that characterizes human thought and that James Joyce began adopting into literature found its musical flow in the lyricism of the symphonic poem.

Herein lies *En saga*'s deepest mystery and possibly its most important meaning: self-absorption in an era of collective aspiration. In a certain and very deep sense, the national awakening was about the self. Nationalism is nearly always a means of achieving self-definition along with the collective goal. In depicting and cultivating what was Finnish, nineteenth-century Finns were striving to identify themselves, seeking and finding value and meaning as individuals in a drastically changing world. And recourse to the cult of the self was the "only possible response to the threat posed to fin-de-siècle man's narcis-sism by the invasion of an autonomous technical world that functioned quite separately from him and that was neither the reflection of his being, nor even the instrument of his power, but the cause of his extinction."[31] In its very privateness, its expression of one man's state of mind, *En saga*, like a lyric poem, "unostentatiously lets us into the secret of a man's life," as Thoreau once observed of poetry; it represents an attempt by its cre-ator to tell us a parable about himself; as has also been said of poets, "Is it not true that what we have is *expression*, and what is expressed is something tissued out of the inner-most being of the poet, and therefore symbolic of that poet?"[32]

Out of the stuff of national aspirations Sibelius had once again found the materials for weaving a tapestry of superlative quality.

THE SPRINGTIME

The fabric of life, whether a society's or an individual's, warms the mind according to its texture, the quality of its filaments, the richness of its warp and woof. The layers of nineteenth-century Finnish life can be tissued out of a variety of sources, not least its public occasions, which give a distinct feel of its threads. Two public occasions of national importance that took place in the spring of 1894 stand out in the weave, and both involved music.

On April 29, 1894, a splendid ceremony unfolded on Helsinki's Senate Square. In the early morning hours scores of university students in their distinctive white caps (the *mössa* adorned with a small lyre) began gathering on the steps of the great Nicholas Church. Hundreds of spectators gravitated to the scene. Officials arrived, musicians grouped, and finally the imposing statue of Emperor Alexander II, the work of Walter Runeberg (1838–1920), a son of the great poet, was unveiled. Music sounded—hymns of Arvid Genetz and Pacius's *Suomen laulu*; impassioned cries rang out—"Eläköön" (Long Live [Finland!]); and speeches droned on by the likes of Leo Mechelin and others. The entire front page of *Päivälehti* was dedicated to reporting the ceremony, complete with the full texts of the eulogies delivered and words to the hymns sung. Gallén had refused to attend a reception being held for the sculptor, citing his overpowering loathing of Helsinki. Still, in justifying himself to Robert Kajanus on May 16, 1894, his tone was unmistakable in its recognition of the historic ceremony in honor of the "good" emperor, Alexander II.[33]

A second public occasion, almost two months later, took place nowhere near Helsinki. All Finland, it seemed, had moved to Vasa, the seaside town where Sibelius's in-laws lived and the province of which Alexander Järnefelt was then governor. The draw was the eighth song festival sponsored by the Kansanvalistusseura, whose promotion of music festivals to advance the national mission was proving outstandingly successful. The driving force behind the festivals was the KVS's evangelical-minded secretary, Axel August Granfelt (1846–1919). (He was also the *primus motor* behind Finnish prohibition; in 1883–84 he had founded the Friends of Temperance.) Granfelt's zeal was amply on display in public exhortations to his fellow Finns: "Let our festivals be patriotic, leading and feeding the pure national spirit, festivals in which an important place is given to singing and playing. Let them first of all be national, and only then let them be song festivals."[34]

Granfelt was as good as his stirring words. He worked diligently to promote the festivals that had been part of KVS's activities since 1884. Sibelius had already participated in one of them in 1889, with his Allegro for brass septet and triangle. Now, in June 1894, Finland's finest in the realm of composition—Wegelius, Kajanus, Sibelius, Armas Järnefelt, and Faltin—were to conduct works of their own for the public's enlightenment. For Sibelius, an added frisson lay in the inevitable comparison that would be made with his brother-in-law, the composer and conductor Armas Järnefelt.

The magnitude of the Vasa Festival lay partly in its sheer length—a full week. The

Helsinki correspondents reported to the capital daily on festival events.[35] The program announced for June 21, 1894, when Sibelius was to premiere his contribution, showed how forcefully the profile of the national agenda was being shaped and reinforced by Finland's musicians and composers.

Vasa Festival Program, June 21, 1894

I.

1. Chorale—Martin Luther
2. Swedish-language Festival Speech—J. W. Runeberg
3. *The Sixth of May Cantata*—Martin Wegelius
4. Finnish-language Festival Poem—Kasimir Leino
5. *Aino*, Symphonic Poem—Robert Kajanus
6. *Landkjending*, for male chorus and soloist—Edvard Grieg[36]

II.

7. *Improvisation for Orchestra*—Jean Sibelius
8. Swedish-language Festival Poem—Gånge-Rolf
9. *Korsholma*, orchestral composition—Armas Järnefelt
10. Finnish-language Festival Speech—E. G. Palmén
11. *Promotion Cantata*—Richard Faltin
12. *Vårt land/Maamme-laulu*

All the elements were in place—and in balance. The Lutheran chorale as the opening number and the hymnlike *Vårt land* at the close established the overall high-minded tone. A judicious equilibrium reigned in the delivery of poems and speeches, which took place in both national languages. On the Swedish side, the speakers included the other son of the great national poet Runeberg (whose brother, Walter, had recently unveiled his sculpture of the emperor) and the fiercely Swedish-Finnish nationalist Gånge-Rolf (a pseudonym for V. K. E. Wichmann). As for the Finnish-language speech and poem, they were delivered by men active in the Young Finns' circle.

Similar equality showed in the choice of musical numbers. Wegelius's *Sixth of May Cantata* had been composed in honor of Runeberg: it was written in 1878 for a university ceremony on the one-year anniversary of the poet's death on May 6, 1877.[37] With a beginning that recalled Wagner's Overture to *Tannhäuser*, the cantata was based on themes both familiar and deeply meaningful to the audience: *Porilaisten marssi* (*The March of the Björneborgers*) and *Vårt land*. For his part, Kajanus, ever oppositional vis-à-vis Wegelius (excepting their shared love of Wagner), conducted his symphonic poem *Aino*, which incorporated a Finnish-language folk song and bore the name of a *Kalevala* figure. Finnish education was also on display, invoked by Faltin's *Promotion*—or *Gradu-ation*—*Cantata*. And not least, Finnish history made a meaningful appearance in a new symphonic poem by Armas Järnefelt.

Its title, *Korsholma*, evoked emotional associations with the land, with Finland's past, and with the people's religious beliefs, for the Swedish name Korsholm designated an ancient fortress and the site of "Old Vasa," the location believed to be the very place where the Christian cross had first been raised on Finnish soil, although only the ruins of a fortress remained. Its significance thus went far beyond its architectural remnants and reached deep into the collective beliefs being promoted by the nationally minded. Järnefelt's music, helpfully explained to the great public in program notes, depicted the struggle between Finnish pagans and Swedish Christians, the victory of the latter, and the Finns' subsequent, tenacious embrace of Lutheran Christianity, the faith that profoundly separated true Finns from Orthodox Russians. The whole subject was highly topical for Finns, whose leaders were deeply involved in establishing their historical roots.[38] A Finn-ish folk song used as the opening theme, an orchestra with no fewer than six trumpets, and a majestic conclusion on *Ein' feste Burg* left no doubt whatsoever about the compos-er's ideological message. A rapturous outburst of applause greeted its final chord, vigor-ous shouts of "Hyvä, hyvä!" (Well done!) rang out, and an audience of thousands sprang to its feet.[39] Järnefelt had scored a splendid national success.

By comparison, Sibelius's Vasa appearance, for which he conducted his new *Impro-visation for Orchestra*, was far lower keyed. "Excellently performed" was the unelaborated comment from the same *Päivälehti* reporter who gushed over the new Järnefelt piece. Sibelius's fascination with exotic *espagnolisme* such as had enlivened his *Scène de ballet*, together with an unabashed desire to incarnate the blatantly provocative, even sensuous, in his music had not been stifled either by the festival's national agenda or by the prospect of having his in-laws on the scene: the composition was a work of pronounced erotic content, wrote *Nya Pressen*'s special correspondent, Karl Flodin, who observed in some astonishment that the music had ended in a Spanish dance rhythm with a spirited jiggling of the tambourine.[40]

All traces of the tambourined *Improvisation* with its erotic Spanish dance seem to have disappeared. So has the autograph manuscript of a second version of the work, variously called *Vårsång, Kevätlaulu, Frühlingslied*, and *Spring Song*, although its un-titled orchestral parts survive in copies made by Ernst Röllig, an orchestra member and dogged copyist. There is also a third version of the piece, which was published after the turn of the century, although its autograph manuscript too has vanished.[41] The eventual programmatic titles all had to do with spring, and the music's major-mode blandishments (the second *Vårsång* was in D major, the third in F major) were invariably described as "fresh," "light-filled," "springlike," "graceful," and "colorful" ("as full of Nordic grace and freshness as Grieg and Sinding, yet so different from both," said Flodin). Even though the composer's original title made no allusion to spring, the theme was "in the air"—literally, June being "spring" in Finland.

Celebrating the awakening spring is an ancient tradition in the Nordic lands, especially among the young, whose Flora Day has gone down in Finnish history as a major national event and a new generation of whom were prominently on hand at the Vasa Music Festival in the form of student choirs. Today it is May 1 that students observe in one of the biggest revelries of the Finnish year, but the date has fluctuated, its exact time being less important than the season when the unaccustomed joys of light and sudden softness fill the northern air.

Spring—*vår* in Swedish, *kevät* in Finnish—a perennial theme in poetry and song, had multilayered resonance in Finland of the 1890s. In Juhani Aho's novel *Kevät ja takatalvi* (*Spring and the Late Frosts*, 1906), "spring" represented the early years of national awakening, while the "late frosts" referred to the political oppression at the end of the 1890s and in the early twentieth century.[42] "Spring" was a safe yet sure means of alluding to the national movement, especially in the context of a Finnish music festival staged for public enlightenment and education. Less blatantly nationalistic than *Korsholma*, *Vårsång* nevertheless had a subtext. One of its later critics invoked a parallel to the morning-psalm that begins

Vak upp min själ, och var ej sen,	Wake up my soul, and be not slow,
Ty solen ren sitt blida sken	Because the soft light of the sun
begynner åter visa.[43]	Begins again to show.

Springtime metaphors were not only biblical; they circulated gladly in the imperial grand duchy. Fredrik Pacius, whose choral setting of *Vårt land* had eclipsed Sibelius's music in generating audience fervor on the occasion of the Pro Carelia lottery, repeatedly took up springtime texts: *Vårvisa* (or *Kevätlaulu*, meaning *Spring Song*) was composed for mixed chorus to a spring poem of Runeberg; another *Vårvisa*, to a different poem, was written for solo voice and piano; *Vårmorgonen* (*Spring Morning*), also to a Runeberg text, was composed for chorus (although apparently only in 1897 for a song festival in Turku). And a *Vårsång* by Pacius was mentioned on the Savo-Karelian lottery's program of March 1891, though perhaps it was a journalist's misreporting of *Vårvisa* (a title that means essentially the same thing but leaves uncertain which work was actually performed). Sibelius's *Vårsång* thus joined a string of light, bright, promising spring poetry and music.

Curiously, the "spring" titles were added only after the Vasa Festival. Why?

The Vasa event had been declared in honor of Zachris Topelius, Finland's revered man of letters, who hailed from the Vasa region. The great man himself attended the affair, modestly dressed in a gray suit, weaving his way among the people, nodding gently and smiling benevolently. Topelius's position in the national movement was the mediating "one nation, two languages." It was not by chance that the music festival had been organized in both languages of the land—the last time the groups would cooperate in this way in a music festival for more than seventy years.[44] The leading men's choirs of each language group were conspicuously on hand: Akademiska Sångföreningen, which insisted on singing only Swedish texts, and Ylioppilaskunnan Laulajat, the anti-Swedish organization founded to sing exclusively Finnish texts. Sibelius's neutral title *Improvisation*, like the impartial name of the national museum, Ateneum, was probably a bid to avoid committing to one group and alienating another (Armas Järnefelt had cleverly used a Fennicized Swedish title that alluded to an emotionally laden Finnish *lieu de mémoire*, meanwhile concentrating on the Finns' embrace of Lutheranism).

It may also have been for this reason that Sibelius further evaded the contentious language issue by contributing a piece for instruments alone, even though the event was primarily a song festival. The later string of titles attached to his work demonstrates the wisdom of such a choice, for interpretations tended to flow according to the persuasions and language of the listener. *Uusi Suometar*'s critic called the piece *Kevätlaulu; Nya Pressen*'s critic referred to it as *Vårsång*. More prosaically called op. 16, the composition acquired still another, more international name on publication: in the edition brought out in 1903, *La tristesse du printemps* appeared in parentheses below the main title *Vårsång*. *Tristesse* misses the work's meaning, as Sibelius himself observed; he blamed that title on a suggestion by the publisher, Breitkopf & Härtel, although he had used it himself as early as 1900.[45]

Not for the first time was it clear that a more skillful diplomat than Jean Sibelius was hard to find.

~11~

Aphrodite and the National Project

SYMPOSIA AND EROS

During those smoky Symposium evenings when the waves of discussion rose to great heights, the relationship of creativity, not just to Wagner, *Gesamtkunstwerk*, and religion, but also to Eros, buoyed passions and palaver. The heady mix of sexuality, religion, art, and Wagnerian grandiosity had clearly captivated Gallén, whose most famous records of those evenings swirled Eros into the ether of decadent opulence, hallucinating musicians, and the religion of art. *The Kajus Painting* suggested those intangible dimensions by the direction of the gaze of both Kajanus and Sibelius—toward something unseen—and by the curiously transparent figure before the moon, placed above and behind them. Meanwhile, Wagnerian bombast about matters erotic spilled over in Gallén's correspondence even as it inflated his art. In the autumn of 1894 he told Pekka Halonen that he was eagerly looking forward "to returning to my art like a young groom to his bride's arms,"[1] an echo of Sibelius's pilfered grandstanding the previous summer. The following day, the artist wrote in the same vein: "How I will take pleasure in the opportunity to create art again. It is like—pardon the expression—a thousand wedding nights to come. Whoever knows that art and religion are one will understand this."[2] The letter was written to his *mother-in-law*. The mind boggles.

Gallén's fascination, it might even be said obsession, with the sacred trinity of art, sexuality, and religion was fed by his fellow comrade-in-arms Adolf Paul, that old rogue whose regular and copious correspondence from Berlin, especially during 1894, harped insistently on the idea of the creative power of man's sexual drive. He elaborated on the theme in letters to Gallén ("the strange feminine element in our imagination") and spun variations on it in letters to Sibelius ("religion is only sexual drive").[3] All three of them seemed to believe these forces were one and the same.

Sibelius's courtship of Eros had already been the subject of literary digression (Paul's) and musical commentary (his own and Busoni's). He had even expressed it openly in such works as *Scène de ballet*, *Kullervo*, and *Till Frigga*. Its expression in his life is something not to be belabored. Now, at a time when he would otherwise have been more or less alone, as he put it, Sibelius had found camaraderie with kindred spirits who strengthened his intentions and gave him confidence. Mercy.

Those spirits, it must be said, were by no means unique in being in thrall to Love (*erōs*) and Beauty, art and religion. These were the very themes of that most famous of all symposia, Plato's, whose dialogues are as important for their philosophical ideas as for their protagonists, among whom was Socrates. *Erōs* itself seems to be desire—"for immortality, for wisdom, and for the contemplation of an object which is not in any way bodily or physical."[4] And desire, appropriately directed, led to a good life.

There were also less rarified and more contemporary symposia than Plato's, and the Helsinki group had direct connections to a particularly fabled crowd in Berlin through none other than the eager Adolf Paul. Making Germany's capital his home, Paul kept company there with the "most unnatural, unwholesome, eccentric, queer and odd" bunch of artists and intellectuals to accumulate since the earth cooled, with "nothing but talent and not a spark of common sense," as Frida Strindberg drily observed.[5] These bewitching characters gathered at the blandly named Tuerkes Wine and Beer Cellar, the "trysting place for the souls of the damned," Mrs. Strindberg styled it. Her tipsy if more inventive husband had another name for it: *das schwarze Ferkel* (the Black Porker), after he mistook the squeaking Bessarabian wineskin swinging over Tuerkes's door for a piglet. Strindberg, who was beloved of Sibelius's group since the music institute days when the Leskovites delighted in his satire *The Red Room*, was among the most illustrious Porker patrons, who, astonishingly, included women: it was there that the femme fatale Dagny Juel sent her photograph "to awaken interest."

The nerve center of the forgatherers, however, was a handsome and unnerving Pole, the art critic, author, piano-playing "satanist," and medical student Stanisław Przyby-szewski (1868–1927), prudently called "Staczu" or simply "Poland." When Paul, all agog, reported to Sibelius that he had made a new, good friend, he described him as a genius, an epoch-making individual in art as well as in science (although he might have been speaking of Strindberg).[6] Before long, Paul was sending the good friend's books to Finland. On October 31, 1893, Sibelius began a letter to Paul, saying, "Thanks for Przy-byszewski! *It was good!* . . . You are now there together with Hansson, Strindberg and consorts—you lucky one! *O terque beata!* [O thrice blessed!]"[7]

The literary pantheon awes the lover of literature. Notably, it had a large Swedish component. Aside from Paul (who in comparison was definitely second-tier), there was Ola Hansson (1860–1925), a writer nearly as famous as Strindberg. And of course, there was Strindberg himself. Yet it was the "genius," whose fairness, sapling-slender form, and delicate nostrils belied his satanic spirit—until, that is, you noticed the mouth, "eternally and painfully yearning after red wine or sweet blood to drink," who dominated much of the group's thinking. Frida Strindberg's first impression of the Pole left her wary:

> He is the only one who has not a wine-glass but a water glass standing in front of him. This large glass is full to the brim with cognac. He is bent forward, his eyes riveted on the glass; greyish-bluish, slanted, half-closed eyes, a greyish skin, a thin blond Henry IV beard: on his blood-red, finely chiselled lips, is a voluptuous and tortured smile. Now he comes closer and slowly kisses the two hands of August Strindberg, who, surprised, and with a blush, withdraws them.[8]

Eros drove Staczu's "genius." The primeval force governing the world, the most basic element of life, Eros represented an inexhaustible font of philosophy, poetry, and rhetoric. "In the Beginning was Sex. Nothing outside it—everything within it," he intoned in his *Mass of the Dead*.[9] Sex was the basic substance of life, the means of development, the eternal essence of human beings. Intelligence was merely an annoying, superficial trait, a later veneer acquired by mankind. Malignancy and death were part of Staczu's sexual philosophizing: in his own poems (for he poeticized along with playing Chopin and doctoring), with their plentiful allusions to sexual motives, a recurrent theme was the unconscious, secret power that sexuality exerted over man's conscious will.

Staczu's ideas resonated with those of the Helsinki denizens, only he worked his out better, cleverly mixing in morsels of Schopenhauer (for whom sexuality represented a malign power).[10] The Finns had a natural affinity with young Poles. They shared an interest in sex. Probably as important, they shared the opposition to a campaign of oppression by an outside ruler. At the end of 1894 Gallén journeyed into the very heart of this darkness for a three-month stay. (K. A. Tavaststjerna had just spent a miserable season with the Black Porker hands, the autumn and winter of 1893–94, made wretched by Strindberg's designs on the Finn's wife, the actress Gabrielle Tavaststjerna.) Gallén staged a joint exhibition with the Norwegian artist (and his rival) Edvard Munch (1863–1944), whose view of womankind was as conflicted and complex as the artist himself. From Munch's Berlin experience emerged the erotic portrayals of the alluring Norwegian Dagny Juel, by now married to the red-lipped satanist, Staczu, though she was hardly one to limit her attentions.[11]

It was at this very moment that a major composition burst forth from Jean Sibelius on the theme of sexuality and creativity: *Skogsrået*.

SKOGSRÅET—THE WOOD NYMPH

Like *Kullervo*, *En saga*, and later *Lemminkäinen*, *Skogsrået* belonged to that collection of works with *Gesamtkunstwerk*-like manifestations in art, literature, and music at the hands of Symposium participants. And like them, *Skogsrået* derived its very essence from the realm of myth: in Swedish folklore the *skogsrå* is a wood nymph, a beautiful, seductive— and dangerous—siren, whose back is as empty as an old tree and who may hide the tail of a fox beneath her come-hither clothing. Fatally, any man who succumbs to her allure and makes love with the *skogsrå* will lose his soul.

This dodgy creature inspired the Swedish poet Viktor Rydberg to write his entrancing ballad *Skogsrået* (*The Wood Nymph*), published in his first collection of verses, *Dikter*, in 1882.[12] The very next year Axel Gallén illustrated Rydberg's poem, embellishing its initial letter in India ink with images any Symbolist would love: lilies, a star, the head of a sphinx, a man's profile, all blooming from the *H* of *Han* ("Han, Björn, var en stark och fager sven"). Around the time Gallén and Sibelius first met, the latter set the poem to music, in a song for voice and piano, in 1888 or 1889. Yet it was during the years he was most deeply involved in the Symposium circle that Sibelius returned to the text and made not one but three additional interpretations: a melodrama, featuring the whole poem; a wordless orchestral tone poem; and a piano transcription of the tone poem's concluding section.

It was not hard to see the appeal of Rydberg's poem. The ballad tells of the strong and handsome Björn, whose narrow waist and broad shoulders arouse envy. But Björn (whose name means "bear") is captivated by a wood nymph, the *skogsrå*, whom he pursues in a mysterious and magical woodland setting, lured by forest dwarves in blackest garb:

> Cunningly, in the heather
> They weave a web of moonbeams
> And shadow from swaying branches and boughs,
> A quivering skein
> In brushwood and thicket
> Behind the wanderer's footsteps
> As he goes forth.
> And they cackle hoarsely at their prisoner.
> Wolf and lynx awaken in their dens.
> But Björn, he dreams with the song
> That sounds among the firs
> And whispers, lures and invites him
> Deeper, deeper into the bewitching woods!

Rydberg's forest teems with Symbolist images—moonbeams, sprites, mysterious undergrowth, winking stars, whispering firs, watery arms, and the specter of death. His vision was exuberantly adopted by Gallén, who later described his notion of art by conjuring up similar elves, cosmically lit webs, and thick undergrowth:

> Art is a great eternal forest where the trees are as densely or as sparsely placed as you wish. The moon, the sun and all kinds of glittering stars rise and set at your will, and when you arrive at a forest lake, it is bottomless if you so desire, and great juicy water lilies and wonderful ruddy waterfowl float in the dark water. If you so choose, the sun is rising from behind a craggy mountain at the far end of the lake, and the golden rays of the sun gleam on graceful spiderwebs hanging between ancient pine trees. If it pleases you, birds may strike up a concert with their piccolo flutes, while the elves in the mountains accompany them on the organ.[13]

Sibelius too had embraced this idea world. Around the time he made his first setting of *Skogsrået*, he composed his programmatic piano work *Florestan* (dedicated, not coincidentally, to Adolf Paul). As in Rydberg's poem, the "hero"—here the sad but passionate Florestan—wanders into a soggy forest of wild moss and humid tree bark. Coming upon rapids perfumed with water lilies, he sees water nymphs in the foaming waves and falls hopelessly in love with the one having wet, black eyes and golden hair. But when Florestan tries to lure the elusive creature to his side, she vanishes. His desire thwarted, Florestan loses his creativity as well as his heart's desire; he has little choice but to leave the forest.

The sensual allure of moist, nymphlike creatures drew Sibelius again and again. Their adventures often interwoven with death, that nineteenth-century euphemism for sexual merging and woman's conquest of man, the nymphs represent one of the central themes of his creative expression. On his honeymoon Sibelius composed into thrilling song Runeberg's balladlike *Under strandens granar*, in which a water nymph lures a happy child and his beautiful mother to their deaths. In Rydberg's *Snöfrid* (ca. 1900), turned into a Sibelian recitation with chorus and orchestra, a forest sylph (she of the title) urges the handsome Gunnar to make a fatal exchange—safety for honorable, if watery, demise, in "hopeless battle unto a nameless death" upon the sea.

The list goes on: an insanely jealous river nymph kills the rapids shooter Vilho in *Koskenlaskijan morsiamet*; *I natten* (op. 38, no. 3) features a naiad beside a fountain; in *Hertig Magnus* (op. 57, no. 6), an enchanting little nymphet beguiles Duke Magnus into casting himself into the billows of Lake Vättern, there to swim in watery pleasures until morning; in *Näcken* (op. 57, no. 8), the silver-haired water sprite has become more abstract, the personification of imagination and creativity;[14] and the watery being called *Luonnotar* (op. 70) is the very font of creation itself. The mystery and seductive-ness of wild sprites still haunted Sibelius as he was composing *Tapiola*, the last line of whose attached programmatic quatrain reads, "Wood sprites in the gloom weave magic secrets."

Yet it was in the context of the Symposium circle that Sibelius composed his larg-est work on this theme, the tone poem he called *Skogsrået*. The French title, *Ballade pour orchestre*, hinted at the work's Symbolist leanings. But it hardly prepared the audience for what was to come. At once a symbol of the eternal feminine and the creative heart of man, the *skogsrå* roused Sibelius to create one of the most erotic of all his composi-tions. A series of scenes, like dramatic *tableaux*, file by: first, the strong and handsome Björn, he of the mighty shoulders and narrow waist, confident and self-assured; then the malevolent forest elves, evilly garbed in black, laughing hoarsely as they weave a net of moonbeams, the better to lure their prey, who now appears in their midst; a noctur-nal interlude; a moment of still silence, and then the beautiful *skogsrå* glides forth. Who could resist her throaty solo cello voice, her sensuously swaying movements, a white limb glimpsed, honey-smooth, beneath a moon-white gown, a sweetly heaving breast? A warning cackle flits through the orchestra, but it is too late: the hero's heart has fled, stolen by the nymph, never to be returned. The finale takes its fatal course, the essence of painful yearning for the Aphrodite of the forest, a deadly conquest and an infinite long-ing that can never be satisfied.

Skogsrået's musical sections are as static as any theatrical *tableaux vivants*: the music shimmers, vibrates—and stays put. And as the last scene unfolds, Sibelius, like a skillful lover sensuously building tension, beguiles his listeners with deliciously controlled repe-titions in the orchestra, stretching out further and still further those potent spans, spinning infinite promise, heightening tension, the theme now sounding an octave higher, now building with a modulation upward, artfully delaying again and yet again the apotheosis for which every listener waits with pounding heart—the deeply craved yet deadly merg-ing of two spirits.

Who would have dreamed that a work of such intimacy would play a role in a Finn-ish national lottery?

SKOGSRÅET AND THE LOTTERY FOR THE FINNISH NATIONAL THEATER

In January 1895, *Päivälehti* began publishing advertisements for a forthcoming lottery.[15] The beneficiary was to be the Finnish National Theater, which had no playhouse of its own. Theater has an obvious role to play in a national awakening; its very nature encourages psychological self-awareness and collective linguistic unity. In Helsinki, thanks to the works of Aleksis Kivi and the skillful ministrations of the brother-sister team of Kaarlo and Emilie Bergbom, theater production had become a key means for promoting Finnish-language literature and Finnish artistic culture. At the same time, it was entirely symptomatic of the 1890s that national goals, at least as envisaged by the Young Finns, intermingled with an international outlook. And the National Theater lottery made that intermingling as clear as a Nordic summer sky.

The evening was billed as the Allegri-Arpajaiset (Allegri Lottery), and true to type, there were *tableaux vivants*, lavish costumes, and music of all kinds—sung, played, and danced. Most of the evening looked beyond Finland's borders for inspiration, sprinkling the zest of *espagnolisme* into a swirl of Italian, French, Germanic, and even exotic Asian flavors. All were served up, *horribile dictu*, like a modern-day academic conference in simultaneous events. Although one *tableau*, *Miranda*, was based on a homegrown poem by Topelius, in general there was a thorough disregard for what was Finnish and what was more broadly European. Another *tableau* portrayed "A Day in Old Rome." Meanwhile, Armas Järnefelt's *Tragi-Komedia*, a three-act drama commissioned for the occasion, looked (not surprisingly) toward Germanic lands for inspiration: it included Schubert's *Erlkönig*, the folk tune *Ach, du lieber Augustin*, and lavish quotations from Wagner's *Tannhäuser* and *Ring* operas.

There was a *tintamariski*, featuring faces peering through cut-out holes of a painted stage decoration while music played, the whole titillatingly titled *Unsuccessful Serenade*. The very word *tintamariski*, lost to most audiences today even in Finland, reflected the evening's commotion—*tintamariski* was a quasi-Russification of the Swedish word *tintamarre*, itself borrowed from French, and meaning hubbub or confusion. For the theater troupe and cognoscenti, the term brought up associations with the bisexual or at least androgynous heroine, Tintomar, featured in Carl Jonas Love Almqvist's masterpiece of Swedish romanticism, *Drottningens juvelsmycke* (1834), a tale about the assassination of Gustav III at a certain masked ball.[16]

Then there was a "French orchestra"—members of Robert Kajanus's ensemble, who also played Italian folk music. A one-act "dance-play" called *In the Doll Shop* featured the steps of the *tyrolienne*, Chinese dances, polkas, Spanish boleros, a "Titania" waltz, a soldierly march, and in a great coda, shepherds and shepherdesses, Spaniards, Japanese, and knights. And of course there was choral music: YL sang Italian folk songs arranged by Robert Kajanus and Oskar Merikanto for mixed choir, soloists, guitar, mandolin, and violin. The choir also sang national student songs and Finnish anthems—*Karjala*, *Suomen laulu*, and, of course, *Vårt land*.

Into this jumble went Sibelius's melodrama *Skogsrået*—a recitation in Swedish

accompanied by piano, two horns, and strings. In the zany multinational whirl of bourgeois and folk cultures, dances and folk tunes, Italian, Chinese, Spanish, Austro-German,
French, and Finnish music, the setting of a Swedish-language poem to benefit the Finnish National Theater fit right in with the cosmopolitan theme—or, at least, it did not jolt.
From a darkened stage one of the theater's most charismatic actors, Axel Ahlberg (1855–
1927), declaimed Rydberg's lines.[17] The "French orchestra" (with Karl Ekman Sr. at the
piano) accompanied the speaker with the strains of Sibelius's music, whose four sections
correspond closely to the wordless ones of his tone poem and express musically the clear
images of its lyrical poetry.[18] The orchestra played, the people danced. The whole thing
was repeated around eleven-thirty in the evening and again the following night. It was as
if the theater members were at pains to demonstrate their versatility and openness to the
wide world of ideas and impulses. Finns may have been living in a remote corner of an
authoritarian empire, but their windows to the world were wide open.

ೞಐಐೞ

When some weeks later Sibelius aired the full orchestral tone poem *Skogsrået*, the critic
known as "Bis" (Karl Fredrik Wasenius, 1850–1920) revealed clearly how every new
musical work was evaluated for its contribution to the larger mission. Finland, wrote
Bis, its education, its social order, its culture, indeed its painting and sculpture, "which
moment by moment spiral up with new pulsating life," had begun to attract attention
abroad.[19] But not Finland's new music. The critic complained of stagnation and the desire
for something new in that quarter. At least in his assessment, the future of the national
project in the realm of tones had been looking far from assured.

Then came the concert on April 17, 1895, and, said Bis, offered hope. Along with
"the fresh breeze" he had recently heard in Armas Järnefelt's inspired *Korsholma*, Sibelius's "rich group of new compositions" gave cause for optimism. (The program had
included parts of the *Karelia* music; the Piano Sonata, op. 12; *Vårsång*; the Serenade for
baritone and orchestra; and *Skogsrået*). From chamber to orchestral, vocal to instrumental, the musical bases seemed to be covered by Sibelius's new crop of works. Only opera
was lacking.

What Bis left unremarked was the significance of *Skogsrået* to Sibelius personally:
with its inspirational sources in Swedish literature, Finnish national pride, symbolist
imagery, and potent sexual metaphors, the tone poem had resolved his "Wagner crisis."
It represented a major landmark on the road away from lottery pieces and into the terrain
of symphonic composition.

~12~

National Aspirations and Symbolist Angst

A SYMBOLIST EXHIBITION

In the autumn of 1895, a new exhibition opened at the Ateneum, Finland's national museum of art. The previous year the Helsinki art world had been scandalized by Gallén's *Symposium* painting. Now the community flamed into controversy anew. Lively arguments were heard in the galleries, on the streets, in private homes. Critics held forth in essays and analyses. The source of the uproar was a display of paintings and sculptures by contemporary Finns—Väinö Blomstedt, Albert Edelfelt, Magnus Enckell, Pekka Halonen, Eero Järnefelt, Berndt Lindholm, Hjalmar Munsterhjelm, Walter Runeberg, Beda Stjernschantz, Ville Vallgren, Victor Westerholm, and others. The theme was Symbolism.

The new -ism created a strong dissonance between the artists and their Finnish public. A spate of reviews, sharp criticisms, and downright confusion mushroomed in the Helsinki papers. One of the earliest was a lengthy endeavor by Johannes Öhqvist (1861–1949), art historian and critic, to define Symbolism. "Not a school, not a rubric, not a label," Symbolism required more subtle treatment:

for this complicated inner life, art seeks expressive outlet in the most diverse spheres: steeps itself in the poetry of the sagas; succumbs to the mysticism of religious ecstasy or deep intimacy. Old legends and myths bring forth wonderful dreams of worlds never before seen, and mysterious, ancient Eastern forms of fantasy increase the tendency for rapturous ecstasy. The occult, the bizarre, the out-of-the-ordinary, cast an irresistible spell. And like the darkness of inner life, the darkness in nature exerts an indescribable power to fascinate. You search for the most delicate and translucent nuances in order to do justice to night, evening, mist, dusk.[1]

Although Finns took a certain pride in the fact that, in the space of a mere fifty years, the homeland artists had demonstrated their keen awareness of the issues in the wider European world of art—romanticism, realism, naturalism—and their ability to compete in these realms, it was now publicly wondered whether the embrace of Symbolism was really such a good thing.[2]

Of course, some of the works were praised: Pekka Halonen's *Kalevala* painting; Albert Edelfelt's Paris landscapes; Ville Vallgren's bronzes. The paintings of Beda Stjernschantz (1867–1910) generated mixed reactions, although the musical resonance of one her works drew favorable attention. Its title, *Öfverallt en röst oss bjuder* (*Everywhere a Voice Invites Us*, or, in Finnish, *Kaikkialla ääni kaikuu*), was taken from the last stanza of *Suomen laulu* (*Song of Finland*), whose Swedish verses (*Suomis-sång*) had been penned by Emil von Qvanten (1827–1903):

Öfverallt en röst oss bjuder,	Everywhere a voice invites us,
Öfverallt en stämma ljuder:	Everywhere a voice resounds,
det är Suomis sång![3]	It's Finland's song!

The text was widely known, thanks to its musical setting by Fredrik Pacius, and often performed during those lottery soirées and on concerts. (By its sweetness the composer himself was vastly impressed; he was heard to remark that never had he composed a more beautiful song.)[4]

Stjernschantz's painting depicted a small band of Swedes living on the island of Vorms off the coast of Estonia. When the artist (herself Swedish-speaking) visited there, she found that the group had kept its language, its customs, even its mode of dress. From this at least one viewer, the admiring (Finnish-language) critic in *Uusi Suometar*, wrested national meaning. As he saw it, Stjernschantz had portrayed an old-fashioned population who, though few in number, had succeeded in preserving their nationality and language amidst a foreign people. The strength of the people's national feeling and perhaps the musical allusions—the title and the prominent position given the national instrument, the *kantele*, being played by one of the girls—spoke to this critic's patriotic heart.

But what set everyone at odds was the work of Magnus Enckell (1870–1925). "Bizarre" was the operative description. His *Melancolia* sent Öhqvist, who was actually sympathetic to the painter, into a dither. Who or what was symbolic in this work showing a naked youth, his so-white body lying face down in the lap of an older woman dressed in deep green and violet, in the background a single man rowing on the open sea? Is it him? Is it her? Is it the landscape? Another Enckell work, *Fantasia*, in which mysterious swans, both black and white, keep an Apollolike "bacchant" company, also stirred up the pundits. It was all too weird, too fantastical, too baroque.

The center of this controversy, Enckell, was one of Sibelius's friends. The previous year, Enckell had produced a portrait of a naked youth entitled *Réveil* (*Awakening*) that had also created a stir. Just what the youth was awakening to, a question left suitably, Symbolistically ambiguous, had set tongues wagging. Yet Enckell had the impression that Kajanus, the Järnefelts, and the Sibeliuses supported him (it was, after all, Eero Järnefelt's wife, Saimi, who had modeled for the dark woman in *Melancolia*).[5] To judge by Sibelius's next big work, Enckell had assessed the composer's sympathies quite accurately.

MUSIC OF THE WATERFALL

The spring after the controversial Symbolist exhibition, on April 13, 1896, Sibelius unveiled a new creation. He preceded it with the innocuous *Vårsång*, whose F major, milquetoast blandishments could hardly have prepared the audience for what was to come, even though the new title was announced on the printed program.[6] It read *Sinfonisia runoelmia (Aihe Lemminkäisen tarusta)/Sinfoniska dikter till motiv ur Lemminkäinen mythen* (*Symphonic Poems to Motives from the Myth of Lemminkäinen*). A program leaflet with appropriate lines from the *Kalevala* (in Karl Collan's translation into Swedish) gave the work's motto:

> Then the lively Lemminkäinen
> Guided to the isle the vessel
> To the island's end he drove it
> Where it ends in jutting headland.

Lemminkäinen had inspired Sibelius before. The year was 1893, memorable for the *Karelia* music, in whose opening *tableau* Sibelius had used words of Lemminkäinen in the runic song performed by Larin Paraske and Selma Tavaststjerna. But his Lemminkäinen interest had not stopped there. Near the beginning of the *Kalevala*'s *runo* 40, which relates the momentous creation of the *kantele*, Lemminkäinen attempts to quell the foaming river with a spellbinding incantation:

> "Stop, O rapids, stop your foaming,
> Stop, swift water, stop your seething!
> Spirit of the cataract,
> Foam Maid, sit upon the midrock,
> Boulder in the seething center,
> Lull the water in your lap,
> Fold the eddies in your fingers,
> Hold the spume back with your hands."[7]

To set these magical words Sibelius penciled a choral work, also in 1893: *Heitä, koski, kuohuminen* (see fig. 12.1). For reasons unknown, the composer left its seventy-three bars in draft form: in four-part harmony, the text placed between the staves, but the ending incomplete and the whole without dynamics, tempo, or other finishing touches. Perhaps one reason he abandoned the chorus was that he had found a better use for its restless theme: the Andantino of the piano sonata eventually designated op. 12.[8] Subjected to variations, the theme, now changed from the G minor in the choral draft, makes its entrance in F minor, after which it alternates with a sparkling episode over ostinato eighth notes. Yet its final statement is the choral version incarnate.

Also in 1893, Axel Gallén was engaged in a new project of his own: painting the rapids called *Mäntykoski*. The work is known today as an abstract waterfall whose foaming waters spill through golden strings suggesting a lyrelike instrument, perhaps even a *kantele*. But in March 1893 a visitor to the artist's studio reported that the canvas depicted a female "spirit of the waterfall" posing in the rapids.[9] Gallén ultimately painted over his *kantele*-playing nymph and sublimated his art into a less figurative and more reflective form.

The parallels between piano sonata and painting are striking. Both artworks appear to have had their beginnings in a common *Kalevala* source. Both artists moved away from a too-literal rendering of the myth toward an abstraction that enabled a wider, collective interpretation.[10] Once again parallels among Symposium group members indicate the communal nature of their creations and show the power of the group, not only in inspiring one another, but also in shaping the national art.

In Sibelius's case, the sublimation of national ideas into more abstract form achieved two things. One was that by choosing an instrumental genre instead of a vocal one, he avoided favoring either of the perennially squabbling language groups. Another was that the choice instantly moved his work from a purely national context into an international one. The piano sonata has a long tradition in European music history. Whether consciously or not, Sibelius was reaching out through the national to embrace the all-European.

LEMMINKÄINEN'S REINCARNATION

It was three years later when Sibelius unveiled four full-blown orchestral works on the darling boy himself. None other than Flodin had suggested the idea. After *Kullervo*'s premiere, Flodin had written: "Were Mr. Sibelius to write a new symphonic poem, for example a Lemminkäinen portrait, he would doubtless have to create a completely different

Figure 12.1. Sibelius, *Heitä, koski, kuohuminen.* HUL 0689/2.
© Breitkopf & Härtel, Wiesbaden.

illustration for the Finnish milieu in order not to repeat what he has already said, once and for all, in *Kullervo*."[11]

However presumptuous Flodin's (and later Axel Carpelan's) directives to Sibelius on what he "should" compose seem today, in nineteenth-century Finland such advice was given for the greater good and belonged to the common cause. Rather than impertinence, those suggestions demonstrated the sense of shared mission among the educated members of a society whose collective goal was to advance the national movement. The many musical and artistic competitions, with their dictated rules for entry, belonged in the same category. So did the individual writers and critics who weighed in with their opinions. The influential Topelius, for one, who in an article entitled "Nordiska taflor" ("Nordic Paintings") published in his newspaper *Helsingfors Tidningar* in October 1858, had outlined some thirty-three subjects for artists to paint; the distinguished Albert Edelfelt was among those who, in all humility, complied.[12]

Sibelius, of course, would probably have come to Lemminkäinen's theme without Flodin. After all, it can hardly be mere coincidence that his *Lemminkäinen Legends* and Gallén's paintings on the same topic were begun at more or less the same time. Or that another prominent member of the Symposium circle, Eino Leino, was writing on Lemminkäinen in the very year the *Legends* were premiered. The close connections among the Young Finns meant that ideas migrated quickly from one to another, materializing first in one art form, then another, leaving unsure precisely from whom the notion had originally sprung.

Lemminkäinen should have been a welcome addition to the fold of Finnish-spirited art. Imbued with a thoroughly national and *Kalevala*-inspired program, *Lemminkäinen* also marked the first time that Sibelius had strung together a series of purely orchestral movements that veered in the direction of a symphony but were in truth symphonic poems. Yet despite the national and musical credentials, Lemminkäinen's musical incarnation fell victim to the pettiness of small-town musical life.

At the rehearsals orchestra members had already turned hostile and argumentative.[13] Aino was reduced to tears; Jean alternately harangued and placated the musicians. The first performance garnered only lukewarm response; Flodin averred that he had heard "nothing new." And when the tone poems were repeated the next year (1897), Flodin objected strenuously and absolutely to the "completely different setting for the new Finnish milieu" that Sibelius had created: "This kind of music seems purely pathological and leaves impressions so mixed, painful and essentially undefinable that they have very little in common with the aesthetic feeling of pleasure that all fine art and, above all, music ought to awaken."[14] Flodin, who seems to have appointed himself Sibelius's musical moral compass, had had enough of bizarre allusions, erotic wood nymphs, Neoplatonist mysteries, and pubescent awakenings. What, after all, did such things have to do with the national agenda?

Sibelius was offered an incomparable opportunity to show his Don Quixote mettle, to fight for his ideals, be they windmills or hogsheads. Instead, he withdrew the offending movements. He may have realized that something—or someone—else was behind the public pummeling: Kajanus.

Suspicion for this unaccountable disparagement of a national composer has recently fallen on the ruthless tactics of the man determined to secure his place in Finnish music history.[15] As part of his campaign to win the appointment of university music director, Kajanus seems to have engineered *Lemminkäinen*'s negative reviews, one of whose bizarre criticisms, in *Nya Pressen* on April 14, 1896, was that there was "too much music" (a remark reminiscent of Emperor Joseph II's criticism of Mozart—too many notes). The young composer Erkki Melartin (1875–1937), in one of his letters home in October 1897, wrote about the "great storm" brewing in Helsinki musical circles: "The critics are set against Sibelius," he wrote, "as they all support Kajanus, and now that Sibelius has a concert next week, there is an intrigue going on to prevent him from getting an audience."[16]

O terque beata! Without consorts, and above all, without the support of Kajanus and his orchestra, no composer could get very far in Helsinki, as Melartin would later learn to his sorrow. Before the wiles of the devil, even the most gifted individuals must give way.

THE LEGEND OF LEMMINKÄINEN

It was Lönnrot, of course, who made Lemminkäinen one of the central figures of the *Kalevala*. Of the epic's leading men, the dashing Lemminkäinen is the most besotted with women, a Finnish Don Juan. In endless pursuit of pleasure, Lemminkäinen comes to an untimely end when he kills the swan of the underworld, one of the three impossible deeds he must accomplish to win the hand of the Daughter of the North (Pohjola's Daughter). The first two were daunting enough: Dame Louhi had required him to ski down the elk invented by the evil demon, Hiisi; that accomplished, Lemminkäinen was to bridle the demon's gelding, Big Brown. But the third and last task was the most formidable:

> shoot the beautiful bird,
> Shoot the swan of Tuonela
> Swimming on the death-dark river
> By the sacred river's whirlpool
> With one shot and one arrow,
> Taking but a single arrow.[17]

Although woman leads Lemminkäinen to destruction, it is also woman who saves the wretch: his mother. With that special magic that infuses myths, Lemminkäinen's mother realizes her son's plight when his comb begins to weep blood. She finds him—hacked into pieces by Wet-hat, the blind cowherd. With the supreme faith of mothers, plus the help of a rake and a honeybee who tirelessly brings magic salves and ointments, the mother makes the rapscallion whole again, bringing about a resurrection, though of a very pagan kind.[18]

There is reckless abandon in the myth of Lemminkäinen, a catalog of Don Juan adventures, a "mission," however perverse, from which Lemminkäinen refuses to be deterred. After being resurrected by those who have taken the most extreme measures on his behalf, he demonstrates neither gratitude nor consideration, but lapses into peevish whining:

> For in truth my heart is yonder
> And my sentiments are there
> Among the little maids of Northland
> With those beautiful lovely-locks.[19]

Fortunately, the myth also includes another, less vocal, character: a majestic and symbolic swan.

THE SWAN OF TUONELA

It was Finland's artists and composers who exploited the swan's role in Lemminkäinen's story. In the *Kalevala*, shooting the swan is only one of Lemminkäinen's three impossible tasks. Furthermore, the killing of the swan had been imported from a source far removed from the fonts of the epic *Kalevala* poems: Lönnrot had found it in the lyric verses of *Millä maksan maammon maion*.[20] The poem answers the question of its opening line, "How shall I pay for the milk of my mother?," with a son's promise to repay with something beyond human reach. The swan thus symbolized the unattainable.

That was reason enough for the audacious Young Finns to embrace its image. What made the swan even more appealing was its resonance, both near and far. Swans came with a long history and bountiful imagery that ranged across countries and even centuries and suggested an array of interpretive possibilities that made them far more tempting to artists, composers, and poets than Demon Hiisi's elk or even his gelding. A rich background thus reverberates through Sibelius's *Swan of Tuonela* and helps to explain its magnified role in Lemminkäinen's musical incarnation. The swan's circuitous course over time embodied the inextricable blend of Finnish and international currents that were the hallmark of Finnish nationalism—and Jean Sibelius's outlook—in the 1890s.

The Swan's International Points of Contact

Swans number among the most familiar of the abundant waterfowl inhabiting present-day Finland's glittering lakes and curving shorelines. But in the 1890s, when they were brutally hunted, the birds were rare, numbering no more than one hundred breeding pairs (in contrast to the several thousands nowadays) of the genus *Cygnus cygnus*—whooper or trumpet swans, swans with voices.[21]

Swans have long inspired admiration and a kind of wonder, their regal whiteness and long, graceful necks intimating a kind of otherworldliness and serenity. At the end of the nineteenth century, their popularity with artists, writers, and composers turned into something of an obsession and gave rise to some of history's best-known swans: those in Wagner's *Lohengrin* and *Parsifal*, Camille Saint-Saëns's *Le cygne*, Edvard Grieg's *En svane*, and countless representations by artists from Arnold Böcklin and Edvard Munch to Max Klinger and Paul Gauguin.

Finland's swans have a secure place in this efflorescence, thanks to Runeberg's swan poetry, Lönnrot's *Kalevala*, Sibelius's music, and Gallén's art. The swan may well be the image most capable of embodying the ambiguous and culturally rich fin-de-siècle intellectual world, an emblem at once national and international, ancient and modern, mysterious and uncomplicated, spiritual and corporeal, innocent and erotic. Not by chance did Sibelius return to the swan theme on numerous occasions. Among his song settings, three of the most exquisite have to do with swans: Runeberg's *Men min fågel märks dock icke*, op. 36, no. 2; *Norden*, op. 90, no. 1; and Ernst Josephson's *Jubal*, op. 35, no. 1. Sibelius turned Josephson's text—

> Jubal saw a swan fly up
> High over the water toward the sky,
> Quickly, he drew his bow.
> Clang! The string rang.
> Like a gust of wind,
> the bird, hit by an arrow,
> fell to its watery death—

into quicksilver, the voice now soaring, now capriciously dipping earthwards in dazzling swoops while the piano alternately holds its breath or thrums an emulated string accompaniment (see ex. 12.1). In his orchestral music too Sibelius composed a number of works in which swans play a central role: *The Swan of Tuonela*, the incidental music to Strindberg's *Swanwhite*, and the glorious swan theme in his Fifth Symphony.[22] And two of these works have been central to his legacy.

EXAMPLE 12.1. SIBELIUS, *JUBAL*, OP. 35, NO. 1, MM. 1–17.

© BREITKOPF & HÄRTEL, WIESBADEN.

Like the birds themselves, the swan as topos has migrated, from one country to another, from one art form to another, from one meaning to another. As far back as the ancient Greeks, Plato had Socrates argue for the soul's immortality by means of swans, who "when they perceive that they must die, sing more and better than ever they did before, glad to be going away into the presence of the god whose servants they are."[23]

The Nordic swans ranged across Scandinavia, through Finland, and into Russia. Around 1859 Henrik Ibsen penned *A Swan*:

> My pure white swan,
> silent and quiet;
> neither wingflaps nor bird's trills
> let your voice be known.[24]

Some years later his countryman Grieg gave the mute creature a voice (one of the *Sex digte* of 1876, which were orchestrated almost two decades later, in 1894).

Despite the importance of the Nordic exchange, a particularly important route for the swans into Finland was by way of Germany. *The Dying Swan* (*Der sterbende Schwan*, 1785), written by that nationalist par excellence Herder and first published in a group of "paramyths," turned up in Suomi in the hands of both Lönnrot and Leino, each of whom made a translation.[25] Runeberg, who composed his own hymns to swans, has been so closely identified with the mysterious bird that some scholars see it as his central symbol. "The swan is already reflected in the sea," begins his *Men min fågel märks dock icke*. In *Norden* he apostrophized the migrating swans:

> Sail, sail, o sail mournfully southward,
> Though longing, seek nourishment;
> Dive into strange lakes,
> Missing ours!

Another of Runeberg's swans, called simply *Svanen*, sits in the fullness of Finland's nature, his voice—for this was a decidedly male swan—also filled with love and longing for the Northland, a poem considered to be as powerful in its landscape patriotism as the same poet's *Vårt land*; significantly, its translation into Finnish transformed the swan's song into yearning, not for the generalized north, but for "the sweetness of Suomi," a reinterpretation strongly in support of the national movement.[26] Still, Runeberg's poetry had overwhelmingly positive associations with swans. The association of the swan with death advanced by members of the Symposium circle—in their poetry, art, and music— gave nineteenth-century Finns a shock (though it was not the first from that quarter).

Consider Eino Leino. Swans captured the attention of that poet quite early. While still a schoolboy in Hämeenlinna, Leino copied out Herder's *Dying Swan* in Lönnrot's Finnish translation. Leino's fascination with swans, and their role in the Lemminkäinen myth, intensified over time. In the year Sibelius premiered his *Swan of Tuonela*, Leino composed a work of the same title whose verses he intended for an opera.[27] In Leino's hands the swan became female, a regal symbol of the mystery of death and a familiar image used to plumb the depths of what was unfamiliar. From the poet's own pen came an interpretation in the decade of their creation (the emphases are Leino's):

> Lemminkäinen has become a Titan, *a hero of faith*, who plunges through all dangers into the river of the underworld, torch in hand . . . The Swan has become the queen of death, *symbolizing the mystery of the hereafter*. Lemminkäinen wants to shoot the Swan with his bow of ideals and to win peace for himself and a message of joy for suffering humanity. . . . He is just about to shoot when an arrow aimed by the Herdsman of Pohja, representing his own misdeeds, strikes him. . . . The man who can shoot the Swan of Tuonela must be free from sin (Jesus).[28]

Lemminkäinen as vital national hero, yet prey to human frailty, and the swan as symbol of death and the hereafter—these were the templates that guided Sibelius's hands.

The Swan as Eros

The glowing whiteness of swans has inevitably caused the creatures to be associated with love and purity. In 1831 Alexander Pushkin penned a verse form of a folk tale entitled "The Tale of Tsar Saltan, of His Son, the Renowned and Mighty Bogatir Prince Guidon Saltanovich, and of the Beautiful Swan Princess." At the turn of the century Rimsky-Korsakov turned the story into a charming opera, *The Tale of Tsar Saltan*, which premiered in Saint Petersburg in 1902. Pushkin's *Tale* features a czarevich, cruelly exiled from his father's court, who falls hopelessly in love on hearing of a beautiful princess in a land faraway. The czarevich has saved a swan from death. Now the swan helps the young prince before transforming itself into his beloved, the Swan Princess. Just as in the *Kalevala*'s swan tale, magic and bees make their appearance: the swan miraculously turns the prince into a bumblebee so that he can return to his father's kingdom, where he hears about the beautiful princess for the first time.[29] The points of contact with similar images used by those in the Symposium circle suggest the ease with which ideas migrated—from art to music to poetry, and from country to country.

Swedish author Strindberg, no paradigm for the writing of cheerful stories, also wrote about a swan princess in his *Svanevit* (*Swanwhite*, 1901). The title character, Swanwhite, is also beset by deliciously wicked persons, in this case, a stepmother, who contrives to make the girl's life miserable, meanwhile manipulating the handsome prince to marry the horrid stepmother's daughter. Strindberg associated Swanwhite with feminine innocence and devotion: it is she who, like Lemminkäinen's mother, brings the lifeless body of her beloved prince back to life. For the idea of artistic resurrection had also entered the currents bearing the swan.

This pure and innocent creature was easily associated with saintly virginity, its white plumage denoting chastity, and its impermeability to water, virginity.[30] But the swan's sinuous movements also flowed easily into a sensuous eroticism. Some poetic swans took on the alluring qualities of Aphrodite and Venus. This meaning too reached far back into antiquity, when swans gave rise to such enduring myths as the story of the lovely Leda, to whom the smitten Zeus, seeking protection from a pursuing eagle, came in the form of a swan. On the shores of the river Eurotes, Leda and Zeus-as-swan begot the exquisite Helen of Troy as well as, according to some sources, Castor and Pollux.

In the late nineteenth century, as ancient myths began to be explored by figures ranging from Freud to Zola for their archetypal meanings and their possibilities for plumbing the depths of the human psyche, Leda the legendary beloved began to give way to Leda the seductive female, an instrument for exploring the mysterious powers of sexuality and enslaving seduction. When Juhani Aho published his poem *Musta joutsen* (*The Black Swan*) in a Kuopio paper, *Uusi Kuvalehti*, in 1894, he was tapping into that darker vein; so had Magnus Enckell when he painted both black and white swans in his *Fantasia* around 1895. The transformation of the queenly white swan into a mysterious black bird signaled one of the great themes of the Symbolists: the archetypal battle between dark and light. The darker allegories gained in prominence in Symbolist hands. While for some the swan represented purity and light, for others, she—and this swan was female—was a portent of death, a recurring image in Symbolist literature. That euphemism for the sexual domination of woman over man, death also provided "a simulacrum of creativity . . . the dark underside of life, which every artist, like a Baroque saint, must conquer."[31] The very plurality of the swan's nature—sensual, innocent, familiar, but unapproachable—made her irresistible.

The Swan in Art

The visual beauty of swans appealed powerfully to artists. The creature's gently curving contours and natural habitat—rippling grasses, undulating waters—embodied the essential elements of art nouveau or *Jugendstil*. And it was swan iconography that most deeply stamped the bird's image in the European mind's eye. Arnold Böcklin, whose exploration of myth, decadence, and sensuality so intrigued his contemporaries, depicted swans in the Elysian fields. Eero Järnefelt, on seeing *Die Gefilde der Seligen* in the Berlin National Gallery in November of 1894, waxed ecstatic: healthy worldliness! a rejoicing in the wonders of nature! And that rare fin-de-siècle thing, healthy optimism![32]

By the end of the century there was seldom any doubt that the swan was female. Munch made the gender unequivocal in the opening line of his prose poem about his canvas *Vision: A Swan*, first exhibited in 1892: "She was a swan."[33] *Vision*, showing a swan and the gruesome head of a man, was to be central to Munch's series of paintings called "Love."

Such were the currents that swirled around the swan as artistic symbol in Finland. And foremost among Finnish swans were Axel Gallén's. In the left panel of the triptych called *The Mary Myth*, Gallén depicted maidens disporting themselves with Lemminkäinen while a red swan floats by.[34] When Gallén wrote to K. A. Tavaststjerna about this canvas in October 1896, he made a remarkable comment: "Dare I even mention that I am still struggling with my bright red swan in the River of Tuonela. Could I but pluck a red feather from its tail! and give it to Lemminkäinen."[35] The dizzying mix of Symbolist imagery and various folk legends (a certain *Firebird* being still in the future) with *Kalevala* myth and Finnish nature impressions indicates with sureness and certainty the wide perspective and outward orientation of the Young Finns. Likewise, in *Lemminkäinen's Mother* (originally called *Lemminkäinen in Tuonela*), in which a glowing, nearly white swan floating on Tuonela's dark waters imprints a numinous image on the mind, Gallén combined images from widely ranging sources. The fallen hero lies "ghostly green by black waters where a swan swims away, its neck scornfully arched. Golden, vibrating rays of sunshine offer the kneeling mother hope, and she sends a bee to draw balm from that golden spring."[36]

Many have remarked on the painting's Christian elements, a kind of secular *pietà*: the positions of the mother and Lemminkäinen forming a cross, the mother tenderly caring for a son who is resurrected from death thanks to special intervention.[37] The symbols suggest the painting's (and the Symposium circle's) metaphysical depths, which united religion, both pagan and Christian; Eros, in the love of a mother and the alluring, erotic, feminine force of the swan; and Death, Tuonela's realm. The ultimate mysteries of life and loss lurked in Tuonela's dark shadows.

OF TIME AND SPACE

It is not certain just when Sibelius decided to compose Lemminkäinen's legends into music. His active involvement with the story went back at least to 1893, the year he used Lemminkäinen's lines in the *Karelia* music, attempted a choral setting of the hero's invocation to the rapids, and endeavored to compose an opera on the similar challenges Väinämöinen had faced with the testy Pohjola and her outlandish demands. Sibelius later put it about that *The Swan of Tuonela* was a remnant of the aborted opera's overture.[38] The following summer (1894) Sibelius renewed his acquaintance with Wagner's swan music-dramas, *Lohengrin* and *Parsifal*, in Bayreuth itself. Whether or not he also visited King Ludwig II's Neuschwanstein, where swans adorn walls, tapestries, chandeliers, cushions, curtains, lamps, dishes, sculptures, stair railings, and spigots in a Disneylike world of adult fantasy would probably have made little difference to his expression of the theme, for swans were "in the air"—in fact, the European atmosphere was downright saturated with them.

Although the swan swims silently through the *Kalevala*'s story only briefly and symbolically, Lemminkäinen's tale has plenty of action otherwise—the hero pursuing his quarry, his being slain by Wet-hat, an improbable rescue by the mother, and the magical intervention of the bee. But the problem for Sibelius had been aptly put by Flodin: how to create a setting that did not repeat what he had done in *Kullervo*. And the artistic products that came from the hands of the Symposium participants show clearly that their discussions included deliberations of just such matters, including questions of time and space.

Zachris Topelius had already floated into the Finnish ether the idea that time and space were one. Yet how were such things to be imagined? How could infinitude be conveyed to the human mind? How could the arts portray such ineffable concepts? In music the challenge was to reconfigure the traditional narrative-type schemes, to reimagine the goal-oriented structures, principally Germanic inventions, on which many European musicians, including Finns, had been raised. Yet music also offered greater innate advantages than the visual arts, for its capacity to allude rather than stating forthrightly, for its polyphonic capabilities, and for its essential nature of flowing through time.

The Young Finns' different solutions to these questions show up in their radical rethinking of time itself. The results are evident on Gallén's canvases and in Sibelius's manuscripts, which bear curious similarities. In the left panel of Gallén's triptych *The Mary Myth*, Lemminkäinen frolics with the maidens of Saari, a swan floats across the foreground, and a herdsman who resembles Kullervo blows his birch-bark horn in the background—a compression onto the same picture plane of disjointed story elements from three different *Kalevala* stanzas (11, 14, and 29). By abandoning conventional narrative flow and eliminating distinctions between time and place, à la Topelius, Gallén achieved a "new, anti-naturalistic conception of epic space."[39]

Sibelius proceeded in a strangely similar way. The parallel emerges most obviously from his program texts for the *Lemminkäinen Legends*, for which he selected events from different passages and even different *runo* verses, then reassembled them in his own, imaginative fashion.[40] The process is especially striking when compared with *Kullervo*, composed only four years earlier. For *Kullervo*'s premiere, Sibelius had also provided the audience with appropriate *Kalevala* texts. Yet those texts were quoted directly from the two stanzas (*runo* 35 and *runo* 36) that relate the Kullervo story, and Sibelius's setting of their verses flowed in a straightforward, narrative fashion. By contrast, for his *Lemminkäinen* program, Sibelius picked and chose among different lines and even different stanzas. He began with *runo* 29 for the first movement (*Lemminkäinen and the Maidens of the Island*), skipped backward to *runo* 15 for the second movement (*Lemminkäinen in Tuonela*), left off any verse at all for *The Swan of Tuonela*, and compressed events from two stanzas (29 and 30) in *Lemminkäinen's Return*. As long ago as 1957, Harold E. Johnson had pointed out the curious nature of these program texts, a finding he made widely known in the leading Finnish daily, even identifying the *Kalevala* lines from which the composer had constructed his narrative.[41] The implications, however, went unappreciated.

What Johnson did not have access to was another programmatic text for *Lemminkäinen*. It surfaced only in the 1980s among the composer's effects deposited in the National Library. The document consists of an unsigned typescript, headed "Lemminkäinen sarja suurelle orkesterille. Säveltänyt Jean Sibelius Op. 22 (1895)," and its texts are somewhat different from those in the printed program.[42] They even include four programmatic lines for *The Swan of Tuonela*:

Tuonen mustassa joessa,	In the murk of Death's black river
pyhän virran pyörtehissä	In the sacred river's whirlpool
liukuvi vihanta lintu,	Green bird, passing lightly,
joutsen Tuonelan joluvi.	Swan of Tuonela gliding.

Sibelius's mosaic process of creating his program shows up even more markedly here than in the "official" texts. Although apparently based on the *Kalevala*'s *runo* 14, only line 1 has an exact correspondence to the printed epic (at line 459). Line 2 resembles a phrase that recurs throughout *runo* 14, although it is transformed here into a different grammatical case. The other two lines seem to have been the composer's (or someone else's) creation out of elements borrowed from the epic's formulations. Their color imagery strongly recalls Gallén's description of his canvas on the same subject.

The piecing together and transformation of segments for *Lemminkäinen*'s programmatic text was not the only aspect of the symphonic poems to benefit from a mosaic process. Intriguingly, the music too has been described in the same terms: in Joachim

Schwarz's happy formulation, "mosaic technique" is *Lemminkäinen*'s central principle of melodic organization, a description that arises both from Sibelius's own linguistic formulation and from his artistic process.[43] Whether Gallén or Sibelius came up with the notion or, as is perhaps more likely, it arose out of mutual discussion and debate, what was clear in the works of both was the attempt to reshape, rethink, and restructure conventional notions of time and space.

Arguably, it was Sibelius who achieved the most radical—and the most successful—of their experiments to suspend time altogether. Perhaps it was the focus on the timeless qualities of myth that prompted him to shift the traditional goal-directed logic of Western music away from its usual trajectory leading to apotheosis and triumph.[44] It may also have been the qualities of the real revolutionary figure among the musical *Legends*, not the frivolous Lemminkäinen, but the mysterious Other who leads the lout to his fate: the swan. For in his *Swan of Tuonela* Sibelius tapped into the very essence of myth and Symbolism. All the experience of the preceding years and with those static works composed for lottery *tableaux*; all the angst of coming to terms with Wagner's vast sense of time, space, and scintillating orchestration; all the values, national and universal, buried in myth and such mysteries as Death—all of this was distilled into a mere 102 extraordinary bars. That exquisite moment of stasis was the opposite of the reigning Germanic idea of music, with its scurrying, developing, improving, advancing, progressing, apotheosing. It was the opposite of modern life and its clattering technology, frenetic activity, and scientific-minded positivism. Instead, a Zenlike quieting, a time-space entity of deep serenity and mystery opens up, and the star—the swan—makes an entry as dramatic as any operatic prima donna, unforgettable in its very stillness.

The exquisite paradox was that in creating the most effective evocation of *Kalevala* imagery that has ever been composed, Sibelius distilled its concentrate from a volatile swirl of *Kalevala*-esque, Symbolist, mythic, Wagnerian, Austro-Germanic, and Russifying elements. At that moment, Jean Sibelius showed his real genius.

∽13∽

The Politics of the Theatrical

CORONATION SPLENDOR AND SORROW

On May 26, 1896—only one month after the premiere of the *Lemminkäinen Legends*—one of the most splendid ceremonies of the entire nineteenth century took place in Moscow: the coronation of Nicholas II as emperor of all the Russias. To the ringing of bells and the firing of cannons, Nicholas, who had ascended the throne in 1894 upon the assassination of his father, now received the symbols of the power of his realm. The spectacle unfolded in red, white, and gold on a brilliant spring day. Gilded carriages rumbled through the streets, bearing the dowager empress, the young czarina, and members of the nobility. Court officials and servants, including the four Africans always attached to the imperial suite, processed forth. So did *les gardes chevaliers*, a body of huntsmen, the khan of Khiva, and the emir of Bokhara, those two on superb steeds. Here was Tolstoy, in full court dress, among the thousands who gathered to gape in awe. There was Albert Edelfelt, sketching and even photographing events with his newly purchased "snapshot camera."[1]

Coronation standards fluttered in the breeze. The emperor himself, mounted on a magnificent white Arabian stallion, rode into the Kremlin and up to the Cathedral of the Assumption.[2] Mighty as the Swedish kingdom had been, no Scandinavian Lutheran court could compare in opulence with that of the Russian czars. What other regime could boast such a glorious mingling of East and West? Who else possessed such dazzling symbols of power? A sparkling grand imperial crown created for the coronation of Catherine the Great, encrusted with 4,936 diamonds and weighing 2,858 carats; an imperial scepter encasing the famous Orlov diamond, whispered to have been wrested from the eye of a Hindu idol; and the golden imperial orb, wreathed in diamonds and surmounted by a gargantuan sapphire.[3] Nicholas, garbed in flowing, fur-trimmed robes and wearing the crown, received the scepter and the orb as the people looked on solemnly. One of the two chevalier guards who immediately preceded the newly crowned ruler as he processed through the streets was a Finn: the six-foot, four-inch Carl Gustaf Mannerheim.

Nicholas seemed to be cut from a different cloth from that of his father. As chairman of the Trans-Siberian Railway, he was well traveled about his realm. He had even journeyed abroad and thus was believed to bring a wider understanding of international relations to the throne. In his finance minister, Sergei Witte (1849–1915), he had a dedicated servant committed to expanding Russia into a modern industrial society. In his marriage to Princess Alice of Hesse-Darmstadt, granddaughter of Queen Victoria, who presided over Europe's most stable monarchy, Nicholas had made what seemed to be an auspicious liaison. No one realized just how disastrous would be the combination of a reluctant emperor and a zealous German. Transformed into Empress Alexandra Fyodorovna, the princess would exhibit depths of religiosity and heights of fervor that made her calamitously susceptible to the pretender Rasputin and his soothing promises to heal her only son, the heir to the Russian throne.[4]

Even at the coronation ominous portents already chilled the air. Officials had arranged a public festivity in the large park outside Moscow known as the Khodynskoe. Thousands flocked to the grounds. By early morning, some 500,000 people had gathered to receive a share of the imperial largesse commemorating the spectacle. But no care had been taken to keep order in such a throng. As officials began to dispense coronation mugs, coronation cakes, and coronation candies, the human mass surged forward until suddenly pandemonium erupted. Trampling like stampeding animals, the crowd crushed some 3,000 fellow humans to death and injured hundreds more. In retrospect, it seemed a ghastly forewarning.

INSPIRATION AND ACADEMIA

In Helsinki, the Finns also celebrated the coronation, albeit months later and far more decorously. The date chosen was November 2, the anniversary of Nicholas's ascension to the throne in 1894. The place was the Imperial Alexander University, of which Nicholas II had been chancellor until he was crowned emperor. It fell to Jean Sibelius, at that moment the university's acting music teacher, to compose a cantata in the emperor's honor. The text had been prepared by another of Hämeenlinna's sons, Paavo Cajander (1846–1913), who made his greatest contributions to his country's national awakening as a translator; between 1879 and 1912 he rendered all of Shakespeare's plays in Finnish, thereby enabling frequent performances of the bard in Finland. None of that glorious literature made the first dent in Cajander's repetitious drivel for the *Coronation Cantata*:

Hail! Hail, young Prince,
Dawn of a new morning!
Hail, hail!
The cloud of yearning goes away,
Day indeed again triumphs!
A morning of new hope dawns.
Bright day again triumphs,
Our young Prince.
Hail, young Prince!
With joy of hope in its breast
The people of Finland salute you!

The musical setting of this text, for mixed choir and full orchestra, performed in the Festival Hall of the university, sounded every bit as pedestrian as the text. It was providential that the only imperial presence was in bronze. Would the real imperial ears have caught the dissonance between Mother Russia and her grand duchy in the Luciferian tritone sounded between the G-major key of the first movement and the D-flat key of the second movement? With himself, Sibelius was brutally honest: "It seems as if I am sleeping my life away," he muttered into his diary, followed by a theme from the cantata that was the tonal embodiment of slumber (see ex. 13.1).

EXAMPLE 13.1. SIBELIUS, THEME FROM THE *CORONATION CANTATA*, WITH A DIARY ANNOTATION ON AUGUST 22, 1896. HUL 1472A, P. (4). © BREITKOPF & HÄRTEL, WIESBADEN.

Despite the indifference of the imperial music, Sibelius was just then seeking to strengthen his ties with the Imperial Alexander University. The central position of this academic institution in Finland's history, national life, and politics is difficult for outsiders to grasp. In the annals of national histories, the role of this university may well be unique. As the Finnish historian Matti Klinge observed, it is unlikely that any "university in any country has been more important to society or has played a more significant role in building up national unity."[5]

Emperor Alexander I had invested the institution with the task of raising the national spirit, which his imperial eye viewed as being in Russian interests, and he nearly doubled its budget. His brother and successor, Nicholas I, also granted lavish resources to the university when it was moved from Turku to Helsinki in 1827. Nicholas had imposing new buildings erected and gave the institution the right to bear his brother's name, and so it became the Imperial Alexander University in Finland. As time went on, the university became increasingly central to the country's political life. Its students and their "nations" played decisive parts in awakening national sentiments, and its faculty performed leading roles in shaping the national agenda. No Young Finn could afford to be indifferent to its possibilities and influence.

Sibelius's personal ties with the institution ran deep.[6] Both his father and brother had been graduated from its hallowed halls. Although he had abandoned his own university studies in favor of the music institute, he had been a member of the university's Academic Orchestra, conducted by the widely respected Richard Faltin. In fact, it was Faltin's position that Sibelius was filling that May of 1896, his predecessor having taken a leave of absence. Composing and conducting for official events belonged to the responsibilities of the position, which was how Sibelius came to write another university cantata, this one for the graduation ceremony held on May 30, 1897, to festive texts by A. V. Forsman (later Koskimies; 1856–1929).[7] One of its numbers, *Soi kiitokseksi Luojan* (*We Praise Thee, Our Creator*), was taken up into church services, sung throughout the land in praise of the heavenly—and, by extension, the earthly—creators of modern Finland.

Faltin had announced his decision to retire. As a result, from May 1896 until July 1897, Sibelius filled his place while the university conducted an official search for a full-time replacement. Sibelius, under pressure from his mother, applied for the position. In exchange for a yearly income and considerable prestige, the duties were far from onerous: two hours of orchestra rehearsal per week, a similar amount of time spent teaching either music theory or music history, and the responsibility of composing and directing the music for university ceremonies. Meanwhile, the music director was permitted to earn additional fees through private tutoring.

As with university searches today, there was the inevitable paperwork, including curricula vitae and audition lectures, and these have proved a great boon to scholars. The composer's curriculum vitae, dated May 30, 1896, listed thirty-one compositions.[8] Although the position was artistic, the context was academic, and Sibelius, who was competing with Ilmari Krohn and Robert Kajanus, had to come up with a lecture as part of the application process. A little more than three weeks after conducting his lackluster cantata, Sibelius held forth on the topic "Some Aspects of Folk Music and Its Impact on Art Music."[9]

His rivals, however, were not without merit. Ilmari Krohn had the strongest academic credentials. Although Krohn had some composing to his credit—his music had figured prominently on the Savo-Karelian lottery program of 1891—and he was steadily advancing the folk music research that would occupy so much of his life, he chose to lecture on Robert Schumann; furthermore, he spoke in Finnish. Meanwhile, the strengths of the other candidate, Robert Kajanus, who was being pressured by *his* mother to seek the position, were well-known. Yet the very qualities that recommended him—experience as a conductor and administrator and a visionary founder of his own music school—also made it clear that Kajanus was already committed in numerous directions. And his lecture, on the Finnish-born composer and clarinetist Bernhard Henrik Crusell (1775–1838), was, like Sibelius's, delivered in Swedish.[10]

Krohn, despite having delivered the best lecture, having the strongest academic credentials, and, not least, having spoken in the tongue promoted by the nationalists, was effectively dismissed from consideration (he, bless him, went on to become Finland's "father of musicology"). Kajanus was judged as having too many obligations elsewhere. In a statement unique in university annals—and probably drafted by Faltin, who had supported Sibelius since his student days—the evaluating committee assessed Sibelius's candidacy in superlatives:

> In Jean Sibelius our country has gotten a musician who with his rich talents exceeds everything our music thus far has been able to produce. As if from an inexhaustible well, he has drawn forth for us in these several years a group of magnificent works bearing the stamp of genius and filled with amazing thoughts never before heard. . . . No one has previously been able to depict the essence of our country as Jean Sibelius has, with tunes so original, so purely Finnish, that even the uninitiated recognizes and is captivated by them. It is true that the incredible rapidity and ease of his creative work has so far meant that there are also boring places, which could have been avoided with a slower way of working, but Sibelius has this fault in common with other unusually productive artists, for instance, Franz Schubert. . . . In our view, an artist on Sibelius's level would be a true ornament to any university.[11]

The only possible result of such an assessment was to place Sibelius first among the candidates. Indeed, he received an overwhelming majority vote, 25 to 3 (Krohn received none). But a series of labyrinthine bureaucratic twists playing out over many months gradually revealed where the real power lay. It began with Kajanus's bitter objection to the decision and his demand for a new vote. He gained one supporter. Sibelius's name then went forward to Saint Petersburg, to the man with the final authority: Carl Woldemar von Daehn (1838–1900), Finland's minister-secretary of state. In a resourceful episode of shuttle diplomacy for which he later became notorious, Kajanus himself visited Saint Petersburg. (Even decades later Kajanus's chutzpah left people aghast, though lobbying in Saint Petersburg was something of a Finnish tradition. Harold E. Johnson reported that when he was in Helsinki in the 1950s, "Professor Ilmari Krohn whispered nervously to me, 'Kajanus went to Saint Petersburg!'")[12] On July 29, 1897, von Daehn overruled the Finns' recommendation and appointed Robert Kajanus to the position.[13]

Had Sibelius lectured to a modern-day academic search committee, his candidacy might well have been set aside on the basis of his teaching. Indeed, the examiners found his presentation "full of original ideas" but, like his *Lemminkäinen* music, "mosaic" in construction, even spontaneously improvised (or, put less positively, not rigorously argued). Said Sibelius:

> One speaks of a personal style in music and of a national style. The personal style would then be—to put it briefly—the stamp a composer gives his own work—it follows that the national style would be the stamp a people imprint upon their composers. How important is the role played by folk music in the latter case we learn in a quite striking way from the history of music. We thus see how great a scope folk music has as an aspect of an individual's education.[14]

The general consensus is that even though Sibelius lost the position, he received the ideal result in the long run: a state pension. More important, the larger picture showed how deeply the Finnish-minded leaders, the educated men "from above"—*culture octroyer*—were committed to the national agenda and to what lengths they would go to ensure that matters of significance to the national project be supported. In this case, it seems to have been none other than Yrjö-Koskinen, the ardent mastermind behind the KVS, who addressed a letter to von Daehn broaching the idea of state support for Sibelius. This was the same Yrjö-Koskinen who, seven years earlier, had opposed a travel grant for the untried, erratic, and still wet-behind-the-ears Janne Sibelius in favor of awarding the funds to a young musician he viewed as far more promising, the baritone Alarik Uggla.[15] In October 1897, however, this opportunist made the case that Sibelius, whose music "is fully imprinted with national features," should be granted a state pension of 3,000 Finnish marks and occasionally, some other, less elaborate support, specifically in order "to enrich our national art."[16] The senate made a statement to the emperor on November 30, 1897. On January 8, 1898, the state secretariat communicated that the emperor had agreed to the stipend: an annual sum of 3,000 marks, renewable for ten years, beginning in 1897 (see fig. 13.1).

Sibelius was the first composer in Finland to receive such support, and the sum he received was equivalent to the salary of a university music teacher. As a point of comparison, full professors at the Imperial Alexander University were earning 6,000 Finnish marks annually; "extra ordinary professors," 5,000 Finnish marks.[17] The decision signaled a decisive acknowledgment of the importance of music to the national movement

WJ

NIKOLAI DEN **ANDRE,**

med **GUDS** Nåde,

KEJSARE OCH **SJELFHERRSKARE**

ÖFVER HELA RYSSLAND,

TSAR AF **POLEN,**

Storfurste till Finland,

&c: &c: &c:

Göre veterligt: Som WI i nåder funnit

godt att tillägga tonsättaren Johannes

Christian Julius Sibelius ett årligt

understöd af tre tusen (3000) mark att

utgå i tio års tid, räknadt från den

1 Januari 1897; alltså vele WI här-

med och i kraft af detta öppna bref

tillförsäkra honom, tonsättaren Sibelius,

att sagda understöd, tretusen mark,

under tio års tid, räknadt från den

1 Januari 1897 af finska allmänna me-

del åtnjuta och detsamma qvartalsvis

Utan afgifter.

Figure 13.1. Imperial edict of 1898 granting a decade of annual stipends to Jean Sibelius, beginning "WE, Nicholas the Second, by the Mercy of God, Emperor and Supreme Ruler of all the Russias, Czar of Poland, Grand Duke of Finland, etc. etc. etc.," 1898.
The National Archives of Finland.

and a commitment to its support. It communicated in an official and tangible way that composition belonged with painting, sculpture, and literature in creating the national identity. For Sibelius, the stipend marked a turning point. It provided a base of financial security. And his creativity began to soar.

OPERA AND NATION BUILDING

Because these matters took time to unfold, the year 1896 was a time of uncertainty for Jean Sibelius. The difficulties over the university position were compounded by personal loss: the death of Aino's father on April 14, 1896, just as the *Lemminkäinen Legends* were being premiered. Meanwhile, Sibelius's life was filled with lusterless commotion—teaching (not his heart's desire) and wastrel goings-on. Yet there were some new works. Despite the animosity generated by the wrangling over the university position, Sibelius composed a piece to benefit Kajanus's orchestra and orchestra school: an opera called *The Maid in the Tower*, which he conducted in Society House on November 7, 1896.

Opera was an obvious choice for giving wings to the spirit of national aspirations. Sibelius had witnessed the results for himself at Bayreuth (although there, the grandiose objectives were somewhat blighted by the sausages and beer on offer during the intermissions and the blaring trumpets calling the faithful to each new act).[18] By giving assistance to the national orchestra with a new opera, Sibelius could doubly serve the national mission. And the theme of an innocent maid cruelly incarcerated against her will offered the perfect subtext to the Finnish minded, who had been personifying their beloved country as "the Maid of Finland" since 1890.

Yet the result showed just how difficult it was for a Swedish-speaking Finnish composer to craft a genuinely Finnish opera. First of all, the text, *In a Maiden's Bower*, allegedly based on a "Finnish ballad," was written—and sung—in Swedish (although there were those who insisted the tale came from Lönnrot's *Kanteletar*).[19] Nor was that the only problem with the libretto, written by Rafael Hertzberg. Far from some Nibelungen-like tale, it was a startlingly silly product even by nineteenth-century operatic standards, its inanities on dreadful display from the opening lines:

Sheriff: Fairest virgin, sweetest damsel, thou my radiant star!
Maiden: Please, merciful sir, let me be!
Sheriff: Oh beautiful child, I love thee.
Maiden: Thou must not speak to me thus.
Sheriff: Thee I love, o tarry with me.
Maiden: Leave me!

The maiden's chirrups at times border on the absurd:

> *Maiden*: O Father,
>   O Father,
>   O Father, do not forsake me![20]

Valiantly, *Uusi Suometar* claimed that the opera (which the newspaper's critic referred to as *Tornissa olija impi*) had a genuinely Finnish stamp and was *yleiseurooppalaisuutta* (all European), and hopefully declared that it had a good chance of becoming known outside the country's borders. Perhaps the best that could be said was that the Swedish-speaking Finns advancing the national project had good intentions. It was telling that Sibelius later misleadingly claimed to Rosa Newmarch that this "ballad, which has been dramatised as an Opera in one act, entitled 'The Maiden in the Tower,' dates from my youth."[21] At the time of its composition, he was thirty-one.

To tell the truth, the circumstances of the premiere were considerably more interesting than the new opera. The occasion was another of those lottery soirées. The evening's events, together with the libretto's problems, help to explain *The Maid*'s failings as an opera, though perhaps not as an endeavor to promote the national spirit. The usual rich lottery soirée mix of homegrown and international music and drama swirled together with dance, food, drink, wafting cigar smoke, rustling silk gowns and bespoke suits, all intermingled in the elegant rooms of Society House, where a glimpse of paradise was offered those who jostled for places.

This time the artistic organization was in the capable hands of Albert Edelfelt, who had arranged three *tableaux* for the Sofia Room alone: "A Folk Song," featuring a peasant girl playing a *kantele* before a seascape; "Church Music," highlighting Cecilia, the patron saint of music, looking like an "inspired nun"; and "Opera Music," showing Venus with her knight, Tannhäuser, the march from Wagner's opera having begun the evening. The stunning visual splendor of these and other *tableaux vivants* spelled the ultimate in hedonistic Symbolism: gilded sphinxes, glittering candelabras, glowing lamps, gleaming bronze decorations, swaths of richly brocaded gold cloth, actors dressed as yeomen of the guard, and above all, a voluptuous Salome, whose "Herod's Dance" took the audience by storm.[22] It was this spectacular event, which had to be repeated, that Sibelius's opera had to follow. Succeeding him in turn was a "concert portion" of the evening, featuring *Adjö, Herr Pantalon!* (*Bonsoir, Monsieur Pantalon!*), an *opéra comique* by the Belgian composer Albert Grisar (1808–1869; his name was misspelled on the program as "Grisard"). Lottery tickets were sold continuously.

When it was Sibelius's turn, some of Finland's leading singers—Emmy Achté, Abraham Ojanperä, and Ojanperä's pupil, the promising blonde Ida Flodin, from Oulu—

sang their parts courageously. The conductor-composer egged on his small orchestra. His idea of a choir behind the stage to create the mood succeeded splendidly, thought Flodin, although the critic observed that for long hours the operatic stage stood empty. (He should not have been surprised: everything about the evening except Salome—and the audience—was static.) But all to no avail. Poor Hertzberg was undone. The Sibelius biographer Erik Tawaststjerna drily remarked that as a librettist, Hertzberg hardly rose "to the mediocre heights of Erkko as an author, [though] he still had a certain sense of what worked on the stage."[23] The mortified librettist died on December 5, 1896, less than a month after the premiere, still in his early fifties. Neither Hertzberg nor anyone else that evening had any idea of the real implications of the events that had taken place in their Society House that year: from June 28 to July 5, 1896, the Lumière brothers had shown the first moving pictures in Finland.

FINNISH HISTORY AND MUSICAL PATRIOTISM

Homegrown operas and theatrical lottery soirées were not the only musical avenues for supporting the national movement. Early in 1898 Sibelius was at work on a different kind of nationalist work, this one a choral composition for a competition sponsored by the men's choir Sällskapet MM (variously called Muntra Musikanter and the Merry Musicians). The texts could be either in Finnish or Swedish. Sibelius chose adroitly. No tender *Rakastava* here (his setting of a love text, which had placed only second in a competition in 1894). Although the verses he selected were in Swedish, the lines were drawn from one of the cornerstones of Finnish identity, Runeberg's *Tales of Ensign Stål*, and they carried an unambiguous patriotic message. The rousing piece eventually called *Sandels* tells of the magnificent General Johan August Sandels's defeat of Russian forces at the Battle of Virta Bridge. Composed for men and orchestra (as its first title, *Improvisation for Male Choir and Orchestra*, made clear), the work earned its composer a first place in the competition. Sibelius signed the score *Homo* (Man), as though to emphasize his own courageous connection to the heroic military figure of Sandels.[24]

The dramatic element in Sibelius's creativity also overflowed into a more theatrical but no less historical work. Adolf Paul, showing up in Helsinki early in 1898, persuaded his friend to compose incidental music for Paul's five-act historical drama *König Kristian der Zweite* (*King Christian II*). Translated into both Swedish and Finnish, this sprawling account of a sixteenth-century Danish monarch enjoyed an astounding success: twenty-four performances in the Swedish Theater's 1898 season alone.[25]

However appealing Sibelius's music, the reasons for the sensational impact of such a rambling and bombastic play probably had a great deal to do with its allegorical possibilities in the politically charged atmosphere of Helsinki. The drama tells of the fall of the Danish king after his beautiful mistress Dyveke was poisoned and of the king's eventual restitution—a story with unmissable opportunities to draw parallels between a historical monarch and a certain unnamed current one. The production thus joined other dramatic presentations, from lottery *tableaux* to plays, put into the service of political protests in Helsinki, including Schiller's *Maid of Orleans*, whose title character had been transformed into the Maid of Finland, dressed in the national colors in Kaarlo Bergbom's stagings in 1887, 1896, and 1902–5.[26] As for Sibelius's music for *King Christian*, conducted by the composer himself at the early performances, the phenomenal number of editions and arrangements that sprang up (a list of which goes on for several pages in his thematic catalogue)[27] gives strong testimony to the impact of the event and the composer's extraordinary ability to gauge the moment.

The *King Christian II* music is usually given short shrift in Sibelius discussions, yet in a number of respects it had considerable importance. For one thing, it introduced Sibelius as an orchestral composer abroad—in continental Europe, in England, and in the United States. Hans Winderstein conducted four of its numbers in February 1899 at his philharmonic concerts at the Albert Hall in Leipzig; in December 1900 Texas-born Frank van der Stucken conducted the music with the Cincinnati Symphony Orchestra;[28] in October 1901 Henry Wood programmed its numbers in a London Promenade concert. For another, with *King Christian II* Sibelius established firm connections with a publishing house abroad. The decision marked a crucial move toward wider dissemination of his music. His fateful choice, which governs the publication of his music to this day, fell on the German firm of Breitkopf & Härtel.

Moreover, *King Christian II*, along with *Carminalia*, composed the same year, represented a work in which Sibelius deliberately evoked historical musical styles at a moment when historical—even ancient—Finnishness was materializing as a key element in national opera and drama. Sibelius told Adolf Paul that the choice of two bassoons and two clarinets in *King Christian*'s musette represented bagpipes and chalumeaux, a kind of pseudo-baroque sound. (Of course, he added, we only have two bassoonists in the whole country and one is consumptive: "But my music won't be hard on him. We'll see to that.")[29]

Carminalia, composed to poems discovered by his Lovisa friend Elise Stenbäck, clearly called for historical treatment: their verses represent what is probably the oldest Finnish poetry to have survived. They derive from the *Piae cantiones*, the famous collection of ecclesiastical and scholastic songs intended for pupils of the Cathedral School in Turku. In 1582 a Finnish student had published the poems in Greifswald with the editorial help of the school's headmaster, Jakob Finne.

However oddly historical styles seem to sit with Sibelius, they reveal the depth of his awareness of the national movement and its precepts and the means with which he engaged in the collective project of building Finland's identity. And out of their music, simply but unmistakably, emerges another kind of awareness. We hear it in his rendering of Paul's unforgettable image of malevolence in the libretto for *King Christian II*: "In the grass sits a spider so big and so black / And there he glares and he gloats." The spider image as a metaphor for czarist—not imperial—Russia was ubiquitous in Finland: it showed up in literature, cartoons, magazines, postcards (see plate 6). In the Spider's sly, shimmering, syncopated song—sung by the Fool—twirl the lethal tendrils even then being spun into fatal arabesques around Finland (see ex. 13.2):

EXAMPLE 13.2. SIBELIUS, "SONG OF THE SPIDER," FROM *KING CHRISTIAN II*, MM. 1–4.
© BREITKOPF & HÄRTEL, WIESBADEN.

He seizes the sunbeams and twists and toils
And spins in darkness and knits a web
So strong and so tight
So airy and light
Its meshes entrap each living soul
whom he pitilessly tortures and torments.

1897–98: OF DEATH AND TRANSFIGURATION

It was in 1897–98 that Karl Flodin began to show a growing disgust with the gruesome fascinations and opiumlike effects of Symbolist thought. Whether prodded by Kajanus's devilry or offended by the lottery that spawned the *Maid in the Tower* and that salacious Salome, or whether he sincerely believed it was his duty to set Finland's great musical hope on the path to salvation and national focus, almost a year to the day after the *Maid*'s lottery debut Flodin attacked the most recent concert of the *Lemminkäinen Legends* from a new angle: *Die Kunst des Erschütterns.*[30] Invoking the example of the "draftsman" Sascha Schneider (1870–1927), an album of whose pictures had just been released in Germany, Flodin gave a hellish picture of Schneider's art: the terrifying and the appalling depicted through gargantuan means. Here were fearful demons, there was Satan's struggle for the soul; canvases were pierced with horrid, burning eyes and painted with monstrous hands that grip a man and cast him to earth. Then Flodin launched a killer thrust of his own: what Schneider means to accomplish with his soul-shaking drawings, he railed, Jean Sibelius evidently wants to achieve with his *Lemminkäinen* music.

But Flodin had a way to go to dampen Sibelius's fascination with Symbolism. Some months later, the composer received a commission from Heikki Klemetti (1876–1953), director of the men's choir YL. An uncompromising Fennoman, Klemetti wanted musical settings of texts by Aleksis Kivi, the author who had elevated Finnish to a language of literary prose. And thus it came about that while Aino was expecting their third child, Sibelius set to music Kivi's sorrowful lullaby, *Sydämeni laulu* (*Song of My Heart*), a poem about a dying child, whose verses come at the end of Kivi's famous novel *Seven Brothers*.

Although death pervaded the literature, art, and music of Symbolism, the theme of the dying child had long before been elevated to respectable art by Goethe in his *Erlkönig* and set to chilling music by Schubert. In the Nordic lands the theme had been made topical soon after Schubert's setting, when twenty-one-year-old Hans Christian Andersen composed a poem called *The Dying Child* (1826). Andersen transformed the usual literary treatment of death in childhood by exploring life's ultimate experience through the eyes and words of the child, not the parents. Translated almost immediately into German and then into French, *The Dying Child* started Andersen on the road to world fame.[31]

Being the voracious reader he was, Sibelius was very likely acquainted with Andersen's poem; he certainly knew *Erlkönig* and Schubert's setting of it. Thus, although he could have mined Kivi's poems rather than selecting the most morbid of lines from a novel that, ironically, is often quite comical, the composer had strong precedents for choosing the death lullaby, whose sentiments also fit supremely well with Finns' famous and, it must be said, cherished melancholic disposition:

Tuonen lehto, öinen lehto!	Grove of death, grove of night!
Siell' on hieno hietakehto	There is a fine cradle of sand,
sinnepä lapseni saatan.	There will I go with my child.

Those lines would return to haunt him.

The long reach of Symbolism extended well into the next century. In 1903 Arvid Järnefelt completed one of the few Symbolist dramas in Finnish literature, *Kuolema* (*Death*).[32] The next year his collection of short stories, *Elämän meri* (*The Sea of Life*, 1904), also drew on Symbolist ideas, a resource that, in combination with his Tolstoyan enthusiasm, led Järnefelt to his life's philosophy of the brotherhood of man. Sibelius's incidental music for his brother-in-law's play once again proved how infinitely inspiring the Symbolist aesthetic was for him and how from the simplest of means he mined Symbolist gold—in this case, the seemingly effortlessly composed bars of *Valse triste*, that melancholic minor-mode echo of a lost century. The work's strangely haunting quality fed easily into dramatic realization: in Saint Petersburg, Georg Balanchine selected *Valse triste* for his choreography of an angst-filled dance for the ballerina Lydia Ivanova. In the stunning climax, Ivanova, in exaggerated horror, mimed *The Scream*, a gesture of deadly silence powerfully uniting Edvard Munch's notorious painting with Sibelius's increasingly celebrated music. Ivanova herself came to a tragic and surreal end: she was drowned in the Gulf of Finland. Her friends believed that she had been murdered for political reasons.[33]

The specter of death that seemed to haunt Sibelius made other intrusions into his life. The deaths of Hertzberg and of Aino's father in 1896 were followed by his mother's death at the end of 1897. Maria was buried early the following January in the Borg family plot in the Ahvenisto cemetery in Hämeenlinna. Afterwards, family and friends gathered at the home of her old friend, Eva Savonius, teacher and mentor to the young Sibelius. Savonius later recalled how the composer had sat at the harmonium and played to his mother's memory; in her recollection, perhaps burnished by time and emotion, there was not a dry eye in the room.[34]

Some weeks later, on March 20, 1898, Karl August Tavaststjerna died, not yet thirty-eight years old. The writer had come down with pneumonia after a too-lengthy encounter with a snowbank one alcohol-drenched evening. He never recovered. Tavaststjerna's death deprived Sibelius of "a friend who could have taught me much," the composer remembered sadly.[35] What his friends never knew, because it was revealed only in 1960, was that it was not pneumonia that had killed Finland's "first modern Swedish-language poet." In a perversion of medicine as bizarre as any Symbolist hallucination, a nurse had mistakenly administered the poet a dose of Lysol.

Yet it was a little-noticed event in 1897 that was destined to make the greatest transformation in the lives of Finns: the resignation of Count Fyodor Logginovich Heiden from the office of Finland's governor-general. The move signaled a death of another kind—the death of an era.

$\backsim14\backsim$

From Russia but Not with Love

A NEW MAN FOR FINLAND: MANIFESTOS AND ADDRESSES

The forces that brought Nikolai Bobrikov to Finland grew out of long-simmering imperial concerns. While the Finns were channeling their nationalistic energies into education, art, and public ceremonies from lotteries to song fests, Russian nationalists were promoting the belief in "Russia, one and indivisible."[1] In an amazingly multinational land, less than half of whose population was considered Great Russian, the meaning of that phrase had ominous implications for all minorities. As early as the 1860s the conservative journalist and ideologue Mikhail Nikiforovich Katkov (1818–1887) was urging the formation of a uniform Russian state, a strong Russian nationality, one language, one religion, one *Russian* community. Be Russified or be crushed! With particular rancor he singled out the Finns: "The worst of enemies could not devise a more pernicious fate for Russia than the spread of the example of Finland. There is nothing more repulsive to the political attitude of the Russian people than federalism, the mere thought of which is enough to make one sick."[2]

Katkov was not alone in bitterly resenting the special status of Finland. Businessmen, bureaucrats, pan-Slavists of all stripes, and, not least, military leaders found fault with having an autonomous entity strategically positioned on Russia's western flank, yet beyond their absolute control. Feeding the resentment was uncertainty over the effects of the European powers in the Baltics, Russia's critical borderlands, whose populations were especially susceptible to Bismarck's Germany. Obsession with imperial unity and Russification grew apace.

Yet Finnish autonomy was writ large in the policies of the Russian emperors. Through generations of honoring the grand duchy's position, keeping the imperial word had become ingrained. Even that cold fish Nicholas I, whose repressive policies no one

239

recalled with affection, commanded: "Leave the Finns in peace. Theirs is the only province in my great realm which during my whole reign has not caused me even a minute of concern or dissatisfaction."[3] The emperors were amply rewarded: Finns showed them unswerving loyalty. The xenophobe Alexander III, whose ear the neonationalists steadily bent and who implemented Russification policies in other imperial borderlands, carried on the tradition. He admitted that "Finland's constitution does not please me. I will not permit its further expansion. But I am just as bound to uphold that which my predecessors have granted to Finland as if I granted it myself. And on ascending the throne I confirmed by my word the inviolability of Finland's special autonomous status."[4]

But in the early 1880s shifting political alliances, most worrisomely the Triple Alliance signed by Germany, Italy, and Austria-Hungary in 1882, began to threaten Russia with powerful and potentially hostile coalitions. More and more often, the "Finnish question" was being asked: why should special status be granted fewer than 3 million inhabitants of an empire whose total population numbered some 130 million?

When in 1897 Count Heiden resigned as Finland's governor-general, smoldering concerns flamed into life, fed by fanatical nationalism, diversionary tactics, and individual agendas in Russia. Worse, heightened revolutionary activity within Russia and the specter of Swedish-German cooperation abroad exacerbated the volatile situation still further. In such a climate it was little surprise to find the Russian newspaper *Moskovskie Vedomosti* (in early January 1897) describing the position of Finland's governor-general as "the most difficult of its kind in the whole empire."[5] The man eventually found to take on the task had come to wider attention expressly through his devotion to imperial unity and imperial security: Nikolai Ivanovich Bobrikov.

Major-General Bobrikov (1839–1904) had taken a dim view of the Finns for more than a decade. Assigned to report on the security of Saint Petersburg in 1886, Bobrikov, then chief of staff of the guards and the military district of Saint Petersburg, had expressed alarm at the dangers posed by Germany, on the one hand, and the weakness of Russian power in Finland, on the other. He proposed measures to strengthen the Russian military in terms that appeared draconian to the Finns, since they would bear much of the cost and furthermore would have their administration centralized. Yet it was his professional experience with military issues in the northwestern part of the empire and antirevolutionary struggle, coupled with his "administrative abilities, industriousness, and Russian way of thinking," that ultimately made Bobrikov, despite his personal reluctance to assume the office, the imperial choice.[6] The decision was likely aided and abetted by the Russian minister of war, A. N. Kuropatkin, whose own position was strengthened by a Bobrikovian appointment. In the summer of 1898, Emperor Nicholas II approved. The date—in Finland—was August 23.[7]

Nicholas II might have been young and a weakling, but Bobrikov was known as a "fox," skilled but stern, organized but obstinate, a ruthless and unscrupulous schemer. More than a whiff of dishonesty clung to his person, for he was reputed to have improved his own financial position with misgotten funds. In fact, his excessive influence in the Russian capital, together with certain irregularities he had committed, made it necessary to remove him from the center of power. Unaware of how Bobrikov was viewed in the empire, Finns saw in him the personification of evil. During his tenure in Finland, he received, in addition to the normal salary, an additional salary from the Russian state treasury—both exempt from taxation.[8] Chauvinistic (regarded by the conservative press as a "true Russian"), speaking neither Finnish nor Swedish, backed by the ultranationalists (whose sentiments were running high and escalating), Bobrikov seems to have viewed his role as upholding "the dignity of Russia" by forcing the Finns to understand their position as an imperial borderland, whatever the cost. Within a week of his appointment, on August 18/30, 1898, Bobrikov presented his emperor with a ten-point interim plan with which to bring the Finns to heel. Worryingly, military reform headed the list.

As outlined by Tuomo Polvinen, the plan addressed the following areas:[9]

1. *Military*: Finland's army was to be integrated into Russia's and the military burden and costs of army maintenance "balanced" (meaning shared by the Finns). Finland's famed Cadet School was also to be reformed "in the Russian spirit" and an officers' club for Finns and Russians (presumably to encourage fraternizing) established in Helsinki.

2. *Office of the minister-secretary of state*: Because the governor-general's insufficient power relative to that of the minister-secretary of state had been an issue of long standing, the office of minister-secretary of state was to be abolished or its authority otherwise restricted.

3. *Legislation*: Finland's laws were to be made to conform to Russian law, and special procedures established to deal with matters of interest to both the empire and the grand duchy.

4. *Language*: Russian was to be adopted in the Finnish diet, in educational institutions, and in administrative offices.

5. *Russian rights*: Russians were to be permitted to serve in the grand duchy's institutions without being subject to legal restrictions.

6. *Education*: Supervision of the Imperial Alexander University in Finland was to be reorganized and the textbooks used in schools inspected.

7. *Monetary questions*: Separate tariff and monetary institutions in the grand duchy were to be abolished.

8. *Press*: An official Russian-language newspaper was to be established, and publication of newspapers by Russians either in Russian or local languages facilitated.

9. *Parliament*: Ceremonies for convening new sessions of the diet were to be simplified.

10. *Office of the governor-general*: The regulations pertaining to this office, set forth in 1812, were to be revised; in Bobrikov's view, it was essential that the governor-general have authority equivalent to that of similar offices elsewhere in the empire.

To these menacing propositions, Nicholas II gave his full consent.

On August 21/September 2, 1898—shortly before Bobrikov's arrival in Finland—an editorial in *Moskovskie Vedomosti* gloated:

> The new era which is beginning in Finland will doubtless have a beneficial effect on the inhabitants of our other borderlands, whom separatists have incited into hostile estrangement from Russia of every kind, including appeals to the idea of "autonomous Finland," which is supposedly subject to the Tsar only by a personal union and is otherwise entirely foreign where Russia is concerned. This pernicious illusion will now be destroyed.[10]

On his arrival in Finland on the unlucky thirteenth day of October, 1898, Bobrikov delivered a speech—in Russian—to the grand duchy's governing officials, making his position clear: "Within the boundless reaches of the Russian Empire, there exists for all those people who stand beneath the mighty sceptre of the czar only *one* sort of allegiance and *one* sort of patriotism"—to which the university's vice-chancellor, on being given the translation, was heard to mutter, "Unpleasant prospects."[11]

The effects of Bobrikov's plan soon became dreadfully apparent. Even before taking office, Bobrikov had helped convince the emperor to sign the conscription bill, intended to make Finnish conscription regulations identical to those elsewhere in the empire. On January 24, 1899, an extraordinary convocation of Finland's diet was assembled, and the imperial will, as written and presented by Bobrikov, was presented: "Indivisibly joined to the Realm and under the protection and security of the entire Russian Empire, Finland does not need a military establishment separate from the [R]ussian army. Therefore the legislation on conscription there must be made to conform to that in force in the Empire."[12]

Slowly at first, but with horrifying predictability, more and more freedoms were circumscribed, and the nightmarish prospect appeared of Finnish men having to serve in the Russian military. Then, on February 15, 1899, after a personal audience with the emperor,

Bobrikov presented the Finnish diet with the ukase known as the "February Manifesto." Its purpose was to declare to the Finns that in an indivisible empire, of which they were a part, imperial legislation applied to all. In a word, the diet could be relegated at any time to a mere advisory capacity, its policies overruled by imperial will.

The impact was devastating. The emperors' sacred vow to Finland had been suddenly, cruelly, acrimoniously broken—and through secrecy and intrigue. Cooler heads today view the manifesto as a decree less revolutionary in governmental fact than in political consequence. Among Finnish historians, Tuomo Polvinen observes that some "200 imperial laws and decrees had been published in the same form in the statute-books of both Russia and Finland since 1808"; as Osmo Jussila puts it, the February Manifesto was in certain respects a codification of the existing order.[13] But in 1899 the people were shocked, not least because Nicholas II had been showing the world another, more humanitarian face (especially for a Russian czar). In August 1898, the very month Bobrikov was appointed to the position in Finland, the emperor had issued an invitation to the nations of the world to join a peace conference devoted to arms control.[14] Across Europe "this flash of lightning out of the North" had gladdened the hearts of men and, with the approaching millennium, given cause for belief in favorable omens, hope for a new era, and the dawn of a new epoch.[15] Only a few harbored suspicions: Rudyard Kipling penned the verses he titled *The Bear That Walks like a Man*.

Now the Finnish lion had felt the brute strength of the Russian bear. People reacted as though death itself had visited the land. Women dressed in mourning. People brought narcissi and white roses by the armful and sorrowfully laid them at the foot of the statue of "the good Czar," Alexander II, in Senate Square. University students, ever the political activists, took more vigorous measures, criss-crossing the country on skis to collect signatures for an appeal.

Heretofore most of the political maneuvering vis-à-vis the Russians had been outside the ken of the vast majority of the Finnish population. The February Manifesto galvanized the increasingly enlightened *kansa*—the people—to consider the meaning of "fatherland," and in this context fatherland meant, above all, the fair-minded laws and institutions from the time of Swedish rule.[16] From the grass roots now swelled a mighty protest. Housemaids and milkmaids, farmhands and crofters, wives and widows, smiths and carpenters lent their signatures to the appeal. Unprecedented in Finland's history, Suuri Adressi (the Great Address) garnered more than half a million signatures, over half the adult population of the grand duchy. The people identified themselves by vocation—"crofter," "maid," "hired hand," "milkmaid"—or status—"wife," "widow," "son." To Bobrikov's shock and consternation, a delegation of 500 Finns ("all crooks in relation to Holy Russia") brazenly conveyed the vile document to Saint Petersburg. The emperor, who had declined to receive an earlier delegation, refused this one too, blaming their "domestic government" for such unheard-of misbehavior.

It was a measure of the national outrage that the Finns, who normally exercise docile Lutheran obedience in the face of authority, took the issue abroad—in the form of the so-called International Cultural Address, or *Pro Finlandia*. Printed in folio in Stockholm, dated July 5, 1899, *Pro Finlandia* contained 131 handsomely produced pages in vivid colors and gilded letters. Its first plate is a deep-red reproduction of the feisty Finnish lion under a crown. Its leaves bear 1,050 signatures from sympathizers in Austria, Belgium, Denmark, England, France, Germany, Holland, Hungary, Italy, Sweden, Switzerland, and Norway. Signatories included such distinguished names as Thomas Hardy, Florence Nightingale, Henrik Ibsen, Georg Brandes, Adolf Erik Nordenskiöld, and Christian Sinding. There were some fourteen folios bearing names of sympathetic Italians (fols. 79–93); eighteen folios bristled with signatures of Germans (fols. 2–19). A statement of solidarity was printed in the language of each of the signatory countries, who expressed uniform disbelief that a ruler who had called for international disarmament and peace would "decree the ruin" of a flourishing people (see plate 7).

The general statement in each of the various languages was followed by individual pleas and declarations from each nation. It is one of history's ironies that in the years of Finland's "first oppression," the world grew closer than ever before. The February Manifesto and *Pro Finlandia* roused awareness of the Finns as perhaps nothing else could have done. It literally put Finland on the world map—Frederick Rose's "Serio-Comic Map," to be exact, in which a sprawling Nicholas II, holding the olive branch of peace in one hand, a faintly ominous spindle in the other, nearly obscures Finland (see plate 8).

Nicholas II shrewdly ignored *Pro Finlandia*. As the Russians were well aware, no foreign power was going to intervene in what was essentially an internal matter.

Although the February Manifesto had finally ignited Finland's grass roots, angry protests were not limited to the man in the street or, more precisely, to *torpparit* (crofters) in their miserable huts. On the day the hated document was made public, February 18, Eino Leino composed the poem *Helsinki sumussa* (*Helsinki in the Mist*). In its lines, the statue of the revered Alexander II, personifying the rights of a free and autonomous Finland, stands shrouded in mist, a silent and, one is led to believe, disapproving witness of orders shrieked at a passing Russian army unit.

Sibelius's most radical brother-in-law, Arvid Järnefelt, accompanied by his brother Eero, betook himself to Russia to put Finland's case before Leo Tolstoy, whose devotee he was.[17] Tolstoy counseled that the issue was a question of light and freedom, that it was the duty of mankind to defend Finland for humanity's sake, and that the circumstances morally justified the use of self defense and passive resistance.

In those heady days of imperial opposition and testosterone-fed titanism, Sibelius too was caught up in the throes of vigorous remonstration. In short order he was making his sympathies known. On February 19, he wrote to Robert Kajanus, "Your 'eläköön rakas isänmaa' [Long Live Our Beloved Fatherland] rings in my heart—yes, long live this poor, poor land."[18] Cries of "Long Live Finland," "Long Live Our Beloved Fatherland," and "Light to the People" had been echoing from the halls of patriotic gatherings, lottery soirées, and association meetings for some two decades.[19] Now the cry had become vitally urgent and painfully topical. Approximately two weeks after this letter, Sibelius's fervent emotions took musical form. Turning to one of his most beloved writers, Viktor Rydberg, he found the words to express Finland's militant mood:

> Glorious is Death,
> When courageously led to the forefront
> You fall in the fight for your land
> Dying for hearth and for home.

Rydberg's idealistic and often rebellious poetry had served Finns before (Rydberg was a noted racist who lauded the strong, blond Nordic male). During the 1880s, his *Den siste Athenaren* was one of the most popular books among educated circles in Finland, according to Juhani Aho.[20] Now *Athenarnes sång* (*Song of the Athenians*), from the poet's *Dexippos*, an epic tale glorifying the Greeks' struggle against the superior might of the Goths, chimed with the hour's chord. Finns, with their broad streak of neoclassical conservatism, had long reveled in parallels with the Greeks, seeing in themselves a similar people also capable of enduring a harsh climate, yet magnificent in their trust in God and belief in fate.[21] Many of the nationalists had entered into this classical theme. Had not Lönnrot himself made the *Kalevala* a veritable Homeric epic? And what of Runeberg, who lectured in Greek and depicted the Finns in his patriotic verses in an idealized, classical manner? The indefatigable Fredrik Pacius had even turned Topelius's *Prinsessan af Cypern* (*The Princess of Cyprus*) into an opera in which Lemminkäinen, of all people, was plunked down in Cyprus, while the Cypriot princess had inspired Martin Wegelius to compose his *Oceanidernas sång*. And Juhani Aho intermingled the worlds of the *Kalevala* and ancient Greece in his short story *Nuoruuden unelma* (*A Youthful Dream*).

Now, in *Song of the Athenians*, the Finns were primed to read a high moral parallel to their plight vis-à-vis the Russians in the story of a small Greek tribe (protectors of culture, defenders of civilization!) fighting for its life against the barbaric Persians. No matter that the poet and his words were Swedish. Not only did the Swedish literary heritage belong to Finnish history, but the very foundations of what it meant to be Finnish had been laid in Swedish. And the Bobrikovian climate was demonstrating clearly that

Sweden's legacy of laws and institutions had been enlightened indeed. It helped that the Swedes showed partiality to the Finns in the wake of the February Manifesto, although, like other powers, the Swedish government declined to interfere.[22]

Sibelius's fair copy of his protest chorus has both Swedish and Finnish titles as well as Rydberg's verses in both languages. The texts, however, were added by someone else: the handwriting is not the composer's. And the Finnish translation grated. Another post-card to Kajanus, dated June 10, 1899, read: "Times are hard. Accept this farthing. I hope Atenarnes sång in Finnish will be all right? Try your best!"[23]

He wrote the music for a unisonous chorus of boys and men (that proud and nation-alistic sound promoted by the Turku Romantics) and a mighty phalanx of brass—four horns, three trumpets, three trombones, and tuba. To these he added timpani and tri-angle as well as pairs of woodwinds, but, with the exception of menacing contrabasses, no strings. On March 12, 1899, the men of Akademiska Sångföreningen sang the new piece in Helsinki's spa park, known as Kaivopuisto. The official premiere took place on April 26: Sibelius conducted a concert in the Imperial Alexander University's Festival Hall; it began with *Skogsrået* and continued with his newly concocted First Symphony and *Athenarnes sång*. The *Song*'s wild popularity surged out of all proportion to its musi-cal qualities. Even the most enthusiastic Sibelian recoils at the stomp of its thudding gait tramping gamely along in the basses between verses of rowdy unison, yet *Song of the Athenians* sensationally captured the spirit of the hour (see fig. 14.1a and b).

The spectacular response—in countless versions that suddenly mushroomed as if overnight—for voices with piano and harmonium ad libitum, for piano alone but printed with the incendiary text, for male voices and brass septet, for violin, for military band[24]—and the *Song*'s near-instant publication (by Helsingfors Nya Musikhandel Fazer & Westerlund) left little doubt that Finnish musical resistance represented a force that no governor-general could ever hope to quell.

ᘓᓚᖂᓫᘔ

On September 21, 1899, the soprano Ida Ekman sang two solo songs newly composed by Jean Sibelius: *Svarta rosor* and *Men min fågel märks dock icke*. Their lilting Swedish syl-lables and their intimate expressions kept their creator in touch with his deepest roots.

CENSORSHIP IN FINLAND

Political matters in Finland worsened. Censorship—of the press and other printed materials—had always been a fact of life under the emperors.[25] Heretofore the Finns had reached a more or less workable accommodation with the Russian overlords. The

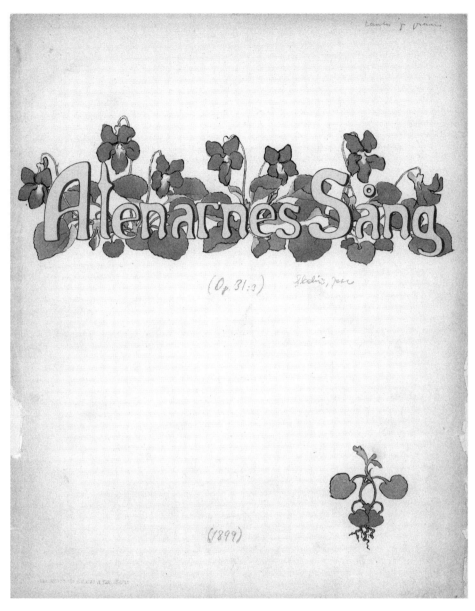

Figure 14.1a. Sibelius, *Athenarnes sång* (*Song of the Athenians*), 1st ed., 1899.
© Breitkopf & Härtel, Wiesbaden. The gently nodding violets, symbolic of Athens, which
authors from Aristophanes to Macaulay have praised as the "City of the Violet Crown," were an
artful Finnish subterfuge deflecting attention from the ferocious passions of the *Song*.

Figure 14.1b.

empire's highest authority for supervising publications was the board of censors of the Ministry of the Interior, with the grand duchy having its own separate, independently functioning board. In 1865 Alexander II had signed into law an imperial decree addressing press regulations.[26] Certain categories of publications were exempt from "preliminary" censorship; regulations for printing houses, etchings, lithographs, the book trade,

Figure 14.1b. (*continued*)

and dramatic works were spelled out. With this decree the emperor gave the press a recognized legal position, a measure that reduced somewhat the government's stringent control. Yet by exposing the often flimsy reasons for the censors' rulings, the decree also contributed to a gradually escalating resentment of those controls. Even so, its fundamental principles continued in effect right up until 1917.

During the 1880s the Finnish diet had frequently raised the issue of press freedom. In particular, the Finns requested that preliminary censorship, which still affected periodical publications in Finland, be lifted. Although the Russians granted more press freedom than has been realized,[27] still, newspapers and magazines had to have the governor-general's special approval to be published, and other kinds of printed materials were subject to inspection prior to publication. Exceptions consisted of official and scholarly works and publications more than eighty pages in length (on the theory that few would read such weighty tomes). And any publication could be banned once it appeared in print.

In 1891 a new decree circumscribed the authority of the grand duchy's board of censors. This edict transferred full power to grant publication permits to the governor-general. At that time Heiden occupied the office, and he continued matters essentially as before. But with the arrival of Bobrikov, who had already singled out the press as a target in his determination to discipline the Finns to his way of thinking, the Finns began to experience the near-dictatorial powers of the new decree. Ironically, the large circulation of low-cost newspapers, a result of the successful educational and enlightenment programs, had made the press an ideal tool for propaganda and therefore an object for censorship as a means of curbing unruly aspirations.

Bobrikov especially despised the Swedish-language newspapers, convinced that they were bent on fulminating separatism; rural Finns, he believed, were likely to be his allies. Consequently, such publications as *Nya Pressen* and *Aftonposten* became his special targets (*Hufvudstadsbladet* meekly adopted a more conciliatory stance and survived; Fennoman papers supporting submissive politics, such as *Uusi Suometar* and *Uusi Aura*, did not even suffer suspensions). Convinced that the best plan would be to shut down recalcitrant newspapers, Bobrikov set about trying to extend his already formidable powers over the press. He obtained an imperial decree allowing him to issue warnings. When these proved ineffective, he simply closed down a publication. He required printing presses to have special permits to take on new projects; he replaced editors willy-nilly; he made the Advisory Committee on Press Affairs permanent. Meanwhile, he pushed forward with plans to establish a Russian newspaper in parallel Finnish and Russian editions in order to "educate" the population about its "benevolent and loving mother [Russia] who does not interfere in their religion, language or traditional ways."[28]

Newspapers with empty columns began to hit the stands. Then, one by one, newspapers began to be banned. By the end of August 1899 the interdict had reached *Päivälehti*, which was proscribed for three months. Before the proscription went into effect, its editors urged readers to show their determination to defend a free press. Defiantly, *Päivälehti* switched names. As *Ilmoittaja*, it published three more issues, including bold declarations of the forthcoming publication of the Young Finns' Christmas album, *Nuori Suomi*, and

announcements of sales of textbooks (bravely signifying that education and enlightenment would continue). But in April 1900 its editor-in-chief, Eero Erkko, was forced to
resign.[29]

NEW LOTTERY SUCCESSES

At this critical moment of heightened restrictions on freedoms of speech and press, the
Savo-Karelian student nation recruited Sibelius for a new lottery event. The students
hoped to repeat the great success of 1891, an occasion made spectacular by Kajanus's
conducting and Gallén's *tableaux*. At the same time they wanted to demonstrate their
commitment to the national awakening and the project of enlightenment.[30] The fantastic
success of *Song of the Athenians* made the choice of star composer obvious. Staged as a
tableau vivant, the *Song* was to serve as the evening's centerpiece. Preceding it was to be
a newly commissioned work: a setting of Topelius's *Islossningen i Uleå älv* (*Ice Breaking
on the Oulu River*).

In a country with few dramatic landscapes, the Oulu River is one of Finland's most
energetic natural manifestations. Because in winter it freezes solid, the river delivers
a never-to-be-forgotten spectacle at the spring thaw. Artists were drawn to its stately
banks. I. K. Inha had photographed its bridge (see figure 9.1). Gallén sketched its streams
(*Uleå elf* [*The Oulu River*]). Topelius, in his epitaph to the stream, penned in 1856, had
used the river and its tributaries as an allegory for loyalty and fidelity to the Russian ruler
then ascending the throne, Alexander II: "the coward who desires to flee danger / Must
die like the trickle dies in the marsh's mire." The poet's dramatic culmination was the
mighty splintering of the river's frozen surface:

> Then—in the hour of speechless terror
> With a thundering boom the ice cracks asunder
> And the collapsing dam bends,
> Breaks, and bursts from the river's swell.
>
> Marching by millions and still millions
> A powerful winter army
> Of white, shimmering splinters
> Is scattered, to vanish in the waves of the sea.

By 1899 that splintering had taken on new meaning. With phrases such as *routa-aika* (time
of frost) and *sortokausi* (period of oppression) beginning to appear in the press, the surge
of that mighty river overflowed with profound connotations for Finns.

On the evening of October 21, 1899, a theatrical build-up launched the new work on its course. E. G. Palmén, rising to give the requisite speech demanded by such occasions, delivered a eulogy in Swedish laden with the code words "education" and "enlightenment," culminating with an invocation to the Finnish people to heed the verses of their poet who had eulogized the Oulu River: "I want air! I want light! My fate I myself will create with my own torrent" (Jag vill ha luft! Jag vill ha ljus! Mitt öde, det vill jag skapa själv med eget flöde). No censor could possibly object: after all, Topelius had penned these lines in honor and admiration of a Russian emperor. Yet veneration for what Finns believed was the good Alexander's fair governance in combination with wild, untamable Finnish nature and flowing water—powerful symbols for political freedom in that climate—gave the poem a subtext evident to every educated citizen.[31]

Sibelius's setting of those words was shrewdly gauged to fit the climate: once again he chose the neutral title "improvisation," *En improvisation för manskör med orkester samt melodram*, for a work anything but neutral.[32] He chose a combination of male narrator and men's chorus, an ensemble that could hardly raise the censors' ire but carried the strongest possible nationalist connotations. The principal role went to the narrator, who led off with ten stanzas of Topelius's poem, beginning with the stanza containing the lines,

> Noble son of Finland's blue lakes,
> Free I was born, and free I want to die.

With the orchestra coloring and punctuating the text with menacing chords, the choir of tenors and basses took over the central portion of the work. They sang in vigorous unison, their syllabic staccatos spitting out the words with rising excitement. The high point came with the bursting of the dam in a thunderous explosion of icy power. Only at that moment did Sibelius temper the aggressive unison voices with harmonization:

> The countryside breathes. The waves lessen.
> Churning over the broken dam,
> Free and victorious, the proud river,
> Majestic, surges on its course.

The narrator returned and on the sixth stanza concluded the work, uttering again the words, now with unconquerable meaning:

> Noble son of Finland's blue lakes,
> Free I was born, and free I want to die.

Sibelius conducted Kajanus's orchestra and the student choir YL. The forceful Axel Ahlberg was the narrator, the magnetic actor who had declaimed *Skogsrået*. The com-

poser penciled in, probably during rehearsals, the various interpretive markings that
stand in the manuscript today; just after the chorus sings "Skingras väldiga vinterhären,
att förgås uti hafvets våg" (A powerful winter army is scattered, to vanish in the waves
of the sea) in the allegro molto section, Sibelius added "Quasi presto—cresc.—molto—
cresc. possibile," building to the powerful moment at the 2/2 presto when the ice splin-
ters. There, between the staves, he scrawled the words "Kolossales pang!" (Colossal
explosion!). A storm of applause erupted.

Only then, with the audience well disposed to impassioned outbursts, did the dramatic centerpiece ratchet up tempers to splendid heights as the choir, now clad in Greek
tunics, raised the rafters with *Song of the Athenians*. The choir sang heroically, the audience clamored, encores were demanded. The entire performance had to be repeated. The
evening's music came to a ringing close with the stanzas of *Vårt land/Maamme-laulu*.

Islossningen is important less for its intrinsic value as a finished composition than
for its place in the sequence of Sibelius's patriotic, thinly disguised protest works that
were created for the purpose of benefiting "public education," building national unity,
and promoting nationalistic fervor through the collective endeavor of national lotteries
and their dramatic manifestations. Sometimes the results remained for domestic use only.
Sometimes they made their way around the world. Such was the case with the music on
which Sibelius was already at work—another lottery commission for something to be
called the Press Days.

~15~

The Finnish Resistance

A LOTTERY FOR THE FINNISH PRESS

The Finnish language makes splendid use of the passive voice. In account after account of the extraordinary efforts that went into raising funds for journalists cast out of work by the strangulating censorship, the newspapers that still could function announced events in the passive voice: "A lottery is planned," "an event called 'Press Days' is being held." Those directly responsible remained safely hidden behind a semantic scrim of obfuscating concealment that avoided pinning action on any single individual. A dominated culture learns quickly the value of artful expression. But for reasons more serious than usual, the primary documents about the Press Days (Sanomalehdistön päivät/Pressens dagar) avoided specifying those who initiated events, while recounting the happenings in considerable detail.

Still, it is clear that among those who harnessed the rising public anger, members of the *Päivälehti* circle loomed large; it was, after all, their mouthpiece that Bobrikov had spitefully silenced. Many were prominent in the events that "were organized" in Helsinki. Meanwhile, all through the land, on November 3–5, 1899, not only Finland's larger towns of Turku and Viipuri but also Oulu, Jyväskylä, Hamina, Naantali, Pori, Mariehamn, Rauma, Kuopio, and Sortavala each staged one or more lotteries and associated happenings. In each case the reason given was to raise money for journalists made redundant by the board of censors, but in reality Finnish leaders were providing outlets for demonstrating resistance and rallying for freedom of speech. The Press Days were thus a nationwide affair, extending far beyond the evening that included Sibelius's music. And for the great public, the high point was almost certainly—sports.

On November 3, 1899, an event at Siltasaari's *manège* or riding school attracted *le tout Helsingfors*. "Living material"—gymnasts, horseback riders, cyclists, fencers, skaters, and wrestlers, all brilliantly attired—flaunted their strengths and skills to the accom-

paniment of music. The affair bristled with meaning. Sporting events, a rapidly growing phenomenon all across Europe with both economic and nationalistic implications,
were proving extraordinarily capable of attracting mass audiences, and Finland was
no exception.[1] There was the sheer physical prowess, the primal power, the stark courage on display. What better way for Finns to demonstrate their aptitudes or to reveal
their willingness to do battle, be it social or military? The rising enthusiasm showed up
in new vocabulary in the Finnish language: a word for sport—*urheilu*, which vibrates
with echoes of *urho* (hero) and *urhea* (brave, courageous). Other new words—*voima*
(strength), *elinvoima* (stamina), and *voimistelu* (gymnastics)—all emphasized the power
imbedded in those two Finnish syllables *voi-ma*. In the very substance of its majority language, Finland was changing.

On the same day as the sports demonstration (and following a popular concert), an
orgy of blooms, bonbons, and artworks enticed an audience with more elevated tastes
(though not much) to Society House, whose rooms had been lavishly decorated by Eliel
Saarinen, Armas Lindgren, and the less well-known architects Werner von Essen, Gunnar Stenius, and one of the Jung brothers (either Bertel or Valter), to make "a beautiful
impression." Program booklets, along with *Det fria ordet* (*Free Speech*), a poem composed
by Ida Lönnbeck of Tampere, were sold out. The crowd vied to purchase reproductions
("framed and under glass") of Albert Edelfelt's pastel drawing of the recently deceased
K. A. Tavaststjerna, despite the steep price of 50 Finnish marks. Helsinki and specifically
Ylioppilastalo (the Student House of the University) was the venue for Maila Talvio's
play *Amerikkaan* (*To America*), directed by the industrious Jalmari Finne, a work that
flaunted the idea of freedoms enshrined in that land's democratic constitution.

It was only on the following evening that the public was treated to the spectacle
that included music commissioned from Jean Sibelius. November days in Helsinki are
among the year's dreariest, and November 4 held true to type. Rain and gloom filled the
night. But in the Swedish Theater, the new electric lights glowed; plush loges and warm
parterre seats welcomed the elite audience crowding in for the evening's entertainment,
whose tickets were at a premium. And entertainment it was—an extravagant if peculiar
mix of homegrown and imported artistry. Kajanus and his orchestra opened the proceedings with Wagner, whose March from *Tannhäuser* set the stage for not just one, but two
prologues, the first in Swedish, read by the poet and zoology professor O. M. Reuter
(1850–1913), and the second in Finnish, read by the prolific Hämeenlinna-born writer
Karl Gustaf Larson, who wanted to be known as Larin-Kyösti (1873–1948). Poems in
both languages followed. No one saw any irony in speeches and poetry being delivered in
Swedish as well as Finnish. The common enemy across the border united them all.

Only after the prologues and poems did the curtain rise on the first of six *Tablåer från Forntiden* (*Tableaux from Ancient History*). These in turn were followed by the expected "concert portion" of the program: Massenet's *Pensée d'automne*, Pacius's *Morgonsång*, and the Andante from Mendelssohn's Violin Concerto, all with piano accompaniment by Oskar Merikanto; and chansons both French and Swedish (Bellman's) performed by Anna Pettersson-Norrie, with Sigrid Sundgren-Schnéevoigt playing on an old spinet built in Turku in 1765. Both women, "charmingly dressed in ancient style," sweetly reinforced the none-too-veiled message: Finns had an ancient history and high culture. Those noble sentiments were somewhat tempered by what followed: a satirical review entitled "Dream or Reality" or "The Great Canard," involving the proscription of a newspaper, which completed the evening's Disneyesque array. Live ducks and real cats waddled and slinked across the stage, flamingos and senatorial chairs whizzed overhead, droll lines were warbled to well-known melodies. During the intermissions sales of lottery tickets continued apace.

The audience could well be forgiven for not immediately conning to the fact that one of the many things they saw and heard that evening would have an afterlife so spectacular that few in their wildest dreams could possibly have imagined it.

TABLEAUX FROM ANCIENT HISTORY: THE TEXTS

It was widely agreed that the evening's high point (*aftonens glansnummer*) was the series of *tableaux vivants*. The reasons seem to have had less to do with the music and everything to do with the dramatic and visual spectacle. The texts had been the work of Eino Leino (1878–1926) and Jalmari Finne (the original commission to Leino having been executed at so slow a pace that the organizers turned to Finne in desperation). As for the staging, the director of the Finnish Theater, "Doctor" Kaarlo Bergbom (né Karl Johan, 1843–1906), had that responsibility. The precocious Bergbom, who had entered the Imperial Alexander University at the age of fifteen, had gone on to earn a doctorate in history, aesthetics, and modern literature—in German, French, English, and Finnish, but not in his home language of Swedish (in which he wrote his dissertation, *Det historiska dramat i Tyskland*, 1868). Like Snellman, Bergbom, an Old Finn, believed that education and art were powerful tools for promoting the national spirit. Together with his sister Emilie he had founded the National Theater. To the dramatic work for his country Bergbom brought "great talent and [an] eye for artistic effectiveness." Despite his longstanding animosity toward Eino Leino, those skills were so prominently on display during the Press Days that people widely agreed that never had such elaborate *tableaux* been seen on a Finnish stage.[2]

As with similar, earlier lottery soirées, the Press Days' *tableaux vivants* were a collaborative artistic effort in the service of political aims. What set the Press Days lottery apart was its elaborate scope and preparation—with events all over the country—and the heightened political tension arising from the loathsomeness of censorship and the curbing of free speech. Nothing drives home that reality more forcefully than the attempt to locate the *tableaux* texts. They vanished. It was not until 1984 that the Finnish historian Tuomo Olkkonen found a copy—in Finland's censorship files.[3] For these texts too, like newspaper articles and all other materials to be made public in the grand duchy, had to be inspected and approved by the board of censors.

Today those texts lie quietly in their hated file box, preserved in full if not quite pristine form (a hole is burned through the title of the second *tableau*). They were copied by someone other than Leino, although they are identified as his (and his alone) and have errors of the kinds all copyists make. On October 31, 1899, the censor had given permission for the affair to go ahead with the proviso that one change be made: the picture of Emperor Alexander II to be included in the last *tableau* would not be permitted.

Tuomo Olkkonen also traced the sources for the Leino-Finne texts. Conspicuously, all the texts had lives beyond their function in the Press Days *tableaux*. They show clearly that their authors had gathered up common themes and given visual and dramatic expression to widely propagated attitudes. The euphemistic use of "spring" was one of those themes. Drawing ideas and even lines from his earlier *Kevätlaulu* (*Spring Song*, 1896), Leino infused spring sentiments into the opening *tableau*, which depicted Väinämöinen charming both people and animals in spring-filled nature. The approaching performance deadline may have induced the poet to appropriate his *Spring Song*'s opening words wholesale for the last *tableau*, a springlike awakening entitled *Suomi Herää!* (*Finland, Awake!*).[4]

Defiance was another theme. Leino and Finne lifted the words for *tableau* IV, which portrayed the Thirty Years' War, right out of the popular *March of the Finnish Cavalry in the Thirty Years' War*, its text by Zachris Topelius, who had died just the year before and whose influential presence was still palpable, especially in the capital.

Yet the overriding theme, as the designation of the *tableaux* made clear, was "history," the more olden, the better. Personifications of true historical figures paraded through the scenes, however fancifully their actions were interpreted: Bishop Henrik, patron saint of Finland, baptized and Christianized Finns in *tableau* II. The conquering spirit of Peter the Great was incarnated in the scene depicting the Great Wrath (as the Great Northern War is often called in Finland), shown in *tableau* V. It is no longer clear just who wrote what in these two scenes. But *tableau* III, set at the court of Duke John (the Swedish ruler considered to be practically Finnish, so devoted was he to Finland), was unmistakably Finne's. The very next year (on April 10, 1901), Finne's four acts of a

poetic "comedy exercise," entitled *Juhana herttuan hovissa* (*In Duke John's Court*), hit the
Finnish stage. Finne returned to the theme in 1917 when his five-act *Juhana herttua* (*Duke
John*) was produced in the National Theater.[5]

Without some knowledge of long-forgotten historical details, Duke John's significance is as lost on the modern listener as was Duke Narimont's in the *Karelia tableaux*.
Yet John's character and reign explain a great deal, both about the attitudes that prompted
the decision to portray him in the first place and also about the music Sibelius composed
to represent the duke and his court. John (1537–1592), later King Johan III, a son of the
powerful Swedish King Gustav Vasa, had been appointed duke of Finland in 1556.[6] The
newly pronounced duke headed for Turku Castle, where he lived in an aristocratic European style such as had never before been seen in Finland. His library contained volumes
not just of ecclesiastical stripe, but also of such classical authors as Plutarch, Aristotle,
Cicero, and Saint Augustine. The duke's attitude toward language was also broad-minded;
he emphasized knowledge of tongues beyond his own (which was Swedish), even promising—an assurance dear to the hearts of later Finnish nationalists—to learn Finnish.

Duke John placed considerable importance on courtly etiquette, ritual, and, after a
trip to England in 1561, the modish style of Spanish dress. He began to wear short tunics
in rich fabrics with padded shoulders; his courtiers dressed likewise. The "improprieties"
of Spanish fashion even seem to have spread to the local aristocracy, inciting the bishop
of Turku to rain down Lutheran condemnation on the heads of "the mad members of
the court" for their vulgar Spanish displays, better suited to bacchanalian orgies than
to proper governance. Nevertheless, the duke followed his extravagant and liberal heart
by marrying a Polish princess, Katarina Jagellonica, whose grandmother was Isabella of
Aragon and whose more distant ancestor was none other than Duke Narimont.

With Katarina's arrival in Finland, the budding Renaissance in Turku burst into full
flower. European artisans were brought in to decorate Turku Castle, musicians were
imported from abroad, and distinguished royal guests visited. Although that Renaissance
was short-lived (the duke and duchess were imprisoned in 1563 by Erik XIV, John's genuinely mad half brother), while it lasted Finland had royalty and a Renaissance court,
not to mention direct contacts with European culture and a venue for the flow of liberal, humanistic ideas. The nature of this splendid court, knowledge of which had only
recently been recovered from newly surfaced documents, fed into the historical views
gladly being promoted by late nineteenth-century nationalists.

Thus did the Press Days' *tableaux* play on the themes of the national awakening,
which were displayed in a glorious panorama of the "true state" of Finland, a poetic space
of treasured landscapes and heroic deeds. Across that space trooped some 150 figures in
all (plus an unspecified number of animals, both live and impersonated), including the

baptizing Catholic bishop; persons standing for broad-minded, highly cultured, *European* royalty; representatives of high moral values (for which the Finnish Cavalry was surely fighting in that Thirty Years' War); cruel Russians (who devastated "Mother Finland"— a shrewd gender switch on *Isänmaa*—fatherland); and, in the thrilling culmination, symbols of an "awakening" Finland.

Never had such elaborate arrangements been made for a Finnish lottery program, a program repeated not just once, but several times: on November 6 it was staged again in the Swedish Theater, and on November 11 it was given twice in the Finnish Theater. Reflecting on these events only ten years later, Eliel Aspelin observed that the Press Days were the last time when all—Old Finns and Young Finns, Finnish-speaking and Swedish-speaking, activists and pacifists—united, before the revenge years and internecine war made such cooperation impossible.[7]

TABLEAUX FROM ANCIENT HISTORY: A SYNOPSIS

Tableau I: Väinämöinen Charms Nature with His Singing

THE PEOPLE OF KALEVA AND THE NORTH

The Finnish Orpheus Väinämöinen (played by Benjamin Leino), seated on a stone, mesmerizes the people of Kaleva and the north by playing his *kantele*, enchanting even the animals and nature itself.[8] A jumble of *Kalevala* characters crowd around. Rising from the sea is Ahti, the Finnish Neptune (and another name for Lemminkäinen). Tapio (the forest god) comes from the woods, Ajatar and Metsähiisi (the forest devil) crouch impishly in a cave, and Sinipiika (another forest spirit) and Sampsa Pellervoinen (the god of growing things) arrive. Aino, Aallotar, Ilmarinen, Louhi, Lemminkäinen's mother, Vellamo—all gather to listen to Väinämöinen. Overhead, the Maid of Pohjola whirls her golden spinning wheel.

(The not-so-subtle subtext unmistakably linked ancient history, Old Finland, Finnish nature, and Finnish literary and folk culture.)

Tableau II: The Finnish People Are Baptized

BISHOP HENRIK, KING ERIK, MONKS, PRIESTS, CHOIRBOYS, FINNS, AND THREE ANGELS

The twelfth-century Bishop Henrik of Uppsala, patron saint of Finland, baptizes a young Finnish chieftain. (Finland has been notably unlucky in its saints and heroes: like poor

Torkel Knutsson, Bishop Henrik too was murdered, by a peasant on frozen Lake Köyliö.) Other Finns await baptism, some willingly, some with reluctance. King Erik IX and a procession of knights, priests, monks, and choirboys look on. An excited girl spies three angels, each bearing a sacred gift: a cross, a palm leaf, and a book (the Bible). They present these to the Finnish people as tokens assuring a bright future.

(All the symbols were weighted with meaning. As baptized Lutherans, the Finns relied on the Bible as the ultimate authority, a reliance the *tableau* emphasized as extending far, far back in time.)

Tableau III: Duke John's Court

DUKE JOHN, KATARINA JAGELLONICA, COURTIERS, AND A
FOREIGN TROUBADOUR

The great castle at Turku where Duke John (played by Kaarle Halme) holds court. Surrounded by ladies-in-waiting, pages and other courtiers, Finnish nobles, guards, and, not least, the foreign troubadour, Duke John declares his love for Finland and commits to its well-being, sentiments of which his duchess, Katarina Jagellonica, noddingly approves. In the Leino-Finne text the duke reassuringly asserts: "The court would speak the native Finnish tongue, / And love of native soil would there be sung."[9] Katharina Jagellonica and the others mingle in a festive bolero.

(The Duke's fascination with *espagnolisme* was emphasized by the use of castanets when Sibelius later revised the movement.)

Tableau IV: The Time of the Thirty Years' War (1618–48)

THE SPIRIT OF WAR, KING GUSTAV II ADOLF, AND SOLDIERS; THE MARCH
OF THE THIRTY YEARS' WAR IS SUNG

Along with officers and soldiers bearing weapons, four allegorical figures—Austria, Germany, Sweden, and Finland—ring the stage. Meanwhile, young Finnish peasants hasten to join the righteous struggle. At center stage, the Swedish King Gustav II Adolf sits upon his war steed. The Spirit of War bestows the banner of religious freedom upon the peasants.

(It never hurt to remind the Russians of how the Finns had fought for religious freedom, especially alongside the fierce Swedes.)

Tableau V: The Time of the Great Wrath

The Great Wrath (Isoviha), also known as the Great Northern War, fought between Sweden and Russia, was marked by Peter the Great's seizure of Viipuri in 1710 (depicted in the Pro Carelia lottery's *tableaux vivants*). The ensuing Russian occupation, lasting until 1721, resulted in the ravaging of Finland. It was a time of great woe; both Swedes and Russians wreaked havoc and destruction on the people and the land. The *tableau* shows "Mother Finland"—in the person of Saimi Järnefelt—seated among the ruins of charred homes, freezing snowdrifts, frozen cattle, and starving children. Personifications of war, hunger, cold, and death (by Axel Ahlberg, Eino Salmela, Emil Falck, and Otto Härhu, respectively) threaten the Finns with total destruction.

Tableau VI. Suomi Herää!—Finland, Awake!

EMPEROR ALEXANDER II, THE SPIRIT OF HISTORY, THE SPIRIT OF THE
NEW CENTURY, RUNEBERG AND HIS MUSE, SNELLMAN AND UNIVERSITY
STUDENTS, AND A SCHOOLTEACHER AND CHILDREN

Despite all threats and difficulties, Finland has not merely survived, it has awakened. The shade of the benevolent Alexander II, his picture forbidden, is invoked instead, significantly, by the Spirit of History, who rises to declare that Alexander's enlightened rule assured the Finns' propitious future. The revered triumvirate of founding fathers "awakens" the Finns: young Runeberg listens to his muse, Lönnrot diligently records *runot* from two folk singers, and Snellman motivates his students. Along with an array of ethnographic objects spilling around these figures—cheese molds, rakes, shovels, and what not—stand other symbols of industrially and culturally progressive Finland: the first folk school, where children are being taught to read by their young teacher, the four speakers of each estate from the first diet, and workers who surround a papier-mâché reproduction of the first locomotive engine (the cause of considerable amusement).

❧❧❧❧

What the synopses leave out is the silent, visual imagery, which lent sanctity and still further ideological meaning to the scenes. The first *tableau* was framed by an old Finnish pine forest; the second, by a stately forest of spruce trees; the third unfolded in the impenetrable and culturally splendid stronghold of Turku Castle; the fourth featured ferocious weapons and flags, including the flag of religious freedom; the fifth showed a frigid winter landscape, a metaphor for Finland and the pitiless cruelties Finns had to endure; while

the sixth was ringed with that quintessential image of the Finnish spring, a forest of delicately budding birch trees. The symbolism of the seasons together with the images of
Finnish trees—evergreen emblems of new growth and renewable resources—conveyed
powerful messages for which no words were needed (and which no censor could forbid).

It was above all the last scene, whose awakening spring reinforced a metaphorically
awakening Finland, that stayed in the minds of onlookers. Echoes of springtime and
veiled references to Russian oppression—the frost—filled the *tableau*, which rang with
the injunction:

Kyntäkää, kylväkää,	Now to plowing! Now to seeding!
toukojen, toivojen aika on tää.	The time for planting and hopes is nigh.
Toivehet milloin toteutuu,	Sometimes hopes are fulfilled,
milloin halla ne syö.	Sometimes nipped by the frost.
Nyt on Suomen toukokuu,	Now is spring in Finland,
nyt on kynnön ja kylvön työ;	Now for the work of plowing and sowing,
leikkuu, korjuu—kaikki muu	Cutting and tying—May everything else
jääköhön Herran huomaan.[10]	Be with God!

A SPRINGLIKE AWAKENING: *HERÄÄ SUOMI!*

With the *Tableaux from Ancient History*, the Finnish-minded elite had once again imposed
their historical visions and political attitudes upon their compatriots. Their evocation of
Finland's history began in mythic time and unfolded chronologically, culminating in the
all-too-real and rather frightening present. It incorporated the idea of the Finnish people
(*Suomen kansa*), oppressed and threatened (by frost and bitter cold, with all of their allegorical meanings), but doggedly determined to fight for freedom of religion and speech
and for justice. That determination did not waver, even in the face of impossible odds
dictated by severe and unforgiving nature, not to mention offensive Russians. Instead,
it would survive and even flourish, thanks to Finland's literate and musical culture and,
increasingly, Finnish high technology.

The organizers also shrewdly played on those tried-and-true ingredients that past
lotteries had shown to guarantee spectacular results: *Kalevala* heroes, the Thirty Years'
War, and the unjust and undeserved oppression of the people. The Thirty Years' War
alone was a guaranteed hit. Not unexpectedly, its *tableau* was one of the two that drew
repeated curtain calls, the other being the sensational finale.

For the real coup was to have culminated the "history" with an awakening. Cannily
plucked from the zeitgeist (or more properly, in Finnish, *ajanhenki*), the phrase *Herää*

Plate 5. Axel Gallén, *En saga*, 1894. Watercolor. Ainola (Järvenpää, Finland). The portrait of Sibelius comes from the artist's Kämp series depicting Young Finns. The empty space at the lower left was reserved for musical notation. Ainola Foundation/Central Art Archives. Photo: Hannu Aaltonen.

Plate 6. "The Empire's Tarantula—The Empire's Nightmare." Postcard
caricature by "ESS," 1906. The National Museum of Finland, Department of
Prints and Photographs, Helsinki.
Photo: Saara Salmi.

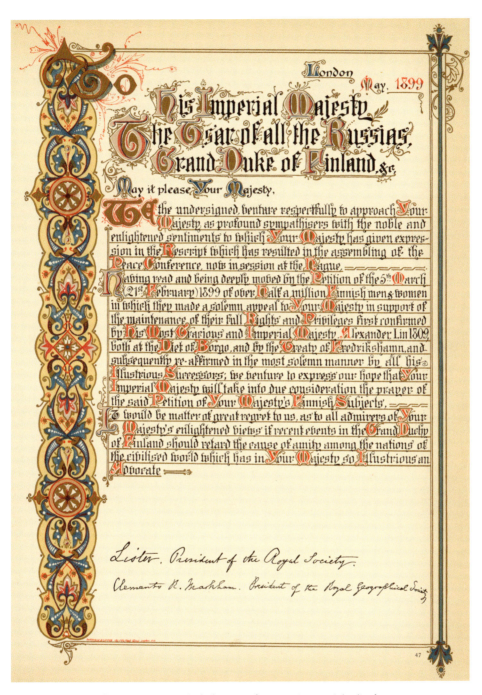

To

**His Imperial Majesty
The Tsar of all the Russias,
Grand Duke of Finland, &c.**

London May. 1899

May it please Your Majesty,

We the undersigned, venture respectfully to approach Your Majesty, as profound sympathisers with the noble and enlightened sentiments to which Your Majesty has given expression in the Rescript which has resulted in the assembling of the Peace Conference, now in session at the Hague. —————. Having read and being deeply moved by the Petition of the 5th March (21st February) 1899 of over half a million Finnish men & women in which they made a solemn appeal to Your Majesty in support of the maintenance of their full Rights and Privileges first confirmed by His Most Gracious and Imperial Majesty Alexander I in 1809, both at the Diet of Borgo, and by the Treaty of Fredrikshamn, and subsequently re-affirmed in the most solemn manner by all his Illustrious Successors; we venture to express our hope that Your Imperial Majesty will take into due consideration the prayer of the said Petition of Your Majesty's Finnish Subjects, —————. It would be matter of great regret to us, as to all admirers of Your Majesty's enlightened views if recent events in the Grand Duchy of Finland should retard the cause of amity among the nations of the civilised world which has in Your Majesty so Illustrious an Advocate ———

Lister. President of the Royal Society.

Clements R. Markham. President of the Royal Geographical Society

47

Plate 7. Great Britain's declaration of support, in *Pro Finlandia*, the
International Cultural Address (Stockholm, 1899).
The National Archives of Finland.

Plate 8. "Angling in Troubled Waters: A Serio-Comic Map of Europe." Matt. B. Hewerdine, from a design
by Frederick W. Rose (London: George W. Bacon, 1899). The National Museum of Finland,
Department of Prints and Photographs, Helsinki. Photo: Ritva Bäckman.

Suomi! (Awake, Finland!) had for several decades been the widely used metaphor for the national movement. Topelius had opened his *Boken om vårt land* with a "Morning Song" in whose five stanzas the injunction *vak upp* (awake) appears no fewer than eight times. The Kansanvalistusseura had long put to good use ideas of awakening and dawning light. These showed up in the KVS motto "Light to Our People" and its goals of "enlightenment," specifically calibrated to awaken an unaware populace to a national consciousness—and, not incidentally, to keep out the weeds of socialism.

Images of awakening abounded in Finland by the 1880s, including in revivalist movements. The zealotry of the Pietists, sometimes called "the Awakened," coalesced into a kind of national movement of its own.[11] Religious revivalism had swept much of northern Europe in the 1830s and 1840s. Today the Finnish figure most remembered in this connection is Paavo Ruotsalainen (1777–1852), thanks to Joonas Kokkonen's opera *Viimeiset kiusaukset* (*The Last Temptations*, 1972–75). On the outer fringes of conservatism, the Awakened had little respect for the higher clergy or the bureaucratic state: the kingdom that interested them was the kingdom of God, and their evangelism was partly fomented in opposition to the national movement. Their brand of fanaticism was reignited during the 1880s, the heyday of Finnish organizational activities. When in 1894 Juhani Aho published *Heränneitä* (*The Awakened Ones*), a collection of allegedly accurate short stories about the Pietists, he was portraying the Finnish religious awakening in his own parish of Iisalmi, where his father was a Pietist pastor.

Awakening had permeated other aspects of society. By the 1890s it widely evoked the extraordinary cultural and educational renaissance, the miraculous "awakening" to a unique Finnish identity and Finnish potential that was spreading throughout every layer of the community. As a motto, *Herää Suomi!*, familiar from lottery programs, lines of poetry, choral concerts, and artworks, tapped into a deep, deep well of emotions, symbols, and swelling Finnish patriotism. The image suffused literature—the pessimistic *Heräämätön* (*Without Awakening*), by the short-lived Oulu poet, Kaarlo Robert Kramsu (1855–1895), which had as its cheerful theme "Suomen kansa on nuorena kuolemaan tuomittu" (The people of Finland are doomed to die young); and the same writer's *Nukkuva Suomi* (*Sleeping Finland*, 1886), whose theme was "awakening":

Nosta ukko, raivoon ilmas, pane	Raise a thunderstorm of rage, old man,
nuolet satamaan,	Let arrows rain down,
ehkä herää Suomen kansa kerran	Maybe the Finnish people will awaken once
ennen kuoloaan.[12]	before death.

Nor was Finland's awakening lost on the wider literary world. James Joyce would give it his own clever variant: *Finnegans Wake*—Finn Again Wake.[13]

The awakening illumined art. In the same year that Aho published his *Heränneitä*, Magnus Enckell painted *Réveil*, known in Finland as *Herääminen* (1894). This portrait of an awakening youth, probably the artist's best-known canvas, gave "awakening" a Symbolist interpretation.[14] Although Enckell had left ambiguous exactly *what* his youth was waking up to, Gallén made no bones about what was waking up in his art: his glass painting called *Herää Suomi/Vakna Finland* (1896) showed a sun rising behind deep forests, casting its pure light on the lake beyond. No ordinary orb, this ascending sun has the shape of the white rose of Finland. Similar images turned up in Sibelius's manuscripts. In a sketch dated 1899 he painted a sun rising over still waters in vivid red, pink, blue, and black; at its center, musical notes (see plate 9).

Similar images were cultivated in passionate, patriotic speeches. One such had been delivered during the Pro Carelia lottery when Sibelius's *Karelia* music was heard for the first time (1893). The alleged purpose of that lottery had been "enlightenment" (in the form of promoting public education), and the prologue (by Gabriel Lagus) that opened the events had radiated images of dawning light. In their wider campaign to raise money for adult education and establish a people's high school, the lottery's sponsors, the Viipuri students, had delivered many speeches and engaged in public debates, and their language, too, overflowed with metaphors of light and awakening. One of the students, U. T. Sirelius (1872–1929), who went on to become a diligent ethnologist, gave an address that went on record for its fervor: waving a flag with the Finnish lion and proclaiming "Long live the people's college," Sirelius had uttered an impassioned oration crammed with visions of a "temple of light" and "our Karelia's awakening." *Rise*, he exhorted the people of Karelia. *Wake up!* "Lift your voices in the refrain 'Life to Karelia for ever and ever.'"[15]

Sirelius's speech had even alluded to the *singing* of *Herää Suomi*, for very quickly the phrase had migrated from poetry to song. Arvi Jännes was the poet who in 1881 had penned verses that began: "Herää, Suomi, niin loppuu yö, / Nouse jo pois, jalopeura!" (Awake, Finland, the night will end, / Rise up, O noble lion!). Jännes's poem addressed the dual-language issue in Finland, which, despite the growing enthusiasm for Finnish, he hoped to see resolved without divisiveness; after all, everyone faced the same fate under the Russian emperors.[16] Soon the strophes written by "Arvi Jännes," whose real name was Arvid Genetz (1848–1915), were set to music by the poet's brother, Emil (1852–1930). Submitted to a composition contest sponsored by the choir MM, *Herää Suomi!* had been nominated for first prize. Choosing among the nominees, however, had taken an exceptionally long time. While the winner was being deliberated, Genetz's chorus was sung in honor of Elias Lönnrot's eightieth birthday in 1882 and published in an accompanying celebratory album. Using the bizarre logic that Genetz's piece "had already been performed," MM awarded the prize to someone else.[17] But *Herää Suomi!* was destined for greater things than a prize from the Merry Musicians. The newly founded and determinedly Finnish-language university men's choir Ylioppilaskunnan Laulajat took up the chorus and soon made it a standard part of their repertoire. YL gave *Herää Suomi!* potent associations of rising, youthful radicalism. There was even talk of adopting the chorus as the national anthem.

In short, the events unfolding in the Swedish Theater that dark November night did not at all take place in a vacuum; they had historical, musical, poetic, and political resonance going back decades, as the Finns who planned the evening were well aware. The calculated efforts they made to capitalize on that resonance would pay off splendidly.

MUSIC FOR THE *TABLEAUX FROM ANCIENT HISTORY*

However skillful the imagery conjured up by Leino and Finne and staged by Bergbom, it is the music to the Press Days *tableaux* that has endured. Yet astonishingly, the full scores of four of the seven numbers composed for that signal event have vanished. Today only the overture, entitled Preludio (HUL 0837); the music to *tableau* II, with Bishop Henrik baptizing the Finns (HUL 0002); and the music to the solemn *tableau* V, depicting the Great Wrath (HUL 0003), are known to exist in their original manuscripts. (Either by fluke or subconscious force, Sibelius notated the Preludio and the baptismal scene in ink of vivid Finnish blue; the music of the Great Wrath, in black.)

Some of the scenes were probably plundered in the course of revision, because Sibelius, on Kajanus's advice, revised and published three of the movements as a suite, named, à la Topelius, *Scènes historiques I*. These included "All'Overtura," "Scena" (portraying the Thirty Years' War), and "Bolero" (Duke John's music, renamed "Festivo"). However, it seems to have been Sibelius's own carelessness that led to the loss of the *Suomi Herää!* score, the one that became *Finlandia*. On November 2, 1900, he wrote to his most trusted copyist, "Dear Herr Röllig! Think of the scandal! My score of *Patrie* (you know, *Vaterland*) is lost. It's supposed to be published—what to do?"[18] The fortuitous survival of the orchestral parts, some of which preserve the composer's corrections, enabled the sorely tried Röllig to rescue *Finlandia* and resurrect the full score, printed in 1901 in Helsinki.[19]

Although overshadowed by the later fame of *Finlandia*, the rest of the Press Days music well repays the listener. The Preludio, for instance, unfolds in woodwinds along with brass and percussion, no string timbre whatsoever tempering its brittle texture. To accompany the baptism of the Finns in *tableau* II, Sibelius created a broad and peaceful expanse of Finnish waters, as moving an evocation of Finnish landscape as he ever composed. As for the transition motive designed for use between the *tableaux* of the Great Wrath and *Suomi Herää!*, Sibelius would one day find another use for it (see ex. 15.1).

EXAMPLE 15.1. SIBELIUS, MOTIVE TO BE REPEATED DURING THE PRESS DAYS' *TABLEAU* V–VI, "ISOVIHA." HUL 0003. © BREITKOPF & HÄRTEL, WIESBADEN.

Yet it is, of course, the music for the last *tableau*, the phenomenally celebrated and renamed *Finlandia*, that has circled the globe in hundreds of guises. While the music that went into *Scènes historiques* still passes for an effective theater score, it was in *Suomi Herää!* that Sibelius united all the strands of his multifaceted heritage and integrated them into an altogether unconventional structure capable of endless transformation.

Against the background of the 1890s, those strands are rather easily teased out. There was realism, at which Sibelius had had a decade of practice. It had burst forth in *Kullervo*: the symphony's love scene between the hero and his sister had unfolded in shockingly realistic terms (by the standards of the 1890s). In the Press Days' music, the composer's skills at realistic portrayal attached not to moments of sensuality, but to a familiar industrial image that had radically changed Finland and was known to him from childhood: the railroad.[20] To a boy from Hämeenlinna—destination of the country's first railroad tracks—the symbolic presence of a locomotive onstage must have been irresistible. Sibelius opened the music to the last *tableau* with the "blue notes" of a train's lonesome whistle undergirded with the mighty sounds of a wheezing steam locomotive revving up its

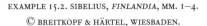

EXAMPLE 15.2. SIBELIUS, *FINLANDIA*, MM. 1–4.
© BREITKOPF & HÄRTEL, WIESBADEN.

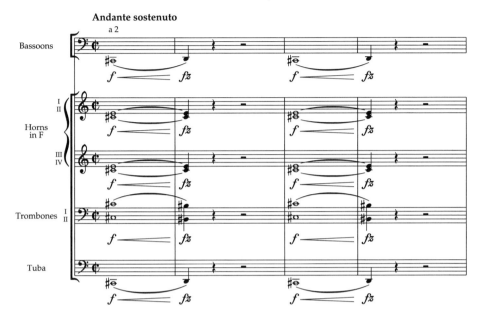

engine for departure (see ex. 15.2). Some ninety-five bars into the work, lurching contra-basses and contrabassoons in powerful, displaced accents reinforced by the indomitable tuba (which plays a last, mighty role in this score before Sibelius relegated it to the back of beyond) vehemently emulate that first iron horse, the Lemminkäinen, steaming forth on its initial journey northward (see ex. 15.3). (Although one of the earliest program-matic evocations of a railroad in music's history, Sibelius's depiction was not the first—not even in Finland. Frans Hoyer had that honor.)

Yet for all its programmatic and populist effects, the underlying structure bespeaks how sharp was the intelligence at work. In a perceptive analysis, James Hepokoski shows how the composer's dutiful acknowledgment of that well-worn convention the sonata form gives way, before even a hundred bars have elapsed, to the quintessential Sibelius, the one whose conversation "darted about like a hare in the undergrowth" (to use Flo-din's words), who juggled not only colors and sounds, but standards and practices, keys and forms.[21] And suddenly, in the middle of the locomotion, the instruments begin a hymn! Its serious and powerful, peaceful yet victorious melody moved even the critics—impossible to describe, they said; the theme awakened new hope and filled the audience with a new mood full of light (see ex. 15.4).[22]

EXAMPLE 15.3. SIBELIUS, *FINLANDIA*, MM. 95–100.

© BREITKOPF & HÄRTEL, WIESBADEN.

EXAMPLE 15.3. (*CONTINUED*)

EXAMPLE 15.4. SIBELIUS, *FINLANDIA*, MM. 132–39.
© BREITKOPF & HÄRTEL, WIESBADEN.

In that lucid chorale, the musical incarnation of Finland's religious heritage, reverberated decades of meaning. Sibelius knew firsthand how spectacular was the success of the hymn in national life. Armas Järnefelt had won the day at the Vasa Song Festival by dramatically ending his *Korsholma* with *A Mighty Fortress Is Our God*. The country's national anthem was a hymn: Pacius's *Vårt land*, invoked at every imaginable public occasion and incorporated into works from Wegelius's *Sixth of May Cantata* to Sibelius's own *Karelia* music, was capable of bringing audiences singing and stamping to their collective feet (an event concluding the Pro Carelia evening in 1893 that Sibelius would not forget).

There were also other hymnlike choruses raising Finnish rafters in the last two decades of the nineteenth century, including the one called *Herää Suomi!* Sibelius knew its creators personally, the Genetz brothers, because they had been teachers in Hämeenlinna. Sibelius had studied with Arvid Genetz, a noted scholar of Finno-Ugric languages who was passionate about Karelia. And his connections to YL, national lottery soirées, and stirring choruses leave no doubt that he knew the musical setting of Arvid's poem

Herää Suomi! by brother Emil. Sibelius had even appeared on the same program with Emil Genetz—in competition.

The time was 1894, the occasion a contest for best male choral composition. YL had awarded the first prize to Genetz for his rousing *Hakkapeliitat* (for TTBB and orchestra, written in the same style as *Herää Suomi!*), relegating Sibelius's tender *Rakastava* (composed to lyrical verses of the *Kanteletar*) to second place.[23] Genetz's success no doubt benefited from the political climate and the enduring enthusiasm of Finnish men for their ancestors' role in that Thirty Years' War: the title refers to those selfsame cavalrymen whose name derived from their blood-curdling yell, *Hakka päälle!*—"Hack 'em down!" Genetz, cleverly tugging on all the emotional strings, had coupled his thrilling text with a seventeenth-century Finnish cavalry march, then, at the crucial moment, launched the tenors into a few bars of *A Mighty Fortress*. (The musical quotation could not be missed: if one ear failed to catch the notes, the other would surely realize that the Finnish-language words had broken off and the choir had shifted into Swedish.)

EXAMPLE 15.5. EMIL GENETZ, *HERÄÄ SUOMI!* MM. 36–41.
BY PERMISSION OF FENNICA GEHRMAN OY, HELSINKI.

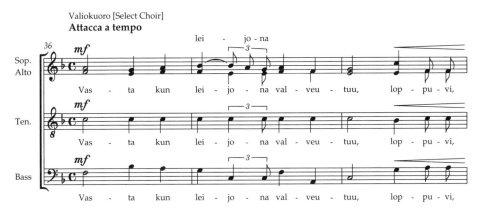

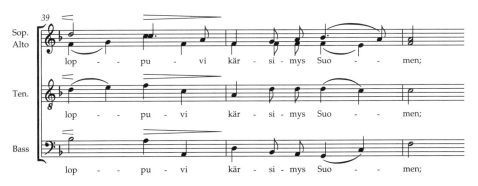

Now, five years later, Sibelius, deliriously composing music for the *tableau* called *Suomi Herää!*, faintly echoed Genetz's chorus—just at the words "Only when the lion awakes will Finland's suffering end" (see ex. 15.5). The resemblance could hardly have been unintentional, given Genetz's textual association and the climate.[24] In Genetz's chorus, the passage follows a cadential "ending," and its instruction "Attacca a tempo" changes both the key (from A minor to F major) and the choral distribution—from full choir to *valiokuoro* (selected voices). Sibelius too reduced his forces for the hymn, paring down the full orchestra to woodwinds alone underpinned by triple-piano tremolos on violins and violas. Was there a sly attempt to go one better, to show his superiority to the less gifted, yet hugely popular Emil Genetz and Fredrik Pacius?[25]

Whatever his intentions, Sibelius now penned his own anthem to the fatherland. Within it lay pure inspiration: no words divided Finnish speakers from Swedish speakers. At this moment, "awakening" transcended language, class, and political party. It was bound instead to a shared sense of place, history, and Lutheran values. At the conquering age of thirty-three, Sibelius achieved the most convincing synthesis of Finnishness that would ever be written.

✁16✁

A New Millennium
Helsinki, Paris, the World!

NEW CURRENTS BRING A SYMPHONY

The new century that was to bring such unimaginable changes to Finland dawned with hope and an outward orientation. On its first day, Sibelius was home alone, taking care of his daughters. Aino had gone to Rantala to help her brother Arvid and his wife, Emmy, nurse their little Anna Katarina, who was sick with typhus. Sibelius wrote to his wife, first about their girls' health and then about wider matters: "Let's see now what the new century brings with it for Finland and Finns. History's condemnation certainly will not fall on us Finns. And the fact that our cause is right lends us dignity and equanimity."[1]

The belief in the "cause" aided by ideas and impulses from far-flung parts commingled democratically in that small but cosmopolitan capital city. The mix echoes not only from correspondence, but also from the pages of contemporary literature and periodicals. Nowhere does its atmosphere come more vividly to life than in the art journal *Ateneum*. To open its covers, embossed with a full figure of the warrior goddess Athena poised to hurl the javelin clasped in her right hand, is to step into Finland's turn-of-the-century cultural and intellectual world. The ideas teeming within those covers have left their traces in golden words, artistic fonts, elegant borders. Faraway travel destinations—Capri, Greece, distant European capitals—beckon from alluring photographs. Reproductions of intriguing new art—Alphonse Mucha's posters, Edward Burne-Jones's paintings, Hans Olde's head of Nietzsche rumbling from its pedestal—greet the hungry eye. Knut Hamsun's stories jostle Verlaine's *Spleen*; Hugo Simberg's sinister, snakelike borders twine around the margins.

Here the architect Armas Lindgren waxes eloquent on Finland's medieval churches. There the Belgian A. W. Finch enlightens the reader on modern ceramics. Sergei Diaghilev expounds on questions of art. Joseph Mandelstam explains Tolstoy. Illustrated reports on the ornamental use of plants by the Japanese, on the women's movement in America, on the insects of antiquity fill volumes whose pages are graced with William Morris's type fonts and stylish *Jugendstil* borders, including one on which a swan leaves a gilded wake in Tuonela's black waters. Finland may have been on the periphery of the world, it may have been ruled by stern and increasingly oppressive dictators, but intellectually and artistically, its borders were porous. Ideas flowed in and out as easily as the tides rise and fall.

Indeed, nothing stood still. While political changes were moving at a swift and frightful tempo, the world of music had been mutating as well, both at home and elsewhere. Sibelius, in the flow of creative endeavor, those large ears like Aeolian harps tuned to the directions of the winds, his ambitions scaled to the peaks of foreign accolade, was responding to those shifting currents. At the same time he officially unveiled his patriotic *Song of the Athenians*, he had conducted another brand new work: his Symphony no. 1.

What turned Sibelius back to the symphony? Almost a full decade earlier, arriving in Vienna that autumn of 1890, he had been burning with desire to compose a symphony. In a sense he succeeded splendidly with *Kullervo*—in scope the most ambitious symphony he ever completed. But *Kullervo* was too idiosyncratically Finnish to succeed outside the country; it was strictly for domestic consumption. Sibelius knew its daunting text and strange tale (with its representation of "a raw Finnish mob," as he had described it to Adolf Paul)[2] would not readily find either performers or sympathetic listeners elsewhere. He also well knew that the marketplace for real success lay not with the small and provincial audiences in Helsinki, but abroad—above all, in Germany. His repeated journeys there speak powerfully of this need; why else would he return time and again, not to Vienna, a city he loved, but to Berlin, full of Germans who "don't understand the first thing about new directions either in art or literature,"[3] but boasting star conductors, fine orchestras, renowned choruses, and publishers of symphonic music? Central Europeans, while they might find swans, Kullervos, and Lemminkäinens momentarily exotic, would hardly sustain a wild enthusiasm for such explicitly Finnish works. As one of their most popular art critics, the esteemed Julius Meier-Graefe (1867–1935), observed, "In Finland, art is a cry of oppressed self-confidence. We do not understand the pictures because we do not have the time to read the *Kalevala* or the other Finnish epics."[4]

Sibelius himself knew this limitation, and knew, too, that his nationalist works needed streamlining and revising. And their mix of early 1890s realism, Karelian fervor, and dark, Symbolist sensuality was gradually becoming dated as the fascination with Symbolism began to wane. Some, like Albert Edelfelt, had never caught the Symbolist fever: "I don't quite understand this symbolism, but the fault may well be mine," he had complained to Gallén; "The strangest thing is that all the ones who have been painted are fas-

cinated by the idea, which they think is so epoch-making."[5] Edelfelt was barking up the
wrong tree. His sympathizers were not Axel Gallén or Jean Sibelius, but Martin Wegelius
and, of course, Karl Flodin, who had made his opinion glaringly plain. Yet their opposition had not deterred Sibelius one whit from further Symbolist meanderings and languid,
waltzy rhapsodizing, at least not at first. Still, the world was turning, and Symbolism was
gradually being relegated to the dark side of the moon.

There were also other changes afoot. One of the surest symptoms was the gradual
fading away of the lottery soirées. With their sumptuous *tableaux*, live music, student
choruses, historical costumes, authentic furnishings, and other trappings, the lotteries
began moving out of town, to summer festivals.[6] For evening entertainment there was
more and more of that novelty which had invaded Society House in 1896: movies. Cinema was becoming a regular fact of Helsinki life. Films were shown at Society House, at
the Hotel Kämp, and before long, on Mikonkatu, where in 1901 Helsinki's first permanent
movie theater would be established. The opulent evenings in the capital city with Sibelius starring as conductor and composer of new patriotic works while stirring speeches
resounded and Salomes whirled began to be outmoded. Something new was needed. And
something new arrived: a baby-faced composer by the name of Ernst Mielck (1877–
1899).

Born in Finland's cosmopolitan city of Viipuri, Mielck was a sickly child who
learned to talk only at the advanced age of seven.[7] Yet from the time he began piano lessons three years later, his musical progress was astounding. His supportive family sent
him to Berlin for study. Accepted into the prestigious Stern Conservatory, he was soon
making appearances as a concert pianist. Then, barely twenty years old, Mielck burst into
Finland's musical arena with a clutch of his own compositions, including a substantial—
and classically structured—symphony. On October 20, 1897, Kajanus created a minor
sensation when he conducted the young man's Sinfonia in F Minor and String Quintet in
F Major together with Grieg's Piano Concerto, in A minor. Mielck himself was the featured pianist. The musicians repeated the program four days later. Within a year, Mielck,
fresh from studying with Max Bruch (to whom he brought "nothing but joy"), had given
a concert in the capital of the musical empire itself, Berlin, in December 1898. No less
an orchestra than the Berlin Philharmonic played his symphony. On a program that also
included two more of his works, *Dramatic Overture* (1898) and *Konzertstück für Klavier
und Orchester*, Mielck again appeared as the soloist. Suddenly, Finland's "foremost composer" had a serious competitor.

Thanks to Flodin, Sibelius was brought face to face with the breakthrough of this
gifted young upstart. Who else could the critic have had in mind when he reviewed
Mielck's symphony?

With good reason, one has lamented the disappearance of a sense of form in our young composers today. They all write rhapsodies, symphonic poems, and suites, but few venture onto the majestic edifice of the symphony for the reason that so few command the difficult art of thinking a musical idea through to the end, logically and comprehensively, allowing it to expand into universal meaning, spiritualizing the form and giving flights of fantasy a definite goal.[8]

Sobering thoughts for a man who wanted to be first on the musical scene. And what did Sibelius have to offer abroad? Conspicuously, *Kullervo* was never performed outside Finland during Sibelius's lifetime. Two of the four *Lemminkäinen* movements were taken off the concert circuit. *Skogsrået* remained in manuscript; neither it nor *Vårsång* interested the Saint Petersburg magnate Belyayev enough to publish them. *The Maid* was left inanely yelping in her tower. With the exception of two suites of dramatic music—the jolly *Karelia* and the trendy *King Christian II*—and the tone poems *Swan of Tuonela*, *Lemminkäinen's Return*, and the sprawling *En saga*, Sibelius really had very little to offer on the international bazaar. And everything he had was stamped "national."

A symphony presented a solution. Its monumentality and its currency in the hallowed Germanic musical world offered the possibility of combining the ideals of nationalism with internationalism. A symphony offered the chance to fulfill that Järnefelt ideal, "through the national to the all-European." And if a mere twentysomething could write a successful symphony, surely an experienced composer of nearly thirty-five could manage something better. After all, there were excellent models to hand. Kajanus and his men had presented one of them, Tchaikovsky's Symphony no. 6, the *Pathétique*, as recently as February 18, 1897.

In formulating the Finnish identity, the country's cultural leaders—its historians, music critics, writers, and influential academics—from the late nineteenth century until well into the twentieth went to considerable lengths to portray Sibelius as utterly original, influenced neither by foreign ideas nor by conscious borrowings, even from Finnish folk music. Instead, he was promoted as the spontaneous, eternal, unquenchable spirit of the Finns manifested in genius form.[9] Particular repugnance was directed toward any influence from Russia, to which no Finn should be indebted. But it was quite natural for Sibelius, living in the Petersburg orbit, having a Russian-Baltic mother-in-law, and keeping an eye on events and yes, opportunities in the nearby imperial capital, to emulate Tchaikovsky—to employ his idea of a "motto theme," to try out the Russian's harmonic idioms and triplet flourishes, to embellish his themes with oriental-sounding chromatic passing tones.[10]

Likewise, a composer so deeply immersed in Symbolism and music for dramatic *tab-*

leaux and other patriotic festivities would be hard pressed suddenly to switch off all those sources of inspiration. It is thus not really surprising to find Sibelius sketching out a plan for his symphony in programmatic terms. In a sketchbook from the years 1896–1900, on the page where ideas for Symphony no. 1 begin (and containing material for *Sandels*, *King Christian II*, and *Athenarnes sång*), appears the following annotation:

Musical Dialogue
I. "The wind blows cold, cold weather from the lake," motto for the Symphony's first movement
II. Heine (The northern fir dreams of the southern palm)
III. A Winter's Tale/Jorma's Heaven[11]

To anyone who had read Flodin's reviews of the previous year, the opening of Sibelius's new symphony might have sounded defiant: it was not a straightforward statement of a main theme, with antecedent and consequent ripe for development to which the imagination could logically and comprehensively strive as toward a definite goal, to paraphrase the critic's recipe. Instead, a near-motionless opening—a lone, melancholy clarinet over a trembling timpanic wave—creates a dreamlike state as mystical as any Symbolist work. Without any obvious concessions to classical construction, the long, slow melismatic themes give the impression of the freest possible approach.

For a listener as sophisticated as Flodin (who, after all, was a composer himself), there was a further taunt: the fluid interplay between keys a mere third apart: E minor and G major in the first movement; E-flat major and C minor in the second; and C major and A minor in the fourth. As if to demonstrate that out of the most numinous and ambiguous of dreamlike substances "spiritualized form" could be created, Sibelius began the symphony with a trancelike melody and returned to it in the finale. Yet in between he packed the symphony with plenty of muscle (see ex. 16.1). Nothing was quite as it seemed—not the meandering opening, not the keys, not the meter, notated one way in the Scherzo but sounding another in performance.[12] Once again a Mozart had cocked a snook at a Salieri.

OLD HANDS STAGE A FESTIVAL

At this crucial juncture nothing better demonstrates the Finns' outward orientation than their plans to take their national orchestra through central Europe. The ultimate destination: Paris and the World's Fair. Kajanus rehearsed his men in a swashbuckling, all-Finnish program: his own *Kesämuistoja* (*Recollections of Summer*) and *Finnish Rhapsody*

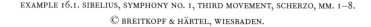

EXAMPLE 16.1. SIBELIUS, SYMPHONY NO. 1, THIRD MOVEMENT, SCHERZO, MM. 1–8.
© BREITKOPF & HÄRTEL, WIESBADEN.

no. 1; Armas Järnefelt's *Korsholma* and a prelude; songs by Mielck, Wegelius, Melartin, and others; and, the centerpieces around which all the rest revolved, Sibelius's *Swan of Tuonela, Lemminkäinen's Return, King Christian II* music, *Finlandia* (under the title *La patrie*), and Symphony no. 1. Sibelius was to accompany the musicians as associate conductor. But before their departure, the orchestra and its composer-conductors participated in a colossal national event: a huge music festival staged over three days in Helsinki, June 18–20. Its sponsor? That ideological organization for the people's enlightenment, the KVS.

With patriotic fervor running high in a climate of severe censorship and amid the hoopla swirling unchecked that Russian was soon to become the grand duchy's official language, people thronged to Kaisaniemi Park and surged across the city's great square.[13] At seven o'clock each morning the square ricocheted with silvery blasts as the brass bands (*soittokunnat*) welcomed the day from the steps of the Nicholas Church. There were the by-now-inevitable sports competitions. There were "historical concerts," featuring *runo* chanting, *kantele* playing, and folk singing. And there were men's choirs, women's choirs, mixed choirs, a capella choirs, and choirs with instrumental accompaniment competing for approval, applause, and prizes. Altogether some seventy-six choral groups, nineteen bands, and nearly three thousand participants strummed, sang, tooted, blew, served up homilies, and, at the crowning moment, lifted up their voices in *Vårt land / Maamme-laulu.*

That moment, June 20, 1900, resounded with extravagant addresses and a florid poem composed and read by Juhani Aho before the Nicholas Church. Then the crowd trooped a short distance westward to witness the laying of the cornerstone for the new Finnish Theater. More lofty orations filled the air; there were eulogies to the Finnish language as the embodiment of the living Finnish spirit and yearnings to hear its monotones echoing from the soon-to-be-built national stage.

Surpassing to an unheard-of degree all previous festivals in the land, this momentous occasion blossomed with the sights and sounds of Finnishness: brightly colored Karelian dresses, the haunting recitation of *runot*, the piquant thrumming of *kanteles*, the hooting of birch-bark horns. Ingrians and Estonians, Jews and Russians, rural and city Finns circulated among the crowds. The theater director Kaarlo Bergbom had even hoped for a full *Kalevala* procession through the streets, though the plan was mooted for lack of funds.[14]

In this massive festival Sibelius, Kajanus, and their music played a central role. Indeed, by the late 1890s it was perfectly evident that, although Robert Kajanus ruled the orchestra, Jean Sibelius was the compositional hope of his country and the essence of its national spirit. The staging of the "historical concerts," for instance, was attributed to both men. And the historical concerts were not Sibelius's only contribution to the KVS festival: his orchestral works figured prominently in the concert on June 20, Kajanus's run-through of the coming Paris programs. Moreover, Sibelius had composed not one, but two works specifically for the festivities: a vigorous brass septet with percussion, meaningfully entitled *Tiera*—the javelin thrower in the *Kalevala*'s *runo* 30 and Lemminkäinen's brother-in-arms—and a nationalistic chorus for mixed voices called *Isänmaalle* (*To the Fatherland*), its patriotic words by Paavo Cajander celebrating Finnish strength and force—*voima*: "Yks' voima sydämehen kätketty on, / Se voima on puhdas ja pyhä" (One power is hidden in the heart, / That power is pure and holy). Within months the KVS had published both pieces.

In this assortment of *Kalevala*-esque and patriotic music, the high point came not with the new contributions, but with the wildly popular *Song of the Athenians*. The chorus was sung and, once again, lavishly staged. Against a backdrop of classical columns and Greekish trees, the men clad in tunics, the women wearing graceful white robes, all brandished swords, shields, or forearms (see fig. 16.1).

On that very day, the emperor signed a degree making Russian the official language

Figure 16.1. Sibelius, *Athenarnes sång* (*Song of the Athenians*), performed at the National Song Festival in Helsinki, 1900. The National Museum of Finland, Department of Prints and Photographs, Helsinki. Photo: Emil Rundman.

of the grand duchy. For his part, Bobrikov callously outlawed the further staging of such cursed events as music festivals.

À PARIS!

In 1900 the Paris World's Fair was the biggest celebration of consumerism the modern world had ever seen. The benefits of colonialism and foreign trade swirled together with the marvels of science and technology in a grand, multicolored, multicultural mix, meant above all to glorify *la France*. "France will emerge . . . yet more splendid, at the vanguard of civilization," declared the fair's director, Alfred Picard.[15]

Le grand rendez-vous colonial was the Parc du Trocadéro. On its grounds, temples, markets, huts, even entire villages, complete with residents, materialized overnight. There was a Congolese village. There was a North African street. Some residents lived in their artificial communities for up to six months. "Natives," clothed in exotic, indigenous garb, strolled authentically through the marketplaces. Visitors, on the other hand, were conveyed from place to place by machine-driven walkways, a marvel of mass movement that left some giddily swooning and others seriously nauseated. Technology reigned: there was the world's largest telescope; there was *le globe céleste*, which offered a voyage through space via a series of scrolling panoramas. The Russian exhibition left guests agape at the "Trans-Siberian Railroad," where a visitor could enter a full-size railway car, sit before a table set with crystal and onyx, and luxuriate in a fur lap rug while traversing Siberia's great rivers, forests, and vast deserts, which glided past the windows on painted canvases—an eighty-seven-yard journey to the gates of Peking at the Chinese exhibition.

The commercial importance of the Franco-Russian Alliance meant that the French made considerable exhibition space available for Russia, of which they viewed Finland as an inseparable part (the Finns' portion even had to be labeled *la section russe*). And the Finns played into the ethnic distinctiveness that made the fair such a fabulous show. Indeed, Finnish success in Paris is surprising only when viewed anachronistically. The Great Cultural Address had brought approving attention to the Finns from around the world. "There is more sympathy in Paris for Finland than there ever has been before," Albert Edelfelt wrote to his mother.[16]

Although Finnish music subsequently proved difficult for the Gallic soul to love, in 1900 its exotic sounds inspired awe at the unexpected accomplishments of a tiny, freedom-loving population living in harmony with nature in an ancient land. That at least was the image Finns sought to portray of themselves. A booklet called *La musique en Finlande* (*Music in Finland*), prepared by "Charles" Flodin and translated into both French and German, served up a Runebergian image of a modern Arcadian idyll with an ancient history—the land of a thousand lakes, of quiet, solitudinous forests that nevertheless echoed with poetry and song, a land where a man answers only to himself, and where all these characteristics tinge his thoughts and feelings with that prized Finnish melancholy. Not a word was printed about the inner discords, the *klang* of Swedish words against the Finnish ear, the rising fear of the lower classes, the tension between the conductor Kajanus and the "assistant conductor" Sibelius (who never got the chance even to lift his baton in public). Instead, peaceful great men with the support of their entirely silent women living harmoniously in an independent nation—such was the image purveyed to the world.

In his *Notices sur la Finlande*, written on the occasion of the fair and intended for French distribution, the influential Finnish senator Leo Mechelin publicized the position he had declared for Finland nearly fifteen years earlier in his *Précis du droit public du grand-duché de Finland*. He opened the chapter entitled "Political and Administrative Organization" with an astonishingly provocative subtitle: "The Grand Duchy of Finland is a Constitutional Monarchy Whose Throne Is Indissolubly United with the Throne of the Russian Empire."[17] The building of the Finnish identity had entered a new, global phase.

Music was neither the only nor the most apparent Finnish commodity on offer in Paris. Industrial and commercial interests belonged to the nature of world expositions, and it had been the grand duchy's Board of Industry that launched the initiative for Finnish participation in the Paris event. Four representatives from wood-processing industries (one of which was the Nokia mill) turned up at the fair along with some representation from engineering and chemical production. Finnish industrial achievements were on display—in the Russian Pavilion. Elsewhere, there was an exhibit of Albert Edelfelt's paintings.

The main Finnish exhibit, however, was the Finnish Pavilion. And once again the educated upper strata of Finnish society—artists, architects, composers, conductors, sculptors, craftsmen—took charge of designing the Finnish image to be shown abroad. Thanks especially to Albert Edelfelt at the helm as the Finnish Art Commissioner (whose multiple Russian contacts eased many potential problems) and Leo Mechelin, prominence was given to the uniqueness and value of art and culture in an autonomous land, which in multiple subliminal ways was portrayed as a sovereign nation.

Visitors were treated to Finnish sculptures, paintings, reliefs, textiles, and handicrafts rich with subtexts: Magnus Enckell's *Kansakoulu* (*Primary School*); Väinö Blomstedt's ancient castle at Savonlinna; Juho Rissanen's *Jäämurtaja* (*The Icebreaker*); and Emil Halonen's wooden reliefs depicting rural life.[18] The Finnish Antiquarian Society and the Friends of Finnish Handicraft showed pictures of national landmarks and student works; the association of fisheries displayed some of its most outlandish equipment; learned societies, social institutions, and the Imperial Alexander University paraded their publications and dissertations; and a riotous hodgepodge of Finnish nature, from stuffed bears and desiccated wolves to a model of a tar pit and a meteorite fragment the size of a three-year-old that had fallen to Finnish earth (a papier-mâché reproduction of the so-called Bjurböle meteorite) threatened to overwhelm the touring crowds. Somehow, the weird jumble succeeded in projecting a sense of the "authentically Finnish" and convinced onlookers that they had truly "experienced" the land and its people. "The Land of the Thousand Lakes is full of poetry," one commented, although adding sourly, "all we get to see of it is a gigantic bear, an ice-breaker, some amusing furniture and the practical side of life in the North."[19]

What most enchanted the fair's visitors was the pavilion itself ("the strangest and quaintest" of them all, one visitor was heard to remark; Sibelius thought it was the most artistic).[20] Designed by Eliel Saarinen (alone, not together with his partners, as was formerly thought), the pavilion was built of wooden boards and gypsum over which plaster was added to give the illusion of thickness and texture. The result implied that the building had been hewn from the very bedrock of Finland. It seemed to hold the spirit of *sisu* (that Finnish equivalent of stubborn determination) within its immovable walls, which silently conveyed the strength of a people who refused to be broken even by the most grueling of trials. Those swollen palisades, those arched portals, those natural details allegedly owed their inspiration to an American architect, H. H. Richardson (how better to distance Finland from Russia?). The roof's supporting ribs, however, portrayed the rays of Nordic sunlight (visitors being counted on to know Nordic sunlight when they saw it). The bears, squirrels, pinecones, and other flora and fauna adorning the outer façade represented Finnish, not Russian, nature, and the unrealized plan to paint those gypsum bears, which were left white, may have fed the persistent myth that polar bears roam the streets of Helsinki.

Within the pavilion was a special room for the Finnish press as well as the Iris Room, the latter furnished with items from Louis Sparre's like-named furniture factory in Porvoo and from the Friends of Finnish Handicraft. Just inside and above the main door, an array of Finnish skis splayed out like the rays of the sun. Glass panels in the roof let in light, although the interior remained quite dark. At approximately the roof's midpoint, the glass was replaced by a solid covering on which Axel Gallén's cartoonish ceiling frescoes depicted scenes from the national epic. These had clearly been chosen for their allegorical possibilities: *The Forging of the Sampo*; *The Defense of the Sampo*; *Ilmarinen Plowing the Field of Vipers*; and *Christendom and Paganism*, the latter combining the building of a church with Väinämöinen's *kantele*. The figures painted there, men one and all, glorified the Finnish cult of masculinity and delivered a message of unconquerable defiance (in *The Defense of the Sampo* one enemy soldier had the face of Bobrikov; in the *Field of Vipers* a crown painted on the head of the leading viper bearing the Russian colors—red, white, and blue—audaciously mocked the emperor himself).[21]

And what fused all those disparate elements into a winning national whole was the exhibition's overall conception: the Finnish Pavilion—with nobility in every line, with style in every detail—was nothing less than the physical re-creation of a Lutheran country church.

MUSIC AT THE WORLD'S FAIR

Against such a backdrop Kajanus unveiled Finland's music.[22] Posters by the country's leading artists—Magnus Enckell's winsome lass enthralled by a songbird as she reclines on a lakeshore in the fullness of Finnish nature and Gallén's version of the blonde Maid of Finland sacrificing her golden locks to provide strings for Finland's *kantele*—had helped to attract audiences, though in August in Paris, authentic Frenchmen were thin on the ground. Flodin's booklet prepared listeners for what they were to hear, emphasizing Finland's history and the country's nature: "Finnish songs emanate from a sorrowful inspiration and go back to remotest antiquity. From the most ancient pagan times, the *runot* were on the lips of the people."[23] Describing composers from Armas Järnefelt to Kajanus, Mielck, and the critic himself, Flodin nevertheless made it clear that "the most remarkable" of the Finnish crop was "without question Jean Sibelius . . . more than anyone else, he has been able to give his compositions the cachet of Finnish nature and national character";[24] Sibelius was the *true* creator of Finnish music. Flodin avoided unseemly talk about rogue Symbolist works and instead singled out *Kullervo*, Sibelius's "great symphonic poem, the text of which is from the *Kalevala*," and his "Suites pour orchestre" (presumably *Lemminkäinen* and *King Christian II*) as works conveying better than word or pen "the peaceful, profound, serious, and melancholy splendors of Finnish nature and the national epic."[25]

If nothing else, the Finns presented a unified front of a people bound to their natural surroundings and immersed in their folk music and poetry, "a poor people who have suffered and *sung* themselves to this simple beauty,"[26] said one of them. And their musical presentation was nothing short of electrifying. In the hall of the Fêtes de Trocadéro, the "excellent Monsieur Robert Kajanus" revealed to those present composers of whom the French had been "profoundly ignorant: Sibelius, Jârnefeldt, H. Halonen [*sic*]."[27] Although Monsieur Gustave Babin, who wrote those words, was unsure of how to spell those odd Finnish names and blithely mixed artists with composers, he was nevertheless smitten with "Monsieur Sibilius's" *La patrie*. On this first rendition of *Finlandia* in France, "*La patrie* . . . roused an indescribable enthusiasm. There were before us Finlanders who literally shook with musical power, and thereby roused the entire audience. It was an especially imposing patriotic manifestation. The soul of Finland itself was palpable in that enormous hall."[28]

The orchestra in general and Sibelius's music in particular were praised and admired (the public evidently accepted without batting an eye that leading Finns had such French names as "Charles," "Robert," and "Jean," although there was some concern about the misrepresentation of "Jean").[29] Sibelius wrote buoyantly to Aino, "The pro-Russian papers are bound to heap abuse on us, above all on me, as I am supposedly nationalist."[30] He seemed to be enjoying his anarchical role. Sibelius was made a *chevalier* in the Légion d'honneur (eventually), although, inexplicably, the orchestra brought home no medals despite every visual artist and his brother's having received one, including the Swedish orchestra—a particular blow. Still, the response was highly satisfying, given that the "separatist" Finns were performing in a highly charged political atmosphere. That a measure of Gallic reserve marked their reception should have come as no surprise. What was important was that the windows to the world were wide open. And Sibelius was poised to fly right through them.

DISCIPLES

At this point in the story, a most curious, even weird, yet wonderful figure steps onto the stage: Axel Carpelan (1858–1919). The supporting role of this character in Sibelius's life has long been calmly accepted, yet were the tale fiction, Carpelan would appear to be an author's contrivance, an operatic deus ex machina who bears little resemblance to real life, yet saves the day. Axel Carpelan was no man of the people. He had a title—that of baron—and refined tastes, although no money. He was a cultured, if hypochondriac, aesthete, extremely well read on international doings. And he was a Swedish-speaking Finn.

At the time he befriended Sibelius, Axel Carpelan had mounting frustrations, no gainful employment, and only thwarted aspirations.[31] A serious-looking, dandified type (he was known to dress in polka-dot ties and bowler hats), Carpelan sprouted sideburns and a walrus mustache, hirsute compensations for a rapidly receding hairline. Rimless eyeglasses perched beneath prominent eyebrows gave him the effete look of an overindulged youth. Axel Carpelan was also a frustrated violinist. When his parents opposed his urge to devote himself to music, he smashed his violin in fury, flung the pieces into the Aura River, and indulged in an aristocratic sulk. He refused to enter the university or to pursue composition or to make himself into a reputable critic. Instead, like Adolf Paul, he endeavored to become "a friend of great men," or those he believed destined for greatness. He took up writing to Swedish poet Viktor Rydberg. He corresponded with the wealthy Axel Tamm, a Swedish patron who sometimes supported Carpelan (for what reason was never clear). Sometimes he wrote anonymous letters—a sure sign of a desire to exert control—hiding behind such corny signatures as "X." He showed his real face when Kajanus's orchestra departed for the World's Fair in July 1900: wearing his bowler hat and twitching his bushy mustache, Carpelan appeared at the harbor bearing flowers for the musicians.

It was not the first time Sibelius had attracted a disciple. "You were born to be praised," Strindberg had written of the genius artist in *The Red Room*, and Sibelius was not one to shirk his birthright. Probably the first devotee was Walter von Konow (1866–1943), the friend from Hämeenlinna days who had supplied Sibelius's first "opera" libretto (*Ljunga Wirginia*). Later, along came Adolf Paul, who remained a lifelong follower. Around 1905 Rosa Newmarch took Sibelius under her ample wings. Meanwhile, across the Atlantic, the young Olin Downes had discovered the Finn and his music just the year before; Downes's half century of earnest advocacy on behalf of Jean Sibelius earned him the title "Sibelius's Apostle."[32]

Each of the apostles had a hand in promoting Sibelius's career, yet Carpelan was different: he insinuated himself into Sibelius's inner creative life. It was Carpelan who, when he materialized in March 1900 with his "X" letter addressing the forthcoming Parisian tour, directed Sibelius to adopt the title *Finlandia*.[33] As he became bolder, Carpelan urged Sibelius to compose a violin concerto, to write a *skogssymfoni* (a "woods symphony," ultimately realized in the symphonic poem *Tapiola*), to publish *Kullervo*. Not least, Carpelan launched a scheme to send Sibelius to Italy "where *cantabile*, moderation, and harmony are learned [along with] plasticity and symmetry of line, where everything is beautiful—even the ugly."[34] Carpelan's advice certainly seemed sound. Even better, he was prepared to act on it: he convinced a donor to fund an Italian journey for Sibelius and his entire family, which now included a second daughter (Ruth, born in 1894). Suddenly, Sibelius had a new patron.

Because the sonic and visual dimensions of the national spirit are so gloriously evident today, it is easy to forget that these were not the sole or even the principal goals of the majority of Finns. To be viable, a people had to be economically stable. The Russian emperors' interest in industrialization fostered the mercantile interests of Finnish businessmen, and their success was the arts' gain. Prospering businesses and flourishing arts proceeded hand in hand. Little has been written about this commercial side of the patronage that enabled Finland's composers, painters, sculptors, writers, and dramatists to thrive; such matters have the air of being faintly unclean.[35] Yet commerce was absolutely essential to the ongoing building of the national identity. The evidence lies all around: in those who commissioned Sibelius to write pieces for them and later purchased his manuscripts for untold prices; in the portraits of the wealthy by artists of the caliber of Albert Edelfelt, Axel Gallén, Eero Järnefelt, and others; and in private arrangements quietly made by businessmen to defray expenses for their artistic compatriots.

One of these men, the fabulously successful Hämeenlinna-born Colonel Hugo Standertskjöld (1844–1931), believed to be the richest man in Finland, had made his fortune manufacturing arms in Russia. Numerous others, people such as J. K. Paasikivi, the Paloheimo family (né Brander), Jacob von Julin, Magnus Dahlström, and many more, were central in shaping the Finnish national idea. They were men who saw what the national awakening, national unity, and Finnish identity meant for the economy and for strengthening Finland ideologically and politically, and many of them gave generously to support education and the arts. Their role has not always been fully appreciated. Patronage of the arts was seen as something "high" and clean, as it is in Finland still. The mindset shows in the Finnish attitude toward the entrepreneur, something hardly considered a profession and certainly not respectable (the Russian entrepreneur Sergei Diaghilev was never understood in Finland). Until the twenty-first century, the very word used in Finnish for entrepreneur, *yrittäjä*—a tryer, someone who tries—contained an element of disparagement, not respect for the ingenuity and creativity that the term *entrepreneur* conveys to people elsewhere. Yet as the Russian artist Ilya Repin, living in Finland after the revolution, observed, "Art loves wealth and flourishes only in its presence."[36]

Entrepreneurial wealth was a key factor in assuring Jean Sibelius's success, although sometimes the wealth was Sweden's. It was a Swede, Axel Tamm, who, prompted by Carpelan, was the reason that Sibelius found himself in the winter of 1900 with Aino and their daughters on a train headed through the Italian Alps, his only obligation being to compose.

Sibelius adopted what was perhaps the only stance he could in this situation and still preserve his dignity: from this time forward, he made it clear that he regarded his patrons' generosity as a patriotic duty directed toward his music and thus toward Finland.[37] It was now that the formulaic phrase, "Thank you for all the interest you have shown in my music," entered his correspondence. Fifty years later it was being used still.

∽17∽

Italian Classicism and Finnish Nationalism

MEDITERRANEAN IDYLL

Italy's seductive effect on the creative mind is a truism. Robert Browning, Johann Wolfgang von Goethe, Edvard Munch, Valentin Serov, Percy Bysshe Shelley, Pyotr Ilyich Tchaikovsky, Richard Wagner—the list of those who have plundered the Italian peninsula for artistic ideas seems endless. Yet although Italy's ability to set inspiration alight is something of a platitude, there has been rather little appreciation of its mighty effects and lustrous results on the Finnish imagination. One of Axel Gallén's most famous and most Finnish works—the fresco *Kullervo Departs for War*—owes a clear debt to fourteenth-century Italian techniques.[1] The shapes and colors of Oiva Toikka's plump and winsome glass birds were found in ancient Pompeii (Toikka's predecessors are preserved today in the National Museum in Naples). Alvar Aalto built his Finlandia Hall of Italian marble, material so utterly unsuited to the northern climate that within twenty years of its construction, chunks of the stone were falling lethally to earth.

That Jean Sibelius too would be stirred by Italy's soft nights, ancient architecture, and enchanting colors hardly merits belaboring. What intrigues is how that stimulus played into the composer's personal development and into the construction of a Finnish identity. Olin Downes, tongue in cheek, once observed, "A composer born in Finland who goes to Italy had better be careful. If he doesn't, he'll find that he has composed *Il Trovatore*."[2] It is often in difference, in encounters with other worlds, that personal identity is crystallized. And in most ways Italy could hardly be more different from Finland.[3] Catholic, whereas Finland is Protestant; riotously colorful, whereas Finland has a limited, albeit highly nuanced, color spectrum; a glorious antiquity, whereas Finland's was just being invented; an atmosphere of classical proportions, whereas Finland was burgeoning with *art nouveau*—all these contrasts and more assailed the senses.

Sibelius, together with Aino and little Eva and Ruth, had departed Finland on

October 27, 1900.[4] The family traveled through Germany to Basel, the wonderful old Swiss town of beautiful buildings and quaint passageways on the Rhine, host to Erasmus, Brahms, Nietzsche, and Wagner. They continued on to Lucerne, as dazzling as its pictures, with its clear blue lake and white peaks, crossing one mighty mountain after another. Through the Gotthard tunnel they went, at last coming to Milan, whose Duomo, encountered in the half light, was the most beautiful structure Aino had ever seen. As they headed even further south toward Genoa, the snow gave way to orange groves, olive trees, palms, and cypresses.

Finally, they arrived by moonlight in the little coastal village of Rapallo, installing themselves in the Pension Suisse. As if in a dream, almond trees, cactus, agaves, magnolias, cypresses, vines, palms, and even flowers filled the countryside. The sun shone; the Mediterranean lapped. The setting in which Sibelius's countrymen had sent their national genius to work could hardly have been more poetic, especially in the eyes of those escaping the numbing gray and unremitting cold of the far north. The contrast with February in Finland could hardly have been greater. Aino's mother wrote that snow and sleet were falling by turns in the homeland and the temperature was minus 19 degrees.[5]

Those born with the sea in their ears often find it difficult to live without it. But for Sibelius, who grew up near a lake, that noisome motion was the first of Rapallo's annoying distractions. He rented a workroom, the villa of Signor Molfino, high above the infernal sloshing, reached by a long set of stone steps, set in a garden filled with scarlet camellias, and blessed with stunning views and a piano. "It was the season for violets—the woods were filled with their scent. I used to take long walks from the town of Rapallo along the hills on the shore covered with pines, olive trees and cypresses, to Zoagli, Santa Marguerita, Santa Miguela and Portofino," he told his biographer Karl Ekman years later.[6] But at the time, he was writing to Adolf Paul, "Here it's wonderful—full summer—sea cliffs, palms, flowers, heaven and hell."[7]

In that mix of extremes Sibelius began to sketch out his ideas. In jottings dated "February 2, 1901, Rapallo. Ligure. Italia Villa del Signor Molfino," Sibelius notated a theme together with what appears to be a lyrical scenario featuring a "Don Juan":

In the enchanted garden when Juan is away
Balletto in minore
Serenata dell' estero
(She asked me to send pressed leaves from Italy. I sent fig leaves. "Are they so
    small," said Augusta.)[8]

And still, in this Italianate setting, the strong identification with Finland's Swedish literature inspired him as much as Signor Molfino's enchanted villa and the sweetness of Italian orange blossoms: startlingly, Augusta is a character in Runeberg's *Julqvällen*, the work in which Runeberg gave clear and explicit voice to a patriotic consciousness.[9] And Sibelius's writing of "Juan" is so uncertain that it could easily be "Jean." On the verso of this sketch, his pen traced another scenario, "In der Fremde": "Don Juan / [I] am sitting in my castle in the twilight; a guest enters. More than once I ask who he is.—No answer. I make an effort to entertain him. Still no answer. Finally, the stranger breaks into song and then Don Juan notices who he is—Death."[10]

DEATH IN ITALY

Death? Its specter seems a strange figure indeed to introduce into paradise. Visitors to Italy most often wax eloquent about the sunshine, the blue sky, the exquisite light, the landscape, the art, the architecture. But the unwelcome guest hovered at the Sibelius family's door. Only ten months earlier, their youngest, two-year-old Kirsti, had contracted typhus. The disease had taken Arvid Järnefelt's little Anna Katarina, and then it claimed Kirsti. Aino and Jean each mourned in their different ways. Christmas with the Adolf Paul family in Berlin had been hard because the Pauls' smallest son reminded them so much of Kirsti.[11] Jean's grief found musical outlet. On January 22, 1901, in Berlin, he sketched an innocent-sounding F major nursery tune, its triadic shape and lilting three-beat bars evoking a child on a rocking horse (see ex. 17.1a). But the regular phrases unexpectedly turn dark. The theme veers into D minor, and deadening repetitions of the new tonic transform innocent happiness into numbing depression (see ex. 17.1b). He labeled the sketch *Memento mori*.

The family encountered death afresh in Basel: a torchlight parade in memory of the town's recently deceased native son, Arnold Böcklin, who had allegedly inspired *En saga*. Now in Italy the journey that began so hopefully took an unexpected turn, as the Fates

EXAMPLE 17.1A–B. SIBELIUS, SKETCH, BERLIN, JANUARY 22, 1901. HUL 1547.
© BREITKOPF & HÄRTEL, WIESBADEN.

cut short the hope of idyllic bliss. The winter was the bitterest in the inhabitants' memories, the rooms impossible to heat, the mornings all of six degrees inside.[12] Six-year-old Ruth, already sickly in Berlin, turned seriously ill. Her parents at first feared that typhus had struck again, but the doctor diagnosed gastric fever.[13] Aino was frantic.

For some two weeks she nursed the child. Gradually, the fever subsided, and Ruth's health began to return. But the illness of their youngest was not all. Word came from Finland that Aino's sister-in-law Emma (her brother Kasper's wife) was also sick. Although initially the family was hopeful, Emma was soon diagnosed with tuberculosis, and a flurry of letters discussed the need for a sojourn in Italy—the kind of "place where the Sibeliuses are now," Kasper wrote pointedly.[14] But no one had the means to finance such a trip for the deathly ill Emma. Sibelius was so shaken that the flow of his work dried to a trickle.[15]

Thus the pressures mounted. Even the weather conspired in the dismal turn of events: as if in a romantic novel, storm clouds gathered, and rain blew in from the sea. And in the midst of Ruth's illness, once the Italian doctor had pronounced some improvement, Sibelius did the unthinkable: he took off for Rome, leaving only a note and some lire for Aino. It was neither the first nor the last time that Aino's magnificent strength held the family together. Aino's explanation to her mother was that the family was too cramped, Sibelius was too nervous, and he could not compose. To put the best face on it, Sibelius may have believed that the only way to meet his obligation to his patron was to remove himself to a place he could work in order to bring something fruitful back to Finland.

However fraught the personal dilemmas, it is clear that the classical designs of the Forum and the Pantheon, the moonlight on the ancient Colosseum, even the baroque glory of Saint Peter's had a profound effect on his thinking. The immediacy of classical antiquity everywhere apparent in the Holy City resonated powerfully with Finnish neo-classic ideals and also with Sibelius's personal bent. In Florence, where the family eventually reunited, Michelangelo's *David* sent him into ecstasy.[16] The experience of reading the proofs of the *Lemminkäinen Legends* between visits to the Uffizi Gallery sparked a decided tension that further energized his thinking. The seeds of a deep stylistic change were being sown.

OVERWHELMING PROTEST: SYMPHONY NO. 2

The family had hardly been back in Finland two months when in July 1901 the Russians slammed their Finnish subjects with a sickening blow, no less appalling for being expected: an official edict conscripting young Finns into the Russian military. Forced service in the emperor's troops was a horrifying prospect in the best of circumstances. It was worsened by the widespread belief that Russians inflicted severe corporal punishments on soldiers. Oskari Tokoi (the labor leader who would become Finland's first prime minister) described the edict as the first to strike the Finnish people to the heart.[17] It was the working class who bore its brunt, yet the elite gave vent to a widespread sense of grievance, some of them in artistic protests. Many, Sibelius included, signed a petition against the edict.[18] Meanwhile, there were more personal losses. Aino's sister Elli died, only in her early thirties, a suicide. Such was the atmosphere in which Sibelius managed to complete the work he referred to as his *S[ch]merzens Kind*. How extraordinary then that this was the symphony "with sunshine and blue sky and exuberant joy."[19]

When the symphony was unveiled on March 8, 1902, Sibelius conducting, the Finnish public seems to have heard just what it wanted to hear in the poignant chant of the woodwinds, the angry pizzicatos of the contrabasses, and the militant interjections of the trumpets. Some detected the ring of the revolutionary march *Kuullos pyhä vala* (*Listen to the Holy Oath*) in the Scherzo.[20] For the uncomprehending, Robert Kajanus explained the symphony's "program," which he had all worked out. The Andante contained "the most broken-hearted protest against all the injustice that threatens at the present time to deprive the sun of its light and our flowers of their scent."[21] That alone should have reassured the cynical of how valuable was the investment in sending their foremost composer to Italy. Kajanus's picture of the Scherzo was a bit more puzzling; it "gives a picture of frenetic preparation. Everyone piles his straw on the haystack, all fibres are strained and every second seems to last an hour. One senses in the contrasting trio section with its oboe motive in G flat major what is at stake." For the Finale, however, Kajanus again came up triumphant: a "conclusion intended to rouse in the listener a picture of lighter and [more] confident prospects for the future."

Kajanus's "program" was echoed in considerably more detailed and Germanic terms by Ilmari Krohn, the third applicant for the university position some six years earlier. Krohn designated the Second Symphony *Finland's Struggle for Freedom* (*Finnlands Freiheitskampf*) and analyzed the work specifically in terms of awakening national consciousness and class difference.[22] In Krohn's scheme the first movement was "the Development before the Conflict" ("Die Entwicklung vor dem Konflikt"); the second, "the Storm" ("Der Sturm"); the third represented "National Resistance" ("Nationaler Widerstand"), while the fourth depicted a "Free Fatherland" ("Befreites Vaterland"). Nor was that the end of it: the formal structure of each movement, said Krohn, could be understood in patriotic, programmatic terms. The introduction to the first movement's exposition, for instance, sounded the conscientious daily toil of the lower classes, while the main idea (*Hauptkern*) depicted the foreign culture of the upper class. Then a unifying transition, ringing with love of the fatherland, heralded a secondary idea called (would you believe it?) "national awakening" ("Nationale Erweckung"). Krohn provided an extensive table of leitmotifs with all the symphony's motives labeled—including Aspiration, Struggle, Blossoming, Patriotism, and Awakening—and traced in the score. Although he published these views only in the mid-1940s, the ideas had their unmistakable roots in the 1890s.[23]

That the interpretations were culturally influenced is made clear by the very different reactions from Americans, whose political environment was quite another: introduced to the Second Symphony a mere two years after its Finnish premiere, American listeners during the decade 1904–14 found the work "grewsome," even "neurotic," with too much meaningless repetition, although one critic complimented its "attractive weirdness"; Olin Downes, ever ready with *le mot juste*, pronounced it "gloriously rude."[24]

What Sibelius intended is, of course, more difficult to grasp. His correspondence showed that being in the world of the ancient Romans had affected his thoughts deeply. A postcard sent to Carpelan from Rome on April 4, 1901, read: "Here one gets strange ideas about the essence of music."[25] On returning to Finland, the composer elaborated on some of those "strange ideas," which expressly concerned the national in music, for his disciple:

> I have come, I believe, to another view of the national in music. We worship and
> have worshipped the "ethnographic in music," if I may express myself so. But
> the real national lies still deeper. Compare Verdi and Grieg, for example. The
> former is perhaps the most national and still European; the latter—I cannot hide
> it from myself—speaks country speech. It will be interesting to see what you
> think of my music now.[26]

The issue clearly occupied his mind, because he took it up again in the selfsame letter. After telling about his travel plans, he went on in a long parenthesis: "Earlier I wrote that 'we worship the ethnographic in music': I actually mean that when it comes to progressions and such we think only that ethnographical rightness is true. Understand me correctly!"[27]

Three months later, Sibelius still seemed to be dealing with the implications of those revelations. On August 27, 1901, another letter to Carpelan confessed: "The thing was that I've had to undergo a difficult struggle in my art—now I'm again in the clear and proceeding full sail ahead."[28]

The sailing tactic he adopted proceeded naturally out of the large works he had composed heretofore, those nationalist *tableaux* with their processions of personified symbolic events, historical characters, and Finnish aspirations, and out of the symphonic poems in which he had wrestled with the personal expression of a national consciousness. What was more natural than to adapt the same methods to the symphony, using the flow

of states of mind, within the guideposts of symphonic structure?[29] More than in the previous symphony Sibelius availed himself of fermatas and grand pauses. With ambiguity
he veiled those traditional articulation points, the section changes, the movement end-
ings. More shrewdly than ever did he obscure the sounding pulse and the notated one.
Conventional "themes" gave way to distinctive textures: an eleven-note chant in the slow
movement, evocative of Gregorian plainsong; a pizzicato "walking bass"; voicelike dialogues; and choralelike passages. All promoted flow and all suggested a succession of
states of mind. Those furiously rebelling ostinati in the final movement have no *Kalevala*
name, no Runebergian equivalent. Rather, seared in the refining fires of the "national,"
Sibelius's maturing sense of the meaning of "symphony" took on far more precision in
sonic form than words would ever convey.

ഇരുരുര

The Finnish political situation remained tense. There were those who accepted the
emperor's conscription decree with stoic sorrow—to do otherwise was condemned by
the church and, worse in Lutheran eyes, stigmatized as unpatriotic. The impact on the
Finnish population, however, was profound. In 1898, the year of Bobrikov's appointment, 3,500 Finns emigrated to the United States.[30] The following year, the number was
more than 12,000. And in 1902, when over 25,000 Finns were called up for military service, emigration swelled to the highest peak ever: more than 23,000. Those numbers
included liberals and socialists, workers and intellectuals, men of various ages and record
numbers of young women. It was said that Finns could be found in each of the United
States and in every province of Canada. "America's Finland" was the nickname given
the area stretching west from Sault Ste. Marie in northern Michigan through Wisconsin
and around Lake Superior. In honor of these departing brothers Sibelius would compose
a vigorous men's chorus, *Veljeni vierailla mailla* (*My Brothers in Foreign Lands*)—also
known as *Song of Exile*—to a text of Juhani Aho in the spring of 1904. Yet already in the
summer of 1901, Axel Carpelan was writing to Sibelius, "Your name and your success are
a sustaining force for many."[31]

    Some, however, heard a composer undergoing difficulty. Perhaps the strange and
wonderful *På verandan vid havet* (*On a Balcony by the Sea*) contributed to the concerns,
the song to words of Viktor Rydberg that Sibelius wrote during September 1903 and Ida
and Karl Ekman performed on October 16.[32] No glorious patriotic display this, but an
intimate dialogue between piano and singer. Its expressionistic recitative, made up of
twisting half steps and tritone leaps, conveys a heart-wringing personal angst, an aural
equivalent of Edvard Munch's tormented canvases from this same time (see ex. 17.2).

    Perchance such private expression should have no place in Finland's public sphere, a

EXAMPLE 17.2. SIBELIUS, *PÅ VERANDAN VID HAVET*, MM. 1–10.

© BREITKOPF & HÄRTEL, WIESBADEN.

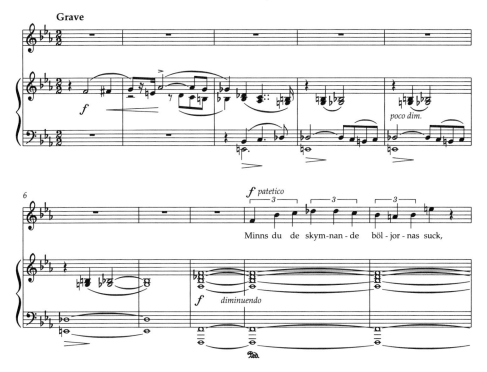

dimension in which many Finnish-minded leaders believed, à la Snellman, that individual concerns should be suppressed for the greater good. But although Sibelius's patriotic choruses and symphonic compositions with Finnish titles and programmatic implications grandly proclaimed the national identity, his songs composed to texts in Swedish laid bare his soul—as he did in these mere fifty bars, in which he achieved a remarkable level of emotional and musical nuance. The contrast of his notation with the huge *Kullervo* choral symphony and its *Kalevala* texts is startling. In that work he provided virtually no expression marks for the solo voices, not even dynamics. In *På verandan*, however, the vocalist's every entry is carefully shaded: forte patetico, mezza voce, mezzo piano poco crescendo, poco forte. And when the singer reaches the poet's culminating words:

Minns du en tystnad,   Do you remember a stillness,
då allt var som sänkt i   When everything lay as though sunk in
  oändlighetsträngtan,   longing for the infinite,
stränder och himmel och hav,   The shore and sky and sea,
allt som i aning om Gud?   All as if in presentiment of God?

the combination of the voice—a benumbed monotone, which then shrieks upward nearly to the top of its range—with a nine-bar sustained fortissimo chord in the pianist's right hand and a deeply ominous tremolo in the left carries such anguish and despair that the listener is left shaken.

In this time, but for the help of his nearest and dearest, above all his brother, Christian, together with Aino, who in turn leaned on Carpelan, these years would have been lost ones for Sibelius. Again and again, Christian bailed him out financially. Again and again, Aino was left with the children, including the newborn Katarina (1903), while Jean drank his evenings away in Helsinki. Sometimes when Aino finally, in desperation, came calling for him, he refused to see her.[33] Carpelan counseled getting the composer away from Helsinki and the "dregs of Helsinki 'culture'" in order to get him to focus on his work. Gradually, a plan began to emerge.

~18~

Country Living and the
Finnish National Movement

FLIGHT FROM THE CITIES

Like many upper-class residents of Helsinki, the Sibelius family's habit was to rent a city apartment in the winter and move to a country villa for the summer months. In the opening years of the twentieth century, the call to country life strengthened audibly. It was amplified by several factors, not the least of which were the housing problems brought on by the growing metropolitan population.[1] The problem was not unique to Finland: modernization was feeding urban expansion all over Europe. Even as Finns were chafing under the heavy hand of censorship and other repressive policies, the need for new housing in the grand duchy's capital, combined with the healthy economy, generated an enormous boom in the building industry. Evident by the mid-1890s and lasting nearly two decades, the surge gave national architects and artisans abundant opportunities for work as well as for self-expression. The sensational results remain evident to this day: magnificent *Jugendstil* edifices throughout Helsinki distinguish the city as the leading place of such townscapes in all the Nordic lands.

The price of that distinction included not only dust and noise, but also social and ethical problems and crowding, at least by Finnish standards. "There are many people of the kind one does not like to associate with," young Sibelius had written to Uncle Pehr about Lovisa in 1885.[2] Increasingly, that sentiment applied to Helsinki. Flight to the clean countryside ("clean" socially as well as physically), a yearning to live close to nature, and the belief that the natural environment would engender higher morals and happier family lives exerted strong appeal. Indeed, in the view of many, living in natural surroundings belonged to the very essence of being Finnish. Such sentiments were aided and abetted by the Fennomans, who were promoting the idea that the development apparent in the cities should be expanded to rural areas to sharpen the specifically Finnish profile there and benefit the wider economy.

And so those with means were lured into the Finnish hinterlands. The most celebrated outcome may well be Hvitträsk, built in 1903 by a trio of architects—Eliel Saarinen, Armas Lindgren, and Herman Gesellius—whose communal living and unusual family arrangements raised eyebrows and lowered voices. But these architects were not the first prominent Finns to forsake city living. In 1897 Juhani Aho and his artist wife, Venny Soldan-Brofeldt, started an exodus of Helsinki artists to Tuusula, a parish just twenty-three miles from Helsinki. Distinguished for its lakeside beauty and excellent transportation connections, Tuusula soon attracted others: the poet J. H. Erkko, the artists Pekka Halonen and Eero Järnefelt, and, before long, the Sibelius family, now expanded with little Katarina. If closeness to nature equated with happy family life, Aino may have been hoping to effect some improvement in that direction. At least Jean would have farther to go to squander his evenings in drink.

Thus in 1903 Sibelius, with the help of the bank and the services of one of the country's leading architects, joined the rush, and, in the fullness of nature in fields not far from Lake Tuusula, built the "villa" known as Ainola. The word *villa* used in English and Swedish, *huvila* in Finnish, is misleading, at least in English. Ainola was a simple log home set deep in the forest—there was no running water, no electricity, no central heating, no indoor facilities (although there was a telephone, "Järvenpää 22"). Yet Ainola stood for more than a change in the life of composer Jean Sibelius. It represented a countrywide reaction against urban culture, "the flight from the city of the artist collective." Moreover, the house itself represented one of the earliest manifestations in Finland of an architectural style that wedded the national vernacular to classicism and modernism.[3]

Ainola's foundations were laid in late 1903, building began in the spring of 1904, and the family moved into their new home on September 24, 1904. The architect responsible for Ainola's design was Lars Sonck (1870–1956), just thirty-three years old at the time he agreed to design the Sibeliuses' new home, yet already distinguished in his field. Sonck had established his reputation as a builder of churches. He had planned Saint Michael's in Turku and the marvelous sanctuary in Tampere, adorned with Hugo Simberg's startling and touching frescoes of naked youths bearing garlands. Around the time Ainola was being built, Sonck designed some of Helsinki's most notable landmarks: the hospital in Eira, the Helsinki Telephone Association Building, and Kallio Church.

Prior to the turn of the century, Sonck had made use of national historical features in his designs. Although he tapped into various architectural traditions (Nordic dragons and whatnot), he endeavored to use characteristically Finnish techniques of construction, especially those found in the architecture of Karelia, that unfailing font of Finnish inspiration. But around the time Sibelius's concept of nationalism in music was deepening, so

Figure 18.1. Lars Sonck, sketches for the north, west, and south façades of Ainola, 1904.
The National Archives of Finland.

was Sonck's concept of architectural history. In 1903 Sonck moved to cleaner lines, more symmetrical planning, and smooth surfaces—in short, to a kind of personal classicism. Ainola was among the first manifestations of this change. Whereas a number of Sonck's country houses had previously been distinguished by the rough-hewn logs and highly decorative exteriors evocative of Karelian architecture, Ainola had a cleanly sloping roofline, symmetrically balanced windows, unextended corner joints, and light-colored siding. Only the balconies, with their round logs, hinted at the vernacular (see fig. 18.1). The plan is all the more astonishing in that the location—a pristine natural setting—and the new owner—a man who had come to personify the national cultural aims—would seem to have called for "a building of archaic forms derived from real and imagined vernacular architecture."[4] Instead, Ainola reflected the new international trends.

It has never been established to what degree Sibelius himself affected Sonck's planning, or vice versa, but there was clearly some dynamic interchange of ideas between these two artistic and intelligent men (as Sibelius's own sketches of some of the interiors show). That Ainola exemplified the "simplicity and authenticity" which was the modernist ideal was surely as much Jean and Aino Sibelius's wish as Sonck's. In architecture, to which Sibelius was supremely responsive, as his recent Italian experiences had demonstrated, national elements in combination with aspects of international design could be transformed and regenerated to deliver a uniquely modern result. Out of living traditions, something modern was born.

Sonck, five years younger than Sibelius, was fully in tune with modern trends. Looking back on this time, the Russian literary historian Viktor Zhirmunsky (1891–1971) observed a fatigue with

> going to the Golgotha of mysticism; [poets] wanted to be simpler, more direct, more human in their experiences. They were tired of so much lyricism, spiritual excitement. . . . They did not feel a sacred obligation to proclaim divine truths, but wanted to speak about objects from external life simply and clearly, stories about intimate ordinary life. They continued the Symbolists' focus on artistic technique, but produced not so much melodious lines, a musical effect, as the pictorial, graphic clarity of visual images.[5]

Graphic clarity and classical impulses were streaming in from many directions, and Saint Petersburg was one. A number of that city's artists, among them Valentin Serov, had begun to rethink their styles. Solomon Volkov, a former resident, recalled that the city's culture

> tended toward neoclassicism even before the revolution; for example, there was a strong classicist tendency inside *Mir iskusstva*. The manifestoes of the acmeists in the years before World War I called for simplicity, clarity, precision, and economy in the selection of words; many of the poems of Kuzmin, Gumi-lyov, and Mandelstam were quintessentially classical. Before the revolution this orientation was presumed to be primarily aesthetic, with reference to Petersburg traditions. After the Bolshevik seizure of power the political underpinnings of neoclassicism suddenly became much clearer.[6]

Sibelius may have withdrawn to the Finnish countryside, but in the artists' colony of Tuusula and the extended artistic family of the Järnefelts, he was fully in touch with the new currents of thought (Pekka Korvenmaa put it aptly in the title of his Ainola essay: "Back to Nature—but in a Civilized Manner"). And those currents brought Sibelius out of the slough of his wastrel lifestyle.

LIVING TRADITIONS

In September 1902 Sibelius had written to Aino from the Finnish archipelago, "I've gotten some wonderful themes for the violin concert [*sic*]."[7] Truth be told, some of those themes had occurred to him long before. The melody ringing through the concerto's first movement had floated out to him a few years earlier; it appears on a page sketched in Rapallo, one of whose themes is labeled "Allegretto Klockorna i Rapallo" (Allegretto, the Bells of Rapallo).[8] Although it was only in 1903, as Ainola was going up, that Sibelius was well and truly at work on a concerto, the bells of Italy lent their resonance to the new work (perhaps not coincidentally, he and Aino named Ainola's orchard "Rapallo"). Carpelan, who had egged Sibelius on in this as well as other projects, had been writing to friends about a Sibelius violin concerto as early as the previous July.[9] Meanwhile, Ainola had gotten under way, and its construction enabled Sibelius to experience in a direct and personal way interconnections between national form and classical and modernist ideas: all interweave tradition, universality, and renewal.[10] The manifestation of these connections in architecture seems to have worked as a catalyst for Sibelius, who of all people understood the parallels with musical genres. And not least among those genres was the solo concerto, which in the early twentieth century was very much a living practice.

Mendelssohn's Violin Concerto in E Minor, which Sibelius had studied and played, had been composed only sixty years before. Tchaikovsky's Violin Concerto in D Major had been available in full score only since 1888. That work was dedicated to Leopold Auer, the violinist who in 1905 would premiere yet another new violin concerto, this one by Alexander Glazunov, in Saint Petersburg. Sibelius, who had played various concerti in the course of his violin studies, was fully aware of these traditions.

Was it an encounter in Berlin with the violinist Willy Burmester that finally prompted Sibelius to follow through with a concerto? The need for something to be performed easily? The new ideas in the air? All this and more? What is clear is that Sibelius's violin concerto acknowledged the living traditions in multiple ways.[11] His overall structure recalled Mendelssohn: an Allegro moderato in sonata allegro form; a slow movement, Adagio di molto (in lied form), and a rondo finale, Allegro, ma non tanto. Mendelssohnlike, too, was the soloist's role in opening the concerto. The virtuosic flamboyance expected of solo concerti, the dazzling cadenzas, the deep-throated and muscular themes, the glittering figuration—all were in place. He added teasers: themes in "wrong keys"—recapitulating the first movement's opening theme not in its tonic, D minor, but in G minor. He infused the demonic undercurrent with incisive Beethovenian gestures.

Yet along with tradition, Sibelius added his own national vernacular. The "Bells of Rapallo" ring out the "Sibelian triplet" (which might as well be called the "Petersburg triplet," because it decorates many works in the Petersburg orbit). The dark, brooding themes bespeak Finnish melancholia. Most striking, in the concerto's structure, while clearly alluding to custom, he created his own innovation. In a solo concerto, the moment for which every audience waits is the first-movement cadenza. The more extravagant, the more breathtaking, the more dizzying, the better for the great public. Cadenzas often give the feeling of being tacked on. Seldom had they been integral to the work. Usually, they served simply as a vehicle for the soloist to awe the public. The orchestra sits and waits (occasionally giving a bark of admiring support), the audience gapes, and the soloist makes extravagant gestures and fiddles flamboyantly. Mendelssohn had begun to tamper with the problem of the tacked-on feeling, incorporating his cadenza into the end of the first movement's development section. Sibelius was prepared to go even further: he composed a cadenza to *replace* the development. The entirety of this crucial structural moment was given over to the soloist, whose role was thus to further the drama.

A striking parallel was taking place in Russian ballet. The choreographer Mikhail Fokine (1880–1942), with no small help from the innovative Sergei Diaghilev, was renewing dance not by renouncing its tradition, but by treating it in such a way that the formality gave way to the dramaturgy. Classical ballet has an analogy to the concerto's cadenza in the *pas de deux*, the moment the prima ballerina flaunts her most dazzling skills, served by a partner whose sole function is support. Fokine brought that tradition to an end. The results burst forth in stunning glory in 1909–10 with Stravinsky's *Firebird*, in which the *pas de deux* between the feathered prima ballerina and her prince became a true dance of partners and one that furthers the drama—an integration of music, choreography, and new ideas about traditional events.[12]

Engaging in a similar living tradition, Sibelius was not prepared to minimize the soloist's role, however much he wanted to integrate its peak moments into the concerto structure. He conceived the entire first movement from the point of view of a broken-hearted, thwarted violinist longing for the virtuoso career that would never be: the soloist plays almost nonstop from the first bar to the last. As the work's harshest critic, Flodin, put it: "[Sibelius] knew about the fate of these modern concertos: to be played once and then put aside. He preferred to choose the other alternative, to let the soloist become a sovereign ruler all the time with all the traditional pomp and circumstance."[13] Even more surprising, the soloist had not one, but *two* cadenzas. The second drew considerable attention, because it seemed to sit oddly in its surroundings: a Bachlike chaconne.[14]

The extravagant daring of Sibelius's construction took some time to appreciate—especially after that first performance, which charitably could be called a flop. Flodin severely chastised not the performer, but the composer. The cruelest, and most demonstrably undeserved, swipe was surely the words "the concerto is boring."[15] Yet even Sibelius found it unworkable architectonically. By the next year, in an effort to streamline, he eliminated the Bach chaconne cadenza. The result was that the balance shifted: the cadenza—the true moment of violinistic flamboyance—became the centerpiece of the entire movement.[16] Sibelius had not renounced the concerto's formal tradition. Rather, he had found a way to reinterpret its structure so that its formality receded and the drama shone through. Form and function were one.

Sibelius's revisions to his concerto clearly belonged to the modernizing taking place in the wider aesthetic discussion. Eliminating the cadenza à la Bach, despite its potential resonance for Finland's Lutheran audiences, seemed, in retrospect, the obvious thing to do. In fact, the question could well be asked, why on earth did he include this kind of jolting disconnect in the first place? And the answer seems to be Willy Burmester.

THE BURMESTER CASE

Despite his long virtuoso career, Carl Adolf Wilhelm Burmester (1869–1933) never once performed the violin concerto that holds the record for being the most frequently recorded in all the twentieth century.[17] And yet Burmester's name is inextricably bound to the work. In addition to Sibelius's chance encounter with Burmester in Berlin in 1902, the composer himself had sent Burmester the concerto's piano arrangement at the end of 1903.[18] The press announced that Sibelius would dedicate the piece to Burmester. But no such dedication was ever forthcoming. Nor was any occasion ever made convenient for Burmester to premiere the work, in either its initial or its revised form.

It has been remarked that the insensitivity the composer too often showed to Aino spilled over into the relations with Burmester, with whom Sibelius had been connected since the Symposium days. Indeed, despite the prior discussions with Burmester, Sibelius, with staggering lack of acumen, prevailed upon Viktor Nováček (1873–1914), a mediocre Hungarian violin teacher at the Helsinki Music Institute, to give the work's premiere in the autumn of 1903, with predictably unhappy results.

Meanwhile, Burmester, who was concertizing in Copenhagen, heard rumors that the concerto's premiere was to be given by Henri Marteau (1874–1934). Burmester reacted with haughty emphasis: "If this is in fact the case, then *I* will *never* play the concerto."[19] Sibelius frantically explained that he was in desperate financial straits, made semantic ditherings, and promised Burmester an "official" performance in Helsinki. Burmester calmed down. Responding in his supercilious way, he told Sibelius that he would put "*all* his twenty-five years of concert routine, his art, his understanding" into interpreting the work—the very fact of which, he pointed out condescendingly, showed the importance of Sibelius's new concerto. In his forceful style he continued (the emphases are all his): "Strauss's *Ein Heldenleben* played by a small city orchestra would have exactly the same ridiculous effect as a *Bismarckian* speech from a proletarian. Do not allow yourself therefore to be irritated by anything; stroll peacefully on your way and trust me. I will play such a concert for you in *Helsingfors* that they have to forgive you."[20]

As it turned out, the autumn premiere had to be postponed—to February 1904. In a few weeks Burmester could have introduced the piece. Instead, the disastrous Nováček rendition took place. A year later, after Sibelius had revised the score and sent it to Robert Lienau for publication, a discussion ensued about a German premiere. Lienau favored

Karl Halíř (1859–1909), concertmaster of the Berlin Philharmonic and, like Burmester, a Joachim product; Halíř had given the first German performance of Tchaikovsky's violin concerto. Moreover, an occasion was at hand—a concert to be conducted by Richard Strauss. Sibelius could hardly refuse such a glittering opportunity, despite the inevitable consequences: the death blow to his relationship with Burmester.

Why Sibelius treated Burmester so shabbily has long been a puzzle. Although there are no completely satisfactory answers, as usual there is more to the situation than meets the eye. When Burmester played his Berlin debut in the 1890s, the audience at the Singakademie was dazzled. At least, so Adolf Paul recalled, for he was there. Burmester eventually came to Helsinki, by way of Saint Petersburg. In the Russian capital his duties had included rehearsing and directing the Aquarium Orchestra, not exactly one of Russia's finest. On one occasion when Burmester detained the violin section to work on a particularly feeble passage, making the players rehearse it again and again, he was suddenly confronted by an exasperated musician, shouting, "If I could play the passage perfectly, I would not be a member of the Aquarium Orchestra!"[21]

Fortunately for Burmester, Kajanus got hold of him, probably when the Finn was doing a stint with the Aquarium ensemble in the summer of 1892. Lured to Helsinki, the violinist served as concertmaster and soloist of the Helsinki Philharmonic for three years, from 1892 to 1895. During one of Burmester's first performances in Society House, the corpulent critic of *Hufvudstadsbladet*, "Boulot," caught the violinist's attention as he fiddled away and was immediately rewarded with a couple of well-aimed harmonics that hit the bull's-eye; Boulot chortled with delight, and Burmester's success in Finland was assured.[22]

Burmester's tenure in Helsinki coincided with the Symposium's high point, and he joined fully in its revelries. His marathon performance with Alfred Reisenauer, playing ten sonatas of Beethoven, three of Brahms, and two of Grieg, lasted from eight o'clock one evening until five o'clock the next morning and lived in legend—his own, at least.[23] He spoke Swedish. He entertained his companions. He courted the local ladies. He even made his connection to Finland deeply personal by marrying the pianist Naema Fazer (1869–1951), sister of the Helsinki music publisher Konrad Fazer. Though Burmester sometimes composed (small virtuoso works and a serenade for string quartet and double bass) and arranged (a five-volume set entitled *Pieces by Old Masters*), it was for his gifts as a performer that he was widely praised in Finland. His picture, taken by the Helsinki photographer Daniel Nyblin, repeatedly ran in *Program-bladet*, the capital's entertainment rag. With his head proudly tilted, chin held high, full hair precisely coiffed, and plaid silk cravat stylishly bowed, "Willy" won the hearts of the Helsinki public: "May we long have him with us!" echoed from the pages of *Program-bladet*. When he eventually left Finland, he made Berlin his home. And to events there Sibelius had a direct pipeline: Adolf Paul.

Through Paul and personal experience, Sibelius would have known that Burmester had a certain temperament, not to put too fine a point on it. His disposition frequently steps off the pages of the self-congratulatory autobiography *Fünfzig Jahre Künstlerleben* (with no fewer than eighteen immodest leaves of laudatory press clippings). In Copenhagen, greeted by an audience of only some sixty persons, Burmester proceeded to chastise those present—in Swedish—for the little interest in music shown by Danes (!); on dining with the famous Georg Brandes in the Danish capital, the violinist silenced an entire dinner party with the wet blanket of his arrogance.[24] And although Adolf Paul praised his talents (if Paul's letter included in Burmester's autobiography can be believed), others begged to differ. Some branded him "a mere technician." The Berlin correspondent for the *Musical Courier*, Arthur M. Abell, describing him as "phenomenal," at the same time admitted that the bowing suffered from an elbow raised too high, a wrist held too stiff.[25] Rapid legatos and spiccatos muddied into indistinction; vibratos reverberated everlastingly.

A fellow violinist, Carl Flesch (1873–1944), callously cut him down to size. Burmester's style was "distinctly unmusical, arbitrary, inconsistent and unbeautiful; his tone was cold, his bowing angular and mixed with scraping noises. In later years, moreover, he played intolerably out of tune."[26] Flatly rejected by almost everybody but the Germans, the inexplicability of his success gave the French their chief argument against their Teutonic neighbors; posterity, sniped Flesch, "will pass on him the harsh judgment that he was of no significance whatever to the development of violin playing."[27]

Even allowing for personal jealousy, Flesch's criticism finds some corroboration. Posterity has accorded Burmester no entry in either *Die Musik in Geschichte und Gegenwart* or the 2001 edition of *The New Grove Dictionary of Music and Musicians*. Even during his lifetime, Burmester had foundered in the United States. He had hoped for success in Japan, but on the voyage over, in an instant of monumental stupidity, he challenged a sailor to a wrestling match. His burly opponent gave Burmester the unforgettable opportunity of becoming acquainted with Japan's hospitals rather than its concert halls. Even the Germans found fault. On December 5, 1902, Rudolf Buck commented in the *Allgemeine Musik-Zeitung* that Burmester's recent performance had been fidgety and that the artist had failed to bring out any of the music's progressive tendencies. Only in playing Bach did he succeed.

Ah. Burmester's Bach had merit. German audiences applauded it enthusiastically. It earned a mention in Alberto Bachmann's *Encyclopedia of the Violin* (New York: 1925): "a remarkable interpreter of Bach and Spohr."[28] Sibelius's initial conception of his concerto with its Bachlike cadenza seemed inspired: it combined Lutheran tradition and musical universality with the forte of the soloist for whom the work was ostensibly being written. Yet on hearing the performance the composer realized that the cadenza did not work— it overbalanced the first movement. His usual way of proceeding was to revise a work after its first performance, and the violin concerto was true to type. The work attained an increasingly modernized and tautened form, like the simplified new structures being built in Finland. With the elimination of the Bachian appendage, Burmester's weaknesses may have begun, in Sibelius's mind, to outweigh his strengths. The stiffness of his wrist, the scrapings of his bow, the problems of his tunings (even one of his admirers claimed, "Burmester never plays off the key unless his strings are out of tune")[29] hardly boded success before the rapier-sharp pens of music critics.

There is still another factor to be considered in the Burmester affair: it is suggested by the rumors that the work would be given to a French violinist. The man in question, Henri Marteau, had made his debut at the age of ten. Concertizing widely around Europe, Marteau had also appeared in Russia, in 1897–99, and in the United States. Just as Sibelius was launching his *Kullervo*, in 1892, Marteau was winning first place in a competition at the Paris Conservatory. Jules Massenet composed a violin concerto for this virtuoso. Eventually (on Joachim's death), Marteau became head of the violin department of the Berlin Hochschule für Musik. Was it the dazzling Frenchman who reminded Sibelius of his boyhood dreams of becoming a virtuoso performer and of those heady days when Wasiljeff had nurtured him on the French and Belgian violin repertoire? It was a dream that lingered. As late as June 1914, on his visit to North America, Sibelius was pointedly reminding his hosts that he had been a violinist.[30] Some months thereafter, awakening from sleep on February 2, 1915, he recorded in his diary a dream: "was 12 and a virtuoso."

For various reasons, the heaviness of German culture lost its appeal. In this scheme of things, the German Willy Burmester's "twenty-five years of concert routine, his art, his understanding" really amounted to very little.

EUTERPE: FRENCH CLASSICISM

The Finns' French sympathies have often been underestimated, and the importance of their French connections for advancing the national movement has gone largely unrecognized. Recently, however, Kristina Ranki's study of Finnish Francophilia demonstrated how profoundly French culture wielded its allure over an entire generation of Finnish elites.[31] For a multitude of Finnish poets, novelists, painters, and sculptors, as well as musicians, critics, and composers, French liberalism served as a European elixir: when drunk, it heightened Finnish patriotism, while opening the drinker's eyes to a new, more global love. Its residue remains in correspondence and travel journals, in Finnish periodicals and newspapers, in lectures and society proceedings, in artworks and musical compositions. Prominent among Finnish Francophiles were the Järnefelts, including Aino and her sister, Elli. They studied the French language, borrowed books in French from the library of the Alliance française in Helsinki, and translated from French to Finnish (an endeavor in which Aino worked at the behest of another notable Finnish Francophile, Juhani Aho).

Some of the clearest manifestations of the Helsinki French connection surfaced in a group and a periodical, both named for the musical muse Euterpe and both indicative of how tightly interwoven were the threads of the national fabric, in this case, Francophilia with classicism.[32] Euterpe the group was a loosely defined collection of writers, artists, critics, and activists united by friendships extending in some cases back to childhood. Although women sometimes joined in, the Euterpists were almost exclusively male, the sons of aristocrats. Camaraderie was evidently their chief goal, pursued in long and leisurely evenings at the Robber's Den, their own upstairs room in Lundqvist's in central Helsinki. That a portrait of Jean Sibelius, not Johan Ludvig Runeberg, adorned the wall indicated something about the men's ideals: a weariness of the nationalism that had elevated Runeberg to a cult figure, yet abhorrence of the increasingly oppressive, police-state atmosphere in Finland.

Caught politically between patriotism and cosmopolitanism, without being able to find a truly satisfactory position, the Euterpists looked abroad for inspiration and found it above all in France. Through the writings of Maurice Maeterlinck and Anatole France, they gained entrée into the world of French intellectual ideas. Those who lived or studied there encountered sensual visual beauty, the wider world of orientalist thought then captivating French intellectuals, and, not least, the clear, classical orientation of the French spirit, a classicism embodied in the group's name. The Euterpists' most famous portrait shows the men dressed in Greek tunics, no less, laurel wreaths perched rakishly on their heads.

In 1902 the Euterpists found an outlet for disseminating their views: Karl Flodin's music journal, *Euterpe*. Founded the previous year, *Euterpe* had introduced Finns to Claude Debussy with articles about *Pelléas et Mélisande*.[33] Flodin had a personal connection to Paris: his wife, the soprano Adée Leander-Flodin, had studied and performed at the Opéra-Comique. Now, in the hands of some of the many Söderhjelms (Werner and Torsten) and Gunnar Castrén, the journal's focus widened. The new full title, *Euterpe: Veckoskrift för musik, teater och skönlitteratur* (*Euterpe: Weekly for Music, Theater and Belles Lettres*), showed the fleshed-out orientation of those aspiring to "new paths of thought, new values in emotional life."[34] Emphasis gravitated to the development of the individual personality, a point on which the Euterpists agreed: "The personality was for them the highest thing in life as in teaching. If this was decadence, they were decadents with all their heart and soul."[35]

Euterpe's editors published the poetry of the Swedes Oscar Levertin (1862–1906) and Gustaf Fröding (1860–1911). They wrote reviews and criticisms of new literary works. They presented biographical information about leading artists. It was in *Euterpe* that the first list ever published of Sibelius's compositions appeared.[36] *Euterpe* was short-lived, lasting only until 1905. Yet in those few years it breathed new life into Finnish intellectual debates and kept Finnish windows open to the literary and artistic breezes wafting northward from France.

Although Sibelius's name does not appear among the group's official members, evidence from various quarters securely links him to its company and their ideals—significantly, just at the time he was composing his violin concerto.[37] It was in the company of Euterpe, in May 1903, that Sibelius, seated at the piano, improvised as the Norwegian actress Johanne Dybwad declaimed members' poetry. In later years the composer attended the group's reunion (1922). Meanwhile, his travel itinerary, formerly focused on Berlin, now broadened to include France. Having visited Paris for the first time in connection with the orchestra's appearance at the World's Fair in 1900, he returned on his own in 1905, and he would journey there again—in 1909, 1911, and 1927. Sibelius even began speaking some French and entertaining the bizarre (for him) notion of moving to France, as many of the Euterpists were doing.[38] Their admiration for French art, literature, and aesthetic ideals reflected and reinforced his growing classicism.

Sibelius also began composing to poems and translations by the Euterpists as well as by the authors they promoted. In 1904 he was writing incidental music to Maurice Maeterlinck's *Pelléas et Mélisande*, in a Swedish translation by the Euterpist Bertel Gripenberg. The same year he turned Oscar Levertin's *En slända* (*A Dragonfly*) into scintillating quiverings and made that setting of Gustaf Fröding's *Jag ville, jag vore i Indialand* (*I Wish I Were in Indialand*). Two years later (1906) he was writing music for the play *Belshazzar's Feast* by another Euterpist, Hjalmar Procopé (1868–1927). And he composed music for a *tableau* on a classical theme, *Pan and Echo*. His terse comment about the piece was heavy with meaning: "Not one note of Finnish music in it!"[39]

In the years 1904 to 1914, Euterpist texts and Gallic ideas stand out sharply in Sibelius's music. In 1908 the composer turned Gripenberg's *Teodora* into one of the most sensuous and ravishing miniatures he ever created. *Romeo* (1910), whose tart humor might be mistaken for a Debussian cabaret song, and *Oceanides* (1914), whose swirling glissandos and flowing thirds, coupled with the suggestive title, prompted critics to use the label "impressionism" and make comparisons to *La mer*, all belonged to these impulses. In 1910 Sibelius again reached out to Gripenberg, setting the poem *Vårtagen* (*The Spell of*

Springtide) and, in 1915, his *Evige Eros* (*Eternal Eros*) and *På berget* (*On the Mountain*).
He eventually composed Gripenberg's *Ett ensamt skidspår* (*A Lonely Ski Trail*) and, in
1925, *Narciss* (dedicated to Nylands Nation). But it was during the desolate decade from
1904–5 to 1914–15 that these writers had the greatest importance for him. Their language—Swedish—and their outward and classically oriented precepts offered reassuring
company on that melting ice floe where Swedish speakers in Finland were marooned.

It may well have been an Euterpist play, *Ödlan* (*The Lizard*), written by one of the
group's members, Mikael Lybeck (1864–1925), that had the greatest single importance
for Sibelius's creative thinking in the years after the violin concerto. In the wake of K. A.
Tavaststjerna's death in 1898, Lybeck was considered "the entire Swedish literature of
Finland." Lybeck's style—unostentatious and elegantly reserved—was as strongly
symptomatic of the Euterpists' isolation and withdrawal from Finnish society as was his
home, a handsome villa in the exclusive surroundings of Kauniainen, a Helsinki suburb.

In his important article "Sagan om Satu," Rabbe Forsman has discussed the significance of Sibelius's connection to Lybeck, and particularly to *Ödlan*, both of which have
too often been glossed over; in 1908, Forsman observes, Sibelius was not shy about telling Lybeck that *Ödlan* had gripped his very soul: "It's poetry, and above all, there is style.
I'll certainly compose the music you desire. To the best of my ability! Naturally!"[40] Even
years later Sibelius was describing *Ödlan*'s music as "among the most full of feeling that
I have ever written."[41] Although at one time he thought of turning its final theme into
a set of symphonic variations, the composer ultimately decided that the music was too
closely bound to the theater—or, more accurately put, to the drama, which it exquisitely
balances—to be extracted and arranged into an independent suite.

Lybeck's biographer, literary historian, and critic Erik Kihlman (1895–1933) believed
that for Lybeck, the association of dramatic events with Sibelius's musical language
resolved an artistic crisis.[42] As for Sibelius, Lybeck's prose in turn stirred something deep
in the composer. Shorn of the philosophical musings characteristic of Arvid Järnefelt or
the prolix historical details characteristic of Adolf Paul, *Ödlan*'s text moved Sibelius to
compose some of his darkest, most minimal, yet most gripping expressions.

On the surface of things, the story, a love triangle, would hardly seem the stuff of
great musical inspiration: its action takes place in an old mansion, whose atmosphere
would, along with the bizarre Tennessee Williams–like characters, fit right into a macabre
tale from the American South.[43] The characters are Alban, scion of the Eyringe estate;
Elisiv, Alban's sweet cousin, with whom he is in love; and Adla, a temptress with a name
strikingly similar to the Swedish word for lizard—*ödlan*—and a weird penchant for
dressing up like one. Startled by Adla/Ödlan in her green get-up, Elisiv trips, falls, and is
killed. Meanwhile, Alban has fallen prey to Adla's temptations. But when Alban sees his

EXAMPLE 18.1. SIBELIUS, *ÖDLAN*, FIRST MOVEMENT, MM. 12–20.
BY PERMISSION OF FENNICA GEHRMAN OY, HELSINKI.

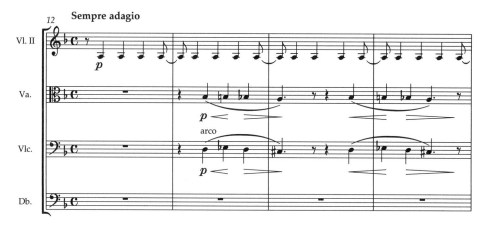

beloved don the lizard gear—*voilà*! He comes to his senses and shoves the creature off a balcony. Then he goes mad.

Yet beneath the surface of that tale currents run deep. Sibelius captured them in musically shadowy forebodings (see ex. 18.1). Some of the drama's most important currents for the composer, Rabbe Forsman suggests, are the views expressed by Alban, who says, "All great music strives to surpass the borders between life and death"; Alban further expresses the belief that "the religion of the future is music."[44] Such reflections sound deeply familiar to anyone conversant with Jean Sibelius's ideas and music. And nowhere would those ideas find more profound expression than in Sibelius's Fourth Symphony, begun the year after *Ödlan* was composed (see ex. 18.2). But as Forsman observes, it

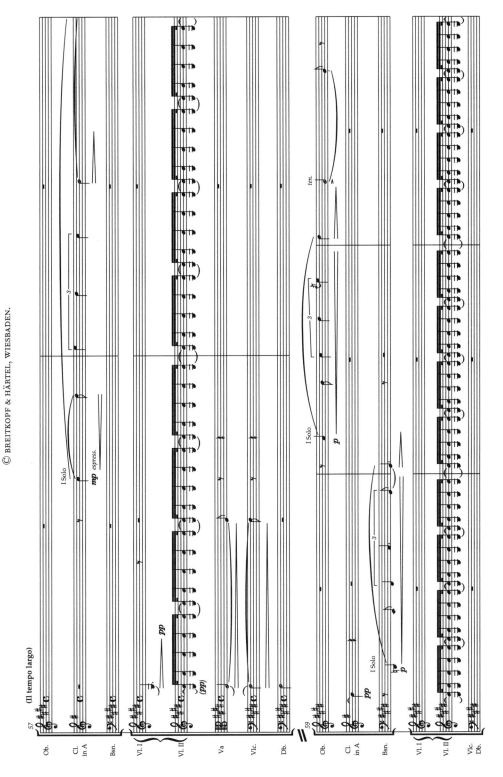

EXAMPLE 18.2. SIBELIUS, SYMPHONY NO. 4, THIRD MOVEMENT, MM. 57–61.

© BREITKOPF & HÄRTEL, WIESBADEN.

would be heresy to claim that Finland-Swedish drama rather than Finnish nature inspired this great composition. And so *Ödlan*'s—and Euterpe's—importance have been relegated to a mere blip on the screen of Sibelius's life and work.

ASSASSINATION!

Helsinki is not the calm classical town where the learned and government convene
and where their representatives reign with unbridled autocracy as in the mid-19th
century. Helsinki is a febrile, restless modern town where everything that is new stirs
one's blood, where youth prevails, political parties fight, competition abounds and
where everything changes, lives and moves.

JAC AHRENBERG, "DET NYA HELSINGFORS," *VK-SYDVÄST*, 1904,
TRANSLATED BY VILLE LUKKARINEN

So Jacob Ahrenberg described the atmosphere in Finland's capital in 1904, the year that would be the most dramatic of Finns' entire lives. On February 8 the fate of Sibelius's new concerto would be decided, at least in the short term. But far more calamitous fates were sealed in 1904. The "time of oppression" (*sortokausi*) was upon Finland, and those responsible would be called on to pay the price. Bobrikov was one. Since coming to office, his shenanigans had rewarded him with near-dictatorial powers. He ruled the entire civil administration. He could eliminate any entity perceived as dangerous. He could expel any individual suspected of troublemaking—and he did. Prominent figures began to be cast into exile. Some went willingly, as in the case of *Nya Pressen*'s Axel Lille. Less willing were Eero Erkko, founder of *Päivälehti*, and Wenzel Hagelstam, editor of *Ateneum*.[45]

The dissolution of the Finnish army and the imminent conscription of Finnish men into the Russian military preoccupied the populace. So did the escalating press censorship. One by one, Finland's newspapers, both in Finnish and Swedish, were silenced, including those oriented toward cultural issues, *Päivälehti* and *Nya Pressen*. There were more language manifestos, a particular thorn in Finnish flesh, and other onerous decrees. One mandated the use of the Russian language in administrative offices in Finland. In October 1903 Russian had become the language of the plenary sessions of the senate, the government's administrative body; this meant that Bobrikov could preside as chairman and thereby directly influence the resolutions of the Finnish government. There were a declaration requiring permission of the governor-general to hold public meetings and a decree permitting peddlers free movement throughout the grand duchy (enabling Russian agitators to circulate freely). Meanwhile, since the meeting of the Finnish diet in the summer of 1900, that supposedly representative body had not convened again.

Legal objections and open protests appeared futile. The only recourse was refusal to obey illegal orders. Earlier, passive resistance had had a measure of success. When the conscription calls had gone out in 1902, fewer than half (according to Bobrikov's reckoning) showed up; among university students, the proportion was thought to be lower still.[46] Emigration swelled to a point so mortifying for the empire that it seems some consideration was given to transferring Bobrikov to another post. But now the situation had changed, and Bobrikov reigned imperious. The resistance movement went underground. The secret society called Kagaali (Kagal, the name of the resistance organization of Russia's persecuted Jews), had formed as early as August 1901. Its members, including some of the leading figures in the national movement—Eero Erkko, Carl Gustaf Mannerheim, and P. E. Svinhufvud, who would later become president of the republic of Finland—illegally distributed information at home and abroad and incited opposition among the people.[47] A corresponding group for women had, as its principal goal, awakening opposition among their countrywomen and preventing children from learning the Russian language. The clergy meanwhile largely bowed to authority and from pulpits all over Finland read out the emperor's new decrees to their parishioners.[48]

The tension was palpable. At the end of August 1903, Albert Edelfelt, returning to Finland from France, wrote to Bertel Gripenberg:

> When on that icy summer evening we sailed in between the first low Finnish rocks [of the archipelago], conversation and noise on deck suddenly ceased—the expressions of all the Finnish men and women showed rigid dread and resignation. In Åbo where I had landed, I noticed nothing other than the usual summer drowsiness but—in Helsingfors! The new police, the Tartars . . . absolutely hideous, multitudes of them and armed (among other things, they are always carrying handcuffs); they give our previously peaceful city a new character.[49]

By the following June, things were, if anything, worse. Yuri Belyayev, in Finland for *Novoe Vremia*, reported that it felt like war in Helsinki, only without the weapons.[50] Edelfelt was heard to remark, "*Mod* is a beautiful word in Swedish, but more beautiful still resounds the French word *courage!*"[51] Sibelius evidently shared his friend's sentiments: he twice turned Josef Julius Wecksell's poem *Har du mod?* (*Do You Have Courage?*) into a militant men's chorus, once with orchestra. The choir and orchestral version (op. 31, no. 2) premiered on the same program as the violin concerto, February 8, 1904.[52] Exactly one month later, he was writing to Carpelan: "What do you think about the war[?] The official accounts!! Japan owns 23 battleships and according to Bobba [Bobrikov] 40 have been destroyed. *Sic itur ad gehennam!* [So it's going to Hell!]"[53]

But the resistance movement did not have the full support of the populace; instead, a rift developed among the Finns, all too predictably, along the old rancorous lines of language difference. The so-called compliance wing of the Old Finnish party revived the rhetoric of Snellman, who was said to have gotten close to the czar and who had advocated "a strong folk-spirit [as] the surest defence against external oppression."[54] Led by that polemicist Yrjö-Koskinen, their most extreme members seized the chance to promote language unity above all else and rid themselves of the Swedish party, the caustically named "Vikings." Young Finns and others balked at such maneuverings. "Better to join the Swedish party in making common cause against the perceived assault on Finland's constitutional legitimacy," ran their thinking. These "Constitutionalists" maintained that preserving the country's autonomy depended on maintaining Finnish rights unconditionally. They should simply refuse to obey illegal laws and decrees. One of their number, Viktor Magnus von Born (1851–1917), invoked the stalwart pillars of God and Runeberg, declaring: "In life there are many collisions of duty, but for us there can be only one course. Read *Ensign Stål*, if you have forgotten your Bible, and the answer will be clear."[55]

The unease echoing through the capital ripples through Sibelius's *Kyllikki*, composed in 1904. The feminine name of its title has inevitably led to associations with one of Lemminkäinen's brasher exploits in the *Kalevala*, but the composer always denied any such connection. "Three lyric pieces for piano," he called his work, and his *Kyllikki* sobs and shudders with deep-throated voice—if Chaliapin had been a piano, he would have sounded like *Kyllikki*. The lyric personae who populate *En saga* and Symphony no. 2 show up here too, in the imperious octaves of the first movement, with its sustained pedals and dissonant outcries, the caws of gulls or the cries of humans; and in the folklike melody of the slow movement, filled with foreboding and sorrow. But there is a strange disconnect, a jolt, in the character of the third movement: its Commodo superficiality— "easy, comfortable" with emphasis on the piano's upper register—conjures up a salon style à la Pushkin. In the tranquillo section, however, the anxiety returns, a switch from a banal B-flat major to a haunting G-flat minor, with syncopated undercurrents threatening the salonlike glitter of the outer parts. In a strong sense *Kyllikki* expressed what could not easily be put into words about the ominous atmosphere of 1904.

June 16, 1904

There were those who contemplated measures stronger than covert musical responses to the threats to Finland. At least as early as 1901, murmurings about doing away with the great evil himself, Bobrikov, had flitted through some of the more radical circles. In the winter of 1903–4 university students and workers formed an activist group based on the Russian Socialist Revolutionaries' model of "propaganda by deed." The initial plan was to select a collaborator to kill as a warning to the other "moral traitors." But one plan after another fizzled—until June 16, 1904.

Shortly before eleven o'clock in the morning, an athletic young man walked unnoticed into the senate building on Helsinki's great Square. In one pocket he carried a note to the emperor; in another, a Browning pistol. Bobrikov was scheduled to open the senate's session, and within minutes, his reviled figure, clad in Russian uniform and carrying cane and briefcase, was mounting the steps. The young man, Eugen Schauman, strode swiftly forward. When the target advanced into close range, Schauman lifted the Browning and fired. Five shots rang out: three for Bobrikov, two for the assassin, one piercing his already broken heart.

Schauman died instantly. Unbelievably, Bobrikov continued into the assembly hall before he collapsed. He was taken to the Finnish Surgical Hospital (rather than the Russian hospital, at the wounded man's own request), where Richard W. Faltin (son of the musician) operated on his torn intestines. Gendarmes and police stood at all the entrances and doors checking everyone who entered or left. The hospital corridors swarmed with handsome soldiers and fine ladies. Spurs jingled. Tears flowed into lace handkerchiefs. The family was in despair. Madame could not understand how such a fine man, who only wanted the best for the people, could be so poorly rewarded: "He always forgave those who approached him repentantly." The daughters sobbed and wailed repeatedly, "Warum? Warum?" (Why? Why?), although one was heard to add, "Aber ich weiss, dass Papa in Finnland nicht geliebt ist" (But I know Papa is not loved in Finland).[56] Bobrikov, sixty-five years old and having already suffered several heart attacks, expired during the small hours of the night.

It seems that Schauman was bent on suicide for personal reasons: there was an unrequited love. There was also a public humiliation of his father, Waldemar Schauman, a Finno-Swedish officer in the Russian army who had succeeded Alexander Järnefelt as governor of the province of Vasa in 1894: Bobrikov had summoned the father to a dinner on the very eve of the February Manifesto, and this show of friendship, sealed with a moist and highly visible Russian kiss, widely observed through the windows on Fabian Street, "became the talk of Helsingfors."[57] To make the son's humiliation complete, he had been whipped by the emperor's Cossacks during a protest skirmish on the steps of the Nicholas Church in 1902.

Whatever drove him to such a desperate measure, to the nationalists Schauman was a hero.[58] They erupted in rejoicing. Flags flew, champagne flowed. (Alma Söderhjelm wrote tartly that never had so much champagne been poured in Helsinki; while Bobrikov lay dying, she said, they were toasting freedom and peace; she and her crowd thought decency might have called for waiting until his struggle was over.)[59] Sibelius joined the jubilation. Along with Armas Järnefelt and Jost von Qvanten, he was hauled into the local police station for unseemly behavior, charged with *omotiverad glädje* (unwarranted happiness).[60] Sibelius's sympathies at the time were clear to people other than the police. On New Year's Day 1905, visiting his brother-in-law Eero Järnefelt, he told another guest, Tekla Hultin (1864–1943), leader of the women Kagaalists, of his intention to compose a requiem to Schauman's memory; the work, he said, was already under way.[61] Meanwhile, Eero Järnefelt was commissioned by the Kagaali organization to do a portrait of the martyr—a difficult task, Hultin recalled, since Järnefelt had never actually seen Schauman in real life.[62]

Yet even though some Finns venerated the fallen Schauman as the hero who committed the first-ever political murder in the land, Finland's pernicious language divide showed among those who called the deed a "Swedish act." Even among Finnish-speaking Finns, some still called it murder, and there was serious concern about the consequences. J. K. Paasikivi, at that time director of the Finnish treasury (and later president of the Republic), expressed the conflicting feelings that circulated among the populace: some held that "murder is not acceptable, not even for political reasons," he wrote in his memoirs, yet many felt Bobrikov had gotten his just deserts. Paasikivi counted himself among the first group, although he admitted that "there was no doubt that Bobrikov belonged among the bad rulers."[63] *Päivälehti* made no mention of Schauman in its extensive coverage of the funeral cortege that slowly made its way from Helsinki's Uspensky Cathedral to the railroad station on the first leg of the journey bearing its loathsome burden to Saint Petersburg.

Just over a month later, an assassin murdered the Russian secretary of the interior, von Plehve, in Saint Petersburg. The crucial hour was at hand.

1905
The Crucial Hour

Thursday, January 19, 1905. Sibelius writes to Aino: "Now is the crucial hour when I still can take myself in hand and be something really great."[1]

Sunday, January 22, 1905. On Sunday, January 22 (January 9 in Russia), Father George Gapone leads a peaceful crowd of men, women, and children toward the Winter Palace in Saint Petersburg. Bearing religious icons and pious banners, the people wish to present a petition to Emperor Nicholas II.[2] Nicholas is not in his residence. But his Cossacks have been called out. Suddenly, with little warning, they fire upon the crowd, killing over a hundred and wounding as many as a thousand. The bloodbath splatters the myth of benevolent sovereignty. The dead and injured are largely workers and their families. The artist Valentin Serov is among those who witness the horrible massacre. From that day forward his rejection of imperial autocracy does not waver. The shock waves of Bloody Sunday reverberate through artistic and intellectual circles across Russia, through the grand duchy of the Russian Empire, and around the Nordic world.

Heretofore, the Finns had heaped all their fury upon Bobrikov's head. Now, with the personification of evil gone, the myth of a benevolent emperor shattered, and the grass roots ignited, Finland veers toward a dangerous pass. Demonstrators stone the windows of the Helsinki newspaper *Uusi Suometar*. Protests erupt in Turku.

February 5, Runeberg Day, 1905. Robert Kajanus leads the men of the Philharmonic Orchestra in a concert of all Finnish music. Along with Kajanus's saber-rattling arrangement of *Björneborgarnas marsch*, also called *Porilaisten marssi* (*The March of the Men from Björneborg/Pori*), the audience hears—for the first time in a dozen years—Sibelius's *Kullervo*. Kajanus chooses the militant movement called "Kullervo Departs for War," the one with the motto:

Kullervo, son of Kalervo,
Old man's son in blue stockings,
Went off piping to the war,
Went rejoicing to the battle.
He sang and piped on marsh and moor,
High-hallooing on the heather,
Quaking, shaking grass and greensward,
Booming over stump and stubble.[3]

February 6, 1905. A young Finn dresses in the crisp uniform of a Russian Lifeguards' Light Infantry officer. "A splendid swimmer, strong as a bear, and a first-rate sailor," a Russian-speaker, Lennart Hohenthal strides down Helsinki's fashionable Boulevard. At no. 12 he enters the residence of Eliel Soisalon-Soininen (né Johnsson). The fancy name designates the grand duchy's procurator, a man widely believed to have been a Bobrikov stooge. Hohenthal pulls a revolver and shoots the man dead.[4]

April 2, 1905 (March 21 in Russia). Rimsky-Korsakov is "relieved" of his duties at the Saint Petersburg Conservatory, a victim of his liberal sympathies with the true cause. Less than a week later Rimsky's *Kashchey the Immortal* is staged, with strong parallels to the year's political issues. In the allegory the real victors against the emperor and his rule are the people.

May 28, 1905. Russia suffers a humiliating defeat at Port Arthur, on the Liaotung Peninsula.

July 19, 1905. In Helsinki, an attempt is made on the life of the governor-general's aide-de-camp, one Deutrich, as he comes from a plenary session of the senate. At three-twenty in the afternoon a bomb thrown on Senate Square shatters over a hundred windows and seriously damages the police station and town hall. *Hufvudstadsbladet*'s reporter observes unsympathetically that Deutrich holds essentially the same views as did Governor-General Bobrikov.

July 20, 1905. Sibelius sells his Finnish copyrights to a German firm, Breitkopf & Härtel.

August 18, 1905. Albert Edelfelt dies, age fifty-one.

September 3, 1905. Axel Carpelan writes to Sibelius: "The connection with Europe broken! *You* are now our great hope and our pride."[5]

October 30, 1905. The general strike roiling Petersburg and Moscow erupts in Finland. People are thrown into turmoil. Finland grinds to a halt. Two years before, at the Forssa Conference, Finnish workers had transformed themselves into a legitimate political party, the Social Democrats. Now workers march through the streets of Helsinki. They bear belligerent placards reading "Käy eespäin väki voimakas" (Onward, You Powerful People). The words are taken up into the anthem for the Social Democratic party. Meanwhile, Axel Gallén makes the drawing called *Vallankumous* (*Revolution*): an old, bearded Russian worker leads a crowd of men over the barricades, an allegorical fantasy with similarities to Delacroix's famous *Freedom over the Barricades* (1830).

November 1, 1905. In Tsarskoe Selo, "the Czar's Village," today called Pushkino, Nicholas and Alexandra meet Rasputin for the first time.

November 28, 1905. A popular concert in Helsinki, conducted by Selim Palmgren, presents Palmgren's *Serenade*, Dvořák's *Bohemian Dance no. 1*, Tchaikovsky's *Andante for Strings*, and Sibelius's *Vårsång*.

December 1905. In Tampere, Finland, labor capital of the grand duchy: Lenin meets Stalin for the first time.

PART III

TAIDE KUULUU KAIKILLE— ART BELONGS TO ALL

A POLITICAL SEA CHANGE

The decade launched by Schauman's deed and the revolutionary upheaval of 1905 was the most politically charged Finns had ever experienced.[1] After it, Finland was forever changed. Within a year of each other, not one, but two political assassinations eliminated hated figures, Bobrikov and Procurator Soisalon-Soininen, from the streets of Helsinki. Blood also ran in the squares of not-so-faraway Saint Petersburg and across the greenswards of Sveaborg, the islands that appeared to be part of Helsinki but which were under Saint Petersburg's direct control: in July 1906 a revolt erupted in the Russian garrison there, led by one of Arvid Järnefelt's school friends.[2]

Within Finland's political ranks a watershed had been reached. Whereas previously the national awakening had served to unite the Finns, more or less, now, with the sudden and spectacular growth of the labor movement, national awakening had metamorphosed into class struggle. Numbers tell something of the tale: from a little more than 16,000 members in 1904, one year later the new Social Democratic Party counted more than 45,000; the year after that, the ranks more than doubled, swelling to nearly 100,000.[3] Antagonistic to the upper class, agrarian and industrial, the labor movement depended heavily on the rural proletariat, and its rhetoric trumpeted the rural sentiments of *herraviha*—class hatred.

It was in connection with the growth of labor that the most radical reform in all of Europe was carried out in Finland: in one fell swoop, the Parliament Act that came into force on the first day of October 1906 replaced the country's antiquated diet with a representative, unicameral parliament. "Universal suffrage" had become a reality. Voting rights were now granted to many who previously had none, among them women, largely because they made up a substantial component of the labor force. The number of voters multiplied tenfold, from 126,000 to 1,273,000.[4] The hard work of awakening the people through national enlightenment—fostering education, defining Finnish identity, and defending national rights—had succeeded brilliantly. It had also unleashed forces unforeseen by its promoters. The following spring, when the first elections with the newly enfranchised population were held (1907), these nationalists experienced an awakening themselves—of another, ruder, kind.

Heretofore, two of the former diet's four estates (nobility, clergy, bourgeois, peasants) had been dominated by Swedish speakers. The election changed that balance irrevocably. It broke the power of the Swedish factions, but it was not the liberal Young Finns who emerged victorious. It was the Social Democrats. The cultural and political elite were stunned. Gallén began to lament that the political landscape was no longer the same; "my people" have left me and become Social Democrats, he mourned. (He was always saying things like "my people.") After the election, he packed up and went to Africa.

And where were the other young lions who had thrilled audiences in politically charged concerts, exhibitions, poems, newspaper columns, sculptures, poetry, and drama? Where were those men and women who had created such an outpouring of art, music, drama, architecture, and sculpture that a golden age had gleamed from Finland's stages and concert halls, squares and museums? Men and women such as Sibelius, the Järnefelt brothers, the Erkko brothers, the Brofeldt brothers, the Leino brothers, Helene Schjerfbeck, Beda Stjernschantz, Eliel Saarinen? For one thing, those lions were no longer young: they had reached middle age—and a hundred years ago, middle age was much more aged than it is today. For another thing, most of the pride had been dangerously decorated, accoladed, idolatrized, and rewarded with lifetime stipends; in short, they had been transformed from wild-haired, rarin'-to-go bohemians into comfortable, increasingly hairless members of the bourgeoisie. And they were isolated. Part of it was their own fault. Sibelius, Aho, Eero Järnefelt, Eino Leino, and J. H. Erkko were figuratively circling the wagons in their elite community around Lake Tuusula. Saarinen, Lindgren, and Gesellius were doing the same around Hvitträsk. Armas Järnefelt had taken a position in Sweden. Gallén had marched off to hunt manly game. The artist Helene Schjerfbeck was living in isolation with her mother. Within a few years Beda Stjernschantz shot herself.

But in another sense the events that this generation of prominent, considerably privileged, mostly Swedish-speaking Finns had helped to put into motion overtook them and cruelly cut them off from their sources of greatest inspiration. Their language, for example. The stridency of tone and heightening prejudice against the Swedish speakers in the population, always a distant drumbeat, thrummed with new intensity. In the unicameral parliament, what now became the Swedish People's Party had to weld disparate social classes into a unified whole based on their common "nationality." Early in the spirited year of 1890, Thiodolf Rein, musing on matters from Finns' enormous strides in education to the hated arguments of the Russian nationalists, had observed: "Those two 'cultures' about which so much is spoken, Swedish and Finnish, are, in our opinion, simply useless fine words. In our country there is only one culture, even though it sometimes dresses in Finnish, sometimes in Swedish garb."[5] Yet Rein ignored certain realities. In 1894, when Yrjö-Koskinen rose in the House of Nobles and spoke in Finnish—the first time the language had been used in debate in that hallowed space—he was met with incomprehension. Anger swiftly followed. Within two decades, the ethnonym *finlandssvensk*—Finland-Swede—had entered the language, deepening a divide by giving it a name.[6] Eino Leino recognized the profound and sickening shift: "Our Swedish upper class are no longer Fennicized as they were during the years of growing national self-consciousness but rather the opposite . . . We have two cultures and nations, one Finnish, the other Swedish, which are moving fast apart."[7] And one of those cultures was fast being marginalized.

Other rifts were beginning to fracture Finnish society. In 1906 the divisions suddenly assumed something more than metaphysical form. Svenska folkpartiet—the Swedish People's Party—was founded. So was Brage, an association named after the Nordic Orpheus initiated by Otto Andersson to preserve and encourage Swedish folk poetry, music, and dance in Finland. Battening down the cultural hatches and deepening the "us versus them" divide, the Fennomans came up with Suomalaisuuden liitto—the Finnish Alliance, the association of Finnish culture and identity. And rising above them all was a new building: the House of the People. It was being erected in the workers' district of Helsinki, a part of the city whose very name meant rock (*kallio* in Finnish, *berghäll* in Swedish). The foundations were being blasted out of Finnish stone. The symbolism was not lost on contemporaries: from the bedrock of Finnish granite "the abode of the oppressed was defiantly growing."[8]

THE NEW ORDER

In the summer of 1906 Sibelius was in Helsinki. Its streets felt forbiddingly calm. "Emotions have become so red hot that I haven't been able even to imagine such class hatred," he told Aino; "eyes just blaze."[9] Throughout Finland, the sea change was profound, and no one, least of all the country's artists and composers, could escape the tide.

When the new parliament began to meet the following year, it soon became clear that it was less sympathetic to the arts than the old diet had been.[10] Its lack of enthusiasm translated into fewer legislative bills to support cultural endeavors. The deeper significance of parliamentary inaction meant that the former integration and unity between art and politics had begun to weaken. Political disputes about the arts gradually disappeared from the parliamentary forum, to be taken up instead by art clubs and various societies. Art was no longer a vital means of promoting national aims.

It took time, of course, before the full effects were felt. One of the very few who foresaw what the changed order might mean was Jac Ahrenberg (the architect who had directed the Pro Carelia lottery). Although admittedly extreme in his conservatism, Ahrenberg sharply criticized the abolition of the diet with its four estates: "It is a heritage from an aristocratic nation and a time of great men. It is like a great shield of noble material from the time of Nordic greatness, wreathed with garlands and wrought in iron." Invoking the concept of *Ragnarök*—the end of the world, in Nordic myth—Ahrenberg warned that "our world-famous single-chamber parliament, given to us by heaven in its wrath in a moment of imposing terror," boded the ills of "state socialism, poverty, and destruction of the arts and sciences."[11]

For all their promotion of education and enlightenment among the great public, many nationalist leaders took a patronizing view of the masses. The founding fathers had often assumed the patriarchal role of telling the people how they should behave and how they should think (a mode of expression that has been labeled the "discourse of the bovine masses").[12] Topelius was a case in point: in *Boken om vårt land* (1875), in which he had authoritatively instructed the Finns to work hard for the sake of the fatherland, Topelius had constructed a patronizing stereotype, "Matti," personifying "ideal" Finnish characteristics. Snellman was another; he wrote one way for cultivated society, another way for the people. These leaders' view of the people, like that of many others in the upper classes, was that of "a mindless herd of cattle" over which Finland had charge. Without proper instruction and control, the people could morph into a dangerous mob, a bunch of socialists with working-class egalitarian ideas (the very weeds Yrjö-Koskinen specifically wanted to keep out of Finland's working-class soil).

Fear of proletarian mobs was exacerbated by episodes like that in the Paris Commune in 1871, when Parisians were massacred by workers. The riot unleashed a wave of hysteria at the specter of proletarian revolution, which gripped rulers and their middle- and upper-class subjects alike.[13] The overriding fear of the masses—the poor, unprivileged, often uneducated populace—terrified respectable society and gave rise to crowd theories by psychologists from Sigmund Freud to Gustave Le Bon. In 1895 Le Bon had published his *Psychologie des foules*, translated into English the very next year as *The Crowd: A Study of the Popular Mind*.[14] In his view, crowds were possessed of a collective mind, whose inferior reasoning (if a crowd could be said to reason at all) and mindless convictions showed blind submission, fierce intolerance, and overpowering emotions akin to religion. The "soul of the masses" could wreak violent upheaval, and the Paris Commune episode proved it.

Yet the masses—whether in demonstrations, electorates, or markets—were an unstoppable tide. As they grew, so did fear. And fear of democratic governance—heresy in a world bent on equal rights—was voiced not only by Ahrenberg, but also by other, more famous men: Nietzsche, for instance. The radical German had piqued European imaginations with the seductive notion of a new aristocracy whose members would lead humanity to the higher plane of the *Übermensch*. Nietzsche rejected the democratic idea of equal rights for all men. In his view, such a myopic plan would simply hamper natural leaders from realizing their full capacities; mass opinion, mass taste, and mass prejudice amounted to nothing less than "slave morality."[15]

Ahrenberg articulated perfectly the qualms in Finland, where the symbiotic connections between art and ideology had been amply demonstrated throughout the 1890s. What would happen to these connections in the changed circumstances no one really knew. As early as 1903 Ahrenberg had warned of "the frightening parallel" in the evolution of art and "the evolution our society is now experiencing. [Artists] Holmberg, Lindholm, Edelfelt, Berndtson, Järnefelt, representatives of the educated classes, are disappearing or gradually retreating, and the bearers of the new epoch, the sons of peasants, the men of the first generation step forth."[16] By 1908 Ahrenberg was claiming: "Our times are democratic throughout, even social-democratic. All democracy is basically hostile to art. All art is basically aristocratic in the same way that all science is basically plebeian."[17] For artistic and intellectual Finns, these worries added to the frighteningly swelling threat of Russification.

Jean Sibelius's saving grace—and simultaneously his curse—was that both at home and abroad, he was widely seen as the representative of "his people." The French critic Maurice Touchard, writing in *La revue bleue*, incongruously described Sibelius as having "dressed the folk song in a toga. He is simple and unsophisticated: he is the people."[18] In the first decade of the twentieth century, the real Sibelius, always an elusive creature, became increasingly difficult to pin down. What was genuine can best be gauged by his music. With his retreat to the Tuusula art colony in 1904, he had already joined the exodus of the educated. In 1906 he composed into song the despairing words of Georg Busse-Palma, *Erloschen* (*Burned Out*), with their putrefying metaphors for depression—black roses and black butterflies:

Wüsst ich ein Land für mich und meinesgleichen	If I knew of a land for me and my kind
wo schwarze Rosen an den Stöcken blühn,	Where black roses bloom on their boughs,
wo breitgeflügelt Trauermantel streichen,	Where broad-winged black butterflies flutter
Und blasse Sterne durch die Wolke glühn.	And pale stars glimmer through clouds
. . . Herz und Augen schliefen mählich ein,	. . . my eyes and heart would gradually shut
und mit der Welt würd ich dich vergessen.[19]	And along with the world I would forget you.

The voice thuds numbly in a nearly inert chant, the key rejected as surely as both poet and composer have rejected the world.

May 12 of the same year (1906) marked the one hundredth birthday of the great nationalist Snellman. Sibelius dutifully composed a cantata for the patriotic celebration, for mixed choir and full orchestra, to words by Paavo Cajander. *Vapautettu kuningatar* (*The Liberated Queen*), an allegorical ballad alluding to Finland's struggle for identity, could hardly pose a greater contrast to *Erloschen*, either in its poetry or its music. On the program, which Sibelius conducted, the title appeared as *Siell' laulavi kuningatar* (*There a Singing Queen*). A queen imprisoned in a gloomy castle hears a youth singing beneath her window, and he spreads her story throughout the land. Eventually, a deliverer, a hero from the ranks of the people, frees the queen and returns her to the throne. The chorus rejoices in the light of a new day:

Ja on kuin laulua hellää	And it seems like a song
ja vienoa taaskin sois,	Tender and gentle, sounded again,
Mut aamulaulua on se,	But a Morning song it is,
yö on iäks mennyt pois.	Night is forever banished.

Strings, brass, and timpani thump along, repeating uninspired D minor chords for what seems like ages. The disconnect between the outer Jean Sibelius and the inner Janne was audible to anyone with ears to hear.

For the tin-eared, it might have been possible to gauge the composer's true feelings by his actions—or more accurately put, his inactions. In connection with the Snellman celebrations, an appeal went out to the people to "Fennicize" their names. Thousands complied. In many cases, Finnish appellations long ago discarded for more "favorable" Swedish names were revived, Snellmans returning to Virkkunens, Branders to Paloheimos. Blomstedts became Jalases; Eliel Aspelin became Aspelin-Haapkylä. Around the same time Gallén exchanged the accent in his surname for a hyphen and added "Kallela" after it, thereby covering both Finnish and Swedish bases.

Jean Sibelius remained Jean Sibelius. Neither that French nor that Latin name was changed one whit.

∽19∽
Connections East and West

ven though the Russian Empire's political policies felt oppressive, travel abroad had never been impeded. In 1905 Sibelius not only journeyed to Paris, he also made his first trip to England, as the guest of Granville Bantock (1868–1946).[1] He made other important connections—with that English matriarch Rosa Newmarch (1857–1940), and with England's most celebrated critic, William Roberts (1868–1959). Everyone knew him, but not as Roberts; his public face was that of "Ernest Newman," a pseudonym derived from his rational outlook, "a new man in earnest." In 1905 the New Man was transported by Sibelius's First Symphony and earnestly proclaimed that fact in the *Manchester Guardian*. Newmarch was also living up to her new (married) name, marching on the London Concert Goers' Club armed with lectures about Sibelius. Breitkopf & Härtel published her immortal words the following year as *Jean Sibelius: A Finnish Composer* (1906). All three individuals—Bantock, Newman, and Newmarch—helped to assure the composer's reputation in the British Isles.

But 1906 stands out in Sibelius's life as the year he made his first professional journey into the heart of the Russian Empire. He had traveled through Saint Petersburg before— probably for the first time in 1898, when he and Aino were headed for Berlin (in winter the overland route was the way to travel from Finland to central Europe). In May 1903 Sibelius had visited another part of the Russian Empire: Reval (today known as Tallinn), Estonia, directly south across the Baltic from Helsinki. There he conducted two programs, which included the First Symphony, *King Christian II Suite*, *The Swan of Tuonela*, and *Finlandia* (under the neutral title *Impromptu*) in the popular resort park Catharinenthal (named after Catherine I).[2] The following spring the ritual was repeated. On May 24, 1904, Sibelius led more than fifty musicians of the Warsaw Philharmonic Orchestra in his Second Symphony. The program, which this time included *En saga*, *Vårsång*, the *Karelia Suite*, and *Valse triste*, showed off a new, quite Tchaikovskyan Andante for strings (later called Romanze in C Major; it had been premiered in Turku and was dedicated to that orchestra's conductor, José Eibenschütz).

Now, in 1906, in the darkest month of the year, Sibelius traveled to the Russian capital, arriving by rail. He could hardly have gone without trepidation. Barely four months earlier, a coach and pair had drawn up outside the villa of Russian Premier Pyotr Stolypin on Aptekarsky Island. Its nervous occupants, bent on murder, achieved a perverted result: accidentally dropping his bomb, the chief assassin blew up himself, his companions-in-arms, and a major-general, decapitated the court chamberlain, destroyed the rear of the villa, and injured Stolypin's daughter so gravely that both her legs had to be amputated.[3]

Against the atrocious background of that grisly deed, Sibelius bravely made his way to the Concerts Siloti.

THE SILOTI–SIBELIUS CONNECTION

Alexander Ilyich Siloti (1863–1945), a cousin of Sergei Rachmaninoff and a product of the Moscow Conservatory, had studied with Tchaikovsky as well as with Nicholas Rubinstein. Siloti had made a most favorable marriage, to Vera Pavlovna Tretyakova, daughter of the celebrated art patron Tretyakov.[4] With the fabulous Tretyakov fortune, Siloti financed his own concert series, which he inaugurated in Saint Petersburg in 1903; the series continued until just after the revolution. The Concerts Siloti featured symphonic programs with the Mariinsky Theater orchestra, international guest conductors, piano recitals (Siloti's own), and chamber music. The high quality of the performances and Siloti's personal magnetism won an increasingly large public for the musical avant-garde.

Siloti spent many summers in Finland's beautiful port city of Viipuri, where he participated in that lively town's musical events. He also visited Helsinki. On November 15, 1900, he was the featured pianist with Kajanus's orchestra; among his offerings was a Romance by Sibelius (presumably from op. 24) on a program featuring *Snöfrid*. Siloti thus knew about Jean Sibelius and his compositional activities, and in August 1906 he approached the Finn with an invitation.

Russian artistic figures had long cultivated ties to their Finnish counterparts. As early as 1896 ten of Gallén's works, including the *Aino* triptych, had been exhibited at Nizhni-Novgorod, prompting Ilya Repin to declare the Finn's ideas "the hallucinations of a madman, his works like a magpie's track."[5] (Repin later apologized.) In 1898 Diaghilev and his associates staged a joint exhibition with Finnish artists, some of whom had substantial ties to Saint Petersburg, which was, after all, not so far away.

(Elisabeth Järnefelt's brother Constantin was known to zip over—on his motorcycle—from "Piter," as the locals styled it, to visit Finnish relatives.)[6] Both Eero Järnefelt and Albert Edelfelt had lived in the city at times: Järnefelt studied with an uncle, and Edelfelt drew and painted Emperor Nicholas II and his family and even became engaged to the charming Sophie Manzey.[7] Eliel Saarinen had also lived there: his pastor father, Juho, administered to the Finnish-speaking congregation in Saint Petersburg, much as Hermann Kajanus did to "Piter's" Swedish-speaking Finns. With his partners Gesellius and Lindgren, Saarinen later took in Russian students at Hvitträsk.

Despite the linguistic obstacles, there were even literary ties. Arvid Järnefelt's devotion to and visits with Tolstoy were well-known. Meanwhile, such Russian writers as Maxim Gorky ("the Bitter One," 1868–1936) came to Finland, arriving in 1906, hosted by Eero Järnefelt and Eliel Saarinen; it was during this visit that Gallén made his dark and evocative portrait of the writer. In the realm of music, it was, above all, Robert Kajanus who kept the tracks well oiled between the Russian and Finnish capitals.[8] Robert's music-loving brother Herman regularly organized musical events at his church, Saint Catherine's.

Given these and many other connections, particularly between Sibelius's in-laws, the Järnefelts, and the city of their mother's birth, the only surprising aspect of his artistic contact with the Russian capital is that it was so long in coming.[9] That it arose just at this time and that Sibelius would continue to cultivate connections to the imperial capital over the next several years suggests not only opportunity, but also Sibelius's desire to find the kinds of outlets and audiences that were beginning to be eclipsed in Finland.[10]

In a sense, then, his appearance on the program of December 29, 1906, had been foreordained. That evening, Eugène Ysaÿe played Mozart, Bach, and Beethoven, and Sibelius conducted the Mariinsky Theater's splendid, dark-toned orchestra—sixteen violins, twelve violas, ten cellos, eight contrabasses—in two works based on the *Kalevala*: *Lemminkäinen's Return* and the newly composed *Pohjola's Daughter*. Less than a year later, in November 1907, Sibelius returned to the Siloti concerts, this time to conduct his newest symphony, the Third. Aino herself came for the performance. The young Sergei Prokofiev was in the audience. The next day Prokofiev went for his orchestration lesson with Rimsky-Korsakov, whom the younger man evidently relished baiting. Rimsky was full of criticism:

"What's this? Why do you use only one cello to play this theme?"
"I didn't care for the effect when all the cellos played together," said Sergei
      Sergeyevich coolly.
"You didn't, eh? Have you ever heard them?"

"Yes, I heard them yesterday in the Sibelius symphony."

"Heavens! Sibelius!" Rimsky-Korsakov snorted. "Why listen to Sibelius? What about *Ruslan*? What about the secondary theme in *Ruslan*?"[11]

Rimsky was not completely hostile to the Finn. Although on hearing the Second Symphony he memorably remarked, "Well, I suppose that is also possible," he found something to praise in the Third. "He rather liked the first and second movements," V. V. Yastrebtsev, Russian banker and faithful chronicler, recalled Rimsky saying; "'it sounds different, somehow, not like our music, and this is good. . . . I'm beginning to value originality in a composer.'"[12] After divesting himself of this novel idea, Rimsky proceeded to criticize the First Symphony by his pupil Igor Stravinsky (1882–1971) for imitating Glazunov too closely in the last movement. Written in the key of E-flat, Stravinsky's un-Stravinskyan symphony is filled with Italianate lyricisms—an oddly Sibelian sound, particularly in the Largo—the sounds being cultivated in the Saint Petersburg orbit.

In November 1908 Sibelius completed a new tone poem, *Night Ride and Sunrise*, for a concert in the Russian capital. His plan was to dedicate it to Madame Siloti (of whom he had once written to Aino, "The wife is extremely prattlesome. It's a bit tiresome—but what can you do?").[13] But in a classic mix of cultural misunderstanding and Sibelian mismanagement, the plan went awry. Unusually, Sibelius himself turned prattlesome, offering first one explanation and then another for *Night Ride and Sunrise*. He told Karl Ekman that its principal idea had come to him in Rome during that Italian journey of 1901.[14] He told Rosa Newmarch that the music concerned "the inner experiences of an average man riding solitary through the forest gloom; sometimes glad to be alone with Nature; occasionally awe-stricken by the stillness or the strange sounds which break it; not filled with undue foreboding, but thankful and rejoicing in the daybreak."[15]

These "explanations" are so out of character that one wonders what was behind them (this was, after all, the same composer who coyly evaded talk about his compositions, affectedly comparing them to butterflies—"you touch them only once and the powder on their wings is gone").[16] Possibly the fiasco of the premiere had something to do with it: instead of returning to Russia, he had allowed Siloti to conduct the new piece in January 1909. But Siloti made merciless cuts and changed the tempi. The press excoriated not the conductor, but the composer.

Yet the real explanation may have been encoded in the music and its title, a ride through the darkness followed by the rising of the sun. With the dawning light the listener expects a new compositional world to open to the mind's eye and ear; instead the dawn leads directly into the coda.[17] The awakening day heralds the beginning of the end. Had Sibelius's innermost self perceived a truth too terrible to contemplate?

POHJOLA'S DAUGHTER AND THE SAINT PETERSBURG ORBIT

The difficulty with tracing the work of a creative personality in its historical context is that great works often require lengthy periods of gestation. Particularly when creative persons live in swiftly changing times, the impetus for a major work might well be found in an era rather different from the time the piece was finally completed. The works connected with Saint Petersburg are a case in point. The roots of *Pohjola's Daughter* seem to lie as far back as the 1890s; those of *Night Ride and Sunrise* and probably the Third Symphony began germinating in Italy in 1901.

Pohjola's Daughter emerged out of the abandoned opera project that Sibelius once planned with his fellow Symposium participant J. H. Erkko. The tone poem's title character and its appended verses are the very ones from which the *The Building of the Boat* had taken its outline, a tale related in the *Kalevala*'s eighth *runo*: smitten with the beauty of the Daughter of the North (*pohjola* in Finnish), Väinämöinen receives a promise of her hand if he accomplishes various impossible tasks. The exasperating Daughter, together with Luonnotar (the nature spirit), Kuutar (the Daughter of the Moon), and Väinämöinen, never lost their appeal for Sibelius; rather, they evolved and assumed new forms over time. Their sounds and shapes glided toward him through the moonscape of Italy in 1901; they floated to him as he worked on his symphonies and his various *Scènes historiques*.

When the work entitled *Pohjola's Daughter* was at last completed, at Ainola in 1906, more than a decade had passed since the opera based on her story had been envisioned, and the climate in Finland had changed dramatically: Bobrikov was dead, the unicameral parliament was just months from becoming a reality, and *Kalevala* topics were losing their currency. The lip-twisting title *Väinämöinen*, which Sibelius had proposed, was (not surprisingly) rejected by his German publisher, Robert Lienau, so the composer suggested instead *The Adventure of a Hero*. Lienau opposed this suggestion too. Sibelius's symphonic poem, he said, was not "heroic" in the German sense of "mighty, tremendous."[18] But why not "Pohjola's Daughter"? And so *Pohjola's Daughter* the work became.

Sibelius's heroic titles and his encounter with *Ein Heldenleben* in Berlin in 1905, conducted by Richard Strauss himself, have fed speculation that the tone poem conceals an autobiographical program, with Sibelius casting himself as a kind of Väinämöinen, the bringer of music to Finland, a hero who, like Strauss, defies his critics and

> once more his head he raises.
> Never can the hero falter,
> All his grief is put behind him.

Gentle tones from his remembrance
Bring him hope and lighten sorrow.[19]

Indeed, what better role for a musician deeply rooted in classicism and striving for its modern sonic version than that of heroic Orpheus leading the doomed from the underworld of Philistines (those of "auntie tastes") into the bright day of enlightenment?

The only thing that grates in this rendition of things is the title character: in Finland Väinämöinen was ritually portrayed as an old graybeard, with billowing robe and flowing hair. The hoary image was the *Kalevala*'s: its verses repeatedly describe him as *vaka, vanha Väinämöinen*—"old and steady Väinämöinen," or "old, reliable Väinämöinen," or just "old Väinämöinen." The antithesis of a titanic young lion, the aged seer might have wisdom and inventiveness, but no style, and certainly no sex appeal. Väinämöinen was not a figure to set a girl's heart aflutter or her eyes alight. Indeed, in one of the *Kalevala*'s tales, the winsome Aino preferred death by drowning to betrothal to this elderly specimen. Even with a stretch it is difficult to imagine the modish skirt chaser Sibelius (see fig. 19.1) typecasting himself in Väinämöinen's shuffling shoes.

Perhaps Sibelius had someone else in mind when he suggested these titles. After all, he dedicated the piece to Robert Kajanus. Kajanus was old, or at least older than Sibelius, by nearly a decade. He represented a far better candidate for Väinämöinen (or Christ or the devil, depending on whom you asked) than Sibelius. Kajanus could afford being viewed as *vaka, vanha Väinämöinen*. No one could doubt his role as a bringer of music to Finland or question the virility of a man—so slim, so erect, so supremely confident!—who had had four wives. Perhaps the harp in the score also inclined Sibelius's thoughts toward his colleague, who at that time had not just one, but two harp-playing daughters (he eventually fathered a third).

Indeed, even the orchestra for *Pohjola's Daughter*—an ambitious conductor's dream—suggests Kajanus. One of the largest Sibelius ever required, it included, besides the harp, other instruments he had begun to abandon—the contrabassoon, the tuba ("I do not like this instrument . . . it is far too heavy—what the Germans call *schwerfällig*"), the bass clarinet ("an elderly gentleman; you mustn't ask him to run too fast!").[20] And it was a happy "coincidence" indeed that Sibelius premiered this "Symphonic Fantasy for Orchestra" in Saint Petersburg, the city where Kajanus had been cultivating strong musical connections for more than two decades, through his brother and with the emperors themselves. Sibelius had reason to hope that both its dedication and its rich, dark orchestration would find favor in the Russian capital.

It may have been in anticipation of that first professional visit to Saint Petersburg

Figure 19.1. The stylish composer at home, ca. 1908.
Photograph by Ernst Ovesén/Otava Publishing Company.

that Sibelius created the Canzonetta, a work he composed in 1906 entirely for strings
(even though the piece was not unveiled until 1911).[21] Long afterward, Saint Petersburg's
native son Igor Stravinsky, who arranged the Canzonetta for a different ensemble and
who could wither any compliment, was heard to remark, "I like that kind of northern
Italianate melodism—Tchaikovsky had it too—which was part, and an attractive part,
of Saint Petersburg culture."[22]

A NEW SYMPHONY FOR "PITER"

As early as September 21, 1904, Sibelius had written to Axel Carpelan that a third symphony was under way, yet a full three years elapsed before the work was completed.
The composer premiered Symphony no. 3 on September 25, 1907, in Helsinki. In his
Sibelius biography, Erik Tawaststjerna remarked, "Of course, the Third Symphony
was totally out of step with the times. Its Viennese classical orchestration could hardly
be at greater variance with the ethos of Mahler and Strauss."[23] Both in its genre and in
its pruned-down, classical structure, the Third Symphony might well be seen as being
in the vanguard, signaling a resurgence of the classicism forecast by Lars Sonck's simplified architectural designs. Neoclassical theory galvanized major debates in Finland,
fought out publicly between Juhani Aho and Thiodolf Rein.[24] Rein viewed the national
as being wedded to the universal; the model for Finnish national art, declared he, should
be classical Greek art. The Euterpists too were promoting the classical—the idea was
reflected in their name as well as in their ideology.

There were other aesthetic tremors in the Nordic air. It was during these years that
Sibelius had begun to develop his ties to Siloti and the Russian capital. And in several
important respects, his new symphony's features seemed gauged to suit the Saint Petersburg milieu. For one thing, there was that theme in the first movement, undulating sensuously over brass drones sounding the perfect fifth in the strange key of B minor (see ex.
19.1).

Vladimir Vasilyevich Stasov (1824–1906), dogged champion of native Russian talent, fingered "the Oriental element" as one of the distinguishing features of the so-called
New Russian School.[25] (Sounding familiar, striving for the national in art, and an inclination toward program music were among the other attributes.) Richard Taruskin has characterized orientalism as "a syncopated undulation that is sounded in conjunction with two
other distinctive musical gestures to complete a characteristic semiotic cluster: a drone
(or drum) bass such as even Glinka had suggested, and—most important of all—a chromatic accompanying line that . . . steadily descends along with the sequences of undulating melismas."[26] Characteristic of the man, Sibelius's appropriation of this idea is compressed: the syncopated undulation is itself chromatic, while ostinato strings add their
vibrant drone.

Fascination with the oriental element had spread to Helsinki. It rippled in the air
around the Euterpists, who delighted in Oscar Levertin's oriental-themed and fantasy-
filled poetry. Sibelius knew Levertin's work, because he composed the poet's bewitching
En slända (*A Dragonfly*) into music just as he was beginning his Third Symphony. The
Euterpists were also exploring oriental themes in their own writings—Hjalmar Procopé

EXAMPLE 19.1. SIBELIUS, SYMPHONY NO. 3, FIRST MOVEMENT, 10 MEASURES BEGINNING AT REHEARSAL NUMBER 3. © 1907 BY ROBERT LIENAU, FRANKFURT/MAIN.

in his play *Belshazzar's Feast* and Bertel Gripenberg in poems such as *Teodora*. It was to a declamation of *Teodora*, whose highly charged verses brimmed with erotic, Byzantine images, that Sibelius improvised at the piano in the Euterpists' company:

Nu nalkas Teodora min lustgård i natten,	Now in the night Teodora draws near my pleasure garden,
när österlandets rosor stå röda som blod,	when roses of the East bloom red as blood,
och svagt sorlar springbrunnens plaskande vatten,	and splashing water purls faintly in the fountain,
och månljuset dallrar kring Astarots stod—	and moonlight shimmers around the statue of Astarot—
kejsarinna, jag vill kyssa din hånande, kalla	Empress, I will kiss your scornful, cold,
och törstande heta, förrädiska mun	thirsty, hot, and treacherous mouth—
jag vill dricka dina blickar, som tvinga och suga,	I will drink in your glances, which seduce and lure me,
jag vill smeka ditt eldröda, doftande hår.	I will caress your fragrant hair, red as fire.

Teodora's rustling silk, her lustrous lips, the insatiable fire of her blazing desire roused Sibelius to create one of the most heated of all his song settings. Its notated version dates from 1908, although the improvisation took place in 1903.

With the connections to the Euterpists and the travel along the Saint Petersburg and Paris axes stimulating the composer's thinking in new directions, oriental aspects of his music became remarkably pronounced. One of the clearest manifestations was the incidental music to *Belshazzar's Feast* (premiered on November 7, 1906). The numbers included an "Oriental March," "Khadra's Dance," and a "Jewish Girl's Song." The tension between the narrow constraints of nationalist aims and wider currents could not have been clearer.

Those around the Saint Petersburg orbit shared other ideas, such as were easily traded through the conduits of personal exchange. Not least was an aversion to Germanic symphonism. Musorgsky, writing to Rimsky-Korsakov on August 15, 1868, had put it in famously flavorful terms:

> And another thing about *symphonic development*: I tell you, our cold kvass soup is a horror to the Germans, and yet we eat it with pleasure. And their cold cherry soup is a horror to us, and yet it sends a German into ecstasy. In short, *symphonic*

development in the technical sense is just like German philosophy—all worked out
and systemized. . . . When [an artist] revises although satisfied, or worse, adds
to what already satisfies, he is *germanizing*, chewing over what has been said. We
are not cud-chewers, but omnivores.[27]

In Musorgsky's view, a German reasons his way to a conclusion, whereas a Russian will
begin with the conclusion and amuse himself with reasoning.[28] Sibelius, whose position
was closer to Musorgsky's than to the hypothetical German's ("I even distrust my way of
working—this 'plein air' way—so far removed from the German working method!"),[29]
put it rather more elegantly: the crowning moments of his new symphony, emerging in
the finale from nimble themes in 6/8 time, "crystallized out of chaos."[30] Both men owed
more to the Germans than they admitted.

The concept of "the thought crystallizing out of chaos" was even then being seriously discussed in contemporary German aesthetics. In 1907 the German art historian
Wilhelm Worringer (1881–1965) took up the complicated notion of *Kunstwollen*. Initially
advanced by the influential Austrian Alois Riegl (1858–1905) in *Stilfragen: Grundlegun-
gen zu einer Geschichte der Ornamentik* (*Problems of Style: Foundations for a History of
Ornament*, 1893), "art will" seems to have been one of those ponderous Germanic con-
structs meaning something along the lines of a nation's tendency, contingent upon historical factors, to develop its art without regard to imitation or technology.[31] Worringer
developed the idea further in his doctoral thesis, *Abstraktion und Einfühlung* (*Abstraction and Empathy*, 1916), specifically linking spirituality and depth in art to "crystallized"
abstract forms. In his view, such a profound, otherworldly mentality set Germans and
other northern peoples apart from lesser mortals.

What listeners discern crystallizing out of the chaos of the Sibelius symphony is a
hymn. Filled with determination and grandeur, it steps forth in the last movement *con
energia* (see ex. 19.2). Sibelius had already been exploring the means he now used for
treating that theme (in *Skogsrået* and *Lemminkäinen's Return*). There was also a Saint
Petersburg precedent: Mikhail Glinka's *Kamarinskaya*, a "fantasy on two Russian Folk
Songs." At first hearing, those folk songs, a wedding song and a dance (the *kamarinskaya*), seem to contrast sharply, yet as his one-movement work unfolds, Glinka proceeds
to demonstrate their underlying unity in a series of ostinato variations (103 bars).[32] Strikingly, Sibelius too began his symphony's sonata-form first movement with two sharply
differing themes that, in the course of development, are revealed as springing from the
same fundamental idea.[33] Although Sibelius's work sounds altogether different (after all,
his was a full-blown symphony, not a one-movement fantasy), he too brought his work
to a close with a set of powerfully accumulating ostinato variations. Rather than being

EXAMPLE 19.2. SIBELIUS, SYMPHONY NO. 3, THIRD MOVEMENT, MM. 4–17 AFTER REHEARSAL NUMBER 13.
© 1907 ROBERT LIENAU, FRANKFURT/MAIN.

"developed" in any systematic, Germanic way, his theme revolves, its circular iterations driving the symphony to a close in a triumphal C major.

That quality of C major was itself a rare and pure-sounding phenomenon, the opposite of the degenerate, clattering, dissonant modern world, and a sound that was also ringing around the Saint Petersburg orbit. Rimsky had chosen the key for *his* Third Symphony. And it was Rimsky's *Shéhérazade* that reminded Stravinsky that there was "still a great deal to be said in C major."[34] For his part, Stravinsky, too, showed a strengthening interest in C-scale melody.

These various strains came together in Saint Petersburg in a weird and wonderful way. From the vantage point of today, it is clear that it was Saint Petersburg's most famous émigrés—Igor Stravinsky, Georg Balanchine, and Vladimir Nabokov—who developed, independently of one another, the most talked-about aesthetic precepts based on classical principles of the twentieth century and made them resoundingly, quirkily modern.[35] Jean Sibelius's Third Symphony may have been out of sync with the gargantuan Germanic fulminations of Strauss and Mahler. But it was fully in tune with the Saint Petersburg orbit.

～20～

Proletarians versus Bourgeoisie

THE SINKING SHIP

I f art can be a means of fathoming the world from which it comes, then early twentieth-century Finland appeared to be slipping into deepening gloom. In 1898 Robert Stigell (1852–1907) had created a statue called *Haaksirikkoiset* (*The Shipwrecked*), showing a stranded family whose heroic father was crying out desperately for help. The work was installed on Observatory Hill, overlooking Helsinki's eastern harbor. A decade later images of foundering ships, storm-swept seas, and Finland itself whipped by gales began to appear regularly in the press, metaphors for the increasingly turbulent psychological air.[1]

Social developments deepened the gloom, and not just in Finland, but throughout Europe. Anxiety about overall moral degeneration darkened the atmosphere in restaurants and private parlors. Many people, especially among the upper echelons, feared that primitive urges and violent passions were destined to overwhelm civil society and wreak havoc on them all. The abhorrence of moral decadence that Flodin had unleashed on *Lemminkäinen* now envenomed critics in the plastic arts, their anxieties exacerbated by the increasing numbers of artists from working-class backgrounds. Any questioning of the tradition of the previous century's golden age, that "cornerstone of the old moral order," around which fantasies of security and perfection began to be spun, aroused extreme reactions.

Heightening the unease were fears of political tyranny. Despite the apparent victories of the 1905 strike and the passive resistance against imperial conscription, the Finns were still ruled by an emperor with a will of his own. And the flames of Russian nationalism were fanning his policies. "Finis Finlandiae!"—the triumphal cry of the Russian nationalists—echoed through the Russian Duma. The emperor himself increasingly exhibited an implacable determination to curb Finnish autonomy. By 1909 Finland's senate was filled with Russians or with Finns who had served in Russia. Meanwhile, increasing numbers of decisions affecting the grand duchy were being transferred to the imperial administration.

In Finland, the cry "Finis Finlandiae!" was heard and heeded, yet the most perceptive recognized that a greater danger lay within. In 1910 an essay appeared in *Nuori Suomi* entitled "Finis Finlandiae?" Its author, Ilmari Kianto, sounding like a Finnish evangelist, asked the pointed question: Was the end of Finland, that is, the end of the *Kalevala* people, truly happening at the hands of the *Russians?*

> *Finis Finlandiae* is connected to our public, petty bickering over party politics, our inability to merge honestly, even in the hottest melting pot. "The end of Finland" shows up as wretchedly in our daily hatred of Swedes and Russians as in our own Finnish suspiciousness and hatred of our neighbors, which tears families asunder; in a word, our whole patriotism is half asleep and is awakened by no stimulus. . . . Everywhere that the humanity of our people appears low and flat, everywhere that the customs of the Finnish people appear poor, ugly, clumsy, everywhere that the Finnish citizen lives and acts like a spineless creature, whether he be senator or tramp—there is reflected "the end of Finland," *Finis Finlandiae.*[2]

In this climate Sibelius the composer seemed to draw more and more into himself. Already removed from the ferment of Helsinki, he turned inward in a manner so extreme that his music almost seemed to come from another world. By the end of the decade 1904–14 a kind of introspective neoclassicism had gained the upper hand in his most personal works. Sibelius liked to present this position as an independent one, "a protest against present-day music. It has nothing, absolutely nothing of the circus about it," he wrote forcefully to Rosa Newmarch about his Fourth Symphony.[3] But in point of fact, as he well knew, his position coincided with many ideas in the debate about art, architecture, and aesthetics, even futuristic ones. Sibelius is specifically mentioned in the "Manifesto of Futurist Musicians 1910." While calling on the young, its author, the Italian composer Balilla Pratella, nevertheless singled out the forty-five-year-old Sibelius in praising what he called the futurist evolution of music in countries other than Italy: "In Finland and Sweden, also, innovatory tendencies are being nourished by means of national musical and poetical elements, and the works of Sibelius confirm this."[4]

Meanwhile, Sibelius the man experienced more than his usual measure of emotional anxieties, exacerbated by his drinking. By 1907 even *he* was recognizing that *suputen Sibb* (boozing Sibb) had gone too far.[5] The usual trail of letters to Axel Carpelan dried up. Only one letter to Adolf Paul survives from that year, its contents extremely unhappy:

"Everything going to hell."[6] Things worsened. In the summer of 1908, as Aino awaited
their fourth child (Margareta, born in September), a tumor was found in the composer's
larynx. Apparently biopsied for testing, it was eventually removed by a Berlin specialist.[7] It proved to be the proverbial blessing in disguise: it was not malignant, yet the very
threat it posed frightened the intemperate and hypochondriac composer into abstaining
from alcohol and tobacco for a biblical seven years.

The excessive behaviors reflected the wider circumstances. On December 29, 1909,
Sibelius wrote in his diary: "I've also turned down music for the lottery." His composi-
tions for national lotteries had dwindled drastically. In 1904 he composed *Musik zu einer
Szene* for a lottery to benefit the Helsinki Philharmonic Society. In 1906 he conducted
Pan and Echo at a lottery to benefit a new concert hall in Helsinki (it was never built).
But the lottery concerts held less and less interest for him. So did other fonts of national
inspiration that had seemed bottomless—men's choruses, for instance. In the summer
of 1910 he told Carpelan that he had grown away from the male voice choir.[8] Most troubling of all was his relationship to the country's national epic: "Picked up the *Kalevala*
and it struck me how I've grown away from this naive poetry," he wrote disgustedly in
his diary on December 3, 1910. The exclamation that followed, "Fan vete förresten" (I
don't know, but maybe the devil knows), mitigated the determined certainty initially
implied.

Those essential springs of inspiration had not only failed him; worse, they had
pigeonholed him. The next day, he was again grumbling in the diary, "A 'well-known
name.' Ja! That's all." Already on November 14 he had pinpointed the real trouble: "Am
I really nothing other than a 'nationalistic' curiosity?" The same year he composed into
song the words of K. A. Tavaststjerna, *När jag drömmer* (*When I Dream*):

Ju mera mitt sinne veknar	The more mellow I become
i sommarnätternas svala ro,	in the cool quiet of the summer nights,
ju mera min tanke jag lyckas sno	the more I am able to unwind my thoughts
ur härvan av tunga bekymmer . . .	from their tangle of heavy burdens . . .
jag slår av de klaraste toner en bro	Out of the purest notes I make a bridge
till världen, sorgen och kvalen.	to the world, to sorrow and to anguish.

But who would cross that bridge of notes? The music began with a long-held
D-sharp on the piano, the wrong note in the alleged key of G. The voice is left to sing
alone, an abstracted, aristocratic Finn isolated in the forest, as Sibelius himself increasingly appeared.

Gradually, the piano plays a more and more harmonizing role—first gracing the
voice with arpeggios and finally shifting into rocking chords. But the voice flits from key

EXAMPLE 20.1. SIBELIUS, *NÄR JAG DRÖMMER*, OP. 61, NO. 3, MM. 68–74.
© BREITKOPF & HÄRTEL, WIESBADEN.

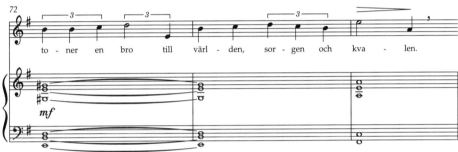

to key, like the nightingale in the poem's final line, the bird of happiness that seemed to elude the composer (see ex. 20.1).

ഇ‍ഇ‍ഇ‍ഇ‍ഇ

Much has been written about Sibelius's inward turn.[9] It was galvanized in part by developments on the international stage. The Russians, Stravinsky and Scriabin, and the Austrian Arnold Schoenberg were blazing the trails that the musical world judged to be pioneering. Sibelius realized that younger men were passing him by in works of such ultramodernity that his own looked painfully dated. Meanwhile, the leading symphonic composers of his generation, Strauss and Mahler, were just then pursuing grandiose, even sensationalist aims (works like the former's *Salome*, *Elektra*, and *Ein Heldenleben* and the latter's *Symphony of a Thousand*, although this Barnum and Bailey–style title was not Mahler's). The most extreme of their expressions appeared histrionic to Sibelius and affronted his Finnish reserve and classical bent.

Then, late in October 1907, Mahler himself visited Helsinki, arriving by train from Saint Petersburg, where he was conducting a series of concerts.[10] The guest was himself exuberantly conducted around the city and its environs by Axel Gallén, whom he had met in 1904 when the artist exhibited with the Vienna Secessionists. The Finn, who had fixed Mahler with a gaze "like a hunter does with a hare," painted an exceptionally fine portrait of the composer-conductor during this stay. Mahler in turn was hugely impressed by "Galén," his boat, and his robust "twelve schnapps before the soup" masculinity. On November 1 Mahler conducted Kajanus's orchestra in a serious program— Beethoven's Fifth Symphony and *Coriolan* Overture, plus Wagner's Vorspiel and *Liebestod* from *Tristan* and the Overture to the *Meistersinger*. Two nights before, in company with Gallén, Mahler had heard the same musicians in a typically light popular concert, featuring Belgian pianist Arthur de Greef (Liszt pupil and friend of Grieg). Sibelius had been unfortunately on the program—with *Vårsång* and, as an encore, *Valse triste*.

The star-crossed encounter between the two symphonists during this visit has gone on record for the opinionated views each held about the other. Although he found Sibelius the man "extremely sympathetic, like all Finns," Mahler made a pungent and brutally honest assessment of the music: "*Pui Kaki!* They are the same everywhere, these national geniuses. You find them in Russia and Sweden—and in Italy the country is overrun by these whores and their ponces."[11]

Sibelius's much later, sanitized version has often been quoted, beginning with the improbable claim that "Mahler and I spent much time in each other's company":

> When our conversation touched on the essence of symphony, I said that I admired its severity and style and the profound logic that created an inner connection between all the motifs. This was the experience I had come to in composing. Mahler's opinion was just the reverse. "Nein, die Symphonie muss sein wie die Welt. Sie muss alles umfassen" (No, [a] symphony must be like the world. It must embrace everything).[12]

Sibelius had not yet begun to keep a regular diary, and his immediate impressions of Mahler have gone unrecorded. He related this episode—to Karl Ekman for that celebratory biography—only in 1935, distilling into dogma each famous man's approach to a shared musical problem. Sibelius went on:

> I respected [Mahler] as a personality, his ethically exalted qualities as a man and an artist, in spite of his ideas on art being different from mine. I did not wish him to think that I had only looked him up in order to get him interested in my compositions. When he asked me in his abrupt way: "Was wollen Sie dass ich von Ihnen dirigiere?" (What would you like me to conduct of yours?) I therefore only answered: "Nichts (Nothing)."[13]

In truth, Mahler's "ideas on art" had powerful points of similarity with Sibelius's. Aside from the obvious—a shared commitment to symphonies—Mahler too appreciated "the profound logic that created an inner connection between all the motifs"; his Sixth Symphony (1904) demonstrated that.[14] And what could be more Mahlerian than Sibelius's gigantic *Kullervo*, which swirled a world of folk song, mythic archetypes, Finland's male-choir traditions, and Freudian conflict into a Germanic symphonic structure?

In 1907, however, Sibelius was having a particularly difficult time, while Mahler, whose conducting emphasized "the masculine element, cruelly honest and characteristically robust," was being acclaimed in Helsinki as "undoubtedly the world's most famous conductor," a "personality and a character . . . with the wild hair, the elongated face, the black eyes behind their gold-rimmed spectacles."[15] The great man had entered the Helsinki concert hall to a special fanfare and exited to thunderous applause. In Saint Petersburg too, the influential critic Alexander Ossovsky also waxed euphoric about this "hero who bends everything to his will, and has the mentality of an eagle": "Powerful emotions. Mighty ideas. And above all, the stamp of majestic mastery. That is Mahler."[16]

The next month it was Sibelius's turn to appear in Saint Petersburg, to conduct his newest symphony, the Third. The music was met with hostility. Comparisons with Mahler were inevitable. As the one critic in his favor wrote, "he is very different indeed from a composer like Mahler, whose whole aim is to astonish us with everything he can think of. Herr Sibelius is a serious and sincere artist, without the newest Jewish composer's offensive circus tricks and the pretentiousness that one finds with Strauss and Mahler."[17] It was three years later, wrestling with his Fourth Symphony, that Sibelius, angrily scribbling into his new diary, gave vent to his real feelings about Gustav Mahler: "It's a matter of life or death! Stand before the orchestra and public as that one who makes art and pretend to carry it out the most pious way you possibly can. Mahler, Berlioz, bah!"[18] Exalted pretensions and circus tricks seemed to be winning the day.

By then Sibelius was beginning to realize the consequences of his musical choices. In *Pohjola's Daughter*, less than a third the length of Strauss's *Ein Heldenleben* (a work Sibelius seemed to be "answering"), and especially in the Third Symphony, a streamlined C-major concentrate of modern classicism, the very antithesis of Mahler's sardonic and sprawling symphonies, Sibelius had struck out on a very different path from these contemporaries, and the ramifications on the international stage would be profound.[19] Already on the home front, audiences and critics no longer found in Sibelius the fascinating young radical whose stirring male choruses and dazzling *Kalevala* interpretations had set Finland alight. He was caught—as were other creative men and women of his generation—in the crisis affecting society at large. The face of nationalism had changed, and its new visage no longer inspired their intense and impassioned outpourings.

European society as a whole "was in the process of destroying the bases of its existence, the systems of value, convention and intellectual understanding which structured
and ordered it."[20] In Finland that destructive process had its own peculiar linguistic,
social, and political features, but the elements that were undermining the traditions—
mass consumption, mass production, mass sporting events, and rapidly evolving tech-
nologies that were spawning films, faster-moving presses, public broadcasting, and pho-
nograph recordings—were becoming apparent everywhere. These factors were throwing
the oppositions of modern/antimodern, avant-garde/conservative, elitist/democratic,
nationalism/internationalism, and classic/reactionary into utter disarray.

Sibelius's musical response was not to stop composing. Instead, his music reveals a
man with even greater conviction of the rightness of combining classical precepts, diatonic melody, and triadic writing in mystical, authentically Finnish designs. Reaching
within, he drew on resources that were quintessentially Finnish because they were so
intimately his own. The poignant *Voces intimae*, completed in April of 1909, was such
a work. A chamber composition—a rare occurrence in his maturity—it harked back to
days of innocent hopefulness and infinite possibility, to a time when he had made music
with his Hämeenlinna friends and with his brother and sister, a sister who was then well
and happy. In 1906 Linda Sibelius, intelligent and talented, a teacher of mathematics, had
been hospitalized for a mental disorder. From that time forward, she spent her life in and
out of mental institutions. It was a fate that deeply affected her brothers, to whom she was
devoted. About Linda as an adult, Jean Sibelius said little, but it is clear he felt much.

These and other life experiences were in the background of *Voces intimae*. The first
movement begins with a dialogue as evocative of a pair of Finnish *runo* singers as if two
Karelian shamans had stepped into the room (see ex. 20.2). Yet the intensifying process,
that ever more focused concentration increasingly in evidence since the Second Symphony,
had further matured. This was not music for the masses; it was a meditation for the select
few. It arose from the deepest wellsprings of the composer's personal life: those three out-
of-key chords over which he wrote the words "Intimate Voices" utter a cry of personal
isolation so identifiable that it communicates instantly across time and cultural difference.

೧೧೦೧೧೦

In April 1910 a petition sponsored by a group of internationally oriented Finns including
Yrjö Hirn, Sigurd Frosterus, and Werner Söderhjelm began quietly circulating among
wealthy businessmen (it was marked "Not for the public"). The appeal was a bid to ease
Sibelius's financial difficulties in the aftermath of his throat surgery, and its wording was
powerful: "If his countrymen could contribute to alleviating his circumstances, they
would thereby, in our view, be serving the interests of their own country, and at the same

EXAMPLE 20.2. SIBELIUS, *VOCES INTIMAE*, FIRST MOVEMENT, MM. 1–8.
© 1909 ROBERT LIENAU, FRANKFURT/MAIN.

time *fulfill their duty toward international cultural life* in which it is both our right and our duty to participate" (emphasis added).[21] Sibelius's identification with Finland and its well-being could not have been clearer. The "obligation" was sealed with success: a debt of 51,000 Finnish marks was eliminated from the composer's accounts. The balance due now shifted in a different direction. It would be called in, but not for over a decade.

FINNISH TOURISM AND *LA MONTAGNE*

O altitudo!
Have you sometimes, calm and silent,
Climbed the mountain, in the presence of heaven?

VICTOR HUGO, *CE QU'ON ENTEND SUR LA MONTAGNE*, TRANSLATED BY HUMPHREY SEARLE

Sibelius meanwhile served the interests of his country in other ways. In September 1909 he and Eero Järnefelt journeyed to northeastern Finland, where they climbed *la mon-*

tagne, as Sibelius called it, the modest fell named Koli situated beside Lake Pielinen (Pielisjärvi) in northern Karelia. The brothers-in-law thereby joined in a relatively new, but increasingly popular national activity: tourism.

The Finnish Tourist Association had been established in 1887 by a group of scholars and university faculty members; "knowledge of one's country [is] the sine qua non of truly loving it," insisted one early enthusiast.[22] Mount Koli was one of the major attractions being promoted, along with the Imatra waterfall, Punkaharju and other famous ridges, and Aulanko Park, outside Hämeenlinna, in which Sibelius had played as a child. One might need public assistance to alleviate one's debts, but home tourism fulfilled a duty to king and country.

When Sibelius's new Symphony no. 4 was unveiled on April 3, 1911, in the university's Festival Hall with Kajanus's Orchestra at the ready, the critic Bis, aided by "a friend"—Eero Järnefelt, to whom the symphony was dedicated—interpreted the new work in terms that would have delighted the hearts of the Finnish Tourist Association— superb mountain views, the glittering lake touched with rays of gold, Koli bathed in moonlight, a veritable painting with poetry—except for the appalling fact of the music. A stunned silence met the final bars. "Where were the instrumental colors? Where was the grand gesture, the heroic challenge of the preceding works?"[23] The triumphal, patriotic, *Finnish* sounds had vanished. The powerful rapport with our people and its epic *Kalevala* poetry no longer exists, said Bis sadly:

> Here [Sibelius] is no longer the . . . artist who reaches out and instructs all people, nor is he Nietzsche's Übermensch who descends to the people. In Symphony no. 4 he appears to be a personality who sets himself apart and develops and whose aristocratic music reflects only his private thoughts, his latest stage of development.[24]

What Sibelius heard on that sacred Finnish mountain was not music for the people, but music for himself, a world of bleak soundscapes, the call of unknown, nearly atonal territory, a weird "joke" of a scherzo, and a disconcerting finale with overtones of Mozart that ended mezzo-forte dolce (who ends a symphony mezzo-forte dolce?)—in a word, aristocratic music. Nevertheless, like a true patriot, Bis deflected his criticism by insisting that Sibelius had still created a distinctive work of Finnish music literature.

A preview written three days before the symphony's premiere, by Axel Carpelan of all people, in "a Swedish newspaper," had attempted to place its music in a broader context:

> One has nothing to compare it with . . . not even among Sibelius's own works. . . . In its entirety the symphony may be regarded as a protest against the

prevailing style in music . . . above all, in Germany the home of the symphony, where instrumental music is on its way to becoming mere technique, a kind of musical engineering that tried to cover up its own inner emptiness with an enormous mechanical apparatus.[25]

But the fact was, the Helsinki public was simply not ready for a work so stringent, so psychologically exposed, so infinitely lonely. In no other orchestral composition had its creator succeeded in pruning away the extraneous better than in Symphony no. 4: a sonata exposition of a mere fifty-three bars, a scherzo without a repeat, a distillation of inner voices in the slow movement, a disintegration into musical chaos in the closing movement, out of which a tonality—A minor—is somehow retrieved. Sibelius seemed here his most authentic. All was thoroughly integrated; not one superfluous note remained.

But a gap had opened between Sibelius and his audience. "Rumor had it that . . . [he] had turned his back on all previous music and . . . reduced his musical statement to an economical, essential style just sufficient to say what he meant": Otto Luening's words seemed a perfect description of Jean Sibelius at this moment—they were written about Igor Stravinsky.[26]

MODERN ART VERSUS THE ANTIMODERN: THE SALLINEN WARS

> Despite how my "stock," so to speak, has risen with the people, I feel completely uncertain about myself. I see how the young lift their heads—Madetoja higher than others—and I have to admire them, but my inner self needs more egotism and callousness than I am presently capable of. And my contemporaries are dying.
>
> SIBELIUS, DIARY ENTRY, MARCH 9, 1916

In retrospect 1912 stood out for many reasons across the Far North. In Russia the advent of the Acmeists made it a year to remember. For sports fans it was the time of the Stockholm Olympic Games, which generated great excitement among the Finns. In art the year marked the moment when Magnus Enckell, Sigurd Frosterus, and Alfred William Finch established their group Septem, whose cosmopolitan outlook viewed "painting as an art and not just an expression of national sentiments."[27] More concerned with technique (on which they lavished gay colors) than with topic (which was often French), their goal was to create "harmony out of chaos," not to overturn tradition. Rejecting trends of the previous decade, they advocated reforms based on tradition instead. Some art lovers complained that the "foreign-derived" bright colors evoked feelings utterly alien to the Finnish character—joy and lightness, for example. Frosterus did his best to deflect that charge with an essay on the "victorious procession of the colors of the rainbow."

Above all, 1912 was the year that modernism burst forth in Finland in a clear, dramatic, and very public way. In April a hotheaded young tailor-turned-artist exhibited some of his work in a show sponsored by the Finnish Art Society. Tyko Sallinen (1879–1955) approached the art of painting with a cubist's sense of space and a working man's sense of roughness. Portraits of the artist's wife, looking more pig than paramour (see plate 10), and brutally honest paintings of Finnish society's working-class citizens (including distinctly unlovely washerwomen) defiled the sacred galleries of the national museum, Ateneum.

Helsinki's upper crust, already congratulating itself on its cultural superiority in the wake of the 1907 elections, was not ready for these "grotesqueries," those distorted— some said perverted—expressionist images depicting "us Finns." The reviewer for *Hufvudstadsbladet*, "Publicus," squealed:

> Of Mr. Sallinen's pretentious collection of people and landscapes with their ghastly caricatures of people and nature there is nothing to be said other than that Mr. S. apparently has come to the wrong career in life. Of all the excesses of which the so-called expressionist school (if that is what Mr. S. embraces) is guilty of up to now, here Mr. Sallinen certainly documented some of the worst. One of these "pictures" was bought for the lottery drawing. I can tell you, the winners are not to be congratulated.[28]

The previous day Pekka Halonen's dreary, shopworn, but thoroughly national landscapes had been on view, bringing praise and glory.

Reactions to Sallinen were vicious. In the ensuing polemics, the meanings of art and modernism were widely and publicly discussed. Many felt they had been betrayed (especially *Uusi Suomi*'s art critic, Onni Okkonen, later Gallén's biographer). It didn't help that Sallinen showed the bad manners his rough upbringing had given him. Or that he was a Finnish-speaking son of working-class parents. He was the child of Laestadians, a fundamentalist Lutheran sect with intolerant, extremist ideas—opposed to joy on earth, opposed to art. Sallinen had started out as a tailor, like his peripatetic and severe father. He had been stabbed in Tampere, had studied in Helsinki, and had been schooled in Paris, where French ideas of color and shape left their mark on his work. But unlike the polished, French-oriented artists of the Septem group, he brought to his art something darker, earthier, a passion for life, and a sense of *elämänvoima*—Bergson's *élan vital*— that revealed dark forces in the national soul.

The older generation thought they saw what they most feared: art infected by the same proletarianism that was overtaking the whole of society; they were determined to fight it.[29] The first step was to get rid of the "yobs and socialists," people like that expressionist Sallinen masquerading as an artist. The cocky Sallinen was not about to go without a fight. At a meeting of the artists' guild he publicly called Gallén some very bad names, was ignominiously evicted, and promptly left the country. He headed for the United States, where among sympathetic Finns of Upper Michigan he found work as a cartoonist for *Työmies* (*The Laborer*). But he soon returned. In 1915 Sallinen exhibited *Kääpiö* (*The Dwarf*), a portrait of a hunchbacked cigarette vendor in Helsinki. That did it. The combination of poverty and disability with modernist form and urban decadence tripped a new wave of hysteria. The very degeneration the upper class most loathed was disgustingly there for all to see; it infected art, it was spreading through society! A new Sallinen "war" erupted.

In 1916 Sallinen exhibited his works with Marcus Collin, Alvar Cawén, and Juho Rissanen—the so-called Novemberists. The group came to be viewed as the opposite of the French-inspired Septem artists that had formed around Enckell. Yet despite their international contacts, the young extremists' deviant colors, Finnish themes, and under-lying mentality embodied a core of Finnishness—a kind of coarseness, closedness, and humor.[30] It was a core that artists of the "educated classes" simply did not recognize.

For all the class warfare being waged on the surface of the Sallinen exhibitions, the expressionist and cubist forces erupting in his portraits were spewing their firestorms over the other arts. In the year of the first Sallinen war, 1912, Huugo Jalkanen (1888–1969) turned to a kind of Finnish *vers libre* to write his *Kevät* (*Spring*).[31] Although Eino Leino had experimented with free rhythm, now other poets of Finland—Viljo Kojo (1891–1966), for one, and the writer of real significance, Edith Södergran (1892–1923), for another—began using this radical means more and more. All were part of the new idea of what it meant to be human. Vitality—*elämänvoima*—came from the earth, the water, the sun. No longer was any distinction made between spirit and matter. Even the older generation understood this: Gallén's glowing *Aallottaria* (*The Oceanides*), painted in 1909, was at once a manifestation of a golden age of Finnish art and an embodiment of *élan vital*.

While some of the older artists (not least Eero Järnefelt) inwardly sympathized with the young iconoclast Sallinen and his new ways of thinking,[32] Sibelius, ever adroit in avoiding confrontation, seems to have remained out of the domestic fray. After all, the war was being waged in the visual arts. But the question cut far deeper than a few Finn-ish art shows. It was also going on across the other arts and in many lands. In the autumn of 1911 Sibelius had witnessed a glittering performance of *Salome* in Paris. He knew of Mahler's *Das Lied von der Erde* and late symphonies, of Scriabin's musical genius, and he was increasingly aware of Arnold Schoenberg, whose name shows up for the first time in Sibelius's diary on May 8, 1912. Although Sibelius was not present at the Berlin premiere of *Pierrot lunaire* in October 1912, a year and a half later he was in the German capital, where a "song of Schönberg made a deep impression" on him; where the same composer's *Kammersymphonie*, played the next week, hurt his ears, yet had "something great behind it"; and where a few days after that, Schoenberg's op. 10 string quartet gave him much to think about.[33] The musical landscape had altered every bit as much as the visual terrain, and the composer's diary revealed an increasing preoccupation with his place in this strange world.

Until around 1905, for Sibelius and his contemporaries in Finland "through the national to the all-European" had meant that to embrace the national was to attain the international. Now the forces had realigned and the ground was tilting perilously. The meaning of things was no longer the same. In Finland, the more artists distanced themselves from international modernism, the more praise they received. The worst of the confusing crisscross of competing issues and metamorphosing meanings was that the new urban radicals were making the generation of the 1890s—Sibelius, Gallén, and company, those who had shaken, stirred, and revolutionized the world of Finnish music and art—look like staid, old-fashioned aristocrats who had settled contentedly into bourgeois comfort. The ironies abounded: it was Gallén who, more than any other visual artist, had celebrated the life, look, and spirit of Finland's Finnish-speaking rural and working-class citizens. That it was one among their numbers who was flinging down the gauntlet of artistic challenge was not lost on him.

Sibelius was honest enough to acknowledge his bourgeois comforts, albeit with a caveat: "I'm quite certain I've gotten more comfortable," he wrote in his diary on March 5, 1911, "but—and this is sure—not intellectually lazier." He even looked the part of the settled bourgeois: he had exchanged his untamed hairstyle for a more conventional coiffure, and his proud, slim figure had begun to thicken. In 1911, in an article for *Nuori Suomi*'s *Christmas Album* feting Juhani Aho, Ilmari Kianto snidely described Sibelius as *mehevä porvari*—a juicy burgher.[34]

A decade later, in an interview given in Rome to Alberto Gasco, the music critic for *La tribuna*, Sibelius referred to the confusion roiling through these years. In response to the question, "Are there musicians who have been susceptible to foreign influences?" he replied, "Eh yes, too many. Among the young, one notes a tendency toward an internationalism that I believe is pernicious. Debussy is a *conquistatore* [*sic*]." Gasco prods, "And Strauss, Stravinsky, and Schoenberg?" "They too have their followers," says Sibelius, "but fewer than Claude Debussy."[35] It was not clear exactly what or whom Sibelius had in mind, but among the younger composers, Ernst Pingoud (1887–1942), born in Saint

Petersburg, stands out as a strong candidate. Pingoud had fled to Finland after the revolution, where his statements on behalf of cosmopolitanism and against nationalism set him apart: possibly the only composer in Finland at the time who produced no works whatsoever inspired by the *Kalevala*, Pingoud had the effrontery not only to claim that "national art represented the infancy of all art," but even to criticize, albeit mildly, Sibelius himself.[36]

Although it took some time for these events to play out, in 1912 a dangerous pass had already been reached: the push-pull of nationalism/internationalism, so closely bound up with modernism/antimodernism, avant-gardism/archconservatism, and, perhaps most dangerously, Marxism/capitalism had begun to sabotage and disrupt the meanings that Sibelius's generation had taken for granted.

Finnish society had also been changing in other ways. On October 6, 1913, just months after that Paris audience had famously rioted at the premiere of *Le sacre du printemps*, Helsinki's Apollo Theater presented—for the first time in Finland—the sultry tango.[37] The sensuous Argentine dance, transformed into a specifically Finnish product, took Suomi's population by storm. Meanwhile, mass entertainment of another kind was cutting a swath through the city: movies. Silent films were being shown regularly in Helsinki by 1910. By 1915, when Charlie Chaplin films arrived, the town boasted twenty-five movie theaters, their names endearing personifications of those favorite Finnish themes: classical antiquity—in theaters called Apollo, Arcadia, Helicon, Lyra, and Venus—and *Kalevala* myths—in others named Ilmarinen, Kaleva, Kantele, and Sampo.

And Sibelius—what does he do? At his concert on March 29, 1912, which included a repeat performance of his Fourth Symphony, he premiered a new work: *Scènes historiques II*.[38] The title—*Historical scenes* (its individual numbers called "The Hunt," "Love Song," and "At the Drawbridge")—and the romantic tonal language gave the whole a quality so regressive as to be embarrassing. A year after the Fourth Symphony, after the debut of the delightfully quirky *Petrushka*, after the radical works of Arnold Schoenberg (including *Drei Klavierstücke*, op. 11), after the stringent pieces of Anton Webern (*Fünf Sätze*, op. 5, for string quartet), both in 1909, this second set of *Scènes historiques* seemed well and truly out of step with the times. What on earth could Sibelius have been thinking?

The domestic scene offers some answers. In January 1912 Sibelius had been offered a position in Vienna's Akademie für Musik und darstellende Kunst as successor to none other than his earlier teacher, Robert Fuchs. The offer had its temptations, and his reflections in the diary (on January 17) are revealing: "It would be wonderful if one could be spared these low-class people, 'one's' compatriots, whoever, wherever and however belittle my life's work any way they can."

Sibelius has often been portrayed as hopeless with monetary matters, but his actions at this juncture show him to be as shrewd as the next man in improving his financial position: he delayed making a decision, meanwhile allowing the offer to be publicly known. His most influential friends saw to it that sufficient pressure was brought to bear on the Finnish senate. But pressure had also been put on Sibelius. His former pupil, Leevi Madetoja, wrote from Berlin to say that his absence would be "an irreparable loss" for Finland's culture and voiced the hope that Sibelius would remain at home.[39] In his diary on March 8, 1912, Sibelius put down his refusal of the Vienna offer to patriotism and love of his independent mode of working (meaning, in effect, no responsibilities other than to compose). It was hard to know which had the upper hand. Yet the episode helps to put *Scènes historiques II* in perspective. In the wake of the dismal reception of his Fourth Symphony, the new *Scènes* may have been meant to reassure his countrymen that their most important cultural symbol still had the will and the means to engage fully in the national project, "to reach out and instruct all people," as Bis had put it, and create works of truly Finnish, historical, and wide public interest.

His countrymen responded: the senate raised his annual pension from 3,000 to 5,000 Finnish marks.[40]

MODERNIST BREAKTHROUGH: THE MEANING OF ART

In light of the aesthetic polemics going on at home and abroad, the work that now emerged could not have been more significant: *Luonnotar*, a tone poem for soprano and orchestra. That in the midst of all the discussion of modernism Sibelius should have returned to the *Kalevala*—selecting the epic's very first verses, the ones having to do with birth, creativity, and loneliness—sent a powerful message to anyone open to receiving it. While Tyko Sallinen was finding a visual "core" of Finnishness in unconventional deviations of color, form, and subject matter, Sibelius returned to the Finnish source that had never failed to nourish his art and plumbed its depths in a new way.

The character on whom Sibelius centered his new work was no swashbuckling Lemminkäinen or knife-wielding Kullervo. It was a nature spirit, one of those mysterious feminine beings who had often served as the composer's muse. In the *Kalevala* story, after enduring a superhuman seven-hundred-year pregnancy spent in desperate loneliness swimming aimlessly around in the sea, the nature spirit gives birth to Väinämöinen.[41] At the same time another act of creation takes place. On the spirit's raised knee a goldeneye builds its nest and lays seven eggs, six of gold and one of iron. When the eggs break, they are transformed into sky, earth, sun, moon, and stars. With the creation of the cosmos, Väinämöinen, the bringer of music to the Finns, emerges.

Sibelius altered the story, omitting the birth of Väinämöinen and emphasizing the seven hundred years as a deeply forlorn period for the nature spirit. And in his version the broken eggs are transformed only into sky, moon, and stars. But in his creation of the nature spirit, the *luonnotar*, he at last mastered two fundamental principles, rotation and teleological genesis, to borrow James Hepokoski's apt terms. The composer had long grappled with these principles, and now he put them into the service of a new modernism, with a newly invented structure that unified form and content. Within those cosmic circulations, their revolving forms so reminiscent of mythic and particularly *Kalevala*-esque repetitions, a new idea is incubated (see the clarinets in ex. 20.3). Gradually, "the new" expands and matures until it ruptures forth, suddenly materializing as the goal toward which the composition has been heading all along, a twist on the old romantic apotheosis (see ex. 20.4). With the revelation, the gestational matrix that it nourished gradually falls away, placentalike, and the work comes to an end.

The "feminine" and nurturing principles show up most dramatically in the *Kalevala* phrases that Sibelius had set before, in another orchestral song, *Kullervon valitus* (*Kullervo's Lament*, which closes the *Kullervo* symphony's third movement). There Kullervo utters the anguished cry "Voi, poloinen, päiviäni," at the realization that the maiden to whom he has just made love in the sledge is his sister. To that cry Sibelius had composed a piercing wail of musical pain befitting this primitive. Written in common time, the words are punctuated by fortissimo roars from the full orchestra (see ex. 20.5). Thirty-three bars later, "Parempi olisin ollut" (It would have been better [had I not been born]), Kullervo howls to the barely heard whispers of the oboes and clarinets (see ex. 20.6).

Part of the *Kalevala*'s charm is its repetitive use of words and phrases, and these same expressions appear in the *luonnotar*'s story. Setting the same words more than two decades later, now uttered by the nature spirit, Sibelius underpinned them with sustained pedal points in the harps and low strings, but conceived them as "misterioso, piano" (see ex. 20.7). Whether he recalled his long-ago setting of those words in *Kullervo* is less important than is the difference in the way in which he now treated them: where Kullervo brays like a member of a "raw Finnish mob," the *luonnotar*, an impenetrable being who represents the mystery and source of life itself, sings a rarified, cryptic meditation.

One wonders for whom Sibelius was writing *Luonnotar*. Ostensibly, it was the beautiful soprano Aino Ackté (1876–1944), to whom the tone poem was dedicated. Myrrha Bantock, the sharp-eyed offspring of composer Granville, recalled that Aino Ackté "made a very strong impression on the Finnish composer, who, according to my mother, was deeply attracted to her."[42] It was something of a love-hate relationship that had been despoiled when Sibelius backed out of a promise to compose an orchestral song for Ackté. It was to be on Edgar Allan Poe's poem *The Raven*, and the pair of them would

EXAMPLE 20.3. SIBELIUS, *LUONNOTAR*, MM. 77–80.

© BREITKOPF & HÄRTEL, WIESBADEN.

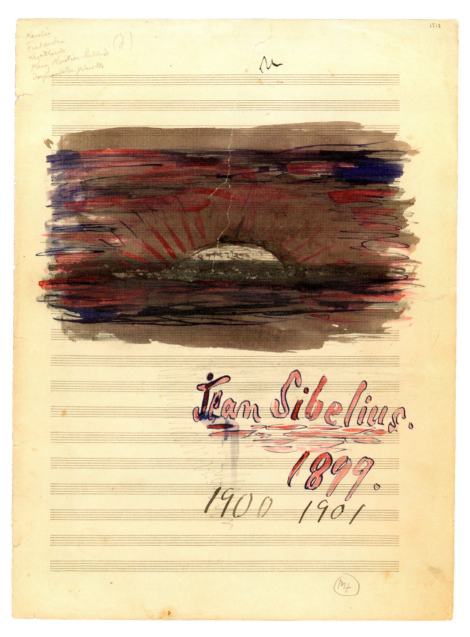

Plate 9. Jean Sibelius. Watercolor. Music manuscript HUL 1512.
Photo: Kari Timonen.

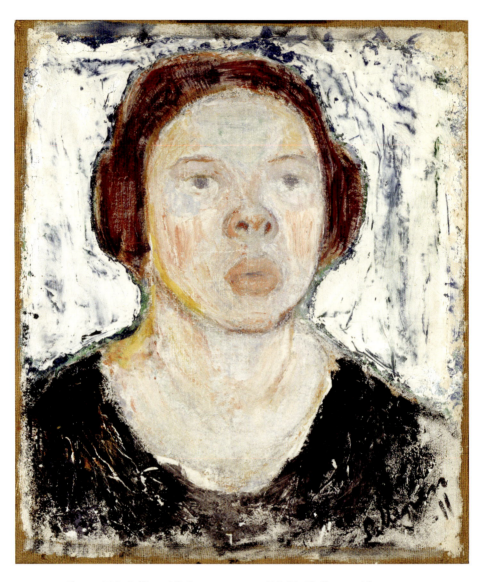

Plate 10. Tyko Sallinen, *Mirri mustassa puvussa* (*Mirri in Black*), 1911. Oil on canvas.
Ateneum Art Museum/Central Art Archives. Photo: Jukka Romu.

Plate 11. Helene Schjerfbeck, *Espanjalainen* (*The Spaniard*), 1881. Oil on canvas, Ateneum Art Museum. Photo: Janne Mäkinen.

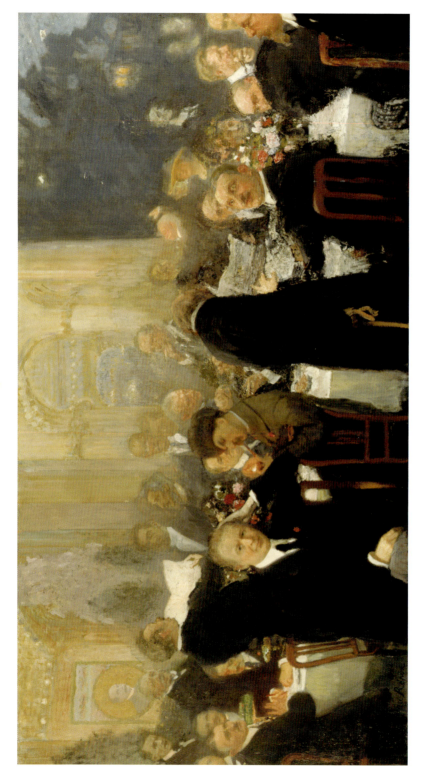

Plate 12. Ilya Repin, *Suomen suurmiehiä* (*The Great Men of Finland*), 1922. *Left to right:* Viktor Jansson, Vilho Sjöström, Harald Gallen, Woldemar Toppelius, Jean Sibelius (seated, writing), Eino Leino (standing and declaiming), Eliel Saarinen (facing the viewer), Robert Kajanus (directly behind Saarinen), J. J. Tikkanen, Emil Cedercreuz, Pekka Halonen, Akseli Gallen-Kallela (in the fur hat, lighting a cigar), Eero Järnefelt (just above the fur hat), Antti Favén, Ilya Repin (standing), Felix Nylund, Ville Vallgren (with raised and gesturing arm), C. G. Mannerheim, Hilda Flodin-Laitinen, Viivi Vallgren, Torsten Stjernschantz, Viktor Malmberg, and Bertel Gripenberg. Oil on canvas. Ateneum Art Museum/Central Art Archives. Photo: Antti Kuivalainen.

take the new work on a central European tour.[43] That was in 1910, and Ackté made her diva displeasure crystal-clear at such unheard-of abandonment. *Luonnotar* offered Sibelius some kind of redemption. Ackté gave its first performance, at the Three Choirs Festival in Gloucester, England, on September 10, 1913, without Sibelius in view (the work was conducted by the British composer Herbert Brewer).

Did Sibelius truly expect so personal, so esoteric, so mystically Finnish a work, to succeed abroad? At the first performance, the audience, even with an English translation in hand, found the text nearly incomprehensible. As one reviewer bravely declared, "The orchestral undercurrent seemed more interesting than the vocal part, but . . . one has to exert faith that there is more in the music than is apparent on one hearing."[44] And aside from Ackté, who could be expected to perform so demanding a composition? Not only are its formidable language and its weird and wondrous tale far removed from Western thought traditions, but so too are its musical demands. The most well-known is the cry *Ei!* on a high C-flat (bars 125–30), the first time poco forte, the second time—heaven forfend!—pianissimo. Cecil Gray later described it as "one of the highest pinnacles in the whole range of Sibelius's creations, and consequently in the entire range of modern music."[45] And he was not just talking about that C-flat.

Even in Finland, there is a serious question of who in 1913 would have appreciated a work such as *Luonnotar*. The audience for so abstruse a composition, never large, had dwindled further. And *Kalevala* topics seemed increasingly dated in a world of expressionist urban paintings, supple tangos, and moving pictures. Mass audiences of proletarian workers were not likely to feel sympathy for a sensitive spirit of nature who brandished no grand, heroic, or nationalistic rhetoric. Nor were Swedish-speaking Finns likely to relate to the tone poem, any more than they had related to *Kullervo*, which most had appreciated only on a national and patriotic level.

There is also *Luonnotar*'s strange genre: a tone poem with a soprano solo. Even though Mahler had composed an aria in his Fourth Symphony and had written for voice and orchestra in his magnificent *Das Lied von der Erde*, in the international musical bazaar these combinations were not easily marketable items. Add in a Finnish text, and the possibilities plummeted.

Coming on the heels of the Sallinen war, with its barbs and fears about proletarian art, *Luonnotar* could hardly have delivered a stronger message: the embodiment of *elämänvoima*—vitality both feminine and *Kalevala*-esque—*Luonnotar* conspicuously demonstrated that a great composer could still derive creative passion and *élan vital* from the *Kalevala*. By moving away from the "heroic" in national, male-defined terms and toward the natural, more feminine processes of rebirth and creativity, Sibelius found highly original solutions to the issues plaguing him and other artistic contemporaries.

EXAMPLE 20.4. SIBELIUS, *LUONNOTAR*, MM. 148–59.

© BREITKOPF & HÄRTEL, WIESBADEN.

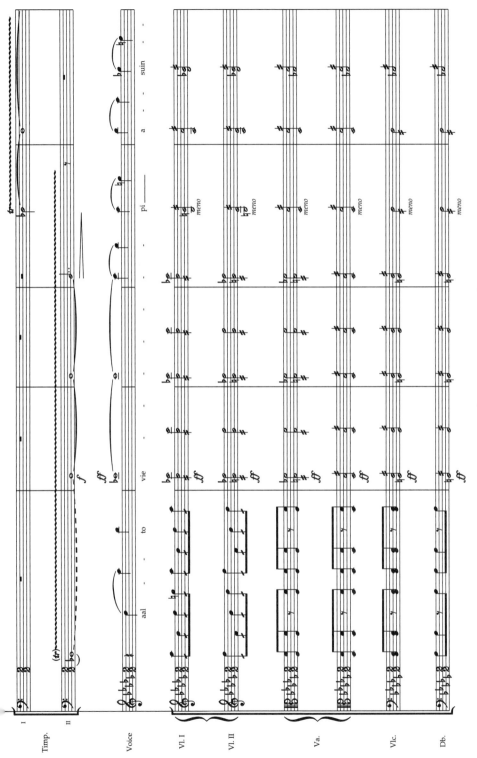

EXAMPLE 20.4. (CONTINUED ON NEXT PAGE)

EXAMPLE 20.4. (CONTINUED)

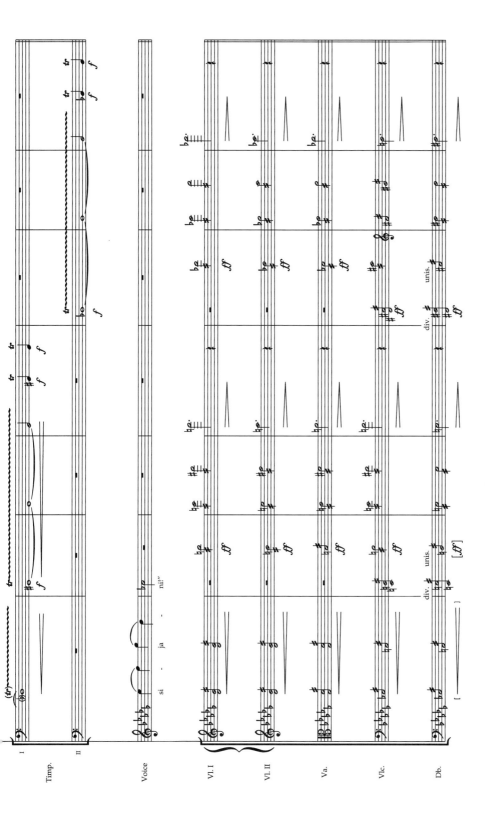

EXAMPLE 20.5. SIBELIUS, *KULLERVO*, THIRD MOVEMENT, MM. 508–11.

© BREITKOPF & HÄRTEL, WIESBADEN.

EXAMPLE 20.6. SIBELIUS, *KULLERVO*, THIRD MOVEMENT, MM. 544–48.
© BREITKOPF & HÄRTEL, WIESBADEN.

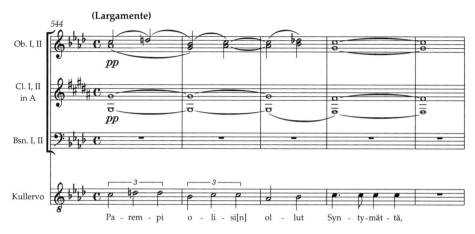

But he also found himself moving further away than ever from "the people." In a certain sense, *Luonnotar* is a tragically beautiful testimony to isolation and loneliness. However crucial it was for his musical path, *Luonnotar* is so deeply personal a work that hearing a performance comes too close: it is like witnessing a human soul stripped bare.

STRIKE A BLOW FOR EVERYTHING FINNISH!

Till America! Avay!

SIBELIUS, *DAGBOK*, MAY 1914

As if there were cosmic forces at work to balance the experience of *Luonnotar*—the most extreme retreat into nature mysticism Sibelius had ever made—the Finn now received an invitation to travel out of his isolation and embrace the world. The forces took the shape of an American composer, Horatio Parker (1863–1919), one of the so-called Boston classicists and a professor at Yale University.[46]

Parker had contacted Sibelius in the summer of 1913 with an invitation to write *Three Songs for American Schools*. The charming results—*Autumn Song, The Sun upon the Lake Is Low*, and *A Cavalry Catch*—are all too seldom heard. Parker published the pieces in his instructional Progressive Music Series (Boston: 1916), a project for which he had also engaged Max Reger and Gabriel Pierné. At the same time, the professor was playing a far more important role in Sibelius's life: he recommended the composer to Carl and Ellen

EXAMPLE 20.7. SIBELIUS, *LUONNOTAR*, MM. 57–67.
© BREITKOPF & HÄRTEL, WIESBADEN.

Battell Stoeckel, wealthy music lovers who had established a music festival in Norfolk, Connecticut, for which they sponsored such world-class figures as Ralph Vaughan Williams, Max Bruch, and Samuel Coleridge-Taylor.[47] The Stoeckels, too, had connections to Yale University: Ellen was the daughter of Robbins Battell, a Yale graduate and well-to-do amateur composer. Carl's Bavarian-born father had been Yale's chapel organist and music instructor and eventually became the Battell Professor of Music.

EXAMPLE 20.7. (*CONTINUED*)

EXAMPLE 20.7. (*CONTINUED ON NEXT PAGE*)

It was thus through divine intervention of a certain kind that Sibelius found himself on a ship sailing for America in May of 1914, leaving behind Aino and his daughters, now five in number with the birth of Heidi in 1911. He had in hand the manuscript of a new work commissioned for the Stoeckels' festival. Given a choice of writing for chorus and orchestra or for orchestra alone, Sibelius had wisely chosen the latter: his command of English was hardly up to giving the language adequate, much less inspired, musical set-

EXAMPLE 20.7. (*CONTINUED*)

ting.[48] The piece he envisioned was in three movements, and he had announced its title to Parker in an odd mixture of French and German, *Rondeau der Wellen*.

But first the title changed: by the end of April 1914, it had become *Aallottaret* (*Oceanides* in English), those seductive feminine life forces whom Gallén had only recently depicted in a glowing canvas of radiant pink and gold, and for which there was also a Finnish musical precedent: Wegelius's *Oceanidernas sång*, composed in 1868. In the course of the voyage, the composer's first transatlantic crossing, Sibelius found that not only had his view of the sea altered (as he told the Stoeckels, he had learned more about the ocean on the crossing than he had previously known from gazing at it from Finland's shores), but so had his view of the piece, which he now reduced to a single movement, "a composition for grand Orchestra," befitting the grand country to which he was traveling.

In 1914 the United States of America was undergoing unprecedented expansion. In the two short decades from 1880 to 1900, the population had boomed from 50 million inhabitants to 75 million and was still burgeoning. Those millions teemed with white, black, Indian, European, Asian, and Hispanic citizens, with workers, Wobblies,[49] cowboys, cattle barons, robber barons, railroad kings, abolitionists, educators, soldiers, suffragists, professors, prohibitionists, muckrakers, and millionaires. Like Finland, America was changing from agrarian to industrial, but the sheer size of the country, the wealth of its resources, and the dynamism of its collective immigrant populace fostered the building of an industrial empire that by 1918 would be second to none.

Along with the practical inventions and capitalistic endeavors pouring forth in these years (from the likes of Thomas Edison and George Pullman, George Westinghouse and Orville and Wilbur Wright), the *nouveaux riches* were fostering a Gilded Age of extravagant cultural display. Andrew Carnegie (1835–1919) and John D. Rockefeller (1839–1937) were giving lavishly in support of education, public libraries, and foundations to foster research and artistic endeavors. Robber barons such as J. Pierpont Morgan (1837–1913) tried to soften their images by flaunting an interest in the arts. Morgan, who was involved with the Metropolitan Opera and served as president of the Metropolitan Museum of Art, had amassed the largest private collection of medieval and Renaissance manuscripts in the world by the time he died in 1913. Along with beautiful gems, *objets d'art*, and Old Master drawings, Morgan hungered for autograph manuscripts and acquired such items as Keats's *Endymion*, Dickens's *Christmas Carol*, and original correspondence of the American nation's founding fathers. His library would eventually purchase several of Sibelius's autograph manuscripts as well.

The journey to America was the farthest away Sibelius had ever been, yet Finns had been traveling there at least since 1638, when with Swedes they sailed up the Delaware River.[50] The most famous of these travelers was undoubtedly Pehr Kalm, a naturalist and assistant to the celebrated Carl Linnaeus, sent by the university in Turku to study plant life in the New World in 1747. By the end of the next century, with the curse of Bobrikov visited upon Finland, large numbers of Finns began immigrating westward. The vast majority were working people looking for refuge, jobs, and sometimes adventure. Even though Pehr Kalm had met Benjamin Franklin, no Finn had ever been welcomed, feted, and honored as Jean Sibelius was about to be—nor had any seen the America he was about to be shown.

The United States is not, in principle, a class society. But it has great social unequalizers; education, money, race. The impressions of America that Sibelius received were those orchestrated by the well-educated, comfortably moneyed, upper-crust Stoeckels: dinners at the elegant Ritz-Carlton and pricey Delmonico's; rehearsals at Carnegie Hall on Manhattan Island; private automobiles; a battery of personal servants—"Negroes, whites and maids of every color,"[51] reported Sibelius; the company of Yale professors, many of whom spoke fluent German or French; and dinner companions of the likes foreigners rarely encounter, including the twenty-seventh president of the United States, William Howard Taft (1857–1930), who had just completed his presidential term.[52] There was also the Stoeckels' distinguished circle of musical friends: composers such as Henry Hadley, Horatio Parker, and others among the Boston classicists; performers such as Maud Powell, who had given the American premiere of Sibelius's violin concerto and who recorded his music for the Victor Talking Machine Company (Stoeckel had even commissioned a violin concerto for Powell, from the African Englishman Coleridge-Taylor); singers such as the soprano Alma Gluck, whom Sibelius heard at Norfolk in the summer of 1914 (the year Gluck married Efrem Zimbalist and also made that recording of "Carry Me Back to Old Virginny" that would eventually sell a million copies for Victor);[53] and not least, accomplished conductors such as Arthur Mees, who was also a music editor and a writer of program notes for the Boston Symphony.

In short, it was the conservative, cultivated, and moneyed America of Connecticut, New York, and Pennsylvania to which Sibelius was introduced. (Notably, Horatio Parker did not introduce his Finnish guest to his most original composition student, Charles Ives, Yale class of '98.)[54] Sibelius felt right at home; as he had told Aino during the Vienna year, "There is a natural aristocracy who have sensibility and a view of life that the ordinary masses don't understand," and he discovered that that aristocracy extended to America.

Stoeckel appears to have been the most thoughtful of hosts. Endeavoring to grant his guest's every whim, he arranged for Sibelius to experience some of North America's most dramatic natural resources: he not only paid for the ocean voyage, he also organized trips to majestic Niagara Falls and the beautiful Housatonic River (one of Charles Ives's *Three Places in New England*), whose soughing winds and euphonius Mohican-derived name captivated Sibelius. The Finn meanwhile was making indelible impressions on Americans. There were those fastidious personal habits: he required a barber; he never, he averred, shaved himself (did he distrust his already shaking hands?). Americans remarked on his distinctly blonde hair, his immaculate dress, his shopping extravagances. He dressed elegantly and purchased expensively—a new white summer suit, having brought only warm clothes from Finland, he said; new patent leather shoes, his fine Finn-

Figure 20.1. Sibelius posing with Arthur Mees in Connecticut. *Musical America*, June 13, 1914.

ish ones not being exactly what was needed, he insisted; a summer straw hat and cane, an American "look" in which he was photographed with Mees (see fig. 20.1). Repeatedly, he reminded the company that he had been a violinist.

They complied with his request to attend church (!)—as a matter of observation, he explained. He told them that his family religion was Lutheran, though the subject seemed too vast to discuss. He was interested, he said, in the old New England hymns, about which he appeared surprisingly well informed. The true religious experience, however, was Niagara Falls, "the nearest to true religion of anything I have yet felt and I believe music comes next to it."[55]

People praised his unfailing good manners. They were impressed with his massive girth, his large features, his manner of speaking: "a man that threw out jerky sentences and abrupt, energetic phrases in [French], and usually bit them off before they were concluded," reported Olin Downes.[56] They delighted in his funny stories and showered him with gifts. Stoeckel recorded that everyone grew very fond of the composer during his few weeks; "it was remarkable to see how all kinds of people were drawn to him," he wrote.[57]

But the highest honor of all they bestowed on Sibelius was the doctor of philosophy degree, *honoris causa*, conferred by Yale University. On June 17, to the strains of *Finlandia*, *Vårsång*, and *Valse triste*, Sibelius marched in the university's academic procession clad in a flowing black silk robe, the blue velvet bars of the doctoral degree on its sleeves, a black mortarboard incongruously clamped on his head. He had come prepared with a short speech in Latin, which he rehearsed for the Stoeckels with schoolboy precision. But the only words spoken were those addressed to him, and they specifically made tribute to both the national and the international dimensions of his music: "What Wagner did with Teutonic legend, Dr. Sibelius has done in his own impressive way with the legends of Finland as embodied in her national epic. He has translated the *Kalevala* into the universal language of music, remarkable for its breadth, large simplicity, and the infusion of a deeply poetic personality."[58] Not to be outdone, the Imperial Alexander University, on learning of the coming tribute to their native son, hastily conferred a similar degree in absentia, Sibelius already having left for North America.

Most impressive of all, everyone agreed, was his Norfolk concert, featuring *Pohjola's Daughter*, the *King Christian II* Suite, *The Swan of Tuonela*, *Valse triste*, *Finlandia*, and, of course, the new work, *Oceanides*, whose main title was given only in Finnish, inevitably misspelled on the program—"Aalottaret," but with the intriguing subtitle "Nymphs of the Ocean." Two mighty blocks of sound currents circulated in slow motion, their daring proto-minimalist design veiled in luscious orchestral garb—harp, glockenspiel, and clarinet over shimmering string tremolos here, glittering woodwind colors there. Sibelius's conducting of these immense currents was graceful yet forceful, Stoeckel observed, his motions reminiscent of someone reading a mighty poem and unfettered by the necessity of giving anything so obvious as a beat.[59] Another eyewitness reported that Sibelius had

> at least one characteristic gesture, when he wishes an effect peculiarly characteristic of his music. This effect is the attack of a chord sforzando by the brass, an immediate pianissimo and a wide crescendo from this pianissimo to an angry fortissimo. The gesture is an opening of the arms gradually farther and farther apart so that the conductor seems to pull the tone from the instruments.[60]

What Sibelius pulled from the instruments caused the waves of sound to accumulate in power, building and building until they mounted in a final shock that left the audience agape, then brought it excitedly to its feet, shouting and stamping with enthusiasm.

When afterward the chorus, orchestra, and audience performed *Vårt land* (its words—in English—printed in the program as "The National Air of Finland"), Sibelius appeared greatly moved: "Finland thanks you and your wife," he said, turning to Stoeckel; "I regard the singing of this anthem as an honor not to me but to my native land."[61]

The American journey has too often been treated as a mere speck on the horizon of Sibelius's more important European circuit. Yet to do so is vastly to underestimate just how profound is the impact upon the imagination of discovering a new continent, a new world. Sibelius's American experience was not a touristic seeing, but a deep encounter with a new culture on many levels. Once in America he found old prejudices vanishing. Convinced, as were many upper-class Europeans, that he would find only superficialities ("the foxtrot and the Boston"), he discovered instead that "the orchestra [was] wonderful!! Better than anything we hear in Europe."[62] Moreover, he found that in America he was numbered among the great composers, a position that contrasted sharply with his situation in continental Europe. That very April, in Montreux, Ernest Ansermet and L'orchestre du Kursaal had announced the following program:[63]

Thursday, April 16, 1914

I.

1. Ouverture to *Magic Flute*
2. *Concerto in ut majeur pour violon et orchestre*, Haydn
3. *Scherzo de la Symphonie in mi bémol*, Strawinsky, sous la direction de l'auteur

II.

4. *Finlandia, Poème symphonique*, Jean Sibelius
5. *Poème pour violon et orchestre*, Chausson
6. *L'apprenti sorcier*, Dukas

It seems unlikely that Sibelius, grouped with the programmatic and romantic Frenchmen rather than the classic Austrians and the one neoclassic Russian, was appreciated for the progressive qualities of his *Finlandia* as a technologically inspired piece of program music. As the British critic Percy Scholes remarked the very month Sibelius sailed for American shores, "In these present days the storms rage most fiercely, perhaps, around the heads of the three S.'s of the most modern music—Schönberg, Scriabin, and Stravinsky. Here are the men who have apparently cast aside all the accepted canons of musical art and evolved, each in his own way, something new and strange."[64]

It was true that many Americans viewed Sibelius as "a nationalist in art," as the Yale encomium declared. Yet among those nationalists were two King Richards—Strauss and Wagner. And most encouraging of all, American critics were praising his most "advanced" music, the Fourth Symphony. Arthur Farwell, anointing Sibelius "a Musical Redeemer," demanded to know why critics dwelled on the Finn as "a product of the wild and sombre north, and [have] nothing to say of the manner in which he grapples in his works, with the great musical questions of the day?"[65] Reassuring words for a man who had been feeling marginalized.

As the American trip was coming to a close, Sibelius noted in his diary, "I have struck a blow for everything Finnish!"[66]

~21~

Turning Points

On June 28, 1914, as Jean Sibelius was steaming homeward across the Atlantic Ocean, Gavrilo Princip fired that devastating shot igniting the Great War. It took some time before the world situation affected the Finns directly. In Sibelius's case, he had to confront instead the dangerous pass he had reached at home, though it came in the devil's guise. Internationally celebrated, in demand from Karelia to Connecticut, Sibelius had reached an undisputed pinnacle of success. He should have been wary: those whom the gods wish to curse, they first make famous. And famous he had been made. Buoyed by his overwhelmingly positive reception in America, he set about composing a new symphony.

A BIRTHDAY SYMPHONY: "HIER STEHE ICH, KANN NICHT ANDERS"

In a sketchbook begun immediately after his American journey, Sibelius began to develop ideas that would ripen into his last compositions: the Fifth Symphony, the Sixth Symphony, the Seventh Symphony, and *Tapiola*. On October 26, 1914, he made an annotation in his diary: "Begun in earnest with Symphony no. 5. . . . In a truly glorious mood forging these themes." He followed this observation with Martin Luther's famous but here imperfectly recalled words: "Hier stehe ich, kann nicht anders, Gott helfe mich, Amen!'"

Despite (or because of) that religious blessing, or perhaps because he was back again in Aino's arms, or, yet again, maybe because the work came to fruition in the spring, the Fifth Symphony contained some of the most sensuous music Sibelius ever created. In the spring of 1915, on April 10, he made that famous diary entry:

In the evening [worked] on the symphony. On the disposition of the themes. The importance is done with this mystery and enchantment. As if God the

375

Father had thrown down the shards of a mosaic from the floor of heaven and asked me to find out what it had looked like. Perhaps a good definition of "composing." Perhaps not. What do I know!—Warm outside, and winter is receding. Once again there is a fragrance in the air of the spring thaw, of youth, and of breaking—of change.

What immediately precedes that much-quoted description was a sense of wonder at himself as a man: "I'm sensitive again. How is it possible?"[1] And lo, the opening of the symphony is nothing so powerful as a delicious, sensuous awakening—to spring, to feelings of youth, to the voluptuousness of life in all its earthy glory. This symphony is filled with vigor, *elämänvoima*, the affirmation of life that comes in the springtime with its fever of love and energy. Even though Sibelius was turning fifty, he was experiencing the life force in a personal way. Three days later, he added: "You, Jean Sibelius, certainly know that ecstasy and sweet talk never die! The sap indeed rises in you as in another fifty-year-old tree. Ah! Der rüstige Alte! [Ah, the vigorous old!]."[2] One of the sketchbook pages of the Fifth Symphony's finale bears the rubric "Bacchus Procession" (after a poem of Rydberg entitled *Love of Life and Weariness of Life*), with all the lascivious implications that Bacchic celebrations imply.

The glories of springtime nature filled the symphony's pages. On April 21, 1915, ecstasy overflowed into the diary:

Today at ten to eleven I saw 16 whooper swans. One of the greatest experiences in my life! Lord God, what beauty! They circled over me for a long time. Disappeared into the solar haze like a gleaming, silver ribbon. The call the same woodwind type as that of cranes, but without tremolo. The swan call closer to the trumpet, although it's obviously a sarrusophone sound. A low-pitched refrain like the cry of a small child. Nature mysticism and life's Angst! The Fifth Symphony's finale theme:

Legato in the trumpets!! . . . That this should happen to me, who have so long been the outsider. Have thus been in the sanctuary, today 21 April 1915.[3]

It was Axel Carpelan, a kind of Boswell to the composer-as-Johnson during the work's creation, who committed to paper the name "the swan hymn beyond compare,"[4] but the idea of a swan theme seems to have been Sibelius's. Its glorious wings soar across the orchestra in a heart-stopping evocation of swans in flight, a stunning mastery of time and space that erased any ostensible difference between them and brought those esoteric discussions of the Symposium years to unimagined heights (see ex. 21.1).

Of course, acknowledgment of the sensual and Symposium aspects of the new symphony could hardly be thought, much less publicly said, about a great national composer, and the Fifth Symphony was about to play a very public role. Its premiere was to be used to celebrate Jean Sibelius's half century of life. In Finland, a fiftieth birthday is cause for great jubilation in ordinary people's lives. In the case of a national figure, the milestone approaching on December 8, 1915, fueled a national frenzy: concertizing, poetry writing, speech making, gift giving, genealogy tracing, and even serious biographical activity attended Sibelius's turning fifty.[5]

The extravagant coverage and lavish sentiments expressed in the Helsinki newspapers alone make the head swim. On December 7, December 8, December 9, and December 10, the presses unrolled full-page congratulatory announcements; photographs showing Sibelius, his family, and Ainola; contents of speeches given in his honor; drawings of the festival banquet; programs of concerts honoring "the Master"; reviews of those concerts; and laudatory poems wreathed in decorative laurel borders. The celebratory mood was not limited to the capital. Newspapers from all over the country—in Finnish and in Swedish, "Red" (Social Democrat) and "White," liberal and conservative, from north and from south, from eastern parts and western provinces—joined in the salutations, publishing lengthy tributes, most of them with one or more photographs, and most of them for several days running. The well-wishers included those in the composer's hometown: *Hämetär* devoted nearly an entire page to the great occasion; *Hämeen Sanomat* ran a front-page, four-column article with a photograph of Hämeenlinna's native son and a separate story on "Jean Sibelius as a Hämeenlinna boy." Not for Sibelius the role of prophet despised in his own land.[6]

The moment inspired Otto Andersson, a folklorist and a leading musical figure in the Finland-Swedish movement, to publish genealogical tables illuminating Sibelius's ancestry.[7] Meanwhile, Erik Furuhjelm, composer, critic, and pedagogue, published the first full biography of the composer—in Swedish: *Jean Sibelius: hans tondiktning och drag ur hans liv*.[8] "The people" lavished gifts on the hero (*päivän sankari*, as every birthday boy is in fact called in Finland): some twenty paintings from Finnish artists arrived at Ainola. A Persian rug. A Steinway grand piano. A leather-bound formal address from Breitkopf & Härtel. Meanwhile, enough money was being collected that some 30,000 Finnish marks would eventually be presented to the composer—enough to pay off his debts and leave a substantial balance.[9]

In the concerts organized to celebrate the event, the premiere of the new symphony was to mark the high point. It was to be played on December 8 and repeated on Decem-

EXAMPLE 21.1. SIBELIUS, SYMPHONY NO. 5, THIRD MOVEMENT, REHEARSAL LETTER D, MM. 1–12.
© WILHELM HANSEN, COPENHAGEN.

ber 12 and 18. Sibelius even scheduled a concert in the headquarters of the labor movement, on January 9, 1916.

On December 6 the Helsinki Music Institute staged a chamber concert of his works
(with the composer's new Violin Sonatine in E Major, movements from the youthful
op. 4 String Quartet in B-flat, the piano work *Kyllikki*, and *Voces intimae*). On December 10 Georg Schnéevoigt and Robert Kajanus conducted the first two symphonies,
and Ida Ekman performed a group of songs. And on December 14 MM sang their way
through a Sibelius evening.

On the birthday morning, December 8, Sibelius portraits appeared in shop windows.
That evening the composer conducted his *Oceanides* and Symphony no. 5, both new to

EXAMPLE 21.1. (*CONTINUED*)

the Finnish public. The two Serenades (op. 69) were played. Kajanus presented a wreath of honor, "from his old fellow comrade-in-arms." Sibelius received a "civic address" with an astonishing fifteen thousand signatures. He was feted at a banquet where cultural leaders vied to outdo each other in the glory of their eulogies. Robert Kajanus held forth in lofty tones: "Barely had we begun to till the barren soil when a mighty sound arose from the wilderness. Away with spades and picks. Finnish music's mighty springs came bursting forth. A mighty torrent burst forth to engulf all before it. Jean Sibelius alone showed the way."[10] Mikael Lybeck's grandiose Swedish words echoed through the banquet hall: "The soil in which your art has its roots has already become a whole country; now the country is becoming a world—and the world yours."[11] Not to be outdone, Finnish poetry likewise celebrated Finland's "lord of music." Otto Manninen (1872–1950), poet, translator, and the university's lector in Finnish, spent his judiciously conserved creative energy on verses in honor of the great occasion: "Hail to you, craftsman, master of sweet music!" On and on he went, until—

In triumph you arrive, and castles quake
and bosoms yield to beauty in your wake.
None can resist the sceptre of your sounds:
your empire grows apace and knows no bounds.[12]

Gad. At least Sibelius had the grace to grumble into his diary, "Difficile est satiram non scribere" (It's difficult not to parody all this).[13]

Sibelius was not the only mortal being celebrated by the Finns. The need for heroic figures to validate the strongly awakened Finnish identity and the modern cult of celebrity fed the zeal. The reading public snapped up other biographies of "great men": in 1917 the life stories of Aleksis Kivi and Leo Mechelin were published; so was the book *Suomalaisia sankareita* (*Finnish Heroes*). The previous year a volume entitled *Suurmiesten seurassa* (*In the Company of Great Men*) had been released.[14] In 1918 a biography of Helene Schjerfbeck appeared. Meanwhile, on his fiftieth birthday, in April 1915, Axel Gallén had also been lavishly feted: he was even given credit for Finnish music. Similar acknowledgment had been accorded Robert Kajanus. Those accolades lavished on his compatriots sent Sibelius into a frenzy of his own, suggesting that he was a little too wedded to his overinflated image. The fatal allure about which he knew well—had he not composed it into *Skogsrået*?—seems to have had him in its thrall.

The drawbacks were already apparent. The new symphony was seen as a retreat (and even, to some, a relief after the astringent excursions of the Fourth Symphony), far from the cutting edge of modernism. Even with its revisions over the next few years and the eventual structural innovations that reduced the number of movements from four to three, the symphony was not really understood.[15] Its bold confrontation with "the great musical questions of the day" was lost on public and critics alike.

THE SHIFT

That whole birthday business was a product of years of educating a public, composing for it, building its self-image, and whatnot. And in the course of those activities other seeds had begun to flourish unnoticed. The process was not unlike the design of Sibelius's *Luonnotar*, in which within a gestating matrix a new idea is born. And this new idea began threatening to take over, to the ruination of all that had brought it forth.

The thing was, while Sibelius had been creating musical images of Finland, Finns had been making Sibelius into an image of their own. Their formulation, too, belonged to the project of national awakening, in the course of which Finns "awoke" to the need for great men and musical, artistic, and literary traditions the equal of other great nations'.

Sibelius was not alone in being made into an icon by the Finnish people; the artists Albert Edelfelt and Axel Gallén were idolized at different times by different groups. The writers Topelius and Runeberg were admired, then venerated, then turned into monuments. But Sibelius's case has become the most notorious, because its effects were so spectacular and so heartbreaking.

The seeds of idolatry had put out shoots in the 1890s. In Sibelius's case they came to public notice on January 14, 1898, when the then brand-new art journal *Ateneum* had published Karl Flodin's article "Jean Sibelius." Beneath an impressive *Jugendstil* border and beside a flourishing decorative capital, Flodin's words, which at times had been clearly geared to keeping the capricious composer to a nationalist line, set forth the view of Sibelius that was held—or being promoted—by the country's cultural leaders:

> Even if for some reason or another the young composer should change his musical physiognomy or if, by contrast, he stays at the point of development he has presently reached, still *he has already made such a significant contribution to Finnish music history and so sharply defined his profile against the background of the cultural phenomena of his fatherland* that he can with reason be considered an individual artistic personality in his own right worthy of the very greatest attention.[16] (Emphasis added.)

A portrait of a curly-haired, serious-looking young man sporting a bushy mustache and high collar, showing one trademark dish-shaped ear, occupied the center of the page. Only a week earlier, efforts put into motion by other Finnish-minded leaders had come to fruition when the emperor approved that annual stipend for Jean Sibelius.

The composer himself contributed to his great-man image (a phenomenon he had observed with distaste with respect to Wagner during his trip to Bayreuth in 1894). His withdrawal from Helsinki in 1904 facilitated the myth making that turned him into a public symbol and his concerts into national institutions.[17] And pressures from his family, who were supremely conscious of their position in Finnish society, added to the situation. Aino Sibelius's influence on her husband's professional life has yet to be systematically explored, but it is clear that her opinions mattered tremendously to Sibelius and that he accepted her view of his prestigious social standing and public importance as a symbol of the nation.

However human was the confluence of factors, on the one hand, and yet far beyond human control, on the other, it is clear to anyone trying to write about Sibelius that by the time he reached fifty, his story has altered. The tapestry being woven of a creative personality fully committed to his country's awakening has begun to unravel; the threads knot and tangle. The unity and balance of the picture, with Finland poised vis-à-vis Sweden and Russia, and Sibelius and his music twining through, is disturbed. The ground gives rise to unwelcome figures that grow out of all proportion to their assigned place, and they begin to take over. However skillfully the weaver unravels and then reweaves the threads, unpicks and plaits again, the result is the same. Something both implacable and irrevocable has taken place: the creative mind has begun to recede, and the public icon and its uses for the public good has started to take over—to the point that the disruption itself becomes the story. As though a parody of his own brilliant solution to questions of musical structure and design, the composer's life has ceded to a kind of teleological genesis whose trajectory cannot be altered.

It is difficult to pinpoint exactly when the shift took place, because it was a gradual and cumulative process. But the manic activity that erupted around Sibelius's fiftieth birthday left no doubt that it had indeed occurred. From the tale of a human being emerges the story of a people. And the people must now step forth to claim their rightful role.

"THE PEOPLE"

It was the Turku Romantics who introduced the ethnic concept of "the people" into Finland, for, after all, the people were a cultural construct.[18] Runeberg had featured the Finnish people in his poetry, idealizing them as tough, enduring, classically sublime in their faith in God and Fate. Topelius had envisioned the people as humble, satisfied, obedient, and God-fearing, personified in his ideal peasant, Matti. *Kansa* in Finnish, *folk* in Swedish, the term translates only roughly into English as "people." Whereas in English, one can speak of "people in the street," neither *kansa* nor *folk* would be used in such a way. The Finnish concept is laden with emotion and near-sacred meaning, akin to the German idea of *Volk*. If Runeberg, Topelius, and Finnish artists such as Gallén were to be believed, "the people" were agrarian peasants, typecast exotics from the lower classes toiling in peaceful landscapes. "The people" manifestly excluded the Sámi, however; these residents of Finnish Lapland failed to show up in golden age canvases or to win an equal place with other Finns in Topelius's *Boken om vårt land*.

"The people" were stepping forth elsewhere across Europe. As Jürgen Habermas has written in connection with this era, a bourgeois public sphere—a realm where private people come together as a public—were becoming a force to be reckoned with.[19] Early on Fennomans realized the value of that force and harnessed the concept of the people for political purposes. It was the people whom the Finnish national movement intended to "awaken" through education, transforming the masses into civilized participants in a civic community. "The People's Holy Will" and "From the People" became sacred slogans of the national movement. Yet matters went a good deal further: "the people" became part of the very identity of the educated classes. Class distinctions were pushed deep into the background before the greater concept of being unified as Finns vis-à-vis everyone else (especially Russians and Swedes). The leaders placed the people—*kansa*—at the very core of the Finnish nation, the newly invented term for which was *kansakunta*; a citizen was called *kansalainen*. That Finnish, rather than Latin, supplied the basis for the word "nation" and its associated concepts demonstrated an unmistakable linguistic assumption. It also set Finland apart from other Nordic countries, where the comparable political term is *nation* and where the people as a unit are not similarly emphasized in political thought.

The idea of the people was thus central to the Finnish national awakening. And with the elections in 1907, it was clear that the awakening had succeeded. But now "the people" appeared to have changed. No longer peasants, they had turned into Social Democrats. And the balance of political power was on their side. It is thus the people's story that rightly, in a sense, grew to overwhelm its creators—like Sibelius—whose lives cannot be fully exhumed without considering the people's role therein. That role has been given superficial acknowledgment—in 1931 Cecil Gray dedicated his biography *Sibelius* "To the Finnish People in sympathy and admiration"—but the Finnish people have never been accorded their rightful place in Sibelius's life. Even though a history of the people of Finland belongs elsewhere, as a character the Finnish people indisputably must be joined to a full recounting of Jean Sibelius's story.

Curiously, rather detailed chapters about Sibelius vis-à-vis American people, British people, German people, and even the seemingly unreceptive French people have been written, but the most important chapter, Sibelius and the Finnish people, has yet to find its full chronicler.[20] Perhaps one reason is the story's friction. As a well-educated, well-traveled, Swedish-speaking Finn, Sibelius might represent Finns, but he was manifestly not "of the people." An aristocratic bearing was an inseparable part of his persona. During his engagement, he had addressed letters to his fiancée in the polite form of the time, "High, well-born [*Högvälborna*] Aino Järnefelt." Later he would say, "My wife is an aristocrat and I the artist—the equivalent."[21]

Yet in 1916, when geneticist Eeli Granit-Ilmoniemi enthusiastically began publishing the results of his research into the composer's ancestry in *Uusi Suometar*, lo, the people's great composer was revealed as one of them, descended from solid Finnish peasant stock. The equilibrium of a composer who saw himself as an aristocrat was shattered.[22] In 1919 Granit-Ilmoniemi was again in action, publishing a photograph of a distant carpenter cousin. "Compares me with Kuula, Merikanto, and Klemetti—we all come from peasants," Sibelius fumed in his diary:

It's not enough that one is branded a peasant abroad (that is, a former serf—
they don't know abroad that we never had serfs). I am made impossible in the
society to which I actually belong by education as well as genetically . . . A
refined suffering for so sensitive a soul as I am. Here I am alone in the dark—the
only one who will come to me is my sister—the madwoman. She laughs.[23]

His sister, Linda, left him feeling particularly vulnerable; her mental illness had become
acute and, to the narrow-minded eugenicists, represented a potentially weak link in his
genetic chain. By February 9, 1920, the composer had worked himself into a royal lather,
spewing ink over a number of diary pages in his outrage. It all seemed rather like a tempest in the proverbial teapot, but it demonstrated unmistakably Sibelius's self-image—an
aristocrat in a land increasingly dominated by proletarians.

   Against this backdrop, the incidental music Sibelius composed to *Jedermann* (*Everyman*, 1916) cries out for mention. The text was Hugo von Hofmannsthal's German version of the English morality play translated into Finnish (as *Jokamies*) by Huugo Jalkanen; the linguistic circuitry seemed to bear out the common property of the drama.
In 1955 Hans Keller, reviewing a broadcast of *Everyman* with Sibelius's music ("the first
work of Sibelius which I can stand and understand"), observed that it was an open secret
that Hofmannsthal's "sham morality" "is archaizing *Kitsch* with a powerful snob appeal
for the naive mass of empty-heads in search of culture (criterion: boredom)."[24] It is thus
all the more striking that the Viennese Keller, known for his penetrating and often acid
criticisms and general dislike of Sibelius, found this incidental music to be inspired. Its
composer, said Keller, unfolded a "musical organism" under the guise of conventional
sound effects; he expressed Everyman's progress through a continuous, albeit far from
straightforward, development from chromatic to diatonic language in general and to the
tonic minor in particular. In the course of that development Sibelius made the most of
the age-old musical associations of the devil with the tritone and chromaticism and of the
heavenly with the Dorian mode and the diatonic, associations simple enough for every
man and woman to grasp. Sibelius himself had grasped that this music, meant for *simultaneous* accompaniment to the stage actions (not preliminary to them, as his incidental
music had previously been), required precise timing, of the sort necessary for film compositions.[25]

   "Everyman"—the people—belonged to Sibelius's life as well as to his musical development. The people must thus be considered here, at least in scenes of crucial overlap,
for the ways in which they most profoundly shaped Sibelius's story. The most shattering
episode was "the People's War." Yet that might not have happened if Finland's independence had not come about first.

THE PEOPLE'S REPUBLIC

The backdrop against which "the people" had been elevating their national composer to impossible heights had begun to darken with the ominous war clouds overshadowing Europe. Unbelievably, some in the artistic world saw in the war an opportunity for aesthetic rebirth. Thomas Mann, for one: "War! We could feel it meant purification, liberation and an enormously great hope."[26] The Finnish architect Sigurd Frosterus, for another: he penned essays with titles such as "Modern Weapons: Their Origin and Development" ("Moderna vapen, deras uppkomst och utveckling," Helsingfors, 1915), peppered his prose with admiring comments on the beauty of the war machine, and praised the splendidly functional, rational technology that made the machine possible. "Steel" became the byword. Steel stood for the bravery of the soldiers, the helmets of the military, the shields of the victors.

As it turned out, no hostilities were fought on Finnish soil during World War I. To be sure, the people suffered hardships—along with the aggravation of hearing Russian spoken by the increasing numbers of troops on Finnish streets and ever more street names appearing in Cyrillic, there were the real difficulties of food shortages, widespread unemployment, and a commercial blockade. Still, in general Finnish economic interests were doing very well, thanks to the Russian presence. Where Finns felt the war's adversities most was in the cessation of life as they knew it and in their isolation. The Finnish parliament was suspended. It did not meet a single time between August 1914 and the spring of 1917. International travel came to a halt. Artistic activities ceased. The disruption of connections to Germany cut off many economic contacts; for Sibelius, it meant isolation from his publishers, Breitkopf & Härtel. When the firm's ability to produce musical scores came to an end, so did its ability to pay its composers, terminating a key source of income for Sibelius. By the war's end the firm was thoroughly bankrupted. It was then he turned to the Danes.

Sibelius's plaints in his diary record the loneliness and isolation that he felt were his own, but that in truth afflicted all artistic Finns. On July 30, 1914, he wrote, "The war begins. . . . And we here in Finland? Shall we become Philistines for want of leadership? Effeminate as we are. I trust the Swedish element more. But our Finns?" On August 18 he was writing, "War! Probably the end of our civilization." On September 30, 1914, his "complete isolation from people" had continued to grow. He felt that his time was running out. Two years later, little had changed: "Anyway, this disastrous war will still go on for a long time. And thus my isolation as well," he lamented on December 17, 1916. In earlier years he had noted crossly, "Damn it! Don't ever let yourself be without an orchestra for a long time. *N'oubliez pas!*"[27] Now that lack was enforced.

Remarkably, concerts continued to be heard in Finland, and the country's composers continued to write new music, in particular symphonies: while Sibelius was composing and twice revising his Fifth Symphony during the war years, Robert Kajanus was completing a sinfonietta, Erkki Melartin composed his Fifth Symphony, and Leevi Madetoja wrote his First Symphony. It was as though Finnish composers wanted to make a point of showing musical solidarity with Germany's still-admired civilization.

But the series of events that unfolded at the war's end, in connection with the Bolshevik Revolution in Russia, proved to be far worse than isolation. Retrospective accounts have treated Finnish independence as a preexisting condition to which "the nation" unwaveringly aspired, a kind of teleological genesis toward the revelation of an eternal truth. The reality was rather different.

During the Great War, Finland had officially backed Russia.[28] There were even Finns who volunteered for the imperial army to fight the Germans. The majority of the Finnish people harbored no separatist aspirations. With some exceptions (such as the Svecoman leader A. O. Freudenthal, who as early as 1863 was propagating the idea of Finland's liberation from Russia, presumably in the form of reintegration or union with Sweden), the notion of Finnish independence stood on no political party's agenda prior to 1917.[29] Accommodation with Russia, if not contentment, had been the operative assumption and had prevailed.

The reasons ran deep and included economic, political, and even cultural factors. At the war's outbreak the grand duchy was a stable and prosperous land. Statistics tell something of the story. A railroad that had begun with 67 miles of tracks in 1862 had spread to some 2,600 by 1914.[30] Between 1885 and 1913, imports and exports had increased fivefold. Finns benefited enormously from the trade with Russia, and the Sibelius families were no exception. Arvi Paloheimo, the husband of Sibelius's oldest daughter, Eva, had business connections in the city now called Petrograd, the city where Arvi and Eva were living in 1916 and where Aino Sibelius came to visit. From businessmen to arms makers to owners of homes and seaside villas, few had reason other than national pride to wish the Russians gone, and, as Anthony Upton has pointed out, "good hard currency is a great salve of injured pride."[31]

A manifestation of the reigning attitude was the art exhibition that opened in Petrograd in April 1917, after the overthrow of the czar, featuring some forty Finnish artists.[32] Paintings of the Septem group went on display, as did those of Tyko Sallinen, whose works were particularly successful in the Russian capital. Feelings of goodwill ran high. Maxim Gorky sent the Finns an effusive telegram, ending with "Eläköön Suomi" (Long live Finland). In turn, the Finns sent their Russian comrades a greeting through Gorky— "you, the representative of the spirit of freedom"—that was even more expansive: its signatories included Juho Rissanen, Axel Gallén, Eero Järnefelt, and Jean Sibelius. On the very day that Lenin returned to Russia from exile, Sergei Prokofiev, Robert Kajanus, Alexander Benois, Eero and Saimi Järnefelt, Nikolai Roerich, Ville Vallgren, Tyko Sallinen, and still more Finnish and Russian cultural leaders were gathering in Petrograd to mark the opening of the Finnish exhibition and celebrate "freedom, culture, and brotherhood." The fulsome speeches on every side, the fervid expressions of fraternity and sodality gave little indication that these aristocratic and intellectual-minded Finns harbored visions of independence from their "brothers." (Sibelius was not present on that occasion, having broken his seven-year abstinence from alcohol. Already in January he admitted that he had been trying to cultivate "a highly aristocratic" tone at the familiar watering holes.)[33]

Yet the seeds of separatism had not only been sown, they had also been fertilized and watered by Nikolai Bobrikov and his harsh policies. Some activists had begun to nurture real hopes for Finland's freedom in a Russian defeat. As Finnish composers clearly demonstrated through their music, there were many in Finland with pro-German sympathies, admiring of the land of Bach and Beethoven, Luther and Goethe. Among the most politically involved were students and faculty of the Imperial Alexander University. In the autumn of 1915 student activists had organized the Jaeger movement (Jääkäri in Finnish), a clandestine and soon to be notorious daredevil vanguard meant to provide Finland with a national liberation army. Over the next two and a half years, some 2,000 Finns slipped into Germany to join the 27th Prussian Jaeger Light Infantry Battalion.

As the war began coming to a close, the Jaegers represented a problem. In the grand duchy of an empire increasingly shading to Red, their militant, fascist-backed power made them traitors. Rumors flew. Word went around that the battalion would be disbanded. To boost morale, in August 1917 the Jaegers, who were bivouacked in Latvia, held a competition for words to a new marching song. The winner, Lieutenant Heikki Nurmio, had penned in Finnish a screed of *ryssänviha* (Russian hatred). It began:

> Deeply we strike, our hate unconquered,
> We have neither mercy nor homeland.

And as the lines came to a close, the poet invoked the vengeful Kullervo:

> We rise as Kullervo's vengeance
> It is sweet to try the fates of war.
> A new tale of Finland will be born,
> It grows, it attacks, it conquers.[34]

Then the Jaegers prevailed upon Jean Sibelius to set the poem to music. He agreed.

It was a startling assent. There was the personal danger: association with the Jaegers at this point could have meant a prison sentence.[35] Indeed, the text had to be smuggled into Finland. Nor did the composer dare to put his name to the finished composition, at least not right away. There was also the political statement: with the *Jääkärimarssi* Sibelius abandoned his famous ambiguities and dithering equivocalities. Now he positioned himself firmly on the non-Russian side of the issue engulfing all of Finland.

Not least there was the changed approach to the symbolism of Kullervo, a topic he knew well. Twenty-five years earlier Sibelius had made a profound reinterpretation of Kullervo's story by ignoring the emphasis on revenge and shifting the focus to a love scene (albeit one admittedly fraught with psychological complexity). Now, in October 1917, he set the stamp of his sympathies upon the hatreds that began to cleave Finland in two. Both the musical results and the song's fate suffered from this rancorous choice. Although the march had momentary success in the early days of the new republic, it was *Porilaisten marssi* (*The March of the Pori Regiment*), not the *Jaeger March*, that eventually became the Finnish army's signature piece.

Around this time, Sibelius pulled out the arrangement of the baritone aria in the *Kullervo* symphony (from the end of the third movement). He had arranged that solo, *Kullervo's Lament*, in the winter of 1892–93 to a German translation, *Kullervos Wehruf*, evidently in hopes of generating revenue from central Europe. Now, in the militant climate at the war's end, *Kullervo's Lament*, with its original Finnish words (*Kullervon valitus*) but in readily singable form for voice and piano, was arranged anew and published as a supplement to the periodical *Säveletär* (1918).[36] By contrast with the listeners who had filled the auditorium to hear the *Kullervo* symphony's premiere—refined, perfumed, Swedish-speaking, upper-class Finns—the potential audience for *Kullervo's Lament* was drastically different.

ഡ്രൊ

However brotherly the bonds between artists, as the Russian Empire disintegrated, Finland was inexorably drawn into the vortex.[37] As matters worsened, the gulf between Finnish socialists and Finnish nonsocialists deepened. With the October Revolution (November 7 by the Western calendar) and the Bolshevik seizure of power, events in Finland plunged toward a dramatic pass. There were configurations and reconfigurations of internal political alliances, with former enemies joining forces against new enemies. Finland's leading parties changed positions: the bourgeois now refused to recognize the Lenin-led Russian government; they plumped for independence. The Social Democrats in turn decided to support the Russian government, being, as they were, on good terms with the Bolsheviks. The socialists argued that independence could only arise through cooperation with Lenin's people. Sibelius's reaction was visceral: on November 23, 1917, he wrote in his diary, "Terrible happenings concerning the socialists' progress, [which are] crushing us patriots."

A week after the dramatic events of the October Revolution, the Finnish parliament resolved to assume the governing authority over the country, a de facto declaration of Finland's independence. Yet it took several weeks more to draft a document with appropriate wording and sufficient heft, a formal declaration of Finland as a free nation. Even then, the bitter animosities whose malicious energies had poisoned the Swedish and Finnish language groups against one another degenerated into petty fighting over wording. This profound moment in Finland's history was achieved with only a narrow margin of the governing bodies assembled (the senate acted as "the government," then sent its decisions to parliament for ratification). And its public announcement was equally laconic. On December 6, 1917, a statement in the country's leading newspaper, *Helsingin Sanomat*, addressed "To the People of Finland" ("Suomen kansalle") announced "an administrative change" in Finland, followed the next day by a slightly more expansive statement. With neither pomp nor circumstance, Finland became a free and separate nation.

Why did Lenin acquiesce to Finnish independence?[38] Ideologically, Lenin evidently believed each nation had the right to secede from Russia, certain that once the revolution spread, the secessionists would voluntarily and enthusiastically return to the fold. Independence would be merely a temporary stop on the road to a federation of Soviet republics. Realistically speaking, the Bolsheviks simply had too few resources to be able to carry on military operations. Convinced of Finland's eventual return, thanks to their Finnish Red brothers, Lenin and company took the pragmatic course of directing their limited energies elsewhere.

In November 1917, as these events were unfolding, Sibelius once more turned to Mikael Lybeck and made a setting of this poet's Swedish words, this time using *I systrar, I bröder, I älskande par!* (*O Sisters, O Brothers, O Loving Couples!*)—"one of the best *music* texts I've ever had!" he exulted.[39] A strange song, it portrays ordinary men and women at the tasks of weaving and plowing. Three musical strophes correspond to the three verses of the poem. The piano keeps up a near-constant, shimmering D-sharp, with repeated ostinato eighth notes (see ex. 21.2), reminiscent of *Gretchen am Spinnrad* (perhaps it was inspired by Schubert: Lybeck's first verse tells of three sisters weaving). But the words of the final stanza burn into the mind, reinforced by those relentless eighths and the poet's color imagery:

EXAMPLE 21.2. SIBELIUS, *I SYSTRAR, I BRÖDER, I ÄLSKANDE PAR!*, MM. 37–42.
© WILHELM HANSEN, COPENHAGEN.

Får elden i blodet	If the fire in the blood
bli flammande röd,	Turns flaming red,
den bränner till liv,	It burns you to life,
den bränner till död, till död.	It burns you to death, to death.

On New Year's Eve, 1917, Sibelius wrote in his diary, "Is it wise to isolate myself so completely? I've not heard an orchestra for nearly a year. Not met anyone, in fact. But— how to do otherwise?" As the composer wrote these lines, Lenin was recognizing Finnish independence.

☙❧

The dominant tone of the newly independent republic—militaristic, white, German-oriented—reverberated through the solemn "academic celebration . . . [in an] impassioned patriotic mood" held in the Festival Hall of the university on January 19, 1918.[40] Standards of the Imperial Alexander University and the Technological University stood side by side with banners of the Jaeger Battalion and Finland's coat of arms, where the

Finnish lion (the nation's flag at that moment) on a light blue iron cross was surrounded by black German eagles. J. J. Mikkola, a professor of Slavic philology, delivered a speech promoting Greater Finland—with German assistance. Celebration poems were read: V. A. Koskenniemi's Finnish poem dithyrambed in the sacrificial vein of *Song of the Athenians*, and Arvid Mörne's Swedish-language verses portrayed a direct connection to the Jaegers.

And there was militaristic music—Sibelius's. The evening began with *Finlandia*. The Swedish-language choir Akademiska Sångföreningen performed the *Jaeger March* with orchestra, in Swedish, directed by Olof Wallin. The audience stood. The chorus was repeated. The men's voices were then raised in *Die Wacht am Rhein*, the German anthem widely identified with hostility (to the French). It too had to be repeated. YL sang the Hungarian national song, *Sezozat*. Eino Välikangas gave a speech of lavish gratitude to our "Jaeger brothers." Heikki Klemetti conducted YL in the *Jaeger March*, this time in Finnish. It too had to be repeated.

What jars about the evening were the deep divisions in Finnish society clearly on display, even on such an intensely symbolic occasion as this, when the new and, one would presume, unified nation was being celebrated. One rift showed between the language groups. Even Finland's musicians contentiously refused to sing as one people. Another rift showed between Reds and Whites. The Social Democrats, who had voted against independence, were conspicuous by their absence. Their spokesman insisted that their place was with their "Russian comrades." The oppositional positions of the great powers, Germany and Russia, stood inalterably behind the occasion, to the point that the French consul took offense and exited in high dudgeon. "From the poems and speeches, one would almost have thought that it was really our 'Jaegers' who defeated Russia—albeit with Germany,"[41] Juhani Aho muttered into his diary.

The same year Breitkopf & Härtel published Sibelius's *Jääkärimarssi* in a dramatic cover. Against a black German cross, a fearsome imperial eagle, crowned with the diadem of the Hohenzollerns, clutches thunderbolts and a sword in its talons. The words *Pro Gloria et Patria* ring its head.

"THE PEOPLE'S WAR"

On January 28, 1918, Finland erupted into the unmitigated horror of civil war.[42]

Few had foreseen the coming strife between brother Finns. Yet the course had been set during the Great War. At that war's height, a massive Russian military presence had accumulated in Finland, well over 100,000 troops (estimates ranged as high as 150,000). Warships loomed menacingly in Helsinki's harbor. Russian soldiers tramped through the city's streets. The Finns, lacking an official armed force of their own and having only a weak police force, became increasingly apprehensive. Out of their fears arose the defense organizations that would play a terrible role in their lives: the White (or Civil) Guards, from the nonsocialist ranks of society; and the Red Guards, formed of Social Democrats and other leftists.

When fighting erupted between Reds and Whites, the populace was stunned. The elite—artists, composers, poets, writers, and others who had built the national image and fostered the national movement—had enjoyed being in the national limelight, but the sad truth was that they were largely indifferent to the serious problems of the working class. Having created an idealized and unrealistic image of "the people," suddenly they were faced with a working-class uprising that threatened to overthrow an order they had taken for granted. The upper classes' worst nightmare—murderous mobs of uncouth proletarian hooligans unleashed on a civilized society—seemed to have materialized.

But the elite were not the only members of society to be rudely surprised. So were most of the combatants. Without Russia to maintain order, the solidarity of the proletariat with the educated class—a basic tenet of Finnish national ideology—collapsed. With that collapse went the myth of a united Finnish people. The new power holders announced the formation of a Socialist People's Council to the Bolshevik government in Petrograd. A new Red government, the "People's Commission," took charge of the more populous southern part of the country, where some three-quarters of the population supported their cause. The Reds took control of telephones, telegraphs, and railroads; they banned such newspapers as *Helsingin Sanomat*, *Hufvudstadsbladet*, and *Uusi Suometar*. Only the workers' papers—*Työmies* (*The Laborer*) and *Kansanvaltuuskunnan Tiedonantolehti* (*The People's Herald*)—were allowed to continue. Meanwhile, the White "government in exile" was forced to base its operations in the north and west (in Ostrobothnia).

Although the battles of the Great War had taken place elsewhere (and were still), Finland's Civil War rolled out horrifically close to home. No one was immune. Gallén skied from his home to the front and fought for two weeks for the Whites until he was discovered by Mannerheim, who put him to work designing uniforms and insignias. ("But how will I be paid?" Gallén allegedly asked. "Paid?" barked the general. "I thought you were rich!") Sibelius has often been portrayed as essentially apolitical, and it is true that, like many highly creative people, he lived in a world of his own. Yet no one had the luxury of ignoring contemporary events in a land riven by fraternal conflict. His home at Järvenpää was in territory held by Reds, and people feared for their lives. "Murder after murder," the composer scribbled into the diary on February 2, 1918; "proletarian mob power grows like an avalanche."

Statistics can represent the scale, but not the horror, of the killings. Gösta Schyberg-son, just twenty-four years old, a physician and a member of the choir Akademiska Sång-föreningen, was seized at work and marched off to be executed on the very day Sibelius made that murderous diary entry. Erik Hernberg, a close friend of Sibelius's daughter Katarina, was shot. The brother of the composer Leevi Madetoja was killed at the hands of Reds. The poet Juhani Siljo, a Red sympathizer, died of wounds sustained in the fight-ing. The greatest single loss to Finnish music was Toivo Kuula, only thirty-five, who had played the piano for the victors, then was murdered in an altercation between Reds and Whites just after the war's end. Others were imprisoned: the composer Aarre Merikanto, son of Oskar. And Christian Sibelius, now a supervising doctor at the mental hospital Lapinlahti in Helsinki, although he was incarcerated only briefly, having refused Red sol-diers beds at his hospital.

As in civil wars everywhere, families were divided. Aino's brother Arvid Järnefelt sympathized with both Whites and Reds. His sermonizing on the message of love got him arrested and a night in prison. Aino, by contrast, was a zealous White. Not even the children of Reds were welcome at Ainola, nor were they allowed to play at her brother Eero's home, Suviranta.

The Sibelius family's difficulties during this time are well-known:[43] how Ainola was searched by Red Guards; how that self-appointed savior Kajanus turned his Christ-like face outward and obtained permission to bring the family into Helsinki to live with Christian and Nelma Sibelius; how the food shortages began to take their toll. Sibelius lost some forty-five pounds during the two months in Helsinki, and his hair began to thin. Already at the time of the "Sallinen wars" in 1912, Sibelius had begun looking like a set-tled, self-satisfied aristocrat. But by the end of the People's War, the increasing loss of his hair led him to shave his head.[44] The solid, granitic look of conservative militarism fit the stern, ascetic image of the new nation. But like Samson, with his hair went his strength.

THE AFTERMATH

Finland's civil war was brief—some three months. But the damage inflicted on the young nation persists even as these words are being written. The Sibelius family returned to Ainola, and as elsewhere in Finland, a semblance of normality returned. But that normal-ity was a façade. In countless personal documents, from diaries to correspondence, the state of shock in which the war left the Finns keens from tear-stained pages. The wounds ran so deep that even now, early in the twenty-first century, reconciliation has not yet been fully achieved.

True, Finland was a free and independent republic.[45] Yet nearly half of its population—40 percent—belonged to the losing side in the Civil War. And treachery had been exacted on every side. Outside Finland, it has been difficult to appreciate the depth of the bitterness, how far its poison seeped into Finnish soil, and how deeply divided was society. No one went unscathed. The victorious White Finns saw themselves in highly moral terms; they viewed the Reds as anarchists who had consorted with the enemy and connived to undermine Finland's newly won independence. Resentment rankled, festered, and leached into the war's subsequent accounts. Because the victors write the histories, historical descriptions blamed Red Finns for the war.[46] Reds were portrayed as traitors; Whites, as the just and incorruptible people of Finland who had fought for home, faith, and fatherland. The racial theories circulating widely in the period fed into the image of Reds who were seen as a symptom of an infected plague, somehow not even Finnish.

Although class differences were clearly part of this picture, division into Reds and Whites was by no means strictly along class lines. There were members of the educated classes who supported the proletariat; there were crofters who had supported the emperor. The dissensions showed at Tuusula, where the Sibelius neighbors were far from unified in their views of the conflict. Juhani Aho opposed amnesty for Red "traitors"—and made his sympathies publicly known in a densely packed, four-column article headed "Armahdustako?" ("Amnesty?") in *Helsingin Sanomat*; meanwhile, Eino Leino was insisting, "Where would we be without the Social Democratic movement?"[47]

The immediate aftermath to the shock of the war was the horror of retributions. It has been estimated that some eighty thousand Finns died, a huge number from a population of fewer than four million people.[48] Many Reds were shot in the act of surrendering. Many more perished in prison camps, where appalling conditions bred disease and caused starvation. The sorrow reached deep into people's lives in unimaginable ways. For a time, it was a crime for the living to honor fallen Reds. It was symptomatic that by 1929, there were over three hundred memorial stones or markers for the victors, but fewer than twelve for the defeated. It was even forbidden to put flowers or names on Red graves—assuming these could be found. Many soldiers lay where they had been executed, in woods, bogs, or gravel pits, their graves unmarked. Knowledge of their whereabouts spread only by word of mouth.

Even though officially the government reversed this ruling as early as 1918, in practice people feared to honor their dead; flowers left on graves were destroyed by nightfall; memorial stones were removed. The men bore the brunt of the horrible behavior, yet wives and girlfriends of Red soldiers came in for their share of ill treatment. They were ostracized, accused of having consorted with the enemy. Widows of Red soldiers had little recourse in the new state; many were reduced to begging. And the children suffered: some twenty thousand were orphaned, of whom most were the offspring of Red families.

Not even religion offered the people comfort. The Lutheran church was associated with the victorious Whites, and many parish priests treated the Reds as Antichrists; some even refused to sanction Christian burials for Red soldiers. The two Finlands that had been divided by language—Finnish and Swedish—were now further splintered into irreconcilable Red and White factions. And those factions lived in different conceptual worlds, perhaps best epitomized by their differing perceptions of the Whites' general, Carl Gustaf Mannerheim: for the Whites, he was a hero; for the Reds, a beast.

Those different worlds had existed for a long time, but the overwhelming pressures of the Russian "oppression" had blurred their borders.[49] Even at the beginning of the twentieth century, the fissures had been clearly visible everywhere in daily life, reinforced by where people shopped, where they banked, where they socialized. The forced choices fostered oppositional attitudes in subliminal ways, a dualism that the war starkly magnified. As early as 1900 food cooperatives had grown up along ideological lines. The cooperative Suomen Osuuskauppojen Keskuskunta (SOK, whose S-Markets still exist in modern Finland and whose department stores have been called Sokos since the 1950s), represented a right-wing organization; its bright green cards differentiated the members unequivocally from leftist, "Red" groups who had a cooperative of their own, Osuustukkukauppa (OTK; their stores were later called Elanto). Banks too divided the populace. So did newspapers. Red sympathizers banked with Työväen säästöpankki, read *Työmies* (which changed its name to *Uutispäivä Demari*), and voted for the Social Democrats. Those who identified with "pure" Finnishness did their banking at such establishments as Kansallis-Osake-Pankki (KOP) and read the now-defunct newspaper *Uusi Suomi*, which had used the Civil—White—Guard as its logo. They voted for the Kokoomus (Coalition) Party; their elite patronized Suomalainen klubi (the Finnish Club), founded as a political organization for urban Fennomans in the 1880s. Swedish-speaking Finns had their own banking establishments (Nordiska Föreningsbanken, the present Nordea), newspapers (*Hufvudstadsbladet*), and clubs. Children learned early "not to go" where the other part of their society shopped, banked, or gathered.

Along with separate banks, political parties, and newspapers, there were also separate insurance companies, separate farmers' associations, separate choral groups, and separate youth organizations. Among the ones for educating young people, those called Nuorisoseura, or Ungdomsförening in Swedish, advocated patriotic and Christian ideals and opposed the radical workers' movement in the countryside. The Nuorisoseura built their own halls and the Social Democrats built theirs, segregating even social activities along ideological lines.[50] The People's War caused those social fractures to rupture, leaving critically wounded hearts and minds and devastated lives.

Although in the context of a composer's life it might seem tangential to dwell on a civil war and its sorrows, this conflict was one of the cataclysmic events precipitated by the Bolshevik Revolution, which in turn was the most calamitous upheaval any European nation had experienced in modern times. Furthermore, Finland's Civil War was intricately bound up with the issues unleashed by its national awakening. Not only was Sibelius not immune, he was as profoundly and irrevocably affected as was everyone else in the former Russian Empire.

The new status of independence was destabilizing enough. However glorious it sounded, no one knew which of the many alternatives for the future would be realized or how. Some thought the Bolsheviks would not last and a new emperor would emerge to take control in Russia, with clear consequences for Finland. Meanwhile, the links to Germany remained strong. Many viewed the Germans as the best hope for protection from the newly created communist monster lurking on the eastern border (hence the plan, thwarted by Germany's defeat at the war's end, to appoint a Finnish king to be recruited from German aristocracy; a monarchy was seen by many as the means to strengthen and stabilize the new Finland).[51] Personal as well as political hopes ran to extremes in those circumstances.[52] The awfulness of that climate of uncertainty, the demoralizing effects of not knowing where your allegiances should lie, the inability to make firm plans for a future that no one had any way of knowing how to conceptualize affected all Finns.

For artists and intellectuals, the People's War was the ultimate blow. As Risto Alapuro writes, "the 'people' had stabbed a *puukko* [the knife widely carried by rural Finns] into the back of its own intelligentsia."[53] With the Civil War, it became clear that the golden-age awakening had gone horribly awry. Instead of the benign image so many had imagined of them, "the people" turned out to be infected with the red plague of communism, unruly and uncouth members of an impossible-to-educate class. Instead of a unified and benevolent stratum of gentle Finnish folk to glorify through music, art, and literature, there were now snarling factions whose unity had to be forcibly maintained by the militaristic might of a new republic, the very survival of which was far from guaranteed.

The whole demoralizing atmosphere bred a deadening spiritual depression. Even before the war, Sibelius's generation had begun to lose its bearings in a world of tango, two-step, moving pictures, and expressionist art. Now the Civil War did away completely with their former stimulating lives. Borders were closed to travel and to ideas from afar. Within those borders, ideals had been turned upside down. Nothing and no one was as it had seemed. The "powerful feeling of expansiveness" that had prevailed from the 1890s well into 1914 turned inward. It was as if the population had to gather its innermost resources unto itself and batten down simply to survive.[54]

The consequences were enormous—and for creative minds, devastating. The effect

Figure 21.1. Helene Schjerfbeck, *Ompelijatar* (*Työläisnainen*) (*The Seamstress [Female Worker]*), 1927. Oil on canvas. Mikkeli Art Museum/Central Art Archives. Photo: Janne Mäkinen.

can partially be gauged by the situation of other composers, those born in Sibelius's generation but who lived outside this closed world. In fact, most had died by the mid-1920s: Busoni, Debussy, Mahler, Puccini, Wolf. But Richard Strauss and Carl Nielsen, though changed, were very much alive and busily composing. Even more telling is the fate of those who, like Sibelius, were at the epicenter of people's war and revolution, those on the eastern side of the Russia-Finland border. For a border it was. Its gates slammed shut, forcing Finnish exports to a screeching halt, freezing artistic exchange to a standstill. In isolated Petrograd, Glazunov, born in 1865 like Sibelius, left off composing, turning to administration instead. Feodor Chaliapin (1873–1938), also living in Petrograd, although acknowledging "that at the very basis of the Bolshevik movement there was a striving for a real restructuring of life on a more just footing, as it was perceived by Lenin and some of his comrades," felt that the "robot would choke me if I didn't get out of its inanimate embrace."[55] Chaliapin left for the West.

And there was the poet Alexander Blok, born in 1880. Blok stopped writing poetry. "All sounds have disappeared," he would say when asked. "Can't you hear that there are no sounds?" When Blok died, on August 7, 1921, it was clear to his friends and contemporaries that he had suffocated—as he had often told them: "I'm suffocating, suffocating, suffocating! We're suffocating, we will all suffocate. The world revolution is turning into world angina pectoris!"[56]

On the western side of the border, in the former grand duchy, the airlessness of the new, closed-down, wounded regime brought on spiritual asthma there too, extinguishing creative life. Those like Eliel Saarinen who went abroad found that their art was rejuvenated. Those who stayed behind to contribute to the nation they had created paid dearly. Two paintings by Helene Schjerfbeck give eloquent voice to Finland's changed atmosphere. During the 1880s Schjerfbeck had created a vibrant oil painting called *Espanjalainen* (*The Spaniard*). Alive with lustrous colors, *The Spaniard*'s seductive dark eyes and vital, masculine energy make the blood race, more than a century after he posed proudly before the canvas (see plate 11). In stark contrast is the artist's bloodless, sexless portrait of a seamstress from the 1920s (see fig. 21.1)—a neurotic, minimalist rendering of a worker from whom all life has been drained.

In that climate Gallén was reduced to designing flags and uniforms. Eino Leino drowned himself in drink. Juhani Aho faded into obscurity. And Jean Sibelius slowly lapsed into a silence from which he never emerged.

～22～

Onward, Ye Powerful People!

Pontevasti [Energetically]

Käy ees - päin, vä - ki voi - ma-kas, äl' or - ja - jouk - ko hal - pa

THE DISPLAY ON THE NATION'S CABINET

The people meanwhile were oblivious to the creative fate of their artists.[1] The Finns have a saying: "kansakunnan kaapin päällä" ([display the emblems] on the nation's cabinet). With the birth of the Finnish republic, the people began to lavish attention on that display.

No better example can be found than the plans for a "Kalevala House." The idea came from the Kalevala Society, one of the first associations established in independent Finland, organized in December 1919. Among the founding members were Axel Gallén and his student, the Hämeenlinna-born Alpo Sailo (1877–1955), whose sculpture of the *runo* singer Larin Paraske sits today in the park between Finlandia Hall and the Opera House. The purpose of the Kalevala Society, whose first honorary member was Jean Sibelius,[2] was to advance scholarly and artistic activities in connection with the national cultural tradition, particularly the *Kalevala*. In fact, the Society's *raison d'être* was to build a monumental Kalevala House for the nation in which to immortalize Finland's great men and their magnificent deeds.

The idea was for a vast complex, a museum combined with a research institute, "for Finnish people and [Finnish] culture."[3] Eliel Saarinen offered to design the structure, and his grandiose plans reflect the scale of the founders' dreams and aspirations as well as the

399

meanings now invested in the *Kalevala* and the reverence accorded the creative personalities linked to it. Saarinen's design called for a tower almost 280 feet high, surrounded
by two enormous concentric circles. There was to be a courtyard for the main building,
encompassing the museum, a two-story-high concert hall, an art gallery, a lofty crypt for
burying famous men, a domed memorial hall ("the Pantheon"), rooms for the Kalevala
Society, space for working artists and composers, and not least, archival vaults and library
facilities where scholars could study Sibelius's manuscripts and Gallén's sketches.

Kalevala House was never built; its plans were gradually abandoned owing to financial difficulties and other problems. But like the melting of the ice on the Oulu River,
it signaled the bursting of an energy stream that inexorably swept Sibelius up in its
powerful currents. Sibelius had an important role to play in the new republic, but his was
a part invented by the people, not a character truly his own. Rather like a royal family
member whose duties are peripheral to the real work of governing, Sibelius was trotted
out to open official functions, grace state proceedings, and lend his illustrious name to
institutes, schools, and musical ensembles. That activity reached its zenith in the 1930s,
when the Sibelius Quartet was christened with his name (1933) and "the master's" former
school, the Helsinki Music Institute, became the Sibelius Academy (1939)—a particularly
ironic choice, given that the institute's driving force and longtime director had been Martin Wegelius, not Jean Sibelius.[4]

The Finnish people further saw to it that their great composer's name was seen and
heard abroad. In 1930 the Finnish Government took an unprecedented step for a national government: it helped to subsidize recordings of its national composer's music.[5]
The Columbia Graphophone Company produced the recordings in London, where Robert Kajanus was brought for the purpose of conducting the First and Second Symphonies. Fifty thousand Finnish marks from the nation's coffers went into these recordings
so that "Finnish music would receive a stimulus all over the world."[6] Five years later the
composer permitted an "official" biography to be written (by Karl Ekman, Jr., son of his
friends the musicians Karl and Ida); it was translated into English by Edward Birse and,
kitted out with an introduction by the eminent Ernest Newman, also distributed from
London, by the firm of Alan Wilmer. One of those life histories of great men romanticized to depict a solitary genius struggling against impossible odds, the biography
simply left uncomfortable truths, such as Sibelius having studied with a Russian violinist,
unstated; for the nation there should be an unsullied, fully republican hero.

Along with being put on display, Sibelius was needed to help create that display. There
was no shortage of opportunity. The same month that the Kalevala Society was founded,
the opening of an art gallery, Stenman and Hörhammer's, marked the first art event in
the new republic of Finland. Gösta Stenman was the entrepreneur who had championed

the rascal Tyko Sallinen, and the inauguration of his new showrooms on December 1, 1919—Helsinki's largest art salon and "the Nordic countries' handsomest"—was turned into a state occasion.[7] The new nation's first president, K. J. Ståhlberg, was conspicuously on hand. So were government officials, members of Helsinki's diplomatic corps, and some six hundred invited guests—politicians, university faculty, artists, socialites, foreigners, and representatives of the art market who crowded into the showrooms. A stylish standard with a red "S" on a golden background fluttered in the breeze before the gallery doors. On view were hundreds of paintings by the new nation's old artists: Pekka Halonen, Magnus Enckell, Helene Schjerfbeck, Fanny Churberg, Juho Rissanen. An entire room was devoted to works of Gallén, who now was called Gallen-Kallela. Another was given over to Albert Edelfelt. Afterward a lavish dinner was staged for the new republic's artistic "establishment" (for there already was one): Sibelius, Gallén, Eero Järnefelt, Mikael Lybeck, Emil Wikström, Hjalmar Procopé, and all the rest. Its atmosphere was captured by the Russian artist Ilya Repin (whose villa and studio on the Karelian isthmus had remained on the Finnish side of the border) in the enormous canvas called *Suomen suurmiehiä* (*The Great Men of Finland*; see plate 12).[8]

Sibelius had accepted a commission to compose music for the occasion. The text he was given was not in Finnish, but in Swedish: *Ej av jaktens lekar*, written by Procopé (one of the classically oriented Euterpists). Even at the dawn of the republic, Swedish continued to be the language widely used for administrative purposes and the tongue most comfortable for its leaders. Sibelius, however, gave his new composition a French title, *Scène pastorale*, later calling it *Autrefois*. No nod to the proletariat there; French was the language of culture and refinement and had also been the language of the Russian court.

Autrefois has been seen as reflecting the neoclassicism and nostalgia widely evident in the arts after the Great War. Yet coming from the composer of the Fourth Symphony, its artificially gay, eighteenth-century-styled allegretto sounds anything but genuine: it pretends, it placates. The turn from major to minor after the glib opening introduces two solo voices, directed to sing *con sentimento*: the orchestra accompanies with a weird combination of Debussyesque, half-step oscillations in the violins and Sturm und Drang–like syncopations throbbing in violas and cellos.[9] The whole effect is one of preciosity, contrivance, and mockery. Behind it is bitterness: it sounds as though Sibelius has lost his way.

The composer knew it. Almost a year later, he exclaimed into his diary, "If only *Autrefois* were good—but it isn't. Oh, woe!"[10] "The people," however, reacted as if they had heard the angels themselves: "a sublime and captivating composition that, like a genuine pearl, shall radiate with immortal luster" was the far-fetched reaction of *Hufvudstadsbladet*'s critic.[11] Some said Sibelius had composed another *Valse triste*. "But I don't believe it," Sibelius wrote with affected modesty to his publisher, Wilhelm Hansen; "still, I had to play it three times in a row at a concert."[12] With those words Jean Sibelius revealed himself to be a master of spin; the truth was, the "cantata," as it was being called, had to be repeated simply to give different members of the huge circulating crowd a chance to hear it. Was he succumbing to the danger Busoni had seen long years before? "Nothing appears [in Finland] that is not *good* or *talented*," Busoni had written; "if I were to get into the habit of assessing my ability in relation to my surroundings, what kind of a figure would I *actually* cut?"[13]

Sibelius was too intelligent to believe the preposterous critical reactions, because they only confirmed what he himself knew at some level: he had lost touch with his audience. "The people" for whom he believed he had been composing no longer existed— if ever they had. The plaints in his diary show it clearly: "I have no success with the masses," he had written early in the war years. A later entry sounded bitter: "Here at home the public's interest is certainly no longer in me."[14] When in March 1919 his faithful advocate, Axel Carpelan, died, the news struck him like a hammer blow. His outburst, "For whom shall I compose now?,"[15] was the cry of a man whose lifeline had been ripped from his grasp.

POWER FOR THE PEOPLE

Sibelius's artistic life had changed. Instead of being fired by lofty goals to awaken the hearts and enlighten the minds of the Finnish *kansa*—the people—in thrilling events that combined art, theater, historical trappings, and music, all affirming an ancient and powerful Finnish identity, more and more often he was relegated to appearances in the service of growing mass consumerism—trade fairs, industrial exhibitions, commercial ventures. In the summer of 1920, when independent Finland held its first industrial fair as a nation, there was Sibelius, conducting no fewer than five concerts. Even though the fair had an artistic component (the planners had included Finland's leading architects Eliel Saarinen and Armas Lindgren, Carolus Lindberg, and Alvar Aalto) and even some political resonance (the previous April, Poles had attacked Russians, raising national sympathies with the "brothers" across the Baltic), the happening was first and foremost a commercial and trade event. Nearly a thousand exhibitors attended, of whom some two hundred were foreign businesses and associations. Above the summer straw hats, fedoras, bowlers, and workers' caps, Sibelius's patrician top hat stood out as prominently as the flying Finnish flags.

Then there was that episode of the "Imatra Symphony." Imatra, where the Vuoksi River rushes into its magnificent rapids, had for some decades been promoted by the

Tourist Association as one of the jewels in the grand duchy's crown of natural beauties. The site had attracted the elite of Finland and especially of Russia (Igor Stravinsky had famously honeymooned beside its foaming waters). Now this nationally promoted landscape was to be industrialized for the benefit of the nation's democratic and commercial needs: an ambitious development project was launched to harness the waterfall's power.[16] Between 1922 and 1927, to the tune of some 400 million Finnish marks, a hydroelectric plant was constructed at Imatra.

The Finnish tenor Wäinö Sola (1883–1961) began promoting the idea that Sibelius should be commissioned to compose a symphony of one hundred players for the plant's inauguration. Sola even wrote out a program for an "Imatra Symphony." The plan was for the composer to premiere the work in the great turbine hall, the president of Finland would open the sluice gates, and the waters that had given such inspiration to Finnish art and music would plummet forth, bringing power to the people.

Sibelius went as far as to make a trip to Imatra, spending a day with Sola and the CEO of the Imatra Power Company, Hugo Malmi (1878–1952). Together they toured the plant, visited the rapids, and discussed inaugural plans. But when the plant was christened by the president of the republic, Lauri Kristian Relander, on May 25, 1929, there was no symphony—and no Sibelius.

The reasons the composer gave for declining this opportunity were profoundly revealing. One was the expense of a big Helsinki orchestra. This was another of those diverting spins: Sibelius had rarely if ever been known to worry about expense. But the other reasons struck the chords of truth: one was that his recent works (*Academic March*, *Hymn of the Earth*, and *Väinämöinen's Song*, all composed for national purposes) had not been performed after their commissioned events and had found no publisher (meaning the composer had recouped little or no financial return). But the third reason was the most telling: "I doubt if the festival audience," said Sibelius, "would have enough patience to listen to nothing but the orchestra for such a long time."[17]

MUSIC FOR THE PEOPLE

Clive Bell (1881–1964), a British art critic and philosopher, writing in 1914, may not have known Sibelius and Finland personally, but his words hit uncannily close to home. "Society," he said,

> can affect Art indirectly because it can affect artists directly. . . . The one good thing Society can do for the artist is to leave him alone. Give him liberty. The more completely the artist is freed from the pressure of public taste and opinion,

from the hope of rewards and the menace of morals, from the fear of absolute starvation or punishment, and from the prospect of wealth or popular consideration, the better for him and the better for art, and therefore the better for everyone.[18]

Finnish society and its people had changed, and not just in their less docile and more belligerent self-image. The fabulously successful educational programs and people's concerts, to which Sibelius had contributed splendidly through the 1890s and beyond, had appealed to larger and more eager audiences. But the problem was that "the people will pay the piper and call the tune," as Bell remarked. "In the choice of politicians the method works well enough, but to art it would be fatal. . . . When all works of art are public monuments, do you seriously expect to have any art at all?"[19]

In Finland, musical standards and public taste seemed indeed to have gone the way forecast by the architect Jac Ahrenberg almost two decades earlier. In 1918, in an article entitled "The Future of Our Musical Cultivation" ("Musiikillisen viljelyksemme tulevaisuus"), Gallén's son-in-law, the ethnomusicologist A. O. Väisänen (1890–1969), publicly posed the question that haunted the pages of Sibelius's diary:

> Are our people artistically mature enough to bring about a new peak any time soon, to produce a new crescendo? An honest answer seems to be no. We do not think we err badly in making the claim that Sibelius has permanently captured at most only half the concertgoing public with his first three symphonies. The large part of the Finnish public "understands" only choral music and claps heartily only for small orchestral pieces. That such is apparently a developmental prerequisite, however, is affirmed by those "names," among whom many have risen straight out of humble origins. Our older educated classes who go in for music have the great credit of having provided the necessary favorable climate for fostering Finnish music. But more than one young Finnish composer who today seeks comparable circumstances groans upon realizing that such a climate is difficult, if not impossible, to find. The broad educated public is slipping away to operettas.[20]

The role prescribed for Jean Sibelius was beginning to take its toll. In the decade after the People's War, the quality of his music meant for public monuments diminished: the works he wrote for the nation—*Academic March*, *Hymn of the Earth*, and *Väinämöinen's Song*—had been quickly forgotten for the simple reason that they weren't very good. And his music was not the only thing that changed. His appearance changed as well. Sibelius had always dressed meticulously, even at home: bespoke suits, handmade shirts, the finest leather shoes. Now, if anything, he became even more fastidious: sharply creased cuffs, elegantly finished buttonholes, stylishly pressed collars. It was as though, faced with an awakened proletariat whose plebeian tastes bred mass production and mass consumerism, he found a way to rebel in the most personal of ways. While his granite-like shaved head proclaimed his White sympathies, his very mode of dress insisted on his elitist position, even in his private domain.

Outsiders looked askance at what was happening. In 1923 the Swedish critic and composer Wilhelm Peterson-Berger (1867–1942), whom Sibelius despised for his scathing criticisms, described the Finn during a Stockholm concert appearance:

> Many a young lady may well have attended in order to set eyes on the creator of *Valse triste* [expecting] to find him slim, pale, handsome, fashionable and with perhaps a touch of the bohemian, as she had imagined him from his portrait and his music. But, oh, dear! Instead, she beheld a rather thickset and bald gentleman, who indeed behaved like a man of the world, but on the program officially bore the title professor. (How can you *do* that when you are Jean Sibelius!) Such a note from the world of institutionalized, systematized vanity sobers and saddens not only teenaged girls.[21]

However cruel his remarks, the critic had shrewdly recognized what was behind the change in Jean Sibelius, a change his Finnish compatriots did not wish to see: the nation had placed its icon on its collective cabinet, and the institutionalization of their national composer was effectively complete.

At some level Sibelius realized what was happening. In a litany of complaints about schedules, commissions, art, and his "aristocratic" past as well as his own foibles, including the return to the whiskey that was guiding his hand on that day, the composer confided to his diary:

> Can't be alone. Drinking whiskey. "The constitution" can't take it.—Painters— the more they decorate the walls of the riffraff, the better. Altar pieces, family tableaux! To hell. Anguish—anguish! Ja, ja. *Perhaps Gallén's life and mine have gone for the fatherland.* I was someone else in 1896. But the critics and the public. Dumber than God is wise![22]

In vino veritas.

∾23∾

The Militaristic State

FEATURES OF THE NEW FINLAND

For conceptualizing the changes in the new republic of Finland, there is no better visual aid than Helsinki's architecture.[1] The city's imperial center gives grandiose testimony to the benevolent aspects of Russian rule. Around Senate Square, the Nicholas Church, the statue of Alexander II, and the Imperial Alexander University bespeak pure Saint Petersburg. Down Alexander's Street into the business district, the Pohjola Building and other stone structures testify to the "stone movement" (1890–1910), whose enthusiasts had embraced Finnish granite and soapstone as a means of expressing national "truths." The street ends at Stockmann's department store, a bow to German architecture. Representing the ultramodern when it was built between 1916 and 1930, that temple of materialism offered a plethora of goods from books to bicycles to satisfy the mass consumer wants increasingly in demand in Finland. It does so still today.

With independence and the deep changes in Finnish society, architecture had followed suit. Nineteenth-century Helsinki was a city of growing bourgeoisie and a swelling proletariat. In the 1920s, in the aftermath of the wars and the rise of a new middle class, a "pure Finnish" quarter called Töölö began going up around the National Museum. There white-collar families and independent women came to live. The contrast with the old nineteenth-century capital could hardly have been more pronounced. Consciously avoiding the faintest whiff of anything Russian by looking westward to Scandinavia and, even farther, the United States, Finnish architects began constructing a new district built along neoclassical and new urban ideals: the Italianate Taidehalli or Konsthallen (Art Hall) in Töölö, built in 1928; and the monolithic Parliament House, constructed between 1926 and 1931, boasting fourteen columns on its façade, each crowned with a Corinthian capital. The political statement was unmistakable: that enormous cube of reddish Kalvola granite represented an unbreachable stronghold of republican values.

During the 1930s Finnish architects borrowed structural features from international functionalist ideals. Trademark white surfaces, for example. "White" functionalism, initially employed for institutional buildings such as military barracks and hospitals, gradually became the de facto official style of the Finnish republic. Those clean surfaces, standing in stark contrast to the red brick buildings of the imperial army, symbolized purity and authenticity, eerily incarnating the division into red and white that had played out so tragically in the People's War. In postwar Finland, the victors sanitized the country with dazzling white structures, the very incarnation of the "purity of the Finns," an injunction still being taught to Finnish schoolchildren after World War II. "White" radiated simplicity and self-discipline, good hygiene and cleanliness, health and sunlight. Its impact endures: Alvar Aalto's Finlandia Hall, designed in the 1960s, was finished in radiant white marble; the walls of the National Opera, completed in 1993, soar heavenward in gleaming white. White Finland saw itself as patriotic and righteous, defenders of a nation that, according to Hegelian theory, had existed as an entity for centuries and was immortal.

Architecture makes concrete the more difficult-to-grasp aspects of the new Finland, where ideological positions metamorphosed and hardened and where the arts were starkly politicized—a place where, as the art historian Olli Valkonen has observed, "Modernism in art was not a cornerstone of the new nation."[2] It was an atmosphere that favored proletarian tastes and a desire to build a unified and militarily strong state in a spirit of cooperation. Works of prose favored as "classics" in that climate—Johannes Linnankoski's *Laulu tulipunaisesta kukasta* (*Song of the Blood-Red Flower*, 1905), Ilmari Kianto's *Punainen viiva* (*The Red Line*, 1909), F. E. Sillanpää's *Hurskas kurjuus* (*Meek Heritage*, 1919), Joel Lehtonen's *Putkinotko* (a title designating a place, 1919–20)—were powerful metaphors for creating a unified national literature that reached across class difference.[3] Conditions fostered a stern conservatism. Criticizing and idolizing the new age in the spirit of futurism were hardly acceptable in a new nation that needed unifying monuments to liberty and fallen war heroes.

In painting, palettes darkened. In Alvar Cawén's (1886–1935) *Venäjän laivasto Helsingin satamassa* (*The Russian Fleet in Helsinki's Harbor*, 1918), the cubic shapes of the fleet and the black smoke of their engines occupy the canvas front and center, although their ill-omened force does not obscure the church on the Great Square, clearly seen in the upper left background, bathed in radiant "White" light. Cawén's contemporary, Marcus Collin (1882–1966), an artist who had studied with Eero Järnefelt at the Imperial Alexander University as well as in Paris, was one of the few Finns to depict the struggles of the working class. In somber, dismal-colored canvases, Collin portrayed immigrants, factory workers, farmhands—not as individuals, but as faceless members of a social class.

In sculpture the new conditions were even more starkly set forth. In Tampere, the seat of Finland's labor movement and the city where Lenin and Stalin first met, Wäinö Aaltonen (1894–1966) was commissioned to create statues for the new bridge spanning the Tammerkoski rapids, Uusi Hämeensilta. The four figures Aaltonen sculpted in 1927 are outstanding examples of the right-wing political ideology that held sway and with which the artist was closely identified: monumental in size—each figure is more than twelve feet high—these nude sculptures embody archetypal Finnishness. Their "racially" identifiable Finnish features and robust physiques symbolized the militaristic atmosphere of the new Finland and uncomfortably evoked ideas being promoted in the Third Reich and Italy.[4]

An advancing tide of racial theories, already on the rise before the war, flooded Finnish society, causing further anxieties and strains. Darwinism was being widely discussed around Europe, and racial studies, including eugenics, the idea of "the nobility of race," flourished. Among the self-conscious Finns, long concerned with determining the antiquity and nobility of their people and now struggling to establish their position as an independent nation in the wider European community, these questions were deeply felt and widely discussed. Nietzsche's doctrine of the Superman exerted its seductive allure in Finland as it did in other Nordic lands; as Janne Gallen-Kallela-Sirén has observed, the "projections [of social and political utopias] and the subsequent success of the social welfare state tend to mask the chauvinist underpinnings of turn of the century Nordic art and thought."[5]

During the 1920s the Finnish economy began to recover, and businesses began to prosper. So did some of the creative personalities in the younger generation. But Sibelius and other golden-age artists had had the pillars of their identity ruinously damaged, the props knocked out from under them. On what foundation stones were they now to build?

PILLAR I: "MOTHER" RUSSIA

Throughout the nineteenth century dynamic tension vis-à-vis the Russian Empire had been a powerful force driving business and artistic creativity alike. Imperial coffers had made possible travel stipends for study abroad and ongoing state support for artists and intellectuals. Many Finns had cultivated not only business and artistic connections with Russians, but also personal relationships. Finnish children were named for the emperors and for famous Russian generals. On their deaths the emperors appeared to be genuinely mourned: Alexander II was the most deeply lamented, but there were those who recalled that the people had also grieved when Nicholas I died in 1855. And plenty of icono-

graphic and other evidence survives to show that the Finns royally welcomed the emperors on their imperial visits to Finland, even as late as the summer of 1889.[6]

But the new republic of Finland belched poisonous fear and loathing of Russians into
the Nordic air.[7] Many Finns, General Mannerheim included, held the Russians responsible for the Civil War. Bitter memories of the "time of frost" and "time of oppression"
were stirred into blame and laced with worry about further Russian aggression, brewing
a deadly mix of hatred that threatened to boil over. In the view of alarmists, a Russian
attack on Finland was only a matter of time, a perception exacerbated by the eight hundred miles of "long, unnatural border" the countries shared. The Finns saw themselves
as an outpost of the West against Russia, the "steel wall . . . protecting [the West] from
Moscow"; to this perception was joined the desire to liberate from the Russians the Finns
and other Finno-Ugric peoples east of the border and the aspirations for a Greater Finland: "Let there be joined together what God intended to be united. Let there be formed
one and only [one] Finnish nation—Greater Finland."[8]

To defend against the eventuality of Russian aggression and achieve a Greater Finland required military force. And militancy there was aplenty in the aftermath of the
Civil War. As Sibelius had groaned in his diary on June 9, 1918, "All Finland is in the grip
of war, that is, militarism." The war had profoundly changed the people's self-image: the
peaceable, nonaggressive Finn ready to defend hearth and home had given way to a snarling, antagonistic fighter. Conscription was now required of Finland's youths, whether of
Red or White persuasion. By the 1930s approximately "one out of nineteen males—
regardless of age—was a member" of the Civil Guard Organization, whose weekly publication, produced from 1925 to 1944, was given the aggressive war cry of Thirty Years'
War fame: *Hakkapeliitta*—"Hack 'em down!"[9] And much of the antagonism was chan-
neled into *ryssänviha*—hatred of Russians.

In 1922 a pamphlet entitled *Ryssästä saa puhua vain hammasta purren* (*One Can Speak
of the Russki Only with Grinding of Teeth*) formalized Russian hatred by its very title
and its pejorative use of "Russki" for the neighbors.[10] How quickly familiar symbols
metamorphosed into badges of hateful aggression showed in the title of its revision: it
was called *Herää Suomi—Awake, Finland*. The following year another fervent pamphlet
appeared: *Suursuomi on yhtä kuin isänmaa* (*Greater Finland Is the Fatherland*), fanatical in
tone and revisionist in historical outlook. Those dubious qualities were elsewhere in evidence, too, such as in the article "Vihakin voimaa" ("Even Hatred Is Strength"):

> But we who once drove the Russians out of this country, we who know what
> marks they have stamped on this land, we must learn and teach others to hate the
> Russian so deeply and strongly that the roots of that hate will not wither even at

the moment of death. Let us remove the name of the devil from our curses and put *ryssä* in its stead.[11]

The force driving Russian hatred and galvanizing support for Greater Finland was Akateeminen Karjala-Seura—the Academic Karelia Society (AKS).[12] Founded by three university students on February 22, 1922, the AKS dominated the Finnish-speaking student world for a full decade. The organization's stated purpose was to provide aid for east Karelians. But its real agenda quickly surfaced: militant activism on behalf of Greater Finland and passionate hatred of Russians (which, in the view of some scholars, was essentially an aversion to communism). For this, armed conflict was the only viable option.

Because of the university's importance in Finnish political and cultural life, the impact of this militant group in its ranks, uncompromising and moralistic—no atheists allowed!—spread far. As one of its leading members, Martti Haavio (1899–1974), boasted, "What the students think today the entire nation will think tomorrow."[13] It was easy to accept the truth of Haavio's claim: students in the AKS remained members for life and went on to occupy leading professional, business, and military positions in Finland.

Although there were many Finns who quietly refused to engage in such hatred, a diligent "de-Russification" process now ensued.[14] Institutions, streets, and buildings were shorn of their imperial names and given designations more fitting to the new republic. In 1919, in an episode of tar-bucket nationalism, the young Urho Kekkonen (1900–1986) and his companions glopped sufficient tar over the monogram of Alexander I ("A I") to obliterate the hated Russian initials completely from the façade of the Imperial Alexander University. The institution was renamed and given a more democratic appellation—the University of Helsinki. Street names such as Nikolai, Vladimir, and Andrei disappeared, replaced by Snellman, Kaleva, and Lönnrot. People no longer referred to the Nicholas Church, but to the Great Church (Suurkirkko). Only a few street names from the Russian time—Alexander, Maria, Elisabeth, and oddly, "Union," which had commemorated Finland's annexation to Russia in 1809—survived the grim hand of hatred. Even the bust of the university's namesake, Alexander I, was eventually removed from the university's Festival Hall after repeated demonstrations in the 1930s; in 1957 it was finally hauled outdoors, where it still stands in an obscure corner of a tiny park, subjected to the indignities of snow, sleet, and rain.

The hatred was a festering canker in the heart of the new republic. Yet matters concerning the Russians had rarely been black and white in Finland. Finns had long intermarried with Russians, Alexander Järnefelt being one of the most prominent examples. Finnish artists, musicians, and intellectuals had cultivated exchanges with their Russian counterparts throughout all the years of Sibelius's life. Those with business and even family connections to Russians kept a low profile. For many Finns like Sibelius (who had a Russian-Baltic mother-in-law, a wife and children in whose veins that same blood flowed, and family connections in the city then called Petrograd), the acid drip of poison burned deep.

PILLAR II: THE SWEDISH LANGUAGE

As toxic as was the Russian hate fomented by members of the AKS, their rigid position on the issue of language represented a still greater threat to their fellow Finns: Finland's Swedish-speakers, the AKS insisted, would have to concede Finnish to be the nation's only language.[15] Such a measure would consolidate the military forces and enable the building of a strong national state. Into the turmoil of socialist versus nonsocialist, communist versus conservative, and Russian versus Finn was tossed the grenade of language hegemony.

Both Finnish- and Swedish-speakers started from the idea of language as the basis for nationality. Yet the Swedish-speaking faction, declaring themselves a separate ethnicity, wanted autonomy, with separate Swedish-speaking army units, Swedish-speaking departments within the government, and so on. The desires for such far-reaching separatism fed the True Finnish movement (*aitosuomalaisuus*) zealously being promoted by the AKS. With increasingly rabid nationalism the AKS members forced the University of Helsinki into a "pure Finnish" stance. In 1923 a law was enacted requiring the language of university instruction to be in proportion to the students of the language groups enrolled in a given class. Then Lauri O. Th. Tudeer issued an astounding decree: he forbade university library officials even to *speak* to one another in Swedish. The absurd lengths to which petty men were prepared to go had effects on matters from the practical (which language one might speak where) to the philosophical (how to write the history of Finland).

Two concepts of history had already been evident in the 1880s.[16] Now their oppositional viewpoints hardened: the Finnish nationalists consciously distanced themselves from the Swedish past and took the view of a subjugated preexisting nation destined "to awaken" and claim its rightful independence. The Liberal-Swedish view emphasized Finland's distinctive history within the Swedish realm as a whole. The difference was summed up in the phrase "the period of Swedish rule" (implying a time of foreign domination) versus simply "the Swedish time."

It was the language conflict that came closest to Jean Sibelius and the core of his identity. Swedish was his "mother tongue," the language in which he wrote his diary and most of his vast correspondence. After his marriage to Aino, Sibelius spoke and even wrote to her in Finnish (though in long letters, whole sentences and even paragraphs would shift into Swedish). Yet expressing himself in Finnish meant searching for words, speaking with a Swedish-speaker's logic, seeking the correct accentuation. Swedish remained the mode of his most intimate expressions. Five of the six Sibelius daughters bore Swedish, not Finnish, names—Eva, Ruth, Katarina, Margareta, Heidi (only little Kirsti, who died before she turned three, had been christened with a Finnish name). Finnish may have been the language of the home, but Swedish was the language of the bedroom.

That a Swedish speaker in Finland would rise to the position of national hero was inevitable in the nineteenth century, when the leaders of Finland's awakening were nearly all "Finland-Swedes": Snellman, Topelius, Runeberg, Mannerheim, Gallén, Kajanus, and many others. But after the 1907 election and the drastic change in the country's linguistic complexion, it was easy to forget this reality, just as it was easy to overlook how profoundly the imperial reign and patronage of the Russian emperors had provided unparalleled opportunities, engendered a sense of dynamism, and fostered the development of Finland's economy and its very identity as a nation. Now those Swedish-speaking Finns who had been at the forefront of creating that identity were being rudely pushed aside, their language scorned, their history revised.

Sibelius revealed this crucial part of his identity to very few. One of the elect was Axel Carpelan, who in the last year of his life had arranged a commission for Sibelius in connection with the inauguration of Åbo Academy—the new private university being established in Turku by those promoting the interests of the Swedish minority in Finland. A letter to this friend in connection with the commission indicated how deeply the Swedish-language culture thrived in the composer: "When I first read the words 'Åbo Academy' on the envelope, I experienced the same sensation I had in Italy when the train conductor called out Rome for the first time. It's really as if we make contact again with *our culture* before the 'fire'" (emphasis added).[17]

The importance to Sibelius of preserving that culture in Finland surfaced a year later in the episode of the Åland Islands question. In the wake of Finland's declaration of independence, the determinedly Swedish-speaking Åland Islanders wanted to secede from Finland to reunite with Sweden. Sibelius, evidently prompted by the unconventional Sigurd Wettenhovi-Aspa, who was lobbying for a "friends of Åland" committee, unusually made his political position clear, sending a telegram—in Finnish: "Will do anything for our country."[18]

The marginalization of his identity in the new Finland contributed to personal crisis and profound feelings of loneliness. "Ensam, ensam" (alone, alone), the composer mourned again and again to his diary. The early 1920s show him falling into the deepest depression he had ever experienced. He even called the gray days of October 1923 "the darkest hours of my life." Throughout that life, it had been his music that spoke most truly, often revealing what his words left ambiguous or altogether unsaid. But this time the revelations were coming not through what he composed, but through what he did not. The most heartrending symptom emerged in connection with one of Sibelius's most essential means of creative expression—solo songs to Swedish-language texts. They stopped. The break is precipitate—and deeply disturbing.

The very first composition Sibelius had ever published, in the long-ago year of 1888, had been a solo song setting of a Runeberg poem, *Serenad*. Twenty-nine years later he saw out the year 1917 by completing the six Runeberg settings that make up opus 90, led off by the exquisite *Norden*. In between, scarcely a year had passed without the creation of more such songs, nearly a hundred in all, to Swedish-language texts. But from the time the People's War erupted in January 1918, with all its social, linguistic, and political onslaughts, until the end of his life—a span of nearly forty years—Sibelius abandoned that activity. Only twice in all that time did he again set a Swedish-language text as a solo song: the frivolous *Små flickorna*, written in 1920 to a poem by the Euterpist Hjalmar Procopé; and *Narciss*, composed in 1925 to verses by the right-wing poet Bertel Gripenberg.[19]

The great Runebergian texts that had nurtured and sustained him as had verses by Swedish poets of the likes of Viktor Rydberg were utterly irrelevant in the new Finland. By the end of the 1920s student activists in Turku were even attempting to have the Runeberg-texted *Vårt land* replaced as the national anthem.[20] The students were plumping for some Finnish-language verses by V. A. Koskenniemi (1885–1962), the rector, from 1924, of Turku's Finnish-language university (it was symptomatic that two linguistically separate universities had arisen in that smallish town). Like Aaltonen, the highly esteemed Koskenniemi was identified with right-wing ideology. He supported the ultranational Lapua movement. He cultivated close ties with the Germans: during World War II he accepted an invitation from Joseph Goebbels to become vice chairman of the Europäischer Schriftstellerverbund in the Third Reich. That move harmed him not at all in the homeland: after the war Koskenniemi was elected to the prestigious Academy of Finland.

For Jean Sibelius, however, something precious had been lost. His anxieties and despair only deepened. On May 4, 1934, on hearing a London broadcast of his works, Sibelius reacted to what he saw as the dismal state of affairs in Finnish society by comparison with the enlightened goodwill of the British in the one and only diary entry he made for the whole of that year: "Our coarseness—which has increased to an alarming degree since they demolished everything Swedish—our conceit over these sporting events. Uneducated, our claims to civilization are in their infancy—everything shows the language squabbling." One of the most vital parts of his creativity had been snuffed out.

PILLAR III: *THE KALEVALA*

Why, oh, why, when all else was closing in on him, did Sibelius not go back to the *Kalevala* for rejuvenation, to drink from the creative wellsprings that had nourished him for decades?

He tried.

During the 1920s he made sketches for a projected tone poem, *Kuutar*, and he pondered settings of *runes historiques* (in a diary entry on March 4, 1920). But *Kuutar* remained only a dream; wisps of her enchanting music went into his Sixth Symphony. The few compositions he did complete to *Kalevala* texts, such as *Väinön virsi* (*Väinämöinen's Song*), a cantata for mixed choir, based on the *Kalevala*'s forty-third *runo*, demonstrate just how arduous was the task of reinventing his *Kalevala*-esque musical style for the new society and a new musical order: the result sounds like the most unctuous of church choir music.

Unsuccessful in reinterpreting the *Kalevala* for a changed world, Sibelius did the next best thing: he began hauling out those fabulously successful *Kalevala*- or Karelian-based works of the golden age for public performance, an activity that conspicuously began as his own creativity waned. On Kalevala Day in 1921, at a celebration in the Finnish National Theater, a bizarre mix swirled a medley of *Karelia* numbers into the Press Days' lottery music: the All'ouvertura followed by Bishop Henrik baptizing the Finns; the troubadour's ballade succeeded by the *grave* music of the Great Wrath, weirdly culminating in the Promotion March, all accompanying a series of pompous *tableaux* (planned by Eero Järnefelt, Eero Snellman, and Oskari Salo). "National romanticism," spat one of those present.[21]

Yet the most striking occasion was the Kalevala Jubilee in 1935, when two long-suppressed movements of the *Lemminkäinen Legends* and one of *Kullervo* were again heard. Fifteen years later Sibelius negotiated the much-postponed publication of the two withheld *Lemminkäinen* movements. *Kullervo*, too, had its day. Although Sibelius refused a personal request to allow the symphony to be performed in North America, he did agree to one of its movements' being played several times in Turku.[22]

Meanwhile, both in public and in private, he propounded the creative importance of his Finnish folk heritage. To Alberto Gasco in Rome he claimed that his *Swan of Tuonela*, like his other symphonic works, represented "the expression of a national art": "I am imbued (so to speak) with the poetry, with the legends of my homeland, and have sung in my way, inspired by one or another Finnish texts, especially the *Kalevala*, which is a bottomless well of emotion for a Finnish artist who has not been seduced by the mania for exoticism."[23] As late as 1953 he was telling family members that for him "the *Kalevala* was something holy. Not motives, nor sagas of heroes. I felt the religion in it deeply, loved it. It lights up all of Lemminkäinen."[24]

The difficulty with the *Kalevala* was that, like the "national," the "modern," and even Sibelius himself, it was being sharply politicized in a very disagreeable way, acquiring empty new meanings in the republic of Finland.[25] No longer a source for building up the positive image and affirmative character of the nation, the *Kalevala*, long an ideological tool, had become an instrument of militaristic propaganda, appropriated both by the political Right and the political Left.

The Right, especially the more vocal supporters of a Greater Finland, commandeered folk traditions, particularly research into such sources as the *Kalevala*, to justify their militaristic goals of extending the country's borders. Those infected with *ryssänviha* saw folklore as an instrument to fuel the flames of hatred for communism and rouse the ultranational spirit of White Finland. How drastically national symbols had altered from their meanings in the 1890s was clear in a speech given on Kalevala Day, 1923. The orator was Elias Simojoki, a theology student who became, significantly, both a Lutheran priest and a right-wing politician: "On this 'Kalevala Day' . . . let a rousing cry of holy love and hate travel through the tribe of Kullervo and through our beloved birthland."[26]

As for the Left, the labor movement had initially distanced itself from the various nationalist activities associated with Finland's folkloric heritage.[27] The proletariat viewed such pursuits as attempts by the elite and propertied class to divert attention from society's real problems by glorying in a romanticized past. But after the Civil War, the light began to dawn on the Left too, and its proponents began to awaken to the propaganda value of folklore. The Left and especially the communists were in a difficult position in Finland, associated as they were with Bolshevism, the defeated Reds, and such "dirty" activities as labor strikes. Finnish communists who wanted to affirm their national loyalties (they were often accused of spying for the Soviets) realized that cultivating Finnish folklore was a sure means of demonstrating their national allegiance.

The figure of Kullervo offered especially apt possibilities: here was a serf, a *worker*, who, during his entire short life, had waged constant battle against upper-class oppression. Kullervo's story, especially as presented in Aleksis Kivi's play, became a favorite with Finnish workers' theaters (*työväen teatterit*).[28] In the volatile year of 1917, the charismatic Aarne Orjatsalo (1883–1941), a handsome actor and political activist known for his booming voice, a man who incited admiration and scandal in more or less equal measure, organized a performance of Kivi's *Kullervo* in Tampere, the center of Red activity in Fin-

land. Orjatsalo, himself a member of the Red Guards, had arranged the performance as
a political demonstration for the working class—practically an incitement to rebellion.
(Orjatsalo later fled to the United States, where he died in obscurity.) During the 1920s
Kivi's play *Kullervo* was repeated numerous times in the Tampere theater as well as elsewhere throughout Finland.

The Left also attempted to press music into the service of political ideals. In 1927
Knut Kangas, one of the central composers in the Suomen Työväen Musiikkiliitto (Workers Musical Organization), praised Finnish folk music as classical, masterful, eternally
fresh. A genuine Herderian, Kangas sounded like a Turku Romantic gone communist:

> It is as is though [our folk songs] are spewed from nature's breast. Bubbling
> bogs, in whose nature descriptions one surely finds nothing comparable in the
> folk songs of other nations. . . . If you look through the folk-song collections
> of our western neighbors, the Swedes, for example, you will see that their songs
> are clumsier and less colorful.[29]

Folk song and folk dance offered ways to combat the scourge of Western popular culture,
whose corrupt "foreign dances" were bound to waylay innocent, unsuspecting Finnish
young. As a writer for the workers' music journal put it in 1929, "[Folk] music educates
the people, it takes away their widespread coarseness, it even makes life more enjoyable in
the countryside and is more likely to keep young people there close to home."[30] Remaining close to home, shutting out all foreign influences, justifying self-absorption by means
of the *Kalevala* and the rest of the "pure" Finnish folk heritage—all this belonged to the
changed and repressive attitudes in the new Finland.

The *Kalevala* thus turned out to be a useful source for leftist political ends. Leftist
wits penned lyrics to workers' songs in trochaic tetrameter (the so-called *Kalevala* meter)
with instructions that they be sung by seated couples holding hands, swaying to and fro
(the now discredited practice by which it was long believed the *Kalevala* verses were performed). Sometimes the performers donned folk costumes. Across the barricaded border,
the *Kalevala* was being used to advance the cause of communism in Karelia. Communist
Party members objected to folklorists who reached "artificial" conclusions that "fit the
dirty purposes of capitalistic imperialism"; they wanted the Soviet Karelians to understand that the *Kalevala* depicted a world of peaceful workers laboring together for the
greater communal good. Even Otto Ville Kuusinen (1881–1964), founder of the Finnish Communist Party and the man who in 1920 dismissed the Republic of Finland as an
"extremely transitory phenomenon," eventually published his own Marxist view of the
Kalevala (Moscow, 1949): *Kalevala ja sen luojat: Kalevalan alkulause* (*The Kalevala and
Its Creators: Introduction to the Kalevala*).[31]

Like so much else in Finland, the *Kalevala* had become "hot," an ideological battle-ground. As a source for creativity, it no longer "burned you to life," but "burned you to death, to death."

THE LAST PILLAR: RELIGION

Perhaps Sibelius could have overcome one or even some of the losses. But the convergence of social, political, aesthetic, and life forces hit him with shattering might.

Part of it was age. Today it is easy to forget that in 1915, when Sibelius celebrated a half century of life, fifty was old. He had already been sobered on the marriage of his firstborn, Eva; when he became a grandfather in his fiftieth year, the passage of time further brought him up short. And like other mortals, he was not granted the gift of foresight to see how many years still lay ahead. There were also personal sorrows. The youngest of the Sibelius siblings, Christian, on whom Jean had always counted to be the "rock," the "beloved brother," fell ill. It gradually became apparent that his illness was incurable. His incomprehensible death in 1922, following on Carpelan's in 1919, left Sibelius in emotional darkness.

In the wake of the People's War his drinking resumed. Then it worsened. His hands began to shake more and more. His correspondence tapered off. His diary entries thinned out. His conducting career came to a halt. His relationship with Aino deteriorated. The problems converged in that appalling episode at Gothenburg, Sweden, when on an April evening in 1923 he was found consuming champagne and oysters when he should have been readying himself to conduct.[32] The concert, which he began in a seriously inebriated state, then broke off, then began again, was nearly a disaster. Aino's patience was at an end. A few months after this appearance (which she had witnessed firsthand), she wrote a letter of such severity to her husband that he was finally shaken to the core.[33]

It is clear from the composer's diary that the 1920s were the nadir of Sibelius's life. Afflicted with bitter feelings of aloneness (his *Alleingefühl*) and numbing depression, he alternated between alcoholic binges ("alcohol—my truest friend") and a kind of manic euphoria that never lasted. He cranked out bloodless piano pieces. In desperation, in 1922 he offered to sell the autograph manuscript of his *Kullervo* to the Kalevala Society.[34] Meanwhile, the wider aesthetic discussions and the changed musical landscape intensified his discouragement, his feelings of isolation, and the despair of seeing his works eclipsed abroad by "the three S.'s of modern music—Schoenberg, Scriabin, and Stravinsky." At home, with his language and its culture derided, the *Kalevala* reinterpreted one way by the fascists, another way by the communists, the national awakening perverted in directions he could never have imagined, only one pillar was left to him: the faith of his fathers.

This faith was far from the rigid Lutheran strictures of his youth, yet it had been awakened by that childhood exposure, shaped into a core of deep personal beliefs, and transformed into artistic expression. Sibelius's association of religion (in the spiritual sense) and music was lifelong. In 1882 he had written to Uncle Pehr that playing Haydn's sonatas filled him with a strange feeling that was "almost holy"; in the 1930s he was telling Karl Ekman that "it is impossible to define a religion—least of all in words. But perhaps music is a mirror."[35] Even in explaining his musical structures he invoked a higher power: "The final form of one's work is, indeed, dependent on powers that are stronger than oneself. Later on one can substantiate this or that, but on the whole one is merely a tool. This wonderful logic—let us call it God—that governs a work of art is the forcing power."[36]

Now, in the 1920s, as though with the last reserves of his strength, Sibelius gathered up all the strands of his experience, sublimated them into exquisite musical shape, and, reaching far above the petty politics of daily life, composed the most moving, uplifting, and deeply spiritual of all his works, his two last symphonies. One senses in those calming and profound expressions—one in the grieving aftermath of his brother Christian's death in the summer of 1922, the other in 1924 in the midst of the bitterest hatreds and most mean-spirited arguments in Finland's public life—an extraordinary ability to reaffirm a deep faith in humanity and life's vitality—*elämänvoima*.

In a climate in which experimentation and modernist gambits were frowned upon as seriously un-Finnish, Sibelius availed himself of unprovocative tonal language, yet radically exploited its possibilities in ways so profound that those symphonies still inspire the world's leading conductors and intrigue the most thoughtful analysts.[37] Already in the incidental music to *Everyman* Sibelius had made clear his awareness of the age-old associations of the heavenly and faith with diatonic melody and the ancient church modes; the earthly and the devil, with chromaticism. Now, in the Sixth Symphony, the composer put those hallowed associations into play on a vast scale to craft a work of unimaginable purity. Incredibly, both the principal key areas are "pure": the first, an incorruptible Dorian mode; the second, a clean C major. The Sixth Symphony's ebb and flow between diatonic and chromatic and between the harmonic poles of D and C invests divine meaning in that Dorian mode. At the close of the first movement, when a D-flat scale ascends to C major and the orchestra swells to fortissimo, the conclusion seems to have arrived. But a Haydnesque fermata is poised over the bar line: a breath is drawn. Then, poco tranquillo, strings and woodwinds elevate the orchestra heavenward—into D Dorian (see ex. 23.1).

Throughout the symphony the composer alternated between these tonal regions with enviable fluidity until, in the final measures, the theme is transformed into an ineff-

EXAMPLE 23.1. SIBELIUS, SYMPHONY NO. 6, FIRST MOVEMENT, LAST 10 BARS.
© WILHELM HANSEN, COPENHAGEN.

EXAMPLE 23.1. (*CONTINUED ON THE NEXT PAGE*)

EXAMPLE 23.1. (*CONTINUED*)

able hymn that reaches aloft for such startling realms as D-flat, E, and C-flat major. In its glowing white-note transparency, its consonant "goodness," its upward-bound farewell gestures, its wondrous ability suddenly "to make everything clear," Symphony no. 6 intimates that the shining memory of Christian Sibelius—"the lamplighter in the night of ideas" (*lykttändare i tankens natt han var*), as Topelius's words read on his tombstone—was not far from the composer's own dark night as he worked.[38]

Yet now to compose a four-movement symphony? The very genre was a holdover from the nineteenth century. And a symphony so unmistakably, unshakably tonal? This was the work "out of step with the times." Jean Sibelius seemed to be affirming principles that the modernists found deeply suspect for the simple reason that those principles were anything but neutral: they represented the very culture that had brought "civilization" to global conflagration.[39] The principles that Sibelius was challenging—his reassessment of the meaning of "symphony" in a new world order, his redoubled commitment to an intuitive way of composing and allowing the musical content to determine the form (like water, he said, "which, after a hard frost, crystallizes into beautiful ice flowers, according to eternal laws"),[40] his exploration of the very essence of sound in circular, meditative constructions—went unappreciated by proponents of the new music in their rush to resolve the crises of modernism.

In that atmosphere the consonance and tonality of the Sixth Symphony and the joyfully C major world of the Seventh Symphony misled the uncomprehending into casting Sibelius as "regressive." Indeed, few outside Finland had any idea of the terrible discords in Finnish society or of the internal conflicts tearing at the people's collective heart. Can it be coincidence that in his Seventh Symphony Sibelius virtually erased the distinctions between symphony and symphonic poem, the artificial divide between absolute and program music, and created an encompassing symphony in one movement? Such a move was not only the logical trajectory of a composer who had steadily worked to link symphonic movements (the third and fourth of his Second Symphony, with the direction *attacca*; the fused movements in the Third and Fifth Symphonies; and the intimate links between the movements of his Fourth Symphony, each ending on a unison note that pivots effortlessly into the following key). It was also the intuitive move of a man who deeply desired the remerging of a society whose factions into Swedish and Finnish, communist and fascist, worker and aristocrat, had profoundly splintered them all.

In the 1920s names, words, and labels invited risk and censure, from the hardline nationalists at home every bit as much as from the ultramoderns abroad. "I could not very well provide [my symphonies] with labels that would give a wrong impression of what I aimed at," Sibelius told Ekman; "the current idea had to be extended."[41] The enlightened caliber of his reach showed in the vast difference between the new one-movement work and that long-ago symphony *Kullervo*; its sprawling movements—five in all—had been based on conventional symphonic structures and infused with the essence of Finnish-Russian folk songs. The new symphony flowed forth as from a spring of clear water, its patterns crystallizing like frost on a windowpane, shaped by the musical ideas themselves.

The reassessed vision showed in the very title of this symphony: "Fantasia sinfonica I" was how he referred to it in his diary (on March 2, 1924), and *Fantasia sinfonica* was how it appeared on the program at the premiere three weeks later (in Stockholm, on March 24). Symphony no. 6 had also started life as a fantasia. Still, even these words were too confining. Just as the next year he devised a wordless chorus for *The Tempest*, thereby avoiding the anguished linguistic issue, so now in the Seventh Symphony Sibelius conveyed the stunning solutions to his reassessment of formal and symphonic questions solely through the transformative poetry of musical instruments. And he gave the most unforgettable role to the trombone, whose historical associations powerfully evoke the mysteries of religion and the supernatural. When its deep-toned pronouncements make their sonorous entrances—a mystical three in all—no one with any religious instruction of any kind can doubt that they have heard a voice from another world (see ex. 23.2). Thereafter, the strings soaring into the ether—reaching for "joy of life and vitality, with appassionato passages"[42]—leave an indescribable sense of the air thinning, of time running out, of Aida in the tomb.

EXAMPLE 23.2. SIBELIUS, SYMPHONY NO. 7, MM. 7–14 AFTER REHEARSAL LETTER C.
© WILHELM HANSEN, COPENHAGEN.

"Confessions of Faith"

Sibelius once observed to Karl Ekman, "These symphonies of mine are more in the nature of professions of faith than my other works."[43] More than two decades earlier, on November 5, 1910, he had recorded the same thought in his diary: "A symphony is not just a 'composition' in the ordinary meaning. It's rather a confession of faith at different stages of one's life." Yet it was not only the symphonies that bore those confessions: a number of "religious" compositions are sprinkled among the lackluster "sandwich pieces" of the 1920s: several works for organ, called *Präludium*, *Postludium*, and *Intrada*, composed in 1925 and 1926; the *Three Introductory Antiphons* and *Herran siunaus* (*God's Blessing*), composed in 1925 at the request of the Fennoman Heikki Klemetti, who was making a standardized edition of liturgical melodies; and *Musique religieuse* (the *Masonic Ritual Music*), much of it written in 1926–27.[44]

Other works of the 1920s, although not explicitly religious, have a deeply spiritual character. Among them is *Andante festivo* (1922). Later used endlessly as the predictable opening at state and ritual occasions, *Andante festivo* embodies something far deeper than the lifeless *Academic March* of a few years before (1919). Significantly, Sibelius had initially composed *Andante festivo* not as a work for the masses, but for that most highbrow and intimate of music ensembles, a string quartet. And he conveyed something of its meaning for him in still another work, a piano composition called *The Village Church*, one of the miniatures in the *Five Characteristic Impressions* (op. 103).

Their titles alone indicated the nostalgia spilling through an old man's fingers onto the keys: *The Fiddler*, *The Oarsman*, *The Storm*, and *In Mournful Mood*. Jointly published in 1924 by Carl Fischer in New York and Wilhelm Hansen in Copenhagen, each of the *Impressions* suggests something reflective about this moment in Sibelius's life, and none more than *The Village Church*, its title reminiscent of Runeberg's poem *Kyrkan* (*The Church*). All the wistfulness of a lost past saturates its bars. A majestic hymn marked largo, its homophonic stateliness underpinned with long pedal points, alternates with

EXAMPLE 23.3. SIBELIUS, *THE VILLAGE CHURCH*, OP. 103, NO. 1, MM. 1–7.
© WILHELM HANSEN, COPENHAGEN.

Bachlike arpeggios, coming to its final amen with a plagal cadence that affirms the key, a pure C major. Memories of a long-ago childhood of Runeberg's poetry and Lutheran chorales, of lost innocence and youthful idealism, well up from its pages. Yet the most piercing moment comes in the three bars (mm. 5–7) that peal out the theme of the creator's own *Andante festivo* in that "village church" (see ex. 23.3). Sibelius's personal awakenings and volcanic nationalism had been transmuted into something so deep, so complex that it seemed to have been made of the very fiber of his soul.

ᔎᒍᔕᔎᒍᔕ

If music is a gauge—and for a composer, it must be—then Sibelius in the 1920s was a man divided. There were the inevitable small pieces, which earned the family's bread and butter. There were the dutiful and mostly uninteresting public works, written for official state occasions: graduation ceremonies, a song festival organized by the ever-energetic KVS, choruses for the Civil Guards and a Viipuri choir, a flag song for an immigrant chorus. And there were the *real* works, private compositions not meant for "the people": Symphony no. 6, Symphony no. 7, *Tapiola*, music for *The Tempest* (to a Danish translation of Shakespeare's play). It has not escaped notice that of these, only the Sixth Symphony was premiered in Sibelius's homeland.[45] Nor that by 1924 the great symphonies that had been incubating since the American journey had been delivered into the world.

Thereafter came the inexorable fade into silence. It came gradually. In 1925, from May to September, Sibelius was at work on *The Tempest*. During the spring and summer of the next year he composed *Tapiola*, part of which was composed in Italy, where he had gone with Walter von Konow to visit Rome and Capri. And he began working on a new piece that, in retrospect, was identified as an eighth symphony.[46] Yet these compositions show that all was not well in Sibelius's musical world. *The Tempest* is no symphony. Nor is it a tone poem. Despite flashes of brilliance, it is not a work of sustained inspiration. In its turn, the alleged Eighth Symphony was never completed, for all the supposed work on it over the next seven or eight years. As for *Tapiola*, named for the forest god, its slow-moving tonal and rhythmic ostinato personified an inertia that was all too real in the composer's life.[47] Its shape and sway (see ex. 23.4) had been used in the golden age's headiest days, oscillating in the Press Days' *tableaux* during the scene of the Great Wrath that led up to *Finlandia*. Now, recast for a new, "victorious" Finland, these bars, too, had acquired different meaning. Around them swirls the new atmosphere the country had engendered—an ominous beginning, followed by sweeping storms of social unrest.

EXAMPLE 23.4. SIBELIUS, *TAPIOLA*, MM. 64–71.
© BREITKOPF & HÄRTEL, WIESBADEN.

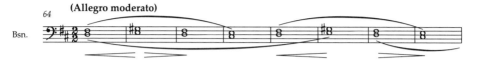

The motto affixed to Sibelius's score, as published by Breitkopf & Härtel, is misleading:[48]

> Wide-spread they stand, the Northland's dusky forests,
>
> Ancient, mysterious, brooding savage dreams;
>
> Within them dwells the forest's mighty god,
>
> And wood sprites in the gloom weave magic secrets.

Those lines suggest the world of German fairy tales, in which the forest is a dark, threatening, terrifying realm. There monsters lurk, wolves gobble up unsuspecting children, and witches lure the lost into dank dens from which they never escape. But for Finns, the forest is a place of safety, a haven of peace. Among the composer's effects, two versions of the poem, both ironically in English, come closer to the Finnish spirit:

Tapiola

> A wild northern forest,
>
> the home of the god of forests and his wood-nymphs.

"Tapiola"

> A deep and dreamy northern forest,
>
> where the god of forests and his wood-nymphs live.[49]

"Deep and dreamy" rather than "brooding and savage," "nymphs"—enchanting, inspirational—rather than "sprites" with their overtones of mischief making and wicked ways—the differences are significant. In the sheltering forests around Ainola, the composer had found a haven of safety. There he sculpted the leanest, most minimal symphonic piece he had ever written. Like Giacometti, who ultimately chiseled his art out of existence, Sibelius too reduced his music until, in the end, there was none.

BRAVE NEW WORLD

Sibelius could have slipped away from the closed atmosphere of Finland and headed for a brave new world, because he was handed the opportunity. In January 1920 an old acquaintance from his Berlin student days, the Norwegian musician Alf Klingenberg (1867–1944), made the composer a tantalizing offer: the post of composition professor at the Eastman School of Music in Rochester, New York. Klingenberg was its new director. He realized that his proposition might seem outlandish—after all, he wrote, the Americans are really *fraekke djevlar* (impudent devils)—yet he wanted Sibelius to consider the possibilities: "You come to Rochester for the opening of the school; stay a year, or if possible longer; you teach composition to the up- and-coming geniuses in America at the school; the number of those will certainly not make your workload too heavy."[50] More-over, Sibelius would have free time to travel as a guest conductor, performing his own works with the many fine orchestras in the United States.

Here was a chance to break out of the iconic role prescribed for him, free himself of the constraints of militaristic Finland, encounter fresh ideas, and experience with new musicians the "orchestral baths" that had always revitalized his music. Sibelius, who made indecision a way of life, left his answer dangling. But on January 3, 1921, he noted in his diary that he had cabled an answer to Rochester: "Yes."

Now human forces entered to deflect Sibelius from this decision. Rosa Newmarch, née Jeafferson, the staunch British matron who had written one of the earliest biographical essays about Sibelius, had been "looking after" the composer since 1905 when she began preparing that memorable lecture. Her interests had taken concrete form—personal correspondence, visits to Ainola, and the promotion of Sibelius's music in England. Newmarch objected strongly to the Eastman decision. As it happened, early in 1921 Sibelius made his first trip away from Finland since 1914, to Berlin and thence to London, from where he would return home via Norway.

From the moment the composer set foot on Albion's green shores, the stalwart Newmarch crusaded to prevent him from accepting the American offer. Her reasons are not altogether clear. Whether it rankled that the upstart "colonists" would be able to boast of having one of the world's leading composers or that Newmarch herself risked losing her measure of control ("he would have no one to look after him in America," she exclaimed, aghast), or something else, Rosa was a new woman on the march. She spared no words, begging him not to squander his energies on "young Americans," whom she seemed to view as a kind of infected strain of low life. She even took her crusade to Aino: "I hope your husband will not go to America. I do not see him giving lectures and teaching. I do not think his nervous system would endure the life for a year. . . . I have seen so many artists fail after America: Dvořák, Safonoff, and others. The life is too strenuous and inartistic."[51] However well intentioned, Newmarch may have done Sibelius a terrible disservice, but she was not alone. Aino herself had no desire to leave her children and grandchildren or to leave the national "position" in society that Sibelius had attained for them. Yet it could have helped Sibelius, who was increasingly withdrawing into his narcissistic cocoon, to come out of his self-absorption from time to time and extend a hand to younger aspirants in the art of composition. More important, it would have given him new stimulation at a time when Finland was turning so decidedly inward. Klingenberg had assured the composer that his teaching duties would be light and opportunities to conduct plentiful. A year "in that hurried, excitable race for life" would hardly have been ruinous for Sibelius and might have proved his creative salvation. He vacillated. He dithered. First he said yes. Then he said no. With that decision, his fate was sealed.

We who see his future want to cry, "Go, go!"—we who know that the new orchestras, the stimulation of young minds, and the currents and ideas from afar had never failed to feed his innovation and creative genius. Together with having something to push back against, these things had given his art its vitality. But like Snellman, who twice was invited to accept a professorial chair in Sweden but declined because he believed it his moral obligation to remain in his native land,[52] Sibelius turned down the offer.

All the reasons may never be known. Newmarch had convinced him that his creative life was at stake. In his heart, however, Sibelius knew there was something else, though he steadfastly refused to specify what. The decision haunted him for a long time. In a diary entry on February 23, 1922, he was still bitterly regretting having turned down the Eastman offer the previous year, but added, "I will not write down the reasons." Two years later, among the very few diary entries in 1924 (on May 14), he was once again chastising himself for refusing the American offer. It may have been that to leave Finland felt too much like betrayal. Or he may have lost heart at the prospect of leaving a steady pension, national status, and a life of idolization for the great unknown. His first response to Klingenberg alluded to these reasons. He wrote, "My position here as 'poeta laureatus' (♩) with an artist's salary, etc. is such that I can't simply bid adieu."[53] He was fully aware of his patriotic role: a later missive in which he discusses frankly the benefits for him of the financial considerations ends with the ironic exclamation, "Aren't I a good patriot!"[54]

Yet there were also important family considerations. For all the tension at home, it is clear that Sibelius deeply loved Aino. And he was a devoted father. He worried over his daughters' growing pains, their social problems, their marital decisions. Three of the girls were still living at home: Heidi was only ten; Margareta, thirteen; and Katarina, eighteen. They suffered from influenza and pneumonia (with which Katarina fell ill in

December, at the time the American offer was being considered). After Kirsti's death, the fear of losing another child lingered. Would Sibelius leave the girls and Aino to cope on their own? After all, in those days, moving an entire family to a new life in a faraway land was rare, though not unheard of. The initial plan, such as it was, had evidently been to leave them, because on January 5, 1921, when Sibelius wrote to Klingenberg that he had just telegraphed "Yes" to the Eastman School, he said that his wife would probably not be coming.[55]

The same letter indicates that Aino was not well. "My wife has been and is sick— confined to bed for 2½ months," Sibelius wrote. This was apparently not just a Sibelian feint, because his letter to Aino, written from England in February 1921, also reflected concerns for her health.[56] When he well and truly gave his final answer to Klingenberg, the reason was "health," though just whose health he meant was left unspecified: "Owing health unable come America next season. Greetings. Sibelius."[57]

The last letter on the subject in the Klingenberg file was written by Sibelius to Klingenberg's wife, the feisty Alexandra, who had tried to persuade the composer to come after all: your name has gone out all over America, everything is in full flame and can't be stopped, she had told him frankly.[58] She even suggested that he come just for a month! But Sibelius would not now be deflected from his path. He wrote her a polite and typically evasive epistle: "I think it's best to leave the thing as it is, that is, everything is still just between us. When there is time, we'll find the means."[59]

Ultimately, the momentous decision of whether to accept the Eastman offer was bound up with issues profoundly, incommunicably personal. In making that decision, Sibelius appeared at his most authentic and his most reassuringly human.

⤳24⤳

Might Makes Right

The 1930s

I n the 1930s the people of Finland carried on with their daily lives as people do everywhere. Nevertheless, the worldwide economic depression made its inevitable impact. Not least, travel abroad, crucial for the rejuvenation of small societies, was again difficult; to the east, it was prohibited. In the domestic sphere the extremist positions hardened further. White Finland's fear of a communist resurgence was exacerbated by labor strikes and other socialist activities. Widespread anxiety over securing the borders and preserving the democratic order fed an increasingly defensive and autocratic national position to the point that extreme leftist activity was proscribed. Even freedom of speech, that treasured liberty for which Finns had passionately and imaginatively demonstrated against Bobrikov, was curtailed. Its loss was mocked in verses of an agitation song that admonished salaried workers to "sing nice songs," since otherwise "the law would plug your mouth up."[1] The song was confiscated by the security police.

A few scenes from that time will suffice to illustrate the spirit of the decade and Sibelius's place in it. The scenes are tinged with fascist colors, although in hues less deep than elsewhere in Europe. Indeed, for all the fear-of-the-communists hype, the real threat to Finland's internal stability was from the far right. Around 1929, the widespread fear of the communists gave rise to an organization called the Lock of Finland. The organization quickly metamorphosed into the Lapua Movement, a near-fascist conglomeration of peasant farmers and extremists who went from coordinating mass marches to wreaking violence. There were beatings and kidnappings (including of the former president K. J. Ståhlberg and his wife), even political murders.

Matters came to a head in February 1932, when Lapua militants opened fire on a meeting of Social Democrats in the town of Mäntsälä. Attempting to mobilize the Civil Guards, the militants threatened to bring Finland to the brink of another civil war. Fortunately, the Civil Guards responded not to the Lapua mobilization orders, but to an appeal from the president of the republic, P. E. Svinhufvud, to avert further violence. On the strength of a law its members had themselves helped to enact, the crisis was defused and the Lapua Movement ultimately suppressed.[2]

Unfortunately, Sibelius was drawn into taking sides openly, pressured, it seems, by Aino, who was known for her extreme right-wing views. On July 7, 1930, the couple attended a Lapua demonstration in Helsinki, a huge affair in which some twelve thousand zealots marched, and the president, the prime minister, and General Mannerheim addressed the nation. Sibelius was photographed at the event and was asked to compose a march for the movement. He responded with *Karjalan osa* (*The Fate of Karelia*). He made not one but two fair copies (HUL 1011 and 1012). In both, the writing of the music is sure and quick: pressed firmly in black ink upon the withering yellowed paper, the chords stride briskly (*Reippaasti*) across the page, musical soldiers in parade formation. Oddly, the text, added only in one copy (HUL 1011) and in pencil, looks frail. The hand is not sure, the words cramped. The world of tones seemed secure; the world of words and politics did not.

The Fate of Karelia, composed for unison men's voices and piano, was first performed two months later on a September evening arranged by the Lock of Finland in Sortavala.[3] The march was quickly taken up by militant groups. Someone arranged it for voices and brass, because on November 28, 1930, the Finnish-language men's choir, Ylioppilaskunnan Laulajat, gave the work a lusty rendition in the university's Festival Hall. A little over a week later, on the anniversary of Finland's independence, December 6, a large military band played the piece in an instrumental arrangement during a grand celebration in the National Theater. The full score and choral parts were almost immediately made available in print (see fig. 24.1), brought out by a small Helsinki firm called Musiikkikeskus (the Music Center). Yet the piece later proved something of an embarrassment. It was one of the very few Sibelius works for which no recording was listed in the composer's massive thematic-bibliographic catalog published in 2003.

The Fate of Karelia has an alternate title: *Patriotic March*. There was no question as to how Sibelius saw himself.

THE KALEVALA JUBILEE

Of all the scenes from the 1930s, the defining display "on the nation's cabinet" was, without doubt, the Kalevala Jubilee. As fate would have it, 1935 marked both the seventieth birthday of Jean Sibelius and the 100th anniversary of the *UrKalevala*'s publication. A host of celebrations unequaled in the nation's admittedly short history were mustered up

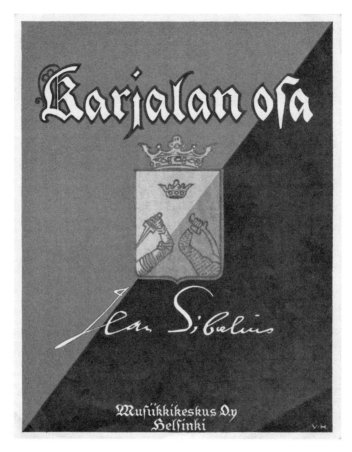

Figure 24.1. *Karjalan osa* (*The Fate of Karelia*) (Helsinki: Musiikkikeskus, 1930).
Sibelius Academy Library. Scan: Mikko Ikkala.

to pay homage to these national anniversaries. The elaborate media outpourings on the birthday, December 8, 1935, surpassed even those of 1915, thanks in part to the greater sophistication of the provincial papers. This time *Hämeen Sanomat* had several pages of illustrated articles. The cruelest and most telling photograph showed baby Janne on his "mother Mary's" lap—all traces of four-year-old Linda (on their mother's right side in the original picture) completely erased.

Yet it was the scope and zeal of events for the *Kalevala* Day, February 28, that surpassed anything ever seen in the new republic.[4] There were happenings all around the country—sports competitions, theatrical presentations, concerts, radio broadcasts, festivals, art exhibitions, eulogies, orations. A *Kalevala* Memorial was erected at Tampere. A *Kalevala* songfest was held at Sortavala. Wreaths were laid at the grave of Elias Lönnrot. Speeches and radio programs were held in the great bard's honor. *Runot* were sung, *kanteles* played. The University of Helsinki held an essay competition on two themes, both around the *Kalevala* and "the people": "Miten saisi Kalevalan lähemmäksi koko kansaamme" (How to bring the *Kalevala* closer to all our people) and "Mitä Kalevalalla on nykyiselle nuorisolle sanottavana" (What does the *Kalevala* have to say to young people today). The prize was the unbelievable sum of 15,500 Finnish marks, and its award ceremony attracted a wildly enthusiastic public.

In a nation that seriously valued its academics, the centennial prompted scholarly reassessment of the *Kalevala* as a pillar of Finnish identity. In 1935 Martti Haavio, the former AKS activist, now a poet and prominent scholar, announced his new conception of the *Kalevala*: "The heart of the *Kalevala* poetry is simply war poetry."[5] In militaristic Finland, society's highest ideal was war, and the sword was the means of assuring its rights. The *Kalevala* represented a uniquely Finnish source for educating young Finns into a warfare that, it was now believed, the epic showed to be their heritage. The Kullervo *runot*, for example, which had inspired Sibelius to such artistic heights in 1892, were cited to prove that for centuries the Finns had been capable of fearsome, aggressive deeds.

Martti Haavio was an increasingly influential voice in the land, thanks to his position as director of the Finnish Literature Society's extensive folk archive, his teaching of folklore research at the University of Helsinki, and his participation in the group of writers called the "Torch Bearers" (Haavio published his poetry under the pseudonym P. Mustapää). Now, in the year of the Kalevala Jubilee, Haavio was elaborating on the new meanings of the *Kalevala*. In his volume *Suomalaisen muinaisrunouden maailma* (*The World of Ancient Finnish Poetry* [Porvoo, 1935]), he answered the perennial question of whether the *Kalevala* represented history or myth with the claim that, of course, "folklore is historical because it reflects the culture, the way of life, of past ages," but the authors of the *Kalevala* had surely exercised poetic license.[6] Nor could those authors have been "the people," as Sibelius and his generation had been taught. Instead, Haavio claimed, a small group of professionals from the aristocratic classes of society, "comparable to the scaldic poets of Scandinavia," had created these heroic poems. "The people," it seemed had not after all been the originators of those verses that had inspired the golden age, as its artists had deeply believed.

The Kalevala Jubilee was thus anything but a politically neutral set of celebrations. On the home turf, its events polarized a number of issues swirling through the domestic ether—right-wing autocracy versus socialist collectivism, aristocratic traditions versus the newer popular mass culture, and not least, the meaning and importance of folklore. Nor had its frenzied activities gone unnoticed by the totalitarian state to the east.[7] The

belligerent rhetoric, the militaristic skiing events, and the pro-Finlandia events staged as
nationalist propaganda—all were viewed as provocations fanning the flames of chauvinistic hatred. The leftist press screamed such headlines as "Folklore and the Imperialistic
Aims of the Finnish Bourgeoisie," "The Attempts of the Finnish Bourgeoisie to Force
the *Kalevala* into the Service of Nationalism and Chauvinism," and "To What End Has
the Finnish Bourgeoisie Used and Is Now Using the *Kalevala*."[8] The *Kalevala*, whose
poetry had inspired such magnificent artistic outpourings, was now being used to justify
the Greater Finland aspirations and as an excuse for promoting a fascist dictatorship.

To counter the "fascist propaganda," the communists organized their own *Kalevala*
Jubilee, staged in Petrozavodsk (called Petroskoi and, later, Äänislinna by the Finns), in
Soviet Karelia. The Finn Edvard Gylling (1881–1938), chairman of the People's Com-
missariat, proclaimed: "We have before us the especially important task of exposing the
use of the *Kalevala* poems as the ideological foundation of the Finnish bourgeoisie's
imperialistic ambitions, in the service of their Karelian-conquest enterprises and their
daydreams of a Great Finland."[9] (Two years later Gylling was arrested by the Party as a
spy, and in 1938 he was shot.)

In Helsinki the celebration's central occasion was a memorial exhibition of some
five hundred paintings by Axel Gallén (who had died in 1931) launched with four days of
musical events; representatives of no fewer than twenty-five nations attended. The very
space in which the Helsinki event took place showed how profoundly Finland's cultural
life had changed. In the 1890s concerts had been held in the solemn academic setting of
the university's Festival Hall or in chic Society House or in the acoustically excellent
hall of the Volunteer Fire Brigade (*Palokunnantalo*). The *Kalevala* Jubilee concerts were
not staged in any such intimate, upper-class setting; they took place in Helsinki's newly
completed Fair Hall (Messuhalli, today renamed Kisahalli).[10] This vast exhibition space,
Finland's first, was finished just in time to pitch its inaugural festivities into the Kalevala Jubilee. Fair Hall was not designed for the elite; it was meant for the multitudes.
Some idea of its mammoth scale can be appreciated from the sheer numbers it accommodated during its inaugural weeks: along with the scads of *Kalevala* paintings on display
(Gallén's hundreds supplemented by another hundred fellow artists'), some thirty thousand people visited during the jubilee's celebrations; another sixty thousand attended the
exhibition.

The jubilee's central musical events consisted of no fewer than seven concerts of
orchestral, choral, and piano music. And during these occasions not one new work of
Jean Sibelius was heard. Oh, there was a great deal of his music performed, all inspired
by the *Kalevala*: overtures to the *Karelia* music and the first set of *Scènes historiques*;
Pohjola's Daughter; choral works from *Tulen synty* and *Rakastava* to *Venematka*, *Sortunut*

ääni, *Terve, kuu*, and *Väinön virsi*; and for piano, *Kyllikki*. There were even performances of works long set aside: three of the four movements of the *Lemminkäinen Suite* (all but *The Swan of Tuonela*), and part of the *Kullervo* symphony. But to this long-planned celebration, the music for which had been discussed in meetings of the Kalevala Society at least three years earlier, the composer had contributed not one jot of new music, not so much as a patriotic fanfare, not a men's chorus, not a piano miniature.

How far the creative artist had diverged from the idol that the nation had placed on its collective cabinet could hardly have been clearer. Sibelius had even lost control of the manner of performance. In 1934 the Kalevala Society had budgeted the costs of making orchestral parts for all five movements of *Kullervo*, an almost certain indication that Sibelius was willing to allow the full symphony to be performed.[11] But the final decision was taken out of his hands. Georg Schnéevoigt, then conductor of the Helsinki Philharmonic Orchestra, briefly examined the score and perfunctorily announced that only the third movement would be suitable.

Schnéevoigt's lack of enthusiasm may have contributed to the lackluster result, for it was *Lemminkäinen* that overshadowed *Kullervo* in the concert played on March 1, 1935. In the archconservative atmosphere of the 1930s, the stalwart Lemminkäinen and his adventures had more appeal to the moralistic far right than the serf Kullervo, who had unwittingly even committed incest, an act portrayed in the very movement (the third) that Schnéevoigt chose to perform. Probably worse was that Kullervo had become tainted with proletarian red: there were those frequent performances of Kivi's play *Kullervo* in the workers' theaters. And there was that variant of a Russian folk tune permeating the third movement of Sibelius's symphony. Not least, there were problems with the soloists. The baritone Oiva Soini (1893–1971) had rehearsed the title role. When Soini was suddenly taken ill, Kullervo had to be sung by a substitute, the tenor Wäinö Sola. In the regimented martial climate of 1930s Finland, warbling tenors did not have the same cachet in the role of national hero as did those magnificent baritones and basses.

Jean Sibelius's creative life was at an end. Only, sadly, it was now plain for all to see, a monument entombed in Finnish granite in Wäinö Aaltonen's interpretation (see fig. 24.2; significantly, Aaltonen was deaf).

In the summer of 1936 the *New York Times* music critic Olin Downes paid a visit to Finland. Downes engaged the composer in conversation about the much-ballyhooed Eighth Symphony. Could Sibelius tell him if the work was complete? Well, two movements were written, Sibelius answered nervously; the rest remained in his head. But could the composer say something about the kind of orchestra required, the number of movements, the formal design? Downes reported sadly, "Sibelius recognised my need. . . . [He] wanted to do something for a friend, and he was the picture of misery. He mumbled

Figure 24.2. Wäinö Aaltonen, *Sibelius*, ca. 1935. Marble bust.
Ateneum Art Museum/Central Art Archives.

incoherent words. His features worked. Then he turned to me in sheer desperation. 'Ich kann nicht,' he exploded in German, and sighed deeply."[12]

The most cataclysmic occurrence in Sibelius's entire career happened not with the proverbial bang, but with a heartbreaking Lutheran cry from the heart of childhood—an echo of the great reformer's "Ich kann nicht anders."

⁓ 25 ⁓
The Close

WAR REVISITED

E ven in the midst of extreme ideological passions, optimism and economic prosperity can flourish, and the late 1930s in Finland was such a time. Preparations were under way for the 1940 Olympics. But on November 30, 1939, a day that began as ordinarily as any other, the heavens suddenly rained down incendiary bombs on Helsinki's citizens. Finland was again at war.

Sibelius's role was scripted for him, although he had auditioned for it for decades. It was romantically expressed by the conductor and pianist Martti Similä after a birthday visit with Sibelius at Ainola on December 8, 1939:

> The image I have formed of the composer of Finlandia had assumed ever clearer features. That image is, even externally, like a wondrous combination of a gigantic force and a mysterious sensitivity. A large presence which, at the same time, includes a surprising vivacity and an intensively staring intensity. A powerful, proud head, supported by a sturdy neck, strangely radiating gray-blue eyes which seem to see the invisible, large, beautifully formed ears, which seem to hear the inaudible; a powerful, elegant, captivating and considerate person.[1]

Politicized and desiccated, the icon served its country exceedingly well. A few months earlier, as world events were threatening to make Finland a pawn in the hands of larger powers, J. K. Paasikivi had made a telling entry in his diary:

> The Russian requirement to "guarantee" Finland in the negotiations with England and France has worsened our position. It has placed us in a different position from the other Nordic countries. We certainly get sympathy from many quarters, but our future is doubted. We are now also "being comforted" and our

position is found to be improving, since Germany made an agreement with Russia. It shows our weak position. *The sympathy for us rests* [on the following]: *we have athletes and Sibelius, we have paid our debt to the USA, we have won against difficulties in our struggle for independence*, and more of that sort of thing. We are seen as an honorable people, who deserve independence. Our Nordic orientation has also notably influenced this.[2] (Emphasis added)

By the 1940s Paasikivi's image of Sibelius had solidified—one might as well say ossified. Composer Sulho Ranta (1906–1960) garbed it in flowery extravaganza, emphasizing the composer's significance to "the people":

A people which has produced and added to the ranks of the great such a mighty master of composition, this almighty seer, charmer, and magician and, what is more, a powerful spiritual giant such as Sibelius who gathers everything around his person and his art—this people may be proud even if it is small and apparently isolated. Sibelius's country and people cannot be forgotten.[3]

Sibelius's terrible fate was to see all he had worked for turned on its head, drained of its substance and meaning for him, and then to be himself transformed into an institution, a hollow shell of what he had once stood for. Had he left Finland, he might have been able to salvage his creative life. But his self-image was too bound up with the nation's, too well entrenched in his iconic status, too strongly reinforced within his family, for him to leave the kingdom whose crown he wore. Indeed, the very idea of Sibelius as the figure of the people's spirit harked back to those golden-age endeavors he had so enthusiastically joined: the central figures of the *Kalevala* were believed to have their origins in the "collective spirit of the nation."[4] Jean Sibelius was widely seen as embodying that spirit.

FAUSTIAN BARGAIN OR HEROIC SACRIFICE?

In Finland World War II is known by its three phases there: the Winter War, the Continuation War, and the Lapland War. Their mind-numbing events have been told in innumerable ways, recounted in the words of survivors, analyzed by historians and journalists, military officers and political leaders. That story belongs elsewhere. Here it will be observed only that Sibelius's role was to remain with his people and to endure the fears and deprivations suffered by all the Finns. As Aino remarked incredulously when offers of refuge began streaming in from abroad, "Those foreigners just do not understand that a Finn doesn't leave his homeland in a moment of danger."[5]

One day during those terrible years, Sibelius walked purposefully into the dining room of Ainola, a basket of manuscripts in his arms. He strode to the fireplace, where flames gently warmed its green tiles. With grim relentlessness he began feeding pages into the blaze.

It is impossible to know exactly all that was destroyed that day. Most believe that the Eighth Symphony went up in smoke, since few traces of it have ever been found. Aino remembered that there was something else: pages savagely ripped from the *Karelia* music. Among them were the ones containing *Vårt land.*[6]

Aino described the period thereafter as "a happy time." Such a dubious description convinces only if one believes that at last, *at last*, Sibelius was making his own Kullervo-like act of defiance. For this was no destruction in order to create anew, such as Michelangelo had done with his Florence *Pietà.*[7] This fire was a destruction to erase the traces of a vision that would no longer cohere and to rage, *rage* against fate, which had given so much and taken so much away. Jean Sibelius had been forced into a role that was not of his choosing and that was not true to himself. Whether he had made a Faustian bargain for a life of fame and security and simply lacked the courage to break free, or his choice to remain in Finland represented an act of supreme heroism, will forever be a question of interpretation. The price, however, is not: his creative life.

HERO OF THE FINNISH PEOPLE

For the Finnish people Sibelius continued to play the part expected of him. After the war, on Finland's Independence Day, December 6, 1948, he granted a rare interview for radio broadcast. He was probably persuaded by a combination of coaxing from the interviewer, Kalevi Kilpi, who was married to Sibelius's granddaughter Merike Ilves; a sense of duty; and the need to bolster the nation's spirit at Christmastime in the sorrowful aftermath of a ghastly war. Even though hostilities had ended, the Finns had retained their independence and their identity only by agreeing to punishing reparations on top of the unimaginable human sacrifices they had already made.

Yet the torch had long ago been passed, and the younger generation had its sights set on other things. Even during the war most of the men at the front wanted to hear popular music, not Sibelius symphonies, in the broadcasts from the one national radio station. Now, only a certain amount of deference to an aging symbol was required. In portions of the documentary not aired until much later, it is possible to hear Kilpi setting up for the interview in the library at Ainola. Patronizingly, he addresses the composer, not with the customary and deferential "Master," but as "Pappa." Aino, monitoring the proceedings like a hawk, quickly objects. Both Sibeliuses adamantly refuse to allow any discussion of a new symphony. Sibelius tentatively brings up the issue of whether he might speak in Swedish. An immediate response, from both Aino and Kilpi, squelches the idea. Wouldn't it be nice, Kilpi placates unctuously, for the public to know that Pappa speaks Finnish; everyone thinks he speaks only German.

When the interview proper begins, the conversation seems anything but genuine. Even allowing for the language question and the fact that Sibelius was, after all, eighty-three years old, his responses seem like carefully scripted sound bites. Most of them, in fact, can be read in interviews, his diary, or the biographies by Karl Ekman or former Sibelius pupil, Bengt von Törne, all written decades earlier.

"Where have you composed most of your works?" he is asked. "At Ainola. Here at Ainola silence speaks."

His advice to young composers? "Never write an unnecessary note. Every note must live."

The majority of the questions were demeaning by their utter inanity. "Do you have a favorite composer?" Sibelius refuses to be drawn: "That is difficult to say, there are so many." "Have there been successful performances of your works recently?" The expansive answer: "Yes."

Kilpi asks Sibelius what sorts of gifts he has received. "What," he prompts, "has come from India?"

JS: A rather strange gift came from there: it was a grain.

KK: A grain of rice?

JS: A grain of rice, engraved with my name.

KK: So it had been written in small letters then?

JS: And it was microscopic.

KK: Indeed.

JS: But they showed up clearly. They have that kind of folk art there.

Then Kilpi turned to matters of somewhat more musical interest.

KK: Would you like to say whether you listen to the radio very much, Professor Sibelius?

JS: Yes, I do, very much.

KK: Well, to what?

JS: Above all, to new music.

KK: From the radio's point of view, of course, it is interesting to know your opinion of the importance of the radio for music, Professor Sibelius.

JS: It is of great importance.

And then—

> *KK*: Could you talk, for example, about current contemporary Finnish com-
> posers? Are there some whom you especially like?
>
> *JS*: There are many of those, and I believe that Finnish music has a great
> future.
>
> *KK*: Certainly, all music lovers will be glad to hear this. And could I ask the
> question, which of your own works do you love the most?
>
> *JS*: I love them all in the same way I love my children.

To paraphrase a Finnish saying, those phrases look good, they sound good, but they don't taste.

ଈଓଈଓ

Jean Sibelius was not the only Finnish icon displayed on the nation's cabinet and dusted off for ritual occasions. By this time, the *Kalevala* and its gods had also undergone further changes. Tapiola, for instance, a name appropriated for something quite other than the mystical evocation of the sheltering forest that rules Sibelius's last great tone poem. For most Finns today, "Tapiola" brings to mind the rather ordinary suburban city in Espoo (the town neighboring Helsinki), but Tapiola had been intended as a garden city, a carefully planned social utopia that would epitomize a classless and equitable society.[8] With a mix into one community of inhabitants of different types, dwellings of different kinds, and nature itself, Tapiola was envisaged with the people's welfare and democratic integration in mind.

In 1950 the indefatigable Martti Haavio published a new volume about the *Kalevala* heroes: *Väinämöinen: Suomalaisten runojen keskushahmo* (*Väinämöinen: The Central Figure of Finnish Poems*). Departing from his earlier, militant interpretation of the *Kalevala* poems and their history, Haavio now wrote that it was not Väinämöinen's combative nature that had made him the font of Finnish *runot*. Rather, it was "his qualities as a sage . . . of far-off days." Two years later Haavio elaborated on his latest interpretation in *Kirjokansi: Suomen kansan kertomarunoutta* (*Kirjokansi: Narrative Poetry of the Finnish People*). In a sharp departure from nationalist dogma, Haavio now argued that it was foolish to seek in the heroic poems a unified golden age of the past and a unified national spirit. Those poems, he maintained, reflected many ages, many spirits. After all, the *Kalevala* was the creation of just one man, Lönnrot. It was not genuine folklore. It was not even genuine history:

> The concept of folk poetry has been overturned. The epic idea of the roman-
> tics has collapsed; the contention of these same romantics that folk poetry is the

product of a mysterious folk spirit has collapsed; the claim that the poems represent only one cultural period, the time of greatness of the southwestern Finns, has collapsed; the illusion that a certain part of our narrative poetry is heroic poetry, etc., has collapsed.[9]

These latest theories must have fallen like hammer blows on Jean Sibelius. In September 1952, Otto Andersson was visiting Ainola with a view to writing the composer's biography (a project he never completed). Again and again Sibelius returned to Haavio's new theories.[10] What did Andersson think of them? How could they be genuine? What had happened, one reads between the lines, to the "inexhaustible source of inspiration"? Sibelius's diary lay nearby, its last entry made in January 1944. Sibelius had written: "What enormous musical possibilities the *Kalevala* offers." Haavio's terrible words summed up the collapse of all the illusions of Jean Sibelius's creative world.

THE FINAL CALL

The curtain did not ring down for some years. And when it did, Sibelius himself was not present. Appropriately, the actions were played out by the Finnish people. It was they who accompanied their "master of composition" on his final journey, he who "was called to eternity" on Friday, September 20, 1957; at that moment "the sorrow of the Finnish people unite[d] the entire civilized world." Such were the phrases heard across the land.[11] (The one slight bit of levity in a nation repeatedly described as sorrowing and filled with mourning citizens was a cartoonlike sketch in one of the national papers: outlines of three aged figures, clearly recognizable as Sibelius, Kajanus, and Gallén in their poses from the famous Symposium portrait, bask in the light of heaven radiating from the right, angel wings welcoming them on the left. The caption read, "Together again.")[12]

Ten days later a state funeral of epic proportions unfolded in Helsinki, the likes of which only heads of nations or celebrity royals are normally accorded. The moment was politically strategic. The "nation was on its belly" before the Soviet Union (the colloquialism in the title of Timo Vihavainen's study of this period),[13] struggling to rebuild after the devastation of the wars while trying to master the delicate art of having the Soviets for neighbors. In 1955 Finland had joined the United Nations. The following year Urho Kaleva Kekkonen (whose first name means "hero," and whose middle name needs no elaboration), a former AKS member, had been elected president of the republic. During his reign (the word is used advisedly—it would last a quarter of a century), the controversial Kekkonen cannily pressed into service a variety of means to maintain Finland's independent and neutral status and demonstrate diplomatically but unequivocally the Finns' position.[14] The passing of Jean Sibelius afforded the optimal occasion for impressing that message upon the global community.

Kekkonen and his ministers were thus conspicuously on hand to give meaning and symbolism to the *scène historique*. At noon on the day following the composer's death, September 21, 1957, the president had gone on Finnish National Radio to speak to the nation in its time of sorrow. Sibelius, he told the people, who "was Finnish to the innermost depths of his heart," composed music that "was and is national in the best sense of that word," although the works had also become common property to music lovers the world over.[15] It was thanks to Sibelius's music, said Kekkonen, that the Finns' national character was known, understood, and respected throughout the entire civilized world. Then he ratcheted up the national rhetoric and myth making a notch further, according Jean Sibelius true visionary status: "In his music [Sibelius] has described the difficult periods in our nation's history, but the works that have made the greatest impact are those telling in monumental tones of Finland's undaunted faith in her future. He was fortunate to live long enough to see his dream of a free Finland come true." The gigantic legacy of this "great son of our people," the president concluded, "will strengthen the faith of generations to come." In death as in life, Jean Sibelius was serving the greater good of the people.

In keeping with the glorious speechifying, the solemn pageantry of the funeral itself surpassed anything the historic *tableaux* of the golden age had ever staged. The church on the Great Square—the Nicholas Church—was cloaked in mourning, lighted only by candles. Seven burned on the altar—one for each of the numbered symphonies (*Kullervo* not yet having received its due recognition in that pantheon). The composer's black-draped coffin had arrived the day before, watched over through the night by an honor guard of students from the university "nations," formally dressed in black tuxedos, their white student caps in hand. On the day of the funeral, Monday, September 30, flags were lowered to half mast throughout the land. Black-draped pictures of "the Master of Ainola" appeared in shop windows. An unaccustomed silence fell on the capital.

Floral tributes had already begun pouring in—from schools, associations, towns, organizations, orchestras, theaters, choirs, societies, and individuals, and from every imaginable corner of Finnish life and far beyond the country's shores. The colors and fragrances of the carnations, chrysanthemums, irises, lilies, and autumn leaves somewhat tempered the stark mood. At one o'clock in the afternoon, events began to move toward their dénouement. Bells tolled. Mounted policemen stood watch, their dark steeds dressed with ribbons of Finnish blue. Already assembled inside the church were leading figures in the nation's musical and cultural life, including such distinguished foreign guests as Sir

Malcolm Sargent, who had been in Helsinki conducting Sibelius's Fifth Symphony the night the composer died.

Newsreels show members of the establishment arriving in their somewhat threatening black luxury automobiles. The British ambassador made his entrance with a wreath of red carnations from the *corps diplomatique*. The ambassador of the Republic of China brought a wreath from his land. The Bulgarian legation arrived with a bouquet so enormous it took two men to carry. Representatives from many other nations came to pay tribute: ambassadors from Czechoslovakia, Denmark, the Netherlands, Norway, Poland, Sweden, Turkey, and the United States; chargés d'affaires from Austria, Canada, France, Hungary, and the Soviet Union; and delegations from East Germany, West Germany, and Switzerland.

At this moment the Finnish nation was in the world's eye. And its leaders played their parts superbly. The prime minister of Finland and the minister of education brought laurel wreaths, tied with a ribbon of the senate in the national colors, blue and white. The speaker and the secretary of the Finnish parliament arrived bearing symbols of farewell from the freely elected members of parliament. Then President and Mrs. Kekkonen descended upon the scene in a deftly orchestrated appearance. Accompanied by their adjutants, they entered the church with a wreath of white lilies and autumn leaves. As the president and his wife approached the catafalque (the only ones allowed to do so), the people rose and listened solemnly as he laid the flowers upon the bier and said in a quiet voice, "In honor of the memory of Professor Jean Sibelius, Finland's great master of composition."

From Aino Sibelius there was a simple wreath of lilies of the valley. It was now to Aino that the nation looked to symbolize their departed composer. The image of the widow arriving at the funeral, dressed in mourning, her face veiled in sheer black silk, led news commentators to murmur, "Mrs. Aino Sibelius bore her great sorrow with great dignity." The photograph of the grieving widow was immediately swept up into the iconic imagery and endlessly reproduced.

Within the church, Tauno Hannikainen (1896–1968) led the assembled Helsinki Philharmonic Orchestra in Sibelius's music: the Intrada and Berceuse from *The Tempest*; *Soi kiitokseksi Luojan* (*We Praise Thee, Our Creator*), from the cantata for the Imperial University's graduation ceremonies but well-known to the people as a psalm, now sung by the choir Suomen Laulu; and *Il tempo Largo*, the slow movement from the Fourth Symphony. Sitting near the coffin was Yrjö Kilpinen (1892–1959), composer and honorary member of the Kalevala Society, poised to give the commemorative speech. The choice of speaker for this role also had its subtext: Kilpinen was known chiefly for his hundreds of songs, many in the mold of German lieder, and he had successfully pursued his career in Hitler's Germany. Like Koskenniemi, Kilpinen's choices caused few problems in right-wing Finland, where in 1942 he was made an honorary professor and, in 1948, a member of the Academy of Finland.

Kilpinen's words played on the theme of Sibelius the man of the people: "Jean Sibelius was truly Finnish, a Finn who faithfully loved his country and his people throughout his whole life."[16] He became the hero of our people, said Kilpinen; his compositions lay close to the people's heart, a precious spiritual treasure that the people cherish and from which in ages to come they will draw strength and new belief to accomplish the tasks that the people as a nation have been bequeathed. It was thus the people themselves whom this extraordinary ceremony was honoring.

As the coffin was borne, to the strains of *In memoriam*, from the church to a waiting hearse and the long slow journey to the burial place at Ainola began, Finland's citizens thronged, gathering along the lengthy procession of black automobiles. Leading the way were the massed standards of Finland and thirty-seven other nations. At the center was the flower-bedecked hearse, somberly rumbling through the streets of Helsinki. Over all, deep silence reigned.

As graphic as are the pictures of the funeral procession, the starkest images of that day are of the people, thousands upon thousands of them. A seemingly endless flood—some seventeen thousand—had streamed into the church to bid farewell. Now university students in their white caps lined up along the departure route in farewell salute. Solemn professional people gravitated there. Shopkeepers, workers, professors, businessmen, bankers, schoolchildren, scouts, homemakers, blind people, disabled people, the Tuusula neighbors—they all came, "the many grief-stricken people who had arrived to accompany Sibelius on his last journey." Every window had faces pressed outward, every balcony held onlookers. Old eyes were wet with tears; young faces showed genuine grief. "The people" stretched across the Great Square, through the city, along Unioninkatu, down the Esplanade, beside Mannerheimintie. Out at Järvenpää they had assembled by the hundreds, waiting patiently for hours while the procession slowly wended its way from the capital to Ainola.

The news commentator spoke for them all, giving the people a collective voice: "It was, of course, *Finlandia* that [Sibelius's] people loved perhaps most of all of his ingenious music. This powerful tone poem of Finnish nature was one of those works that already in the master's lifetime had brought the halo of immortality to his name."

Now that halo of immortality had forever imparted its luster to them.

NOTES

Preface

1. *Jean Sibelius Works*, as the edition is somewhat oddly named in English (referred to as JSW), is the largest and most important humanistic project of its kind ever undertaken in Finland, although its tremendous potential significance is still not widely understood there. The project by the Swedish recording company BIS to make all the composer's music available on CD and billed, equally oddly, as "the Sibelius edition," is a separate, unrelated undertaking.

2. For a review of these biographies up to 1994, see Goss, *A Guide to Research*, 59–74.

3. *Amerikan tiellä—route 66* ([Helsinki]: Alfamer, [1998]).

4. *Dance of Life*, especially chapter 4, "High and Low Context Messages."

5. As Carmen von Boehm Tawaststjerna makes clear in her charming memoir, *Elämän kultareuna* (Helsinki: Otava, 2005).

6. Marja Pohjola describes the National Archives' materials in "Cream of Composer Collections." Gitta Henning's indispensable catalog of the Sibelius family correspondence is available in the Archives.

Introduction

1. "Natursympatien ter sig som det primära, det urkarakteristiska hos Sibelius"; Furuhjelm, *Jean Sibelius*, 13. The first chapter of Nils-Eric Ringbom's biography, published in English translation in 1954, bears the title "Apprenticeship of a Nature Lover."

2. Conflating two different episodes in the composer's life, the text goes on: "It is no wonder that Sibelius' compositions are full of the natural vigour of the forests; once he even took a grand piano with him in the midst of [the] forests and hills of Koli"; http://virtual.finland.fi, accessed January 4, 2006.

3. Finland's land mass is 130,559 square miles; the United Kingdom's, 94,251; see Sjöblom, *Finland from the Inside*, 120, 185.

4. "Och ytlig är den så det förslår. Men jag älskar denna ytlighet ty det är som att marschera med tiaran i nacken öfver sorger m.m. och lifvet blir så dramatiskt. Icke detta gråa." Jean Sibelius to Christian Sibelius; the letter is undated but was probably written in the autumn of 1903.

5. *Dagbok*, December 1918, 280; emphasis added.

Chapter One

1. These and other statistics may be found at http://virtual.finland.fi/, accessed January 4, 2006.

2. Edelfelt's article "Sketches in Finland" includes the artist's drawings of people and landscapes; on Gallén's view, see Gallen-Kallela-Sirén, "Axel Gallén," 45.

3. Auer, *My Long Life*, 11–12.

4. Quoted in Mead and Smeds, *Winter in Finland*, 28; the authors' treatment of the topic and numbing personal experience are the bases for the information here.

5. J. L. Runeberg, *Borgå samlingen*; quoted in *Winter in Finland*, 15.

6. Ibid., 16, 17.

7. Busoni, *Selected Letters*, 30.

8. For a short history of Finland in English, see Kirby, *Concise History*.

9. Klinge, "Finland blir till," in *Finlands historia 3*, 11–49. In Finland the Russian rulers bore the titles of emperor (*keisari* in Finnish, *kejsare* in Swedish) and grand duke (*suur ruutinas* and *storfursten*); the word *czar* (*tsaari* in Finnish), demeaning in its very sound, had a pejorative connotation and when used was intended to make the ruler look as dreadful and non-European as possible. The title *emperor* will be used here as it was by nineteenth-century Finns until the Russian rulers became insupportable.

10. See Klinge's essay in his book *Let Us Be Finns*, and Alapuro, *State and Revolution*, especially 19–39.

11. Alexander Pushkin, "To the Slanderers of Russia"; quoted in Volkov, *St. Petersburg*, 101.

12. On Hämeenlinna, see Vuolio, *Putkesta putkeen*, 29–31; Koskimies, *Hämeenlinnan kaupungin historia, 1875–1944*, 441–44; and Lindeqvist, *Hämeenlinnan kaupungin historia*.

13. Christian Sibelius had worked as a doctor in Mikkeli, a town in eastern Finland, as a military and town doctor in Turku, and as a physician in Tampere before coming to Hämeenlinna; see *Uusi sukukirja*, 222–23.

14. See Yrjö S. Koskimies, "Hämeenlinnan poika Janne Sibelius ja hänen kotikaupunkinsa," in Örlund, *Sibeliuksen Hämeenlinna*, 9; and the episodes related by Ilmi Koponen and reprinted in Sirén, *Aina poltti sikaria*, 15–22.

15. Otto Andersson, Anteckningar, SibMus.

16. "Vill han heta Johan Christian Julius & vi börja kalla honom till Janne, till minne af vår aflidna broder." Christian Gustaf Sibelius to Pehr Sibelius, January 4, 1866; SFA, file box 118.

17. Count Uspensky's words, quoted in Andrew, *Russian Writers and Society*, 3–4.

18. The famine, during which the Finnish population declined by 8 percent, is discussed in Klinge, *Finlands historia 3*, 237–43, from which these statistics are cited.

19. The details of this sorrowful event are drawn from the *Hämeenlinna Letters*, 13.

20. *Dagbok*, July 30, 1912; the translation is Robert Layton's, ETL 1:10.

21. "Gud vår Gud hjelpe! och ledsage! oss till det r[ä]tta i allt görande och låtande samt gifve helsa och krafter till arbete." Maria's undated letter to her son Christian; SFA, file box 118.

22. "Wår Herre Jesu Kriste frid vare med Eder alla! Nåd, Barmhertighet och frid af Gud vår Fader och af Jesus Christus vår Herre! Amen." October 18, 1879; SFA, file box 118.

23. "Hvad hans religiositet beträffar, så är det en sak, som jag alltid skall värdera hos honom." Otto Borg to Maria, February 21, 1879; ibid.

Chapter Two

1. In a letter to Teuvo Pakkala, March 1892; in Heikkilä, *Sanoi Minna Canth*, 120, 256. I am indebted to Rainer Knapas for many of the ideas in this chapter. Schoolfield, *History of Finland's Literature*, has also been an invaluable guide.

2. As of this writing, in the summer of 2006, Finland is the only country in the European Union in which, along with the Evangelical Lutheran Church, the Orthodox Church is an official state church.

3. The percentages were reported in "Presidentti Halonen saa kansalta aiempaa huonommat arvosanat," *Helsingin Sanomat*, July 9, 2006, when a dip in the president's approval rating to a mere 81 percent made national headlines.

4. November 30, 1884; *Hämeenlinna Letters*.

5. *Fantaisie finnoise* was composed in 1909; the *Sketches*, op. 89, in 1912; the hymn is heard in the movement called "Solemn Procession."

6. Söderhjelm, *Min värld*, 1:377.

7. A theme to which he often returned during his engagement to Aino Järnefelt. On this occasion, he continued: "They are, like everyone in my family except me, very religious. I like it so much. Yet they are so sensitive. Their religiosity (especially my Mother's and Aunt's) is also not of the doctrinaire kind, from what I understand. They don't talk of the cold, dogmatic—but they are a little bit like Topelius [meaning childlike]" (De äro, som alla i min familj, utom jag, mycket religiösa. Jag tycker så om det. De äro ändock så känsliga. Deras religiositet [i synnerhet min mors och fasters] är ej heller af det rätta slaget, enligt hvad jag kan förstå. De tala ej det der kalla, dogmatiska—men de äro så litet à la Topelius). Sibelius to Aino, November 22, 1890.

8. Levas, *Sibelius: A Personal Portrait*, 44.

9. For a concise examination of Finland's national literature in English, see Pirjo Lyytikäinen, "Birth of a Nation: The Literary Inscription of Finnishness," in Lehtonen, *Europe's Northern Frontier*, 138–65.

10. Excellent discussions of Runeberg are Schoolfield, *History of Finland's Literature*, 301–17, and Wrede, *Finlands svenska litteraturhistoria*, 1:242–63. See also Wretö, *J. L. Runeberg*. For a review of current research on Runeberg, substantially augmented in the bicentennial year of 2004, see Schoolfield's review of Michel Ekman's *Kaos, ordning, kaos: Människan i naturen och naturen i människan hos J. L. Runeberg* (Helsingfors: Schildts, 2004), *Scandinavian Studies* 78 (2006): 198–203.

11. *Blommans död*; Sibelius set the poem to music as *Blommans öde*, op. 88, no. 6.

12. See Klinge, *Let Us Be Finns*, 74–80.

13. Merete Mazzarella has recently published a biography of Runeberg's wife, *Fredrika Charlotta född Tengström: en nationalskalds hustru* (Helsingfors: SLS; Stockholm: Atlantis, 2007).

14. Ahokas, *History of Finnish Literature*, 44.

15. Johan Wrede, "Runeberg and the Tales: The Voice of the People," in *Albert Edelfelt ja Vänrikki Stoolin tarinat*, 22–28; the quotation is on 26.

16. Topelius, *Boken om vårt land*; quoted in Wrede, "Runeberg and the Tales," 22.

17. Forslin's indispensable *Runeberg i musiken* lists twenty-four Runeberg settings by Sibelius (116–29, 307–9, et passim), nearly one-third of the composer's entire solo song repertoire.

18. The work has been recorded by Astrid Riska (mother of Monika Groop) and the Jubilate Choir as *Sibelius: Music for Mixed and Female Choir* (BIS, 1999; CD-998).

19. See Schoolfield, *History of Finland's Literature*, especially 334–46, on Topelius as writer and poet. Fewster has a discussion of Topelius's role in shaping the "manifest destiny of Finland"; *Visions of Past Glory*, 127–42.

20. Ekman, *Jean Sibelius* (1936), 4.

21. Ibid., 53–54.

22. SWV, 3–6.

23. Composed in 1906, *The Countess's Portrait* was first performed as a *tableau* for a lottery to benefit a college in Kronoby. On the question of opus numbers, see Kari Kilpeläinen, "Opus Numbering and Lists of the Works of Jean Sibelius," in Tarasti, *Proceedings from the First International Jean Sibelius Conference*, 88–97, as well as Kilpeläinen's more extensive discussion in *Tutkielmia*, 167–215.

24. Fewster discusses the book's impact in *Visions of Past Glory*, 133–37. Knapas and Koistinen, *Historiallisia kuvia*, trace the development of Finnish landscape images through handsomely reproduced old lithographs and explanatory texts.

25. Hedvig Rask, "Topelius Boken om vårt land," in Wrede and Zilliacus, *Finlands svenska litteraturhistoria*, 1:424–25, and Fewster, *Visions of Past Glory*, 139–42.

26. Linna's relationship to Topelius was recently highlighted in the nation's leading newspaper, *Helsingin Sanomat*, in an article entitled "Elämä siirtyy kirjoihin ja kirjat elämään," October 25, 2006.

27. Quoted in Schoolfield, *History of Finland's Literature*, 346.

28. My text here is indebted to discussions with Rainer Knapas and Derek Fewster, and to Beijar, Ekberg, Eriksson, and Tandefelt, *Life in Two Languages*.

29. Beijar, Ekberg, Eriksson, and Tandefelt, *Life in Two Languages*, 69–70.

30. In *Über die Wichtigkeit der deutschen Sprache für gründliche Bildung, insbesondere in Finnland* (Saint Petersburg, 1813); quoted in Wuorinen, *Nationalism in Modern Finland*, 247.

31. Varpio's lavishly illustrated *Suomen kirjallisuushistoria* addresses these issues, as does William A. Wilson, "Sibelius, the *Kalevala*, and Karelianism," in Goss, *Sibelius Companion*, especially 44–45. Schoolfield discusses the effect of the dual-language situation on literary historiography in *History of Finland's Literature*, xiv–xxx; and Engman considers its effect on historiography in "National Conceptions of History in Finland."

32. Fewster, *Visions of Past Glory*, 14–16. On Russian imperial policy à propos language, see Klinge, *Let Us Be Finns*, 80–83.

33. Ekberg, *Uppslagsverket Finland*, s.v. "Svenskfinland."

34. Useful sources on Snellman include Fewster, *Visions of Past Glory*, 116–20; Pertti Karkama, "The Individual and National Identity in J. V. Snellman's Young-Hegelian Theory," in Branch, *National History and Identity*, 141–52; and Rainer Knapas, "J. V. Snellman och nationallitteraturen," in Wrede and Zilliacus, *Finlands svenska litteraturhistoria*, 1:280–88.

35. See Schoolfield, *Helsinki of the Czars*, 145, and Fewster, *Visions of Past Glory*, 45, on the vertiginous permutations of this nationalist's name.

36. Schoolfield, *Helsinki of the Czars*, 79, 144, 149.

37. See Branch, "Invention of a National Epic," and William A. Wilson, "Sibelius, the *Kalevala*, and Karelianism," in Goss, *Sibelius Companion*, 43–60. Branch portrays the *Kalevala* as being among the Finns' invented traditions; the statistics cited are on his p. 206.

38. Kirby, *Concise History*, especially 59–67. On the Turku patriots, see Söderhjelm, *Åboromantiken*; Joachim Mickwitz, "Åboromantiken och A. I. Arwidsson," in *Finlands svenska litteraturhistoria*, 1:216–19; Klinge, "'Let Us Be Finns': The Birth of Finland's National Culture," in the same author's *Let Us Be Finns*, 66–95; and Wuorinen, *Nationalism in Modern Finland*, 47–76.

39. See the chapter "The University of Helsinki," in Klinge, *Finnish Tradition*, 81–90.

40. Söderhjelm quoted Gottlund's words in *Åboromantiken*, 144; the translation is from William A. Wilson, "Sibelius, the *Kalevala*, and Karelianism," in Goss, *Sibelius Companion*, 48.

41. Adolf Ivar Arwidsson is supposed to have uttered this famous phrase, although the first recorded mention is Snellman's, from the 1850s.

42. Henrik Stenius, "Körens röst: Den profana körsången som forum för den allmänna opinionen," in Smeds, Knapas, and Strömberg, *Boken om vårt land 1996*, 286–96; and Otto Andersson, "Adolf Iwar Arwidsson och Svenska fornsånger," in Andersson, *Studier i musik*, 1:326–46.

43. For the impact of Herder's ideas on the Finns, see Wilson, "Herder, Folklore and Romantic Nationalism."

44. Ekberg, *Uppslagsverket Finland*, s.v. "Fennomani."

45. Quoted in William A. Wilson, "Sibelius, the *Kalevala*, and Karelianism," in Goss, *Sibelius Companion*, 48.

46. Ibid.

47. Ibid.

48. For those interested in the history of this enormous labor, useful starting points include Kai Laitinen and George C. Schoolfield, "New Beginnings, Latin and Finnish," in Schoolfield, *History of Finland's Literature*, especially 45–59; and Wilson, *Folklore and Nationalism in Modern Finland*. Michael Branch provides a specialized study of one of the early Finnish scholars against a broad background of folkloric research in *A. J. Sjögren: Studies of the North* (Helsinki: Suomalais-ugrilainen seura, 1973).

49. Published by the Finnish Literary Society (SKS) in 1835–36. Lönnrot's historical awareness is discussed in Fewster, *Visions of Past Glory*, 92–98.

50. *Book of Our Land*; the translation is from Wilson, *Folklore and Nationalism in Modern Finland*, 47.

51. For discussions on the *Kalevala* as a historical source, see Hannes Sihvo, "Karelia: A Source of Finnish National History," 181–201, and Anthony F. Upton, "History and National Identity: Some Finnish Examples," 153–65; both in Branch, *National History and Identity*.

Chapter Three

1. On Hämeenlinna, see Poutanen, *Hämeenlinna*; Örlund, *Sibeliuksen Hämeenlinna*; and Koskimies, *Hämeenlinnan kaupungin historia, 1875–1944*.

2. Koskimies, *Hämeenlinnan kaupungin historia*, 442.

3. In 1819 Alexander I called attention to the weakness of the army band's wind power when the troops were practicing at the Parola drilling fields near Hämeenlinna. As a result, by 1820 the Hämeenlinna battalion band was augmented to twenty players; see Vuolio, *Putkesta putkeen*, 19–40.

4. Andersson, Anteckningar, SibMus; for a translation of this recollection into Finnish, see Sirén, *Aina poltti sikaria*, 39.

5. Vuolio, *Putkesta putkeen*, 41–42, considers some of the Russian families in Hämeenlinna and their contributions to the town's life. Sibelius recalled some of his Russian playmates for Ekman in *Jean Sibelius* (1936), 11–12.

6. Lindeqvist, *Hämeenlinnan kaupungin historia*, 169–73.

7. Ina, whose married name was Lange, went on to teach music to the princesses at the Danish court. She also became a writer; using the pseudonym Daniel Sten, Ina Lange published various collections about Finns and Finland, including the essays brought out in 1913 entitled *Skilda tiders musikmästare: Händel, Beethoven, Chopin, Sibelius, Studier över deras liv och verk* [*Music Masters of Different Periods: Händel, Beethoven, Chopin, Sibelius, Studies of Their Life and Work*] (Stockholm: Norstedt & Söner, 1913). See Schoolfield, *A History of Finland's Literature*, 386–87, and Goss, *Jean Sibelius: A Guide to Research*, 114–15.

8. "Säveltäjämestarin lapsuusvuodet ja koulu-ajat," SHS arkistokokoelmat IV: 4, NA.

9. Ibid.

10. March 17, 1883; *Hämeenlinna Letters*.

11. A useful overview of this development is given in Markku Kuisma, "Europe's Wood Basket Transformed: Finnish Economic History in a Long Perspective," in Lehtonen, *Europe's Northern Frontier*, 50–85.

12. Ibid., especially 54 and 58–59. Kuisma observes that tar was strategically important to the British navy, and its supply is what Napoleon tried to cut off as part of his Continental Blockade.

13. Sirén, *Lovisa stads historia*, is the source for the Lovisa details.

14. *Uusi sukukirja*, 221–222. Pehr Unonius moved to Sweden in 1815.

15. Elise Stenbäck gave this vivid description of Captain Jean Sibelius in a letter to composer Jean Sibelius, January 3, 1911; HUL Coll. 206.36.

16. SKB, s.v. "Kingelin, Abraham."

17. Pehr Sibelius's central role in young Sibelius's life was first examined in the *Hämeenlinna Letters*, on which this account is based.

18. Jussila, Hentilä, and Nevakivi, *From Grand Duchy to a Modern State*, 59.

19. Sibelius told this and other stories to Einari Marvia in 1955; Marvia published the interview ten years later as "Kymmenen vuoden takainen käynti Ainolassa."

20. July 6, 1889; *Hämeenlinna Letters*.

21. *Den lustige Nötknäpparen eller En utvald samling af 101 Nöjsamma Gåtor till tidsfördrif vid lediga Stunder afskrifven af Pehr Ferdinand Sibelius*; SFA, file box 119.

22. The story of Pehr's violins was told by the violinist Satu Jalas, granddaughter of Jean Sibelius, in her lecture-recital at the Sibelius birthplace, Hämeenlinna, August 14, 2003.

23. So Helsinki's *Hufvudstadsbladet* related, February 20, 1880.

24. "Sanomaton suru on kohdannut Suomen maata. Aleksanteri II, meidän jalo, rakastettu hallitsijamme on kuollut"; *Hämeen Sanomat*, March 18, 1881.

25. On Alexander III, see Volkov, *St. Petersburg*, 129; *Encyclopedia Britannica* 2005, s.v. "Alexander III"; and Auer, *My Long Life*, 227. Valkenier discusses Valentin Serov and this emperor in *Valentin Serov*, 122–25.

26. Taruskin has dealt with these three principles extensively; see his *Oxford History of Western Music*, 3:327–41, and *Defining Russia Musically*, 25–26, 43–44.

27. A reversal that destroyed a life's work for the composer and chemist Alexander Borodin, who had developed programs for young women doctors and chemistry students; see Redepenning, *Geschichte der russischen und der sowjetischen Musik*, 316; and Billington, *Icon and the Axe*, 435.

28. The description is Kiril Fitzlyon's, transcribed from the documentary film *Stravinsky*, dir. Tony Palmer (n.d.; Paul Sacher Stiftung, Basel, Switzerland).

29. Quoted in Volkov, *St. Petersburg*, 129.

30. Söderhjelm, *Min värld*, 1:378.

31. Valkenier, *Russian Realist Art*, xii.

32. In point of fact, the family owned a violin, but Sibelius told Uncle Pehr in a letter that he had loaned it to a poor classmate and could not bear to ask for its return. June 19, 1881; *Hämeenlinna Letters*.

33. Sibelius described his and Kitti's "debut" to Uncle Pehr, November 30, 1884; *Hämeenlinna Letters*.

34. The role of pharmacists in the musical life of small nineteenth-century towns was not unusual. Leopold Auer recalled that during his early concert tours, he and his father "followed the custom and applied to the town pharmacist, who was invariably a man of more or less education, so that it became his duty to attend to all the details of arranging a concert and provide us with the addresses of the local music-lovers." *My Long Life*, 28.

35. August 1, 1882; *Hämeenlinna Letters*.

36. July 10, 1885; ibid.

37. As he told Ekman years later, in *Jean Sibelius* (1936), 35.

38. August 14, 1885; *Hämeenlinna Letters*.

Chapter Four

1. And honored in the title of the most engaging book ever written about the city, Schoolfield's *Helsinki of the Czars*, to which this chapter is greatly indebted.

2. In the words of artist Albert Edelfelt, "after the manner of the Isaac Cathedral at Saint Petersburg, a sort of little Paris Pantheon flanked by four little towers." "Sketches in Finland," 341.

3. Like Saddam Hussein's statue in 2003, the hated Russian eagle was toppled in 1917, breaking into pieces in the process. However, the pieces were preserved, and in the late twentieth century the symbolic bird was restored to its perch.

4. For a history of this university, see Klinge, Knapas, Leikola, and Strömberg, *Helsingin Yliopisto, 1640–1990*, especially, in the present connection, vol. 1. A brief discussion in English can be found in Klinge, "The University of Helsinki," in *Finnish Tradition*, 81–90.

5. So Ferruccio Busoni observed; *Selected Letters*, 39.

6. "Sketches in Finland"; the quotations are on 341–42 and 343.

7. June 2, 1885; *Hämeenlinna Letters*.

8. "Ich habe Riesenkräfte ins russische Neujahr herübergenommen. Aber bin ich denn noch in Rußland? Hier wird nach europäischer Zeit gerechnet, hier wird so viel Deutsch, Finnisch und Schwedisch gesprochen, auch nicht mehr nach Rubeln gerechnet, sondern nach Mark und Penniä [*sic*], die aber nur den Wert der französischen Franken und Centimes haben—auch die Postmarken sind, wie Du siehst, andere. Enfin, die Stadt ist wunderschön originell—meine Fenster gehen auf den Markt und das bunteste Volksgewühl—im Hintergrund zahllose festgefrorene Schiffe. Hotel höchst elegant, luxuriös, dabei nicht teuer—Verpflegung erträumbar verlockend. Aber ein Mangel an Zeit, der unerhört. Die Leute verfolgen mich mit Respekt, Anbetung. Weißkravattierte Deputationen des Orchesters, der Musikschule usw. Gastfreundschaft bis zum Exzeß. Dabei in den Konzerten eine Andacht und dann ein Getobe." Bülow, *Ausgewählte Briefe*, 441.

9. Sibelius to Uncle Pehr, September 17, 1885; *Hämeenlinna Letters*. Most of what is known about Wasiljeff comes from Sibelius's correspondence to Uncle Pehr, preserved in the Hämeenlinna letters. With the exception of some teaching records in the archive of the Helsinki Music Institute (today in the National Library) and a few newspaper reviews, the documentary collections in Helsinki have yielded virtually nothing about this Russian, not even his dates; the evidence was set forth in my presentation, "Mitrofan Vasilyev, Sibelius's Russian Violin Teacher," at the Finnish-Russian Musical Relationships conference, Sibelius Academy, April 7, 2003.

10. Sibelius to Uncle Pehr, October 28, 1885; *Hämeenlinna Letters*.

11. A photograph labeled "Wasilieff" in the archives of the Helsinki Music Institute is misidentified: the picture shows one Prof. J. Smit, a violinist who appeared rather often in the pages of the theater-and-art newsrag *Program-Bladet*.

12. Sibelius to Uncle Pehr, November 7, 1886; *Hämeenlinna Letters*.

13. November 14, 1885; ibid.

14. November 7, 1886; ibid.

15. Jaakko Kuusisto and Folke Gräsbeck have recorded the E minor composition along with other early works for violin and piano as *Jean Sibelius: Complete Youth Production for Violin and Piano*, vol. 1 (BIS, 1999; CD-1022).

16. For recent research on the Franco-Belgian "school," see Suchowiejko, "Franco-Belgian School of Violin Playing," and Woźna-Stankiewicz, "Compositions of the Franco-Belgian School of Violin Music"; the latter includes a list of the repertoire of these composers heard in Poland up to 1914.

17. See Quitin, "Un grand violoniste belge." Sibelius performed those *Souvenirs* on a concert in Lovisa in 1885; see *Hämeenlinna Letters*, 77–78, 161.

18. *Eugene Onegin*, 196.

19. The letter, with its postscript bearing Sibelius's decision to change his name, is shown in facsimile in the *Hämeenlinna Letters*, 85. The traditional explanation of the name's origin and the reason given in the

Hämeenlinna Letters are not at all mutually exclusive. From Karl Ekman's biography through Erik Tawast-stjerna's, the origin of "Jean" has been attributed to Janne's discovery of calling cards bearing the name in French of his uncle, Captain Johan ("Janne") Sibelius. Young Sibelius's enthrallment with the Franco-Belgian violinists gives more convincing justification for such a profound decision than simply happening upon some calling cards; as he explained to Ekman, "Jean" was "originally intended as a kind of artistic name"; see Ekman, *Jean Sibelius* (1936), 9.

20. September 27, 1887; *Hämeenlinna Letters*. Why Wasiljeff disappeared and where he ended up are questions that currently remain unanswered.

21. See Antony Beaumont's indispensable edition of Busoni, *Selected Letters*, 35.

22. Ibid., 38.

23. Sibelius to Uncle Pehr, September 27, 1887; *Hämeenlinna Letters*. The celebrated Ferdinand Laub (1832–1875) became violin professor at the Moscow Conservatory in 1866, after a brilliant European career; the year before his death he played in Helsinki. Tchaikovsky dedicated his third string quartet, op. 30, to this artist.

24. In 1922 Karl Flodin penned a thorough but uninspiring biography, *Martin Wegelius*. More up to date is Lappalainen, "Martin Wegelius." Both inform the text here.

25. The music history was entitled *Hufvuddragen af den Västerländska Musikens Historia* (1891–93). Its fundamental premises are examined in Huttunen, *Modernin musiikinhistoriankirjoituksen synty Suomessa*. Wegelius's history, along with his writings on Wagner, is discussed in Salmi, *Wagner and Wagnerism*, 164–67. Among Wegelius's various theoretical texts were *De första grunderna i allmän musiklära* (1887), *Lärobok i allmän musiklära och analys* (1888–89), *Lärobok och läsebok i tonträffning* (1893), and *Kurs i homofon sats*, 2 vols. (1897, 1905).

26. "I Finland måste en musikhistoria först *göras*, innan den kan skrifvas." Martin Wegelius, *Hufvuddragen*, 3:584.

27. "Och sannolikt skall det nu uppväxande släktet i detta afseende både få upplefva och kunna uträtta vida märkligare saker än vi." Ibid. Philip Donner and Juhani Similä, "Jean Sibelius," in Donner, *Idols and Myths*, 69, point out that in 1904, when Wegelius revised his history, he added to the Finnish version a statement that his "prophecy" that Sibelius would become a European star had been fulfilled: "the recently established Finnish tradition of classical music may now demonstrate at least one name which is famous in Europe: Jean Sibelius."

28. *Hämeenlinna Letters*, 64, 149.

29. Ibid., 96, 175. Although Sibelius's "facts" must always be checked, his historical claim was, for all practical purposes, correct—oddly enough, given the lively chamber music activity in small Finnish towns such as Hämeenlinna. String quartets had been composed earlier by a Finn—a set of six, written around 1780 by Erik Tulindberg (1761–1814)—but they had been forgotten and were not rediscovered until 1923.

30. See Busoni, *Selected Letters*, especially those on 33–35, the basis for the account here.

31. Ibid., 33. Despite his fault finding, Busoni found the love of his life in Finland: Gerda Sjöstrand, daughter of Swedish sculptor Carl Eneas Sjöstrand, who had made the famous statue *Kullervo Speaking to His Sword*.

32. Ibid., 34.

33. "En liten smärt italienare med brunt helskägg, grå ögon, ung och glad, med lång grå överrock med långa skört på, en liten rund mössa käckt tronande på de yviga konstnärslockarna och en jättestor bernhar-dinerhund, som låg och såg så allvarligt på eleverna under lektionerna att det aldrig var värt att spela falskt. Hans herre skrattade så han fick hålla sig för magen, när han såg vår fingerexercis." Paul, *Profiler*, 46–47.

34. Luening recalls these remarks in *Odyssey of an American Composer*, 175.

35. Flodin, *Martin Wegelius*, 400. The translation—"You are certainly a master of punctuality,

Busoni!" "And you are a master of counterpoint"—does not capture the pun on *Pünktlichkeit* and *Kontrapünktlichkeit*.

36. Luening, *Odyssey of an American Composer*, 175–76.

37. *Dagbok*, November 3, 1910. The exasperation was expressed after studying Busoni's *Fantasia contrappuntistica*.

38. This experience took place between 1917 and 1920, as recounted in Luening, *Odyssey of an American Composer*, 175–76.

Chapter Five

1. *Den lilla sjöjungfrun*, 1887–88; SWV, 526.

2. "Mångt och mycket rent af genialt. Men mycken cynism!" Sibelius to Axel Carpelan, March 12, 1917; quoted in ETS 4:203.

3. Wilson, *Tolstoy*, 66. On literary impulses during *Kullervo*'s genesis, see my introduction to *Kullervo*, in JSW I/1.1, and "Vienna and the Genesis of *Kullervo*: 'Durchführung zum Teufel!,'" in Grimley, *Cambridge Companion*, 28–31.

4. Thurman, *Isak Dinesen*, 60–63; and *The New Encyclopedia Britannica* (2005), s.v. "Brandes." Burmester's description was given in *Fifty Years as a Concert Violinist*, 99.

5. Strindberg, *The Red Room*, 65, 74, 95.

6. Frida Strindberg quotes Hamsun in *Marriage with Genius*, 278. Hamsun's poem to Sibelius appears in facsimile in ETF 1 (among the unpaginated photographs).

7. Aspelin, "Itkusta ja naurusta Kalevalassa." Gallen-Kallela-Sirén observes that the *Kalevala* paintings by his great-grandfather Axel Gallén conformed closely to Aspelin's interpretation: the men tend to look grave, with only the women indulging in smiles and laughter; see Gallen-Kallela-Sirén, "Axel Gallén," 266.

8. The issue was brought to wider public attention as recently as 2004, when Johanna Korhonen, under the headline "Virallisen mollin maa" (The Country of Official Minor Mode), interviewed the popular-music researchers Pekka Jalkanen and Vesa Kurkela, *Helsingin Sanomat*, May 16, 2004.

9. Bax, *Farewell, My Youth*, 61; the date of Bax's encounter with Sibelius was 1909.

10. For an entertaining discussion of Paul, see Schoolfield, "Sibelius in Finland-Swedish Literature," in Murtomäki, Kilpeläinen, and Väisänen, *Sibelius Forum 1995*, 27–28, to which this section is indebted, along with Johnson, *Sibelius*, 34–39.

11. ETL 1:40–41. Tawaststjerna also discusses the similarities between the Sibelius and Schumann "Florestans."

12. The words are put into his relative's mouth by Bo Carpelan in the historical novel *Axel*, 104.

13. SKB, s.v. "Järnefelt."

14. Arvid Järnefelt, *Vanhempieni romaani*, 3 vols. (Porvoo, Helsinki: WSOY, 1928–30).

15. Of the other girls, Sigrid died as an infant, Hilja died in early childhood, and Ellida and Ellen (Elli) perished as relatively young adults.

16. Kopponen examines the Järnefelts' philosophy in "Järnefeltit."

17. See *Eero Järnefelt, 1863–1937*, from which Järnefelt's quotation is taken (4), and *"Mir iskusstva."* Lindqvist gives biographical particulars about Järnefelt in *Taiteilijan tiellä*.

18. Strindberg's description of Falander in *The Red Room*, 131.

19. Karl Flodin's description, quoted in Ekman, *Jean Sibelius* (1936), 40.

20. As can be heard in a radio interview given by Sibelius, December 6, 1948.

21. So Busoni told Adolf Paul in a letter written November 10, 1921; quoted in ETL 3:212.

22. Quoted in Ekman, *Jean Sibelius* (1936), 39.

23. "'Se on kumma, mutta kyllä Jean herättää kaikissa vaan ihastusta, vaikka hän niin vähän sitä varten tekee.'" Aino Järnefelt reported both her father's and Hanna Wegelius's reactions in a letter to Sibelius, November 19, 1890.

24. Söderhjelm, *Min värld*, 1:378–82.

25. Sibelius related the details of the masked ball in a letter to Uncle Pehr, February 3, 1889; *Hämeenlinna Letters*.

26. The quotation is taken from Couling, *Ferruccio Busoni*, 158; Couling is one of the few scholars to discuss the work. Long unavailable on disk, the *Geharnischte Suite* was finally recorded in 1999, on *Ferruccio Busoni: Brautwahl-Suite, Geharnischte Suite*, by Jean-François Antonioli and l'Orchestre Philharmonique de Timisoara (Timpani; 1C1054).

27. "Kom hit i vår. Wi skola gå till Pratern vifta och lefva. Wi äro ju bägge på sätt och vis konstnärliga Don Quixottes. Det är ju nog så bra så plagierar man åtminstone Cervantes." January 13, 1891.

28. Quoted in Kagan-Kans, *Hamlet and Don Quixote*, 13. See also Billington, *Icon and the Axe*, 380–81, and the chapter "Ivan Turgenev" in Andrew, *Russian Writers and Society*, 1–43.

29. "Minä tahtoisin enemmän ylpeyttä meihin suomalaisiin. Ei 'kaiken kallella kypärin'! Mitä meillä on häpeämistä? Tämä ajatus käy läpi 'Lemminkäisen kotiinpaluun.' Lemminkäinen vetää vertoja mille kreiville tahansa. Hän on ylimys, ehdottomasti ylimys!" Quoted in A. O. Väisänen, "Jean Sibelius vaikutelmistaan," 80.

30. *Dagbok*, August 16, 1912.

31. Quoted in Ekman, *Jean Sibelius* (1936), 104, where the full letter is translated.

32. *Zweite-Orchestersuite (Geharnischte-Suite)*, op. 34, A. (Komponiert 1895, Umgearbeitet 1903) (Leipzig: Breitkopf & Härtel, 1905).

Chapter Six

1. "I mellersta Europa skaffa sig ökad bildning i allmänhet, närmare kännedom af språk, länder och menniskor, stegrad erfarenhet och vidgad horisont för hufvudets blick och hjertats." Quoted in Hjelt, *Stipendier*, 27.

2. As shown in Tuomikoski-Leskelä, *Taide ja politiikka*; the statistics are on 24–26 and 318.

3. Ibid., 319. Support was given not only to men, but also to Finland's women artists (there were almost no women composers). The country's tiny population meant that all human resources counted, especially in building up the national identity. Nevertheless, women often had greater difficulties with funding than the men, and as the male artists became increasingly involved in the plastic arts, the women were often edged out. Where the women could excel without threat of male replacement was in vocal performance and the theater.

4. This phenomenon is discussed in Ranki, *Isänmaa ja Ranska*; see especially 73–82. The quotation, from a letter dated November 2, 1908, written by Hilja Onerva Lehtinen (later Madetoja) to her father, is translated from Ranki's text, 79.

5. "*Il y a trop de musique en Allemagne.*" "Musique française et musique allemande," in *Richard Strauss et Romain Rolland*, 219.

6. Lourié, *Sergei Koussevitzy and His Epoch*, 61.

7. September 8, 1889; *Hämeenlinna Letters*.

8. "Jean Sibelius (utmärkt hygglig och begåvad pojke, speciellt ställd under vårt beskydd)." Quoted in Söderhjelm, *Werner Söderhjelm*, 87.

9. The translation is Johnson's, in *Jean Sibelius*, 35.

10. They were "saddled with a sense of social, cultural, and legal inferiority and emerging from their provincial narrowness onto an art scene that lacked tradition (except the discredited one of service to the Court)," as Valkenier observed in *Russian Realist Art*, 16.

11. October 3, 1889; *Hämeenlinna Letters*.

12. And "every other nose is Jewish," as Aino wrote to Elisabeth Järnefelt, December 12, 1900; Talas, *Aino Sibeliuksen kirjeitä*, 194. To her brother Kasper, Aino complained, "Money is god for them, their daily bread and always the subject of talk"; the fervent materialism "we gladly left at last"; letter transcribed in Sirén, *Aina poltti sikaria*, 198–200.

13. "Jag har, som du lär veta, syff," September 19, 1889; HUL 206.62.

14. This discussion is based on Häkkinen, *Rahasta—vaan ei rakkaudesta* (*Money—but Not Love*), and an interview with the author, May 25, 1996. I am grateful to Mr. Häkkinen for his generous advice, information, and his insights incorporated here. See also Schoolfield, *Helsinki of the Czars*, 114, 122.

15. Häkkinen, *Rahasta—vaan ei rakkaudesta*. The author's chart on p. 81, showing social groups of women who contracted venereal diseases from February 1905 to October 1907, indicates that 76 percent of the diseases were found among women who were prostitutes, with the remaining 24 percent distributed among the upper class, middle class, working people, and servants.

16. Hayden, *Pox*, 319–20.

17. Quoted in Tramont, "*Treponema pallidum* (Syphilis)," 2769.

18. Berättigad till dimissionsbetyg, 1889, "Herr Jean Sibelius," Helsinki Music Institute Archives, HUL.

19. September 8, 1889; *Hämeenlinna Letters*.

20. "Kära Broder gå icke den väg jag gått, lek icke med eld. Detta är min ruin, såsom så mången annans," November 9, 1889; SFA, file box 118.

21. "Det är något af 'rus' och 'lår' i den," May 4, 1891. See Tomi Mäkelä, "'Mein Kopf ist voller Walzer: Jean Sibelius und der Umkreis Pauline Luccas in Wien,'" in Krones, *Jean Sibelius und Wien*, 70, for the difficulties of interpreting this passage; Mäkelä outlines Sibelius's symptoms and indiscretions during the Vienna year in detail.

22. Paul, *En bok om en människa*, 193; the translation is from Schoolfield, "Sibelius in Finland-Swedish Literature," in Murtomäki, Kilpeläinen, and Väisänen, *Sibelius Forum 1995*, 28.

23. Quoted in Johnson, *Jean Sibelius*, 28.

24. Tramont, "Impact of Syphilis."

25. December 24, 1889, *Hämeenlinna Letters*.

26. According to Dr. Edmund C. Tramont of the National Institutes of Health in Bethesda, Maryland, to whose studies and personal consultation, on December 12, 2006, about Sibelius's case I am indebted. As Tramont explains in his detailed article "*Treponema pallidum* (Syphilis)," syphilis is most infectious when it is acute, i.e., when there is an ulcer. It can also live in the blood and be transmitted by means of blood transfusion. But four years after contracting syphilis, virtually no one is infectious. The majority of people—as many as 90 percent—self-cure and never go on to develop the disease's late-stage complications.

27. February 29, 1892.

28. Tramont, "*Treponema pallidum* (Syphilis)," 2769.

29. For an overview of the 1889–90 season, see Muck, *Einhundert Jahre Berliner Philharmonisches Orchester*, 31–37.

30. "Då Adagiot föredrogs tyckte jag mig vara i en pelargång. Det var månsken. På venstra sidan var en fast vägg, på den andra en härlig trädgård med paradisfåglar, snäckor, palmer, m.m. Allt var dött och stilla, skuggorna voro långa och skarpa och det luktade som i ett gammalt bibliothek. Ingenting annat hördes än suckar. Det var Beethoven som suckade. Då themat i Fmoll för andra gången återkommer suckade han ofantligt djupt.—Efter en stund förvandlades allt till stora sjöar med rödt vatten och ofvan dem spelade Gud violin. Småningom märkte jag att Joachim dock förde stråken, de Ahna och de andra kommo också fram, och slutligen var jag sjelf J. Sibelius." Sibelius to Wegelius, November 6, 1889. This extraordinary description is quoted in ETS 1:129, but not in the biography's English translation.

31. Wegelius seems to have recommended Leopold Wirth, but Wirth charged a fee Sibelius could not afford. Uncle Pehr heard from Aunt Evelina that their nephew had begun violin lessons with a "Schultze." A

violist by the name of "I. Schulz, Lottumstr. 11N" appears in the city's *Adress-Kalender* for 1889, and various other musical Schulzes show up in the city, but which, if any, of these might have taught Sibelius is not clear. See n. 34.

32. Leichtentritt, *Das Konservatorium der Musik Klindworth-Scharwenka*, 6.

33. As he mentioned in a letter to Kåre Foss in Kristiania (Oslo), May 30, 1921; private collection.

34. In the first biography about Sibelius, Furuhjelm stated that the young composer had taken violin lessons in Berlin "with Sachse and Struss" (*Jean Sibelius*, 104). "Sachse," a name as common in Berlin as sausage, has proved as elusive as "Schulz." One wonders if perhaps they are the same shadowy figure, the correct name simply misapprehended in the family's literary round robin.

35. Schellenberg, "Overview," 1–6, reviews some of the biographical sources. Becker also appears in Hermann Abert's *Illustriertes Musik-Lexikon* (1927) and *Biographisches Jahrbuch* (in an entry written by Robert Eitner).

36. So Eitner observed of Becker in *Biographisches Jahrbuch*.

37. Their son Theodor Albert, born the following year, became a cellist. Becker's grandson was the composer Günther Raphael (1903–1960).

38. Schellenberg examines *Selig aus Gnade* in some detail in "Overview," 47–66.

39. *Neueberliner Musikzeitung* 34 (1880); the translation is Schellenberg's, "Overview," 10.

40. October 3, 1889; *Hämeenlinna Letters*.

41. "Vet Du Becker det är då en peruk[stock] från hufvudet till fotabjellet. När han såg min qvartett, så höll han på få slag (isynnerhet kunde han icke nog förundra sig öfver att jag begagnat samma tons dur och moll treklang omvexlande)," September 29, 1889.

42. October 4, 1889.

43. "Försök att vara man. Tänk alltid på att du har ansvar. Låt aldrig en passion få välde öfver dig. Utveckla harmoniskt det hvad du fått. Inbilla dig ej ha annat än du har. Tänk icke att blifva en storhet. Arbeta med förstånd. Si male nunc et olim sic erit. Du är så många förb[ö]ners och böners barn att du omöjligen af Gud lemnas"; SFA, file box 1.

44. "Att han krassar Dig i den stränga stilen är ju just för att ge Dig kraft för den *fria*," October 4, 1889.

45. Schellenberg, "Overview," 67.

46. Quoted in Ekman, *Jean Sibelius* (1936), 68.

47. As Sibelius reported to Uncle Pehr, "[My] landlord is from Alsace and talks a language which is more like yelling; he often has friends over and then they drink, shout, and sing loudly. I too have been part of the latter sometimes," October 3, 1889; *Hämeenlinna Letters*.

48. These manuscripts, preserved in Finland's National Library, are described in Kilpeläinen, *Jean Sibelius Musical Manuscripts*, 358–66. They have yet to be systematically examined for what they might tell about a budding Finnish composer in the context of Berlin's late nineteenth-century musical world.

49. SWV, 482–83.

50. Wegelius to Sibelius, May 6, 1890. This letter, containing detailed criticism of the quintet, is translated in ETL 1:64.

51. "Janne skall blifva något stor[t] för sitt fosterland!" Aunt Evelina reported Uncle Pehr's words to their nephew in a letter dated January 16, 1890; SFA, file box 28.

52. As Sibelius had told Uncle Pehr, August 25, 1885; *Hämeenlinna Letters*.

Introduction to Part II

1. Quoted in Schoolfield, *Helsinki of the Czars*, 199.

2. On these developments, see Kirby, *Concise History*, 75–76, 124–25; Klinge, *Finlands historia 3*: 316–21; and Paasivirta, *Finland and Europe: International Crises*, 166–69.

3. Kirby, *Concise History*, 75. The essay was also published in Russian and English.

4. Hroch, *Social Preconditions*, 22–24. Hroch considers the Finns' specific case in his chapter 10, "Integration without Revolution: The Finns."

5. See "Introducing Early Finland," in Fewster, *Visions of Past Glory*, 50–114; and William A. Wilson, "Sibelius, the *Kalevala*, and Karelianism," in Goss, *Sibelius Companion*, 43–60.

6. Snellman to Castrén, October 1, 1844; quoted in Kirby, *Finland and Russia, 1808–1920*, 39.

7. Hroch, *Social Preconditions*, 14–17, discusses the complex problem of defining the structure of class societies.

8. On Flora Day and the astonishing quantities of alcohol available, see Klinge, *Finlands historia* 3:152–53.

9. Klinge has an entire chapter on *Vårt land* as the national anthem in *Den politiske Runeberg*, 355–74. Runeberg apparently wanted to set one of the *Ensign Stål* poems to the tune of "Yankee Doodle" and was influenced in the writing of his *Vårt land* by S. F. Smith's "My Country 'Tis of Thee."

10. Hroch, *Social Preconditions*, 23.

11. See Liikanen, *Fennomania ja kansa*, and Kirby, *Concise History*, 135, 137.

12. Kirby, *Concise History*, 130–31; and Stenius, "Breakthrough of the Principle of Mass Organization."

13. For useful discussions of the Kansanvalistusseura, see Fewster, *Visions of Past Glory*, 158–63; Liikanen, *Fennomania ja kansa*, 166–74, 350–52; and Ekberg, *Uppslagsverket Finland*, s.v. "Kansanvalistusseura."

14. Klinge, *Finnish Tradition*, 111.

15. "Mikä velvollisuus on siis suurempi, pyhempi kuin palvella tätä kansaa, parantaa sen asemaa, jakaa sen suurelle joukolle sitä valistusta ja sivistystä." Gebhard, "Kirje Helsingistä," 70.

16. See Rainer Knapas, "Liberalism och fennomani," in Wrede and Zilliacus, *Finlands svenska litteraturhistoria*, 1:356–61.

17. The Finnish library system is discussed in Fewster, *Visions of Past Glory*, 161–63, from which the statistics here are taken.

18. Undated, although its contents show the letter to have been written in the fall of 1889.

19. "Skada att Du har så kort tid på Dig, annars kunde du ju komponera t.ex. en kör-cykel till någon episod från Kalevala eller dylikt. Äfven skall jag söka att skaffa dig finska folksånger och danser." Ibid.

20. The anthology's full title was *Mäntyharjun Kansanlauluja koonnut sekä kvartetille ja sekaääniselle köörille sovittanut* (Porvoo, 1887). Karjalainen identified these tunes in "Sibeliuksen Allegro torviseptetille"; see also Saari, "Sibeliuksen Allegron jäljet johtavat Mäntyharjulle." For facsimiles showing the Allegro's folk tunes, see *Kullervo*, JSW I/1.1, xvi. The energetic Sivori promoted music for the masses, collected the songs of the people, and arranged them for various groups.

Chapter Seven

1. Adolf Paul, "From a Friend of Sibelius," *New York Times*, December 29, 1935.

2. Albert Becker's letter confirming Sibelius's study and progress, May 5, 1890; SFA, file box 1; emphasis added. The letter is transcribed in Gleißner, *Der unpolitische Komponist als Politikum*, 43–44.

3. "Meillä on kultaa keskellämme," *Päivälehti*, March 6, 1890.

4. "Jag älskade Dig då redan," February 26, 1891. The title of this section comes from a line Sibelius wrote in a letter to Aino from Berlin on April 11, 1898: "Se rakkautemme on kuitenkin elämämme."

5. The Norwegian-born Nyblin (1856–1923) established a studio in Helsinki in 1877 and became Finland's foremost portrait photographer; he was also well-known for Finnish landscapes (see fig. 4.1) and interiors. Nyblin was the *primus motor* behind both the Finlands Fotografers Förbund in 1897 and the first general photography exhibition, held at the Ateneum (1903). Nearly all the Young Finns posed for Nyblin at one time or another.

6. Sibelius to his mother and Aunt Evelina, November 10, 1890; *Hämeenlinna Letters.*

7. Ibid.

8. December 2, 1890; ibid.

9. December 26, 1890; ibid.

10. Sibelius to Wegelius, April 9, 1891.

11. So Minna Canth told Elli Canth, June 14, 1892; *Minna Canthin kirjeet*, 555–56.

12. Sibelius to Aino, December 26, 1890. On the ironies of Sibelius's use of this passage, see Goss, "Vienna and the Genesis of *Kullervo*," in Grimley, *Cambridge Companion*, 30–31.

13. Ingelius was not only Finland's first symphonist, he was also the country's first music critic and the creator of Finland's first *Künstlerroman*. Sometimes these musical and literary interests entwined in productive ways, but at other times this "brilliant bungler" (Topelius's description) was thwarted by his own carelessness and egocentricity; see Schoolfield, *History of Finland's Literature*, 329–30. Details of Ingelius's short but engrossing life can be found in Öller, *En finländsk romanskrivare*, and Sarjala, *Poeettinen elämä.*

14. See the introduction to *Kullervo*, JSW I/1.1, on which the text here is based and where passages from the original letters are transcribed.

15. "Jag tänkte sist i dag då jag satt vid pianot och komponerade att då Du, engel, är hos mig sitter Du bredvid mig eller i min famn och hjelper till med kyssar," February 3, 1892.

16. Goss, "Backdrop for Young Sibelius," 70–72. *Halu* first showed up in the composer's piano-vocal arrangement of movement 3, completed in February 1892. The arrangements of *Kullervo*'s two choral movements (the third and fifth) have recently been published for the first time, in JSW I/1.4.

17. "I går läste jag för tror jag tionde gången Yksin." Sibelius to Aino, February 25, 189[1].

18. "Du tycker kanske att jag är en narr, en Don Quixote," Christmas Eve, 1890.

19. "Om han vore en välmående handelsman med fett om hjärtat skulle jag skratta, men, Finland behöver dylika som han och derföre detta," ibid.

20. The title of this section comes from a letter Sibelius wrote to his mother, December 26, 1890; *Hämeenlinna Letters.*

21. "Denna luft gör mig galen. Walser fara i hufvudet på mig och alla likna de Schuberth's," October 25, 1890.

22. March 28, 1891.

23. "Jag har aldrig gråtit så mycket som då jag lagade den." Sibelius to Wegelius, May 4, 1891. In the background of the *Scène*, he wrote, lay "ett sorgligt, sorgligt minne." Tomi Mäkelä believes that this "sorrowful, sorrowful memory" involved Pauline Lucca; see "'Mein Kopf ist voller Walzer,'" in Krones, *Jean Sibelius und Wien*, 65–78. Runeberg is quoted in Schoolfield, *History of Finnish Literature*, 307.

24. "För mycket 'Machen.'" Sibelius to Wegelius, February 12, 1891.

25. "Nu har det redan något lagt sig och min gamla antipati för det tyska börjar röra på sig." Sibelius to Werner Söderhjelm, January 19, 1891; HUL Coll. 469.

26. December 26, 1890; *Hämeenlinna Letters.*

27. "Blef presenterad för en massa personer alla hörande till aristokratin här," January 6, 1891.

28. "Det går igenom verlden en aristokratie, jag menar icke den med förnäma namn utan den hvilken känner fint och har vyer hvilka ej andra förstå. Denna älskar jag så." Sibelius to Aino, February 10, 1891.

29. See Goss, "Backdrop for Young Sibelius," where these ideas have been more fully explored, and "Vienna and the Genesis of *Kullervo*," in Grimley, *Cambridge Companion*, 22–31.

30. The two-part article, "Kirjailijain muotokuvia, XXIII: Leo Tolstoi," appeared in the Finnish periodical *Valvoja* (*The Watchman*).

31. "De äro båda så radikalt emot publik- och tante-smak att jag fröjdas." Sibelius to Adolf Paul, April 24, 1891.

32. The contest and its importance for Sibelius's *Kullervo* project are more fully discussed in Goss, "Backdrop for Young Sibelius," 60–63, where some of the relevant Kullervo artworks are reproduced.

33. Rein, "Muutama sana Kalevalan kuvittamisesta," 227; translated in Goss, "Backdrop for Young Sibelius," 62. See also "Kalevala-kuvien näyttely Ateneumissa," *Päivälehti*, April 3, 1891; and, on Rein as philosopher, Ripatti, "Filosofi apologeettana."

34. See Gallen-Kallela-Sirén, *Minä palaan jalanjäljilleni*, 148.

35. Writing to Rosa Newmarch in 1906, Sibelius explained in stilted French that his *Kullervo* "est une symphonie pour soli, chor et orchestre; le text de 'Kalevala.'" Then he asked her to correct an error frequently found in the foreign press: "Jusqu'à présent je n'ai jamais employée que des temata absolument de moi même," February 8, 1906; SFA, file box 121; emphasis added. Newmarch published this claim in her *Jean Sibelius: A Short Story*. It was only with the production of the symphony's critical edition in the early twenty-first century that *Kullervo*'s folk-song sources began to emerge: see the introduction to *Kullervo*, JSW I/1.1, which includes pertinent transcriptions and facsimiles; and Goss, "Jean Sibelius's Choral Symphony" and "Jean Sibelius and Finnish Nationalism."

36. The Lvov-Prach anthology, first published in Saint Petersburg in 1790, went through further editions in 1806 and 1815. See Mazo, introduction to Lvov and Prach, *Collection of Russian Folksongs*.

37. The tune is *Ai, vo polye lipin'ka* (*A Linden Tree Is In the Field*); see Taruskin, *Stravinsky and the Russian Traditions*, 1:695–717.

38. An opera based on a novel by Dostoyevsky about life in a Siberian prison. The tune, which is especially prominent in the opera's prelude, is the well-known *Vo polye beryozyn'ka stoyala* (*In the Field Stood a Birch Tree*), no. 39 in Rimsky-Korsakov's *100 Folk Songs*. Janáček had his own copy of Lvov-Prach, which, according to John Tyrrell, was a valuable resource for his operatic inspiration; see Tyrrell, *Lonely Blackbird*, 352–53. Prach, incidentally, was probably Czech.

39. A poignant letter to Sibelius from Rimsky's widow after the revolution implored the Finn's help in the return of their Karelian home.

40. *Päivälehti*, April 28, 1892.

41. See the critical commentary to *Kullervo*, JSW I/1.1, 132–45.

42. Merikanto's words appeared in *Päivälehti*, April 28, 1892; the banner's words are from the *Kalevala*, *runo* 50; quoted in *Kullervo*, JSW I/1.1, xii, xv.

Chapter Eight

1. Väisänen, "Jean Sibelius vaikutelmistaan," 78.

2. These descriptions are reprinted in Sirén, *Aina poltti sikaria*, 111, 132.

3. The portrait remained in Jean and Aino Sibelius's possession until the 1930s. In that decade Sibelius returned the painting to his brother-in-law, informing Järnefelt that he really didn't like it at all. See Lindqvist, *Taiteilijan tiellä*, 125.

4. See the provocative chapter "Shocking as a Fine Art," in Jackson, *The Eighteen Nineties*, 113–20.

5. "Våra politiska strider—bara ras- och språkfejder—äro outhärdliga. Ryssarna chicanera oss vad de kunna, och ju mera vi strida inbördes, desto gladare äro de"; quoted in Hintze, *Albert Edelfelt*, 2:96.

6. See Liikanen, *Fennomania ja kansa*, 150–74, and Klinge, *Finnish Tradition*, 111–14.

7. Konttinen examines the Young Finns in *Sammon takojat*. Also valuable are Gebhard, "Kirje Helsingistä," and Gallen-Kallela-Sirén, "Gallén and the Circle of Young Finland," in "Axel Gallén," 298–307.

8. "Käsitykset 'fennomania' ja 'svekomania' eivät minulle enää eksisteeraa. Ne ovat menneitä. Aika on nyt toinen, ajan tarpeet ovat toiset. Ruotsalaisia ei meistä millään mahdilla enää tule, mutta meidän on katsominen, ettei meistä tule venäläisiä." Kannila, *Minna Canthin kirjeet*, 577. The letter is transcribed in full on 574–79.

9. "Se vaati puhtaampaa ilmaa, nuorempaa, europalaisempaa [*sic*] elämänkäsitystä, uskonnollista vapaamielisyyttä ja suvaitsevaisuutta, valtiollista ja yhteiskunnallista kansanvaltaisuutta." *Nuori Suomi* 24 (1914); reprinted in Mällinen, *Nuoren Suomen ytimessä*, 69. Gallen-Kallela-Sirén translates a substantial portion of this important recollection in "Axel Gallén," 303–4.

10. "Nuori Suomi," *Nuori Suomi* 1 (1891); reprinted in Mällinen, *Nuoren Suomen ytimessä*, 63.

11. October 28, 1883; quoted in *Emil Wikström*, 94.

12. Gallen-Kallela-Sirén, "Axel Gallén," 297–98.

13. The publication continues today as *Helsingin Sanomat*.

14. The photograph, dated 1889 in Vihola, *Keuruun ja Pihlajaveden historia*, 389, is reproduced in ETF 1:157.

15. Liikanen, "Light to Our People," especially 421–22.

16. Notably, Topelius himself was involved in arranging *tableaux vivants*, staged with appropriate dress and other requisites, sometimes with classical sculptures, sometimes accompanied by music, as described in his *Finlands krönika* (for an illustrated and annotated edition, see Topelius, *Finlands krönika, 1860–1878*). Such living montages were also popular in France and Germany as well as in Saint Petersburg, where famous paintings were "enacted." The vivid stagings, which satisfied a deep visual and theatrical need in an age before cinema or television, prompted many participants to requisition hand-colored photographs of themselves onstage. For other background and the importance of *tableaux vivants* to music, see Grey, "*Tableaux vivants.*"

17. See Hobsbawm, "Mass-Producing Traditions: Europe, 1870–1914," in Hobsbawm and Ranger, *Invention of Tradition*, especially 270–72.

18. Gallen-Kallela-Sirén describes the Savo-Karelian lottery and its importance for Axel Gallén in "Axel Gallén," 307–12; his discussion has informed this account, as have contemporary press reports, especially *Päivälehti*, March 12 (where the full program was published) and March 14, 1891.

19. Exactly which Pacius work is meant is not clear; on this question and the title's meaning, see chapter 10.

20. Heiden's letter is translated from the citation (in Finnish) in Polvinen, *Valtakunta ja rajamaa*, 171. On the Russian position vis-à-vis Fennoman activities, see Klinge, *Let Us Be Finns*, 80–81.

21. Pacius had died just two months before the lottery event, on January 8, 1891. His son-in-law, Karl Collan (1828–1871), a song composer and specialist in Serbian poetry, and the first translator of the *Kalevala* into Swedish, and whose music was also heard that evening, had died twenty years before, only forty-three years of age.

22. Lauri Kivekäs (né Stenbäck, 1852–1893) was a radical agitator who, in a bid to promote his agenda of the supremacy of the Finnish language, tried to seize control of *Päivälehti*; see Hannes Sihvo, "Valta vai kulttuurihegemonia," in Tommila, *Herää Suomi*, 368–71. It was Kivekäs's corpse that Gallén eerily painted in its casket, at the bidding of the dead man's widow, Ida Aalberg.

23. Bohlman, *Music of European Nationalism*, 83–84. Regeneration and continuity are especially vital questions where such small populations as Finland's are concerned (today only a little over 5 million), since births are essential to perpetuating the nation. Currently, at least a page or more of every weekend edition of the country's major newspaper, *Helsingin Sanomat*, is given over to birth announcements, many accompanied by photographs.

24. "Silloin ei enää katsottu taitavasti järjestettyä kuvaelmaa, vaan elettiin ja tunnettiin itse mukana." *Päivälehti*, March 14, 1891. "Tuomas" was one of Juhani Aho's several pseudonyms.

25. Ahlqvist's original poem read, "Red is the region of the *southeast*," ostensibly a reference to Saint Petersburg, situated south and east of Helsinki. Autio suggests that the word was changed from *kaakkon kulma* to *pohjan kulma* to avoid offending Russian sensibilities; *Savo-karjalaisen osakunnan historia III: Roudan aika*, 182. The alteration remained in Kajanus's setting long after Finland was no longer a Russian grand

duchy; see, for example, *Sotamarssi*, in *Isänmaallisia Lauluja*, vol. 1, ed. A. E. Taipale (Helsinki: Otava, 1946), 58–60.

26. In his *Cartas finlandesas*, printed posthumously (and translated into Finnish as *Suomalaiskirjeitä* in 1964). After his service in Helsinki, Ganivet, who was born the same year as Sibelius, was posted to Riga, where in 1898 he drowned himself in the Dvina River.

27. Mustonen, *Ravintolaelämää*, 9–48, provides details and illustrations of Society House.

28. Matti Huttunen, "The National Composer and the Idea of Finnishness," in Grimley, *Cambridge Companion*, 10–11.

29. Sillén speaking, in Paul, *En bok om en människa*; quoted in Johnson, *Jean Sibelius*, 38–39.

30. Up to 1917 Viipuri served as a key transit point for revolutionary literature, arms, and agitators moving into Russia.

31. Teperi, *Pro Carelia*, 15.

32. On the complex question of defining Karelia, see Hannes Sihvo, "Karelia: A Source of Finnish National History," in Branch, *National History and Identity*, 181–201. Sihvo investigated both the region and the topic in numerous fine studies; see especially his *Karjalan kuva*.

33. Anttonen, *Tradition through Modernity*, 140, 172–73.

34. The article was entitled "Karjala ja sen taiteellinen merkitys" ("Karelia and Its Artistic Significance"). The translation is Michael Wynne-Ellis's, in Valkonen, *The Golden Age*, 52–53.

35. Quoted in Janne Gallen-Kallela-Sirén, "Akseli Gallen-Kallela and the Pursuit of New History and New Art: Inventing Finnish Art Nouveau," in *Now the Light Comes from the North*, 43.

36. Quoted in William A. Wilson, "Sibelius, the *Kalevala*, and Karelianism," in Goss, *Sibelius Companion*, 57; Wilson provides an excellent discussion of Karelianism. Fewster, *Visions of Past Glory*, 184–88, addresses the distinctions between the Karelian drive in the 1890s vis-à-vis the enthusiasms in Lönnrot's time.

37. Kajanus, "Vanha runosävelmä"; quoted in Goss, "Backdrop for Young Sibelius," 55.

38. In the chapter "Kalevalaromantiken och Axel Gallen-Kallela: Jämte några betraktelser över Carelianismen i Finlands kulturliv," in Hirn, *Lärt folk*, 189–225.

39. See *Kanteletar*, xxv. In *Lärt folk*, Hirn tells of visiting Paraske in Sibelius's company in the chapter "Larin Paraske, den stora runosångerskan." Hirn reports the time as "the summer of 1891" (p. 243); however, the composer's letters to Aino speak of visiting Paraske in the late fall of 1891. It is uncertain today whether Hirn's recollections were off by a few months or whether Sibelius in fact made several trips to hear this performer.

40. Sketches showing the evolving lullaby theme are shown in facsimile in *Kullervo*, JSW I/1.1, xvii–xix.

41. The bill from Röllig, dated November 13, 1893, indicates a total of nine musical numbers: "Festmusiken af Jean Sibelius, Overture, 7 Tablåer och Intermezzo för stor orkester," reproduced in facsimile in Teperi, *Pro Carelia*, 47.

42. Teperi has provided a detailed study of the lottery and its background in *Pro Carelia*. In addition to this source, the present account is based on *Nya Pressen* and *Päivälehti*, November 14, 1893; Roiha, "Sibeliuksen Karelia-sarjan historiallista taustaa"; Erlund Wirkki, "Kertomus Wiipurilaisen osakunnan vaiheista ja toiminnasta lukuvuonna 1892–93," HUL ViO Me:2; and Sibelius's manuscript of the *Karelia* music, HUL 0833. Some of these findings were first published in Goss, "Jean Sibelius and Finnish Nationalism."

43. The full speech, read by Werner Söderhjelm, was printed in *Uusi Suometar*, November 14, 1893.

44. For a discussion of Schvindt's work, including contemporary photographs of his costumes, see Fewster, *Visions of Past Glory*, 188–91, 199–200.

45. The music for this *tableau* was cut from Sibelius's manuscript.

46. Although the event was not depicted in the *Karelia* music, Torkel Knutsson met a tragic end.

Betrayed by jealous dukes who turned the king against him, he was arrested in the year 1306 and beheaded. Some three hundred years later, apologetic Swedes belatedly erected a statue to Knutsson in Stockholm.

47. The first four pages of the *tableau* are missing from Sibelius's manuscript.

48. Duke Narimont is hardly a household name today, even in Finland. For his identification and importance, I am indebted to Matti Klinge, "Narimont," *Hufvudstadsbladet*, May 9, 2001, and to Rainer Knapas's detailed e-mail message, July 27, 2007.

49. The Nordic blonde maid personifying Finland, whose first known press appearance is depicted in figure II.1, was destined to become a familiar icon in art, literature, and music. She is the central figure in Edvard Isto's painting *Hyökkäys* (*Attack*, 1899), and she shows up frequently in art and literary journals. In 1901 she appeared, dressed in flowing Finnish folk dress, on the cover of *Nuori Suomi*, a torch in one hand, a spear in the other, the sun rising over the horizon. Sibelius too used her image: she is presumably the Captive Queen in his choral piece of that title.

50. Fortunately, Sibelius's full *Karelia* music has been reconstructed. In 1965 Kalevi Kuosa made a partial restoration for the Sibelius centennial using the surviving orchestral parts. In 1997 the composers Kalevi Aho and Jouni Kaipainen separately reconstructed the missing portions from the surviving orchestral parts and, in Aho's case, beginning from the work begun by Kuosa. The full *tableau* music was recorded by Osmo Vänskä and the Lahti Symphony Orchestra in 1997 (*Karelia [1893]: Kuvaelmamusiikkia Viipurilaisen osakunnan juhla-arpajaisiin kansanvalistuksen hyväksi Viipurin läänissä*, BIS, CD-915) with Aho's reconstruction, and by Tuomas Ollila and the Tampere Philharmonic Orchestra in 1998 (*Sibelius: Complete Karelia Music/ Press Celebrations Music World Première Recording*, Ondine, ODE 913-2) with Kaipainen's.

51. The composer's transcription has been published in *Kullervo*, JSW I/1.1, xxiv. For the *Karelia* music Sibelius raised the melody a half step. To judge by the preserved oral sources, however, the sung melody was far from precise. In 1905, when Shemeikka was eighty, the composer Armas Launis recorded the ancient shaman singing a variant of this tune, "Tulen synty," to relate the charms of fire and its origins. The results can be heard on *The Kalevala Heritage* (Ondine, ODE 849-2, 1995), an excellent example of the indeterminate pitches and mutating nature of *runo* songs.

52. See the *Hämeenlinna Letters*, February 1, 1888, where one version of the song is transcribed on p. 93.

53. November 21, 1893.

54. Dahlström, "Jean Sibelius' Beiträge," 7. A table (p. 8) lists the *tableau* scenes and subsequent performances of their music, from November 1893 until their publication in March 1906. According to Teperi, the *tableaux* were repeated twice on November 18, 1893, but without Sibelius's music (as happened again in 1894 and 1898).

Chapter Nine

1. Bell and Hietala, *Helsinki*, 77–99, provides the facts and figures here. See also Schoolfield, *Helsinki of the Czars*, 200–201, and Pedersen, *Urbana odysséer: Helsingfors*.

2. Private companies had begun providing gas for street lighting only in 1860, nearly thirty years later than in Saint Petersburg and almost fifty years later than gaslight service elsewhere in Europe.

3. Schoolfield, *Helsinki of the Czars*, 128.

4. Sibelius to Uncle Pehr, October 24, 1888; *Hämeenlinna Letters*.

5. Quoted in Andersen, *Hans Christian Andersen*, 417.

6. So Frida Strindberg recalled in her engaging memoir, *Marriage with Genius*, 117, 125.

7. Hobsbawm, *Age of Empire*, 232.

8. These ideas, articulated by Sigmund Freud, are summarized here from the excellent discussion in Clair, *Lost Paradise*, 17–22.

9. Stanislavsky, *My Life in Art*, 344. The actor identified Ibsen, sometimes Maeterlinck, and Knut Hamsun, among others, as Symbolists.

10. See René Wellek, "What Is Symbolism?" in Balakian, *Symbolist Movement*, 17–28; and Roderick Conway Morris, "The Elusive Symbolist Movement," *International Herald Tribune*, March 17–18, 2007.

11. Clair, *Lost Paradise*, 21.

12. Gilles Genty, "The Homeland Regained," in Clair, *Lost Paradise*, 252.

13. Salme Sarajas-Korte, "The Finnish View of Symbolist Painting from Antinoüs Myth to *Kalevala* Mysticism," in Clair, *Lost Paradise*, 285–92; and Irma Rantavaara, "Symbolism and Finnish Literature," in Balakian, *Symbolist Movement*, 595–601, have examined symbolism in Finland, from which my text takes its point of departure.

14. *Päivälehti*, March 6, 1890.

15. Quoted in Salme Sarajas-Korte, "The Finnish View of Symbolist Painting from Antinoüs Myth to *Kalevala* Mysticism," in Clair, *Lost Paradise*, 286. Those Egyptian currents fed the often overworked imagination of Sigurd Wettenhovi-Aspa, who eventually put his theories about common Fenno-Egyptian roots into his *Fenno-Ägyptischer Kulturursprung der alten Welt: Kommentare zu den vorhistorischen Völkerwanderungen* (Amsterdam: Genius-Verlag, 1935).

16. "Sfinxen[,] modren till våra andliga barn[,] kommer då för ett ögonblick som en främmande fogel i underbar, öfvermättad färgprakt,—sitter ett ögonblick vid vårt bord, färdig att i nästa nu flyga bort igen. Och den berättar och ljuger halft på hån för oss de grannaste sagor, tyder de underligaste gåtor, gycklar de äfventyrligaste framtidsbilder för oss, den är den hermafroditiska själen i hela underhållningen, ett sinnesrus endast som kommer och flyger—med alkoholen," undated, but ca. January 1894; Akseli Gallen-Kallela Säätiö, VA Y 3544, letter 567, NA.

17. "Rauhaa [crossed out] Onnea etsivä sielu. Etsii eikä löydä. Tila k[ä]y tuskastuttavaksi. Heitt[ä] ytyy ja koettaa tappaa ilo[n]. Baccanal. Menen yksinäisyyteen kaukaisen metsä järven luo. On ilta. Yksin[ä]inen vesilintu laulaa surullisesti." HUL 1220, p. [14]. Either Sibelius has written a number of *a*'s where there should be *ä*'s, or the marks have faded over the years.

18. Canetti, *Crowds and Power*, 31. On the "circle" among the Russian intelligentsia, see Pipes, *Russia under the Old Regime*, 262–65.

19. "Symposionkvällarna gåvo mig mycket på en tid då jag dem förutan hade stått mer eller mindre ensam. Möjligheten att byta tankar med besläktade själar, livade av samma anda och samma mål, utövade ett i högsta grad stimulerande inflytande på mig, befäste mig i mina uppsåt, gav mig tillförsikt." Ekman, *Jean Sibelius* (1956), 152.

20. For an excellent discussion of the Symposium group see Gallen-Kallela-Sirén, "Axel Gallén," 361–99. His findings inform my text, as do the accounts of Ekman, *Jean Sibelius* (1956), 151–54, where rather more is related than appears in the English translation of this biography; Mustonen, *Ravintolaelämää*, 192–215; and Schoolfield, *Helsinki of the Czars*, 189–90.

21. Hagelstam, *Personer och minnen*, 149.

22. Ekman, *Jean Sibelius* (1956), 151. The passage does not appear in the English translation.

23. Most recently, in Kirby's *Concise History*, 155, in whose version it is Sibelius who departed (in this case, to Saint Petersburg), returning to find his friends still seated at their drinking table two days later.

24. *Dagbok*, February 17, 1925. A perceptive short story about Sibelius at the Kämp is "The Silence," in Barnes, *The Lemon Table*.

25. April 18, 1885; quoted in *À Paris!*, 19–20.

26. According to Gallen-Kallela-Sirén, "Axel Gallén," 362.

27. Hanna Rönnberg (1862–1946), a Finnish artist who hailed from Hämeenlinna, tells this story in her *Konstnärsliv i slutet av 1880-talet*; quoted in *À Paris!*, 21.

28. The caricature is reproduced in Martin and Sivén, *Akseli Gallen-Kallela*, 9.

29. "Timo" relates this far-fetched tale in "Pika-kuvia XII: Akseli Gallén [*sic*]," *Päivälehti*, November 9, 1892.

30. Gallen-Kallela-Sirén, "Axel Gallen," 55.

31. "Vaikka hän olisi puettu viimeisen englantilais-pariisilaisen muodon mukaan leveihin housuihin, väljään takkiin, hienoihin hansikkaihin, suureen kravattiin ja kädessä paksu hopeahelainen merenruokko, taikka pitkävartisiin pieksuihin, lammasnahkaturkkiin, naapukkalakkiin, käsissä rukkaset ja roskulakeppi— tietää heti käynnistä, pitkästä vartalosta, kauas näkyvistä isoista kasvoista ja terävistä vilkkuvista silmistä, että se on Gallén, joka sieltä tulee." "Timo," "Pika-kuvia XII: Akseli Gallén," *Päivälehti*, November 9, 1892.

32. I am indebted to the James Joyce scholar Hans Walter Gabler for pointing out this resemblance. In fact, Gallén had studied the fresco; see Gallen-Kallela-Sirén, *Minä palaan jalanjäljilleni*, 285.

33. "Våra seanser voro oerhört givande, något överdåd i bruket av Bacchi håvor var alls icke av nöden för att skänka dem innehåll och färg. Man lät fantasin flyga, tanken spela. Diskussionens vågor gingo mycket höga. Vi dryftade allt mellan himmel och jord, problemen stöttes och blöttes, men alltid i en optimistisk och frigjord anda. Det skulle banas väg för nya idéer på alla områden." Ekman, *Jean Sibelius* (1956), 152. The passage does not appear in the English translation.

34. Adolf Paul, "From a Friend of Sibelius," *New York Times*, December 29, 1935.

35. Edelfelt is quoted in *À Paris!*, 20; the other descriptions appear in Ekman, *Jean Sibelius* (1956), 151.

36. Gallen-Kallela-Sirén, "Axel Gallén," 371–72.

37. *Dagbok*, May 3, 1922.

38. "Lemna nu, Bäste Bror[,] all antipatiska känslor för mig.—Jag är verkligt Din vän var Du det äfven! . . . Jag lefver ej länge mera, så Du kan riskera," March 14, 1891, SibMus.

39. Yrjö Suomalainen, *Robert Kajanus* (Helsinki: 1965), 98; quoted in Philip Donner and Juhani Similä, "Jean Sibelius," *Idols and Myths*, 69. For a more recent biography, see Vainio's *"Nouskaa aatteet!"*

40. Suomalainen, *Robert Kajanus*, 87; quoted in Donner and Similä, "Jean Sibelius," *Idols and Myths*, 69.

41. A file labeled "Tankar om Kajanus" ("Thoughts about Kajanus"), SFA, file box 1, preserves these distressed outpourings.

42. "There is no more obvious expression of power than the performance of a conductor." Canetti, *Crowds and Power*, 394. "Timo" described Kajanus in admiring and graphic terms at the time of the Symposium brotherhood in "Pikakuvia VI: Robert Kajanus," *Päivälehti*, April 23, 1892.

43. Helena Tyrväinen has resurrected the details of this extraordinary series of concerts in scholarly presentations as well as in articles in the Finnish press. In this concert series Sibelius had only a passing and somewhat controversial role: after the performance on April 28, 1895, he presented the conductor with a laurel wreath bearing ribbons of red and gold, sparking some sniping in the press about "Finnish colors" (blue and white being associated with the Fennomans, red and gold with the Svecomans, "Vikings").

44. "På min tafla har jag målat Dig som mästaren och oss som elever," wrote Gallén to Kajanus, May 16, 1894; Taiteilijakirjekokoelma, Central Art Archives, Finnish National Gallery. Portions of the letter appear in Finnish and English translations in Ilvas, *Sanan ja tunteen voimalla*, 42–43, 124–25. As for the dual titles of the second portrait, *The Symposium* and *The Problem*, Gallen-Kallela-Sirén believes they may have been simultaneously conceived, even though in 1894, when Gallén exhibited the painting in Helsinki, it was called *Problem*, while in 1914, it was displayed in Stockholm as *Symposion*; see Gallen-Kallela-Sirén, "Axel Gallén," 369–70.

45. Gallen-Kallela-Sirén analyzes the painting, its various incarnations, and its deeper meanings in "Axel Gallén," 367–95, on which the discussion here is based. The author also deals with the importance of Christian imagery to Gallén's *Kalevala* paintings, 412–44.

46. Quoted in ibid., 491; see also Kai Laitinen, "The Rise of Finnish-Language Literature," in Schoolfield, *History of Finland's Literature*, 102–3.

47. According to Gallen-Kallela-Sirén, "Axel Gallén," 434.

48. These plans are discussed in Virtanen, "Pohjola's Daughter," in Jackson and Murtomäki, *Sibelius Studies*, 156–60; and Virtanen, "Jean Sibelius, Symphony no. 3," 127–40.

49. Kajanus recalled this episode in "Ristiäismatka," 83. The connections between Kajanus and Gallén were manifold. The men designed a country house together in the Karelian spirit, which they called Hevonpää (Horse's Head), completed in 1897. Their relationship eventually became even more deeply personal when their children married each other: in 1928 Elvi Kajanus wed Jorma Gallen-Kallela.

50. Pastor Herman Kajanus's (1852–1913) importance for artistic links to Finland was brought to light by Janna Kniazeva of the Russian Institute for Fine Arts History, Saint Petersburg, at the conference Finnish-Russian Musical Relations, Helsinki, April 7, 2003.

51. See ETL 3:156, on Danish reactions to Kajanus's appearance.

Chapter Ten

1. See Väisänen, "Jean Sibelius vaikutelmistaan," 78. Sibelius told Karl Ekman: "When I got to work I found that some notes I had made in Vienna were very suitable for adaptation. In this way 'En saga' appeared"; *Jean Sibelius*, (1936), 112. For a comparison of the composer's inconsistent *En saga* recollections, see Barrett, "In Search of a Lost Chamber Work."

2. Sarajas-Korte, *Vid symbolismens källor*, 263. The author's discussions in this volume, especially "Axel Gallén och Adolf Paul," 248–51, and "Symbolistiska försök," 262–67, have been especially valuable here. The time frame is based on Gallen-Kallela-Sirén, "Axel Gallén," 378. Gallen-Kallela-Sirén regards the panels' differences in style as indicating their separate dates of execution: the landscape was probably painted soon after the premiere, and the portrait conceived later as a study for the *Symposium*. The watercolor hangs today in the library of Sibelius's home, Ainola.

3. The correspondences among composition, painting, and story are examined in Karila, "Uusi näkökulma."

4. As Tawaststjerna observed in ETF 1:310, but not in the English or Swedish editions of his biography.

5. Lindqvist, *Taiteilijan tiellä*, 39–40.

6. Fewster, *Visions of Past Glory*, 142.

7. The episode is discussed in Sarajas-Korte, *Vid symbolismens källor*, 250–51, 356. This "collaborative" story was first published in German in a collection called *Ein gefallener Prophet*; in 1895 Paul brought out the same tale in Swedish, in the volume *En saga ifrån ödemarken och andra berättelser*.

8. "I världen, i livet, och i naturen finns det ingenting annat än *vackra sagor* och då dörren öppnas, träd in och ta för dig för hela din själ." Sketchbook XI, November 12, 1894; quoted in Sarajas-Korte, *Vid symbolismens källor*, 255, 356.

9. Sarajas-Korte has an insightful discussion of Finnish artists and their saga ideas vis-à-vis the celebrated Danish teller of fairy tales in "Sadun ulottuvuuksia."

10. *Symphonic Broadcasts*; quoted in Goss, *Jean Sibelius and Olin Downes*, 105. See also p. 118 in the same source for Downes's other dramatic images of *En saga*.

11. "Jag har en 'Saga' för orkester färdig. Du borde anslås af den. Den är *rausch*. Jag har tänkt på Böcklins taflor. Han målar ju där för klar luft, för hvita svanor, för blått haf, med m."

12. According to none other than the leading contemporary Swedish writer and critic Viktor Rydberg (1828–1895) in "Något om Arnold Böcklin," *Vintergatan* (1894): 207; quoted in Facos, *Nationalism and the Nordic Imagination*, 123.

13. "'Satu on psykologisesti kaikkein syvällisimpiä teoksiani,' hän selitti. 'Voisinpa melkein sanoa, että siihen sisältyy koko nuoruuteni. Se on erään sieluntilan ilmaus. Niihin aikoihin, jolloin kirjoitin Sadun,

sain kokea paljon järkyttävää. Missään muussa teoksessani en ole paljastanut itseäni niin täysin kuin Sadussa. Kaikki Sadun tulkinnat ovat minulle tietysti jo senkin vuoksi aivan vieraita.'" Levas, *Muistelma*, 1:139.

14. Although this Finnish term is rich with Symbolist associations, its German counterpart, *Seelenzustände* (soul states), was already being used in the early nineteenth century: *Seelenzustände* was a key point in A. B. Marx's three-stage schema of Beethoven's symphonic development, whose first stage Marx characterized as "the succession of soul states portrayed with deep psychological truth"; see Burnham, "Criticism, Faith, and the *Idee*," especially 188–92; the quotation is on p. 191.

15. "Jag har hört Meistersinger och Tannhäuser och är alldeles ursinnig.—Nog är den musiken styf. När vi träffas skall jag närmare tala om för Dig mina intryck och hvad jag kände. Det var i mitt inre en sådan egendomlig blandning af förvåning, missräkning, jubel m.m.," September 29, 1889. Such phrases as "When we meet, I'll tell you more," liberally strewn through Sibelius's correspondence, make a scholar weep for the lost details.

16. Eero Tarasti, "Sibelius and Wagner," in Goss, *Sibelius Companion*, 61–75. In this article Tarasti also traces the mythical Wagnerian links to Finland. The most extensive research on Wagner and Finland is Hannu Salmi's; in *Wagner and Wagnerism*, Salmi devotes all of chapter 8 to "the campaigners for Bayreuth," in which Wegelius and Richard Faltin played leading roles; see especially 203–14.

17. Quoted in Eero Tarasti, "Sibelius and Wagner," in Goss, *Sibelius Companion*, 63.

18. For instance, in a letter written to K. A. Tavaststjerna, on October 6, 1896; quoted in Salme Sarajas-Korte, "Axel Gallén's Swan Symbolism," in Ilvas, *Akseli Gallen-Kallela*, 57. For some of Gallén's Wagnerian views, see Gallen-Kallela-Sirén, "Axel Gallén," 349 n. 127.

19. "Aino kultani! Nyt juuri olen kuullut Parcival. *Ei* mikään maailmassa ole tehnyt sellaista vaikutusta minuun, se ihan liikuttaa sisimpiä sydämen kieliä. Luulin olevani jo kuiva puu, mutta eipä olekkaan niin," July 19, 1894.

20. "Se on kohonnut kuin ainakin uusi oksa vanhan hongan kylestä"; reprinted in Mällinen, *Nuoren Suomen ytimessä*, 62.

21. As Sibelius recounted in Ekman, *Jean Sibelius* (1936), 116.

22. "Minun täytyy muutamin sanoin ensiksi selittää mihinkä vakuutukseen musiikin suhteen, suurien surujien perästä, olen tullut. Uskon että musiikki yksinänsä, se on absoluuttinen musiikki[,] ei voi tyydyttää. Se herättää kyllä tunteita ja mielentiloja mutta aina jääpi jotain ei tyydytettyä sieluumme, sitä aina kysyy 'minkätähden tämä.' Musiikki on kun vaimo, sen täytyy tulla miehestä raskaaksi. Tämä mies on Poësis. Säveleet pääsevät oikeaan voimaansa vasta silloin kun niitä ohjaa runollinen tarkoitus. Toisin sanoen kun sana ja sävel yhdistyy." Sibelius to J. H. Erkko, July 8, 1893; J. H. Erkko Collection, SKS Letter Archive 212. The similarity to Wagner's turgid ponderings on this topic has often been remarked; cf., for example, *Oper und Drama*, ed. and commentary Klaus Kropfinger (Stuttgart: Philipp Reclam, 1984), 1:116, where Wagner wrote: "*aller musikalische Organismus ist seiner Natur nach aber—ein weiblicher*, er ist ein nur *gebärender*, nicht aber *zeugender*; die zeugende Kraft liegt *ausser ihm*, und ohne Befruchtung von dieser Kraft vermag sie eben nicht zu gebären.—Hier liegt das ganze Geheimnis der Unfruchtbarkeit der modernen Musik!—."

23. Salme Sarajas-Korte, "The Finnish View of Symbolist Painting from Antinoüs Myth to *Kalevala* Mysticism," in Clair, *Lost Paradise*, 286.

24. As Minna Canth shrewdly observed, "[Ida Aalberg's] nervous system was quite the same sort as Sibelius's" (Hänen hermostonsa on hyvin samaa sorttia kuin Sibeliusen [*sic*]), January 6, 1894; Kannila, *Minna Canthin kirjeet*, 646.

25. The first national operas to Finnish texts, beginning with Oskar Merikanto's *Pohjan neito* (1897), were composed to *Kalevala* themes or other, equally solemn medieval subjects. It was only with Armas Järnefelt's sensational Wagner performances in 1904–6 that Finnish activists began to see national operas as viable; for a discussion of the importance of antiquity and Wagner to Finnish music, see Fewster, *Visions of Past Glory*, 262–66.

26. Samson considers tone poems and nationalism in "Music and Nationalism."

27. "Minä olen luullakseni löytänyt itseäni musiikissa taas. Olen niin paljon tosiseikkoja löytänyt. Luulen että minä oikeastaan olen musiikki maalari ja runoili[j]a. Tarkoitan että tuo Listz'in [sic] musiikkikanta on minulle lähintä. Tuo symfoninen runo (sillä tavalla meinasin 'runoilija')." Sibelius to Aino, August 19, 1894. The letter, with all its misspellings, is transcribed in full in Talas, *Tulen synty*, 83–86.

28. Sibelius's comment, in a letter to Alf Klingenberg, February 28, 1920, HUL Coll. 206.62, characteristically resonated on many levels: the last major work of one of his favorite poets, K. A. Tavaststjerna, was *Laureatus* (1897), in which the title character visualized himself as the suffering Christ; see Schoolfield, *Baedeker of Decadence*, 135.

29. Quoted in David Haas, "Sibelius's Second Symphony and the Legacy of Symphonic Lyricism," in Goss, *Sibelius Companion*, 83; Haas's insightful discussion informs much of mine.

30. Ibid., 78.

31. Clair, *Lost Paradise*, 21.

32. This perceptive remark is from Leon Edel, "Symbolic Statement: A Psychological View," in Balakian, *Symbolist Movement*, 662, from where the Thoreau quotation is also taken.

33. Gallén to Kajanus, May 16, 1894; Taiteilijakirjekokoelma, Central Art Archives.

34. "Olkoot meidän juhlamme isänmaallisia, puhtaan kansallishengen johtamia ja elähyttämiä, juhlia, joissa laululle ja soitolle suodaan tärkeä sija. Olkoot ensi sijassa kansallisia, vasta toisessa laulujuhlia"; quoted in Smeds and Mäkinen, *Kaiu, kaiu, lauluni*, 33.

35. *Nya Pressen*, for example, had articles on June 18, 19, 20, 21, 22, 23, and 26, 1894. *Päivälehti* ran lengthy columns on June 19, 20, 21, 22, 23, 26, and 27, 1894.

36. *Landkjending* (*Land-Sighting*), a setting of a text of Bjørnson, was written for TTBB, baritone, orchestra, and organ ad lib.

37. For a discussion of Wegelius's cantata, see Lappalainen, "Martin Wegelius," 149–50.

38. Järnefelt's "explanation" appeared in both Finnish and Swedish; it has been reproduced together with an English translation in the notes to its first recording, *The Orchestral Music of Armas Järnefelt*, Gavleborg Symphony Orchestra, cond. Hannu Koivula (Sterling, 1997; CDS-1021-2). The final struggle between pagans and Christians in Finland figured in Juhani Aho's novel *Panu* (1897), inspired by Viktor Rydberg's *Den siste Athenaren*.

39. *Päivälehti*, June 23, 1894, whose reporter was quite carried away.

40. "'Improvisation' är af ett pregnant erotiskt innehåll. . . . och övergår i en i spansk dansrytm hållen afslutning med ystra knäpp af tamburine[n]." *Nya Pressen*, June 23, 1894. Flodin's text in fact reads "tamburiner," meaning tambourines in the plural, but this was probably a typesetter's misreading of the critic's *n* (Flodin's report would have been handwritten); few works, especially for small orchestra, have two tambourines. Sibelius may have found inspiration in Karl Collan's *Tamburinen*.

41. See SWV, 56–58, and the recent edition of the two surviving *Vårsång*s, JSW I/9, edited by Tuija Wicklund, who believes there were only two versions; for her argument, see xi–xiii.

42. Kai Laitinen, "The Rise of Finnish-Language Literature," in Schoolfield, *History of Finland's Literature*, 102–3.

43. The critic was Bis, writing in *Hufvudstadsbladet*, April 18, 1895. The lines are from a psalm whose eleven verses began appearing in psalmbooks as early as 1695; Wikipedia, accessed July 10, 2007.

44. Smeds and Mäkinen, *Kaiu, kaiu, lauluni*, 44–45. The authors point out that only in 1967, in honor of Finland's fiftieth year of independence, did Finnish-speaking and Swedish-speaking Finns again celebrate together in a similar event.

45. See JSW I/9, xi, and SWV, 57–58.

Chapter Eleven

1. Salme Sarajas-Korte, "Axel Gallén's Swan Symbolism," in Ilvas, *Akseli Gallen-Kallela*, 55.

2. Ibid.

3. "Det underliga qvinliga element i vår fantasi, hvilken man ger sig åt med hela sin könskraft vid en konstnärlig produktion." Paul to Gallén, ca. January 1894; Akseli Gallen-Kallela Säätiö, VA Y 3544, letter 567, NA. "Religion är endast könsdrift." Paul to Sibelius, December 15, 1892, NA.

4. Plato, *Symposium*, especially xii–xiii; the quotation is taken from p. xxii.

5. Strindberg, *Marriage with Genius*, 145. Of the many sources on the Berlin group, memoirs of two participants have been especially important here, Frida Strindberg's and Adolf Paul's (*Profiler*), together with Sarajas-Korte, *Vid symbolismens källor*, 294–300; Sarajas-Korte, "Axel Gallén's Swan Symbolism"; Prideaux, *Edvard Munch*, 136–52; and Schoolfield, *Baedeker of Decadence*, 117–31.

6. "Jag har ändtligen funnit en god vän här. Och då denne gode vän dessutom är ett geni, och hans verksamhet här kommer att göra epok så inom konst som vetenskap—måste jag naturligtvis föreställa honom för dig. Jag gör det genom att sända dig två broschyrer af honom. Håll till godo och läs dem många gånger. Vill du ha mera af samma sort så skrif till din sant tillgifne vän Adolf Paul," September 30, 1892.

7. "Käre! Tack för Przybyszewski! *Det var bra!*. . . . Du är nu der bara med Hansson Strindberg et consortes—lyckliga! *O terque beata!*," October 31, 1892. In *Baedeker of Decadence*, Schoolfield devotes all of chapters 9 and 13 to Przybyszewski, with valuable discussions of the Pole's writings.

8. Strindberg, *Marriage with Genius*, 43.

9. "Am Anfang war das Geschlecht. Nichts ausser ihm—alles in ihm." *Die Totenmesse*, quoted in Sarajas-Korte, *Vid symbolismens källor*, 297.

10. And quite possibly a source of Sibelius's resistance to Schopenhauer, well-known among his friends. In a letter to Sibelius, undated but apparently written after November 1894, Adolf Paul tried to convince his friend to read Schopenhauer: "I don't presume to ask you to read anything nowadays. Otherwise, I would ask you to read what Schopenhauer has written about art. *He is no woman hater* and is the *wittiest* writer I've read. Begin with 'Über das Sehen und die Farben'; you'll get a feeling as if you'd been blind before. The whole of nature and life become so simple, and one has such fun at the least bagatelle. It's marvelous what we are for some idiots—we educated people" (Jag vågar ej be dig läsa något numera. Annars skulle jag be dig läsa hvad Schopenhauer skref om konst. *Han är ej kvinnohatare* och den *morsommaste* skriftställare jag läst. Börja med "Über das Sehen und die Farben," skall du få en känsla som om du varit blind förut. Hela naturen och lifvet blir en så enkelt, och så roligt har man åt den minsta bagatell. Det är förunderligt hvad vi äro för ena idioter—vi bildadt folk).

11. Dagny Juel came to a tragic end: she was murdered by one of her lovers in distant Tbilisi; see Prideaux, *Edvard Munch*, 203–6.

12. The collection was an exceptionally fruitful one for Jean Sibelius; within its covers lie many of the poems he eventually set to music: *Skogsrået*, *Aténarnes sång*, *Snöfrid*, *Vattenplask*, *Vi ses igen*, *Kyssen*, and *Höstkväll*, along with verses he contemplated setting, such as *Goternas sång*.

13. Sketchbook XI, November 14, 1894; quoted in Salme Sarajas-Korte, "Axel Gallén's Swan Symbolism," in Ilvas, *Akseli Gallen-Kallela*, 54.

14. Its poet, Ernst Josephson, painted a striking counterpart to his poem, *Strömkarlen* (of which there are three versions), showing an ecstatic youth playing his violin amidst foaming rapids and water lilies; one is reproduced in Goss, *Sibelius Companion*, 185.

15. *Päivälehti*, January 27, February 17, and March 3, 6, and 7, 1895; see also *Uusi Suometar*, March 9, 1895.

16. George C. Schoolfield provided the etymology and associations of *tintamariski*.

17. Raised and educated to speak Swedish, Ahlberg nevertheless became so forceful a presence on

the Finnish-speaking stage that it was said to be difficult to imagine the Finnish theater without him. The story went around that Ahlberg was heard speaking Swedish in a local restaurant. Confronted by indignant patrons, Ahlberg magnificently quelled their irritation: "Finnish is too noble and fine a language to use in a *tavern*"; the story is related in SKB, s.v. "Ahlberg."

18. This is the work, said *Uusi Suometar*'s critic, writing on March 9, 1895, that every Finn interested in composition will come to hear. One cannot help but wonder if the full tone poem—perhaps even with *tableaux vivants?*—had been intended for performance, and, for whatever reasons—financial, incompleteness, or simple logistics—had been abandoned in favor of the melodrama.

19. *Hufvudstadsbladet*, April 18, 1895.

Chapter Twelve

1. "Och för detta komplicerade känslolif söker målarkonsten efter uttryck i de mest heterogena sferer: den fördjupar sig i sagornas poesi, den låter sig gripas af den religiösa extasens eller innerlighetens mysticism. Gamla legender och myter alstra underbara drömmar om aldrig sedda världar och hemlighetsfulla gammal-asiatiska fantasiformer öka benägenheten för öfversinligt svärmeri. Det ockulta, bizarra, icke hvardagliga utöfvar en oemotståndlig dragningskraft. Och liksom det dunkla i själslifvet, erhåller äfven det dunkla i naturen en obeskriflig tjusningskraft. Man spanar efter de skäraste, finaste, genomskinligaste nyanser för att återgifva natten, kvällen, skymningen, dimman." *Nya Pressen*, November 6, 1895. The exhibition received lavish press attention: *Nya Pressen* carried another lengthy article by Öhqvist on November 8; *Päivälehti* covered the event on November 21; and *Uusi Suometar*, on November 22. *Finsk Tidskrift* included a four-page article in its second issue of 1895. For a modern-day discussion, see Sarajas-Korte, *Vid symbolismens källor*, 189–97.

2. The doubts were voiced in J. A., "Finska artisternas Utställning."

3. Published in *Lärkan: Poetisk Kalender* (Helsingfors: Wasenii, 1845), 33.

4. Modern editions appear in *Stora sångboken* (Jyväskylä: Svenska Folkskolans Vänner, 2001), 9, and with Finnish text in P. J. Hannikainen, ed., *Isänmaallisia Lauluja* (Helsinki: Fazer, 1967), 2–3.

5. The dark and melancholic Saimi also modeled for Enckell's painting *The Black Madonna*; see Sarajas-Korte, *Vid symbolismens källor*, 191.

6. A copy is preserved in the Faltin Collection, HUL.

7. Lines 23–30, quoted from *The Kalevala*, trans. Friberg, 303. The incantation continues to line 82.

8. The sonata appears in JSW V/1, ed. Kari Kilpeläinen, who discusses its connection with the choral draft (x, xii). In 1960 *Heitä, koski, kuohuminen* was completed by the Finnish avant-garde composer Erik Bergman in collaboration with Jussi Jalas and Erik Tawaststjerna; see SWV, 550.

9. *Hufvudstadsbladet*, March 23, 1893; *Mäntykoski* and its versions are discussed at some length in Gallen-Kallela-Sirén, "Axel Gallén," 328–37. Gallen-Kallela-Sirén reproduces earlier studies for the work in an appendix.

10. As Gallen-Kallela-Sirén observes of *Mäntykoski*, "A scene inspired by Kalevalian mythology became a collective, political landscape"; ibid., 337.

11. "Ville hr Sibelius skrifva en ny finsk sinfonisk dikt, t.ex. en Lemminkäinen-bild, blefve han nog tvungen att skapa åt den finska miliön en helt och hållet ny belysning, för att icke repetera hvad han redan en gång, och en gång för alla, sagt i ' Kullervo.'" *Nya Pressen*, April 29, 1892.

12. Tutta Palin, "Picturing a Nation: The Finnish Landscape and the Finnish People," in Lehtonen, *Europe's Northern Frontier*, 230, 232.

13. As Aino Sibelius recalled in *Joulutervehdys, 1935*; reprinted in Sirén, *Aina poltti sikaria*, 151.

14. "Detta slags musik värkar rent patologiskt och kvarlämnar intryck, så blandade, pinsamma och till sin natur odefinierbara, att de mycket litet ha gemensamt med den estetiska känsla af lust, som all skön konst och främst musiken bör väcka." *Nya Pressen*, November 2, 1897.

15. Tuire Ranta-Meyer has uncovered these less heroic aspects of Kajanus's career in her research on Erkki Melartin on which the discussion here is based; see Ranta-Meyer, "Erkki Melartin, Jean Sibelius ja Robert Kajanus" (which includes transcriptions of pertinent correspondence from the original Swedish-language texts) and "Melartin, Sibelius and Kajanus."

16. October 26, 1897; quoted in Ranta-Meyer, "Melartin, Sibelius and Kajanus," 40.

17. *The Kalevala*, trans. Friberg, *runo* 14, lines 376–81.

18. The powerful impact of the emblems of the national movement is still evident in modern Finland. It was a Finnish-minded physician who founded a medical center in the Töölö district of Helsinki and named it Mehiläinen (The Honeybee). This institution of healing remains one of the city's leading hospitals.

19. *The Kalevala*, trans. Friberg, *runo* 15, lines 613–16.

20. This important point is made in Salme Sarajas-Korte, "Axel Gallén's Swan Symbolism," in Ilvas, *Akseli Gallen-Kallela*, 48, 52.

21. Mute swans, *Cygnus olor*, were introduced only in the early 1900s. They bred in northern Finland, from the middle portion of Ostrobothnia northward. I am indebted to Patrik Byholm, of the Department of Biological and Environmental Sciences, University of Helsinki, for the information about Finland's swans.

22. Although the British analyst Arnold Tovey had christened this melody "Thor's Hammer Theme," Hepokoski gratefully restored the composer's meaning in *Sibelius: Symphony no. 5*.

23. Quoted in Heller, "Edvard Munch's *Vision*," 230–31. Heller's impressive study has informed much of the discussion here.

24. Ibid., 230. Heller gives the entire poem in its original and in translation.

25. Sarajas, *Elämän meri*, 46–47.

26. So Pirjo Lyytikäinen observes in "Birth of a Nation: The Literary Inscription of Finnishness," in Lehtonen, *Europe's Northern Frontier*, 145. On Runeberg and swans, see Nummi, "Runebergin kultainen teema."

27. A project realized only in November 1966, to the music of Kaj Chydenius; see Ahokas, *History of Finnish Literature*, 150, 466, to whose interpretive remarks I am also indebted.

28. Quoted in Salme Sarajas-Korte, "The Finnish View of Symbolist Painting from Antinoüs Myth to *Kalevala* Mysticism," in Clair, *Lost Paradise*, 291.

29. The cause for a delightful episode in Rimsky's opera in which the czarevich in his bumblebee disguise becomes incensed at the court's intriguers and furiously stings each courtier in turn before zooming back to his land of exile.

30. Heller, "Edvard Munch's *Vision*," 227.

31. Johnston, *Austrian Mind*, 249.

32. In a diary entry, November 13, 1894, quoted in Finnish translation by Annika Waenerberg in Lindqvist, *Taiteilijan tiellä*, 218.

33. Heller, "Edvard Munch's *Vision*," 228; Heller translates the poem and gives its background and dates, showing that the most complete version dates from 1896.

34. See Gallen-Kallela-Sirén, "Axel Gallén," 426–37.

35. Quoted in Salme Sarajas-Korte, "Axel Gallén's Swan Symbolism," in Ilvas, *Akseli Gallen-Kallela*, 58.

36. The description is Gallén's, quoted in Salme Sarajas-Korte, "The Finnish View of Symbolist Painting from Antinoüs Myth to *Kalevala* Mysticism," in Clair, *Lost Paradise*, 291.

37. See, for example, Hannele Heporauta, "Lemminkäinen's Mother—Conservator's Comments," in Ilvas, *Akseli Gallen-Kallela*, 60. Senni Timmonen discusses this and other aspects of Lemminkäinen's mother in her article of that title in Honko, *The Kalevala and the World's Traditional Epics*.

38. Quoted in Väisänen, "Jean Sibelius vaikutelmistaan," 78.

39. See Gallen-Kallela-Sirén, "Axel Gallén," 424–35; the quotation is on p. 430. Although anachronis-

tically christened the "Maidens of Tapiola" by the art historian Onni Okkonen, this panel, Gallen-Kallela-Sirén shows, is more likely to depict the Maidens of Saari. On the confusion and different meanings of this title in connection with Sibelius's *Lemminkäinen Legends*, see Johnson, *Jean Sibelius*, 71–72.

40. The texts were printed by Päivälehden kirjapaino (1896) in Finnish and in Karl Collan's Swedish translation; a copy has been preserved in the Faltin Collection, HUL.

41. Harold E. Johnson, "Sibeliuksen Lemminkäis-sarja," *Helsingin Sanomat*, May 19, 1957. Johnson included similar information in his *Jean Sibelius*, 66–70, with portions of the program texts translated into English. He seems to have been the only person to have recognized the composer's programmatic innovation.

42. HUL 1786. On this document, the title of movement 1 appears as *Lemminkäinen ja Saaren neidot*. Also included is a separate sheet containing prose explanations of the movements in German and Finnish.

43. Joachim Schwarz, "Structural and Formal Principles in Sibelius's *Lemminkäinen* Suite," in Murtomäki, Kilpeläinen, and Väisänen, *Sibelius Forum 1995*, especially 306–9. Cecil Gray would give those elements the memorable if weirdly biological label "thematic germs," perhaps not altogether inappropriate for a Symbolist work, since to Symbolism belonged the ideas of "growth" and death and arising from and returning to earthy origins.

44. See Daniel M. Grimley, "*Lemminkäinen and the Maidens of Saari*, op. 22 no. 1: Acculturation, Italy and the Midsummer Night," in Murtomäki, Kilpeläinen, and Väisänen, *Sibelius Forum 1995*, 206–7.

Chapter Thirteen

1. Edelfelt reported on the occasion to his mother, May 26, 1896, a letter translated into English in "Dearest Mother!," 51–53.

2. On May 30 and June 6, 1896, the *Illustrated London News* reported these and other details accompanied by full-page illustrations by "our Special Artist in Moscow."

3. The fantastical statistics are given in Clarke, *Lost Fortune of the Tsars*, 7–8.

4. Wilson, *Tolstoy*, 417–18.

5. Klinge, *Finnish Tradition*, 84.

6. The most extensive research on Sibelius and Finland's principal university is Erkki Salmenhaara's: see his "Jean Sibelius ja Helsingin yliopisto"; and Salmenhaara, "Jean Sibelius and the University of Helsinki," in Murtomäki, Kilpeläinen, and Väisänen, *Sibelius Forum 1995*, 22–26. The discussion in Johnson, *Jean Sibelius*, 73–79, still retains its value. Klinge has written extensively about the role of the university in Finland's intellectual life; along with his volumes in *Finlands historia*, see Klinge, *Finnish Tradition*, 81–90; and Klinge, Knapas, Leikola, and Strömberg, *Helsingin Yliopisto, 1640–1990*.

7. Sibelius had composed his first cantata for the university, a work written for its graduation ceremonies to a text by Symbolist enthusiast Kasimir Leino, in 1894. Sibelius and Leino engaged in an unseemly and—for the later Sibelius, uncharacteristic—public dispute over the point at which the poet had (finally) delivered the text.

8. Kanslerinvirasto, saapuneet asiakirjat 9/1897, Helsingin yliopiston arkisto. See Kilpeläinen, *Tutkielmia*, 160–66, for these and other Sibelius work lists.

9. The full text has been published in the composer's original Swedish (Sibelius, "Några synpunkter") as well as in a Finnish translation by Ilkka Oramo, both in *Musiikki* 10 (1980). Robert Layton translated part of the lecture into English; see ETL 1:191.

10. Vainio, "Helsingin yliopiston musiikinopettajan virantäytön vaiheet," examines anew the selection process for the university position and maintains that the oft-repeated charge that Kajanus plagiarized his lecture was false. In the same issue of the journal (*Musiikki* [2007/1]) Vainio published the lecture (which surfaced only in 2006) in a Finnish translation.

11. Asiantuntijalautakunnan lausunto, January 23, 1897, Helsingin yliopiston arkisto; cited and translated from the transcription in Salmenhaara, "Jean Sibelius ja Helsingin yliopisto," 27–28.

12. Johnson, *Jean Sibelius*, 77–78.

13. Exactly what happened in Saint Petersburg has remained conjecture; according to Vainio (*"Nouskaa aatteet!,"* 336–37), no documents survive to confirm the rumors of special pleading.

14. Sibelius, "Några synpunkter," 96.

15. Uggla, who had studied in Paris and in Sweden, had a very active career from the 1880s into the first decade of the twentieth century, when he made some of the first recordings of Sibelius's songs.

16. A copy of this letter, dated October 17, 1897, is preserved in SFA, file box 121. It reads in part: "Redan för någon tid sedan har man på mitt initiativ tagit upp frågan om en livränta för herr Sibelius, kompositören. Även jag anser att hans verk, som har en fullt nationell prägel, äger tillräckligt värde och betydelse för att det skall ligga i det allmännas intresse att tillförsäkra honom något slags existensmöjligheter. Mer än konstnärer i allmänhet tycks han fullständigt sakna allt sinne för det praktiska, t.o.m. i så hög grad att det enligt min mening vore olyckligt att skaffa honom en tjänst vid universitetet. Med ett statsunderstöd på 3 000 mk och mindre, tillfälliga understöd kunde han komma till rätta och fortsätta sitt arbete till fromma för vår nationella konst."

17. Otto Andersson, "Sibelius och Kajanus," in Andersson, *Studier i musik*, 1:85; the details of the financial arrangements are examined throughout pages 78–86.

18. Tuchman, *Proud Tower*, 293.

19. According to *Uusi Suometar*, November 8, 1896. Although Finnish-language newspapers and concert programs referred to the new opera as *Neitsyt kammiossa: Näyttämölle sovitettu suomalainen ballaadi* (*In a Maiden's Bower: A Finnish Ballad Arranged for the Stage*), the libretto read, in Swedish, *Jungfrun i tornet, efter en finsk folkballad*.

20. Hertzberg (1845–96), who was associated with the Swedish-language newspaper *Hufvudstadsbladet*, was an exceedingly versatile man. An early advocate for women's right to vote, Hertzberg also sold insurance and devised inventions ranging from a typewriter for the blind to a cigarette machine.

21. February 8, 1906; SFA, file box 121.

22. The evening was reviewed in *Hufvudstadsbladet*, *Uusi Suometar*, and *Nya Pressen* on November 8, 1896. Oscar Wilde's *Salome* was censored in Finland, but, curiously, the dance was permitted. On the Finnish reception of *Salome*, see Helka Mäkinen, "'Toiseutta' näyttämöllä: Oscar Wilden *Salomen* vastaanotto Suomessa vuosisadan vaihteessa," in Mäkinen, *Lihasta sanaksi*, 124–51.

23. ETL 1:185.

24. The first page of the autograph manuscript is reproduced in facsimile in Ekman, *Jean Sibelius* (1956), 177. Sibelius's classical education was a strong and ever-present component of his makeup, as it had also been for Runeberg. Rosa Newmarch remarked that "it was impossible to converse with [Sibelius] for long without recognizing that the classical scholar was closely linked with the creative musician. 'Homer and Horace had a significance in my development I cannot value highly enough,' he writes of himself." Newmarch, *Jean Sibelius: A Short Story* (1939), 16–17.

25. Johnson, *Jean Sibelius*, 80–82. Fewster, *Visions of Past Glory*, 277, 474, gives the statistics cited here; by 1902 the seasonal number had increased to forty.

26. Hanna Suutela examines Schiller's Maid of Orleans as "national protagonist" in "Orleansin neitsyt—kansallinen protagonisti: Esitykset Suomalaisessa Teatterissa 1887 ja 1896 sekä Suomen Kansallisteatterissa 1902–1905," in Mäkinen, *Lihasta sanaksi*, 169–89.

27. SWV, 121–29.

28. The son of Belgian immigrants, van der Stucken (1858–1929) studied in Europe, including a stint with Edvard Grieg, who took a special interest in him. After serving as principal conductor of the Cincinnati Symphony Orchestra (1895–1907), van der Stucken toured Europe. He died and was buried there.

29. So Adolf Paul recalled in "From a Friend of Sibelius," *New York Times*, December 29, 1935. See also Ekman, *Jean Sibelius* (1956), 175–76.

30. *Nya Pressen*, November 2, 1897.

31. For a discussion of the poem and a translation into English, see Andersen, *Hans Christian Andersen*, 96–100.

32. Kai Laitinen discusses this and other Järnefelt dramas in "The Rise of Finnish-Language Literature," in Schoolfield, *History of Finland's Literature*, 104–7.

33. Volkov describes the choreography in *St. Petersburg*, 304–5, observing that the dance was repeatedly staged in this version in Russia even after Balanchine emigrated to the West. See also pp. 312–13.

34. Savonius's account is reprinted in Sirén, *Aina poltti sikaria*, 123–24.

35. Ekman, *Jean Sibelius* (1936), 102. Schoolfield has a full chapter on Tavaststjerna in *Baedeker of Decadence*.

Chapter Fourteen

1. The events and issues here have been frequently discussed. This chapter is especially indebted to Tuomo Polvinen's *Imperial Borderland* and to his original Finnish text, *Valtakunta ja rajamaa*. Other sources informing the discussion include Jussila, "Historical Background of the February Manifesto"; Schoolfield, *Helsinki of the Czars*, 203–14, and Gallen-Kallela-Sirén, "Axel Gallén," 526–65.

2. Quoted in Polvinen, *Imperial Borderland*, 21. In 1863 Katkov became manager and editor of *Moskovskie Vedomosti* (the *Moscow News*), from which he exerted considerable influence on public opinion.

3. Polvinen, *Imperial Borderland*, 21.

4. Ibid., 22.

5. Ibid., 29; see also p. 33.

6. Ibid., 56, 64.

7. Finland did not officially change to the Julian calendar when it became a part of the Russian Empire, but retained the "new-style" Gregorian calendar adopted in 1753 when the country was part of Sweden. Dates in Russia were thus thirteen days behind those in the grand duchy. Hereafter, when two dates are cited (such as August 18/30), the first refers to the calendar date in Finland; the second, to the Julian calendar.

8. Polvinen, *Imperial Borderland*, 66.

9. Ibid., 67.

10. Quoted in ibid., 70.

11. Quoted in Schoolfield, *Helsinki of the Czars*, 205, 206. Polvinen, *Imperial Borderland*, 73, observes that most senators had some fluency in Russian, although they refused to use it in senate sessions because it was not required by law.

12. Quoted in Polvinen, *Imperial Borderland*, 81; see also pp. 51–60 on these measures.

13. Polvinen considers the manifesto's effects in detail, ibid., 83–85; the quotation is on p. 83; Jussila's observation was made in "Historical Background of the February Manifesto," 146.

14. See chapter 5, "The Steady Drummer," in Tuchman, *Proud Tower*.

15. Ibid.

16. Jussila, "Nationalism and Revolution," 290.

17. Arvid kept a diary of this visit, *Päiväkirja matkaltani Venäjällä ja käynti Leo Tolstoin luona keväillä 1899*, published in Helsinki that same year by Otava. Kolehmainen has written about the encounter in "When Finland's Tolstoy Met His Russian Master."

18. "Ditt 'eläköön rakas isänmaa' klingar i mitt hjärta—ja, Lefve detta arma arma land." Sibelius to Kajanus, postscript, dated February 19, 1899, to a letter written on February 16, which he had forgotten to mail; Kajanus correspondence, SibMus.

19. Liikanen, "Light to Our People," especially 422–23.

20. Smeds, *Helsingfors—Paris*, 288.

21. Klinge discusses the connections between Finnish nationalism and neoclassical conservatism in *Finnish Tradition*, 107–8.

22. Polvinen, *Imperial Borderland*, 100.

23. "Tiderna äro hårda. Tag emot en skärf. Atenarnes sång på finska må väl gå? Bjud till!" Kajanus correspondence, SibMus. For the *Song*'s rapid transformation into a species of "banal nationalism," see Goss, "Jean Sibelius and Finnish Nationalism."

24. A multipage list of these arrangements appears in SWV, 139–42.

25. On censorship in Finland, see Leino-Kaukiainen, *Sensuuri ja sanomalehdistö Suomessa*; Polvinen, *Imperial Borderland*, 190–200; and Ruud, *Fighting Words*.

26. An English translation of the decree is given in Ruud, *Fighting Words*, 237–52.

27. Ibid., 207–26.

28. Quoted in Polvinen, *Imperial Borderland*, 199; see also p. 195 on Bobrikov's measures. The Russian paper *Finliandskaia Gazeta* continued publication until 1917, although its Finnish version, *Suomen Sanomat*, expired with Bobrikov in 1904.

29. Three years later Erkko would be expelled from Finland. He headed for New York, where he founded a Finnish nationalist newspaper, *Amerikan Kaiku*, with distinctively anti-Bobrikov and pro-socialist sympathies.

30. Autio discusses the lottery soirée plans in *Savo-karjalaisen osakunnan historia III: Roudan aika*, 240–41. Further details were related in *Uusi Suometar*, October 22, 1899.

31. The numerous paintings of the rapids of Mäntykoski and Imatra by artists from Gallén to Halonen and Järnefelt served a similar subversive purpose; see Gallen-Kallela-Sirén, "Axel Gallén," 338–39.

32. The work is one of a trio that Sibelius seems to have regarded, at least until the age of fifty, as companion pieces, the other two being *Snöfrid* and *Sandels*; see Johnson, *Jean Sibelius*, 98.

Chapter Fifteen

1. See Eric Hobsbawm, "Mass-Producing Traditions," in Hobsbawm and Ranger, *Invention of Tradition*, especially 287–91. For a consideration of Finnish participation in this production, see Rainer Knapas, "The Landscapes of Ideas," in *Surface and Depth*, 28–43. As for Finland's Press Days, reports were limited because many newspapers had been shut down. The account here is based on those still permitted to circulate in Helsinki: *Hufvudstadsbladet*, *Nya Pressen*, and *Uusi Suometar*, November 4, 5, 7, and 11, 1899. The best of the all-too-few secondary accounts are Fewster, *Visions of Past Glory*, 258–62; Johnson, *Jean Sibelius*, 89–94; and Tawaststjerna, "Sibelius' *Finlandia*."

2. Aspelin-Haapkylä, *Suomalaisen teatterin historia*, 4:129.

3. Olkkonen reported the discovery in "Leinon ja Finnen kuvaelmien arvoitukset," *Helsingin Sanomat*, December 23, 1984, reproducing the texts in full. Olkkonen tracked down the texts along with the censor's decision in Finland's National Archives (Painoasiain ylihallitus III, Ee3 and Da 27, Kirjekonseptit 1899). The discussion here is based on those archival documents, Olkkonen's article, and information he generously supplied in person.

4. In 1906 the poet would rework *Kevätlaulu*, enlarging it into *Kevätkantaatti* (*Spring Cantata*).

5. Later Leino took up the subject: in the spring of 1919 he presented *Juhana herttuan ja Catharina Jagellonican lauluja* (*Songs of Duke John and Catharina Jagellonica*).

6. Kallio, "Duke John and European Culture," in *Finland: Cultural Perspectives*, 45–50, gives these details; see also Ekberg, *Uppslagsverket Finland*, s.v. "Johan III."

7. Aspelin-Haapkylä, *Suomalaisen teatterin historia*, 4:128–29.

8. These summaries are based on Olkkonen, *Helsingin Sanomat*, December 23, 1984, and reports in *Uusi Suometar*, *Nya Pressen*, and *Hufvudstadsbladet*, November 5, 1899.

9. Quoted in Jutikkala and Pirinen, *History of Finland*, 121.

10. *Uusi Suometar*, November 5, 1899.

11. See Kirby, *Concise History*, 99–100; and Stenius, "Breakthrough of the Principle of Mass Organization," 199–200. For an examination of the role of women in the revivalist movements see Irma Sulkunen, "The Women's Movement," in Engman and Kirby, *Finland*, 178–91.

12. Quoted in Hannes Sihvo, "Runoilijat sorron yössä," in Tommila, *Herää Suomi*, 375.

13. W. R. Mead, "Perceptions of Finland," in Engman and Kirby, *Finland*, 9. As the Joyce scholar Hans Walter Gabler observes, "Polyglott punster that he is, [Joyce] will have mustered every opportunity of further linking the Irish predicament to the Finnish one . . . Joyce was, in his way, politically (as well as historically) highly aware"; e-mail communication to the author, June 12, 2008. See chapter 18 for more on Joyce and Finland.

14. Salme Sarajas-Korte, "The Finnish View of Symbolist Painting from Antinoüs Myth to *Kalevala* Mysticism," in Clair, *Lost Paradise*, 287.

15. The speech has been preserved in the Wiipurilaisen Osakunnan historia, v[uosia] 1893–94, Liitte XIV, HUL Vio: Me2. The images and language of the awakening persist in Finland even today, especially in connection with the Finns' cherished freedoms of speech and of the press. In preparation for the World Congress and 58th General Assembly of the International Press Institute (IPI) being organized in Helsinki, the editor-in-chief of *Helsingin Sanomat* (formerly *Päivälehti*), wrote a welcoming address in which he first acknowledged the IPI's vital work on behalf of freedom of speech everywhere and then observed: "Only when people are able to know can they believe in the possibility of change and, for us it goes without saying, *in the sunrise on a time of national freedoms*"; brochure, "Spirit of Helsinki: Welcome" (Helsinki, 2009), [2], emphasis added. The editor-in-chief, Janne Virkkunen, is a great-grandson of Jean Sibelius.

16. Hannes Sihvo, "Runoilijat sorron yössä," in Tommila, *Herää Suomi*, 372–76.

17. F. Krohn, in *Ylioppilaskunnan Laulajat 50 vuotta*, 113–14.

18. Quoted in SWV, 114.

19. The entire program of the Press Days music, including the original version of *Finlandia*, was reconstructed from those parts and presented in an anniversary concert in Helsinki on November 4, 1999. The music was recorded for the first time in 1998: *Press Celebrations Music*, the Tampere Philharmonic Orchestra, cond. Tuomas Ollila-Hannikainen (Ondine, ODE 913-2).

20. The Finnish composer Jouni Kaipainen seems to have been the first to call attention to the locomotive association, in his notes to *Press Celebrations Music*.

21. James Hepokoski, "*Finlandia* Awakens," in Grimley, *Cambridge Companion*, 81–94.

22. A. U. (Alarik Uggla), "Prässens dagar," in *Hufvudstadsbladet*, November 7, 1899; and E. K. (Evert Katila), "Juhlakuvaelmien musiikki," in *Uusi Suometar*, November 7, 1899.

23. Johnson, *Jean Sibelius*, 59–60.

24. Ibid., 93–94. This resemblance has been explored further in James Hepokoski, "*Finlandia* Awakens," in Grimley, *Cambridge Companion*, 92–94.

25. Eight years earlier Sibelius had written to Aino from Vienna, "Well, Pacius has died. I read it in the Swedish newspaper. It said that he had such a pronounced 'Finnish feature' in his music. With all due respect I haven't yet succeeded in finding anything in it other than reminiscences of operas, Italian and German" (Pacius har ju dött[.] Jag läste det på svenska tidningen. De sade att han i sin musik hade ett så utpräglat 'finskt drag.' Med respekt sagt har jag ännu ej lyckats se i den annat än reminiscenser af operor, italienska och tyska), January 27, 1891.

Chapter Sixteen

1. "Saa nyt nähdä mitä tämä uusi vuosisata tuopi mukanaan Suomelle ja suomalaisille. Historian tuomio ainakaan ei lange [*sic*] meidän suomalaisten yli. Ja se seikka että asiamme on oikea antaa arvokkaisuutta ja tyyneyttä," January 1, 1900.

2. "En rå finsk folkhop"; letter postmarked September 20, 1892.

3. "De [Tyskarna] förstå t.ex. ej det minsta den nya riktningen såväl i konst som litteratur." Sibelius, letter to Aino from Vienna, January 6, 1891.

4. "In Finnland wird die Kunst zu einem Schrei des geknechteten Selbstbewußtseins. Man versteht die Bilder nicht, weil wir nicht die Zeit haben, die Kalevala zu lesen oder die anderen finnischen Epen." *Entwicklungsgeschichte der Modernen Kunst*, 2:643. Meier-Graefe was among the patrons of the Black Porker in Berlin and a founder of the cultural magazine *Pan*, to which Finns and Swedes alike contributed; see Brummer and Lengefeld, *En glömd relation*, especially 24–30.

5. "Jag kan inte riktigt förstå denna symbolism, men felet ligger kanske hos mig. . . . Det märkvärdigaste är, att alla avbildade äro förtjusta i idén, som de anse epokgörande." Edelfelt to Gallén, September 2, 1894; quoted in Hintze, *Albert Edelfelt*, 114–15.

6. Teperi, *Pro Carelia*, 73–74.

7. See Salmenhaara, in *Finnish Music*, 34–36, and FMQ (1994/1). As early as 1901, a twenty-page booklet, *Ernst Mielck: ein kurzes Künstlerleben*, was brought out in Leipzig by F. Hofmeister.

8. "Man har med fog klagat över formsinnets försvinnande hos våra dagars unga komponister. Rapsodier, symfoniska dikter och sviter skrifva alla, men få våga sig på sinfonins kungliga byggnad, af skäl att så få beherska den svåra konsten att logiskt och uttömmande tänka en musikalisk tanke till slut, låta den vidga sig till universell betydelse, förandliga formen och gifva fantasiflykten ett bestämt mål." *Nya Pressen*, October 21, 1897.

9. See Huttunen, "Nationalistic and Non-Nationalistic Views of Sibelius," especially 223–24. A different outlook reigns today, exemplified by James Hepokoski's recent analysis of the symphony's "core Finnishness" in "Sibelius Builds a First Symphony: Modalities of National Identity," forthcoming in *Musurgia*, which Professor Hepokoski kindly shared in advance of its publication.

10. For an analytical discussion of the First Symphony vis-à-vis Tchaikovsky, see Joseph Kraus, "The 'Russian' Influence in the First Symphony of Jean Sibelius: Chance Intersection or Profound Integration?," in Murtomäki, Kilpeläinen, and Väisänen, *Sibelius Forum 1995*, 142–52.

11. *Musikalisk Dialog* / I "Det blåser kalt, kalt väder från sjön" / motto till I sats i Sinfonin. / II sats. Heine (Nordens fura drömmer om söderns palm) / III. Vintersaga/Jormas himmel, HUL 1472a, p. [38]. "Jorma's Heaven" refers to Juhani Aho's novel *Panu* about the struggle between Christians and pagans at Korsholm.

12. See Kallio's thoughtful "Metrical Structures in Sibelius's Works," in Murtomäki, Kilpeläinen, and Väisänen, *Sibelius Forum 1995*, 276–81.

13. Smeds and Mäkinen, *Kaiu, kaiu, lauluni*, 53–56, give details and photographs of this impressive event; *Päivälehti* (temporarily back in business) published lengthy reports on the festival, June 19, 20, and 21, 1900.

14. Fewster, *Visions of Past Glory*, 291.

15. Quoted in Garelick, who discusses the fair and its agendas in "*Bayadères, Stéréorama*, and Vahat-Loukoum." Two dissertations, both illustrated, have dealt with Finns' participation in the fair: Smeds, *Helsingfors–Paris*, and Walton, "Swedish and Finnish Pavilions." For additional photographs, see MacKeith and Smeds, *Finland Pavilions*. The pavilion and the event's nationalistic meanings are currently being reexamined by Finnish scholars, including Gallen-Kallela-Sirén, "Axel Gallén," 565–93; and Fewster, whose more recent findings about the structure and building of the pavilion were generously shared for inclusion here.

16. Quoted in MacKeith and Smeds, *Finland Pavilions*, 16; see also pp. 13–23 and 107–12. Also valuable for this discussion have been Nordenson, *Finskt sekelskifte*, especially Marika Hausen's essay there, "Finlands paviljong på världsutställningen i Paris," 27–59; and Kirsi Saarikangas, "Wood, Forest and Nature," in Lehtonen, *Europe's Northern Frontier*, 166–79.

17. "Le Grand-duché de Finland est une monarchie constitutionnelle dont le trône est indissolublement uni au trône de l'Empire de Russie." Mechelin, chapter 2, "Organisation politique et administrative," in *Notices sur la Finland*, 1.

18. A number of the paintings and furnishings are reproduced (in black and white) in Nordenson, *Finskt sekelskifte*.

19. Quoted in MacKeith and Smeds, *Finland Pavilions*, 22.

20. Ibid.; Sibelius recorded his description in a letter to Aino, July 27, 1900.

21. Gallen-Kallela-Sirén, "Axel Gallén," 586–87. Not surprisingly, the author observes, contemporary reproductions were censored.

22. The best studies of the Helsinki orchestra in Paris are Helena Tyrväinen's: "Sibelius at the Paris Universal Exposition of 1900," in Murtomäki, Kilpeläinen, and Väisänen, *Sibelius Forum 1995*, 114–28, and the more detailed "Suomalaiset Pariisin maailmannäyttelyiden 1889 ja 1900 musiikkiohjelmissa."

23. "Les chants finlandais procèdent d'une inspiration triste et remontent à la plus haute antiquité. Dès les temps les plus reculés du paganisme les *runes* étaient sur les lèvres du peuple." *La musique en Finlande*, 3.

24. "Mais de tous les compositeurs finlandais contemporains, le plus remarquable est sans contest Jean Sibelius . . . mieux que tout autre, il a su donner à ses compositions le cachet de la nature finlandaise et du caractère national dans ce qui'ils ont d'essentiel. On peut dire qu'il est le vrai créateur de la *Musique Finnoise* dans l'acception spécifique de ce mot." Ibid., 9.

25. "Son grand poème symphonique avec texte tiré du *Kalevala*, ses Suites pour orchestre, traduisent, d'une manière plus élévée que ne peuvent le faire la parole ou le pinceau, les splendeurs paisibles, profondes, graves, mélancoliques de la nature finlandaise et de l'épopée nationale." Ibid., 10.

26. Albert Edelfelt to his mother, ca. March 28, 1900; quoted in *Ur Albert Edelfelts brev: Kring sekelskiftet*, 108.

27. "Le concert finlandais," *Journal des débats politiques et littéraires* (August 2, 1900): 2.

28. "La Patrie de M. Sibilius a soulevé notamment en enthousiasme indescriptible. Il y avait là beaucoup de Finlandais tout vibrants, et dont la flamme a gagné l'auditoire entier. Ce fut une manifestation patriotique des plus imposantes. L'âme même de la Finlande palpitait dans l'immense salle." Ibid., 2.

29. In *"Nouskaa aatteet!,"* 359–61, Vainio cites instructions from Axel Carpelan that "Jean" Sibelius and "Ernst" Mielck should be represented on programs abroad only by a first initial, to prevent "the crazy French" from thinking that the first was of French origin and the latter, of German.

30. "Wenäjän puoleiset (chauvinistiset) lehdet tulevat haukkuman minkä jaksavat etenkin minua koska olen muka nationelli." Sibelius, letter to Aino from Paris (in Finnish), July 27, 1900.

31. See ETL 1:232–33, and Bo Carpelan, *Axel*, a novel written in 1986 by one of Carpelan's descendants. Bo Carpelan (b. 1926) is one of Finland's most decorated authors. He learned of his unusual ancestor only upon reading Ekman's *Jean Sibelius*, Axel never having been mentioned at home. Fascinated with the relationship of this great-uncle to Finland's leading composer, Bo Carpelan told their story through a fictitious diary, providing a dual portrait of Axel the musical amateur and his idolized friend Sibelius intertwined with a historical portrait of Finland from the mid-nineteenth century until the civil war. The novel, written in Swedish, has been translated into English, Finnish, French, and German. In a stage version, it enjoyed extended runs in both Finland and Sweden; see Schoolfield, *History of Finland's Literature*, 588.

32. A relationship explored in Goss, *Jean Sibelius and Olin Downes*.

33. "X" to Sibelius, March 13, 1900.

34. The original is quoted in JSW I/3, x n. 1.

35. Exceptionally, Valkenier raises this question, in a Russian context, in *Valentin Serov*, 58–59.

36. Ibid., 70. Curiously, despite the high-minded attitude toward the arts, learning, and "clean" money in Finland, access to the student branch of that highly respected bastion of learning, the collection-rich Helsinki University Library, is through the tempting electronic and DVD/CD section of a major department store.

37. ETL 1:242.

Chapter Seventeen

1. Gallén's blue-tinted horseman seems in turn to have made a lasting impression on Wassily Kandinsky (1886–1944), whose *Blaue Reiter* (*Blue Rider*) became his symbol; see Sjöblom, "Russian Avant-Garde Art Shown in Finland."

2. "On Misreading Meanings into Sibelius," *New York Times*, October 24, 1937; reprinted in Downes, *Olin Downes on Music*, 241.

3. Although there is one trait that Finns and at least some Italians, the Sicilians, mystifyingly share: the same high rate of diabetes in the population, a medical conundrum that as yet has no satisfactory explanation.

4. Aino's letters preserve the most detailed impressions of the family's journey; see Talas, *Aino Sibeliuksen kirjeitä*, 186–234, and *Elisabeth Järnefeltin kirjeitä*, 273–78.

5. Elisabeth to Aino, February 11, 1901; Talas, *Elisabeth Järnefeltin kirjeitä*, 274.

6. Ekman, *Jean Sibelius* (1936), 148.

7. "Här är härligt—full sommar—haf-berg, palmer, blommor, himmel och helvete," February 24, 1901.

8. "I den förtrollade trädgården då Juan [Jean?] äro borta / Balletto in minore / Serenata dell'estero / Hon bad mig sända pressade blad från Italia—Jag sänder [r crossed through] fikonlöf. Äro de så små, sade Augusta"; HUL 0145. The page is reproduced in facsimile in Goss, *Sibelius Companion*, 89.

9. Klinge, *Den politiske Runeberg*, 355.

10. "Don Juan / Sitter i skymningen i mitt slott. en gäst stiger in[.] Jag [*will bjuda till att roa* crossed out] frågar mer än en gång hvem han är.—Intet svar. Jag bjuder till att roa honom. Lika stum är han. [*Han gör mig* crossed out.] Slutligen stämmer den främmande upp med en sång. Då märker Don Juan hvem han är—döden"; HUL 0145.

11. As Aino confided to her brother Arvid, December 29, 1900; Talas, *Aino Sibeliuksen kirjeitä*, 202–3; and to Linda Sibelius, December 13, 1900; quoted in part in Sirén, *Aina poltti sikaria*, 197.

12. So Sibelius recalled in Ekman, *Jean Sibelius* (1936), 148.

13. Aino to Elisabeth Järnefelt, March 21, 1901; Talas, *Elisabeth Järnefeltin kirjeitä*, 277.

14. To Elisabeth Järnefelt, March 1, 1901; ibid., 275.

15. As Aino related to Kasper, March 7, 1901; Talas, *Aino Sibeliuksen kirjeitä*, 222.

16. Sculpture and architecture had deep meaning for Sibelius. He once told Aino that, as a boy, he had envisioned a whole new art—half sculpture, half music. Curiously, he added, "I began with sculpture, and, as you know, I made a complete fiasco"; December 18, 1890. If this be more than braggadocio, then these youthful sculptural attempts have yet to be discovered.

17. Tokoi, *Sisu*, 97. In *Imperial Borderland*, 113–32, Polvinen devotes an entire chapter to "the military question."

18. ETS 2:162, 248. The evidence comes from a letter written in 1966 by the man who collected the signatures, Petter Forsström.

19. Sibelius's *Schmerzens Kind* comment was written in a letter to Axel Carpelan dated November 9, 1901. The exuberant description is Carpelan's to Lydia Rosengren, October 9, 1901: "en symfoni med sol-

sken o[ch] blå himmel o[ch] jublande glädje"; quoted from Kilpeläinen's edition of the symphony, JSW I/3, x n. 9.

20. According to Veijo Murtomäki, in a tabulation of "Sibelius's political/patriotic or allegorical compositions in the context of Finland's fight for independence"; "Sibelius, the Composer and Patriot," presented at the conference Finnish-Russian Musical Relations, Sibelius Academy, April 7, 2003.

21. Kajanus's explanations appeared in *Hufvudstadsbladet*, March 11, 1901; quoted in ETL 1:244.

22. Krohn, *Der Stimmungsgehalt der Symphonien*, 1:207–27.

23. Even in the 1950s, Krohn's analysis was polemical; see A. O. Väisänen's sharp criticism in "Sibelius tutkimusongelmana."

24. Quoted in Goss, *Jean Sibelius and Olin Downes*, 34, 37.

25. "Man kommer här på underliga tankar angående musikens väsen."

26. "Jag har kommit till, som jag tror, en annan åsigt om det nationella i musik. Wi dyrka och hafva dyrkat det 'etnografiska i musik['], om jag så får uttrycka mig. Men det värkligen nationella ligger nog djupare. Jämför t.ex. Verdi och Grieg. Den förra [är] kanske den mest nationella och dock europé—den sednare—jag kan ej dölja det för mig—talar bygde mål. Roligt skall det bli att se hvad Du tänker om min musik nu." Sibelius to Carpelan, May 21, 1901; Rosengren Family Archives, Åbo Akademi Bibliotek, Handskrift avdelning.

27. "Jag skref tidigare att 'vi dyrkat det etnografiska i musik,' jag menar egentligen att vi anse för sant endast det etnografiskt rigtiga hvad tongångar och dylikt angår. Förstå mig rätt!" Ibid.

28. "Saken var den att jag hade att utstå en hård kamp i min konst—nu är jag åter på det klara och far för fulla segel."

29. See Haas's insightful "Sibelius's Second Symphony and the Legacy of Symphonic Lyricism," in Goss, *Sibelius Companion*, 77–94, on which my remarks are based.

30. These figures are given in Ross, *Finn Factor*, 48.

31. "Ditt namn och din framgång äro en uppehållande kraft för mången," June 11, 1901.

32. Alarik Uggla, writing in *Hufvudstadsbladet*, October 17, 1903, described the song as "hardly singable and appears to be as philosophical and difficult as Rydberg's text" (*På verandan vid havet* är föga sångbar och synes ock lika filosoferande och svårtydd som den Rydbergska text). However, on the same day Flodin, who was then writing for *Helsingfors Posten* (*Nya Pressen* having been discontinued in the years 1900–1905), observed of the new song that "Sibelius always knows how to surprise and to say something new" (Sibelius vet alltid att överraska och alltid att säga någonting nytt).

33. ETL 1:272–73.

Chapter Eighteen

1. See Riitta Ojanperä, "The City," in *Surface and Depth*, 292–97; Bell and Hietala, *Helsinki*, 162–71; and Kirsi Saarikangas, "Wood, Forest and Nature," in Lehtonen, *Europe's Northern Frontier*, especially 174–82.

2. On September 27; *Hämeenlinna Letters*.

3. Korvenmaa, *Innovation versus Tradition*, 126–27. Korvenmaa's study of Ainola's architect includes valuable observations on the house; this section draws on his monograph (see especially 122–30); Korvenmaa's "Takaisin luontoon—mutta sivistyneesti," in *Ainola*, 26–45; and materials preserved in SFA, file box 12.

4. Korvenmaa, *Innovation versus Tradition*, 126. See also Kirsi Saarikangas, "Wood, Forest and Nature," in Lehtonen, *Europe's Northern Frontier*, 166–69, on appropriating the international as "typically Finnish."

5. "Overcoming Symbolism" (1915); quoted in Reeder, *Anna Akhmatova*, 45.

6. Volkov, *St. Petersburg*, 317. On Serov's change of style, see Valkenier, *Valentin Serov*, 26–27.

7. "Olen saanut ihania teemoja viulu konserttiin," September 18, 1902.

8. HUL 1550, p. [4]; for a transcription of the theme, see Jukka Tiilikainen, "The Genesis of the Violin Concerto," in Grimley, *Cambridge Companion*, 69.

9. See Sirén, *Aina poltti sikaria*, 213.

10. Åman has explored this connection in chapter 6, "National Form," in *Architecture and Ideology in Eastern Europe*.

11. As Erkki Salmenhaara showed in "The Violin Concerto," in Goss, *Sibelius Companion*, 103–19, with examples from the work's first incarnation. See also Tomi Mäkelä, "The Sibelius Violin Concerto and Its Dramatic Virtuosity," in *Proceedings from the First International Jean Sibelius Conference*, 118–33; Mäkelä compares the work to Tchaikovsky's, Brahms's, and Bruch's violin concerti as well as Mendelssohn's.

12. Kirchmeyer, *Kommentiertes Verzeichnis der Werke und Werkausgaben Igor Strawinskys*, 75.

13. *Euterpe*, February 13, 1904; quoted in Erkki Salmenhaara, "The Violin Concerto," in Goss, *Sibelius Companion*, 107.

14. For a facsimile of the Bachian cadenza, see Lindgren, "I've Got Some Lovely Themes," 30–31. Jukka Tiilikainen has raised fundamental questions about just what *was* the first cadenza in the concerto's original form and about its recorded "reconstruction"; see his discussion in "The Genesis of the Violin Concerto," in Grimley, *Cambridge Companion*, 78–79.

15. Flodin, *Helsingfors Posten*, February 9, 1904.

16. Jukka Tiilikainen, "The Genesis of the Violin Concerto," in Grimley, *Cambridge Companion*, 79; for more on the revisions, see Erkki Salmenhaara, "The Violin Concerto," in Goss, *Sibelius Companion*; and James Hepokoski, quoted in Lindgren, "I've Got Some Lovely Themes," 28.

17. Haapakoski, "The Concerto That Holds a Record."

18. In a letter postmarked August 8, 1903, Sibelius wrote in haste to Burmester, "Violinkonserten skall jag snart sända Dig i ett acceptabelt 'Klavierauszug' med skild tydlig hufvudstämm. Jag drömmer bara huru den må låta under dina mästare händer"; HUL 206.61.

19. "Wenn dieses der Fall werde *ich* das Concert *nie* spielen." Postcard from Burmester to Sibelius, October 4, 190[3]; SFA, file box 17.

20. "'*Ein Heldenleben*' v. Strauss von einem Kleinstadtorchester gespielt würde genau so lecherlich wirken wie eine *Bismarcksche* Rede im Munde eines Proleten. Laß dich also bitte durch nichts irritieren, wandle du ruhig deine Bahn und verlasse dich auf mich. Ich werde dir das Konzert in *Helsingfors* so geigen, daß man dir Abbitte leisten wird." February 13, 1904; ibid. Burmester wrote the letter mostly in *Sütterlinschrift* but emphasized certain words either by changing to Latin letters or by underlining. His Latin letters are here rendered in italics and his old-fashioned spellings left unaltered.

21. Burmester related these and other anecdotes in his autobiography, *Fünfzig Jahre Künstlerleben*; the translations are quoted from the English-language edition, *Fifty Years*. The Aquarium Orchestra yarn appears on pp. 60–63.

22. So Adolf Paul recalled; see Burmester, *Fifty Years*, 84. "Boulot" was the pseudonym for the *Hufvudstadsbladet* critic, Leonard Salin (1857–1911).

23. Burmester, *Fünfzig Jahre*, 91.

24. Burmester himself recounted these episodes without compunction; they are included in *Fifty Years*, 99–100.

25. Ibid., 155.

26. Flesch, *Memoirs* (1957); quoted in *Fifty Years*, 152.

27. Ibid., 154.

28. See Jukka Tiilikainen, "The Genesis of the Violin Concerto," in Grimley, *Cambridge Companion*, 79. It was Tiilikainen who perceptively made the connection between Burmester's Bach interpretations and Sibelius's cadenza.

29. Arthur M. Abell, writing in the *Musical Courier* in 1894; quoted in *Fifty Years*, 158–59.

30. Stoeckel, "Some Recollections," 60.

31. Ranki, *Isänmaa ja Ranska*; in connection with the present discussion, see especially 155, 225–31, 254.

32. Olof Mustelin devoted a full monograph to Euterpe and its times, *Euterpe: Tidskriften och kretsen kring den*. Ranki considers Euterpe (as both group and publication) in the broad context of Finnish Francophilia in *Isänmaa ja Ranska*, 265–81. See also Goss, "Interlude II: 1900–1914," in Goss, *Sibelius Companion*, 97–102.

33. See Tyrväinen, "Les origines de la réception de Debussy en Finland."

34. Schoolfield, *History of Finland's Literature*, 401.

35. Mustelin, *Euterpe*, 322; the translation is quoted from ibid.

36. September 13, 1902.

37. Mustelin, *Euterpe*, gives a membership list, 24–25, and recounts various episodes involving Sibelius, 116–17.

38. Conspicuously, his letters to Rosa Newmarch from this time were written in French rather than his usual German.

39. Quoted in Johnson, *Jean Sibelius*, 129.

40. "Ödlan har djupt gripit mig. Det är poesi och, framför allt, stil i den. Jag skall nog komponera den af Dig åtrådda musiken. Efter bästa förmåga! Naturligtvis!" Sibelius to Lybeck, November 25, 1908; HUL 206.62.

41. To Ekman, *Jean Sibelius* (1936), 186. See also SWV, 26–27.

42. Kihlman, *Mikael Lybeck*, 409. Kihlman devoted an entire chapter to *Ödlan*; see 389–412.

43. See Schoolfield, *History of Finland's Literature*, 404, and Ahokas, *History of Finnish Literature*, 390, 515. Johnson summarizes *Ödlan*'s plot in *Jean Sibelius*, 140–41.

44. "All stor musik 'strävar ut över gränserna mellan livet och döden' och att 'framtidens religion är musiken'"; quoted in Forsman, "Sagan om Satu," 5; see also p. 6.

45. This section is especially indebted to the chapter "Bobrikov's Assassination" in Polvinen, *Imperial Borderland*, 254–67; and to "In Bobrikov's Days," in Schoolfield, *Helsinki of the Czars*, 205–14; as well as to Söderhjelm's letters and recollections in "Den 16 Juni," *Min värld*, 3:252–95. For a firsthand account of one man's traumatic flight into exile, dodging armed Russian guards as he fled Helsinki in desperation toward Stockholm, see Hagelstam, *Personer och minnen*, 147–64.

46. Kirby, *Concise History*, 140.

47. Ekberg, *Uppslagsverket Finland*, s.v. "Kagalen."

48. Kirby, *Concise History*, 141.

49. "Då vi i den isande sommarkvällen seglade in mellan de första låga finska klipporna, tystnade pratet och glammet på däck—alla finnar och finskor fingo ett drag af stel fasa och resignation i ansiktsuttrycket. I Åbo der jag landade, märktes ej annat än den vanliga sommarsömnen men—Helsingfors! De nya poliserna, tatariska—, förskräckligt fula, gifva genom mängd och beväpning (de bära bl.a. alltid på sig handklofvar) vår förr så fredliga stad ett nytt tycke"; quoted in Mustelin, *Euterpe*, 144.

50. Polvinen, *Imperial Borderland*, 256.

51. "Mod är ett vackert ord i svenska språket, men ännu vackrare ljuder det franska ordet courage!" Hultin recorded Edelfelt's remark in her diary, *Päiväkirjani kertoo*, 17.

52. The same year he made a keyboard version of *Har du mod?*, placing its verses beneath the melodic line. In 1911–12 Sibelius returned to the text yet again and made a new keyboard arrangement to the choral melody. On the purely choral version, which shares little with these three settings except the text, see SWV, 549–50.

53. "Hvad säger Du om kriget. De officiella rapporterna!! Japan äger 23 krigsskepp och enligt Bobban äro 40 förstörda. Sic itur ad gehennam!" March 8, 1904.

54. Schoolfield, *Helsinki of the Czars*, 207. See also Kirby, *Concise History*, 138–39.

55. Quoted in Jutikkala, *History of Finland*, 360.

56. Matilda Wegelius, a hospital worker, related the family's words to her sister; quoted in Polvinen, *Imperial Borderland*, 262. Schauman seems to have loaded his Browning with "dum-dum" bullets, which explode on entry; Schoolfield reviews the situation in *Helsinki of the Czars*, 211–12, with reference to the memoirs of the assassin's sister Sigrid Schauman, *Min bror Eugen: En gestalt ur Finlands frihetskamp* (Stockholm: Natur och Kultur, 1964).

57. Schoolfield, *Helsinki of the Czars*, 209–11.

58. The parallel between Finland's oppression and Ireland's was not lost on James Joyce, who adopted the day of the assassination, June 16, 1904, as Bloomsday in his *Ulysses*. The deliberateness of his choice is borne out by the mention of Bobrikov in the text; see Joyce, *Ulysses: A Critical and Synoptic Edition*, chapter 7, line 602.

59. Söderhjelm, *Min värld*, 3:256–57.

60. Levas, *Jean Sibelius: Muistelma*, 2:10.

61. Hultin, *Päiväkirjani kertoo*, 73. Completed in 1909, the composition was *In Memoriam*. In 1935 Sibelius claimed, "I did not want to call it 'Marche Funèbre.' Some time later I hit upon its title: 'In Memoriam.' The title may give the impression that I was thinking of the death of some particular person when I wrote it. However, this is not the case." Ekman, *Jean Sibelius* (1936), 187. However, one of the composer's daughters, Eva Paloheimo, reiterated to Erik Tawaststjerna that her father meant the work, or at least its main theme, for Schauman; see ETS 3:13, 360.

62. Hultin, *Päiväkirjani kertoo*, 318.

63. "Murha ei ole hyväksyttävä, ei poliittisista syistäkään"; "Ei ole epäilyä, että Bobrikov kuului pahoihin vallanpitäjiin." *Muistelmia sortokaudelta*, 1:85–89; the quotations are on 85 and 89. See also Polvinen, *Imperial Borderland*, 262–63.

1905: The Crucial Hour

1. "Nu är sista stunden inne då jag ännu kan taga i och bli något riktigt stort."

2. Among the many sources on this episode, see Gonneau, "Le dimanche sanglant," and Figes, *A People's Tragedy*, 173–80.

3. Quoted in *Kullervo*, JSW I/1.3, motto page.

4. Quoted in Schoolfield, *Helsinki of the Czars*, 212–13, where Hohenthal's deeds are dramatically related. Captured, tried, and condemned to life imprisonment, Hohenthal escaped to England and married the woman who helped to rescue him.

5. "Bindelänken med Europa bruten! *Du* är nu vårt stora hopp och vår stolthet."

Introduction to Part III

1. The title of this part is the motto for Juhlaviikot, the Helsinki Festival Weeks, 2006. The slogan, which comes from Communist art manifestos and harks back to the 1917 Revolution, has strong leftist overtones.

2. Järnefelt's novel *Veneh'ojalaiset* (1909) describes the events of the mutiny against a background of rural Finns who had moved to the city, their sense of uprootedness contributing to the uprising; see Kai Laitinen, "The Rise of Finnish-Language Literature," in Schoolfield, *History of Finland's Literature*, 106.

3. Kirby, *Concise History*, 144–49, from where the statistics are cited.

4. These statistics are given in Jutikkala, *History of Finland*, 373–74. As Fewster points out, the vote

was not truly universal: certain categories of persons were exempt, including vagrants, those on welfare, and those bankrupted or condemned for criminal offenses; see his *Visions of Past Glory*, 186–87 n. 5. Still, Finland was the first country in Europe and the second in the world to extend this right to women. It is seldom remarked that this momentous shift had far less to do with any benevolent feelings toward a huge disenfranchised segment of the population than with the need for a strong labor vote. The traditional view of woman in Finnish society is very different from the adoration she has been accorded in southern Europe. Woman's value in Finland has been and still is connected to her capacity for work. In his pioneering research on Finnish proverbs, the folklorist Matti Kuusi found that the oldest peasant maxims embodied a remarkably consistent view of woman as a silent workhorse. Like a beast of burden, woman was valued for her working abilities, good nature, and sturdy build; see Kuusi, chapter 26, "Talonpojan näkökulma" ("The Peasant's Perspective"), in *Sananlaskut*.

5. "Nuo kaksi 'kulttuuria,' ruotsalainen ja suomalainen, joista niin paljo puhutaan, ovat meistä vaan turhia korupuheita. Meidän maassamme on olemassa vaan yksi kulttuuri, vaikka se pukeutuu milloin suomalaiseen milloin ruotsalaiseen muotoon." Rein, "Uudenvuoden mietteitä 1890," 31.

6. Max Engman, "The Finland-Swedes: A Case of a Failed National History?" in Branch, *National History and Identity*, 166–77.

7. *Helsingin Sanomat*, June 26, 1910; quoted in ETL 3:11. In the first decade of the twentieth century, the university became the headquarters for the "new philosophy," influenced by Henri Bergson and William James, whose ideas fueled debates on philosophical and national identity in a Nordic context. The "new philosophers" rejected Rein and opposed national idealism; see Stefan Nygård, "Vardandets världsbild och intuitionens blixtljus: Om receptionen av Bergsons filosofi i Finland," in Nygård and Strang, *Mellan idealism och analytisk filosofi*, 79–110.

8. Ringbom, *Stone, Style and Truth*, 186–87.

9. "Mielet ovat siihen määrin hiiltyneet etten ole voinut kuvailla sellaista 'klass-hat.' Silmät kiiluu vaan"; August 9, 1906.

10. Tuomikoski-Leskelä, *Taide ja politiikka*, 114–15, 319–20.

11. Quoted in Lukkarinen, *Classicism and History*, 61–62.

12. "Karjadiskurssi," Rantanen's term in *Suolatut säkeet*. Rantanen examined the formation of Finnish identity in writings of national figures from the seventeenth to the nineteenth centuries; these remarks are based on her findings. See especially 191–98, 210–17, and 248–50.

13. Hobsbawm, chapter 4, "The Politics of Democracy," in *Age of Empire*.

14. By 1912 it had appeared in a Swedish translation, *Massans psykologi*.

15. Nietzsche first elaborated on these ideas in *Beyond Good and Evil* (1886); see his chapter 5, for example, "The Natural History of Morals," and chapter 9, "What Is Noble?" He worked them out more thoroughly in *On the Genealogy of Morals* (1887). On Nietzsche's reception in Finland, see Marja Jalava, "Lidelse och bragd: Nietzschereceptionen i Finland ca 1890–1910," in Nygård and Strang, *Mellan idealism och analytisk filosofi*, 51–78.

16. Quoted in Lukkarinen, *Classicism and History*, 62.

17. *Hufvudstadsbladet*, July 23, 1908; quoted in ibid.

18. Quoted in ETL 3:62. Sibelius remarked on the article, which was mentioned in the Helsinki newspapers, in his diary on August 15, 1915.

19. The poet, Busse-Palme (1876–1915), a largely self-taught German writer, lived in Berlin, where Sibelius presumably came to know about him. "Erloschen" was published in *Lieder eines Zigeuners* (Stuttgart: 1899); Sibelius set it to music in October 1906. In 1904–5 Busse-Palme's *Furcht* had been set to music by Alban Berg; see Chadwick, "Berg's Unpublished Songs."

Chapter Nineteen

1. On Sibelius's connections to Britain, see Laura Gray, "Sibelius and England," in Goss, *Sibelius Companion*, 281–95; and Peter Franklin, "Sibelius in Britain," in Grimley, *Cambridge Companion*, 182–95.

2. Thanks to Maris Männik-Kirme, "About Sibelius's Unknown Performances in Tallinn," in Murtomäki, Kilpeläinen, and Väisänen, *Sibelius Forum 1995*, 94–99, details of his Estonian visits are known. One of the most popular health resorts in the Russian Empire, Catharinenthal (Kadriorg in Estonian) drew the wealthy of Saint Petersburg. It appealed to Baltic Germans and, to a lesser extent, enticed local Estonians. Summer concerts were a special attraction. The *primus motor* behind the visit was evidently Georg Schnéevoigt (1872–1947), an energetic Finnish cellist and conductor who, like Sibelius, had studied with Robert Fuchs in Vienna.

3. *Herald Tribune*, August 25, 1906; reprinted in *The International Herald Tribune*, August 26–27, 2006.

4. Taruskin, *Stravinsky and the Russian Traditions*, 1:396–97.

5. Sjöblom, "Russian Avant-Garde Art Shown in Finland," 40.

6. Talas, *Elisabeth Järnefeltin kirjeitä*, 284–85.

7. Edelfelt's sweetly pink portrait of Sophie Manzey hangs today in the museum known as Villa Gyllenberg, outside Helsinki. The match was opposed by the Manzey family, who were horrified that their daughter would consider marriage to a "mere artist." But in their opposition, they sealed her fate: Sophie married well, stayed in Russia, and starved to death during the long siege of Leningrad. Their relationship unfolds in Knapas and Vainio's magnificent illustrated edition of Edelfelt's letters, *Albert Edelfelt och Ryssland*.

8. Helena Tyrväinen has been at the forefront of examining the artistic connections among Finns, Russians, and Frenchmen; see her "Helsinki–Saint Petersburg–Paris."

9. Busoni had attempted to forge a Sibelian connection with the Russian magnate and music publisher Mitrofan Belyayev (1836–1903), but it came to naught. For a view of Belyayev in 1918, see Montagu-Nathan, "Belaiev: Maecenas of Russian Music."

10. Sibelius also visited Moscow, with the idea of conducting his violin concerto. At the last minute, when it became clear that the solo violinist could not handle the work, the concerto was omitted. The public heard *Pohjola's Daughter*, Symphony no. 3, *Karelia*, *Pan and Echo*, *Valse triste*, and two numbers from *Belshazzar's Feast*: "Oriental March" and "Khadra's Dance"; see ETL 2:81.

11. Quoted in Hanson and Hanson, *Prokofiev*, 35.

12. Yastrebtsev, *Reminiscences of Rimsky-Korsakov*, 420; the date, according to the Julian calendar, was November 4, 1907.

13. "Rouva on erittäin 'puhelias.' Se minua vähän vaivaa—mutta mitä tehdä," November 13, 1907. For discussions of *Night Ride*, see ETL 2:97 and Daniel Grimley, "Landscape and Structural Perspective in *Nightride and Sunrise*," in Huttunen, Kilpeläinen, and Murtomäki, *Sibelius Forum II*, 248–58.

14. Ekman, *Jean Sibelius* (1936), 187.

15. Newmarch, *Jean Sibelius: A Short Story* (1939), 68.

16. "Enligt min tanke är det med kompositioner som med fjärilar: rör vid dem en enda gång, och stoftet är borta." Ekman, *Jean Sibelius* (1956), 207.

17. As Grimley observes in "Landscape and Structural Perspective in *Nightride and Sunrise*," in Huttunen, Kilpeläinen, and Murtomäki, *Sibelius Forum II*, 258.

18. "Denn das Wort héros schliesst durch die deutsche Bedeutung vor allem den Begriff des Mächtigen, Gewaltigen in sich, und in diesem Sinne ist Ihre sinfonische Dichtung doch eigentliche nicht heroisch," August 30, 1906; SFA, file box 46.

19. Jean Sibelius, *Tone Poems in Full Score* (New York: Dover, 1991), 189. Sibelius's heroic ideas and their implications for the work are considered in Timo Virtanen, "*Pohjola's Daughter*: 'L'aventure d'un héros,'" in Jackson and Murtomäki, *Sibelius Studies*, 139–74.

20. Sibelius's observations on the instruments (recorded by Bengt von Törne and quoted here from "Observations on Music and Musicians," in Goss, *Sibelius Companion*, 224, 225) were those of the later composer. The man of the 1890s held different views, as his music shows.

21. By which time it had been slightly revised; see SWV, 286.

22. Stravinsky and Craft, *Dialogues and a Diary*, 225. It was on receiving the Sibelius prize in 1963 that Stravinsky arranged the Canzonetta, reconfiguring the all-string piece for two clarinets, four horns, harp, and contrabass.

23. ETL 2:67.

24. Gallen-Kallela-Sirén discusses this debate and translates excerpts from its polemics in "Axel Gallén," 275–79.

25. Stasov's essay has been published in English translation as "The 'New Russian School,'" in *Music in the Western World*, 391–94. Richard Taruskin has dealt extensively with orientalism; see especially his essay "'Entoiling the Falconet,'" in *Defining Russia Musically*.

26. Taruskin, *Defining Russia Musically*, 165.

27. Quoted in *Music in the Western World*, 395–96; the emphases are Musorgsky's.

28. As the translation in *Music in the Western World* has it. On the meanings of this letter in the context of Russian nationalism, see Marina Frolova-Walker, "Against Germanic Reasoning: The Search for a Russian Style of Musical Argumentation," in White and Murphy, *Musical Constructions of Nationalism*, 104–22; in translating part of this letter (107), Frolova-Walker avoids the verb "to reason"; instead, when a German thinks (she translates), he first rambles, then delivers the proof, whereas the Russian gets right to the point, then amuses himself with rambling. Significantly, her analysis shows that Russian composers in the Saint Petersburg orbit, despite their antipathies to Germanic "reasoning," had deep roots in Germanic musical language, as did Sibelius.

29. *Dagbok*, July 18, 1911.

30. "Tankens utkristallisering ur kaos," ETS 3:78.

31. Raakel Kallio, "Aesthetics and Emotions," in *Surface and Depth*, 21. The notion was taken up in Finland (*taidetahto*), especially by the art historian Onni Okkonen (1886–1962). Coarsely woven *ryijy* rugs and wooden churches were considered its most important manifestations.

32. *Kamarinskaya*, Eulenberg miniature score no. 834. Marina Frolova-Walker makes these points in "Against Germanic Reasoning: The Search for a Russian Style of Musical Argumentation," in White and Murphy, *Musical Constructions of Nationalism*," 108–9.

33. See Goss, *Jean Sibelius and Olin Downes*, 46–48.

34. According to Taruskin, *Stravinsky and the Russian Traditions*, 1:740. Taruskin further observes (2:1467): "It is a measure of the thoroughness with which Stravinsky had octatonicized his style that major-scale priority should be newsworthy. In fact, all during the Swiss years, alongside the Turanian masterpieces that brought Stravinsky's octatonic practice to a peak, the composer was turning out little pieces, chiefly of a parodistic nature, that heralded a new interest in clean diatonic—no, not just diatonic, but 'C-scale'— melody."

35. Volkov, *St. Petersburg*, 321–22. Joseph Straus suggests that Stravinsky's neoclassicism may have been sparked out of anger—at the continuing tyranny of Saint Petersburg academic music over concert halls, standard repertoire, and even musical imagination. Satirizing and mocking earlier styles, says Straus, Stravinsky may have turned to earlier models as much out of rebellion as reverence, his use of sonata form being the supreme act of defiance; see Straus, "Sonata Form in Stravinsky," in Haimo and Johnson, *Stravinsky Retrospectives*, 141–61.

Chapter Twenty

1. Stigell, *Finländska gestalter: Robert Stigell*, traces the evolution of the work from its classical roots to the final version. For a photograph, see Valkonen, *The Golden Age*, 43. Raakel Kallio discusses the Finnish atmosphere at this moment in "Aesthetics and Emotions," in *Surface and Depth*, 14–27, as does Olli Valkonen, "The Breakthrough in Finland," in *Scandinavian Modernism*, 35–41.

2. "Suomenko loppua, kalevaisen kansanko häviötä todella? . . . *Finis Finlandiae* koskee meidän julkisia pikkumaisia puolue-pyyteitämme, meidän mahdottomuuttamme rehellisesti sulautumaan yhteen kovimmassakaan yhteissulatuksessa. 'Suomen loppu' ilmikäypi yhtä surkeasti meidän arkipäiväisessä ruotsalais- ja venäläis-vihassa kuin omassa suomalaisuuden epäilyksessämme ja perheitä raatelevassa naapurivainossamme, sanalla sanoen—koko kansallistuntomme torkkuvassa, mistään sysäyksestä heräämättömässä . . . . Kaikkialla, missä kansamme ihmisyys ilmenee matalana ja maantasaisena, kaikkialla, missä Suomen kansan tavat esiintyvät huonoina, rumina, tökeröinä, kaikkialla, missä Suomen kansalainen elää ja toimii ryhdittömänä olentona, olkoon hän senaattori tai maantien kulkuri,—siellä heijastelee 'Suomen loppu,' *Finis Finlandiae*." Reprinted in Mällinen, *Nuoren Suomen ytimessä*, 115, 117, 118.

3. "Meine neue Sinfonie ist eine vollständige Protest gegen d[ie] Composition heutzutage. Nichts—absolut nichts vom Cirkus," May 2, 1911; SFA, file box 121.

4. "Manifesto of Futurist Musicians 1910," reprinted in Apollonio, *Futurist Manifestos*, 31–38; Sibelius is mentioned on p. 33.

5. Writing to Mikko Slöör early in 1907 (probably on January 13), Sibelius goes on at length about his drinking (Gallen-Kallela Archive, NA). Tawaststjerna transcribed a substantial portion of this document in ETS 3:74 (translated in ETL 2:64).

6. "Alt går åt helvetet," dated only "Järvenpää 1907," but written late in the year, since he mentions coming home ill from Turku, where he had gone in November.

7. Tawaststjerna gives the details through the eyes of the physician in the family, Dr. Christian Sibelius; see ETL 2:92–94.

8. In a letter dated June 7, 1910.

9. The best of these writings are James Hepokoski's; see "Sibelius," in Sadie, *New Grove*, 332–35; "Sibelius," in Holoman, *Nineteenth-Century Symphony*; and *Sibelius: Symphony No. 5*.

10. The most expansive treatment of Mahler's Helsinki visit is in La Grange, *Gustav Mahler*, 3:744–61, with pertinent correspondence and substantial excerpts from contemporary reviews. See also the perceptive discussion of the Sibelius–Mahler relationship in Vignal, *Jean Sibelius*, 447–52.

11. Undated letter to Alma Mahler from Helsinki; quoted in La Grange, *Gustav Mahler*, 3:752, 753.

12. Ekman, *Jean Sibelius* (1936), 176.

13. Ibid.

14. Vignal, *Jean Sibelius*, 451.

15. Quoted in La Grange, *Gustav Mahler*, 3:745, 747, 756.

16. Ibid., 3:745–47, including the full text of Ossovsky's review.

17. *Novoe Vremja*, quoted in ETL 2:80–81.

18. *Dagbok*, September 6, 1910.

19. Hepokoski, "Sibelius," in Sadie, *New Grove*, who further observes Sibelius's unusual aim—"the defamiliarization of the diatonic and the consonant within a surrounding European context of multiplying dissonance, ironic detachment and high modernism—was easy for audiences and critics to misconstrue" (331).

20. Hobsbawm, *Age of Empire*, 235. His discussion of this critical predicament continues; see especially 236–42.

21. "Om hans landsmän kunde bidraga till lindrandet af denna hans belägenhet, synes det oss som om de därmed skulle tjäna sitt eget lands intressen och samtidigt fylla dess plikt mot det internationella kulturlif, i

hvilket det är vår rätt och vår skyldighet att taga del." This petition, a copy of which is preserved in SFA, file box 1, was a printed circular dated March 15, 1910.

22. Quoted in Eskola, *Water Lilies and Wings of Steel*, 48, a study of the photographic imagery of one of the favorite tourist destinations, Aulanko Park. Lukkarinen and Annika Waenerberg, *Suomi-kuvasta mielenmaisemaan*, explore the construction of "national landscapes," particularly Eero Järnefelt's role in turning Mount Koli into one of the foremost of these; see chapters 4–9.

23. The words are Olin Downes's (quoted in Goss, *Jean Sibelius and Olin Downes*, 55), but the sentiments were international.

24. The critic's first reactions, in *Hufvudstadsbladet* on April 4, 1911, were mild and devoted to the whole concert; he wished to reserve judgment on the new symphony, he said, until after a second hearing. When it was repeated, on April 5, Bis devoted his entire column to the new work: "Den mäktiga rapport, hvari Sibelius ställt sig i många sina tidigare verk till vårt folk och dess nationalepos, och som gjort honom så stark och stor, detta samband existerar ej mer i fjärde sinfonin. Han är här icke komponist i denna bemärkelse, icke en konstnär, som går ut och lärer allt folket, icke Nietsches till detta nedstigande öfvermänniska. Han ter sig i sinfonian n:o 4 som en personlighet, hvilken afskiljer och utvecklar sig och hvars aristokratiska musik återspeglar endast hans enskilda tankar, hans sednaste utvecklingsskede, men hvilken mycket betydande konstyttring dock framkallar vårt stora intresse och som, äfven den, har sin bemärkta hedersplats i den förnämsta finska musiklitteraturen." *Hufvudstadsbladet*, April 7, 1911. For modern analyses, see Elliott Antokoletz, "The Musical Language of the Fourth Symphony," in Jackson and Murtomäki, *Sibelius Studies*, 296–321; and David Pickett, "The Fourth Symphony: Ending and Beginning in Complete Disaster," in Huttunen, Kilpeläinen, and Murtomäki, *Sibelius Forum*, 88–96.

25. Quoted in Johnson, *Jean Sibelius*, 144–45.

26. *Stravinsky: A Composers' [sic] Memorial*, 131.

27. Schoolfield, *Helsinki of the Czars*, 243. In addition to Schoolfield's chapter "The Golden Age of Finland's art," 240–44, Rolf Nummelin, "Maalaustaiteen uusia virtauksia," in *Suomen taiteen historia*, 245–57; Olli Valkonen, "The Breakthrough in Finland," in *Scandinavian Modernism*, 34–41; and Raakel Kallio, "Aesthetics and Emotions," in *Surface and Depth*, inform the discussion.

28. "Om hr Sallinens pretensiösa samling af figurbilder och landskap med deras hemska vrångbilder af människor och natur är intet annat att säga, än att hr. S. synbarligen kommit in på orätt bana i lifvet. Bland alla de utsväfningar, som den s.k. expressionistiska skolan (om det är den som hr S. omfattar) gjort sig skyldig till äro nog hr Sallinens här dokumenterade några af de värsta. En af dessa 'bilder' har inköpts till utlottningen. Vinnarna är minsann icke att gratulera." *Hufvudstadsbladet*, April 28, 1912.

29. See von Bonsdorff, in *Hurmos ja harmonia*.

30. Raakel Kallio, "Aesthetics and Emotions," in *Surface and Depth*, 23.

31. Kai Laitinen, "The Rise of Finnish-Language Literature," in Schoolfield, *History of Finland's Literature*, 143–44; and Knapas, "Kulttuurin tunnuskuvia," 649.

32. Lindqvist, *Taiteilijan tiellä*, 143, observes that for all his revolutionary ideas, Sallinen valued the previous generation and demonstrated the sincerest form of flattery in *Pyykkärit* (*Washerwomen*, 1911), a paraphrase of Järnefelt's *Pyykkiranta* (1889, showing washerwomen on a lakeshore).

33. *Dagbok*, January 28, February 4, and February 9, 1914.

34. "Juhlan kunniaksi Juhani Ahosta," *Nuori Suomi Joulu Albumi* 21 (1911): 118.

35. [*Gasco:*] "Anche da voi ci sono musicisti che soggiacciono ad influenze straniere? [*Sibelius:*] Eh, sì, purtroppo. Tra i giovani si nota la tendenza ad un internazionalismo che credo pernicioso. Debussy è un conquistatore . . . [*Gasco:*] E Strauss e Strawinsky e Schönberg? [Sibelius:] Anch'essi hanno seguaci, ma meno di Claudio Debussy." "La musica in Finlandia: Un colloquio con Jean Sibelius," *La tribuna*, March 18, 1923.

36. Aho, Jalkanen, Salmenhaara, and Virtamo, *Finnish Music*, 65. See also Vignal, *Jean Sibelius*, 852–53, and Pingoud, *Taiteen edistys*.

37. Rainer Knapas, "The Landscapes of Ideas," in *Surface and Depth*, 40–43.

38. According to Nors Josephson, who was preparing *Scènes historiques II* for publication in the JSW, this second set of historical scenes appears to have mainly superficial connections with the three *Scènes historiques I* (arranged from the Press Days *tableaux*), namely, the title, the numbering of the movements (IV, V, VI), and a pair of motives (in "At the Drawbridge") taken from *tableau* III of the Press Days Music.

39. Quoted in ETS 3:277.

40. Andersson, "Sibelius och Kajanus," in *Studier i musik*, 1:82–83.

41. The most insightful and multifaceted discussion that has ever been written about *Luonnotar* is James Hepokoski, "The Essence of Sibelius: Creation Myths and Rotational Cycles in *Luonnotar*," in Goss, *Sibelius Companion*, 121–46, on which my remarks are based.

42. Bantock, *Granville Bantock*, 22.

43. For the correspondence related to this incident, see Savolainen and Vainio, *Aino Ackté*, 310, 315–17, 321.

44. Quoted in Johnson, *Jean Sibelius*, 156.

45. Gray, *Sibelius*, 85.

46. For Parker's role in Sibelius's life, see Goss, *Jean Sibelius and Olin Downes*, 39–44 et passim.

47. McGinty, "'That You Came So Far to See Us,'" examines Coleridge-Taylor's visit with the Stoeckels. Carl Stoeckel's memoirs remain the best account of Sibelius's journey. Preserved in manuscript in the Yale University Music Library, the text has been published by George C. Schoolfield (Stoeckel, "Some Recollections") with excellent annotations and relevant correspondence with both Stoeckel and Parker. Additional details may be found in Andersson, "Norfolk," in *Sibelius i Amerika*.

48. The deficiency is painfully apparent in his setting of the English-language *Hymn to Thaïs*, composed in 1909. When the unsuitability of the music to the text was mentioned to him, Sibelius bafflingly responded, "It is not essential. Any singer can place the English accent correctly"; see Jukka Tiilikainen's edition and discussion of the song in JSW VIII/4; the quotation is on p. x. Paradoxically, Sibelius's acute sensitivity to correct pronunciation was frequently on display during the American trip; after witnessing a choral rehearsal of 525 (!) men and women, he declared that never had he heard "better pronunciation of words"; on another occasion he praised the remarkable diction of the chorus, whose almost every word he understood. See Stoeckel, "Some Recollections," 63, 67; and McGinty, "'That You Came So Far to See Us,'" who discusses the Litchfield Choral Union.

49. As members of the Industrial Workers of the World were known.

50. John Wuorinen traced these travels in *The Finns on the Delaware, 1638–1655* (New York: Columbia University Press, 1938). The previous year Yrjö Kohonen had published the adventure story *Länteen* (*To the West*), in which the (fictitious) Karelian navy discovers America well before the Vikings' arrival; see Fewster, *Visions of Past Glory*, 362–63.

51. "Negrer, hvita och pigor af alla kulörer." Jean to Christian Sibelius, June 10, 1914.

52. Taft was a graduate of Yale. In 1914 he had returned to his alma mater to teach law, continuing until he was appointed U.S. Chief Justice. Sibelius mentions his conversation with the president in his *Dagbok*, June 1914, 190.

53. It can be heard on the Wikipedia site at the entry for Alma Gluck.

54. On Ives and Sibelius, see the essay of that title in Goss, *Vieläkö lähetämme hänelle sikareja?* [Are We Still Sending Him Cigars?]

55. Quoted in Stoeckel, "Some Recollections," 76.

56. Downes, "Creative Genius," 3–4.

57. Stoeckel, "Some Recollections," 83.

58. Ibid., 81, n. 35. The robes and mortarboard are on display in the Sibelius Museum. Sigurd

Wettenhovi-Aspa painted the composer swathed in Yale's academic regalia (reproduced in Goss, *Jean Sibelius and Olin Downes*, 43), although Sibelius allegedly disliked his friend's interpretation.

59. Stoeckel, "Some Recollections," 68. For *Aallottaret*'s structural importance to the Fifth Symphony, see Hepokoski, *Sibelius: Symphony no. 5*, 28–29.

60. Downes, "Creative Genius," 3.

61. Quoted in Stoeckel, "Some Recollections," 69. The English words to *Vårt land* are reprinted in Andersson, *Sibelius i Amerika*, 77–78.

62. "Orkestern härlig!! Distanserar allt hvad vi i Europa får höra," he wrote to Carpelan on June 5, 1914.

63. A copy is preserved in the Stravinsky Archive, scrapbook 1914–15, Paul Sacher Stiftung. André de Ribaupierre was the featured soloist.

64. "Stravinsky at Close Quarters," *Everyman*, May 1, 1914; clipping in the Stravinsky Archive, Paul Sacher Stiftung.

65. Farwell, "Sibelius: A Musical Redeemer," 14.

66. *Dagbok*, June 1914, 190.

Chapter Twenty-one

1. Sibelius's diary entry echoed Ola Hansson, who had shocked polite society with his collection of (morbid) erotic sketches called *Sensitiva Amorosa* (1887).

2. *Dagbok*, April 13, 1915.

3. Sibelius's intriguing reference to the sarrusophone, a brass instrument with a double reed, almost certainly reflects his experiences abroad, since neither the Helsinki orchestra nor Finnish brass bands included it, according to the Finnish brass specialist Kauko Karjalainen (e-mail communication, June 16, 2008). The sarrusophone is especially associated with France, where it was probably invented (by the French bandmaster W. Sarrus), constructed (by P. L. Gautrot the elder in Paris and patented in 1856), and used in the Paris Opéra.

4. In a letter to Sibelius, December 15, 1916. For the swan theme's central, structural role in the work, see Hepokoski, *Sibelius: Symphony no 5*.

5. Tawaststjerna covers the birthday events in detail; for the English version, see ETL 3:69–72. In the SFA two entire file boxes (59 and 60) are filled with materials related to this celebration.

6. Someone took the trouble to preserve these newspapers in their entirety. They are found today in a broadsheet-sized file box (SFA 60), approximately two inches thick, with the tributes, concert reviews, and other articles clearly marked in each.

7. "Jean Sibelius: Biografisk tabell," *Tidning för musik* 5 (1915): 175–82.

8. The biography missed publication in the anniversary year, delayed in the flurry of activity to locate *Kullervo*, the most important but not the only one of his early manuscripts that Sibelius readily supplied Furuhjelm. The author devoted fully half of his text to the youthful compositions. It was only much later that Sibelius became deeply reluctant to show these materials, at one point even threatening (to Otto Andersson) to destroy them all.

9. ETL 3:80.

10. Quoted in ETL 3:71.

11. Quoted in Johnson, *Jean Sibelius*, 165.

12. "Jean Sibelius"; quoted in Bosley, *Skating on the Sea*, 167–68, where the verses appear in their awful entirety.

13. December 1915, 240. Dahlström identified the quotation among the *Satires* of Juvenal; see *Dagbok*, 447.

14. Knapas, "Kulttuurin tuunuskuvia," 636–38. Knapas points out that Finns also began writing biographies of "great men" from other cultures, including Martin Luther, Oliver Cromwell, Victor Hugo, and Milton.

15. It was only in 1993 with Hepokoski's analysis in *Sibelius: Symphony no. 5* that a convincing analytical view of the symphony appeared and one that simultaneously demonstrated its originality.

16. A facsimile of the richly illustrated page with these words is reproduced in Goss, *Sibelius Companion*, 39.

17. See Matti Huttunen, "The National Composer and the Idea of Finnishness," in Grimley, *Cambridge Companion*, 7–21.

18. See Alapuro, "Mihin kansa katosi?" ("Where Have the People Gone?") and Sääskilahti, *Kansa ja tiede*, who examine how "the people" were constituted. Two chapters in Lehtonen, *Europe's Northern Frontier*, also address "the people": Tuija Pulkkinen, "One Language, One Mind: The Nationalist Tradition in Finnish Political Culture," and Tutta Palin, "Picturing a Nation: The Finnish Landscape and the Finnish People."

19. Habermas, *Structural Transformation of the Public Sphere*.

20. What turned out to be the first in this chain was my *Jean Sibelius and Olin Downes* (1995), followed by Laura (Jean) Gray's "Sibelius and England" (1996), in Goss, *Sibelius Companion*, and Gray, "Symphonic Problem: Sibelius Reception in England prior to 1950" (Ph.D. diss., Yale University, 1997). In 2001 Ruth-Maria Gleißner completed her dissertation, *Der unpolitische Komponist als Politikum*, providing the basis for subsequent studies of the composer in Germany. The studies by Tyrväinen (listed in the bibliography) and Vignal, *Jean Sibelius* (2004), have shed considerable light on French reactions to Sibelius, while Mäkelä, *"Poesie in der Luft"* (2007), provides irreplaceable perspective on understanding how Germans have viewed Sibelius and why.

21. *Dagbok*, September 19, 1914.

22. As shown in diary entries on February 2, 1916; August 20, 1919; and January 20, 1920. Granit-Ilmoniemi (1866–1945), founder of the Genealogical Society of Finland and its first secretary (1917–22), researched the forefathers of other great Finns, including Topelius and Lönnrot. Interested in questions of race, racial characteristics, and racial biology, he advocated establishing an institute of racial biology for Finland. In the 1910s he joined the intense debate on whether such leaders of Finnish society as Mikael Agricola had in truth been Finnish-speaking. It was in this spirit that his "research" on Sibelius was undertaken in the wake of the fiftieth-birthday celebrations and Andersson's "Biografisk tabell," which emphasized the composer's Swedish-language roots.

23. *Dagbok*, August 20, 1919, and January 20, 1920.

24. Keller, "First Performances," 141.

25. See Jalmari Lahdensuo's "Jean Sibelius ja 'Jokamiehen' musiikki: Muistelmia vuosilta 1916 ja 1917," *Uusi Suometar Sunnuntailiite*, December 6, 1925; reprinted in Sirén, *Aina poltti sikaria*, 363–64. Lahdensuo was a theater director. The incident is translated into English in Hietanen, *Finland—Musicland*, 56–57.

26. Mann, *Gedanken im Kriege* (1914); quoted in Rainer Knapas, "The Landscapes of Ideas," in *Surface and Depth*, 35. Knapas, "Kulttuurin tunnuskuvia," 698, remarks that by April 1918, a display of Maxim machine guns had sprung up in the very center of Helsinki, on view in the glass restaurant called Kappeli at the end of the Esplanade.

27. *Dagbok*, February 19, 1910.

28. For more on these events, see Rainer Knapas, "The Landscapes of Ideas," in *Surface and Depth*, 29, 34–35; Seppo Hentilä, "Independence between East and West," in Lehtonen, *Europe's Northern Frontier*, 89–90; and Upton, *Finnish Revolution*.

29. "Finnish Russophobia in the Twenties: Character and Historical Roots," in Klinge, *Finnish Tradition*, especially 254–60.

30. The statistics are cited from Upton, *Finnish Revolution*, 3.

31. Ibid., 15.

32. Hellman examines these events in "'Mnogo! Mnogoo! Mnogoo!'"

33. *Dagbok*, January 12, 1917. Tawaststjerna's view, however, was that Sibelius saw "there could be no solution to Finland's problems while the Tsarist Empire survived." ETL 3:87. As for the drinking, Christian Sibelius, who from 1909 to 1920 lectured on alcoholism at the Imperial Alexander University, steadfastly tried to keep his brother from such relapses. The battle was carried on by his son, Jussi, who was an inspector for the Alcohol League in the years 1932–35.

34. The translation of the last four lines is in Wilson, *Folklore and Nationalism*, 152.

35. The Finnish tenor Wäinö Sola, for example, accused of equipping a cousin for the Jaeger Battalion, was imprisoned and threatened with deportation to a Siberian labor camp.

36. Jukka Tiilikainen has edited both arrangements for JSW VIII/4.

37. Seppo Hentilä, "Independence between East and West," in Lehtonen, *Europe's Northern Frontier*, 86–94.

38. Ibid., 90–91.

39. Quoted in SWV, 375.

40. The details were reported in "Akateeminen juhla yliopistolla: Innostunut isänmaallinen mieliala," *Helsingin Sanomat*, January 20, 1918; see also Knapas, "Kulttuurin tunnuskuvia," 641.

41. "Runoista ja puheista päättäen olisi melkein voinut luulla, että ne oikeastaan olivat meidän 'jääkärit,' jotka voittivat Venäjän—tosin yhdessä Saksan kanssa." Aho, *Hajamietteitä kapinaviikoilta*, 115. Aho had not been present, but word had evidently reached him through the grapevine.

42. This war has gone by many names in Finland: Brother War, Civil War, War of Liberation, People's War. For useful discussions in English, see Alapuro, *State and Revolution*, especially 199–202; Seppo Hentilä, "Independence between East and West," in Lehtonen, *Europe's Northern Frontier*, 91–94; and Upton, *Finnish Revolution*.

43. Tawaststjerna has a particularly effective chapter on Sibelius and the Civil War; for the English version, see ETL 3:114–29.

44. The same image was adopted by other leaders in the new republic: Axel Gallén, Frans E. Sillanpää, Urho Kekkonen. See the extensive n. 61 in Goss, *Jean Sibelius and Olin Downes*, 162.

45. See the discussion in Upton, *Finnish Revolution*, 522–23.

46. See Lasse Koskela, "Kansa taisteli—valkoiset kertoivat," in Varpio, *Suomen kirjallisuushistoria*, 2:222–35. It was only in the late 1960s with the novels of Väinö Linna that the civil war story began to emerge from the perspective of Finnish Reds. And only in the 1970s and 1980s did it become possible to identify the names of Reds on monuments to the fallen, laboriously culled from church records, military archives, and prison rolls. Reconciliation has come slowly. Discussion is still going on in Finland about the injustices and the unblessed dead, with religious ceremonies only now being performed at graves of some of the fallen. Newspapers continue to publish articles like the one that appeared in *Helsingin Sanomat*, May 21, 2007: "Monet sisällissodassa kuolleet punaiset ovat haudoissa yhä siunaamatta" ("Many Reds Who Died in the Civil War Are Still in Unblessed Graves").

47. Aho's "Amnesty" had already appeared on November 24, 1917. Leino's "Syvällä tammen juuret" was first published in *Sunnuntai*, December 2, 1917, just four days before the country's independence was officially declared.

48. For a recent consideration of war's immediate aftermath, see "Vuoden 1918 muistot," in Nevanlinna and Kolbe, *Suomen kulttuurihistoria 3*, 192–98, on which much of the present account is based; also valuable here are Alapuro, *State and Revolution*, 197–218; Upton, *Finnish Revolution*, 516–35; and Paasi, *Territories, Boundaries and Consciousness*, 97–102.

49. Jussila, "Nationalism and Revolution," 291.

50. These divisions were transplanted abroad when the Finns emigrated. Throughout North America, Finn Halls were erected along Red/White lines, their segregated clientele refusing to mix. The divide persists even today, a time warp in which both attitudes and language have stood strangely still.

51. In *Finlands kungaäventyr 1918* the journalist and diplomat Anders Huldén (1924–1997) tells the extraordinary story of how Kaiser Wilhelm's brother-in-law, Friedrich Karl of Hesse, almost became king of Finland.

52. Of Paasikivi (1870–1956), for instance, the man from Hämeenlinna who some years later would become Finland's seventh president (1946–56) but who in 1917 was advocating turning Finland into a kingdom, it was said that his children were telling their friends, "If the king comes, then our father will become a count." Sibelius was not the only Finn with a belief in his own essentially aristocratic nature.

53. "'Kansa' oli iskenyt puukon oman sivistyneistönsä selkään." Alapuro, "Mihin kansa katosi?," 8.

54. Olli Valkonen, "The Breakthrough in Finland," in *Scandinavian Modernism*, 38.

55. Quoted in Volkov, *St. Petersburg*, 231.

56. Ibid.

Chapter Twenty-two

1. The title of this chapter is a translation of "Käy ees'päin, väki voimakas," the slogan adorning placards in Finnish labor marches. The musical setting of the slogan is Oskar Merikanto's *Työväen marssi*, arranged by Einari Marvia, and printed here by kind permission of the publisher, Fennica Gehrman Oy, Helsinki.

2. William A. Wilson, "Sibelius, the *Kalevala*, and Karelianism," in Goss, *Sibelius Companion*, 55.

3. Hausen, Mikkola, Amberg, and Valto, *Eliel Saarinen: Projects, 1896–1923*, plan 197. See also Fewster, *Visions of Past Glory*, 330–33.

4. See Matti Huttunen, "The National Composer and the Idea of Finnishness," in Grimley, *Cambridge Companion*, 20–21.

5. On this arrangement, critical reactions to it, and Sibelius's correspondence, see Goss, *Jean Sibelius and Olin Downes*, 98–99, 192–94.

6. Press release, May 30, 1930; quoted in the notes to *Kajanus Conducts Sibelius*, London Symphony Orchestra (EMI Finland, 1988; Finlandia Records, FACD 81234, 1991), 9.

7. The event was reported in *Helsingin Sanomat*, November 30, 1919, and *Hufvudstadsbladet*, December 2, 1919. See also Knapas, "Kulttuurin tunnuskuvia," 661.

8. In 1920 Repin was named an honorary member of the Suomen Taiteilijaseura (the Finnish Artist Society) and feted during a banquet at Society House. His painting of Finland's great men appears to represent that occasion. See Mejias-Ojajärvi, *Venäjän maalaustaide*, 116–17.

9. In the first recording of *Autrefois*, by Neemi Järvi and the Gothenberg Symphony Orchestra (BIS CD-384, 1988), the singers omit the text and vocalise the melody. The composer arranged *Autrefois* for piano, and its first edition included both Swedish and French (but not Finnish) texts, the French in an adaptation by Pierre Chapelle. Sibelius wanted even the translations to be "in the style of the 1760s." For a modern edition of the work, see JSW VIII/1.

10. *Dagbok*, November 4, 1920.

11. "Denna kantat var i all sin strama enkelhet en mäktig och betagande tonskapelse som likt en äkta pärla skall stråla med odödlig glans." *Hufvudstadsbladet*, December 2, 1919 (signed "Pennskaft").

12. A portion of the letter is quoted in ETS 5:58.

13. Busoni, *Selected Letters*, 35.

14. *Dagbok*, November 1, 1914, and December 1918, 280.

15. Ibid., March 29, 1919.

16. Erkki Salmenhaara unveiled the episode in "Sibelius's 'Imatra Symphony,'" in Murtomäki, Kilpeläinen, and Väisänen, *Sibelius Forum 1995*, 15–21.

17. Sibelius to Wäinö Sola, August 7, 1928; quoted in ibid., 16–17.

18. Bell, *Art*, 252.

19. Ibid., 255, 259.

20. "Onko kansamme taiteellisesti kypsä synnyttämään pian uuden nousun, aikaansaamaan uuden crescendon? Rehellinen vastaus näyttää kielteiseltä. Emme luule pahasti erehtyvämme väittäessämme, että Sibelius on vakinaisesta konserttiyleisöstämme kolmelle ensimäiselle sinfonialleen valloittanut vastaanottokykyiseksi korkeintaan toisen puolen. Suuri osa suomalaista yleisöä "ymmärtää" vasta kuorolauluja ja taputtaa sydämellisesti käsiään pikku orkesterisävellyksille. Että, sillä kuitenkin on ilmeiset kehitysedellytykset, sen todistavat ne 'nimet,' joista monet ovat nousseet suorastaan syvien rivien keskeltä. Vanhalle musiikkia harrastavalle sivistyneistöllemme on suureksi ansioksi luettava, että se on suomalaiselle sävel taiteelle tarjonnut sen kehkeytymiselle välttämättömän suotuisan ilmapiirin. Mutta useampi kuin yksi nuori suomalainen sävel taiteilija, joka etsii nykyään tällaista ilmapiiriä, valittaa tulleensa tuntemaan, että sitä on vaikea, ehkä mahdotonta löytää. Laaja sivistyneistö on luisumassa operettiin." Väisänen, "Musiikillisen viljelyksemme tulevaisuus," 2–3.

21. "Mången ung dam hade väl infunnit sig för att betrakta Valse tristes skapare och finna honom så smärt, blek, skön, mondän och lätt bohemaktigt genial som hon drömt efter porträtten och musiken. Ack, hon fick skåda en ganska stadig och skallig herre, som visserligen förde sig som en världsman, men officiellt på programmet bar titeln professor. (Hur kan man det när man ändå är Jean Sibelius!) En sådan ton från den statligt systematiserade fåfängans värld nyktrar och förstämmer inte bara backfischar." *Svenska Dagbladet*, March 2, 1923; quoted in ETS 5:123.

22. September 10, 1926; emphasis added.

Chapter Twenty-three

1. Excellent discussions of the city's architecture include Schoolfield, *Helsinki of the Czars*; Kirsi Saarikangas, "Architecture and the Construction of Finnishness," in Lehtonen, *Europe's Northern Frontier*, 166–207, and Ringbom, who examines the short-lived but hugely impressive stone movement, in *Stone, Truth and Style*.

2. Valkonen, "The Breakthrough in Finland," in *Scandinavian Modernism*, 39.

3. Knapas, "Kulttuurin tunnuskuvia," 651.

4. A further series of symbolic and racially identifiable Finns, sculpted by Aaltonen in 1930–32, rings the plenary hall of Finland's Parliament Building. For more on Aaltonen, see Fewster, *Visions of Past Glory*, 329–30, and Tutta Palin, "Picturing a Nation," in Lehtonen, *Europe's Northern Frontier*, 210.

5. Gallen-Kallela-Sirén, "Axel Gallén," 408.

6. See, for instance, the memoirs of Hällfors, *Äidin muistelmia*, 65–67, and Sjöblom, *Finland from the Inside*, 171. Klinge relates the imperial visit in *Finlands historia 3*, 304.

7. See "Finnish Russophobia in the Twenties," in Klinge, *Finnish Tradition*, 237–61; Wilson, *Folklore and Nationalism*, 132–37; and Max Engman, "The Finland-Swedes," in Branch, *National History and Identity*, 166–77.

8. Quoted in Wilson, *Folklore and Nationalism*, 148; see also Paasi, *Territories, Boundaries and Consciousness*, 101–102. Erkki Räikkönen was among those who sounded the warning about coming war, in *Heimokirja (Book of the Tribe, 1924)*.

9. The statistics on the Civil Guard conscription are given in Fewster, *Visions of Past Glory*, 188, 321.

10. See "Finnish Russophobia in the Twenties," in Klinge, *Finnish Tradition*, 238, on this and the following publications.

11. Quoted in ibid., 239.

12. On the AKS, see ibid., 241–47, and Wilson, *Folklore and Modernism*, 153–61.

13. Wilson quotes Haavio, ibid., 156. Haavio kept a diary of these uneasy years, published in 1972 as *Nuoruusvuodet*.

14. Rainer Knapas, "Derussifieringen av Helsingfors efter 1918," in Gullberg and Sandberg, *Medströms–motströms*, 290–302.

15. On the language quarrel, see "The Evolution of the Linguistic Situation in Finland," in Klinge, *Finnish Tradition*, 149–73; Setälä, *The Language Fight in Finland*; and Hämäläinen, *Kielitaistelu Suomessa, 1917–1939*.

16. See Max Engman, "The Finland-Swedes," in Branch, *National History and Identity*, 167–72.

17. "Då jag på kuvertet läste 'Åbo akademi' erfor jag samma sensation som i Italien då konduktören första gången ropade Roma. Det är ju faktiskt som finge vi åter kontakt med vår kultur före 'branden,'" November 28, 1918. The "fire," of course, referred to the devastating conflagration that had destroyed the old university and much of the town of Turku in 1827.

18. ETS 5:24, and ETL 3:173–74.

19. There may have been a third setting: *Snöfallet* (1927), a lost work known only by its title.

20. Paasivirta, *Finland and Europe: The Early Years*, 334–35. Sadly, even in twenty-first-century Finland, a member of the multination European Union, performances of Sibelius's solo songs in Swedish are rare. For their part, the Swedes have little use for songs by a Finn (with the thankful exception of Anne Sophie von Otter), and all too few singers are willing to take the time to master the pronunciation of the Swedish language. Consequently, a body of moving and beautiful music lies too little performed, too little known.

21. Haavio attended the event and recorded its details in *Nuoruusvuodet*, 341.

22. See the correspondence in Goss, *Jean Sibelius and Olin Downes*, 220, 223.

23. "Mi sono imbevuto (per così dire) della poesie, delle leggende della mia terra natale, e poi ho cantato a mio modo, ispirandomi all'uno o all'altro dei testi finnici, specialmente al Kalevala, che è una miniera inesauribile di emozioni, per un artista finlandese no viziato da manie d'esotismo." "La musica in Finlandia: Un colloquio con Jean Sibelius," *La tribuna*, March 18, 1923. It should be kept in mind that this interesting interview (excerpts of which appear only in the English-language version of Tawaststjerna's biography) was given by Sibelius in French, a language in which he was hardly fluent; it was then published in Gasco's Italian, from which it is here translated into English.

24. "För mig var Kalevala något heligt. Icke motiv, hjältesagor. Jag kände djupt religionen i den, älskade den. Det lyser igenom i Lemminkäinen." Vaxdukshäfte, samtal med familjen, Erik Tawaststjerna Archive, file box 35, NA.

25. Paasi, *Territories, Boundaries and Consciousness*, 101.

26. Quoted in Wilson, *Folklore and Nationalism*, 132–33.

27. Wilson titles an entire chapter "Folklore as Propaganda in Independent Finland," in ibid., 118–203, from which my quotations are taken unless otherwise indicated. See also Vesa Kurkela, "Interest in Folklore and its Myths in the Finnish Workers' Movement," Donner, *Idols and Myths*.

28. Derek Fewster drew my attention to the appropriation of Kullervo by the workers' theaters; see his extensive "Annotated Catalogue of Theatrical Medievalism" in *Visions of Past Glory*, especially 443–44.

29. "Ne ovat kuin itse luonnon rinnasta helskähtäneet. Pulppuavia hetteitä, joista varsinkin luonnonkuvauksille saa turhaan etsiä vertaa muiden maiden kansanlauluaarteistosta. . . . Jos selailee esim. läntisen naapurimme, ruotsalaisten, kansanlaulukokoelmia, niin huomaa, että heidän laulunsa ovat kömpelömpiä ja värittömämpiä." Kangas, "Kansanlaulut," 50.

30. "Musiikki sivistää kansaa, se voit poistaa yleiseksi käyneen raakuuden, saattaa maalaiselämänkin viihtyisemmäksi ja nuoret pysyttelemään paremmin maalla kotipaikoillaan." Vilén, "Kansanmusiikkimme."

31. The study is included in Kuusinen, *Valitut teokset*. Vesa Kurkela, "Interest in Folklore," in Donner,

Idols and Myths, 38–40, observes that works of this kind were highly valued in the Communist movement: they belonged to the creation of a "line of national culture," a phrase originating in one of Stalin's speeches and used frequently in communist writings. Kurkela reproduces a photograph showing Kuusinen's daughter Hertta being presented a large *kantele* by members of a youth association; looming in the background beside the Finnish flag is an enormous photograph of Kuusinen.

32. Tawaststjerna recounted the details; see ETL 3:238–39. The couple had considered separation as early as World War I; ibid., 99–101. Fabian Dahlström's edition of Sibelius's diary gives the fullest documentation of the couple's marital strife.

33. ETL 3:243–44.

34. The society accepted; for details, see Goss, "Sibelius's *Kullervo* after 1892," 66.

35. August 1, 1882, *Hämeenlinna Letters*; and Ekman, *Jean Sibelius* (1936), 217.

36. Ibid., 239.

37. Paavo Berglund, for example, has identified Sibelius's Seventh Symphony as one of the greatest works of symphonic literature (personal communication, December 28, 2001); Colin Davis's belief in these symphonies has repeatedly been made clear in his recordings and interviews. Among recent analyses, see especially James Hepokoski, "Rotations, Sketches, and the Sixth Symphony," in Jackson and Murtomäki, *Sibelius Studies*, 322–51; Luyken, ". . . *aus dem Nichtigen eine Welt schaffen* . . ."; and David Pickett, "Reflections in a Glass of Pure Spring Water: Sibelius's Sixth Symphony," in Murtomäki, Kilpeläinen, and Väisänen, *Sibelius Forum 1995*, 297–302; Pickett writes that the words of the composer Michael Tippett hold the key to Sibelius's late symphonies: the artist's function is to create "images of vigour for a decadent period, images of calm for one too violent" (297).

38. Sibelius's famous description of his symphony as "pure spring water" in contrast to the "cocktails" served up elsewhere also echoed Christian, who worked steadfastly to keep his brother from his dangerous indulgences. The Sixth Symphony was eventually dedicated to the Swedish conductor and composer Wilhelm Stenhammar, another good man who, Sibelius realized, had "done so much for my art!!"

39. See Hepokoski's discussion in *Sibelius: Symphony no. 5*, 19–30.

40. In Levas, *Personal Portrait*, the English translation of this famous observation reads "ice ferns" (83). But what Sibelius said was a bit different, emphasizing water (the metaphor for the national project) and using the word *jääkukka* (ice flower): "Nähdessäni musiikin rakentavan muotoa tulen usein ajatelleeksi, miten vesi kovalla pakkasella kiteytyy ihaniksi jääkukkasiksi ikuisten lakien mukaan." Levas, *Muistelma*, 2:232. The imagery refers to frost patterns on windowpanes and other glass surfaces.

41. Ekman, *Jean Sibelius* (1936), 218.

42. Sibelius's description of the Seventh Symphony, a letter dated May 20, 1918; reproduced in ibid., 238. In 1922 Sibelius had become a member of Finland's newly constituted Masonic Lodge. He would thus have been more attuned than usual to such musical symbolism as Mozart's in his Masonic opera *The Magic Flute*, with its weighty emphasis on things in threes, and *Don Giovanni*, in which the trombone announces the statue's return from the underworld.

43. Ekman, *Jean Sibelius* (1936), 239.

44. On the extremely complex history of the *Masonic Ritual Music*, see SWV, 473–84; Marvia, *Sibeliuksen Rituaalimusiikki*; and Williams, *Sibelius and His Masonic Music*.

45. Sibelius unveiled the Seventh Symphony in Stockholm on March 24, 1924; *Stormen* was first heard in Copenhagen, directed by Johan Hye-Knudsen, on March 16, 1926; and Walter Damrosch premiered *Tapiola* in New York on December 26, 1926.

46. Kilpeläinen, "Sibelius Eight."

47. It was pronounced "avowedly slight" and formless by Olin Downes (*New York Times*, December 27, 1926), who, though an ardent Sibelius champion, was disappointed in *Tapiola*.

48. Studienpartitur PB 3348, ed. Carl Ettler.

49. This leaf is preserved with the correspondence of the Symphony Society of New York; SFA, file box 30. In a letter to the composer, dated June 5, 1926, Walter Damrosch asked, "Would the following title be acceptable to you? 'TAPIOLA,' a wild northern forest, wherein dwell the God of the forests and his wood-nymphs." SFA, file box 19.

50. "Du kommer til Rochester til skolens åbning, blir der et aar, eller om muligt langere; du underviser de opvokomde genier i Amerika i komposition ved skolen; deres mangde skal visselig ikke gjøre dit arbeide tungt," January 19, 1920; SFA, file box 22. Klingenberg's own position as the Eastman School's new director, together with this letter to Sibelius, make it very clear that Klingenberg was inviting his friend to teach, not to be the director of the school, as has often been reported. This misconception arose with Karl Ekman, Jr., who either misunderstood or was misled by Sibelius as to the nature of the offer. See Ekman, *Jean Sibelius* (1935), 251, and Ekman, *Jean Sibelius* (1936), 242.

51. March 6, 1921; SFA, file box 101. Portions of her derogatory "young Americans" letter to Sibelius are reprinted in ETL3:202–3.

52. Jutikkala, *History of Finland*, 312.

53. "Min ställning här som 'poeta laureatu[s]' (♩) med konstnärsgage etc. är af den art att jag ej så utan vidare kan säga adjö," February 28, 1920; HUL Coll. 206.62.

54. "Hvilken god patriot är jag ej!" January 5, 1921; ibid.

55. "Min hustru kan nog ej följa med mig till Amerika"; ibid.

56. The letter is transcribed in Talas, *Syysilta*, 296–99. Newmarch mentioned that Aino suffered from rheumatism. Whatever the nature of the events in 1921, they seem to have been especially serious (*Jean Sibelius: A Short Story*, 64).

57. The English text of a telegram addressed to "Director Klingenberg," March 9, 1921; HUL Coll. 206.62.

58. March 30, 1921; SFA, file box 22.

59. "Jag tänker det är bäst att låta saken ha sin gång d.v.s. allt är ännu oss emellan. Kommer tid så kommer råd," April 19, 1921; HUL Coll. 206.62.

Chapter Twenty-four

1. Vesa Kurkela, "Interest in Folklore and its Myths," in Donner, *Idols and Myths*, 34–35.

2. See Kirby, *Concise History*, 174–84, and Seppo Hentilä, "Independence between East and West," in Lehtonen, *Europe's Northern Frontier*, 95–97.

3. September 7, 1930; SWV, 565–66.

4. Wilson has a valuable discussion of the Kalevala Jubilee in *Folklore and Nationalism*, 161–72, including photographs. More recently, Fewster has discussed the jubilee from the point of view of "the rediscovery of the medieval woman"; *Visions of Past Glory*, 377–84. My text is indebted to both as well as to newspaper clippings in the archive of SKS.

5. Quoted in Wilson, *Folklore and Modernism*, 135.

6. Ibid., 113. Wilson discusses the changing perceptions of the epic throughout his chapter 2, "Folklore Scholarship in Independent Finland."

7. Ibid., 174–81.

8. Ibid., 175.

9. Ibid., 178.

10. Bell and Hietala, *Helsinki*, 204–5.

11. Goss, "Sibelius's *Kullervo* after 1892," 66–67, 72.

12. *New York Times*, September 20, 1936. The interview was titled (in Downes's inimitable style)

"With Jean Sibelius in His Realm of the Sagas: A Portrait of the Thunderous Composer of Finland and a Talk with Him in His Cabin Home Set amid the Pines and Birches."

Chapter Twenty-five

1. Similä, *Sibeliana*, 37–38; the translation is quoted from Philip Donner and Juhani Similä, "Jean Sibelius," in Donner, *Idols and Myths*, 71. Similä dedicated *Sibeliana* to "the 80-year-old master . . . with feelings of admiration and respect."

2. "Wenäjän vaatimus saada 'taata' Suomi neuvotteluissa Englannin kanssa ja Ranskan kanssa on huonontanut meidän asemamme. Se on asettanut meidät toiseen asemaan kuin muut Pohjoismaat. Meillä on kyllä sympatioja [*sic*] monella taholla, mutta epäillään meidän tulevaisuutta. Myös siten, että nyt meitä 'lohdutetaan' ja katsotaan asemamme parantuneen, kun Saksa teki sopimuksen Wenäjän kanssa. Osottaa [*sic*] asemamme heikkoutta. Sympatiat meihin perustuu: meillä on urheilijoita ja Sibelius, olemme maksaneet USA:lle velkamme, olemme voittaneet vaikeudet taistelussa itsenäisyytemme puolesta yms. Meitä katsotaan kunnolliseksi kansaksi, joka ansaitsee itsenäisyyden. Myös pohjoismainen orientoimisemme on tässä huomattavasti vaikuttanut," August 25, 1939. Paasikivi, *"Ei pienillä ole mitään turvaa,"* 311.

3. Ranta, *Sävelten valoja ja varjoja*, 12; translated in Philip Donner and Juhani Similä, "Jean Sibelius," in Donner, *Idols and Myths*, 68.

4. Ibid.

5. "Eiväthän ne ulkomaalaiset ymmärrä, ettei suomalainen vaaran hetkellä maataan jätä." Similä, *Sibeliana*, 37. Aino was speaking to Martti Similä during that visit on December 8, 1939, one week after the Soviet invasion began. The following March, Sibelius's nephew Jussi, Christian Sibelius's son, who had volunteered for service, was killed at Viipuri in skirmishes with the Russians.

6. Aino recalled this dramatic incident to Erik Tawaststjerna; see ETL 3:317. What is left of Symphony no. 8 has been examined in Josephson, "On Some Apparent Sketches."

7. Wasserman, *Michelangelo's Florence "Pietà,"* 68–75.

8. Kirsi Saarikangas, "Wood, Forest and Nature," in Lehtonen, *Europe's Northern Frontier*, 199–200.

9. "Käsitys kansanrunoudesta on mullistunut. Romantikkojen eeposidea on romahtunut; romahtunut on samaisten romantikkojen väite siitä, että kansanrunous on salaperäinen kansanhengen tuote; romahtunut väite, että runot edustaisivat vain yhtä kulttuurikautta, lounaissuomalaisten suuruuden aikaa; romahtunut kuvitelma, että eräs osa kertomarunoistamme olisi sankarirunoutta, jne." Haavio, *Puheita*, 190. Haavio was one of the few AKS members who later publicly repented of his hateful views. His poems *Jäähyväiset Arkadialle* (*A Farewell to Arcadia*, 1945), written under his pseudonym "P. Mustapää," reflected intellectuals' reorientation after the war. Wilson discusses Haavio's postwar theories in *Folklore and Modernism*, 201–203.

10. Andersson, Anteckningar, September 19, 1952.

11. And preserved in two films of the events, both made in 1957 and the sources of this and other quotations here: *Jean Sibeliuksen hautajaiset* (*The Funeral of Jean Sibelius*), released by Suomen Filmiteollisuus; and *Suomen kansan suru: Jean Sibeliuksen hautajaiset* (*The Sorrow of the Finns: The Funeral of Jean Sibelius*), a newsreel of the funeral produced by Oy Filmiseppo. The films were shown in a special Sibelius exhibition at Turku's Sibelius Museum in 2006. In 1957 photographs and extensive coverage of events, including lists of what appears to be every single tribute accorded the composer, were published in the Helsinki newspapers; of principal value here have been *Helsingin Sanomat* and *Hufvudstadsbladet*, both on October 1, 1957.

12. The work of the cartoonist Kari Suomalainen (1920–1999), *Helsingin Sanomat*, October 1, 1957. It had been rumored for some time, however, that the university students, whose duty it was to serve as honor guards at state funerals, had been fervently hoping that Sibelius's time would come not in the winter, but during the warmth of summer, thereby easing their watch along the public thoroughfares.

13. *Kansakunta rähmällään: Suomettumisen lyhyt historia* (Helsinki: Otava, 1991).

14. Kirby devotes an entire chapter to the Kekkonen era in light of the current debate around the man and his policies in *Concise History*, 245–75.

15. Kekkonen's speech was printed in translation in *Nordic Sounds*, an issue commemorating Sibelius's 125th birthday.

16. Kilpinen's eulogy was distributed in print with the title "Mahtava majakka säteilee maailmaan" ("The Mighty Lighthouse Sends Its Light to the World").

BIBLIOGRAPHY

A number of the items below have appeared in multiple editions in Finland and in Sweden, on both sides of the Atlantic, in reprints, revisions, illustrated versions, or abridged editions. Some have been translated into various languages. Because this list is not intended to be a bibliographically comprehensive resource, multiple editions and different translations have been given only when they have served the present volume.

Unpublished Materials

Armas Järnefelt arkisto, NA.

Asiantuntijalautakunnan lausunto, January 23, 1897, Helsingin yliopiston arkisto (Helsinki University Archives).

Erik Tawaststjerna Archive, NA.

Jean Sibeliuksen yksityisarkisto (Jean Sibelius's Private Archive), HUL Coll. 206.

Kanslerinvirasto, saapuneet asiakirjat 9/1897, Helsingin yliopiston arkisto (Helsinki University Archives).

Otto Andersson, Anteckningar, SibMus.

Painoasiain ylihallitus III, Ee3 and Da 27, Kirjekonseptit 1899, NA.

Richard Faltin Collection, HUL Coll. 59.

Robert Kajanuksen arkisto (Robert Kajanus Archive), HUL.

Robert Kajanus, Correspondence, SibMus.

Rosengren Family Archives, Åbo Akademi Bibliotek, Handskrift avdelning.

Sibeliuksen sävellyskäsikirjoitukset (Sibelius Music Manuscripts), HUL Ms. Mus. Sibelius.

Sibelius-perheen arkisto (Sibelius Family Archive [SFA]), MSS 602.248, file boxes (*kansiot*) 1–121, NA; the most frequently cited correspondence files are in the following boxes:

    Adolf Paul to Sibelius, 25

    Axel Carpelan to Sibelius, 18

    Martin Wegelius to Sibelius, 31

    Sibelius to Aino Järnefelt, 1890–92, 94

    Sibelius to Aino Järnefelt Sibelius, 1893–1904, 95

    Sibelius to Aino Järnefelt Sibelius, 1905–15, 96

    Sibelius to Aino Järnefelt Sibelius, 1917–31, 97

    Sibelius to Axel Carpelan, 120

    Sibelius to Christian Sibelius, 118

    Sibelius to Martin Wegelius, 121

Sibelius letters to Adolf Paul, HUL Coll. 206.62 (copies of original correspondence in the Upp-
     sala University Library).
Suomen Historiallisen Seuran arkistokokoelmat (SHS Archive Collections), NA.
"A Traveller's Notebook," 1989, manuscript, private collection.
Werner Söderhjelm Collection, HUL Coll. 469.

Published Sources

À Paris! Pohjoismainen taiteilijasiirtokunta Pariisissa 1800-luvun lopussa/À Paris! Nordic Artists in Paris in the
     Late 19th Century. Espoo: Gallen-Kallelan Museo, 1996. Exhibition catalog.
Adler, Guido. "Internationalism in Music." Musical Quarterly 11 (1925): 281–300.
Aho, Juhani. Hajamietteitä kapinaviikoilta I: Ensimmäinen ja toinen viikko. Porvoo: WSOY, 1918.
Aho, Kalevi, Pekka Jalkanen, Erkki Salmenhaara, and Keijo Virtamo. Finnish Music. Translated by Timothy
     Binham and Philip Binham. Helsinki: Otava, 1996.
Ahokas, Jaakko. A History of Finnish Literature. Bloomington: Indiana University Publications, 1973.
Ahtola-Moorhouse, Leena, ed. Albert Edelfelt, 1854–1905: Jubilee Book. Helsinki: Ateneum Art Museum,
     2004.
Ainola: Jean ja Aino Sibeliuksen koti. Helsinki: SKS, 2004.
Alapuro, Risto. "Mihin kansa katosi?" Kauas on pitkä matka: Kirjoituksia kahdesta kotiseudusta. Kaleva-
     laseuran vuosikirja 72 (1993): 7–12.
———. State and Revolution in Finland. Berkeley: University of California Press, 1988.
Albert Edelfelt ja Vänrikki Stoolin tarinat/Albert Edelfelt och Fänrik Ståls Sägner/Albert Edelfelt and The
     Tales of Ensign Stål. [Mänttä]: Gösta Serlachius Fine Arts Foundation, 1998.
Åman, Anders. Architecture and Ideology in Eastern Europe during the Stalin Era: An Aspect of Cold War His-
     tory. New York: Architectural History Foundation; Cambridge, MA: MIT Press, 1992.
Andersen, Jens. Hans Christian Andersen: A New Life. Translated by Tiina Nunnally. New York: Overlook
     Duckworth, 2005.
Anderson, Benedict. Imagined Communities: Reflections on the Origin and Spread of Nationalism. Rev. ed.
     London: Verso, 1991.
Andersson, Otto. Jean Sibelius i Amerika. Åbo: Förlaget Bro, 1955.
———. Studier i musik och folklore. 2 vols. Helsingfors: SLS, 1964.
Andrew, Joe. Russian Writers and Society in the Second Half of the Nineteenth Century. London: Macmillan,
     1982.
Anttonen, Pertti J. Tradition through Modernity: Postmodernism and the Nation-State in Folklore Scholarship.
     Helsinki: Finnish Literature Society, 2005.
Apollonio, Umbro, ed. and introd. Futurist Manifestos. Boston: Museum of Fine Arts, 1970.
Art Noir: Camera Work by Edvard Munch, Akseli Gallen-Kallela, Hugo Simberg, August Strindberg. Edited by
     Kirsi Kaisla, Kerttu Karvonen-Kannas, Kai Kivimäki, Mikko Pekari, and Tuomo-Juhani Vuorenmaa.
     Espoo: Gallen-Kallela Museo; Helsinki: Musta Taide, 1995.
Aspelin, Eliel. "Itkusta ja naurusta Kalevalassa." Valvoja 10 (1890): 1–18.
Aspelin-Haapkylä, Eliel. Suomalaisen teatterin historia. 4 vols. Helsinki: SKS, 1906–10.
Ateneum internationell: Illustrerad tidskrift för literatur, konst och spörsmål af allmänt intresse. Helsingfors:
     1898–1903.
Auer, Leopold. My Long Life in Music. New York: Frederick A. Stokes, 1923.
Autio, Veli-Matti. Savo-karjalaisen osakunnan historia III: Roudan aika, 1888–1905. Porvoo: WSOY, 1997.
Balakian, Anna, ed. The Symbolist Movement in the Literature of European Languages. Budapest: Akadémiai
     Kiadó, 1982.

Bantock, Myrrha. *Granville Bantock: A Personal Portrait*. London: J. M. Dent and Sons, 1972.

Barnes, Julian. *The Lemon Table*. London: Picador, 2005.

Barnett, Andrew. *Sibelius*. New Haven, CT: Yale University Press, 2007.

Barrett, Gregory. "In Search of a Lost Chamber Work." FMQ (2003, no. 1): 40–41.

Bax, Arnold. *Farewell, My Youth*. London: Longmans, Green, 1943.

Beijar, Kristina, Henrik Ekberg, Susanne Eriksson, and Marika Tandefelt. *Life in Two Languages: The Finnish Experience*. Translated by William Mazzarella. Esbo: Schildts, 1997.

Bell, Clive. *Art*. London: Chatto & Windus, 1914.

Bell, Marjatta, and Marjatta Hietala. *Helsinki, the Innovative City: Historical Perspectives*. [Helsinki]: Finnish Literature Society and City of Helsinki Urban Facts, 2002.

Berlin, Isaiah. *The Crooked Timber of Humanity: Chapters in the History of Ideas*. Edited by Henry Hardy. London: John Murray, 1990.

Bettelheim, Anton, ed. *Biographisches Jahrbuch und deutscher Nekrolog*. Berlin: Reimer, 1900. ·

Billington, James H. *Icon and the Axe: An Interpretive History of Russian Culture*. New York: Vintage Books, 1970.

Bohlman, Philip V. *The Music of European Nationalism: Cultural Identity and Modern History*. Santa Barbara, CA: ABC-CLIO, 2004.

Bonsdorff, Anna-Maria von. *Hurmos ja harmonia: Vastakohtien 1920-luku*. [Tuusula]: Tuusulan museo, 1998. Exhibition catalog.

Bosley, Keith, ed. and trans. *Skating on the Sea: Poetry from Finland*. Helsinki: Finnish Literature Society, 1997.

Bowlt, John E. *The Silver Age: Russian Art of the Early Twentieth Century and the "World of Art" Group*. Newtonville, MA: Oriental Research Partners, 1979.

Branch, Michael. "The Invention of a National Epic." In *The Uses of Tradition: A Comparative Enquiry into the Nature, Uses and Functions of Oral Poetry in the Balkans, the Baltic, and Africa*, edited by Michael Branch and Celia Hawkesworth. London: School of Slavonic and East European Studies, University of London; Helsinki: Finnish Literature Society, 1994. 195–211.

———, ed. *National History and Identity: Approaches to the Writing of National History in the North-East Baltic Region Nineteenth and Twentieth Centuries*. Helsinki: Finnish Literature Society, 1999.

Brummer, Hans Henrik, and Cecilia Lengefeld, eds. *En glömd relation: Norden och Tyskland vid sekelskiftet*. Stockholm: Prins Eugens Waldemarsudde in collaboration with Carlsson Bokförlag, 1998. Exhibition catalog.

Bülow, Hans von. *Ausgewählte Briefe*. Volksausgabe. Edited by Marie von Bülow. Leipzig: Breitkopf & Härtel, 1919.

Burmester, Willy. *Fünfzig Jahre Künstlerleben*. Berlin: Scherl, 1926. Translated by Roberta Franke in collaboration with Samuel Wolfe as *Fifty Years as a Concert Violinist: Recollections and Reflections*. Linthicum Heights, MD: Swand, 1975.

Burnham, Scott. "Criticism, Faith, and the *Idee*: A. B. Marx's Early Reception of Beethoven." *Nineteenth-Century Music* 13 (1989): 183–92.

Busoni, Ferruccio. *Selected Letters*. Translated, edited, and with an introduction by Antony Beaumont. London: Faber & Faber, 1987.

Canetti, Elias. *Masse und Macht*. Hamburg: Claassen, 1960. Translated by Carol Stewart as *Crowds and Power*. New York: Farrar, Straus and Giroux, 1984.

Canth, Minna. *Kirjeitä vuosilta, 1860–1897*. Edited by Irja Harmas, Helle Kannila, Greta Thesleff, and Hilja Vilkemaa. Helsinki: Otava, 1944.

Carpelan, Bo. *Axel: A Novel*. Translated by David McDuff. Manchester: Carcanet Press, 1989.

Chadwick, Nicholas. "Berg's Unpublished Songs in the Österreichische Nationalbibliothek." *Music and Letters* 52, no. 2 (1971): 123–40.

Chipman, Abram. "Janáček and Sibelius: The Antithetical Fates of Creativity in late Adulthood." *Psychoanalytic Review* 87 (2000): 429–54.

Clair, Jean, ed. *Lost Paradise: Symbolist Europe.* Montreal: Musée des Beaux-Arts, 1995. Exhibition catalog.

Clarke, William. *The Lost Fortune of the Tsars.* New York: St. Martin's Griffin, 1994.

Couling, Della. *Ferruccio Busoni: "A Musical Ishmael."* Lanham, MD: Scarecrow Press, 2005.

Dahlström, Fabian. "Jean Sibelius' Beiträge zu den Populärkonzerten in Helsinki in den 1890er Jahren." *Erster internationaler Jean Sibelius Kongress in Deutschland, 25.2.1994.* Meiningen, 1994. 1–12.

————, ed. *Jean Sibelius: Thematisch-bibliographisches Verzeichnis seiner Werke.* Wiesbaden: Breitkopf & Härtel, 2003.

————. *Sibelius-Akatemia, 1882–1982.* Translated into Finnish by Rauno Ekholm. Helsinki: Sibelius-Akatemia, 1982.

Donner, Philip, ed., with the assistance of Hannu Tolvanen. *Idols and Myths in Music.* Special issue, *Musiikin suunta* 7 (1985, no. 1).

Downes, Olin. "Creative Genius in Music Honored at Norfolk." *Musical America*, June 13, 1914.

————. *Olin Downes on Music: A Selection from his Writings during the Half-Century 1906 to 1955.* Edited by Irene Downes. New York: Simon & Schuster, 1957.

Edelfelt, Albert. "Dearest Mother! Extracts from *Niin kutsuttu sydämeni: Albert Edefeltin kirjeet äidilleen, 1873–1901.*" *Books from Finland* (2003, no. 1): 45–53.

————. "Sketches in Finland." *Harper's New Monthly Magazine*, February 1891, 339–53.

Eero Järnefelt, 1863–1937. Helsinki, Ateneum Art Museum; Joensuu: Joensuu taidemuseo, 2001. Exhibition catalog.

Ekberg, Henrik, ed. *Uppslagsverket Finland.* 5 vols. Esbo, Helsingfors: Schildts, 2003–7.

Ekman, Karl, Jr. *Jean Sibelius: en konstnärs liv och personlighet.* Helsingfors: Holger Schildts förlag, 1935; 2nd edition, 1935; 3rd edition, 1936; 4th rev. and enlarged edition, *Jean Sibelius och hans verk*, 1956.

————. *Jean Sibelius: His Life and Personality.* Foreword by Ernest Newman. Translated by Edward Birse. London: Alan Wilmer, 1936.

Engman, Max. *Dagligt liv i S:t Petersburg: Bland kejsarens finländska undersåtar.* Helsingfors: SLS; Stockholm: Atlantis, 2003.

————. "National Conceptions of History in Finland." In *Conceptions of National History: Proceedings of Nobel Symposium 78*, edited by Erik Lönnroth, Karl Molin, Ragnar Björk. Berlin and New York: Walter de Gruyter, 1994. 49–63.

————. *Pietarinsuomalaiset.* Helsinki: WSOY, 2004.

————, and David Kirby, eds. *Finland: People, Nation, State.* London: Hurst, 1989.

Eskola, Taneli. *Water Lilies and Wings of Steel: Interpreting Change in the Photographic Imagery of Aulanko Park.* Helsinki: University of Art and Design Helsinki UIAH, 1997.

Facos, Michelle. *Nationalism and the Nordic Imagination: Swedish Art of the 1890s.* Berkeley: University of California Press, 1998.

————, and Sharon L. Hirsh, eds. *Art, Culture, and National Identity in fin-de-siècle Europe.* Cambridge: Cambridge University Press, 2003.

Farwell, Arthur. "Sibelius: A Musical Redeemer." *Musical America*, March 15, 1913, 14.

Fewster, Derek. *Visions of Past Glory: Nationalism and the Construction of Early Finnish History.* Helsinki: Finnish Literature Society, 2006.

Figes, Orlando. *Natasha's Dance: A Cultural History of Russia.* London: Allen Lane, 2002.

————. *A People's Tragedy: The Russian Revolution, 1891–1924.* London: Jonathan Cape, 1996.

Flodin, Karl. *Martin Wegelius: Levnadsteckning.* Helsingfors: SLS, 1922.

————. *La musique en Finlande.* Paris, 1900.

Forslin, Alfhild. *Runeberg i musiken: Bibliografi med kommentarer och historisk översikt.* Helsingfors: SLS; Copenhagen: Ejnar Munksgaard, 1958.

Forsman, Rabbe. "Sagan om Satu: Jean Sibelius och ett finskt kulturkomplex. Sånger kan jag, som ej konungens maka, ej son av mänska kan. (Eddan)." *Ny tid,* June 23, 2006.

Furuhjelm, Erik. *Jean Sibelius: Hans tondiktning och drag ur hans liv.* Borgå: Holger Schildts förlag, 1916.

Gallen-Kallela-Sirén, Janne. "Axel Gallén and the Constructed Nation: Art and Nationalism in Young Finland, 1880–1900." Ph.D. diss., New York University, 2001.

————. *Minä palaan jalanjäljilleni: Akseli Gallen-Kallelan elämä ja taide.* Helsinki: Otava, 2001.

Garelick, Rhonda. "*Bayadères, Stéréorama,* and Vahat-Loukoum: Technological Realism in the Age of Empire." In *Spectacles of Realism: Body, Gender, Genre,* edited by Margaret Cohen and Christopher Prendergast. Minneapolis: University of Minnesota Press, 1995. 294–319.

Gebhard, Hannes. "Kirje Helsingistä: Palanen 'nuoren Suomen' historiaa." *Valvoja* 12 (1892): 65–72.

Gleißner, Ruth-Maria. *Der unpolitische Komponist als Politikum: Die Rezeption von Jean Sibelius im NS-Staat.* Frankfurt am Main: Peter Lang, 2001.

Gonneau, Pierre. "Le dimanche sanglant." In *Rimski-Korsakov, Le coq d'or: Sous la direction d'André Lischke.* L'avant scène opéra 211. Paris: Éditions Premières Loges, 2002. 70–75.

Goss, Glenda Dawn. "A Backdrop for Young Sibelius: The Intellectual Genesis of the *Kullervo* Symphony." *Nineteenth-Century Music* 27 (2003): 48–73.

————. "A Critical Edition for Jean Sibelius." *Fontes artis musicae* 51 (2004): 358–66.

————. *Jean Sibelius: A Guide to Research.* New York: Garland, 1998.

————. "Jean Sibelius and Finnish Nationalism." *Die Tonkunst* (2007, no. 4): 346–54.

————. *Jean Sibelius and Olin Downes: Music, Friendship, Criticism.* Boston: Northeastern University Press, 1995.

————, ed. *Jean Sibelius: The Hämeenlinna Letters; Scenes from a Musical Life, 1874–1895/Jean Sibelius: Ungdomsbrev.* Translated by Margareta Örtenblad Thompson. Esbo: Schildts, 1997.

————. "Jean Sibelius's Choral Symphony *Kullervo.*" *Choral Journal* 47 (February 2007): 16–26.

————. "Music and Letters for Stravinsky's *Ragtime* for Eleven Instruments." *Mitteilungen der Paul Sacher Stiftung* 19 (2006): 11–16.

————, ed. *The Sibelius Companion.* Westport, CT: Greenwood Press, 1996.

————. "Sibelius Letters in the Helsinki University Library." *Fontes artis musicae* 52 (2005): 145–56.

————. "Sibelius's *Kullervo* after 1892." In *Hundra vägar har min tanke: Festskrift till Fabian Dahlström/ Juhlakirja Fabian Dahlströmille.* Helsinki: WSOY, 2000. 61–72.

————. *Vieläkö lähetämme hänelle sikareja? Sibelius, Amerikka ja amerikkalaiset [Are We Still Sending Him Cigars? Sibelius, America, and Americans].* Translated and edited by Martti Haapakoski. Helsinki: WSOY, 2009.

————. "Worttext und Übersetzungen in Sibelius' *Kullervo-Symphonie.*" *Autor–Autorisation–Authentizität.* Edited by Thomas Bein et al. Tübingen: Max Niemeyer Verlag, 2004. 333–43.

Gray, Cecil. *Sibelius.* London: Oxford University Press, 1931.

Grey, Thomas S. "*Tableaux vivants*: Landscape, History Painting, and the Visual Imagination in Mendelssohn's Orchestral Music." *Nineteenth-Century Music* 21 (1997): 38–76.

Grimley, Daniel M., ed. *The Cambridge Companion to Sibelius.* Cambridge: Cambridge University Press, 2004.

————. *Grieg: Music, Landscape and Norwegian Identity.* Woodbridge, Suffolk: Boydell Press, 2006.

Gullberg, Tom, and Kaj Sandberg, eds. *Medströms–motströms: Individ och struktur i historien; Festskrift till Max Engman den 27 september 2005.* Helsingfors: Söderströms; Stockholm: Atlantis, 2005.

Haapakoski, Martti. "Armas Järnefelt: Refined Pre-Karajan of the North on the 125th Anniversary of his Birth." FMQ (1994, no. 3): 3–8.

————. "The Concerto That Holds a Record: The Sibelius Violin Concerto on Disc." FMQ (1990, nos. 3–4): 32–35.

Haavio, Martti. *Nuoruusvuodet: Kronikka vuosilta, 1906–1924.* Porvoo: WSOY, 1972.

————. *Puheita vv. 1924–1958.* Porvoo: WSOY, 1959.

————. *Väinämöinen: Eternal Sage.* Translated by Helen Goldthwait-Väänänen. Helsinki: Suomalainen Tiedeakatemia, 1952–53.

Habermas, Jürgen. *The Structural Transformation of the Public Sphere: An Inquiry into a Category of Bourgeois Society.* Translated by Thomas Burger with the assistance of Frederick Laurence. Cambridge, MA: MIT Press, 1989.

Hagelstam, Wentzel. *Personer och minnen.* Helsingfors: Söderström, 1923.

Haimo, Ethan, and Paul Johnson, eds. *Stravinsky Retrospectives.* Lincoln: University of Nebraska Press, 1987.

Häkkinen, Antti. *Rahasta—vaan ei rakkaudesta: Prostituutio Helsingissä, 1867–1939.* Helsinki: Otava, 1995.

Hall, Edward T. *The Dance of Life: The Other Dimension of Time.* Garden City, NY: Anchor Press and Doubleday, 1983.

Hällfors, Lydia. *Äidin muistelmia.* Edited by Helmi Krohn. Porvoo: WSOY, 1924.

Hämäläinen, Pekka Kalevi. *In Time of Storm: Revolution, Civil War, and the Ethnolinguistic Issue in Finland.* Albany: State University of New York Press, 1979.

————. *Kielitaistelu Suomessa, 1917–1939.* Translated by Osmo Mäkeläinen. Porvoo: WSOY, 1968.

Hanson, Lawrence, and Elisabeth Hanson. *Prokofiev, the Prodigal Son: An Introduction to His Life and Work in Three Movements.* London: Cassell, 1964.

Hausen, Marika, Kirmo Mikkola, Anna-Lisa Amberg, and Tytti Valto, eds. *Eliel Saarinen: Projects, 1896–1923.* Helsinki: Museum of Finnish Architecture, 1990.

Hayden, Deborah. *Pox: Genius, Madness, and the Mysteries of Syphilis.* New York: Basic Books, 2003.

Heikkilä, Ritva, ed. *Sanoi Minna Canth: Otteita Minna Canthin teoksista ja kirjeistä/Pioneer Reformer: Extracts from Minna Canth's Work and Letters.* Translated by Paul Sjöblom. Porvoo: WSOY, 1987.

Heller, Reinhold. "Edvard Munch's *Vision* and the Symbolist Swan." *Art Quarterly* 36, no. 3 (1973): 209–49.

Hellman, Ben. "'Mnogo! Mnogoo! Mnogoo!' Suomalainen taidenäyttely Petrogradissa 1917." *Idäntutkimus, Östeuropaforskning: The Finnish Review of East European Studies* (2002, no. 4): 27–40.

Hepokoski, James. "Sibelius." In *The Nineteenth-Century Symphony,* edited by D. Kern Holoman. New York: Schirmer Books, 1997. 417–49.

————. "Sibelius, Jean." In *The New Grove Dictionary of Music and Musicians,* 2nd ed., edited by Stanley Sadie and John Tyrrell. 29 vols. London and New York: Macmillan, 2001. 22:319–47.

————. *Sibelius: Symphony no. 5.* Cambridge: Cambridge University Press, 1993.

Hietanen, Sirpa, ed. *Finland—Musicland.* Saint Petersburg: The Finnish Institute in Saint Petersburg, 2007.

Hintze, Bertel. *Albert Edelfelt.* 3 vols. Helsingfors: Söderström, 1942–44.

Hirn, Yrjö. *Lärt folk och landstrykare i det finska Finlands kulturliv.* Helsingfors: Holger Schildts förlag, 1939.

Hjelt, Edv[ard]. *Stipendier och stipendiifonder stående under det Finska universitetets förvaltning.* Helsingfors: G. W. Edlund, 1894.

Hobsbawm, E. J. *The Age of Empire, 1875–1914.* London: Weidenfeld & Nicolson, 1987.

————, and Terence Ranger, eds. *The Invention of Tradition.* Cambridge: Cambridge University Press, 1983.

Honko, Lauri, ed. *The Kalevala and the World's Traditional Epics.* Helsinki: Finnish Literature Society, 2002.

Hroch, Miroslav. *Social Preconditions of National Revival in Europe: A Comparative Analysis of the Social Composition of Patriotic Groups among the Smaller European Nations.* Translated by Ben Fowkes. Cambridge: Cambridge University Press, 1985.

Huldén, Anders. *Finlands kungaäventyr 1918.* [Helsingfors]: Söderström, 1989.

Hultin, Tekla. *Päiväkirjani kertoo: 1899–1914*. Helsinki: Sanatar, 1935.

Hutchinson, John, and Anthony D. Smith, eds. *Nationalism*. Oxford: Oxford University Press, 1994.

Huttunen, Matti. "The 'Canon' of Music History and the Music of a Small Nation." In *Music History Writing and National Culture: Proceedings of a Seminar, Tallinn, December 1–3, 1995*, edited by Urve Lippus. Tallinn: Eeste keele instituut, 1995. 20–30.

———. *Modernin musiikinhistoriankirjoituksen synty Suomessa: Musiikkikäsitykset tutkimuksen uranuurtajien tuotannossa*. Helsinki: Suomen musiikkitieteellinen seura, 1993.

———. "Nationalistic and Non-Nationalistic Views of Sibelius in the 20th-Century Finnish Music Historiography." In *Music and Nationalism in 20ᵗʰ-century Great Britain and Finland*, edited by Tomi Mäkelä. Hamburg: von Bockel Verlag, 1997. 217–32.

———. "Sibelius ja Suomen musiikillinen yhteiskunta ennen toista maailmansotaa." *Musiikki* (1999, no. 3): 262–76.

———, Kari Kilpeläinen, and Veijo Murtomäki, eds. *Sibelius Forum II: Proceedings from The Third International Jean Sibelius Conference, Helsinki, December 7–10, 2000*. Helsinki: Sibelius Academy Department of Composition and Music Theory, 2003.

Hyökki, Matti. *Hiilestä timantiksi: Jean Sibeliuksen Kalevala- ja Kanteletar-lähtöisten mieskuorolaulujen ominaispiirteistä*. Diss., Sibelius Academy, 2003.

Ilvas, Juha, ed. *Akseli Gallen-Kallela: Ateneum 16.2.—26.5.1996/Turun taidemuseo 26.6.—1.9.1996*. Helsinki: Ateneum, 1996. Exhibition catalog.

———, ed. *Sanan ja tunteen voimalla: Akseli Gallen-Kallelan kirjeitä/A Self-Portrait in Words: The Letters of Akseli Gallen-Kallela*. [Helsinki]: Finnish National Gallery, [1996].

———, and Maritta Pitkänen. *Emil Wikström: Delicacy and Strength*. Edited by Helena Hänninen. Translated by Gregory Coogan. [Mänttä]: Gösta Serlachius Fine Arts Foundation, 2002. Exhibition catalog to accompany the exhibition at Gösta Serlachius Museum of Fine Arts, May 17–October 31, 2002.

J. A. "Finska artisternas Utställning." *Finsk Tidskrift* 39 (1895, no. 2): 453–56.

Jackson, Holbrook. *The Eighteen Nineties: A Review of Art and Ideas at the Close of the Nineteenth Century*. Harmondsworth, Middlesex, England: Penguin, 1913.

Jackson, Timothy L., and Veijo Murtomäki, eds. *Sibelius Studies*. Cambridge: Cambridge University Press, 2001.

Jägerskiöld, Stig. *Mannerheim: Marshal of Finland*. London: C. Hurst, 1986.

Jakobson, Max. *Finland Survived: An Account of the Finnish-Soviet Winter War, 1939–1940*. 2nd ed. Helsinki: Otava, 1984.

Jalas, Jussi. *Kirjoituksia Sibeliuksen sinfonioista: Sinfonian eettinen pakko*. Helsinki: Fazer, 1988.

Järnefelt, Arvid. "Kirjailijain muotokuvia. XXIII: Leo Tolstoi." *Valvoja* 12 (1892): 209–27.

———. *Vanhempieni romaani*. Porvoo: Söderström, 1928–30.

Johnson, Harold E. *Jean Sibelius*. New York: Alfred A. Knopf, 1959.

Johnston, William M. *The Austrian Mind: An Intellectual and Social History, 1848–1938*. Berkeley: University of California Press, 1972.

Josephson, Nors S. "On Some Apparent Sketches for Sibelius's Eighth Symphony." *Archiv für Musikwissenschaft* 61 (2004): 54–67.

———. "Die Skizzen zu Sibelius' 4. Symphonie (1909–1911)." *Die Musikforschung* 40 (1987): 38–49.

Joyce, James. *Ulysses: A Critical and Synoptic Edition*, prepared by Hans Walter Gabler with Wolfhard Steppe and Claus Melchior. New York: Garland, 1984.

Jussila, Osmo. "The Historical Background of the February Manifesto of 1899." *Journal of Baltic Studies* 15 (1984): 141–47.

———. "Nationalism and Revolution: Political Dividing Lines in the Grand Duchy of Finland during the Last Years of Russian Rule." *Scandinavian Journal of History* 2 (1977): 289–309.

————, Seppo Hentilä, and Jukka Nevakivi. *Suomen poliittinen historia, 1809–1995.* Helsinki: WSOY, 1995. Translated by David Arter and Eva-Kaisa Arter as *From Grand Duchy to a Modern State: A Political History of Finland since 1809.* London: Hurst, 1999.

Jutikkala, Eino, with Kauko Pirinen. *A History of Finland.* Translated by Paul Sjöblom. 6th rev. ed. Helsinki: WSOY, 2003.

Juva, Mikko, Vilho Niitemaa, and Päiviö Tommila, eds. *Suomen historian dokumentteja 2.* Helsinki: Otava, 1970.

Kagan-Kans, Eva. *Hamlet and Don Quixote: Turgenev's Ambivalent Vision.* The Hague: Mouton, 1975.

Kajanus, Robert. "Bernhard Henrik Crusell." Translated into Finnish and edited by Matti Vainio. *Musiikki* (2007, no. 1): 56–61.

————. "Ristiäismatka." *Kalevalaseuran vuosikirja* 12 (1932): 79–84.

————. "Vanha runosävelmä: Muutamia muistelmia Lönnrotista." *Kalevalaseuran vuosikirja* 1 (1921): 31–38.

The Kalevala: Epic of the Finnish People. Translated by Eino Friberg. Edited and with an introduction by George C. Schoolfield. Helsinki: Otava, 1988.

Kalevala: The Land of the Heroes. Translated by W. F. Kirby. Introduction by M. A. Branch. London and Dover, NH: Athlone Press, 1985.

Kalevalan riemuvuoden näyttely: Akseli Gallen-Kallelan muistonäyttely. Kalevalan 100-vuotisriemujuhlat Helsingin uudessa Messuhallissa 28.2.–17.3.1935. Helsinki: SKS, 1935.

Kallio, Veikko. *Finland: Cultural Perspectives.* Translated by Peter Herring. Porvoo: WSOY, 1989.

Kangas, Knut. "Kansanlaulut." *Työn sävel* (1927, no. 3): 48–52.

Kannila, Helle, ed. *Minna Canthin kirjeet.* Helsinki: SKS, 1973.

The Kanteletar: Lyrics and Ballads after Oral Tradition by Elias Lönnrot. Selected and translated by Keith Bosley. Oxford: Oxford University Press, 1992.

Karila, Tauno. "Uusi näkökulma Sibeliuksen Sadun esteettiseen tulkintaan." *Suomen musiikin vuosikirja* (1964–65): 35–45.

Karjalainen, Kauko. "Sibeliuksen Allegro torviseptetille." *Sulasol* (1987, no. 1): 8–9.

Karni, Michael G., ed. *Finnish Diaspora II: United States.* Toronto: Multicultural History Society of Ontario, 1981.

Kekkonen, Urho. "Jean Sibelius: 125th Aniversary." *Nordic Sounds: Nomus* (1990, no. 4): 2.

Keller, Hans. "First Performances: Their Pre- and Reviews." *Music Review* 16, no. 2 (1955): 141–45.

Kihlman, Erik. *Mikael Lybeck: Liv och diktning.* Helsingfors: SLS, 1932.

Kilpeläinen, Kari. *The Jean Sibelius Musical Manuscripts at Helsinki University Library: A Complete Catalogue.* Wiesbaden: Breitkopf & Härtel, 1991.

————. "Sibelius Eight [*sic*]: What Happened To It?" FMQ (1995, no. 4): 30–35.

————. *Tutkielmia Jean Sibeliuksen käsikirjoituksista.* Ph.D. diss., University of Helsinki, 1992.

Kilpinen, Yrjö. "'Mahtava majakka säteilee maailmaan': Muistopuhe Kalevalaseuran kunniajäsenen Jean Sibeliuksen arkun ääressä Suurkirkossa 30.9.1957." Helsinki: Helsingin Liikekirjapaino, 1958.

Kirby, D. G., ed. and trans. *Finland and Russia, 1808–1920: From Autonomy to Independence.* London: Macmillan, 1975.

Kirby, David. *A Concise History of Finland.* Cambridge: Cambridge University Press, 2006.

Kirchmeyer, Helmut. *Kommentiertes Verzeichnis der Werke und Werkausgaben Igor Strawinskys bis 1971.* Sächsische Akademie der Wissenschaften zu Leipzig. Stuttgart; Leipzig: Hirzel, 2002.

Klinge, Matti. *A Brief History of Finland.* Translated by David Mitchell. 3rd rev. ed. Helsinki: Otava, 1984.

————. *Finlands historia 3: Kejsartiden.* Esbo: Schildts, 1996.

————. *The Finnish Tradition: Essays on Structures and Identities in the North of Europe.* Helsinki: SHS, 1993.

————. *Let Us Be Finns: Essays on History.* Helsinki: Otava, 1990.

————. *Den politiske Runeberg*. Stockholm: Atlantis; Helsingfors: Söderströms, 2004.

————. *Suomen sinivalkoiset värit: Kansallisten ja muidenkin symbolien vaiheista ja merkityksestä*. Helsinki: Otava, 1999.

————, ed. *Suomen kansallisbiografia*. 11 vols. Helsinki: SKS, 2003–8.

————, Rainer Knapas, Anto Leikola, and John Strömberg. *Helsingin Yliopisto, 1640–1990*. 3 vols. Helsinki: Otava, 1987–90.

Knapas, Rainer. "Kulttuurin tunnuskuvia." In *Itsenäistymisen vuodet 1917–1920. 2. Taistelu vallasta*, edited by Ohto Manninen. Helsinki: Valtionarkisto, 1993. 628–706.

————, and Pertti Koistinen. *Historiallisia kuvia: Suomi vanhassa grafiikassa/ Images of Finland in Early Graphic Arts*. Helsinki: SKS, 1993.

————, and Maria Vainio, eds. *Albert Edelfelt och Ryssland: Brev från åren 1875–1905*. Helsingfors: SLS; Stockholm: Atlantis, 2004.

Knuuttila, Seppo. *Tyhmän kansan teoria: Näkökulmia menneestä tulevaan*. Helsinki: SKS, 1994.

Kolehmainen, John I. "When Finland's Tolstoy Met His Russian Master." *American Slavic and East European Review* 16 (1957): 534–41.

Konttinen, Riitta. *Sammon takojat: Nuoren Suomen taiteilijat ja suomalaisuuden kuvat*. Helsinki: Otava, 2001.

Kopponen, Tapio. "Järnefeltit: Suomalaisen kulttuurisuvun elämästä ja ajattelusta." In *Realismista symbolismiin: Kuopio suomalaisen kulttuurin polttopisteenä 1890-luvun taitteessa*. Kuopio: Snellman-instituutti, 1994. 35–45.

Korhonen, Teppo, and Matti Räsänen, eds. *Kansa kuvastimessa: Etnisyys ja identiteetti*. Helsinki: SKS, 1989.

Korvenmaa, Pekka. *Innovation versus Tradition: The Architect Lars Sonck; Works and Projects, 1900–1910*. Translated by Jüri Kokkonen. Suomen Muinaismuistoyhdistyksen Aikakauskirja 96. Helsinki: [Suomen muinaismuistoyhdistys], 1991.

Koskimies, Rafael. "Sortokausien vaikutus kulttuurielämään." In *Venäläinen sortokausi Suomessa*, edited by Päiviö Tommila. Porvoo: WSOY, 1960. 235–54.

Koskimies, Yrjö S. *Hämeenlinnan kaupungin historia, 1875–1944*. Hämeenlinna: Karisto, 1966.

Koskinen, Seppo, ed. *Suomen väestö*. Helsinki: Gaudeamus, 2007.

Krohn, Ilmari. *Der Stimmungsgehalt der Symphonien von Jean Sibelius*. 2 vols. Helsinki: Suomalainen Tiedeakatemia, 1945–46.

Krones, Hartmut, ed. *Jean Sibelius und Wien: Wiener Schriften zur Stilkunde und Aufführungspraxis*. Vienna: Böhlau, 2003.

Kuopiosta Suomeen: Kirjallisuutemme aatesisältöä 1880-luvulla. Kuopio: Snellman-instituutti, 1985.

Kurki, Eija. *Satua, kuolemaa ja eksotiikkaa: Jean Sibeliuksen vuosisadanalun näyttämömusiikkiteokset*. Ph.D. diss., University of Helsinki, 1997.

————. "Sibeliuksen *Metsänhaltijoiden* tähänastiset seikkailut." *Musiikki* (1996, no. 3): 349–61.

Kuusi, Matti. *Sananlaskut ja puheenparret*. Helsinki: SKS, 1954.

Kuusinen, Otto Wille. *Valitut teokset, 1918–1964*. Moscow, 1964.

La Grange, Henry-Louis de. *Gustav Mahler*. Vol. 3, *Vienna: Triumph and Disillusion, 1904–1907*. Oxford: Oxford University Press, 1999.

Lagus, Hugo. "Några musikminnen." *Finsk Tidskrift* 118 (1935): 39–48.

Laitinen, Heikki. "Kalevalan kommentaarin runosävelmäliite vuodelta 1895." In *Paimensoittimista kisällilauluun: Tutkielmia kansanmusiikista 1*. Kaustinen: Kansanmusiikki-instituutti, 1976. 157–92.

Lappalainen, Seija. "Martin Wegelius: musiikkipedagogi ja wagneriaani." In *Siltoja ja synteesejä: Esseitä semiotiikasta, kulttuurista ja taiteesta*, edited by Irma Vierimaa, Kari Kilpeläinen, and Anne Sivuoja-Gunaratnam. Helsinki: Gaudeamus, 1998. 143–55.

Layton, Robert, ed. *A Companion to the Symphony*. London: Simon & Schuster, 1993.

————. *The Master Musicians: Sibelius*. 3rd ed. New York: Schirmer, 1993.

Le Bon, Gustave. *The Crowd: A Study of the Popular Mind*. London: T. F. Unwin, 1903.

Lehtonen, Tuomas M. S., ed. *Europe's Northern Frontier: Perspectives on Finland's Western Identity*. Translated by Philip Landon. Jyväskylä: PS-Kustannus, 1999.

Leichtentritt, Hugo. *Das Konservatorium der Musik Klindworth-Scharwenka, Berlin, 1881–1931*. Berlin, 1931.

Leino-Kaukiainen, Pirkko. *Sensuuri ja sanomalehdistö Suomessa vuosina, 1891–1905*. Helsinki: SHS, 1984.

Levas, Santeri. *Jean Sibelius: Muistelma suuresta ihmisestä*. 2 vols. Porvoo: WSOY, 1957, 1960.

———. *Sibelius: A Personal Portrait*. Translated by Percy M. Young. Lewisburg, PA: Bucknell University Press, 1972.

Liikanen, Ilkka. *Fennomania ja kansa: Joukkojärjestäytymisen läpimurto ja Suomalaisen puolueen synty*. Helsinki: SHS, 1995.

———. "Light to Our People: Educational Organization and the Mobilization of Fennomania in the 1870s." *Scandinavian Journal of History* 13 (1988): 421–38.

Lindeqvist, K. O. *Hämeenlinnan kaupungin historia vuosina, 1809–75*. Hämeenlinna: Karisto, 1930.

Lindgren, Minna. "I've Got Some Lovely Themes for a Violin Concert [*sic*]." FMQ (1990, nos. 3–4): 24–31.

Lindqvist, Leena, ed. *Taiteilijan tiellä: Eero Järnefelt, 1863–1937*. Helsinki: Otava, 2002.

Linna, Väinö. *Tuntematon sotilas*. Porvoo: WSOY, 1955.

Lourié, Arthur. "The Russian School." *Musical Quarterly* 18 (1932): 519–29.

———. *Sergei Koussevitzky and His Epoch: A Biographical Chronicle*. Translated by S. W. Pring. New York: Alfred A. Knopf, 1931.

Luening, Otto. *The Odyssey of an American Composer: The Autobiography of Otto Luening*. New York: Charles Scribner's Sons, 1980.

Lukkarinen, Ville. *Classicism and History: Anachronistic Architectural Thinking in Finland at the Turn of the Century; Jac. Ahrenberg and Gustaf Nyström*. Suomen Muinaismuistoyhdistyksen Aikakauskirja 93. Helsinki: [Suomen muinaismuistoyhdistys], 1989.

———, and Annika Waenerberg. *Suomi-kuvasta mielenmaisemaan: Kansallismaisemat 1800- ja 1900-luvun vaihteen maalaustaiteessa*. Helsinki: SKS, 2004.

Luyken, Lorenz. "*. . . aus dem Nichtigen eine Welt schaffen . . .*": Studien zur Dramaturgie im symphonischen Spätwerk von Jean Sibelius. Kassel: Gustav Bosse, 1995.

Lvov, Nikolai, and Ivan Prach. *A Collection of Russian Folk Songs*. Edited by Malcolm Hamrick Brown. With an introduction and appendixes by Margarita Mazo. Classics of Russian Musical Folklore in Facsimile. Ann Arbor, MI: UMI Research Press, 1987.

MacKeith, Peter B., and Kerstin Smeds. *The Finland Pavilions: Finland at the Universal Expositions, 1900–1992*. Translated by John Arnold. [Helsinki]: Kustannus Oy City, 1992.

Mäkelä, Tomi. "*Poesie in der Luft*": Jean Sibelius, Studien zu Leben und Werk. Wiesbaden: Breitkopf & Härtel, 2007.

Mäkinen, Helka, ed. *Lihasta sanaksi: Tutkimuksia suomalaisesta teatterista*. Helsinki: Yliopistopaino, 1997.

Mällinen, Teuvo, ed. *Nuoren Suomen ytimessä: Näkökulmia nuorsuomalaisuuteen ja Nuori Suomi-albumiin*. Oulu: Helsingin Sanomat; Kaleva, 1994.

Mandelstam, Osip Emilievich. *The Complete Critical Prose and Letters*. Edited by Jane Gary Harris. Translated by Jane Gary Harris and Constance Link. Ann Arbor, MI: Ardis, 1979.

Martin, Timo, and Douglas Sivén. *Akseli Gallen-Kallela, National Artist of Finland*. English adaptation by Satu Salo and Keith Bosley. [Helsinki]: Watti, 1996.

Marvia, Einari. "Kymmenen vuoden takainen käynti Ainolassa." *Pieni musiikkilehti* (1965, no. 6): 33–36.

———. *Sibeliuksen Rituaalimusiikki*. Helsinki: Acta Minervae III, 1984.

McGinty, Doris Evans. "'That You Came So Far to See Us': Coleridge-Taylor in America." *Black Music Research Journal* 21 (2001): 197–234.

Mead, W. R., and Helmer Smeds. *Winter in Finland*. London: Hugh Evelyn, 1967.

Mechelin, Leo, ed. *Finland i 19de seklet: Framställdt i ord och bild af Finska skriftställare och konstnärer.* Helsingfors: F. Tilgmann, 1893.

———. *Notices sur la Finlande publiées à l'occasion de l'Exposition universelle à Paris en 1900.* Helsingfors: Imprimerie centrale, 1900.

Meier-Graefe, Julius. *Entwickelungsgeschichte der Modernen Kunst: Vergleichende Betrachtung der Bildenden Künste, als Beitrag zu einer Neuen Aesthetik.* 2 vols. Stuttgart: Jul. Hoffmann, 1904.

Mejias-Ojajärvi, Iliana. *Venäjän maalaustaide: Ikoneista avantgarden kynnykselle.* Helsinki: WSOY, 2006.

"Mir iskusstva": On the Centenary of the Exhibition of Russian and Finnish Artists, 1898. Edited by Yevgenia Petrova. Saint Petersburg and Helsinki: Palace Editions, 1998. Exhibition catalog.

Moffett, Judith, ed. and trans. *The North! To the North! Five Swedish Poets of the Nineteenth Century.* Carbondale and Edwardsville: Southern Illinois University Press, [2001].

Montagu-Nathan, M. "Belaiev: Maecenas of Russian Music." *Musical Quarterly* 4 (1918): 450–65.

Mosse, W. E. *Alexander II and the Modernization of Russia.* New rev. ed. New York: Collier Books, 1962.

Muck, Peter. *Einhundert Jahre Berliner Philharmonisches Orchester: Darstellung in Dokumenten.* Vol. 1, *1882–1922.* Tutzing: Hans Schneider, 1982.

Murtomäki, Veijo. *Jean Sibelius ja isänmaa.* Helsinki: Tammi, 2007.

———. "Sibelius Caught in a Political Vortex." FMQ (2002, no. 4): 38–45.

———. *Symphonic Unity: The Development of Formal Thinking in the Symphonies of Sibelius.* Translated by Henry Bacon in cooperation with the author. Helsinki: University of Helsinki, 1993.

———, Kari Kilpeläinen, and Risto Väisänen, eds. *Sibelius Forum: Proceedings from the Second International Jean Sibelius Conference, Helsinki, 25–29 November, 1995.* Helsinki: Sibelius Academy Department of Composition and Music Theory, 1998.

Music in the Western World: A History in Documents. Selected and annotated by Piero Weiss and Richard Taruskin. New York: Schirmer Books, 1984.

Mustelin, Olof. *Euterpe: Tidskriften och kretsen kring den; En kulturhistorisk skildring.* Helsingfors: SLS, 1963.

Mustonen, Pertti. *Ravintolaelämää: Kulttuurikuvia, nostalgiaa, kulinarismia.* Helsinki: Tammi, 1990.

Nabokov, Vladimir. *Speak, Memory: An Autobiography Revisited.* Rev. ed. New York: G. P. Putnam's Sons, 1966.

Nationalencyklopedin: Ett uppslagsverk på vetenskaplig grund utarbetat på initiativ av Statens kulturråd. 20 vols, 3 supplements. Höganäs: Bokförlaget Bra Böcker, 1989–2000.

Nevanlinna, Anja Kervanto, and Laura Kolbe, eds. *Suomen kulttuurihistoria 3: Oma maa ja maailma.* Helsinki: Tammi, 2003.

Newmarch, Rosa. *Jean Sibelius: A Short Story of a Long Friendship.* Boston: C. C. Birchard, 1939; London: Goodwin & Tabb, 1945.

Niiniluoto, Marja. *Tapahtui Päivälehden aikaan: Ihmisiä, vuosia, elämää.* Helsinki: Helsingin Sanomat, 1989.

Nordenson, Eva, ed. *Finskt sekelskifte: En konstbok från Nationalmuseum.* Stockholm: Rabén & Sjögren, 1971.

Norrback, Märtha, and Kristina Ranki, eds. *University and Nation: The University and the Making of the Nation in Northern Europe in the 19th and 20th Centuries.* Helsinki: SHS, 1996.

Now the Light Comes from the North: Art Nouveau in Finland. Berlin: Bröhan-Museum, [2002]. Exhibition catalog.

Nummi, Jyrki. "Runebergin kultainen teema: Apollon joutsen." In *Runosta runoon [Suomalaisen runon yhteyksiä länsimaiseen kirjallisuuteen antiikista nykyaikaan],* edited by Sakari Katajamäki and Johanna Pentikäinen. Helsinki: WSOY, 2004. 130–50.

Nygård, Stefan, and Johan Strang, eds. *Mellan idealism och analytisk filosofi: Den moderna filosofin i Finland och Sverige, 1880–1950.* Helsingfors: SLS; Stockholm: Atlantis, 2006.

Okkonen, Onni. *A. Gallen-Kallela: Elämä ja taide.* Porvoo: WSOY, 1961.

Olkkonen, Tuomo. "Modernisoituva suuriruhtinaskunta." In *Suomen historian pikkujättiläinen*, edited by Seppo Zetterberg. Porvoo: WSOY, 1987. 473–543.

Öller, Ragnar. *En finländsk romanskrivare från 1850-talet*. Helsingfors: SLS, 1920.

Örlund, Eino, ed. *Sibeliuksen Hämeenlinna/Sibelius och hans Tavastehus/Sibelius and His Home Town*. Hämeenlinna: Hämeenlinnan Sibelius-Seura, 1990.

Paasi, Anssi. *Territories, Boundaries and Consciousness: The Changing Geographies of the Finnish-Russian Border*. Chichester: John Wiley & Sons, 1996.

Paasikivi, J. K. *"Ei pienillä ole mitään turvaa": J. K. Paasikiven päiväkirjat, 1934–1939*. [Helsinki]: Kansallisarkiston ystävat/Riksarkivets vänner, [2004].

———. *Muistelmia sortovuosilta*. 2 vols. Porvoo: WSOY, 1957.

Paasivirta, Juhani. *Finland and Europe: The Early Years of Independence, 1917–1939*. Edited and translated by Peter Herring. Helsinki: SHS, 1989.

———. *Finland and Europe: International Crises in the Period of Autonomy, 1808–1914*. Translated by Anthony F. Upton and Sirkka R. Upton. Edited and abridged by D. G. Kirby. London: C. Hurst, 1981.

Paul, Adolf. *En bok om en människa*. Stockholm: Albert Bonniers, 1891.

———. *Profiler: Minnen av stora personligheter*. Helsingfors: Söderström, 1937.

Pedersen, Arne Toftegaard. *Urbana odysséer: Helsingfors, staden och 1910-talets finlandssvenska prosa*. Helsingfors: SLS, 2007.

Pekacz, Jolanta T. "Memory, History and Meaning: Musical Biography and its Discontents." *Journal of Musicological Research* 23 (2004): 39–80.

———, ed. *Musical Biography: Towards New Paradigms*. Aldershot, England; Burlington, VT: Ashgate, 2006.

Pierrot, Jean. *The Decadent Imagination, 1880–1900*. Translated by Derek Coltman. Chicago: University of Chicago Press, 1981.

Pingoud, Ernest. *Taiteen edistys: Valittuja kirjoituksia musiikista ja kirjallisuudesta*. Edited by Kalevi Aho. Translated by Seppo Heikinheimo. [Helsinki]: Gaudeamus, 1995.

Pipes, Richard. *Russia under the Old Regime*. 2nd ed. New York: Penguin, 1995.

Plato. *Symposium*. Translated with an introduction and notes by Alexander Nehamas and Paul Woodruff. Indianapolis, IN: Hackett, 1989.

Pohjola, Marja. "The Cream of Composer Collections: The Papers of Jean Sibelius and Family in the National Archives of Finland." *Comma: International Journal on Archives* (2004, no. 1): 173–77.

Polvinen, Tuomo. *Valtakunta ja rajamaa: N. I. Bobrikov Suomen kenraalikuvernöörinä, 1898–1904*. Porvoo: WSOY, 1984. Translated by Steven Huxley as *Imperial Borderland: Bobrikov and the Attempted Russification of Finland, 1898–1904*. London: Hurst, 1995.

Poutanen, Pirjo, ed. *Hämeenlinna*. Hämeenlinna: Tiedotuspalvelu Pirjo Poutanen, 1992.

Prideaux, Sue. *Edvard Munch: Behind the Scream*. New Haven, CT: Yale University Press, 2005.

Pushkin, Alexander. *Eugene Onegin: A Novel in Verse*. Translated with an introduction and notes by James E. Falen. Oxford: Oxford University Press, 1998.

Pushkin's Bronze Horseman. Translated by Wacław Lednicki. Berkeley: University of California Press, 1955.

Quitin, José. "Un grand violoniste belge injustement oublié: Alexandre-Joseph Artôt." *Bulletin de la Société Liégeoise de musicologie* 44 (1984): 1–21.

Ranki, Kristina. *Isänmaa ja Ranska: Suomalainen frankofilia, 1880–1914*. Helsinki: Finska Vetenskaps-Societeten and Suomen Tiedeseura, 2007.

Ranta, Sulho. *Sävelten valoja ja varjoja*. Porvoo: WSOY, 1946.

Ranta-Meyer, Tuire. "Erkki Melartin, Jean Sibelius ja Robert Kajanus: suhteista, vaikutteista ja vallankäytöstä." *Musiikki* (2004, no. 3): 41–63.

————. "Melartin, Sibelius and Kajanus: Connections, conspiracies and collusion." FMQ (2007, no. 2): 36–41.

Rantanen, Päivi. *Suolatut säkeet: Suomen ja suomalaisten diskursiivinen muotoutuminen 1600-luvulta Topeliukseen.* Helsinki: SKS, 1998.

Rantavaara, Irma. "A Nation in Search of Identity: Finnish Literature, 1830–1917." In *The Modern World, II: Realities,* edited by David Daiches and Anthony Thorlby. London: Aldus Books, 1972. 329–61.

Realms of Memory: The Construction of the French Past. Under the direction of Pierre Nora. English-language edition edited by Lawrence D. Kritzman and translated by Arthur Goldhammer. 3 vols. New York: Columbia University Press, 1996–98.

Redepenning, Dorothea. *Geschichte der russischen und der sowjetischen Musik.* Vol. 1, *Das 19. Jahrhundert.* Laaber: Laaber-Verlag, 1994.

Reeder, Roberta. *Anna Akhmatova: Poet and Prophet.* New York: St. Martin's Press, 1994.

Rein, Th[iodolf]. "Muutama sana Kalevalan kuvittamisesta." *Valvoja* 11 (1891): 222–28.

————. "Uudenvuoden mietteitä 1890." *Valvoja* 10 (1890): 28–43.

Richard Strauss et Romain Rolland. Cahier 3: Correspondance, fragments de journal. Paris: Éditions Albin Michel, 1951.

Rickards, Guy. *Jean Sibelius.* London: Phaidon, 1997.

Ringbom, Nils-Eric. *De två versionerna av Sibelius' tondikt "En Saga."* Åbo: Åbo Akademi, 1956.

————. *Helsingfors orkesterföretag 1882–1932.* Helsingfors: Helsingfors orkesterförening, 1932.

————. *Jean Sibelius: A Master and His Work.* Translated by G. I. C. de Courcy. Norman: University of Oklahoma Press, 1954.

Ringbom, Sixten. *Stone, Style and Truth: The Vogue for Natural Stone in Nordic Architecture, 1880–1910.* Suomen Muinaismuistoyhdistyksen Aikakauskirja 91. Helsinki: [Suomen muinaismuistoyhdistys], 1987.

Ripatti, Mikko. "Filosofi apologeettana: Thiodolf Rein idealismin ja naturalismin kriitikkona." *Teologinen Aikakauskirja* 109 (2004): 454–69.

Roiha, Eino. "Sibeliuksen Karelia-sarjan historiallista taustaa." *Kalevalaseuran vuosikirja* 33 (1953): 161–69.

Rönnberg, Hanna. *Konstnärsliv i slutet av 1880-talet.* Helsingfors: Söderstrom, 1931.

Ross, Alex. *The Rest Is Noise: Listening to the Twentieth Century.* New York: Farrar, Straus and Giroux, 2007.

Ross, Carl. *The Finn Factor in American Labor, Culture and Society.* New York Mills, MN: Parta, 1982.

Ruud, Charles A. *Fighting Words: Imperial Censorship and the Russian Press, 1804–1906.* Toronto: University of Toronto Press, 1982.

Rydberg, Viktor. *Dikter.* Stockholm: Albert Bonniers, 1882.

Saari, Raimo. "Sibeliuksen Allegron jäljet johtavat Mäntyharjulle." *Sulasol* (1987, no. 2): 16–17.

Sääskilahti, Nina. *Kansa ja tiede: Suomalainen kansatiede ja sen kohde 1800-luvulta 1980-luvulle.* Jyväskylä: University of Jyväskylä, 1997.

Salmenhaara, Erkki. "Ernst Mielck: Max Bruch's Favourite Pupil." FMQ (1994, no. 1): 2–8.

————. "Finnish Music in the 1920s and 30s: Internationalism vs. Nationalism." In *Music and Nationalism in 20th-Century Great Britain and Finland,* edited by Tomi Mäkelä. Hamburg: von Bockel Verlag, 1997. 175–82.

————. "Jean Sibelius ja Helsingin yliopisto." *Musiikki* (1990, no. 1): 23–38.

Salmi, Hannu. *Wagner and Wagnerism in Nineteenth-Century Sweden, Finland, and the Baltic Provinces: Reception, Enthusiasm, Cult.* Rochester, NY: University of Rochester Press, 2005.

Samson, Jim. "Music and Nationalism: Five Historic Moments." In *Musikvidenskabelige kompositioner: Festskrift til Niels Krabbe 1941. 3. oktober. 2006,* edited by Anne Ørbaek Jensen, John T. Lauridsen, Erland

Kolding Nielsen, and Claus Røllum-Larsen, with the assistance of Sofie Lene Bak and Jakob K. Meile. Copenhagen: Det Kongelige Bibliotek, 2006. 197–210.

Sarajas, Annamari. *Elämän meri: Tutkielmia uusromantiikan kirjallisista aatteista*. Porvoo: WSOY, 1961.

———. *Tunnuskuvia: Suomen ja Venäjän kirjallisen realismin kosketuskohtia*. Porvoo: WSOY, 1968.

Sarajas-Korte, Salme. "Magnus Enckellin joutsenfantasia/Magnus Enckell's Swan Fantasy." *Ateneum: Valtion taidemuseon museojulkaisu* (1994): 6–30.

———. "Sadun ulottuvuuksia: Hugo Simberg, Axel Gallén ja H. C. Andersen." In *Piru, kuolema ja enkeli ateljessa: Tutkielmia Hugo Simbergin taiteesta*, edited by Hanna-Leena Paloposki. Helsinki: Ateneum, 2000. 25–41.

———. *Vid symbolismens källor: Den tidiga symbolismen i Finland 1890–1895*. Translated by Erik Kruskopf. Jakobstad: Jakobstads Tryckeri och Tidnings Ab:s förlag, 1981.

Sarjala, Jukka. *Poeettinen elämä: Biedermeierin säveltäjä-kirjailija Axel Gabriel Ingelius*. Helsinki: SKS, 2005.

———. "Sibelius Euroopan reunalla: Miten nerous puretaan historiaan?" In *Kirjoituksia neroudesta: Myytit, kultit, persoonat*, edited by Taava Koskinen. Helsinki: SKS, 2006. 285–311.

Sarje, Kimmo. *Sigurd Frosteruksen modernin käsite: Maailmankatsomus ja arkkitehtuuri*. Helsinki: Valtion Taidemuseo, 2000.

Savolainen, Pentti, and Matti Vainio. *Aino Ackté: Elämänkaari kirjeiden valossa*. Helsinki: WSOY, 2002.

Scandinavian Modernism: Painting in Denmark, Finland, Iceland, Norway and Sweden, 1910–1920. Produced and edited by Carl Tomas Edam, Nils-Göran Hökby, and Birgitta Schreiber. Translations by Martha Gaber Abrahamsen et al. New York: Rizzoli, [1989]. Exhibition catalog.

Schellenberg, Henry A. "An Overview of the Choral Music of Albert Ernst Anton Becker (1834–1899) with Particular Emphasis on his Mass in B-flat Minor, Op. 16." DMA essay, University of Iowa, 1995.

Schoolfield, George C. *A Baedeker of Decadence: Charting a Literary Fashion, 1884–1927*. New Haven, CT: Yale University Press, 2003.

———. *Helsinki of the Czars: Finland's Capital, 1808–1918*. Columbia, SC: Camden House, 1996.

———, ed. *A History of Finland's Literature*. Lincoln: University of Nebraska Press, in cooperation with the American-Scandinavian Foundation, 1998.

Schweitzer, Robert. "'. . . To Form an Ever More (Im)Perfect Union': Some Suggestions for Further Research on Finland's Position in the Russian Empire." In *. . . Vaikka voissa paistais? Venäjän rooli Suomessa: Juhlakirja professori Osmo Jussilalle, 14. maaliskuuta 1998*, edited by Jorma Selovuori. Porvoo: WSOY, 1998. 493–519.

Screen, J. E. O. *Mannerheim: The Years of Preparation*. London: C. Hurst, 1970.

Setälä, E. N. *The Language Fight in Finland*. Helsingfors: Government's Printing-Office, 1919.

Sibelius, Jean. *Dagbok, 1909–1944*. Edited by Fabian Dahlström. Helsingfors: SLS; Stockholm: Atlantis, 2005.

———. *Improvisation/Vårsång* [Op. 16, 1894]. Edited by Tuija Wicklund. JSW I/9. Wiesbaden: Breitkopf & Härtel, 2006.

———. *Kullervo, Op. 7*. Edited by Glenda Dawn Goss. JSW I/1.1–3. Wiesbaden: Breitkopf & Härtel, 2005.

———. *Kullervo: Piano-Vocal Arrangements, Movements III and V*. Edited by Glenda Dawn Goss. JSW I/1.4. Wiesbaden: Breitkopf & Härtel, 2005.

———. "Några synpunkter beträffande folkmusiken och dess inflytande på tonkonsten." *Musiikki* 10 (1980): 86–105.

———. *Skogsrået* [Op. 15]. Edited by Tuija Wicklund with the collaboration of Peter Revers. JSW I/9. Wiesbaden: Breitkopf & Härtel, 2006.

———. *Solo Songs with Piano*. Edited by Jukka Tiilikainen. JSW VIII/2–4. Wiesbaden: Breitkopf & Härtel, 1998–2005.

————. *Symphony no. 2 in D major*, Op. 43. Edited by Kari Kilpeläinen. JSW I/3. Wiesbaden: Breitkopf & Härtel, 2000.

————. *Works for Piano*. Edited by Kari Kilpeläinen. JSW V/1. Wiesbaden: Breitkopf & Härtel, 2002.

————. *Works for Voice and Orchestra*. Edited by Kari Kilpeläinen and Timo Virtanen. JSW VIII/1. Wiesbaden: Breitkopf & Härtel, 2003.

Sihvo, Hannes. *Karjalan kuva: Karelianismin taustaa ja vaiheita autonomian aikana.* Helsinki: SKS, 2003.

Similä, Martti. *Sibeliana.* Helsinki: Otava, 1945.

Sirén, Olle. *Lovisa stads historia, 1745–1995.* Lovisa: Lovisa, 1995.

Sirén, Vesa. *Aina poltti sikaria: Jean Sibelius aikalaisten silmin.* Helsinki: Otava, 2000.

Sjöblom, Paul. *Finland from the Inside: Eyewitness Reports of a Finnish-American Journalist, 1938–1997.* Edited with an introduction and commentary by Glenda Dawn Goss. Helsinki: NewBridge Press, 2000.

————. "Russian Avant-Garde Art Shown in Finland." *Suomen Silta* (1988): 40–41.

Smeds, Kerstin. *Helsingfors–Paris: Finlands utveckling till nation på världsutställningarna, 1851–1900.* Helsingfors: SLS, 1996.

————, and Timo Mäkinen. *Kaiu, kaiu lauluni: Laulu- ja soittojuhlien historia.* Helsinki: Otava, 1984.

————, Rainer Knapas, and John Strömberg, eds. *Boken om vårt land 1996: Festskrift till Professor Matti Klinge/Juhlakirja Professori Matti Klingelle, 31.VIII.1996.* Helsinki/Helsingfors: Otava/Söderström, 1996.

Smith, Anthony D. *The Antiquity of Nations.* Cambridge: Polity Press, 2004.

Söderhjelm, Alma. *Min värld.* 3 vols. Stockholm: Albert Bonnier, 1929–31.

Söderhjelm, Henning. *Werner Söderhjelm.* Helsingfors: Schildts, 1960.

Söderhjelm, Werner. *Skrifter.* Vol. 6, *Åboromantiken.* Helsingfors: Holger Schildts, 1924.

Stanislavsky, Constantin. *My Life in Art.* Translated by J. J. Robbins. London: Geoffrey Bles, 1924.

Stavrou, Theofanis George, ed. *Art and Culture in Nineteenth-Century Russia.* Bloomington: Indiana University Press, 1983.

Stenius, Henrik. "The Breakthrough of the Principle of Mass Organization in Finland." *Scandinavian Journal of History* 5 (1980): 197–217.

Stigell, Jarl. *Finländska gestalter: Robert Stigell.* Ekenäs: Ekenäs Tryckeri, 1977.

Stoeckel, Carl. "Some Recollections of the Visit of Sibelius to America in 1914." *Scandinavian Studies* 43 (1971): 53–88.

Stravinsky: A Composers' [sic] Memorial. Special issue, *Perspectives of New Music* 9, no. 2–10, no. 1 (1971).

Stravinsky, Igor, and Robert Craft. *Dialogues and a Diary.* London: Faber & Faber, 1968.

Strindberg, August. *The Red Room: Scenes of Artistic and Literary Life.* Translated by Elizabeth Sprigge. London: Dent; Dutton, NY: Everyman's Library, 1967.

Strindberg, Freda [sic]. *Marriage with Genius.* London: Jonathan Cape, 1937.

Suchowiejko, Renata. "Franco-Belgian School of Violin Playing: Techniques—Aesthetics—Didactics." In *Henryk Wieniawski and the 19th Century Violin Schools: Techniques of Playing, Performance, Questions of Sources and Editorial Issues,* edited by Maciej Jabłoński and Danuta Jasińska. Poznań: Henryk Wieniawski Musical Society in Poznań, 2006. 37–47.

Suomen paviljonki maailmannäyttelyssä Parisissa 1900. Helsinki: Wentzel Hagelstam, 1900.

Suomen taiteen historia: Keskiajalta nykyaikaan. [Esbo]: Schildts, 1998.

Surface and Depth: Early Modernism in Finland, 1890–1920. Edited by Riitta Ojanperä; English edition, Timo Huusko. Helsinki: Ateneum Art Museum, 2001. Exhibition catalog.

Talas, SuviSirkku, ed. *Aino Sibeliuksen kirjeitä Järnefelt-suvun jäsenille.* Helsinki: SKS, 2000.

————. *Elisabeth Järnefeltin kirjeitä, 1881–1929.* Helsinki: SKS, 1996.

————. *Sydämen aamu: Aino Järnefeltin ja Jean Sibeliuksen kihlausajan kirjeitä.* Translated into Finnish by Oili Suominen. Helsinki: SKS, 2001.

————. *Syysilta: Aino ja Jean Sibeliuksen kirjeenvaihtoa, 1905–1931.* Translated into Finnish by Oili Suominen. Helsinki: SKS, 2007.

————. *Tulen synty: Aino ja Jean Sibeliuksen kirjeenvaihtoa, 1892–1904.* Translated into Finnish by Oili Suominen. Helsinki: SKS, 2003.

Tarasti, Eero. *Myth and Music: A Semiotic Approach to the Aesthetics of Myth in Music, especially that of Wagner, Sibelius and Stravinsky.* The Hague: Mouton, 1979.

————, ed. *Proceedings from the First International Jean Sibelius Conference, Helsinki, August 1990.* Helsinki: Sibelius Academy Department of Composition and Music Theory, 1990.

————. *Sävelten sankareita—eurooppalaisia musiikkiesseita.* Porvoo: WSOY, 1998.

Taruskin, Richard. "Chernomor to Kashchei: Harmonic Sorcery; or, Stravinsky's 'Angle.'" *Journal of the American Musicological Society* 38 (1985): 72–142.

————. *Defining Russia Musically: Historical and Hermeneutical Essays.* Princeton, NJ: Princeton University Press, 1997.

————. *The Oxford History of Western Music.* 6 vols. Oxford: Oxford University Press, 2005.

————. *Stravinsky and the Russian Traditions: A Biography of the Works through "Mavra."* 2 vols. Oxford: Oxford University Press, 1996.

Tawaststjerna, Erik. *Jean Sibelius.* Edited by Gitta Henning with the assistance of Fabian Dahlström. 5 vols. Helsingfors: Söderström, 1992–97.

————. *Jean Sibelius.* Translated from the Swedish into Finnish by Tuomas Anhava and Erkki Salmenhaara. 5 vols. Helsinki: Otava, 1965–88.

————. *Jean Sibelius.* Translated from the Swedish into English by Robert Layton. 3 vols. London: Faber & Faber, 1976–97.

————. *Сибелиус [Sibelius].* Translated by J. K. Kajav from Robert Layton's English translation of vols. 1 and 2, 1976, abridged. Edited by G. M. Schneerson. Moscow: Muzyka, 1981.

————. *Sibelius.* Edited by Erik T. Tawaststjerna. Helsinki: Otava, 1997.

————. "Sibelius' *Finlandia*: A Symbol of Press Freedom." Helsinki: Helsingin Sanomat, 1971.

Teich, Mikuláš, and Roy Porter, eds. *The National Question in Europe in Historical Context.* Cambridge: Cambridge University Press, 1993.

Teperi, Jouko. *Pro Carelia: Vuosisadan iltama Helsingin Seurahuoneessa 13.11.1893.* Lappeenranta: Karjalan kirjapaino, 1986.

Thurman, Judith. *Isak Dinesen: The Life of a Storyteller.* New York: St. Martin's Press, 1982.

Tokoi, Oskari. *Sisu "Even Through a Stone Wall": The Autobiography of Oskari Tokoi.* New York: Robert Speller & Sons, 1957.

Tommila, Päiviö, ed. *Herää Suomi: Suomalaisuusliikkeen historia.* Kuopio: Kustannuskiila, 1989.

Topelius, Zacharias. *Boken om vårt land.* New illustrated ed. Edited by Helena Solstrand. With an introduction by Matti Klinge. Borgå: WSOY, 1983.

————. *Finland framställdt i teckningar.* Plancherna från Adler & Dietz, Dresden. Helsingfors: A. W. Gröndahl & A. C. Öhman, 1845[–52] .

————. *Finlands krönika 1860–1878.* Edited by Rainer Knapas. Helsingfors: SLS; Stockholm: Atlantis, 2004.

Tramont, Edmond C. "The Impact of Syphilis on Humankind." *Infectious Disease Clinics of North America* 18 (2004): 101–10.

————. "*Treponema pallidum* (Syphilis)." In *Mandell, Douglas, and Bennett's Principles and Practice of Infectious Diseases,* 6th ed., edited by Gerald L. Mandell, John E. Bennett, and Raphael Dolin. 2 vols. New York: Elsevier/Churchill Livingstone, 2005. 2:2768–85.

Tuchman, Barbara W. *The Proud Tower: A Portrait of the World before the War, 1890–1914.* New York: Ballantine Books, 1996.

Tuomikoski-Leskelä, Paula. *Taide ja politiikka: Kansanedustuslaitoksen suhtautuminen taiteen edistämiseen Suomessa*. Ph.D. diss., University of Helsinki, 1977.

Tyrrell, John. *The Lonely Blackbird*. Vol. 1, *1854–1914*, of *Janáček: Years of a Life*. London: Faber & Faber, 2006.

Tyrväinen, Helena. "Helsinki–Saint Petersburg–Paris: The Franco-Russian Alliance and Finnish-French Musical Relations." FMQ (2003, no. 1): 51–59.

———. "Les origines de la réception de Debussy en Finland (1901–1933)." *Cahiers Debussy* 24 (2000): 3–22.

———. "Robert Kajanus and the 'Rimsky-Korsakov Affair.'" FMQ (2004, no. 4): 18–25.

———. "Robert Kajanuksen voimannäyte." *Suomen Kuvalehti* (2007, no. 41): 60–64.

———. "Suomalaiset Pariisin maailmannäyttelyiden 1889 ja 1900 musiikkiohjelmissa." *Musiikkitiede* (1994, nos. 1–2): 22–74.

Upton, Anthony F. *Finland in Crisis, 1940–1941: A Study in Small-Power Politics*. London: Faber & Faber, 1964.

———. *The Finnish Revolution, 1917–1918*. Minneapolis: University of Minnesota Press, 1980.

Ur Albert Edelfelts brev: Kring sekelskiftet. Helsingfors: Holger Schildts, 1930.

Uusi sukukirja II. Suomen sukututkimusseuran julkaisuja XIX. Helsinki: Otava, 1947–51.

Vainio, Matti. "Father of the Finnish Orchestra . . . : Towards the 20th Century." FMQ (1989, no. 3): 27–33.

———. "Helsingin yliopiston musiikinopettajan virantäytön vaiheet 1896–1897 ja Robert Kajanuksen näyteluento." *Musiikki* (2007, no. 1): 43–55.

———. *"Nouskaa aatteet!" Robert Kajanus: Elämä ja taide*. Helsinki: WSOY, 2002.

Väisänen, A. O. "Eräistä säveltäjäin kansansävelmä-aiheista: Vertailevaa tarkastelua." *Kalevalaseuran vuosikirja* 15 (1935): 270–79.

———. "Jean Sibelius vaikutelmistaan." *Kalevalaseuran vuosikirja* 1 (1921): 77–81.

———. "Kalevalaseuran vuosikatsaus 1935." *Kalevalaseuran vuosikirja* 16 (1936): 289–300.

———. "Musiikillisen viljelyksemme tulevaisuus." *Säveletär* (1918, nos. 1–2): 2–4.

———. "Poimintoja Sibeliuksen tematiikasta: Kansanmusiikkia silmällä pitäen." *Kalevalaseuran vuosikirja* 36 (1956): 286–98.

———. "Sibelius ja kansanmusiikki: Muutamia vertailevia poimintoja." *Kalevalaseuran vuosikirja* 16 (1936): 276–88.

———. "Sibelius tutkimusongelmana." *Valvoja* 71 (1951): 60–68.

Väisänen, Maija, ed. *Nationality and Nationalism in Italy and Finland from the mid-19th Century to 1918*. Helsinki: SHS, 1984.

Valkenier, Elizabeth Kridl. *Russian Realist Art: The State and Society; The Peredvizhniki and Their Tradition*. Ann Arbor, MI: Ardis, 1977.

———. *Valentin Serov: Portraits of Russia's Silver Age*. Evanston, IL: Northwestern University Press, 2001.

Valkonen, Markku. *The Golden Age: Finnish Art, 1850–1907*. Translated by Michael Wynne-Ellis. Porvoo: WSOY, 1992.

Vallgren, Ville. *Minnen från mitt liv: Hemma och ute*. Helsingfors: Akademiska bokhandelns distribution, 1931.

Varnedoe, Kirk, ed. *Northern Light: Nordic Art at the Turn of the Century*. New Haven, CT: Yale University Press, 1988. Exhibition catalog.

———, ed. *Northern Light: Realism and Symbolism in Scandinavian Painting 1880–1910*. Brooklyn, NY: Brooklyn Museum, 1982. Exhibition catalog.

Varpio, Yrjö, ed. *Suomen kirjallisuushistoria*. 3 vols. Helsinki: SKS, 1999.

Vasara, Erkki. *Valkoisen Suomen urheilevat soturit: Suojeluskuntajärjestön urheilu- ja kasvatustoiminta vuosina 1918–1939*. Helsinki: SHS, 1997.

Vignal, Marc. *Jean Sibelius*. [Paris]: Fayard, 2004.

Vihola, Teppo. *Keuruun ja Pihlajaveden historia, 1860–1917*. Vanhan-Ruoveden historia III: 3/1. Keuruu: Keuruun ja Pihlajaveden historiatoimikunta, 1983.

Vilén, Helmi. "Kansanmusiikkimme nykyinen tilanne." *Työväen Musiikkilehti* (1929, no. 11): 209.

Virtanen, Timo. *Jean Sibelius, Symphony no. 3: Manuscript Study and Analysis*. Diss., Sibelius Academy, 2005.

Volkov, Solomon. *St. Petersburg: A Cultural History*. Translated by Antonina W. Bouis. London: Sinclair-Stevenson, 1996.

Vuolio, Jukka. *Putkesta putkeen: KTR 1 soittokunnasta Panssarisoittokuntaan 1919–1994, Panssarisoittokunta 75 vuotta*. [N.p.]: Panssarisoittokunnan Perinnetoimikunta, 1995.

Walton, Ann Thorson. "The Swedish and Finnish Pavilions in the Exposition universelle in Paris 1900." 2 vols. Ph.D. diss., University of Minnesota, 1986.

Wasserman, Jack. *Michelangelo's Florence "Pietà."* Princeton, NJ: Princeton University Press, 2003.

Wegelius, Martin. *Hufvuddragen af den Västerländska Musikens Historia från den kristna tidens början till våra dagar*. 3 vols. Helsingfors: K.E. Holm's förlag, 1891–93.

Wennervirta, Ludvig. *Eero Järnefelt ja hänen aikansa, 1863–1937*. Helsinki: Otava, 1950.

White, Harry, and Michael Murphy, eds. *Musical Constructions of Nationalism: Essays on the History and Ideology of European Musical Culture, 1800–1945*. Cork: Cork University Press, 2001.

Williams, Hermine Weigel. *Sibelius and His Masonic Music: Sounds in "Silence."* Lewiston, NY: Edwin Mellen Press, 1998.

Wilson, A. N. *Tolstoy*. New York: Norton, 1988.

Wilson, William A. *Folklore and Nationalism in Modern Finland*. Bloomington: Indiana University Press, 1976.

———. "Herder, Folklore, and Romantic Nationalism." *Journal of Popular Culture* 6 (1973): 819–35.

Wis, Roberto. "Ferruccio Busoni and Finland." *Acta Musicologica* 40 (1977): 250–69.

Woźna-Stankiewicz, Małgorzata. "Compositions of the Franco-Belgian School of Violin Music in the Concert Repertoire of 19th Century Poland." In *Henryk Wieniawski: Composer and Virtuoso in the Musical Culture of the XIX and XX Centuries*, edited by Maciej Jabłoński and Danuta Jasińska. Poznań: Rhytmos, 2001. 215–51.

Wrede, Johan, and Clas Zilliacus, eds. *Finlands svenska litteraturhistoria*. 2 vols. Helsingfors: SLS; Stockholm: Atlantis, 1999–2000.

Wretö, Tore. *J. L. Runeberg*. Translated in collaboration with the author by Zelek S. Herman. Boston: Twayne, 1980.

Wuorinen, John H. *Nationalism in Modern Finland*. New York: Columbia University Press, 1931.

Yastrebtsev, V. V. *Reminiscences of Rimsky-Korsakov*. Edited and translated by Florence Jonas. New York: Columbia University Press, 1985.

Ylioppilaskunnan Laulajat 50 vuotta. Edited by Toivo Aro. Helsinki: SKS, 1933.

INDEX

A note to readers: Titles of artworks, compositions, and literary works are alphabetized by the first main word (ignoring any definite or indefinite article), with the exception of those in Swedish. Thus, for example, *En saga* will be found under *e* rather than *s*. For Nordic readers, please note that the letters *å*, *ä*, *ö*, and *ø* are treated as ordinary *a*'s and *o*'s and alphabetized accordingly, while *v* and *w* are considered separate letters.

When more than three works are cited for a given artist, composer, or writer, the titles appear in a separate entry labeled "works," which immediately follows the main entry. Italicized book titles indicate a published English translation. In the citation of Sibelius's compositions, "JS" plus a number—a designation taken from the composer's thematic catalog, SWV—is given for works without opus numbers.

Page numbers in italics refer to illustrations.